AUTOBIOGRAPHICAL

WRITING

ACROSS

THE DISCIPLINES

AUTOBIOGRAPHICAL

WRITING

ACROSS

THE DISCIPLINES

A Reader

EDITED BY DIANE P. FREEDMAN AND OLIVIA FREY

Foreword by Ruth Behar   Duke University Press Durham and London 2003

© 2003 Duke University Press

All rights reserved

Printed in the United States of

America on acid-free paper ∞

Designed by Amy Ruth Buchanan

Typeset in Bembo by Tseng

Information Systems, Inc.

Library of Congress Cataloging-in-

Publication Data appear on the last

printed page of this book.

CONTENTS

We thank, first of all, our many contributors and would-be contributors, who have been more patient than it is reasonable to ask or expect. Ditto for Reynolds Smith, editor extraordinaire, Sharon Torian, Leigh Anne Couch, and Lynn Walterick. We also continue to be grateful to those many other scholars whose work anticipates, corroborates, complicates, and contemplates the genre and methods represented by this volume. We deeply appreciate the advice and encouragement of the anonymous reviewers of this manuscript.

Diane also thanks the College of Liberal Arts of the University of New Hampshire for funding from the Richardson Fund of the Alumni Annual Gifts Funds; the Center for the Humanities and Burt Feintuch, for additional funding; Dee-Ann Dickson and Stormy Gleason for technical support; and the Department of English, including especially Rochelle Lieber, Rachel Trubowitz, Brigitte Bailey, Tory Poulin, Lisa Feldman, Clare Sullivan, and Jennifer Dube, for various kinds of support. This book would also not have been possible without the support—emotional, intellectual, and/or technical—of Brian and Abraham McWilliams, Martha Stoddard Holmes, Lynn Bloom, Susan Rosen, and Suzanne MacDonald. Thanks also to Jill Gussow.

• • •

The following selections have appeared in other books or journals. Grateful acknowledgment is made to the publishers, agents, and authors for permission to reprint them here:

"Altered States" from *In My Father's House: Africa in the Philosophy of Cul-*

ture by Anthony Appiah, copyright 1992 by Anthony Appiah. Used by permission of Oxford University Press, Inc.

"Juban América," by Ruth Behar, appeared in *Poetics Today* 16, no. 1 (spring 1995): 151–70. Copyright 1995, the Porter Institute for Poetics and Semiotics, Tel Aviv University. All rights reserved. Used by permission of the publisher.

"Introduction," by James H. Cone, is from *God of the Oppressed* (New York: Seabury, 1975; Maryknoll, New York: Orbis Books, 1997). Reprinted by permission of Orbis Books.

"Close Encounters with a CSA: The Reflections of a Bruised and Somewhat Wiser Anthropologist, by Laura DeLind, *Agriculture and Human Values* 16 (1999): 3–9, with kind permission from Kluwer Academic Publishers.

"My Father/My Censor," by Brenda Daly, is reprinted by permission from *Authoring a Life: A Woman's Survival in and through Literary Studies*, the State University of New York Press. © 1998 State University of New York. All rights reserved.

"Gender Tragedies: East Texas Cockfighting and *Hamlet*," by Carlos Dews, appeared, in a slightly different form, in the *Journal of Men's Studies* 2, no. 3 (February 1994): 253–67.

Chapter 9 (pp. 134–55) from *The Broken Cord* by Michael Dorris. With foreword by Louise Ehrdrich. Copyright © 1989 by Michael Dorris. Reprinted by permission of HarperCollins Publishers Inc. Photo credits: 1. From Sterling Clarren et al., "Fetal Alcohol Syndrome," *New England Journal of Medicine* 278, no. 19 (1978); 2. From K. L. Jones and D. W. Smith, "Recognition of FAS in Early Infancy," *Lancet* 2 (1973): 999–1001; 3, 4. From A. P. Streisguth, C. S. Herman, and D. W. Smith, "Stability of Intelligence in the FAS: A Preliminary Report," *Alcoholism: Clinical and Experimental Research* 2, no. 2 (1978): 165–70; 5, 6, 7. K. L. Jones, D. W. Smith, C. N. Ulleland, and A. P. Streissguth, "Patterns of Malformation in the Offspring of Chronic Alcohol Mothers," *Lancet* 1 (1973): 1267–271.

"A Textbook Pregnancy," from *A Not Entirely Benign Procedure: Four Years as a Medical Student*, by Perri Klass, copyright © 1987 by Perri Klass. Used by permission of G. P. Putnam's Sons, a division of Penguin Putnam Inc.

"History of an Encounter" reprinted from Eunice Lipton, *Alias Olympia: A Woman's Search for Manet's Notorious Model and Her Own Desire*. Copyright © 1992 by Eunice Lipton. Used by permission of the publisher, Cornell University Press.

"Personal Thinking" from *The Children's Machine* by Seymour Papert.

Copyright © 1993 by Seymour Papert. Reprinted by permission of Basic Books, a member of Perseus Books, L. L. C.

Parts of "Listening to the Images" by David Richman serve as the introduction to his *Passionate Action: Yeats's Mastery of Drama* (University of Delaware Press, 2000). Grateful acknowledgment is made to Associated University Presses for permission to use this material.

"Maternal Thinking," by Sara Ruddick, from *Maternal Thinking: Towards a Politics of Peace* (Boston: Beacon, 1989).

"Adventures of a Woman in Science," by Naomi Weisstein, appeared in *Women Look at Biology Looking at Women: A Collection of Feminist Critiques* edited by Ruth Hubbard et al. (Boston: G. K. Hall, 1979), and *Biological Woman–The Convenient Myth*, edited by Ruth Hubbard et al. (Schenckman, 1992). © Naomi Weisstein. Reprinted by permission.

"That Disorder," by Alice Wexler, from *Mapping Fate: A Memoir of Family, Risk, and Genetic Research* (Random House, 1995; University of California Press, 1996). Copyright © by Alice Wexler. Reprinted by permission of the Frances Goldin Literary Agency.

"The Death of the Profane" in *The Alchemy of Race and Rights* by Patricia J. Williams, pp. 44–51. Reprinted by permission of the publisher, Harvard University Press, Cambridge, Mass. Copyright © 1991 by the President and Fellows of Harvard College.

Fifteen years ago. I remember the moment vividly. Like it was today. The first time I introduced my personal voice into my anthropology. My son Gabriel had just celebrated his first birthday. I was soon to turn thirty and in the second year of a postdoctoral fellowship. We were living on the corner of McKinley Street in a rented house painted forest-green. The wooden floors were old and warped and we had no rugs to cover them. I had a room where I wrote and dreamed of writing in ways I couldn't write. A deadline was coming up: I needed to prepare a paper for the annual American anthropology conference. But I was finding it hard to write. I was still grieving over the loss of my beloved maternal grandfather, who had passed away over the summer while I was doing research in Spain.

Knowing my grandfather was dying, I had returned to the small village in Spain where I had done my dissertation work, carrying the weight of guilt and uncertainty on my shoulders. Ironically, my reason for going to Spain was to carry out research on attitudes toward death. Even though I'd lived in the village for twenty months, I'd never asked people to tell me stories about death. The research would form the basis of the paper I needed to present for a panel on attitudes toward death in rural Europe.

Shortly before the end of my trip, my grandfather died in Miami Beach. I was overwhelmed with feelings of loss, grief, rage, and moral confusion. Why had I been in Spain talking with strangers about death rather than being at my grandfather's side gently offering my last good-bye? Why was it that over the course of my work as an anthropologist I had become an expert on popular Catholicism and could recite the rosary in Spanish by heart, but I knew nothing of Jewish mourning rituals and had no idea how to honor my grandfather within the traditions of my own heritage?

These questions haunted me, but it wasn't until I began struggling to write my paper for the conference that I realized they needed to be addressed in the very same context as my presentation of my research findings about how Spanish villagers felt about the subject of death. In fact, as I wrote, it quickly became clear to me that what I had come to know about death in Spain had been learned in the space of my grandfather's dying. In turn, hearing stories of sorrow and loss in a small village in Spain had prepared my heart for the ache of death's merciless finality.

With a sense of urgency and necessity, I prepared my paper, and when it came time to read it aloud before my colleagues, I trembled in fear, convinced that I would receive a scolding for speaking so personally and so emotionally at an anthropology conference. I don't doubt that there were people in the room who were made to feel uncomfortable by my presentation, but I didn't notice. I did see that the room fell silent as I spoke and that people were listening. Several colleagues were kind enough to tell me they were moved to tears by my paper. That was all the encouragement I needed. Over the next several months I expanded the paper and turned it into an essay, "Death and Memory," which became the opening piece of my book, *The Vulnerable Observer: Anthropology That Breaks Your Heart* (1997).

After writing that essay, there was no turning back for me. I wanted to approach anthropology with an opening heart. I wanted to treat inter-subjectivity not only as a theory but as a fundamental part of the representation of social reality. And I wanted, maybe most importantly, to discover the deep conjunctures that inform any effort to know the world beyond the self. I'd come to realize that in writing "Death and Memory" I'd mixed together levels of experience that are not usually mixed. I'd created a counterpoint, a *contrapunteo*, between the ethnographic stories of death in rural Spain, which required my objective presence as an anthropologist, and my own grandfather's death in Miami Beach, which had taken place in my pained absence. This unique convergence, with all its friction, poignancy, and contradiction, had a certain musicality, I thought. It conveyed a faith in the surrealist principle that joining together incongruous things could bring about an unexpected awareness, a slant of crooked, sharp light, the most sublime montage, an edgy form of knowing that dared to surprise the knower too. That was what I liked best about this method: that you yourself, the knower, didn't know fully what you knew until you wrote it down, until you told the story with yourself included in it.

Of course, at the time, I didn't know how to describe what I was doing. I kept using this contrapunteo in my writing but assumed it was my own particular idiosyncrasy that was leading me to produce work that didn't fit the classical norms of academic writing. I had no idea, at first, the extent to which my voice was part of a mosaic of voices, which in time would create a vigorous and unsettling interdisciplinary intellectual movement.

I thought I was doing what I was doing because I was too sentimental, or because I was melodramatic, or because I was a frustrated poet, or because I was Cuban and suffered from that terrible Cuban malaise of exceptionalism, or because I was an emigrant and so was always uneasy about my bearings, or because I was the first person in my family to receive an advanced degree and so had to write in ways that my mother could understand, or because I was selfish and wanted everything to connect back to me somehow, or because I was an imposter who'd slipped into the academy through the back door and couldn't do "proper" academic work.

As it turns out, I was not acting out of the needs of my particular ego and personal history but fulfilling my role as a historical actor within an intellectual community that I was helping to create. The entire time I thought I was writing personally, I was actually writing collectively, forming part of the zeitgeist of my time and my generation.

Can it be an accident that the desire which overtook a wide range of American scholars trained in a variety of academic disciplines to write in newly meaningful ways, which refused anonymity and authority and instead sought connection, intimacy, and passion, came as the century was ending? Might it be that all of us, in our respective disciplines, without knowing it, were grappling with the crisis of how to cross the border between the twentieth century and the twenty-first? Were we making history or running from history? I believe we wrote in innocence, from our hearts, and it was a good thing we did so, as if we had intuited how much we were going to need those well-turned hearts in the century to come.

This anthology of autobiographic writing by scholars with a range of ties to the academy, this mosaic of brave, graceful, and compassionate voices, skillfully edited by Diane P. Freedman and Olivia Frey, bears testimony to the strength of an intellectual movement that is changing the way scholarship is being done. Freedman and Frey have brought together people in numerous fields, including literature, music, film, history, anthropology, law, medicine, mathematics, and the natural sciences. They have consciously blurred the illusory line between "hard" and "soft" disciplines. And they have selected forms of first-person writing that are diverse and compelling, never predictable, and at times simply delightful, as when the composer Peter Hamlin offers an easy and delicious recipe for peanut sauce while describing the process of making music. And yet like all anthologies, this book asserts the importance of a common project, a shared commitment to a way of knowing as well as a way of telling.

What exactly is that common project and why does it matter? Having been asked to write a foreword for this volume, I accepted the honor, viewing it as an opportunity to examine how so many of us arrived at this destination. How to describe where we are? Let's says it's an odd and uncharted location, where another kind of truth must be confronted, a location where it would be the worst betrayal and irresponsibility not to confront the intersection of who we are and what we study.

Looked at as a whole, this volume reflects an overall sense of exasperation and frustration with classical forms of uncovering and relaying knowledge. Yet, while there is general agreement that the old paradigms are exhausted, new paradigms have yet to be enshrined. Or more exactly, there is strong resistance to enshrining any paradigms at all. We seem to be a group of scholars who are committed for various reasons to demystifying the intellectual process, to showing how we know what we know and making that comprehensible to the uninitiated. A new epistemology is what we're after, but we might not use that word. We have an aversion to big words and abstractions. We've all at some time been made to feel alien in the academy and consider it a principle of our work that our writing will not be a tool for the alienation of others. We seek, with Brechtian flair, to make our writing accessible to the carpenters who build our cedar decks and the secretaries who sort our mail. At the very least, many of us think it might be nice if our colleagues in other departments could read and understand and perhaps even enjoy what we write. Some of us, too, have attachments to the communities we come from and would be unable to sleep at night if we felt the writing we did was a wall that shut out those who take the greatest pride in our accomplishments. We refuse to classify what we do under the narrow categories of disciplines, even as we continue to labor within those disciplines where we continually confront the taboos against our supposedly self-indulgent pursuits. We are not afraid to take risks. We think it is totally possible to do rigorous scholarship and be personal and personable in our work. We deplore stuffiness and choose to write concretely in the everyday poetry of our speaking voices. Our thinking is not separated from our feeling. We aim, not to put forth heavy arguments, but to move others with our angel-winged words. We have a primitive faith in the power of a story well told. But we ourselves are very sophisticated. We are storytellers with Ph.D.s and academic jobs. We've studied hard and been rewarded for our efforts, but we're not totally satisfied. We are the velvet exiles of the academy, able to comfortably do the work expected of us, but choosing instead the more difficult position, that of the outsider within. The academy would be a dull and complacent place without us. But we aren't merely critics of the academy; most of all, we are chroniclers of the historical moment in which it has been our destiny to be thinkers.

We should not ignore the fact that our intellectual movement, like the memoir boom in general, seems to have taken off primarily in the United States. I am sure that a serious scholar of American culture could provide insight into the particular features of the culture that have inspired such an intense desire to make the personal matter in our intellectual pursuits. Perhaps this concern for the personal in scholarship is rooted in good old American individualism with which we are all too familiar. But it's individualism with a decidedly new twist, as we struggle to understand what happens to the uniqueness of the person in the midst of ever more expansive technologies that make unprecedented demands on our humanity.

Our new world order draws us closer to one another but leaves each of us in peril of becoming ever more anonymous, ever more identified with our social security numbers and our frequent flyer numbers and our e-mail addresses. Such anonymity, I would add, is the price of privilege; the sadder anonymity, the truly painful vulnerability, is that of the large populations around the world mired in hunger, poverty, oblivion, and underdevelopment. And yet despite the finer quality of life for the privileged few, humanity has never been so fragile, so susceptible to massive car crashes and explosions and the killing hatred of the excluded, so susceptible to cruel illnesses like AIDS and cancer, so susceptible to the nasty fallout of an environment that we ourselves have damaged more relentlessly in the past century than in the thousands of years that preceded our existence on this planet. In the United States, we are bombarded daily with too much knowledge to process and too many choices to make about everything, from the shampoo we use to the music we listen to in the silence of the night. In this era of information overload and media saturation, we keep abreast of strife, suffering, and yearnings for liberation in nations scattered about the globe, but compassion fatigue threatens constantly to drain us of sympathy for the struggles of others.

Increasing anonymity, increasing suffering, increasing uncertainty, increasing recognition of too many far-away others who cannot be helped all at once—surely this must weigh on the psyches of the various American intellectuals included in this book, who have chosen deep, critical self-examination, not as an escape from the complexities of the world we live in, but as a way of being more present in this world.

We have arrived in a new century. Wearing our hearts on our sleeves. Yes, that is good. But how much more difficult it is to speak now! But speak we must. There is already, for me at least, a growing sadness as I come to sense that the personal voices we worked so hard to find in our scholarship are rapidly going to have to find another tonality in order for them not to seem frivolous or coy or irrelevant. This is leading many to say that now is the time to return to the detached voice of authority of the past. But that will only give us a false security. I say that more than ever what we are going to need are the strong personal voices we have cultivated, separately and in unison, as outsiders within the academy. I have faith that our voices will rise to the challenges that the future holds.

More than ever, scholarship must cherish the fierce beauty of humanity. More than ever, love must shine in our learning—the love of being able to be there, to fathom what we didn't know before. And then the love of trusting that the words will come to enable us to say what we now know. Trusting that the words will surely come.

—Ruth Behar
Department of Anthropology, University of Michigan, Ann Arbor

DIANE P. FREEDMAN

AND OLIVIA FREY

Self/Discipline:

An Introduction

The "I" implicated here is very precise, yet more than half unspeakable. Its descriptors are not mere political trading chips. They are vectors, interlocked with energy, joy, imbalance, determination, depression—themselves not free-floating emotions, but situated and socially formed.
—Rachel Blau DuPlessis, "Reader, I Married Me: A Polygynous Memoir"

In atomic physics, we can never speak about nature without, at the same time, speaking about ourselves.
—Fritjof Capra, *The Tao of Physics*

WHY THIS BOOK?

In the wake of our book *The Intimate Critique: Autobiographical Literary Criticism* (Duke, 1993), we continued to wonder about the place and impact of autobiography and subjectivity in the work of scholars across the disciplines. What are the relations between life stories and the subjects, approaches, arguments, results, and writing styles of these researchers and scholars? How do personal experience and disciplinary choices intersect? What are some of the bases for the writing conventions in various disciplines and, if these practices have changed, what forces within and among disciplines are precipitating change?

In *Autobiographical Writing across the Disciplines: A Reader*, we explore these questions through writings from the humanities and arts, social sciences, sciences, and the spaces in between. The twenty-six essays and excerpts from books specifically explore the relations between the search for knowledge—in disciplines such as literary studies, theater, ethnic studies, religious studies, history, philosophy, art history, music, film, anthropology, law, education, Africana studies, mathematics, research psychology, biology, and medicine — and the academic writer's own life. In other words, what are some of the ways self and discipline coalesce into and shape one another? To what extent have language, ethnicity, race, class, gender, sexuality, religion, and/or geography, for instance, influenced the choices we made as students and teachers, scholars and writers? And how, in turn, have disciplines, disciplinary communities, and research influenced who we are as persons?

While the disciplinary categories with which we organize this book or identify contributions (and which framed our choices) are themselves conventional, the authors and the pieces, like the autobiographical move in scholarship in general, challenge categories and boundaries and are deeply interdisciplinary. They are integrated in natural, human, organic ways. In these selections we meet a musician who cooks, a mathematician with insights into children's play, a theologian with a historian's eye. We retain the categories we do for convenience and because they are familiar, remaining intact in our collective educational consciousness and in the administrative structures in our schools and colleges, even as these institutional parameters have been challenged and ways of knowing and writing are being deconstructed. We keep the categories in order to beg the question of the assumptions on which their methodologies and rhetoric are based. The writers themselves provide compelling critiques of monolithic methods and writing styles and of the purported objectivity of academic knowing.

By editing this collection, we continue our participation in "the movement to recognize the autobiographical voice as a legitimate way of speaking in academe" (Behar, "Dare We Say 'I'?" B1).[1] We hope the book can serve as inspiration for others writing in the still-emerging genre variously termed "autobiographical criticism," "personal scholarship," "self-inclusive scholarship,"[2] or "cross-genre" writing, and as a textbook for our and others' courses. We see *Autobiographical Writing across the Disciplines* as a further introduction to an increasingly popular, political, and emotionally engaged mode, often belletristic, that "mixes personal elements with research expertise" (Heller A7). Here the personal background is not an incidental fact of the research but that which, quite complexly, shapes the process of searching and discovering. Throughout, the process of thinking through issues is as important as any specific conclusions about those issues. In most cases, this autobiographical knowing directly challenges the methods of the fields and institutions in which the writers work. These selections, then, give us not just new information or new voices but new methods, new means of recognizing, valuing, and circulating information.

The contributors in this book are, in fact, seriously committed to circulating information as widely as possible. Most of them write for nonacademic audiences as well as for their colleagues in the profession. They seek to make their work accessible to all readers. The subjects they have studied and the knowledge they have searched out have *relevance*, often a debased word in academe but one which feminists have long championed in making connections between lived experience and theory, one's work and one's life.[3] As bell hooks has written elsewhere, our efforts to "make sense of everyday life experience," resulting in "critical reflection" and change, constitute the "critical process of theorizing" (*Teaching to Transgress* 70), and this sort of theory and theorizing has relevance no matter who we are and how we spend our days, laborer or professor, within or without ivied walls. We see everywhere the extended possibilities of narrative as a blend of story, interpretation, theory, and praxis—a "female mode of rhetoric" (a helpful label but a mode we realize is now and was historically authorized and practiced by many men and shunned by some women), which influence we also address in our earlier collection.[4] The essays in this book, not distant and abstract but connected to daily life, many times invitingly open-ended and interactive, are accessible to a wide variety of readers.

Among the instances of autobiographical scholarship in the last twenty years, and thus here as well, there is an abundance of literary-critical articles and books. Writing about literature—about stories—seems to be more conducive to the autobiographical-critical than other scholarly pursuits might be.[5] Personal scholarship also borrows the techniques of literature itself. Accounts of the writing and research process or of the reader whose life is different because of what he or she reads unfold dramatically, layer by layer, and through dialogue (internal and external). Such narratives often depend on poetry, the potent shorthand of imagery and metaphor through which writers can argue or propose as well as describe. It is no accident that anthropologist Michael Dorris (a contributor) was also a fiction writer or that Deborah Lefkowitz, a Jewish woman analyzing her marriage to a German and their life together in Germany (and another contributor), is a filmmaker. It is hard to separate modes in such work. Is Dorris's *Morning Girl* children's fiction or ethnography? Is *The Broken Cord* (excerpted here) anthropology, autobiography, or creative nonfiction? Is Lefkowitz's film *Intervals of Silence: Being Jewish in Germany* (about which she writes here) autobiography, ethnography, documentary, or image poem? Moreover, each of the personally situated contributions here are also always so-cially situated, commenting on a larger group, time, and place than that of a lone "self." As anthropologist Ruth Behar argues in an opinion piece in the *Chronicle of Higher Education*, what may begin with a personal inquiry ends in a redrawn map of the social terrain (B1).

• • •

Who is she then? It appears that she locates herself only to disclose that she has no secure location. She writes herself only to falter over the necessity for a stable identity. There are too many categories available to her. The very space of location is indeed a decen-tered one.

—Terry Caesar, *Conspiring with Forms* (on Marianne Hirsch in her book *The Mother/Daughter Plot: Narrative, Psychoanalysis, Feminism*)

Autobiographical criticism has been especially suspect in disciplines other than literature and the arts. In *Social Science and the Self*, Susan Krieger writes autobiographically yet admits that "the social science disciplines tend to view the self of the social scientific observer as a contaminant. The self—the unique inner life of the observer—is treated as something to be separated out, neutralized, minimized, standardized, controlled" (1). Bob Marcus, writing in this volume, reminds us that historians are nervous about as-sertions of the personal, noting that a graduate student once approached him at an American Historical Association conference to say, "I'm so re-lieved, I was afraid history was going the way of English." In general, most in the academy—sociologists, scientists, historians—still suffer a hangover from a potent Cartesian cocktail. Descartes has taught us, and many in aca-deme can't give it up, that knowing requires detachment, objectivity, and depersonalization.

One detractor of autobiographical criticism, Daphne Patai, complains about what she deems a "nouveau solipsism," concluding, "the last time I looked, there still was a world out there" [and that we should attend to it] (A58). We agree. But, we argue, it makes a difference—to our work and to readers—through what lenses we see, how they are shaded by past and present perspectives. We believe it's more human, more politic, more polite, more interesting, more accurate when we acknowledge the extent to which the examined object reflects the examining subject. We need not subsume our research within a continual contextualizing narrative, but neither should we banish the personal narrative completely. Theorizing the personal is a necessary corrective to pseudo-objectivity; more than that, it's part of the double helix of the scholarly enterprise. One of the new so-called public intellectuals, Michael Berube, an English professor, writes elsewhere, "as long as the scholarship in question concerns humans and is written by humans, readers should at least entertain the possibility that nothing human should be alien to it" (1065). Sociologist Laurel Richardson similarly argues in *Fields of Play* that a personal, nonauthoritarian, and creative approach is appropriate in academia today. She adopts her "penchant for mingling the personal, the political, and the intellectual" (12) from anthropologists who describe the present as a period in which we have the "loss of authority of a 'general paradigmatic style of organizing research'" (Marcus and Fisher, qtd. in Richardson 13), and who observe that "ideas and methods are freely borrowed from one discipline to another, leading to a 'blurring of genres'" (Geertz, "Blurred Genres").

The writings in this volume—and many of the now hundreds of autobiographical-critical writings out there—hold our attention in ways that more objective, distanced pieces will not. They are interesting, in the original sense of the Latin *interesse*, "to be in between"; they bridge lives and work, discipline and discipline, reader and author. As feminist scholars have been saying for the last several decades, as reader-response critics have been echoing, as black scholars have argued, we cannot stand outside these discussions, dispassionate, untouched, neither as readers nor as writers. They interest us, in the deepest ways.

WHO ARE WE? THE "I" IN THE TEXT

One day, browsing in her father's library, Diane read with fascination a footnote to Dr. A. A. Brill's introduction to *The Basic Writings of Sigmund Freud*: "Alas! As these pages are going to the printer we have been startled by the terrible news that the Nazi holocaust has suddenly encircled Vienna and that Professor Freud and his family are virtual prisoners in the hands of civilization's greatest scourge." The footnote dramatized for Diane that not only was an author more a part of the text than she had imagined, but so were its editors and readers. Brill alerted Diane, as all of the writers in the volume alert us, to the fact that every book, every reading, is laced and surrounded with personal circumstances worth considering.[6]

Our autobiographies have affected our choices as editors of this collection.

Diane's experience as a poet before she ever became a critic and as a woman writer of mixed Jewish-Catholic and upper-lower-class background makes her privilege the self-consciously meditative product of mixed social histories and hybrid genealogies. And she is also drawn as a nature writer to essays steeped in a sense of place.

Olivia is likewise drawn to writing about actual landscapes, whether the sand, limestone, and marl of South Florida where she grew up or the snow of Minnesota, where she now lives. For any writing to engage her and be meaningful, it needs to render settings, experience, and ideas in concrete ways. The insistence that ideas be situated in the world may also be the bias of her working-class background. Neither of her parents went to college, and her father, originally from Virginia, worked in construction and drove cabs in New York City soon after he left sixth grade. School meant everything to Olivia, until it became impossible to play the academic "objectivity" games any longer. Academic discourse seemed so distant from the world and the real business of living, loving, dying—or driving cabs. Happily, however, the growing practice of self-inclusive scholarship has brought more of us together in and with the academic, though the history of "objectivism" casts a long shadow, as we detail below.

THE CONVENTION OF OBJECTIVITY IN ACADEMIC DISCOURSE

Why in academe do we write the way we do? What are the conventions of academic discourses, and how did they become conventional?

Most of us have been told that academic writing—and by academic writing we mean the books, articles, and reports that we in academe write and publish and the writing that our students produce in advanced courses in our disciplines—should be clear and concise, organized and precise. Such writing should offer consistent assertions supported by evidence. These traits, however, might characterize what most persons consider good writing. What makes academic discourse unique? As compositionist Peter Elbow writes in "Reflections on Academic Discourse," "it's crazy to talk about academic discourse as one thing" (140). Nevertheless, all academic writing shares certain general characteristics.[7]

In *The Writing Scholar: Studies in Academic Discourse*, a collection of essays about the conventions of academic writing, editor Walter Nash notes three general characteristics of this writing: exactitude, modality, and objectivity. Academic writing must be exact and according to the expectations of readers. The writer must support his/her assertions with research data or verifiable views of experts, at least those judged knowledgeable by peers or appearing in discipline-venerated publications and speaking venues. (Note how we too support our statements about academic writing by citing known experts in the field, borrowing the reasoning of authority figures, showing how our claims are spread around.) Central to academic discourse is the "giving of reasons and evidence rather than just opinions, feelings, experiences" (Elbow 140). These reasons and evidence must be rendered via an appropriate "modality," a syntactic and rhetorical way of "suggesting conditions under which [one's claims] . . . be regarded as acceptable in argument or even objectively valid" (Nash 23). Examples are "It would seem" or "It is thought to be." Modality is a way of "saying something without saying it," explains Elbow (145). Modality allows for hedging (the cynical view) and/or for cognitive modesty (the positive view).

Of all characteristics of academic discourse, the most important seems to be objectivity. In fact, exactitude and modality are aspects of objectivity, since exactness means facts or objectively determined truth, and modality acknowledges subjectivity that is as objective as possible within a context ("It would seem from this linguistic pattern"). Even though in the humanities, especially, research does not depend on hard facts, and despite its qualified nature, such phrases/modality reach toward what might be called a "modest objectivity."

As many of our contributors themselves state or imply, as well as many of our previously cited sources, objectivity itself means the importance of being impersonal and, thus, "unbiased." Nash, in phrases echoed through the decades, including by poet-critic T. S. Eliot, asserts, "The topics of academic discourse—commonly summarized as the search for knowledge and truth—are supposed to *transcend personality*" (23, emphasis added). Elbow concurs; "behind . . . academic discourse in general is a bias toward objectivity" (140). In "Exploring Academic Literacy: An Experiment in Composing," Cheryl Geisler writes that, according to academic conventions, a personal account with an "I" "improperly [colors]" the writing. In 1990 Geisler was asked by the Research Network to write an account of her own research. At first, she reports, she included a very personal history but then cut it. Such stories result in "methodological impurity" (41), she felt, and hers was "too personal, too loosely connected to the argument of the essay, and—anyway—too long" (48). And yet, interestingly, Geisler does slip in her personal history, with the following disclaimer, "I can't make the logical account fit in comfortably. My best solution is to append it here as a kind of postscript to the argument and to ask you to consider how it could have been integrated" (48). She's uncomfortable with the story either in or out—"I recognize that a push toward coherence at the expense of the local account is what we should be resisting" (48), though she doesn't completely say why.

Geisler's dilemma epitomizes ongoing tensions within academe about the autobiographical nature of knowledge and the validity of personal experience within academic discourse, with personal stories contributing substantively to knowledge and the relaying of the knowledge process. Especially since academic writing is typically metadiscursive (that is, comments upon itself), attention to process (a movement since the 1970s) cannot but segue to the personal.

We see the reliance on objectivity in the first gatherings of scholars in ancient Greece and Rome and, more recently, the founding of the first colleges and universities in the United States. Before 1870 in the United States, the emphasis in higher education was on speaking rather than writing, and students spoke, read, and translated Latin and, later, Greek, not English. Higher education here was modeled after medieval scholasticism of the early European universities, which provided instruction in the seven liberal arts: the *quadrivium* of arithmetic, geometry, astronomy, and music, and the *trivium* of logic, grammar, and rhetoric; students were prepared to study the works of Aristotle (Rudolph). By the 1740s Yale had introduced an expanded curriculum of more science and math and more rhetoric. Gradually, instruction in English began to replace Latin, Greek, and Hebrew. America was not ancient Greece or medieval Europe. John Witherspoon, president of Princeton, introduced the study of belles lettres in 1768. *Hugh Blair's Lectures on Rhetoric and Belleslettres*, the first English literature textbook, was published in 1783 in London and introduced at Yale by Ezra Stiles in 1785. Colleges continued to train men (not women) for the law, for the church, and for government. But early founders of the institutions and of the nation foresaw a need for men to help build the nation in other ways — through engineering, agriculture, industrialization, and character building. Education was to nurture spirit and moral nature as well as impart skills needed to build a nation.

At no point in the evolution of higher education was the autobiographical or personal as a mode of learning or genre of writing considered valid. Classical disputation and rhetoric did not consider it so. Historian of rhetoric Robert J. Connors has written:

> The technics of classical invention all militated in favor of outward-directed investigation. The Aristotelian topics, which were the point of entry to classical invention, were all based in logos — the nature of the sub-

ject—and much less in questions of ethos, the nature of the speaker. . . .
The lines of argument produced by topical invention are overwhelmingly
impersonal. They take into consideration historical forces, contemporary
feelings, testimony of authorities, class expectations. Everything is useful
to the speaker, but until a speaker had established his own ethos, usually
through community service or previous rhetorical success, his own experiences and opinions were not important to his discourse. (167)

One would think that as college instruction altered to become more relevant to nation building, when literature in English was emphasized as well
as the development of the American ethos, that personal writing would
become a useful tool in shaping the American collective and individual
consciousness. But this was not the case.

Academic institutions in the United States turned to Germany for pedagogy and curriculum. Ten thousand or more Americans studied in Germany between 1815 and 1915 and brought back important aspects of the
German university system: lectures, freedom of inquiry and original discovery, research, and specialization. These replaced recitations, classical and
received knowledge, and an emphasis on breadth (Brereton). Objectivity
was paramount within the new system, and an "ethic of scientific objectivity . . . , an ethic which reinforced the high status accorded science
in modern industrialized society," prevailed (Russell 11). "Good academic
writing" had first to be "an objective rendering of reality" (Russell 11). Contemporary rhetorician James Berlin sees such a perspective as heavily influenced by a Cartesian epistemology: "When the individual is freed from the
biases of language, society, or history, the senses provide the mental faculties with a clear and distinct image of the world. The world readily surrenders its meaning to anyone who observes properly, and no operation of the
mind—logical or otherwise—is needed to arrive at truth" (770). Not only
is coming to know something not personal, it is not considered a process,
and the process itself in no way influences the outcome of understanding.
According to the objectivist perspective, knowing is somehow the direct
experience of reality, reported through language, unmediated by the self
or other circumstances.

As the American university evolved, its leaders were faced with increasing fragmentation and specialization within higher education and a consequent lack of common learning and a shared educational culture. As a
result, Harvard president Charles W. Eliot and his former classmate Adams
Sherman Hill created in 1872 the modern composition program on which

our current programs are based. All students were required to take "English A," a year-long composition course in which students wrote daily essays as well as longer themes on topics of their own choosing. The emphasis was on composition, not the study of literature, though disagreement was constant—at Harvard and at the colleges that adopted its model—over whether good writing was best fostered by reading Latin, Greek, and a little English literature or by writing frequently. Advocates of the Harvard model insisted that writing about and reading literature was not necessary and in fact prevented students from writing about topics with immediate relevance to them (Brereton).

Lane Cooper (who received his Ph.D. from Leipzig in 1901 and taught at Cornell University from 1902 to 1943) lambasted the Harvard composition program in a paper read before the MLA on 28 December 1909. He lamented the "gradual decline of interest in the disciplines of Greek and Latin" and warned that "the concomitant popular demand for a kind of education in the vernacular" would "directly liberate the masses, rather than raise up leaders in scholarship whose paramount influence might elevate and sustain the standards of taste and good usage" (qtd. in Brereton 252). Any education of value, according to him, depended on studying the masters and disallowing writing on subjects of the students' own choosing, much less personal or autobiographical topics. General education meant "a study of particular disciplines in the order of their importance and possibility," not the writing of "immature students" who, "empty witted," did not possess any "valuable truth" (Cooper, qtd. in Brereton 256). For the detractors of the Harvard plan, knowledge was outside the learner, in objective truths, whose significance was determined hierarchically according to objective standards and authority.

Gertrude Buck, who taught at Vassar College, also criticized Harvard, but for opposite reasons. She did not call for the study of classical literature but declared that writing about "pure" composition topics would not promote excellence in writing. In an article in *Educational Review* (1901), Buck argued that students needed to write with "real" motives on "genuine" occasions. Buck thought the writing situations and assignments in English A contrived, devised solely to teach rules and correctness—a correct estimation. Thus her advice sounds very modern; she integrated and applied principles of psychology and ethics and concluded that "every intelligent act is in its freedom responsible—not, indeed, to an arbitrary rule . . . but to the inner law of its own nature, as defined by the end it seeks to reach" (qtd. in Brereton 248–49). In her view, students would write best when they wrote on subjects that had personal meaning for them.

Buck valued personal topics and personal writing, recognizing early that the act of knowing involved the whole learner—body, emotions, spirit, and intellect. Yet hers is the lone dissenting voice among the founders and first teachers in U.S. higher education who shaped the academic discourse of these institutions. The model that has instead dominated is the objective model of incorporating outside, authoritative knowledge and information as a means of discovering truth. Students may write personally in first-year writing classes or in journals in literature or non-English courses but always en route to a more "valid" or "complicated" and objective methodology and prose style. A common final writing assignment in first-year writing courses is the research paper, a sign that students have mastered the important uses and modes of writing in college. Nash reiterates that "the conventions of academic writing have traditionally excluded the authorial personality, inhibiting—almost as a matter of bad form—any attempt at direct conversational dealing between the writer and the reader. The aim is . . . suppression of . . . self and . . . promotion of . . . subject" (21).

That the academy is marked by a dogged insistence on objectivity and received authority is clear from any number of commentators. Parker Palmer, senior associate of the American Association for Higher Education, writing in *The Courage to Teach: Exploring the Inner Landscape of a Teacher's Life*, announces,

> this mode called *objectivism* portrays truth as something we can achieve only by disconnecting ourselves, physically and emotionally, from the things we want to know. . . . For objectivism, any way of knowing that requires subjective involvement between the knower and the known is regarded as primitive, unreliable, even dangerous. The intuitive is derided as irrational, true feeling is dismissed as sentimental, the imagination is seen as chaotic and unruly, and storytelling is labelled as personal and pointless. (51–52)

In its effort to practice objectivity, the academy has adopted "scientific models" for its knowledge practices. Darwinian competition rather than collaboration is valued in classrooms and among scholars, in making the highest grade or writing the award-winning, single-authored article. Palmer identifies " 'atomism' as the dominant cultural metaphor of our time," and one of the most influential metaphors in education: "we and the world we live in are [considered] only an illusion of wholeness, beneath which lies the reality of fragmentation" (96). We may collaborate on articles and attend conferences together, but what is rewarded is exclusively individual achievement, lines on a cv. From literary studies to sociology, the mode of choice is objective research with the subjective self "the enemy most to be feared—a Pandora's box of opinion, bias, and ignorance that will distort our knowledge once the lid flies open" (Palmer 51).

But even scientists would say these tropes for learning and writing misrepresent science and the scientific method and are based on naive views about how the physical world operates. The biological world consists of complex ecosystems, an intricate web of physical dependencies and natural collaborations. Although the grip of objectivity remains tight, previous distortions have been unmasked and things have shifted.

In his book *Local Knowledge*, anthropologist Clifford Geertz summarizes the epistemological shift upon us: "Something is happening to the way we think about the way we think" (20) and "the instruments of reasoning are changing" (23). Neurological scientist Antonio Damasio reports that given how our brains operate, we can't so neatly separate logic from emotion. The brain "centers"—that "complex of somatosensory cortices in the right hemisphere"—of reasoning and emotion are intricately and intimately interconnected (247). Such interconnectedness has ensured survival, according to Damasio, as reasoning, feeling, and biological regulation work together. Both logic and feeling help us organize our sensory experience of the physical world, and logic and feeling determine how we respond. Contrary to the Cartesian model, there is not a singular brain site "feeling" that we can turn off while the "logic" brain site works. Damasio, in analyzing the brain to take on the dominance of Cartesian epistemology, inverts Descartes. Rather than "Cogito ergo sum" (I think, therefore I am), he offers a contrary maxim: "We are, and then we think, and we think inasmuch as we are, since thinking is indeed caused by the structures and operations of being" (248). Thus science itself questions the "scientific"/dualistic model of knowledge making and valuing.

Laurence Veysey, in *The Emergence of the American University*, observes that the goal of the academic researcher has been "certainty—not a labyrinth of tentative opinions true for people of one time and place" (145). Russell has similarly observed that the scholar's project has been "the old Enlightenment project: the progressive accumulation of facts, painstakingly but firmly wrested from nature, revealing immutable, universal laws" (72). The perspective is based on the epistemology of John Locke: "Let us then suppose the mind to be, as we say, white paper, void of all characters, without any ideas" (42). In this schema, truths are objective, and we take them in, unmarked by our places or ourselves. The more we consume, the more expert and knowledgeable we are considered. To be knowledgeable is, after all, to be *full* of knowledge, and quantity matters. Russell concludes that the positivist research idea "narrowed the possibilities for written discourse in the modern curriculum by casting suspicion on genres that were not 'academic,' which is to say, research oriented" (74).

Recent psychological research suggests, of course, that we are not all sheets of blank white paper when we are born. Dr. Rene Baillargeon of the University of Illinois, for instance, has "found that even very young infants share the physical reasoning ability of adults. They understand that objects continue to exist when hidden, that they cannot move through the space occupied by other objects, and they cannot appear at two separate points in space without traveling from one point to the other" (qtd. in Denton 8).

What do babies have to do with the issues of objective and received knowledge and autobiographical scholarship? They show us the mind is not a blank page taking in ideas unmarked by ourselves. We argue that autobiographical scholarship can still be scholarly and critical and that it relates to how we think and think about thinking. This very introduction is a consequence of Lockean conventions in discourse. The legitimacy of autobiographical scholarship is not self-evident (or we cannot assume it is to most); and so, while it is interesting to read about the academy and those conventions of discourse that autobiographical writing challenges, the primary reason for writing about this background is to legitimate and annotate the place of the genre within academic endeavors, which project inevitably includes using the same conventions that the theory and practice of autobiographical scholarship also challenge. However, in some key respects, and at crucial points in the writing, autobiographical criticism assumes that authoritative support and full documentation are not necessary. It assumes that personal experiences are powerful enough sources of insight and knowledge. It finds satisfying certainty in heart, soul, feelings, "intuition." It may not matter that the author is unknown and unreliant on lists and words of other authorities. Beautiful, evocative writing that connects with readers and their understandings and experiences can serve, and has, as a trusted, enlightening source. Evaluating art or architecture, giving coping advice to patients or clients, teaching others to write or work in public life: not all of these always require that feeling, intuition, and personal experience (indeed, expertise) be left behind. In an important study, Evelyn Fox Keller details exactly how "feeling" is what amplified the skills and analyses of scientist Barbara McClintock in a book called, provocatively, *A Feeling for the Organism* (discussed in greater detail below). But far from advocating that we never be traditionally logical again or document with research and corroborators our conclusions, we are suggesting that in our searching and studying we invite in other means of knowing, trusting other facets of ourselves, however suspect they may be in the usual academic venues or routines.

Jane Tompkins, now more than a decade ago, compared academic strictures to wearing a straitjacket. Like Virginia Woolf, who compared the dome of the reading room of the British Museum to a gigantic bald head, and Barbara Ryan, who compared the voice of a typical Ph.D. dissertation to a "voiceover, preferably male," Gail Griffin likened academic patriarchy to the "disembodied bald head" of the Wizard in the Baum tale of Oz. The wizard, or the patriarchal ideal of the intellect, is "purely academic," an abstraction "detached" from the body (63).

For a long while, women in academe have experienced and protested the separation of their lives from their work, their feelings from their thinking, or at least that is what writers such as Carol Gilligan, Mary Belenky, Gertrude Buck, Nicole Ward Jouve, Madeline Grumet, Jane Gallop, Wendy Bishop, Woolf, Griffin, Tompkins—and many contributors to this collection—maintain, with or without traditional and "scientific" proof. Higher education has not always been hospitable to women or to African Americans or Latino/a Americans, or to anyone who comes from a place other than a classroom or laboratory or office. But while the academy has in the past literally closed its doors, today it may only figuratively close its "doors" through financial along with epistemological and methodological exclusiveness.

Objectivism may be about the consolidation of power and protection of the academic status quo and have little to do with the validity of its epistemology. It embodies the commodification and rarified ownership of knowledge (what counts as knowledge). Early on, David Russell writes, scientists and scholars did not "step outside their respective symbolic universes" to share knowledge with a wider, nonacademic group. Exclusivity in the academy was preserved by ever more technical language inaccessible to "outsiders" and, according to Russell, "widespread dissemination of expert knowledge sometimes constituted a threat to professional communities [seeking to maintain] professional jurisdiction over certain social functions" (11–12). We would add that these communities sought to maintain professional jurisdiction over certain economic functions as well.

With the decline in theological authority in the United States came the rise of another kind of authority, the authority of scientific method, with its reliance on deductive reasoning, facts, data, and other quantified information. Objectivity claims to transcend mortal biases, to transcend mortality. Piles of data and the magic of new technologies represent the trappings and tools of the new gods Neil Postman suggests we moderns like better:

> [The theories of the science god] are demonstrable and cumulative; its errors, correctable; its results, practical. The science god sends people to the moon, inoculates people against disease, transports images through vast spaces so that they can be seen in our living rooms. It is a mighty god and, like more ancient ones, gives people a measure of control over their lives, which is one of the reasons why gods are invented in the first place. Some say the science-god gives more control and more power than any other god before it. (9)

Mimicking the sciences, other disciplines depended on scientific tools and apparent values—logic, objectivity, universalism. Susan Miller argues that literary study valued "timelessness, perfection, and spirituality," once the purview of the church and now the science godhead: we and our students would read the *great* books, the *timeless* classics, and *The Great Conversation* (the title of the Great Books course at St. Olaf College), discovering knowledge true for *all time* and *for all men*, not simply a guide within a finite or specific set of contexts.

But what if reading and writing became human again, with truths considered local, linked to a time and place? Perhaps not Truths, but stories. We would have ordinary truths and guidance about living and dying, and they would emanate not from some absolute authority or formula but from authority of experience and shared understandings, even negotiated understandings, and from the meanings and wisdom that our discoveries contribute to our shared lives.

• • •

In Western culture, women have always assumed or been assigned the role of subjectivists at home and in the public sphere, keepers and conveyors of emotions and family ties, of peace and love. And they have been charged with an assumed corresponding incapacity for clear and fair reasoning and all manner of excesses, especially bodily. They have been devalued and maligned when most successful as writers and public figures—recall Hawthorne's invective against the "damned mob of scribbling women" and the way charges of "sentimentalism" relegated inventive lyrical and feisty modernists like poets Edna St. Vincent Millay and Elinor Wylie to the rearguard of modernism (Fried 1). Feminist theorist and poet Susan Griffin ventriloquizes well thoughts and expectations often held about women within a patriarchal society such as ours, among them: "For men must work and women must weep" (30); "women are less objective" (38); and women "are shaped by what we see, it is said [;] there is no objectivity, what we see is shaped by what we are, by our past, and our past has shaped us" (40).

While feminists writing after Griffin's groundbreaking volume *Woman and Nature: The Roaring inside Her* (1978) have usually come to eschew the essentialism or sense of biological destiny they think they may hear in Griffin's jeremiad, many also realize that some combination of the forces of biology, history, society, and individuality are at work in women's and men's ways of being in the world, including their myriad ways of adopting and changing academic scholarly practices. Women's socialized and sanctioned penchant for intimacy and emotion (though often banned from institutional settings of academe, local and national government, industry, and so forth) inevitably must be said to inform—just as feminist recastings of women's capacities and predilections and their awareness of what male-dominated institutions have lacked must be said to inform—current self-inclusive, story-inclusive, emotion-inclusive academic practices. No longer must a dissertation be a giant male voiceover.

In *Autobiographical Writing across the Disciplines*, our contributors, male and female, share a great deal that is meaningful not just to experts in the disciplinary fields they represent but to all of us.

HUMANITIES, ARTS, AND SOCIAL SCIENCES: BACKGROUNDS

When I wrote about *The Godfather* in 1986, I slipped in references to Italian Americans and felt as thought I had put chocolate kisses inside my critical essay—little autobiographical nuggets, pieces of myself. This essay turned out to be a bridge piece for me. . . . Now, for the first time, as I connected my work with my personal history, I saw being Italian American as part of my life as a teacher and writer.
—Marianna Torgovnick, *Crossing Ocean Parkway* (109)

The subject matters and methodologies embraced by the disciplines of literature, writing, art history, music history, theater history, film studies, philosophy, law, religious studies, anthropology, sociology, psychology, communication, education—like those outside these fields—have changed over time. But they have also coexisted over time, so that the so-called new subjectivity has taproots that not only thread through feminism, postmodernism, the new composition studies, and so forth but go down and deep into history. We chart an intensification and validation of various personal approaches in the 1980s and 1990s, but the soil has been fertile a long while. Although a pedagogical or scholarly emphasis on lived experience and its connection to academic inquiry may not have dominated—indeed, the reign of objectivity has been long and loud—it surfaced in teaching and writing; in conferences, lectures, classrooms, especially in women's studies and creative writing; in private, in prefaces, in afterwords.

Thus, though mixed personal-academic texts have been produced and theorized by feminists, deconstructors, French psychoanalytic critics, reader-response critics, and composition teachers in the last two decades, they were also experimented with by past poet-critics from Sir Philip Sidney and Walt Whitman to W. E. B. Du Bois, Gertrude Stein, and Charles Olson along with such anthropologists as Clifford Geertz, James Clifford, Renate Rosaldo, and George Marcus (Freedman, "Creatively Critical Voice" 83), and the "new journalists" Tom Wolfe, Joan Didion, Truman Capote, Norman Mailer, et al.[8] Sherwin Paul, writing on Walt Whitman, Robert Creeley, and David Antin, laments the overinfluence of some criticism on poetry but praises a poetry that is criticism and vice versa as a criticism of "generous attention that, to cite one of Creeley's insistences, opens possibility" (12). Paul finds this "double practice" in David Antin's "talk poems," which Paul terms "remarkable improvised lectures," a criticism "as responsive to the conditions of poetry as we have had it" (12). Like other mixed-genre writers, Antin "talks against boundaries of all kinds."

Now even dissertations are being written in "a narrative, or storytelling, style," the *Chronicle of Higher Education* reports, the goal being to "craft compelling pieces that evoke readers' emotions," at least in fields involving qualitative studies, which "typically involved interviewing or observing subjects" (21 July 2000, A10+). Anthropologist Deborah E. Reed-Danahay asserts that self-inclusive scholarship (which in anthropology she and others term "autoethnography," the title, in fact, of Reed-Danahay's 1997 edited collection) "reflects a changing conception of both self and society in the late twentieth century (Cohen 1994; Giddens 1991). It synthesizes both a postmodern ethnography, in which the realist conventions and objective observer position of standard ethnography have been called into question, and a postmodern autobiography, in which the notion of the coherent, individual self has similarly been called into question" (2). In short, auto-ethnography is "a form of self-narrative that places the self within a social context" (9), and it can be done either by an anthropologist or "by an auto-biographer who places the story of his or her life within a story of the social context in which it occurs" (8). In related new forms and in this book, the self is situated within disciplines and subdisciplines, in relation to key texts, in relation to place, religion, sexuality, ethnicity, dialect practice, and other relevant axes and angles of analysis.

Anthropologist Simon Gottschalk cites S. A. Tyler's account of post-modern ethnography as a "meditative vehicle" and "a different kind of jour-ney" (Tyler 140, qtd. in Gottschalk 205). Gottschalk aligns himself with this postmodern critical approach to ethnography, one that (according to a range of practitioners) "requires its author to remain constantly and criti-cally attentive to issues such as subjectivity, rhetorical moves, problems of voice, power, textual politics, limits to authority, truth claims, unconscious desires, and so on" (207), promoting "purposeful trespassing of boundaries" between the "subjective" and supposedly "objective" (209). This compli-cated traveling is now widely performed in a range of disciplinary fields, each of which cites terms, techniques, and figures of the others as autho-rizing and inspiring their own work.

An additional brief digging into Western literary and philosophical his-tory will serve, we hope, as sufficient illustration of the principle of re-cursive yet innovative practice. The present practice of framing arguments personally or using scholarship to elucidate pressing personal concerns in-evitably relates to the histories not just of particular fields but of the essay and writerly practice more generally, as we note above (and as Diane ex-plores in "Life Work Through Teaching and Scholarship" in a volume titled *Personal Effects*). As literary scholar George Wright insists in an issue of PMLA (October 1998) devoted to the questions of the personal, "If I tell how I chose this topic, what serendipitous encounter with book or friend put me onto this approach, I am only following lines laid down by Augus-tine, Montaigne, Coleridge, Keats, Woolf [and many others]" (1160). In the eighteenth century, rhetorician George Campbell said of persuasive writ-ing, "passion must also be engaged" (113, qtd. in Paley 17). In the nine-teenth century, Alexander Bain praised Plato for his relief of "the severity of philosophical discussion with touches of general human interest . . . dra-matic displays of personal feeling" (202, qtd. in Paley 17). Jules Lemaître and Anatole France "defended the free play of the appreciative mind," the basis of the "impressionistic" criticism much maligned by the "New Critics." In 1910 J. E. Spingarn described such critics as being sensitive to impressions, capable of expressing themselves well, and thus producing new works of art in their responses (5). Spingarn then suggested no one should be alarmed, as "all criticism tends to shift the interest from the work of art to something else" (7). In the 1960s Irving Malin and Irwin Stark claimed that many Jewish-American critics were

> noticeably different in temper from the pure, scientific, rather aloof criticism of the "New Critics" who avoid[ed] committing themselves to any real understanding of sympathy. . . . The refreshing quality of American-Jewish criticism, lies precisely in this involvement with passionate spiritual questions, which is certainly a more humanistic involvement than close scientific explication. This is not to say that American-Jewish critics are merely impressionistic—they think as well as feel. (18)

Speaking of the uses of the personal in the classroom, James Berlin recounts that in the 1920s Richard Reeve drew on dreams for invention in writing personal essays, and in the 1930s J. McBride Dabbs relied on student journals for class reading and Edith Christina Johnson saw writing as forming identity and offering self-knowledge (Berlin, qtd. in Paley 42). In 1938, Louise Rosenblatt brought out *Literature as Exploration*, the text that gained great critical attention when it was reissued in 1976. Rosenblatt had asserted that "the reader counts for at least as much as the book or poem itself . . . through books, the reader may explore his [or her] own nature," and "just as the author is creative, selective, so the reader also is creative" (42). Although our introduction offers a short history of objectivism, clearly there is a long history to its challenge as well.

Diane comments: Part of my own confidence in the rightness of these not-so-new approaches to scholarship comes from vivid memories of undergraduate days in the mid-1970s: In 1974, when I was a student in my first course in ethnography, a seminar offered by the department of anthropology, I read a book titled Never in Anger, *an account of the Inuit peoples by an anthropologist, Jean Briggs, who conducted her research as an honorary daughter of an Inuit family, the only way, she explained, to have been allowed to remain with her subjects. She was thus always already implicated in her research. Her writing style was richly narrative and descriptive. The images that rest with me are of fathers warming their daughters' cold hands on their own bellies, of relations between strangers—like anthropologist and head of family— inevitably being defined bodily, familiarly; Briggs lived and wrote then as "daughter." She also wrote as a writer. Hers was my favorite course reading. Years later, I saw that my penchant for "embodied" writing put me in good company—that of many late-*

twentieth-century feminist writers and scholars, not to mention "the first essayist,"
Montaigne, who "brought his whole body into his writing, inviting his readers to see
his essays not simply as thoughts on a page but as an extension of his physical being,"
according to essayist and editor Robert Atwan (39). Montaigne too was "impatient
with formal philosophy and academic disquisition" and found his way to "a more
flexible and personal discourse" (Atwan 1).

Our professor, however, called Briggs's book "bad anthropology." Why he taught
it, I'm not sure. Most of our texts were in a casebook series, slim, dry as dust except
for the interesting fact of the poison being leached out of manioc and except for Lévi-
Strauss's Tristes Tropiques, *yet another example of "bad anthropology," we were*
warned.

And then, a vindication. Years later I read—and taught, as a central text in my
graduate seminar in American literary nonfiction—Ruth Behar's The Vulnerable
Observer, *where Behar defends just the sort of anthropology I would have practiced*
if I could have continued as an anthropology major. She gives us a new list of writers
(from various fields) to embrace: José Limon, Renate Rosaldo, Kay Redfield Jamison.
By now, as an English professor and writer in just the kind of hybrid, self-inclusive
scholarly mode Behar uses and celebrates, I had already read and discovered the liter-
ary scholars on the list—Carolyn Kay Steedman, Alice Kaplan. But of course, the
borders ostensibly distinguishing disciplines and kinds of scholars blur.

I attribute my hybrid writing and teaching practices in part to my mixed reli-
gious—and mixed-class—heritage, to a historical moment in which "bad" anthro-
pology and "subjective" literary criticism are getting attention from persons both inside
and outside their respective disciplines, and to my reading and classroom histories.
Learning, however, about the professor of psychiatry Kay Redfield Jamison, coauthor
of a standard medical text on manic-depression, I am reminded of another causal agent
in my double-helixed personal and professional identity. Jamison reveals in her mem-
oir The Unquiet Mind *that she herself had the disease about which she is deemed*
expert. My own father studied and treated professionally a disease that he contracted
in his early twenties. He didn't share his history with his patients directly, but he
treated them the more effectively for his own struggle.

HUMANITIES, ARTS, AND SOCIAL SCIENCES: CONTRIBUTORS

The selections included in *Autobiographical Writing Across the Disciplines* position the writer-scholar as an insider-outsider (researcher-informant) in relation to his or her subject and preoccupying themes and questions. The
opening essay of the volume, David Bleich's "Finding the Right Word: Self-
Inclusion and Self-Inscription," describes and demonstrates key practices

and motives of the self-inclusive moment through examining personal-scholarly texts from the fields of linguistics (by Robin Lakoff), social change (by Andrea Dworkin), feminist and Jewish studies and philosophy (by Adrienne Rich and Naomi Scheman), and critical legal theory (by Patricia Williams). Personal scholarship both comes of and fuels interest in writing outside one's ostensible discipline or area of expertise and precipitates true interdisciplinarity and a sense of writing as writing. Bleich quotes Lakoff approvingly, "When the researcher ventures into foreign territory [like the courtroom], it is essential to be engaged, . . . joining the game. . . . True, one loses "objectivity" by taking one side or another, by being involved crucially in the outcome; but only thus is it *possible to truly know*, why certain choices were made, whether change is possible or useful" (emphasis added). Throughout, Bleich reveals his indebtedness to his Yiddish-speaking mother for his commitment to and success at the project of teaching writing and of analyzing language use. Bleich's own practice of self-inclusion shares much with that of the authors he discusses. If, as Lakoff reminds us, "the mission of the university is truth, or knowledge," these essayists, along with the essays in this volume, argue explicitly and implicitly that knowledge and truth in many cases, if not all, depend on human personal involvement, commitment, self-implication, and demarcation.

Carlos Dews's own formative experiences growing up in East Texas male culture help inform his sensitive and illuminating reading of *Hamlet*, in "Gender Tragedies: East Texas Cockfighting and *Hamlet*." Dews explores coming of age in life and discipline while challenging dominant gender, social, regional, sexual, and academic paradigms. He mixes unsent letters and literary analysis with memories of family and cultural dynamics in his native Texas to explore some of the ways in which gender, region, and academic practices are socially constructed.

In "Three Readings of the Wife of Bath," Merrill Black reads her complicated former life as a battered wife through Chaucer's battered character and her own and others' reaction to her. Ultimately Black sees the Wife's tale as a "Chekhovian" victory, with "no clear victor"; "everyone gets something but must give something dear for it." And the Wife of Bath offers Black a substantial something, she argues, an exemplary insistence on "autonomy, . . . freedom of speech, and . . . sexual enjoyment of [one's] partner."

Concentrating on blind characters, blindness as theme, and language over spectacle, blind theater scholar David Richman makes claims to special insights into the verse dramas of William Butler Yeats. And yet Richman also asks himself such trenchant questions as, "Does the fact of my blindness make me old fashioned [in valuing traditional prosody so highly]?" He confesses that his "ear requires the ice or salt, the always varying yet expected beat of traditional lyric meters." "Isn't verse drama itself an old-fashioned form?" he wonders. He concludes that his blindness intensified a "natural" interest in the speaking voice and explores the implications of such a focus in a blind scholar's work given the dominant scholarly emphasis on other issues of performance and textuality.

In "Activist Academic: Memoir of an Ethnic Lit Professor," Bonnie TuSmith, president of MELUS, an organization for the study of multi-ethnic literature of the United States, explains how her life inflects her work, why the ethnic lit professor can't help being an activist. TuSmith evokes the frequent "erasures"—and thus anger—she and others not coded black or white experience in campus and other conversations on "race." She experiences challenges to her pedagogy, to institutional authority, and to professional knowledge, all situations to which she responds not only with frustration but with wit and hope "motivated by the confidence that there are good people who would benefit from . . . mutual exchange through the art of the written word."

Donald Murray, journalist, poet, and founding figure in composition studies' "process" method, writes a powerfully poetic meditation on *voice* in prose and poetry, on the "brown light" dominating his memories of childhood and adolescence and lurking now as a threat that keeps him writing. "Following the Voice of the Draft" is autobiographical in its vignettes and in its metacommentary on the making of those vignettes through the descriptions and pacing and punctuation that add up to *voice*.

Carla Peterson's "Notes of a Native Daughter: Reflections on Identity and Writing" tells the story of Peterson's family's life abroad and retrospectively attributes Peterson's career and present project in African American studies to a summertime visit to her Swiss family home one day by novelist James Baldwin. Estranged from the United States by her father's involvement with the World Health Organization, Peterson only later discerns that many Europeans likely saw her as "a stranger in the village," a positionality she, like Baldwin, comes to accept along with "the fact that this dark and dangerous and unloved stranger [was] part of [her]self forever."

Creative writers are not the only writers striving to find and validate their own voice or voices. In "Journey/man: Hi/s/tory," professor of American history Robert Marcus describes the resistance of his discipline to projects like Martin Duberman's pastiche of traditional historical narrative and experiments in self and his own slowness in making history both more "personally satisfying" and responsive to the lessons of his youth. Marcus, at first "split at the root" by the "cool distance" of his father and the passion of his teacher mother, recalls that his mother's collection of her children's clothes for other elementary school children should have taught her sons that "there is no dividing line between the everyday and what you learn in school"; "education is a form of doing." Retrospectively, Marcus sees how his chosen research projects and even his work in academic administration related to his family history along with changing paradigms in the field of history.

Personal history similarly undergirds academic and writerly practices across the disciplines. Theologian James Cone's *God of the Oppressed* (a chapter of which is reprinted here) reveals some ways in which geographical, cultural, and racial location shaped his theology. Cone asserts, "If Richard Wright is correct in his contention that 'expression springs out of an environment,' then I must conclude that my theological reflections are inseparable from the Bearden [Arkansas] experience." Who Jesus Christ was, the meaning of freedom, liberation, and salvation, God's revelation in the Old Testament, and the meaning of Christ's death are all affected by the fact that Cone was raised where he was, in a town with more whites than blacks but with a strong black church. Cone's method of and desire for writing about these ideas are also affected, of course, by his present situation as a professor of theology. Conversion narratives have perhaps long made the connection between situation and revelation, background and belief, but academic theological theory does not always investigate quite so deeply as Cone does one's early and late perspectives.

In "Beyond Holocaust Theology: Extending a Hand Across the Abyss," feminist philosopher Laura Duhan Kaplan, recalling a visit with a Christian friend to the Jewish cemetery in Worms, tries to move from a focus on suffering and distance to the possibilities of communication across the abyss, of time, of place, of generations, and of religion. She writes of her positions as woman, Jew, moral philosopher, and American, in Germany and beyond.

Sara Ruddick, author of *Maternal Thinking: Toward a Politics of Peace* (from which we reprint the first chapter), at first enjoyed the power and privilege that reason and the objective, impersonal critique bestow in the world of philosophy. In this philosophic world, womanly passion "threatened Reason's calm." By the time she writes *Maternal Thinking*, however, her "love affair" with reason has cooled, while her passions have heated. Moreover, she carefully explains how "maternal work itself demands that mothers think" and such thought—the intellectual capacities developed, the judgments made, the metaphysical attitudes assumed—is worthy of disciplinary attention and is informed as well by disciplinary and professional histories. Thus in *Maternal Thinking* the personal—in this case, being a mother—is inextricably tied to philosophical practice.

"Altered States" by Kwame Anthony Appiah is chapter 8 of *In My Father's House: Africa in the Philosophy of Culture*, a blend of anecdote, memoir, elegy, and—as Appiah himself notes—philosophy, political and intellectual history, biology, sociology, anthropology, and literary criticism and theory. Appiah, a professor of philosophy, views the history of African politics and culture through the perspective of having grown up in Ghana as the multi-affiliated, Western-educated son of a Western-educated man with Asante, Ghanaian, African, Christian, and Methodist identities. In thinking about culture, Appiah maintains, "one is bound to be formed—morally, aesthetically, politically, religiously—by the range of lives one has known." In "Altered States," Appiah writes of the ambiguity and conflict of growing up believing both in constitutional democracy for Ghana and his own Asante heritage.

Eunice Lipton, a feminist art historian, dramatizes her unfolding personal-scholarly response to Manet's famous painting *Olympia* as well as the viewing public's earlier (negative) response. Art history had changed in the wake of Linda Nochlin's controversial dissertation on Courbet, opines Lipton, but just as feminist poet-activist Adrienne Rich in 1976 talked about the necessity of re-vision, Lipton had already been moved to this strategy by none other than the model-painter-icon herself, Olympia/Victorine Meurant, who gazes out from the painting confidently and unflinchingly, refusing to stay serene on the couch. The chapter from *Alias Olympia: A Woman's Search for Manet's Notorious Model and Her Own Desire* excerpted here shows history shaping styles, content, and reception of paintings just as personal histories are revealed as inseparable from Lipton's professional work.

In "Devouring Music: Ruminations of a Composer Who Cooks," Peter Hamlin speaks analogically, enthusiastically comparing—and demystifying—composing and performing music and cooking. He invites the reader to think in a similarly associative mode Hamlin terms "ruminations." Hamlin extols the use of both conscious and sub- or unconscious ruminations in one's practical and theoretical work, concluding, "Composers need to work hard to be successful, but we shouldn't schedule our work time with no margin for a walk in the woods."

Film critic Julie Tharp finds it increasingly difficult to dissociate herself from women who are victims in horror films. The catalytic scene of her self-reflection and critique of film criticism is a professional conference where, after one hour and thirty minutes, the "body count" stands at five women. "Could I disconnect my own body from the body on the screen?" "When the Body Is Your Own: Feminist Film Criticism and the Horror Genre" explains the particular challenges and opportunities for women who are film critics and the resultant form of writing about films, which are largely produced, directed, and plotted by men; which are for male audiences; and in which men predominantly star. Tharp speculates that "many female victims of violence have a better developed analysis of and sensitivity to media violence," thus better understanding "the dynamics of domination enacted there. Identification, in other words, is not inimical to critical thinking."

Deborah Lefkowitz, who writes about as well as creates films, also confronts violence in life and filmic texts. She has lived and worked in Germany and is married to a German, and her Jewish identity, in often uncomfortable relation to place, forms the subject matter for one or more of her personally inflected documentaries. Like Kaplan, who confronts a Jewish cemetery and its silences/absences in the company of a non-Jew, Lefkowitz annotates her memory of an attempted childhood visit to the "yeshiva in Worms where the famous rabbi and Bible commentator Rashi had studied Talmud in the eleventh century."

Michael Dorris's *The Broken Cord* is a factual and informative book about Fetal Alcohol Syndrome (FAS) viewed through the case history of Adam, the author's adopted son. In this excerpt, as in the rest of Dorris's book, the well-known novelist and Dartmouth professor of anthropology (now deceased, sadly, along with his son), cites clinical data about the syndrome. While Dorris gives the facts throughout, however, he also uses his novelistic talent to help dramatize for readers the impact on and symptoms of FAS in his own family. Ultimately, Dorris never lets us forget Adam's and his own familial, ethnic-racial, social, vocational, and medical-clinical situations. In the rest of the book, we see Adam's repetitive behavior, his inability to connect cause and effect and recognize that actions have consequences and individuals have responsibilities; we come to understand Adam's inability to change and Dorris's heartbreak. Adam's condition represents one kind of cognitive lack and Dorris's role as caretaker another. Factual, researched writing combined with autobiographical narrative underscores the limits of each mode alone and their necessary and inevitable interdependence.

Ruth Behar, the "vulnerable observer" who has written so much about and in the form of autobiographical scholarship, is represented here in both our foreword and a reprinted essay, "Juban América," which reveals "the multifaceted construction of Jewish-Cuban identity" while Behar speaks as a "participant-observer" still in the process of forming what she calls a "Juban" identity.

In "Close Encounters with a CSA: The Reflections of a Bruised and Somewhat Wiser Anthropologist," Laura B. DeLind, past president of the Organization for Agriculture, Food, and Human Values, analyzes the allure and failure of a "decentralized, democratized, community-based" farm of which she was a founding member several years ago. Her personal experience with this experiment—where she ran a tractor and rototiller; planted, mulched, and weeded; eliminated pest insects; wrote newsletters; and harvested, washed, and crated pounds of vegetables—teaches us what it taught her: much about community psychology and economics, environmental activism, and the causes of social resistance.

Patricia Williams writes in *The Alchemy of Race and Rights* (chapter 3 of which is reprinted here) that in her analysis of the law, "subject position is everything," a stance contrary to most legal language and practice. "Legal writing presumes a methodology that is highly stylized, precedental, and based on deductive reasoning. . . . [Instead] I would like to write in a way that reveals the intersubjectivity of legal constructions, that forces the reader both to participate in the construction of meaning and to be conscious of that process." "The Death of the Profane" expounds on the lessons found in Williams's exclusion from a Benetton retail store in Manhattan on the basis of her "brown" face. Williams inveighs against both Manhattan store-buzzer scrutiny (the practice of retailers keeping doors locked until and unless a customer judged fit, flush with cash, and safe comes to the plate glass) and the practices of some law reviews intent on banishing certain case specifics.

Brenda Daly's "My Father/My Censor: English Education, Politics, and Status," a version of which first appeared in *Authoring a Life: A Woman's Survival in and through Literary Studies*, is an ars poetica of autobiographical scholarship. It concludes, "Now, whenever I see the kind of academic writing that fails to look within, the kind of impersonal writing that regards the admission of emotion as a weakness, I say to hell with it." A professor of English education at Iowa State University, Daly writes here and elsewhere (in *The Intimate Critique: Autobiographical Literary Criticism* and *Lavish Self-Divisions: The Novels of Joyce Carol Oates*) about the relation of her location as daughter, sister, and incest survivor to her professional locations—as a teacher of a low-status subject in a department that emphasizes literary criticism and theory over teacher training (and denies untenured faculty private offices), as a former secondary-school English teacher, and as an autobiographical literary critic writing about censorship and incest themes in literature.

PHYSICAL SCIENCES, TECHNOLOGY, AND MATHEMATICS: BACKGROUNDS

George Gale dramatizes the autobiographical nature of the scientific endeavor in *Theory of Science: An Introduction to the History, Logic, and Philosophy of Science.* He writes about Antoine Lavoisier, the "father" of modern chemistry, a man among a handful of scientists considered to have instigated a paradigm shift in the thinking about what constituted matter. For those readers not scientists or students of science, who have not opened a chemistry book since high school, a bit of background is needed, though extensive knowledge of chemistry is not needed for grasping the most important point: that Lavoisier drew conclusions inconsistent with the prevailing views on matter because of who he was, because of his personal history.

Until the eighteenth century, when Lavoisier conducted his experiments on combustion, ideas about matter were shaped by Aristotle's theory that four basic elements—fire, earth, air, and water—comprised all that existed. Scientists then judged the composition of matter by observing closely its physical characteristics: Was it hot or cold? Wet or dry? Some combination of these? According to Aristotelian theory, burning objects decomposed, transforming into their elemental parts. Lavoisier and peers believed, for example, that when charcoal burned, three elements would be left: earth, water, and a fiery quality called phlogiston. The prevailing theory, as well as logic and common sense, said that the resultant ashy earth would be less than the original charcoal. However, what Lavoisier discovered was this: that the earthy substance left after he burned sulfur *weighed more* than the original sulfur. This led Lavoisier to conclude that rather than decomposing, the substances must have combined together.

Further experiments ultimately led to the theory that matter is made up of many more elements than the early Greeks had identified, and it consists of various combinations of elements in the form of molecules. Lavoisier also moved chemistry in the direction of quantification—of measuring—from an earlier reliance on simply observing qualities.

What is important to us in the story is less what Lavoisier discovered than why he apparently made the discoveries he did. Lavoisier happened to weigh the sulfur before and after the combustion took place not because it was an expected part of the experimental process but because he was not really a chemist at all by formal training. Instead, he was a businessman who directed the production of gunpowder for the French National Arsenal (and who, by the way, sold gunpowder to Americans during the American Revolution). To facilitate manufacturing and distributing gunpowder, Lavoisier built a superior weight balance, something he used eventually in his experiments in combustion.

Gale relates that Lavoisier's formal training was in business and law: "This preparation had him set up with an expectation that scientific results would have their own 'balance sheets'" (127). Lavoisier's chemistry training came from sitting in on lectures and observing demonstrations set up by Pouelle, infamous for demonstrating "empirical effects which were opposed and, indeed, contradictory to the theoretical conceptions being espoused by the lecturer" (127). Gale argues that because Lavoisier was not a chemistry student per se, he was not pressured to adhere to the dominant paradigm in his own experiments. Gale concludes: "Lavoisier's business orientation as [predisposed to] balanced quantitative representations, his iconoclastic and informal education [under] Routelle, and his thorough grounding in the empirical necessities of weight measurement together provided sufficient conceptual impetus to propel his eventual drive against phlogiston theory" (129). Gale's story may well demonstrate what we mean when we say that science, like other disciplines or ways of knowing, is "socially constructed." While in the popular realm, "scientific" has become synonymous with "objective," and while scientists and their field have often been dedicated to maintaining a presumed "objectivity," there is much—and we do not mean simply inaccurate instruments or procedures—on which science relies that is something else.

In the last thirty years, feminists, social scientists, philosophers, and scientists themselves have vigorously critiqued the conventional notion of all science as objective, empirically based verification of "fact."[9] As Muriel Lederman observes (in her essay in this volume), science is a human activity, and as long as it is human, it can never be completely objective. Science is also a social activity. It is done within the context of society at large as well as smaller societies and groups of scientists. In *Manufactured Knowledge*, Karin Knorr-Cetina similarly explains the various layers of subjectivity in a supposedly objective endeavor. She writes that the "products of science are not only decision-impregnated, they are also decision-impregnating, in the sense that they point to new problems and predispose their solution" (6). The direction of a scientist's research, therefore, is determined by the context in which it is undertaken, the direction that the research has taken up until that point, and the framing of the research questions. The conclusions drawn then determine the next step to be taken by subsequent research/researchers.

Knorr-Cetina claims that we need to "bring space and time back into scientific operations" (33). The shape of research is affected not only by values and personalities but by such things as the equipment and funding that are or are not available and the particular emphases within a given research laboratory. Since the turn of the century, scientific research has taken place mostly within business and industry or in university laboratories funded by business and industry or state or federal government. Because the general public still believes the scientific endeavor to be objective and even altruistic, it/we may miss the ways in which self-interest can be embedded in research that produces wealth for the companies that fund it.

Despite critiques inside and outside the scientific community, the notion that science is objective dominates. Similarly, scientific writing itself (something both of and outside the research) is seen as objective. Oddly, even at those times when the objectivity of the endeavor is questioned, the structure and language of the writing are coded objective. Rhetorician Charles Bazerman tells us that "scientific discourse appears to hide itself. . . . to write science is commonly thought not to write at all, just simply to record the natural facts" (14). But, continues Bazerman, "the human mind stands between the reality it perceives and the language it speaks in" (25). And yet many a scientific article seems to purge the twin endeavors of science and writing of the human mind, of all humanness. In spite of the critiques by feminists, sociologists, and others, the scientific research article and its reception have changed little since the 1800s — except that the articles have become longer, more technically detailed and sophisticated, more inaccessible to the general reader.

Science writing — and science itself — were not always like this. Until the nineteenth century, science existed outside the formal university setting.

Scientists and researchers were funded by individual patrons rather than institutions (Kaysen 155). In tracing scientific writings prior to the eighteenth century, Bazerman has found that these earlier writings were largely descriptive. The scientist recorded what he had done and what he saw, expressing freely his surprise or delight at what nature could produce. Scientists "created marvelous effects" (Bazerman 66). They manipulated nature and then watched what happened, recording their observations in rich detail. These reports frequently included personal narratives. They were a bit like recipes, suggesting "to achieve the effects that I witnessed, follow these steps," with the implication that anyone might produce similar results or make a similar product if he or she followed the directions (although it was unlikely during this period that many "she's" would be reading and replicating scientific experiments).

At one point during the evolution of science and the writing of the scientific article, the goals shifted. Toward the end of the eighteenth century, according to Bazerman, "the definition of experiment move[d] from any made or done thing, to an intentional investigation, to a test of a theory, to finally a proof of, or evidence for, a claim" (65). It would seem that several factors contributed to the shift in tone and purpose of research as well as writing.

Bazerman, reading articles published from 1665 to 1800 in the first scientific journal in English, *The Philosophic Transactions of the Royal Society in London*, noted that until 1800, only 5 to 20 percent of the articles contained experiments and experimental results. The articles were instead quite varied, with the emphasis on "human accomplishment"; one even printed an interview with Mozart. Into the nineteenth century, 39 percent of the articles gave accounts of experiments, and "the language of proof replace[d] the language of discovery" (Bazerman 68). Writers' goals now accorded with what Francis Hauksbee expressed, that "the greatest Satisfaction and Demonstration that can be given for the Credit of any Hypothesis, is, That the Experiment is made to prove the same, agree with it in all respects, without force" (qtd. in Bazerman 67).

Bazerman suggests that it was Henry Oldenberg, the founder of *The Philosophic Transactions*, who was responsible for the shift. Oldenberg believed that science needed to be "agonistically structured" (Bazerman 139). Certainly Oldenberg stressed the importance of proof and verification because he believed such an emphasis would stimulate scientific activity and further science. Could he also have believed such an emphasis would stimulate the sales of his journal? The greater emphasis on verification and proof resulted in more interesting disputes. In any case, the emphasis that Olden-berg required in the articles he published embodied a subjective preference for a certain epistemology over another—a preference for argument as a means of discovering truth rather than for playfulness, accident, wonder, or intuition as valid ways of and routes to knowing.

Sir Isaac Newton's story, like Lavoisier's, is worth repeating. Working in optics, Newton prepared to report on his findings in *The Philosophic Trans-actions* in a letter addressed to the Royal Society of London. In it, Newton speaks of his discoveries as facts even though "the events that made these facts visible to Newton occurred in a private laboratory as the result of speculative ponderings and active experimental manipulations" (Bazerman 90). This letter was read to the Society. To make the findings convincing, Newton established his own personal authority through a "discovery nar-rative" replicating his own process, which would have put his listeners into the moment of discovery and made it seem as if the discovery was "natu-rally found" (95–96).

After the letter was read, however, key members of the Society criti-cized Newton harshly—Sir Robert Moray, the first president of the Royal Society, as well as Robert Hooke and Ignace Pardies. Bazerman reveals that after a series of responses, all met by more criticism, Newton gave up. He didn't publish his findings in *Transactions* or any other journal until he finally published them in *Opticks* and *Principia* (119). When they were published, the form he chose for them was completely different from his letter to the Royal Society. Leaving out the "story" of his discovery, Newton's account is an argument with propositions supported by proof. His opening sen-tence reads, "My Design in this book is not to explain the properties of light by Hypothesis, but to propose and prove them by Reason and Experi-ment" (qtd. in Bazerman 121). Newton conformed to the newer conven-tions of scientific discourse that were becoming the norm. Many would say, though, that he sacrificed a great deal in letting go the wonder and immediacy of his earlier letter.

A contemporary U.S. scientist had experiences that could be described as similar to that of Newton—Barbara McClintock, the botanist and ge-neticist who received the Nobel Prize in science for her work on genetic control and regulation in maize. Her story is fully elucidated in a best-selling book by feminist historian of science Evelyn Fox Keller, *A Feeling for the Organism*. Keller tells us that after teaching botany for five years at the University of Missouri, McClintock set up, with the help of the Carnegie Institute, what was to become a permanent laboratory and research site for her at Cold Spring Harbor, Long Island, New York. For years, McClintock grew corn, studying it at every stage of the growth process. She studied every part of the corn, every cell of every section that she grew. She looked not only for what caused genetic changes in corn but also for the places in the genes that signaled and initiated these changes. Over the years, McClintock gave a variety of papers in symposia held at Cold Spring Harbor. In almost every instance, except toward the end of her career when other discoveries in molecular biology affirmed McClintock's, her findings were dismissed and even ridiculed. McClintock was particularly dispirited at a 1956 symposium, where, Keller reports, a colleague commented, "It may be interesting, but I understand it's kind of mad" (140). Another unsympathetic colleague described McClintock as "just an old bag who'd been hanging around Cold Spring Harbor for years" (141). Like Newton, after repeated criticism and rejection, McClintock stopped publishing anything but her yearly reports to the Carnegie Institute. She spoke to no one about her work except to a few appreciative colleagues—Evelyn Witkin, Royal Brink, and Peter Peterson.

Sexism was certainly the cause of much of the disparagement and indifference McClintock experienced on behalf of her work, as she was consistently the lone woman in the lab or at conferences or symposia. Yet the main cause of McClintock's marginalization among her colleagues and within her profession, according to Keller, was the fact that other geneticists simply did not understand what she was doing and seeing. It was as though she spoke a different language and could see in ways not apparent to others' eyes; her vision of what was happening deep in the corn cell was "internal." Keller writes:

> Through years of intense and systematic observation and interpretation (she called it "integrating what you saw"), McClintock had built a theoretical vision, a highly articulated image of the world within the cell. As she watched the corn plants grow, examined the patterns on the leaves and kernels, looked down the microscope at their chromosomal structure, she saw directly into that ordered world. The "Book of Nature" was to be read simultaneously by the eyes of the body and those of the mind. The spots [she] saw on the kernels of corn were ciphers in a text that, because of her understanding of their genetic meaning, she could read directly. For her, the eyes of the body *were* the eyes of the mind. Ordinary language could not begin to convey the full structure of the reading that emerged. (148–49; emphasis added)

McClintock was called not only an "old bag," but a mystic. While she used scientific method and called what she discovered logical, what and how she learned went beyond any objective method or verification of fact. She herself spoke of getting down inside the organism and looking around; her knowledge was intimate. "In comparison with the ingenuity of nature, our scientific intelligence seems pallid," Keller concludes. We do need other means of knowing. Far from detracting from the scientific endeavor, our subjective humanity can help—our quirky visions, our emotions, our relationships, our predispositions, perhaps our subconscious and our dreams, certainly our "feeling for an organism." How many scientists have made their discoveries because of intuition or a dream? Albert Einstein, Robert Oppenheimer, and Niels Bohr have all advocated other intelligences than the linear, objective mind doing business as usual. And yet the contemporary scientific article still privileges at least the appearance of objectivity and of expected practice.

Keller proposes that there ought always to be a "reciprocal relationship between the agent and object of knowledge" and has hope for objectivity—not "objectivity," she says, which is subjectivity masked as objectivity, but what she terms "strong objectivity." She means by this *reflexivity*, the ability of a researcher to look at his or her own socially situated research and decipher the interplay and impact of human(s) and research subject and content. With "real" or "strong" objectivity, the observer or reader weighs and factors in the subjective context(s) of researcher and research situation. Researcher and audience, then, can become more fully aware of the influence of converging subjectivities. Such work would be honest, reliable, and informative.

Educator Parker Palmer also agrees that "knowledge of truth requires a personal dialogue between the knower and the known, a dialogue in which the knower listens to the world with obedience" (*To Know as We Are Known*). Such a notion, Parker acknowledges, "smacks of anthropomorphism, animism, *argumentum ad hominem*, and assorted other insults to the objectivist sensibility" (64). Yet "in a world devastated by the objectification of everything, including ourselves, the 'primitive' way of personal knowing may turn out to be quite advanced. Perhaps we are ready now to see the wisdom of treating the known as a living self . . . rather than an inert thing over which we can exercise our flawed mastery, our fatal control" (64). To Palmer the act of knowing is relational.

Consider the implications. Researchers may think they know the subject of their research but by listening to what they are studying, they may shift direction. What are the consequences of a researcher allowing the subject to suggest a conclusion or giving over conclusions in favor of contradictory observations? What if what we see expands rather than always narrows to a conclusion, or what we discover can never be verified and we document only confusion? Could it be that we will then be closer to truth and to reality and not further from them?

Most assuredly writing about such processes and acts of knowing requires a different stance, voice, and sense of purpose. And indeed writers in this volume turn to a kind of science and science writing that affirms subjectivities and the productive interaction of knower and known.

PHYSICAL SCIENCES, TECHNOLOGY, AND MATHEMATICS: CONTRIBUTORS

Naomi Weisstein's "Adventures of a Woman in Science," a painful but empowering journey in which Weisstein rediscovers that women are not welcome in science and that the race is rigged, glosses the significance of three social psychology experiments—the experimenter bias experiments, inner physiological state vs. social context, and the obedience experiments (including Milgram's). Her own autobiographical professional history has implications with regard to scientific practice and reveals that methodologies and definitions of excellence and identification of those considered excellent in the profession are not ideologically unbiased. In particular, a study of human behavior must take into account all of the contexts through which subjects as well as researchers themselves move.

Muriel Lederman's "Through the Looking Glass: A Feminist's Life in Biology" charts not only her realization of the ways even "bench work" or laboratory protocols involve and indeed require subjectivity and improvisation but her movement away from laboratory pleasures to the interrogation of objectivity—objectivism—that she began through feminist discussion groups and now makes the centerpiece of most of her university courses.

In her book *Mapping Fate* (the first chapter of which appears here), Alice Wexler writes about both a hereditary disease once known as Huntington's chorea and her family, which has suffered from the disease, her mother succumbing early and her sister and herself holding a fifty-fifty chance of carrying the fatal gene. In dramatic and research-based writing, Wexler explores how her father and sister themselves moved the science of discovering a genetic marker for Huntington's along, a situation that then made possible contemplation of a difficult personal medical option—testing for the gene. In the end, this story may be said to speak to any family with secrets and illness and to the miracles and modern dilemmas of current advances in genetics and in medicine more generally.

Perri Klass, a pediatrician who writes often for a wide audience, describes in *A Not Entirely Benign Procedure* how science and life overlapped for her as a student at Harvard Medical School. In the chapter reprinted here, "A Textbook Pregnancy," Klass offers the double vision of examiner and examined pregnant woman, detailing how her knowledge of both roles changes her work and attitude in the other.

In *The Children's Machine: Rethinking School in the Age of the Computer* (a chapter of which appears here), mathematician Seymour Papert combines educational incidents from his life and the psychologist Piaget's with incidents from the lives of children in contemporary schools and represents an alternative to the method favored by the dominant "scientific" school of thought critiqued or revamped elsewhere in this volume. Papert calls his practice and what he asks of and recognizes in children "personal thinking," the title of this chapter.

The volume closes with a bibliography of books and articles excerpted from or referred to in our introduction and selected other recommended texts that demonstrate or authorize the inclusion of autobiography into scholarship across the disciplines. We hope the volume as a whole, then, will serve teachers and researchers as an expansive source of models and reasons for the new self-inclusive scholarship. The autobiographically inflected ways we inevitably, deliberately, and creatively read, write, and undertake research must be brought forward if we are to achieve Evelyn Fox Keller's "strong objectivity," a complex but readable emotional and rational truth telling, in the academy and for our rich and troubled world.

NOTES

1. Full citations for the parenthetical references in this introduction and for most of the references in its notes may be found in the bibliography at the end of this volume.
2. See Bleich in this volume.
3. Adrienne Rich, for example, in a well-known essay, "Notes Toward a Politics of Location," specifically called for writing informed by "lived experience, particu-

larity . . . life long facts . . . the politics of location" (215). Rachel Blau DuPlessis calls for "situated writing," and Mary K. DeShazer, in "Creation and Relation: Teaching Essays by T. S. Eliot and Adrienne Rich," maps the ways in which Rich and others reject Eliot's traditional valuing of an artistic method of "self-extinction," "separation, detachment," in which "only the 'bad writer' becomes 'personal'" (DeShazer 115). DeShazer resists disciplining the self to remain out of the work area because such a border is in fact illusory. Self-inclusion is the always already of research and writing. In fact, it occurs to us that at the core of subjectivity in the work of all disciplines is the fact that all disciplines involve writing. Since the act of writing of necessity entails reshaping, valuing, and constituting knowledge, subjectivity has a central role in all disciplines. See also Sandra Harding, "Who Knows? Identities and Feminist Epistemology"; Gayle Green and Coppelia Kahn, eds., *Changing Subjects: The Making of Feminist Literary Criticism*; Mary Belenky et al., *Women's Ways of Knowing: The Development of Self, Voice, and Mind*; and Carol Gilligan, *In a Different Voice: Psychological Theory and Women's Development.*

4. This socially constructed/constrained and yet often desired mode, according to Thomas J. Farrell, "seems at times to obfuscate the boundary between the self and author and the subject of discourse" and appears "open-ended, generative, and process-oriented" (910).

5. And yet now, as Liz McMillen points out in an article in the *Chronicle of Higher Education*, even legal scholars are publishing books in which law is viewed as narrative, an enterprise "part of the newfound and widespread scholarly interest in narrative, which has made a comeback in literary studies, history, anthropology, even economics." "The notion of telling a story is very prevalent in our culture today," agrees Peter Brooks, humanities scholar and author of *Law's Stories: Narrative and Rhetoric in the Law* (A10).

6. See Diane P. Freedman, "Border Crossing as Method and Motif in Contemporary Feminist Writing," in *An Alchemy of Genres* (Charlottesville: University Press of Virginia, 1992).

7. See the following writers for further definitions and discussions of the characteristics of academic discourse: David Bartholomae, "Inventing the University," in *When a Writer Can't Write*, ed. Mike Rose (New York: Guilford, 1985), 134–65; Linda Flower, "Negotiating Academic Discourse," *Reading to Write Report* No. 10/*Technical Report* No. 29 (Berkeley: Center for the Study of Writing at the University of California, Berkeley, and Carnegie Mellon); Susan Peck MacDonald, "Problem Definition in Academic Writing," *College English* 48, no. 9 (1987): 315–30; and Patricia Bizzell, *Academic Discourse and Critical Consciousness* (Pittsburgh: University of Pittsburgh Press, 1992).

8. See Sir Philip Sidney, "An Apology for Poetry" (1595); W. E. B. Du Bois, *The Souls of Black Folk* (1903); Walt Whitman, Preface to 1855 *Leaves of Grass*; Charles Olson, "Projective Verse," *Poetry New York* 3 (1950); Clifford Geertz, "Blurred Genres," in *Local Knowledge*; James Clifford, *Writing Culture: The Poetics and Poli-*

tics of Ethnography (Berkeley: University of California Press, 1986); and Renato Rosaldo, "Grief and a Headhunter's Rage."

9. See, for example, Susan Bordo, *The Flight to Objectivity: Essays on Cartesianism and Culture* (Albany: SUNY Press, 1987); Evelyn Fox Keller, *Reflections on Gender and Science* (New Haven: Yale University Press, 1984); and Genevieve Lloyd, *The Man of Reason* (Minneapolis: University of Minnesota Press, 1984).

Language and Literature

DAVID BLEICH

Finding the Right Word:

Self-Inclusion and

Self-Inscription

It is becoming more important for academics to include part of our self-knowledge in work we present for collective endorsement. Many of us want to speak more deeply from personal experience, to add this dimension to the habits of scholarly citation and critical interpretation. Our desire for self-inclusion has led to new genres of writing, new styles of knowledge. We are starting to integrate into professional writing our changing, complicated senses of who we are. Perhaps we can feel more comfortable with "professing" if academic ways of speaking and writing feel connected to the underlying styles of our language use, which have rich affective and intersubjective features not usually found in academic writing. Some of us would like the comfort of affectively relaxed social exchanges, found ordinarily among family members and friends, to be a regular part of scholarly, critical, and scientific exchanges. We have also tried to find new ways for the stories of individual lives to participate publicly in collective interests. Toward these ends, we have begun to include autoethnographic genres in our contributions to academic publications. We have begun to include ourselves in what we know by writing ourselves into what we say.

I had developed academically as a literary-response and hermeneutics "theorist," but that did not seem enough to be called an identity. Now I feel more satisfied with calling myself a writing teacher, but I notice that I use this term *writing teacher* unconventionally enough so that people may not think of me as having that identity. I am really: a student and teacher of writing and language use as they appear in all texts; I teach and learn in a university, but I try to reach anyone who is interested by writing books and essays for public forums. In writing this essay I want to present a basis in autoethnographic reflection and in the study of other people's work for explaining my version of the "writing teacher" identity, to discover what thoughts others in my position may have had. I address those who teach writing, language, literature; I also address those interested in these subjects but who include themselves in a variety of related academic projects.

My mother taught me how to write. Not directly. Not early. But eventually. She did it by communicating what it meant to find and use "the right word": the word that reached you and made you pay attention; the word that changed how you thought; the word that made you want to feel your heartbeat and your backbone when you speak and write. In college, I was surprised to learn that one can get a job teaching others to find and use the right words.

My mother was an immigrant and spoke English with an accent. When I was a boy, she told me to read but I did not take the advice seriously. She did not nag me; she did remind me often. She did not teach me to write until many years into my professional life, after I had written things about which she did not care. When she read an early essay of mine citing the literary responses of an undergraduate student—the topic was lying—she said, "You made this up, didn't you?" My mother read my essay about self-deception and the psychology of lying and said that is what I did. Her view of academic life was that it was mendacious, another understanding (of her view and of the fact) I did not achieve until many years after she reacted to my essay. I started trying to write differently after I understood better what she was getting at. In *Woman Hating*, Andrea Dworkin says,

> Academics lock books in a tangled web of mindfuck and abstraction. The notion is that there are ideas, then art, then somewhere else, unrelated, life. . . . Because there is contempt for the process of writing, for writing as a way of discovering meaning and truth, and for reading as a piece of that same process, we destroy with regularity the few serious writers we have.
>
> Those of us who love reading and writing believe that being a writer is a sacred trust. It means telling the truth. It means being incorruptible. It means not being afraid and never lying. . . .
>
> To keep the sacred trust of the writer is simply to respect the people and to love the community. To violate that trust is to abuse oneself and do damage to others. (24–25)

My mother and Andrea Dworkin thought the same things about academic writing—mindfuck and abstraction. But my mother treated her thoughts with more resignation and the mendacious thoughts of others with a defiant sarcasm. She did not allow herself to get as angry about this situation as Dworkin did. She read all the time, all the time. She loved reading, and believed, like Dworkin, that reading put one in touch with the truth, regardless of lies that were told. When she read the late Meg Greenfield in *Newsweek*, she said (in Yiddish), "She writes with backteeth [the ones that crush and grind]." My translation: Meg Greenfield prepared the food of experience thoroughly for our digestion. Writing is cooking, and has to be done with the same sense of responsibility and duty.

My mother taught me how to write by not getting angry at me, the academy that paid my salary, or "the world" that produced lies and pain. She taught by speaking, by finding the "right word" for everything and everyone, especially those who deserved it. She knew the right words in Yiddish and in English and she taught them to me. In Yiddish, however, the right word sounded better and more authoritative than it did in English. It took me a long time to learn to write because I did not know that I knew the right words in Yiddish but not in English. I am still learning, as from Dworkin, how to find the right word in English. I am still learning from the Yiddish language, now more deliberately.

Sometimes, when you tell a story of your life in this informal way, it seems like either bullshit itself or secondary bullshit, or it makes academic writing seem like bullshit. The writers I discuss in this essay teach that this separation and threat of insincerity need not materialize. By urging us to speak more responsively to those outside the academy, they help us to be better teachers inside our classrooms.

These writers led me to speak in public the way my mother spoke in private. They communicate in a forceful, "backteeth" style regarding a fundamental unfairness in the basic arrangements of society. This is one of the meanings I read in Dworkin's contempt for public lying. Mindfuck and abstraction are derogations of language that amount to political practices that harm most of society. I learned my mother's values through the combination of childhood memories and adult contact, as I was her principal custodian for the last fifteen years of her life. When I informed her (because she did not remember any more) that she turned ninety years old, she said, continuing to find the right word, "That's ridiculous." Her personal generosity, her disciplined values about eating and cooking, her self-sufficiency, her impatience with being dependent on me, her wisecracks communicated her resignation to a situation that should have been different. She walked up the hill until she broke her hip. She walked again until she had a stroke. She ate her dinner until she could not swallow. Her remarkable perseverance is a trait she shared with my father, and it represented, in part, a value she got from being a Jew.

To write, to speak, to use the language, native or adopted, was an inroad to assimilation and to the retention of one's historic identities. That the main language was Yiddish helped dramatize its double role and the flexibility of language use as a means to hold many identities in a heterogeneous society. "The Wandering Jew"? At once a slander, a description of how to survive, and a statement of what happens to all people who necessarily "wander" from one stage of life to the next. There is something to celebrate, I learned from parents who as Jews longed not to fear being public citizens, if you can make your language tell the truth and win you citizenship at the same time. That is what the right word does.

I found myself more deeply involved in this perspective when I found (thanks to Sandra Runzo) Adrienne Rich, who wrote the following in 1972:

> I know that the action . . . of becoming that person who puts signs on paper and invokes the collaboration of a reader, encounters a corresponding check: in order to write I have to believe that there is someone willing to collaborate subjectively, as opposed to a grading machine out to get me for mistakes in spelling and grammar. . . . The whole question of trust as a basis for the act of reading or writing has only opened up since we began trying to educate those who have every reason to mistrust literary culture. For young adults trying to write seriously for the first time in their lives, the question, "Whom can I trust?" must be an underlying boundary to be crossed before real writing can occur. ("Teaching Language in Open Admissions" 64)

At first I read this passage as part of the "movement" toward collaboration, but gradually I felt something different. Here, before political consciousness was widely recognized, Rich is portraying the lived experiences of the disenfranchised coming to school for the first time: a class of people trying to assimilate by coming to our classrooms. People lie (prevaricate) in writing because there has been a failure of trust. My mother must have thought that academics don't trust each other, nor do they trust the public; that is why they lie. Collaboration is an ideal: the practical issue is trust. When my mother said the right word to me, it was because she could trust me, a child, to understand its "rightness."

Cultural assimilation is the process of becoming included into a "mainstream" way of life. It could mean "becoming like everyone else"; mostly it means achieving the status of the established classes of citizens. Self-

inclusion could mean knocking at the door; it could mean entering without knocking; but it could also mean "what applies to others, applies to me
too." It means, "I am responsible for myself, you for yourself, and we for
each other." In coming out as a lesbian and as a Jew,[1] Rich becomes more
candid and forceful and the codevelopment of self-inclusion and political understanding stand out more as themes. Rich's essays are a model of
how to think out of and for oneself, yet also to translate those thoughts
into principles and values whose general applicability create their status as
knowledge.

In one of her later essays, Rich included herself in Rabbi Hillel's formulation of ethical principle, which she then enlarged. She summarizes the tasks
of speaking out and self-inclusion by adding a question to the frequently
quoted three questions asked by Hillel, "If I am not for myself, who is? If I
am only for myself, what am I? and If not now, when?" The appended question is "If not with others, how?" It is the title of an essay that comments
politically on the androcentric Jewish tradition, en-Rich-ing it. However,
before this 1985 essay, the theme of each person's implication in the lives
of other individuals and groups was present in her work. Rich is among
those[2] who regard the collective character of language[3] to account for language use. Rich has combined the priority of ethical collaboration with the
assimilative roles in the study of language. She is thinking through the task
of assimilation and changing the society into which she is to assimilate.

Rich recreates the perspective of what is ordinary to writing—the process of internalizing the collective characteristics of language use.[4] However, this fundamental, prelinguistic process is challenged by the "control"
elements in school that put students in a position to be trapped by the
linguistic cosmeticians—the grammar-and-grades philosophy of writing
pedagogy. Rich rejects the inhibiting teaching conventions by viewing the
scenes of writing in terms of their emotional bases of trust and their social
bases of subjective collaboration.

Rich describes how students achieve this understanding by coming to
"some frontier of self-determination" as part of the project of distinguishing what is indigenous to the self and what is the "not-me." This is the
process of assimilation.[5] It is both an individual and a collective project; it
has been demonstrated, retold, and reviewed repeatedly in the recent past
how various groups of the disenfranchised struggle to find, in spite of the
monotonous enforcement of Standard English, the idiom to correspond
to the thoughts taking the form of many languages in their minds. In the
teaching of writing, Rich observes, one finds the fundamentals of teaching:

Finally, as to trust: I think that, simple as it may seem, it is worth saying: a fundamental belief in the students is more important than anything
else. . . . This fundamental belief is not a sentimental matter: it is a very demanding matter of realistically conceiving the student where he or she is,
and at the same time never losing sight of where he or she *can* be. . . . What
interests me in teaching is less the emergence of the occasional genius than
the overall finding of language by those who did not have it and by those
that have been used and abused to the extent that they lacked it. ("Teaching" 66, 67–68)

Writing and the teaching of writing have in common the need for feelings of trust, the precondition for the "finding of language." Students need
ties to society, to the teacher, and to other students, while teachers and students need to find trust by combining the personal and the professional
in their relationships with one another. Relations of trust are the basis on
which people find language or "voice," as some have put it. The cycle of language and trust connects teaching, language, knowledge, and society and
describes how writing and the teaching of writing contribute to a revised
view of academic life: the abstract ideals of knowledge and truth are present
but are moving out of traditional academic ideology toward a situation in
which there is no separation of teaching and scholarship. Because of the
"flagrant deficiencies" of postsecondary pedagogical practice, one's task in
teaching is to fashion the "tools and weapons for those who may live on
into a new integration":

Language is such a weapon, and what goes with language: reflection, criticism, renaming, creation. The fact that our language itself is tainted by
the quality of our society means that in teaching we need to be acutely
conscious of the kind of tool we want our students to have available to
understand how it has been used against them, and to do all we can to in-
sure that language will not someday be used by them to keep others silent
and powerless.[6] (68)

Rich had been kept "silent and powerless" until circumstances let her
"out." To have gone through marriage and parenthood, to have understood
and publicly identified the meaning of lesbian existence in this society, to
have inquired into the sense in which she was "split at the root" into a Jew
and a Christian, to have added to Rabbi Hillel's perspective on social ethics
—these are examples of "tool-using" in language. Rich's writing is her
weapon in society—the last weapon before weaponry. By inscribing her

own life in her political pedagogy Rich has cast poetry and essay writing as instruments of speaking out and joining in. My mother did not use the term *weapon,* but the right word is also the word as the truth and as a weapon, the one weapon that fights but keeps the peace and the conversation alive.

Rich's autoethnographic essays show the slow pace of self-inclusion. The processes of identifying herself truthfully changed her from one kind of person into another. The processes of self-disclosure were a combination of individual choice, social necessity, and growth. My reading of Rich entered this same slow process in my life, but it had not occurred to me until recently that I was also "split at the root." The "mixed" marriage I refer to was between my parents, a man and a woman. My mother and father were differently oriented as gendered people, as Jews, as social figures, and a strand of my development has been to mix two truthful views of life and society, a project I undertook by exploring subjectivity and socializing it as a pedagogical process.

My father, also an immigrant, celebrated America. He thought that while many non-Jews were hostile to Jews, many were not. But he did not live with a sense of danger. My mother liked America—but only because of the relief it provided from the incessant Jew-hating in her native Poland. The difference in my parents' views was fundamental. My mother thought my father's optimism resulted from his head being in the sand; my father thought my mother just wouldn't let herself enjoy the freedom. But behind this difference was the difference in gendered expectations that could not be reduced to a balance of equally valid perspectives. A man could be optimistic; for a woman, it was much harder. In spite of the obvious equality of my parents, my mother had a lower status, and she was treated that way often enough to keep it constantly on her mind.

My father did not learn English as well as my mother did; he didn't think he'd need it to survive (he was wrong).[7] My mother learned English well because it was needed, yes, but also because she understood the social meaning of knowing the right word. It was a key to survival and as she passed it along to her sons, it was a key to prosperity. But for her, as for Rich, for Dworkin, and for Lakoff and Williams, as I will consider, it was a model of emancipation without war or revolution. Whether this is a "Jewish" trait, or a trait of the disenfranchised, or both, or more, I leave for other discussions.

One thing is clear though. The "right word" is not all that important in most academic writing; it does not seem as important as it does in literature, even though it is as important.[8] For Noam Chomsky's work in linguistics, "finding the right word" was not important; in fact, it was not part of that work, which he defined as conceptualizing language competence. Finding the right word was part of performance, which he said was not eligible for inclusion in the science of linguistics. Following Chomsky, the mainstream custodians of the academic subject of language intensified its identity as a conventionally academic (and distant from experience) subject—linguistics, which tried to devise formal grammars and their logical structures. Even though the spring 1995 presentation of the language-as-Chomsky-sees-it on public television was comprehensible, the substance of what linguists do following this conception of language was not presented. Rather, the questions that Chomsky reported as having instigated his own thinking were repeated during each hourly discussion. These questions were of one sort: why are some language forms permissible, but others, meaning the same thing but following a different rule of formation, are not? For example, one can say "a big red balloon" but not "a red big balloon."[9] The study of language competence is the study of the set of mental operations each person must (according to Chomsky) already have "wired in" in order to comprehend both the rules and their exceptions at a very early age, regardless of which language is spoken. Although Chomsky's is not the only way of studying language, it carries scientific weight as an academic subject.

Others studying language have challenged Chomsky only indirectly.[10] Their proponents have renounced an adversarial style.[11] An especially appealing challenge is Robin Lakoff's, whose many works present a discourse about language habitually using gestures of self-inscription into the subject matter.[12] To her, linguistics was performance, but that term finally is the wrong word for her sense of this subject. By helping us answer our question, Why have you committed yourself to this project?,[13] Lakoff presents a subject that does not divide itself into higher and lower parts. Linguistics is one subject for her, and her own story is part of that subject. Here is one of her more recent self-inscriptions, given in her book about the politics of language, *Talking Power*:

> I probably found my way into the academic world, some twenty-five years ago, as an escape from the anxieties of the real one. The study of language—two removes from that disturbing reality—seemed particularly suitable for this purpose. At first I thought I could play it safe as a transformational syntactician, whose only concern was the arrangement of words in sentences. But in time, several of my colleagues and I were forced to rec-

ognize that sentence structure was not autonomous: you had to know who was speaking, under what social circumstances, and what their assumptions were, before it was possible to assign appropriate form to a sentence, or relate a sentence's form accurately to a meaning. No longer, then, was language a safe refuge.

But we did not know how far we had to go: how much of real experience had to be encoded in linguistic rules. . . . it was . . . clear that not everything we know or could discern about the real context of language use was explicitly encodable into specific linguistic choices.

[In the] late 1960's and early 1970's . . . I realized that [the connection between gender and syntactic decisions] transcended the ivory tower. They arose out of, and gave birth to, disparities in power between the sexes, restricting the options of both.

I tend to get interested in linguistic behavior only after I have been thrust, generally willy-nilly, into direct experience of it. So I got interested in therapeutic discourse because of my involvement in that process; in the language of the courtroom out of a stint on jury duty; and in the discourse of academe, through being around universities for all my adult life, as student and faculty member.

It seems clearer and clearer to me that we cannot understand language except through direct experience, using it or having it used to us. Unless our words make a difference in the outcome, we cannot make valid judgments. Too often the sociolinguist or the pragmaticist still attempt to play the games of the ivory tower, to study some aspect of real language use "objectively." If it's a form of language with which we are all familiar anyway, like conversation, there is probably no harm done. But when the researcher ventures into foreign territory, like the courtroom, it is essential to be engaged, to get a whiff of the adversariality in the air by joining the game, not standing on the surface decorously jotting notes. True, one loses "objectivity" by taking one side or another, by being involved crucially in the outcome; but only thus is it possible to truly know, why certain choices were made, whether change is possible or useful. (ix–x)

These observations represent much of the preface to *Talking Power*. It is a brief history of her professional life and the personal choices that contributed to its present shape. Her subject matter has been language use and whatever went along with it in the situations she studied. This choice of what to write has been steady for those twenty-five years she mentions. The reader will note how unadversarial, relative to colleagues whose views she rejects (certain other linguists), Lakoff is. What she notes offhandedly in the preface as "I was forced to recognize" was in real life a struggle against the transformational in-group of linguists in the early 1960s. Lakoff writes only that she found out something new and followed it. On the other hand, she is more forthright about the material that does not involve conflict with others: she entered the academy to escape, and linguistics to escape even further.[14] The account next suggests not that the subject matter of linguistics itself drew her in a new direction but that some new life experience felt consequential, and since linguistics was a standpoint to her (as opposed to an essentialized discipline that had to be promoted), she read these experiences through linguistics.

The last paragraph I cited is decisive for Lakoff. Characteristically, it is placed where it can be easily overlooked; who reads prefaces? For her, Chomsky's vocabulary (competence and performance) is out of the picture. She tends to use the vernacular, though there is plenty of scholarly discourse in other sections of her book. To understand language, it is essential to have "direct experience" of it. This principle moves away from the transformationalists' use of made-up sentences that present language as independent of social reference. Lakoff observes that some linguists, who are not as detached and rigid as transformationalists, nevertheless try to conform to academic "games" and pursue their project with an attempt at objectivity. While in some cases this may not be harmful (does it ever yield anything good?), she insists finally that one must be able to identify the affective character of a language scene under study, and one must "take one side or another" — be "involved crucially in the outcome" — in order to be in position to achieve understanding of the use of language in that situation. You can't really know anything about language, Lakoff suggests, without having a political stake in the language and in what you know.

As an academic figure, Lakoff has been inspiring for me: her behavior was a model for some of the ideals about academic life about which I was barely conscious. "Agreeing" with her does not describe my early responses to her work. She took the subject of linguistics over from the dozens of equation-loving transformationalists and declared the "obvious": sentences won't yield knowledge if studied out of context. That this idea was related to her social experiences as a woman, a Jew, or a shy person was possible, I thought: but then she announced some of these personal thoughts in her work. She took the additional step of including herself as a way of reaching out to and including her readers. She challenged us to view her work as individual assimilation — coming back to the society from which she was trying to escape—and collective assimilation—developing on be-half of women the voice of full citizenship. My mother's voice and its social motivation, her own love of language and her knowledge of them (she knew six),[15] prepared me to hear Lakoff's.

The figures I have discussed so far, my mother and myself included, are angry at something. We feel a strong sense of injustice, perhaps in "social arrangements," perhaps in response to more individual events in our lives that we might have ameliorated had we known better. Regardless, the feel-ing of anger that may have entered into academic work rarely is identified as such except in certain narrow genres of protest. People writing academic treatises don't say, "I am angry at the constant misreading of this literature, and I'm jolly well going to correct it."[16] I assumed as a matter of course that I could not start with my feelings of anger, present an academic discussion on this basis, and expect it to be admitted to professional consideration. I considered this assumption more critically after I read Naomi Scheman's essays "Individualism and the Objects of Psychology" (1983) and "Anger and the Politics of Naming" (1980). I can summarize the idea these essays communicated to me. Anger is an object of psychology, previously con-sidered to be "located" within each person's body. If the presuppositions of individualism do not obtain in all cases, if there could also be a collec-tive foundational paradigm, then anger as an "object of psychology" could be understood as being "located" in human relationships: in affiliations of two or more people. Therefore, if I feel angry, it would indicate something happening in my relationships, not just in myself.[17] And yet, even in this essay, as I reread it, I notice a certain relaxed quality that does not truly convey my actual anger at the situations about which I am writing. I often feel this is true in the writers I discuss. I imagine that lying in this sense is still taking place on a large scale. I still feel that I cannot discuss either my feelings of others' culpability, or my own. I note how easily the strong voices of Dworkin and Shulamith Firestone (for example) are "included out" of the picture.

Scheman's idea changed my way of thinking. I had been studying people's feelings in response to literature for about twenty years when I read these essays. I had struggled with the intuition that individual feel-ings, associations, and responses alone do not tell enough about literature to account for its almost second-nature status among language-use customs, habits, and tropes. I had tried to document in my first book, *Readings and Feelings* (1975), the collective values working in readers reading the same thing at the same time.[18] But it did not occur to me to locate the feelings themselves "in" two or more people at once. When I read Scheman's essays, her idea provided the missing thoughts and explained why I didn't find them myself.

I do not know exactly why I was open to this idea in 1984 and not in 1974. Reading the essays was a way back to an issue that posed problems for me: the collective character of language and literature. But to put the problem in these terms is still too academic. Reading Scheman's essays alerted me to the concept of self-implication. By not understanding how feelings "reside" in two or more people, I behaved antisocially. As a matter of course, I isolated myself as an individual and protected myself from the claims of those with whom I am affiliated. As ridiculous as it may sound now, I did not really feel the meaning of the formulation I cited earlier: "what applies to others, applies to me too."

My search for intergender solidarity did not take into account my implication in the privileges of men. These privileges were an unconscious assumption. If my mother said in sarcasm and bitterness, "What do I know, I am only a woman," I could note its sarcasm without understanding its social meaning, which was far enough from my thoughts that it was "ridiculous" to consider! Perhaps by hearing Scheman, I was also hearing my mother, who, living in my home and finding the right word every day, made it more likely that I hear what was previously not audible to me. None have asked me as yet to give up my position of higher status. Because status is not a zero-sum game, one doesn't have to give it up so that others can get it. Most men are so deeply implicated in individualism that we don't allow ourselves to think that the ability to contribute given us by our status will not disappear if others also have that status. But we do have to substitute the right words for the vocabulary of mindfuck and abstraction; we do have to stop lying about the social arrangements in public life. Those of us in the academy have to stop participating in its mendacious practices.

Like Lakoff, Rich, and Dworkin, Scheman wants to change the academy by changing the false premises of her discipline, philosophy. Her approach to philosophy, comparable to Lakoff's approach to linguistics, overturns the styles and standards that have been understood as "what philosophy is." Having achieved respected status in the academy, Scheman's self-inscriptions, her success in moving our attention from the philosophy we received to philosophy as it might become more socially engaged, contribute to a perspective capable of changing the academy. Scheman's self-portraiture, appearing in her book *Engenderings*, presents elements that relate her discussions of philosophical premises to her identity as a woman, a Jew, an academic, a daughter, and—a new element in the present discussion—a person living in exile, a stranger. I identify with this element also, as this part of my identity refers back to my identification with my parents struggling with assimilation. Here is one autobiographical passage with which I identify:

> Most of what I write begins life as a talk at some distant place, in response to invitations to address audiences made up entirely or nearly entirely of strangers. I enjoy traveling, and I especially like being places where I'm responsible for nothing except my end of lots of conversations, and where I'm the center of attention for a fixed period of time, fussed over, and then left alone in a comfortable, anonymous hotel room. Writing happens later, when I'm pleasurably alone with my Macintosh. But, as much as I like it (or, precisely because I like it), I have become increasingly suspicious of the effect on my work of such a combination of solitude and life among strangers. ("Who Is That Masked Woman?" 230)

This could well serve as a sample account of the phenomenology of academic life for itinerant faculty members. I have been in the position Scheman describes dozens of times, beginning with my first campus visit to get a job in 1966. Although it almost always feels good, there is no question but that it is peculiar to be a welcomed stranger. The basis on which one is welcomed is, finally, so insubstantial that one can become suspicious of the total cycle. Where, we ask, is the human interaction? We are merely curious experts.

Scheman goes on to explain that, of course, her daily life is "teaching and interacting with friends and colleagues" (230). However, this too is not the ground of the life she is describing. Moving closer to this ground, she says, "I do, usually, write from an insufficiently examined place, in an insufficiently examined voice, and, most important, in insufficiently examined relation to several audiences and communities. I write most easily and fluently from the academy, as a theorist, and for strangers. I want to try to examine some of what I have obscured or elided, some of the voices other than my own, as well as some of my own voices, that I have silenced or (mis)interpreted" (231). This passage is both candid and ritualized. Candid because its substance rings true: how many of us are willing to say that we did not think through the social ramifications of our work, even though we know that is the case? Ritualized because the phrase "insufficiently examined" is a kind of clichéd hedge or euphemism for something that I want to hear differently, and is so presented, later in her essay, where we learn the particulars that lead us to understand this ritual in affective rather than substantive terms. Scheman says, perhaps, "I always have the feeling that I'm not taking so many essential things into account when I write, so I'm going to do some of that in this essay."

In pursuit of this goal, the following thoughts then appear:

> Among the tasks I am best at are those associated with theorizing: seeing connections among apparently disparate things, explaining those connections imaginatively and clearly, and speculating on what holds them all together. I learned to theorize as a student of philosophy, and, before that as my father's daughter, both of which I was very good at and for which I earned a great deal of approval. What it is to theorize as a feminist and as my mother's daughter is both less clear to me and more frightening, and something more important than approval is at stake. Thus, my "home-ophobia": pun, of course, fully intended. (231)[19]

Women who have taken up the received discourse well are not only approved but rewarded, resulting in a sense of bifurcation of loyalty, a misgiving about being so good at handling a discourse considered to act, usually, in opposition to women as a class. This creates the feeling of being a stranger in one's own group. Lakoff said, referring to academic discourse, "We use their language to tout ours—a bit schizophrenic." Similarly, Madeleine Grumet has written in her book, "The very institutions I repudiate for their perpetuation of patriarchal privilege are the ones within which I have found the voice that tries to sing the tune of two worlds" (59). I too belong in this series: I have written a great deal in "academic discourse," and getting paid to use and teach it, I now find it ungainly and, too often, mendacious.

Scheman's essay treats the theme of divided loyalty as being identification with father and separation from mother, which leads to the issue of her seeing herself as her mother's daughter, as opposed to her father's. This also means thinking about why we have left home and why we find stability in the meta-home zone, school. The issue of language emerges in this essay, which Scheman considers to have a special status: it is a "translation" of a talk given orally, "not into a language I can barely read [some of her talks were translated into German] . . . but into my native tongue, what in Yiddish is called the "mame-loshn," the mother tongue. (I do not really know Yiddish. To the consternation of my elderly relatives, what I understand of it comes mainly from what I understand of German. But Yiddish feels natural to me: it sounds like home.)" (232–33).

Through her consciousness of a home language, Scheman relates the theme of Jewish cultural assimilation to assimilation as a stranger and as a woman into the academy. First, she feels the comfort of her native tongue and uses a word to describe it from Yiddish, a language she does not know but that "sounds like home." She does not mention in this essay that while the word *mame* may be familiar to her and others, the word *loshn* is not German but Hebrew. Thus, there is a certain distance already in her description of the "home" language. The issue she raises, however, is not obscure: for a woman to identify with home and mother may mean identifying with a person and an institution that stays in a subordinate situation. However, she expresses this thought with historical reference:

> But, despite the safety, it's become clear to me that home for me is not the stable place from which one sets out into the world, secure that, whatever else changes, it will still be there. Home is where if you can't flee from it fast enough, they will kill you or take you away. Home is where pogroms happen; like most American Jews, I have only the vaguest idea of where my grandparents were born, and there are surely no relatives still to be found there.
>
> . . . In my own life, although I never feared being chased from the home I grew up in, it never occurred to me to remain there, certainly not in the Long Island suburb that felt like a nursery, a place designed to be grown out of, and which I barely remember, though I lived there from when I was two until I started college. (234)

So it is this sense that home is either intrinsically unsafe, as it is for some women who fear the men in their own home, or is the scene of infantilization, a scene that left no impression, and that, in a sense, was made to be repudiated. I contrast Scheman's description with my own. My memories of my mother's home presence remain vivid and important, and they have contributed to my idealism about what can be accomplished in school. My mother provided the kind of model of enlightened, intelligent care that I like to think many of us as teachers have adopted and cultivated in our classrooms.[20]

This is not the case for Scheman. "Part of what I like [about Minneapolis] is precisely that it is not and never will be home" (234). Out of home, there is room for a certain category of public figure: the privileged marginal characteristic of Jews in prewar Germany, of Jews in America, and of philosophers. Out of the home, both the solidarities and the threats may be treated in a public discourse, and to some degree a new home is created.

"When I discovered philosophy, my first year in college, . . . I felt immediately at home with it, as though I was hearing my native tongue spoken for the first time" (235). Is philosophy *mame-loshn,* the mother tongue, for Scheman? Is *mame-loshn* the right word? Subsequently (maybe this means now) the public manifestations of problems are the subject matter of philosophy, the adult professional home: "Thus racism, classism, and gynophobic misogyny are at the heart of the subjectivity whose construction gives rise to the problems of philosophy" (235).

The term *gynophobic misogyny* calls attention to itself and signals a theme that gives an unsettling accent to Scheman's struggle for an honest and clear identity for philosophy. Translated it means "woman-fearing hatred of women." The essay is about "home-ophobia" and why it is an ongoing feeling: fear of women on the part of both men and women. To Scheman it has created an uncertain set of feelings:

> I don't [feel safe] . . . with women. Where, objectively, I am, and know myself to be, safer, I feel frightened, because none of the tricks I have learned will do me any good. They're unnecessary, but without them I feel defenseless, and it does no good to say there's nothing for me to defend myself from. That's just the problem. I don't need the mask, but I'm seized with anxiety that underneath it, there's no face. Politically, personally, and as a theorist I am most comfortable when I feel least at home, when being myself is the last thing I have to worry about. (236–37)

This fear is the continuing factor in Scheman's self-inscription. It is an articulation of the feeling that, perhaps, no one is safe. Her recognition of the loci of androcentrism has, on the one hand, made Scheman conscious that she is wearing a mask, and on the other that she cannot remove it. Not to be able to remove the mask is to recognize a situation of exile, of being locked out of home, even as one is pleased to be away. This feeling is unsettling: Scheman may be seeing herself as inextricable from several collectives in which she claims membership: women, Jews, Americans, philosophers, and men.

The historic action of men, she implies—by understanding objectivity as paranoid—has poisoned the social ecology so as to undermine "home" and create no new arrangement that is safe ("If this be Method, yet there is Madness in it"). It is on this nonground that philosophy is to be rebuilt. It is this nonfoundation that must be acknowledged as philosophy today. So extensive is the destruction wrought by traditional philosophic assumptions that safety is gone from the society of both the privileged and the oppressed. As I read Scheman's essay, it seems as if she were a reporter of a holocaust in which civilization is destroyed, while most people have remained alive but with no safety and only the public language to create sense or stability. The language that once seemed like the mother tongue, the right word, to Scheman is itself the problem.

I read Scheman's essays as parables of exile and assimilation, but not exclusively of Jews or of women or of any particular smaller or weaker group trying to live under the aegis of a dominant group. It is true that for me, assimilation has a more obvious, palpable, present-at-hand feeling and is more clearly related to my identity as a Jew; but Scheman generalizes this problem in a way that makes today's global facts make sense: the excrescence of internecine mass killing, for example, demonstrates the outbreak of anarchy and the lack of safety for all. Similarly, with the reduction in the police presences of global nuclear powers, the level of violence on the part of terrorists or other relatively powerless factions has increased, thus multiplying beyond the actual damage the level of fear among the privileged. Scheman redirects the address of philosophy through her self-inscriptions and self-inclusions. Her new genres of writing let philosophy warn us about changes in societies around the world. In spite of its dire feeling, her philosophy sounds like the right words, like my native language turning my attention to what I was once unprepared to consider. It sends a hopeful message to those, like myself, from other disciplines who thought that philosophy was mindfuck and abstraction and could not see what other choices there were. Writing from exile, Scheman seems at home with the kind of public thinking philosophy had been, before it was overtaken by the obsessions with objectivity and the emphasis on formulations that are isolated from people's living experience.

Writing oneself into existing discussions creates new homes where there were none. I, like Scheman, "lit out for the territory," as I spent twenty-two years in Bloomington, Indiana, feeling, strangely enough, very much at home there. I eventually moved to Rochester, New York, which felt closer to home. I was excited by the words *New York* on the license plates. I went to the new territory to make a life for myself, only to find that lives can only be lived and not made. We Jews have made new lives. Some, like my father, predicted that this movement toward new communities in which new families are not within the Jewish community will lead to the extinction of Jews—an idea Jews might not have considered had it not been considered by others first. If my own life is any indication, my father's fears seem closer to reality now than when he shared this thought with me. This is undoubtedly a principal reason this topic has become important to me in the last decade.

At the same time, if I try to examine my position "sufficiently," I wonder why African Americans would not be concerned about their culture not surviving. The collective concern of this group is that its culture lives on well in spite of the constant derogation and assaults on its individual members. Assimilation seems to have an entirely different meaning for African Americans from its meaning for Jews. Or does it? When I look carefully at the self-inscriptions of Patricia Williams in her presentation of what American law is like, I hear a voice deciding that assimilation is finally not what she wants for herself or for our society. Rather a change in the subject of law is sought, a change in its language, a change that, if it included women, would include every other group with little adjustment.

Legal language, like the academic discourse of linguistics and philosophy, is privileged, even in its informal manifestations—in conversations between lawyers and clients, as well as in the ways in which it is permitted to sum things up or boil things down when particular cases are discussed briefly and off the record. Legal language performs the same functions that academic language does in the university, to conceal secrets and to lie about its actual function. In order to reach a point of what action to take, it gives tacit permission to characterize real situations in exaggerated ways.[21] This amounts to the permission to distort facts in order that a certain action seem more clearly indicated than the alternatives. If the permission to exaggerate were not there, it would be difficult to untangle one right from another. The question of multilingualism is not just a matter of separate languages. Within the same language there are subgenres, customs, registers, habits, all carrying affective and political weight, all subject to the choices of speakers both in individual and professional capacities. Exaggeration and distortion in the service of making certain choices clear takes place within subgenres in individual languages.

Patricia J. Williams's book *The Alchemy of Race and Rights* is an example of how self-inscription helps to render problems of legal language amenable to treatment by interested parties other than lawyers. It also makes legal customs available to public influence. Her several accounts of where she is sitting, where she came from, and how her family's experiences of racism produced her approach to the law provide a buildup of authorization as well as a rationale for challenging received customs of legal education. Her book also shows how the substantive issues of legal language usefully appear in pedagogical sites. She describes those who populate these sites, how they behave, and how they treat challenges to the received languages of legal education. As she describes them, Williams's senior faculty colleagues conceal their commitments to the legal languages they endorse.

Her chapter "Crimes Without Passion," which appears in the "Trial by Text" section of her book, connects the practices of writing with the principles of self-inclusion and social purpose. This chapter has a specimen case from Williams's pedagogical experience. Williams reports a dispute with her sister regarding what the right words will be in coping with the following case. A student, K, comes to her to complain that another faculty member, portraying Shakespeare's Othello as a sample legal case, described the hero as a " 'black militaristic African leader' who marries the 'young white Desdemona' whom he then kills in a fit of sexual rage" (80). The task was to sort out the elements of the murder. The student complained that this was a racist question but the "professor denied it, saying it was not he who had dreamed up the facts but Shakespeare" (81). The student was admonished by the administrator to whom she had complained (before coming to Williams) for being more concerned about how the law is packaged than what its substance is.

Of concern to Williams is the issue of the "unmarked" established language procedures versus the "marked" perspective of the student. The faculty member behaves as if the premise of his posing the question in these terms can be neglected,[22] so that the legal substance of how to conceptualize the murder can be addressed. As shown by the Great Nationally Televised Trial (of O. J. Simpson), it is completely impossible to separate "the murder" from everything else that obviously goes with it: the history of the associated interpersonal relationships and the social and political identities of the suspect and the victims. To say that one is isolating "the murder itself" represents, in the Simpson trial, the defense posture, while including everything else seems to represent the prosecution. However, this is not true either. The defense introduces "nonmurder" considerations in some issues but not in others. In other words, both prosecution and defense, in their actual practice, do not separate the package from the contents. Williams's point is that a separation is not possible no matter what claims are made to the contrary. The pedagogy is mendacious,[23] and the lies were discovered by K, reported to her first teacher and administrator, denied by them, and then brought to Williams, who, only indirectly implicated in the original situation, now deliberately includes herself through this self-inscription.

Her self-inscription has two parts, a discussion of her interaction with her sister, and a report about her struggle to deal with this situation on be-half of the student K and the principle of changing how law practice works. Part of the material about her sister first appears in a memo Williams wrote after K's complaint to her colleagues on the faculty, trying to persuade them to desist from using examples that have racist and sexist premises.

> When my sister was in the fourth grade, she was the only black child in the class. One Valentine's Day, when the teacher went out of the room, all her white classmates ripped up the valentines she had sent them and dumped them on her desk. It was so traumatic that my sister couldn't speak again in that class, she refused to participate: so completely had they made her feel not part of that group. . . . I think the joy of education for its own sake was seriously impaired, in both her and me (for I felt it almost as much as she did; we had made the valentines together). (89)

This analogy does not exaggerate the actual feeling that K had, though in K's case people did not do what the classmates did. K's feeling is that she was ganged up on by teacher, administrator, and the profession, who belittled her "valentine"—her serious professional interest in the laws of white society—by constructing the substance of school work on the as-sumptions of racism. Since "we made the valentines together" Williams's attitude toward (white-governed) education was affected to the extent that she understands the law itself—the substance of what is taught—differ-ently.

The letter to the faculty in which the story appears is written imper-sonally with no names mentioned—no one blamed or accused—just the principles described so they can be recognized. The letter itself got a luke-warm to negative response—"too teacherly," it was said, too much revolv-ing around "personalities and pot shots" (91). Williams writes to her histo-rian sister asking why this happened. Her sister offers back, orally (narrated by Williams), by phone, "She tells me I'm a coward. She thinks I should write up everything Exactly As It Happened and have it published some-where. Otherwise, she says, I open myself up to being dismissed as merely literary. People will be able to say It Didn't Happen." Williams insists she told the truth, but her sister insists that the documentation is essential to go beyond "in principle" and that Williams is fearful of writing in the detail needed to prevent people from denying what happened.

Williams's letter was rejected because it was too nice, perhaps too assimi-lationist and respectful of existing conventions. On one hand, this trans-lates into "too teacherly," which can only be a bad thing in a teacher, and on the other, because it was not nice—"personalities and pot shots"—as a euphemistic presentation of the real concerns. Williams's sister's point of view seems to be that a victory will not be won by rational, negotiable behavior toward the offending forces. Williams's sister was ostracized by her class. The experience did more than teach her to suspect white education: it taught her about fascism and its relentless lying about its violent program. "People will say It Didn't Happen." The sister is angrier and more ready to identify lying at the institutional level.

A contrast is being drawn between Williams's sister's attitude toward writing and her own. The sister, placing the acts of writing in capital letters, sees them in material terms, commanding the events to which they refer. One cannot academicize any longer, she advises Williams, you have to tell it Exactly As It Happened. This lesson was learned by historians of the Holocaust, as they came forth with the many books trying to tell it Exactly As It Happened.[24] Even so, many voices are also saying "It Didn't Happen." The sister, converting Williams's classroom into a historical site, also converts writing into a historical act, something that must be done in such a way as to guarantee that the facts of history will remain as they happened, not vulnerable to the ruthless denial that was taking place in response to Williams's letter.

When Williams describes her own writing, the chapter becomes a combination of her sister's and her own views of writing. She answers one of the faculty critics of her letter:

> Writing for me is an act of sacrifice, not denial. (I think: I'm so glad I didn't try to write this down.) I deliberately sacrifice myself in my writing. I leave no part of myself out, for that is how much I want readers to connect with me. I want them to wonder about the things I wonder about, and to think about some of the things that trouble me.
>
> What is "impersonal" writing but denial of self? If withholding is an ideology worth teaching, we should be clearer about that as the bottom line of the enterprise. We should also acknowledge the extent to which denial of one's authority in authorship is not the same as elimination of oneself; it is ruse, not reality. And the object of such ruse is to . . . empower beyond the self, by appealing to neutral, shared, even universal understandings. . . . But in a world of real others, the cost of such exclusive forms of discourse is empowerment at the expense of one's relations to those others; empowerment without communion.
>
> . . . The other thing contained in the assumption of neutral, impersonal

> writing styles is the lack of risk. . . . I also believe that the personal is not
> the same as "private": the personal is often merely the highly particular.
> I think the personal has fallen into disrepute as sloppy because we have
> lost the courage and the vocabulary to describe it in the face of the enor-
> mous social pressure to "keep it to ourselves"—but this is where our most
> idealistic and our deadliest politics are lodged, and are revealed. (92–93)

Without doing in the situation what her sister advised, she transfers the
Exactly As It Happened idea to this chapter and presents it in more abstract
terms, for example, describing her action as sacrifice without specifying
just what it is. Nevertheless, throughout her book Williams is highly personal without being private. The material relating to her sister seems to be
How It Happened. So does her description of her relation to her student
K. Williams converts this material into two ideas about language.

First, the language of the law exam, in its separation of the "package"
from the legal substance, allows itself to be a vehicle for the perpetuation of
racism and sexism. Unconsciously, students absorb the injurious assumptions of many of the examples, are guided not to pay attention to them,
and learn, instead, to treat what they may be responding to (in this case,
what K responded to) as ancillary to the legal substance. If Williams's point
is taken, however, the personal response will be read seriously as a guide to
what the exam questions say in new legal terms. Both their premises and
the presumed legal point would form a new substance to the issue, so that
what is considered legally substantive changes to include consideration of
the "everything else" features of any case.

Williams's second idea about language is that legal issues may be reported in the context of the personal and the particular (as opposed to the
private). Williams presents the personal as a path for the social and political to be heard. In some homogeneous groups (like the all-white-male or
all-white-law faculties, for example), the personal is excluded by tradition
and by convention; hence the term *impersonal writing*. College students in
most subjects are guided, early on, toward the ideal of academic discourse,
highlighting the skills of abstract, impersonal argument over other kinds
of writing. Some students and writing teachers have chafed at this style,
but the force of its destructive power is outlined by Williams: this style
serves narrow, increasingly questionable forms of understanding.

Williams, like Rich, Lakoff, and Scheman, spells out some paths for
the personal, sharing the personal/historical reasons for her styles of engagement with the law. Like my mother and Dworkin, she is facing the

lying found in formal, institutionally authorized contexts. The material presented through self-inscription was chosen and interpreted in the context of an immediate task. In each case, the reason for self-inscription was a public or collective issue in society, perhaps causing trouble for more than one constituency. Contributing this personal dimension shifts the language emphasis away from its role as a preserver of authority or distance and toward its role as a creator of political and epistemological access for many kinds of people to subjects that matter in their lives.

I include myself in the foregoing group. I am often angry at the bureaucratic ways in which academics engage matters that are urgent to students and colleagues. Like Lakoff, I have been present at meetings where merely to respect the fraternity style of judgment is an uncomfortable feeling. I am implicated even if I sat silently at the meetings and subscribed to their results. To write this essay is to write myself into the positions taken by these figures whose work I discussed and who I admire. If I use conventional academic language I would say that I acknowledged my mother's "input." But that is not How It Happened. A truer way to say what happened is to say that she taught me to write and self-inscribe by showing me *what it feels like* to hear and say the right word. In this way she engaged my trust for things that mattered to her, created a relationship that made me feel trust itself and, further, how to know when it is there. Trust is the ordinary way of identifying connectedness among people. It is a word that describes the subjective element in social relations and that helps to show what Scheman observed about other feelings—their "residence" among people rather than exclusively in individuals. I and many others learned our connectedness from our mothers and our mother tongues and speakers of these languages who treated us as if we mattered.

The academy—sometimes only blindly, sometimes with malice—has tried to perpetuate the superstition of separateness, the falsehood of individual isolation—in many areas, but certainly in the teaching of writing and language use. People are willing to say My Discipline Is Separate from Yours. (That is, "It Is Not Happening"). Self-inscription and self-inclusion are more than taking responsibility and claiming relatedness. Searching for the right word is the willingness to probe the extent of self-implication in both the objects of criticism and the contexts of approbation. This search, conducted through self-inscription into our subject matters, implies a willingness to refrain from the arbitrary and sometimes fearful isolation of self from subject matter, to refrain from claiming the missing Archimedean point and instead writing with the acknowledgment that there is none.

Self-inscription and self-inclusion are ways of teaching one another about our immediate peer presence as well as about the many constituencies to whom our understandings may be addressed. Finally they are ways for us teachers, now sometimes collaborating with movements we resent and even oppose openly, to pass along ways of writing to those who, we hope, won't have to offer this acknowledgment.

NOTES

1. Detailed in "Split at the Root: An Essay on Jewish Identity."
2. They include Andrea Dworkin, Robin Lakoff, Naomi Scheman, and Patricia Williams. Three and a half of these are Jews; all are "minorities." There are others, such as the widely read Deborah Tannen and the many sociolinguists and linguistic pragmatists, such as Lois Bloom, who began on this path about the same time as Robin Lakoff. It is hard to claim cultural regularities. Yet there is an obvious correspondence between the more expressive, disclosing constituencies of women, minorities, and even children, and the values of cultural assimilation. Usually assimilation processes are patronized and inhibited by those who have "successfully" assimilated.
3. In my earlier book, *The Double Perspective*, chapter 3 discusses the collective character of language under the title "reconceiving literacy." The present discussion of self-inclusion is also part of how and why reconceiving literacy is taking place.
4. This description is consistent with the "story" of how an individual acquires language given by Mead and Vygotsky and reviewed in *The Double Perspective*. A multiple or dialogic experience in the preverbal period gets internalized and reemerges as individual language. For Chomsky, this fact does not belong in "competence" and hence does not enter into his universalist theory of language, as mentioned briefly below.
5. As I discuss in *Subjective Criticism* with regard to the acquisition of the symbolization process, and then review in *The Double Perspective*.
6. Rich's perspective is similar to Andrea Dworkin's regarding the political purposes to which language and literature should be dedicated.
7. He was Yiddish actor. He earned his living working in Yiddish. He was blindsided by the precipitous decline in the Yiddish theater in 1945. Because he still spoke with an accent, he was not viable in English venues in spite of his ability to act and his knowledge of the theater, which, as always, was very competitive even among those who knew English perfectly.
8. I think academics don't go along with Mark Twain's view that the difference between the right word and almost the right word is like the difference between lightning and a lightning bug.
9. The program did not entertain the notion that a "red big balloon" is gram-

matically correct and available to be used in some circumstances without being considered ungrammatical. To have entertained that possibility would have reduced the authority of the "rules" that linguists want to establish as "linguistic knowledge."

10. As Hubert Dreyfus did, for example, in the context of artificial intelligence: *What Computers Can't Do* (1972), and his 1992 revision, *What Computers Still Can't Do*.

11. Janice Moulton's 1983 essay "The Adversary Method" contributes this vocabulary, noting the oppositional style of academic work. She suggests that this style is typically androcentric.

12. It loads my discussion incorrectly to call Lakoff's work a "challenge" to Chomsky. While it is historically true that she opposed his views, her public work did not oppose them. I leave this description in my essay to show how the received tropes of oppositional academic argumentation continue to affect my writing. Alternatively, I could write that Lakoff was simply different. Yet that also does not sound "true" because gender issues were involved that were opposed to the social values underlying Chomsky's ideas.

13. My discussion in this essay tries to show in part that the answer to this question must always be of considerable length because it involves the telling of a personal and political history in dialogue or counterpoint with the subject matter. The "answer" to the questions of scientific motivation are like the lengthy answer to the Four Questions in the Jewish Passover Haggadah. The answer to each question requires a recitation of a history, as well as the many commentaries on that history.

14. Other works of hers, such as *Face Value* (1984), give further personal background about why she had such feelings, which, in the present detailing, are remarkable insofar as they are announced though not remarkable in themselves. So few academics would admit they joined the academy to escape anything, though many have done just that.

15. Often, the right word would come in my mother's speech from one of her other languages, as it comes in monolingual speakers from the importation from other registers.

16. An exception is Judith Fetterley, who is angry at men's readings of men's literature and wrote *The Resisting Reader* (1978) to correct them.

17. I note the connection between this idea and Rich's "If Not With Others, How?"

18. The last chapter is titled "Interpretation as a Communal Event," and it discusses a class's reading of Thackeray's *Vanity Fair*. Stanley Fish at the time had the same trouble with a similar idea: the interpretive community, which seemed to stipulate a collective locus for styles of literary interpretation. It was attractive to us academics, but it did not have the social specificity and political backbone it finally got from its use by the identity-politics interest. But by then, Fish did not follow through from that standpoint.

19. This passage is like Madeleine Grumet's presentation of her upbringing and

how she articulated girls being "delivered" to patriarchy by the school system (29).

20. A similar claim might be made by Madeleine Grumet, whose pedagogical philosophy derives from recognizing the influence and generosity of smart, resourceful mothering.

21. Because trials are adversarial—having only two "sides"—they *begin* with the misleading identification of an open mind and two "equal" views. Although we know the difference between finding the truth and deciding who made the better case, one wonders why it would not be correct—as things are done now—to think of all disputed cases being decided by judges and juries solely on the choice of superior arguments. Only the secrecy of jury deliberations and the privacy of judges' minds permits other criteria to be used in deciding cases. The criteria of decisions in legal matters, insofar as these criteria are not mentioned explicitly in statues and precedents, cannot be known.

22. This is comparable, but not identical, to the "neglect" of friction by physicists discussing Newton's laws of motion as ideal cases, none of which exists. The question is whether the practice of concocting ideal cases and situations in order to communicate principles is useful. This is Lakoff's complaint about linguistics and Scheman's complaint about philosophy. The result of this practice is that the *principle* then is taken for ideal, a thought habit that encourages authoritarianism and dogmatism. If, rather, we had been taught about the ubiquity of *approximate* cases, the use of the ideal is then *variable* with the individual or community, thus removing the coercive effect it almost always has now.

23. This style of lying is identical to what a science textbook does to the actual history of science: in the interests of maximum clarity and certainty, the historical ragged edges and loose ends are censored, and science falsely appears to be an ideal collection of unambiguous fact and law. In the present case, the fact and law are just as ambiguous, and the pedagogy censors the ambiguities in the same ways and with the same bad consequences.

24. The best instance of this could be Lucy S. Dawidowicz, *The War against the Jews, 1933–1945*. The more recent film *Shoah*, with a series of personal narratives and no photography, is also an effort of, literally, *telling* it Exactly As It Happened.

REFERENCES

Bleich, David. *The Double Perspective*. New York: Oxford University Press, 1988.
———. *Subjective Criticism*. Baltimore: Johns Hopkins University Press, 1978.
Dawidowicz, Lucy S. *The War against the Jews, 1933–1945*. New York: Holt, 1975.
Dreyfus, Hubert L. *What Computers Can't Do: A Critique of Artificial Reason*. New York: Harper and Row, 1972. Rpt. as *What Computers Still Can't Do: A Critique of Artificial Reason*. Cambridge: MIT Press, 1992.
Dworkin, Andrea. *Woman Hating*. New York: Penguin, 1974.
Fetterley, Judith. *The Resisting Reader*. Bloomington: Indiana University Press, 1978.

Grumet, Madeleine R. *Bitter Milk: Women and Teaching.* Amherst: University of Massachusetts Press, 1988.

Lakoff, Robin Tolmach. *Talking Power: The Politics of Language.* New York: Basic, 1990.

Lakoff, Robin Tolmach, and Raquel L. Scherr. *Face Value: The Politics of Beauty.* Boston: Routledge and Kegan Paul, 1984.

Moulton, Janice. "A Paradigm of Philosophy: The Adversary Method." In *Discovering Reality: Feminist Perspectives on Epistemology, Metaphysics, Methodology, and Philosophy of Science,*" edited by Sandra Harding and Merrill B. Hintikka, 149–64. Boston: D. Reidel, 1983.

Rich, Adrienne. "If Not with Others, How?" In *Blood, Bread, and Poetry: Selected Prose, 1979–1985*, 202–9. New York: Norton, 1986.

———. "Split at the Root: An Essay on Jewish Identity." In *Blood, Bread, and Poetry,* 100–123.

———. "Teaching Language in Open Admissions." *On Lies, Secrets, and Silence: Selected Prose, 1966–1978*, 51–68. New York: Norton, 1979.

Scheman, Naomi. "Though This Be Method, Yet There Is Madness In It: Paranoia and Liberal Epistemology." In *Engenderings: Constructions of Knowledge, Authority, and Privilege*, 75–105. New York: Routledge, 1993.

———. "Who Is That Masked Woman? Reflections on Power, Privilege, and Home-ophobia." In *Engenderings: Constructions of Knowledge, Authority, and Privilege*, 229–38.

———. "Anger and the Politics of Naming." In *Engenderings: Constructions of Knowledge, Authority, and Privilege*, 22–35.

———. "Individualism and the Objects of Phychology." In *Engenderings: Constructions of Knowledge, Authority, and Privilege*, 36–56.

Williams, Patricia. *The Alchemy of Race and Rights.* Cambridge: Harvard University Press, 1991.

CARLOS L. DEWS

Gender Tragedies:

East Texas Cockfighting

and *Hamlet*

I remember pen-sized shafts of light penetrating nail holes in corrugated tin roofs. I remember an indescribable smell of dust mixed with feathers, water, tobacco, and blood. I remember limp necks and the lifeless sway-ing heads of beautiful birds as they were carried by their feet to barrels for burning. I remember perfect drops of blood left behind in the sand. I re-member the many-colored feathers shining in the sun. I was told not to cry, not to remember these things. But we always remember what we're told to forget.

Almost every weekend when I was growing up in East Texas my family loaded a van or pickup truck and went to cockfights. At these derbies, as cockfighting tournaments are called, three-inch steel gaffs (razor-sharp spikes resembling bent ice picks) are strapped on the cocks' legs, replacing their natural spurs. Men carry the opposing cocks into a sand-filled pit, a ring bordered by a two-foot-high wall of plywood or concrete, where the cocks fight. Sitting on bleachers, the audience surrounds the pit and shouts out bets as the cocks are brought into the pit and prepared to fight. Only the two handlers and one referee are allowed in the pit during a match. The men face off across the pit and release the cocks. The roosters fly toward each other holding the gaffs in front of them. After a few hits, or strikes, with the gaffs, a referee shouts "Handle 'em," and the men separate the roosters and return to their corners for a break. After the roosters are in-spected for injury, their heads are sponged off and they are given a drink of water. They are then ready for another round. This process is repeated until one of the cocks dies from loss of blood or from the internal injuries caused by the gaffs. The surviving cock is the winner. Cocks that refuse to fight are killed by their owners to prevent the propagation of scared, or "running," cocks.

Cockfighting is big business; the winner of a derby can take home as much as $50,000. The trophies given to the winners are sometimes eight feet tall. Cockfighters have their own associations and publications, including the bibles of the sport, *Grit and Steel*, *Feathered Warrior*, and *Game Cock Magazine*. The man who wins the most derbies in one year at a single pit is named the "cocker of the year."[1]

Cockfighting is primarily a man's endeavor; however, many women, including both my sisters, participate in the limited roles allowed women in the sport. A woman can be a wealthy supporter of a man's cockfighting career; she can be a devoted fan of her husband or boyfriend, always ready to defend the reputation of her partner; or she can be a shrewd businesswoman who wins money in the wagering. Women cannot compete in the same division with the men. Handling cocks is considered too dangerous for women. Powder Puff derbies are sometimes held in conjunction with the men's derbies during which women and retarded boys are allowed to compete as equals.

As I recently watched a videotaped production of *Hamlet*, I was struck with the similarities between the final fight scene in the play and the cockfights I remembered from my childhood. It all came back to me: the wagering, the poisoned swords, the audience encircling the competitors, the battle to the death.[2] And in *Hamlet*, as so often in cockfights, both competitors die.

As I further indulged my memory, I discovered another reason this association between *Hamlet* and my childhood weekends spent at cockfights was so striking. I recalled that the primary lesson I was expected to learn during these childhood weekends was how to be a man. Cockfighting wasn't the only mode through which this lesson was conveyed to me. There was also deer hunting, fishing, farm work, and participation in my father's logging business. At the same time I was receiving these messages telling me to be a man, I was also receiving a countermessage from my mother, grandmother, and sisters. I was the only boy in the family and spent most of my time with women. I noticed that my mother, grandmother, and sisters behaved differently when the menfolk were around. These women, who would talk and work competently, assuredly, one moment would appear servile, docile, and insecure as soon as one of the men appeared. The women would speak disparagingly about the men behind their backs but never question their authority to their faces. Although I found this confusing, I learned that it was the only way to survive. The women of my family obviously had learned this vital lesson many years before I was born.

With these conflicting lessons of my childhood in mind, I reread *Hamlet* recalling the instructions I received, those from my father about what it meant to be a man, to be masculine, and those from my mother, grandmother, and sisters on surviving in a world where the men were destructive and edged toward paranoia regarding gender. Last summer I realized that I will be the first man in my family to live his life without shooting, if not killing, another person.

When I read the play, I began to identify with Hamlet, to see him as the product of a society similar to my own. We both received irreconcilably mixed messages about gender. These irreconcilable messages led to a sense of dividedness. It is this dividedness I feel in common with Hamlet. I don't like Hamlet and am uncomfortable with my strong identification with him. Although there is a wealth of criticism, written primarily during the last ten years, on gender and sexuality in Shakespeare's plays, there is surprisingly little written regarding the harmful results of society's gender pressure on the male characters in *Hamlet*, or in any of Shakespeare's plays. Furthermore, few, if any, productions of the play have emphasized a gender struggle as the source of Hamlet's indecision.

For a couple of years, when I was between six and eight years old, my father conditioned roosters for a man named Jack Durette. Conditioning is the training process involving a rigorous diet and exercise program cockfighters use to prepare their roosters for fights. At the time Daddy didn't have the thousands of dollars to bankroll his own interest in cockfighting, so he worked for Mr. Durette, who funded the construction of an enviable cock house (the training building to house and condition the roosters) and paid for the travel to derbies in exchange for a percentage of the winnings.

• • •

Dear Jack Durette:

I am not sure how to address you. I don't remember what I called you when I was little. I do remember my parents always called you "Jack Durette." Never just "Jack"; that sounded too familiar. It was as if Daddy called you Jack Durette to avoid sounding as if the two of you were friends. He would probably be mad if he knew I was telling you this, but he often referred to you as "Mr. Durette." He said this with a snide tone implying that you thought a lot of yourself. I think Daddy hated you. He called you a "sissy" — the worst thing he could call a man. He thought you were effeminate and used you as the example of what a man should avoid being. For some reason the anecdote that he most often used concerned you asking your wife to comb your hair. What made this particularly disgusting to him was that it happened at a cockfight, and that you didn't mind that other people heard you ask her to do this. Having your wife comb your hair made you appear too dependent on a woman.

I think Daddy was also envious of you. You had more money than he did and your wife was very beautiful (he thought my mother was not) and you had a mistress on the side who was even more beautiful. Maybe it was this that bothered him the most. He thought you were effeminate, yet you still had two very beautiful women.

I remember once when you and your wife were out of town that Daddy and I went over to your farm to take care of the chickens. While we were there we stopped in at your house for a snack. I remember feeling uncomfortable going into your empty house. Daddy warned me not to touch anything. I remember climbing onto a barstool, which seemed a mile high, where Daddy served me cake that he took from your refrigerator. The glare from the refrigerator cast unfamiliar light on his arms as he reached in and removed the cake. He was awkward, fumbling with the cake on its tray. He had a difficult time cutting pieces and serving them. He cut the cake with a knife that was far too large, and he served it on full-sized dinner plates, not dessert plates or saucers. This was the most awkward I had ever seen my father. He was out of his element. I felt sorry for him. He was unfamiliar with this task, with these surroundings.

Lately I have been thinking about why he disliked you so much. I think you re-minded him of that part of himself that was not allowed to develop fully, that part of himself that he had to constantly deny, that he or someone else had forced to hide deep inside. He had to remind himself, and me, to hold on to the lid of manliness or he/we might accidentally let some of the feminine out. You weren't afraid to show emotions, you were concerned about the way you looked, you admitted feeling pain, you hugged and shrieked and moved quickly. You scared him. You were less afraid to share yourself with others. You were able to let the feminine in you live. He was not. And still is not, although as I see him begin to age (he is 62 now), he seems to be able to let himself go, to be more spontaneous, less in control of his feeling nature.

I got another glimpse of this side of my father the night his father died. As Daddy and his sister left the hospital room after having said good-bye to their father, the rest of the family looked down the corridor to see Daddy walk out of the room carrying his shoes in his hand. He was crying. He had been there beside his father for three days; he was exhausted. He walked with his back bent, stiff from sitting in an un-comfortable chair. Carrying his shoes, he walked tentatively out of the room where his father lay dead. He didn't care who saw him or what they might think. The death of his father had temporarily lifted the lid of self-consciousness and allowed him to be—not to be a man, just to be.

I imagine that you would have described your state of being similarly when you asked your wife to comb your hair. You weren't concerned about what others thought, you just were. You weren't monitoring yourself to be sure you appeared manly at every moment—just like Daddy carrying his shoes out of the room where his father had just died.

. . .

Central to a prescribed gender role for a man is the existence of a masculine ideal, an ideal to which a boy or young man can be encouraged to aspire. The impossible male or masculine ideal against which Hamlet must judge himself is his murdered father.

> See what a grace was seated on this brow:
> Hyperion's curls, the front of Jove himself,
> An eye like Mars, to threaten and command,
> A station like the herald Mercury
> New lighted on a heaven-kissing hill—
> A combination and a form indeed
> Where every god did seem to set his seal
> To give the world assurance of a man.
>
> (3.4.56–63)

> He was a man, take him for all in all,
> I shall not look upon his like again.
>
> (1.2.187–188)

Reviving the myth of his father, the appearance of the ghost reawakens the masculine pole of Hamlet's gender identity. This ghost not only reminds Hamlet of an idealized male/masculine figure but gives him a mission, a quest for vengeance. Hamlet's warring father, appearing dressed in armor, is the ideal male that Hamlet should aspire to be. To be a successful man Hamlet must achieve at least as much as his father. Immediately before Old Hamlet's ghost appears, the young Hamlet speaks of the tragic flaw of "particular men" (1.4.13–38). At first glance it appears that Hamlet is speaking of Claudius, but the speech, coming so close to the appearance of the ghost, can be seen as a reflection on his own potential flaw, his lack of manliness, his "unmanly grief." The mission of revenge asked for by the ghost serves as an opportunity for Hamlet to prove his manliness. In fact, the ghost, in telling Hamlet the story of the murder, says, "If thou hast nature in thee, bear it not" (1.5.81), as if to say, "If you are man enough you will avenge my murder." This ideal man/father has asked his son to prove his masculinity by avenging his wrongful death. More importantly for Hamlet's notion of his own masculinity, the ghost repeatedly asks him to "Mark me" (1.5.2), "Remember me" (1.5.91). Hamlet replies after the ghost exits, " 'Adieu, adieu, remember me.' I have sworn't" (1.5.111–112). Similarly, Laertes has an idealized father in the form of the dead Polonius. In questioning Laertes' resolve to fight over Hamlet's killing of Polonius, the King asks, "Laertes, was your father dear to you? / Or are you like the painting of a sorrow, / A face without a heart?" (4.7.105–107). Laertes' drive to avenge the murder is energized by the valorization of his dead father. Laertes' loyalty to his father, like Hamlet's, appears to be at stake.

. . .

Dear Granny and Momma,

This is a thank you letter. I have only recently begun to realize how thankful I should be for the messages that the two of you gave me when I was growing up. I often saw and heard the two of you acting toward Daddy and Paw Paw in a way that seemed at the time to be hypocritical. You would seem to agree with them but then as soon as they left the room you would talk about how ridiculous they were and disregard what you had agreed to while they were around. For me this often meant that I could ignore the demands that were being placed on me by Daddy regarding what I should be doing as a boy and young man. Your words and actions had a subversive, challenging, contestatory quality. You seemed to say to me, "Give the appearance of complicity but don't compromise what you believe." "Just make it look like you go along." "Go along to get along." "Just pretend and it will be easier." You both distrusted Daddy and Paw Paw but gave the appearance of undying devotion and trust. Your subtle message was that there is another way, an alternate route; the prescribed behavior doesn't have to be accepted. You were very sophisticated.

Daddy's message on the other hand had no subtlety: there was no countermessage; it was simple, less sophisticated. He knew what a man should look like, talk like, act like, and I was to look it, talk it, and act it. I don't know whether you consciously conveyed this message to me or whether I just picked it up. I don't know if I could have survived without your influence; hence the thank you. I love you very much for this lesson. Some people might say that you compromised yourselves, that you were being hypocritical, selling yourselves short, but I respect your ability to use your wit and intuition to make the best of your situation. I admire your ability to empower yourselves in a situation that would seem futile to many. I remember many times when I was in trouble with Daddy, how you seemed to side with him, but as soon as he left the room you would comfort me and tell me not to listen to him. That's the important part, not to listen to him. I use that one almost every day. Yes, it did hurt when it appeared that you sided with him over me, and I often wanted you to stand up to him face to face, not after he left the room, but I guess I learned that was impossible, that your way was actually better. Thanks.

. . .

As I return to a more academic discussion of Hamlet below, I am driven to ask the question, "Can I do this?" Can I continue to use the academic language that I have learned through a process that feels too much like my indoctrination at the cockfights? I feel an uncomfortable shift in my language, style, and approach. I would like to be able to jettison the academic voice in my head and write in a more personal voice. But now, after all those years of graduate school, this academic voice at times feels natural itself and can't simply be ignored. Yet I resist the academic mode because it feels too much like the masculine lessons of the cockfights. This is why writing autobiographical criticism feels so good. I can express my reaction to Hamlet, hopefully providing a unique reading that furthers others' understanding of him, while at the same time use a voice and a method I feel comfortable with. I take great pleasure in using the format of an academic paper to write autobiographically. Like the act of undermining the message of my father, which I was taught by my grandmother and mother, I seemingly can accept the genre and simultaneously mock the rigid conventions of academic writing.

Did Hamlet have a source for a countermessage similar to my own? I think so. Hamlet's great emotional upheaval was caused, in addition to the loss of his father, by what appears to be the betrayal by his mother. This indicates to me that she was the source of his rebellious nature. To see his mother, whom he loved and trusted and who he thought dearly loved his father, betray them both by marrying Claudius was more than Hamlet could take. Like my mother and grandmother, who often appeared to be siding with my father against me, Gertrude was using the resources she had to keep control over her own and her son's fate. Her marriage to Claudius was her only avenue to ensure their survival. What would have been Gertrude and Hamlet's fate if she had not married Claudius?

Ophelia and Gertrude are associated with all that Hamlet's society views as feminine, while Laertes, Polonius, and Old Hamlet are regarded as masculine ideals, having accepted society's predetermined role. Hamlet is in an ambivalent position, suspended between these two poles. Ophelia is perceptive, aware of Hamlet's ambivalence and his mixed feelings toward her.

She doesn't know what to make of him. When asked by her father if Hamlet's interest in her is sincere, she replies, "I do not know, my lord, what I should think" (1.3.104). Ophelia's experience of Hamlet's rage against her and her father's death divide her: "Poor Ophelia / Divided from herself and her fair judgment" (4.5.82–83).

Ophelia innocently receives the brunt of Hamlet's anger against his confused state, his disappointment in his mother, and the death of his father. She reminds Hamlet of his feminine nature. Ophelia is used by the King and her father to test Hamlet's manliness. In addition to the purported aim of observing Hamlet to discern his mental/emotional state, it appears that the King and Polonius, especially Polonius, have a prurient interest in seeing Hamlet perform (sexually, or at least psychologically) with Ophelia. More than a test of his sanity, this observation is a test of Hamlet's manhood. His rage toward Ophelia might be due in part to his rejection of the male control that places him in this situation. The everyday anxiety Hamlet feels regarding his masculinity, or rejection thereof, is concentrated by the presence of Polonius and the King.

Hamlet is only able to ignore the feminine aspect of his own personality when the women around him remain chaste. Evidence of active female sexuality reminds Hamlet of his own feminine nature. He wants his mother to be chaste: "Assume a virtue, if you have it not" (3.4.164) and tells Ophelia to "Get thee to a nunnery" (3.1.119). In this way Hamlet prevents himself from being reminded of both the feminine aspect of his personality and of his expected role as reproductive male. Hamlet's way of dealing with this pressure of prescribed gender is to be genderless, to reject both masculinity and femininity. "Man delights not me; nor woman neither" (2.2.292–293). Hamlet's railing against Ophelia's use of makeup can be read as his anger toward the fluidity of masculinity and femininity evident in the ability to paint another face. "I have heard of your paintings too, well enough. God hath given you one face, and you make yourselves another" (3.1.139–140).

In his rage against Ophelia, Hamlet is driven to an extreme of emotion distancing him from both the masculine and feminine ideals that both attract and repel him. The alternative to this uncentered position is death, which he contemplates in his "To be, or not to be" soliloquy.

Hamlet's and the cockfighters' fear of the feminine is a reaction against being reminded of their own femininity. They must react negatively toward the feminine, except in sexual attraction, in order to prevent the loosening of their grasp on their constructed masculinity. They wish that a person born with male genitalia would naturally become masculine.

Knowing that this doesn't happen because they feel the feminine inside them, and reacting against their own femininity, they must indoctrinate themselves and the males around them. This prescription or indoctrination in its less violent mode takes the form of manly advice about proper masculine behavior, the valorization of role models perceived as ideal representations of all that is manly (especially fathers, e.g., Old Hamlet), and rites of male bonding. Just as importantly, those men who are considered unmanly (Jack Durette) and those activities and mannerisms considered feminine must be condemned.

. . .

Paw Paw,

Writing a letter to you feels very strange because I know you never learned how to read. I remember your driver's license with its "X" for a signature and the words "his mark" written after it. I was always amazed how well you could use numbers. At the cattle auction you could multiply the price per pound by how many pounds a cow weighed faster than I could multiply the first two digits.

Do you remember the calendars you used to get each year from K. L. Barton and Son's Tie Yard? They had pictures of naked women on them. The women were usually in a bathtub or in a bedroom, and the photograph was covered with a sheet of clear plastic which had clothes painted on it so when the plastic was lifted you could see the women's breasts. I am sure you remember them. They were always hung on the inside of the closet door in the spare bedroom, the closet with the circuit breaker.

It may seem strange, but I often think of those calendars. If you remember the calendars at all it might be because of the joking ritual that evolved around them. When I was about four years old you brought home one of the new calendars and showed it to me when you walked in the door. I didn't find the picture of the woman particularly interesting, with or without the plastic clothing. I do remember a strong feeling that this was an opportunity for me to perform and respond in the way I was expected to respond. I very clearly remember thinking that I was supposed to find this picture of a naked woman exciting. I remember shyly walking over to Granny and saying, "When I look at that my heart goes thump thump thump." You were my intended audience but I knew that for the most effect I should pretend to be shy and say it to Granny, knowing that she would immediately tell you what I said. She did, of course. I knew that I was supposed to react in this way to the photograph of a naked woman and that you would be proud of me for reacting this way. It didn't take long for this to become a ritual. Any time I was at your house and a friend of yours or Granny's was there you would go get the calendar, raise the plastic clothing flap and ask me what I felt. My response would always be, "It makes my heart go thump thump thump." I always delivered the lines shyly for effect and immediately ran from the room feigning embarrassment. I remember that Granny would also have me do the same for her friends.

I am amazed that at the age of four or five I already knew what was expected of me. My heart was supposed to go thump thump thump when I saw a naked woman. But I am even more amazed that I performed the expected role knowing that it was just an act. My heart didn't go thump thump thump; it didn't do anything. I often think of those calendars, about the game I was playing, about the women on those calendars, about how they struck me as mothers and sisters. I actually preferred them with their plastic wardrobe.

• • •

Horatio's first line, in answer to "What, is Horatio there?," is "A piece of him" (1.1.19). The men in *Hamlet* are sharply divided within themselves. This division is caused by their society's prescription of their roles. Horatio can answer "a piece of him" because be is exhausted and has left a piece of himself behind in bed but also because only the manly part of himself is needed on the battlements.

The 1948 film of *Hamlet* starring Laurence Olivier begins with a prologue, "This is the tragedy of a man who could not make up his mind." We see Hamlet unable to make up his mind in many ways throughout the play, but perhaps the most fundamental indecision is that of his acceptance or denial of the prescribed gender roles his society dictates for him. This indecision influences all of Hamlet's actions. The indecision surrounding this gender prescription could go a long way toward explaining the ambivalence Hamlet exhibits. Hamlet's tragic flaw is his inability to reconcile the mixed messages he is receiving regarding gender and the options available to him.

Hamlet and those around him seem to accept the inevitability of his station in life, both in relation to his gender identification and his more broadly defined role in life, as prince, heir to the throne, and producer of heirs. "My fate cries out" (1.4.81), Hamlet exclaims to Horatio before following the ghost. Hamlet must follow his father's ghost. Regarding his charge to right his father's murder, Hamlet says, "The time is out of joint. O cursed spite, / That ever I was born to set it right!" (1.5.187–188). Hamlet wants to resist fate but realizes the futility of doing so. "There's a divinity that shapes our ends, / Rough-hew them how we will" (5.2.10–11). In his first soliloquy Hamlet can be seen struggling against what he sees as his inevitable fate. Hamlet's world has been shattered. The two persons in the world that he loved the most, and who appeared to love him unquestionably, are no longer available to him. His father, idealized, is dead. His mother, who he thought adored his father, has taken a new husband only two months after his father's death. For the first time, Hamlet has to face his own individuality. Hamlet wants to escape his own fate, to exchange his identity with another; he addresses Horatio, "Sir, my good friend, I'll change that name with you" (1.2.163). There is an air of inevitability against which Hamlet must toil. He appears to be fated to suffer this indecision. Because of his responsibilities as Prince of Denmark, Hamlet is limited in his choice of roles. As Laertes explains to Ophelia, "For he himself is subject to his birth. / He may not, as unvalued persons do, / Carve for himself; for on his choice depends / The safety and health of this whole state" (1.3.18–21). Hamlet could not follow the advice given to Laertes by Polonius, "to thine own self be true," for "the safety and health of this whole state" depend on his decisions. He is cut off from the option of defining for himself a gender compromise.[3]

Laertes, in contrast to Hamlet, appears to have accepted the prescribed masculine role. His advice to Ophelia regarding Hamlet and his challenging of Hamlet are stereotypical masculine behaviors. Upon hearing of Ophelia's death, Laertes speaks of shameful tears and the purging of the feminine tears from himself: "Let shame say what it will: when these [tears] are gone, / The woman will be out" (4.7.186–187). Polonius's farewell message to Laertes is in fact a catalog of prescriptive male behavior (1.3.55–81). The King's "unmanly grief" speech to Hamlet (1.2.87–117) can be seen as a parallel to Polonius's advice to Laertes. Unlike Polonius's speech, however, the King's advice to Hamlet is more of a scolding, a listing of Hamlet's "unmanly" behavior, which the King looks on suspiciously. The King uses negative examples instead of the litany of "positive" characteristics espoused by Polonius when he speaks to Laertes. Claudius's speech culminates in the idea:

> Tis unmanly grief.
> It shows a will most incorrect to heaven,
> A heart unfortified, a mind impatient,
> An understanding simple and unschooled.
>
> (1.2.94–97)

Claudius's form of chastising Hamlet reminds me more of how the men in Shakespeare's plays typically talk about women, not how a king/uncle would talk about his prince/stepson. These lines appear to push Hamlet further away from the womanly/motherly to the manly/fatherly. It is this pressure regarding what is unmanly that informs my reading of Hamlet. It is also interesting to note that when Hamlet is feigning insanity and reads to Polonius from a book, the section he chooses to read is a list of characteristics of "old men" (2.2.194–200). My father would call Hamlet a sissy. His indecision would be viewed as womanly, his emotional outbursts as weak. According to Daddy, women solve their problems through deception (Hamlet's feigned madness) while men solve their problems directly (violence).

Hamlet's verbosity, which is often discussed in regard to his insanity and indecision, can be viewed as a result of the mixed gender messages he is receiving from his society. His own natural reasonable voice (which I believe to be healthily formed under his mother's influence[4]) struggles against the dogmatic, moralistic (not to mention sexist and homophobic) voice coming from his society and the passionate, angry, vengeful, animalistic voice of the ghost of his father.[5] In Freudian terms the internalized reasonable voice of his mother would correspond to the ego; the dogmatic and moralistic voice of society would correspond to that of the superego; and the energetic, animalistic voice of his father's ghost would correspond to the id. These voices—his own, his father's, and his society's—all vie for dominance. Hamlet's verbosity comes from his alternately giving vent to one of these opposing voices within. His indecision is a symptom of his ambivalence. He is torn between these various conflicting discourses, which can be seen by comparing his speeches in a number of scenes. In lashing out against Ophelia and Gertrude, Hamlet's voice contrasts with the depressed and suicidal voice of the "To be, or not to be" soliloquy. His voice while interacting with the players contrasts with the voice of reverence when he is talking with his father's ghost. The conflicting voices can be heard in cacophony when Hamlet debates whether to kill Claudius as he prays. In addition to, or perhaps instead of, exhibiting hesitancy toward the task of killing his uncle/stepfather/king, Hamlet is more afraid of life and the continued bombardment by the conflicting messages he hears within his head. He is forced to make a decision. Trying to decide which voice to listen to drives him to contemplate suicide.

In this reading of *Hamlet*, the "To be, or not to be" soliloquy takes on a new significance. Hamlet, in addition to considering suicide, can be seen contemplating resolution of the gender conflict within himself. He feels compelled to choose between a purely masculine identity, excluding the feminine, or a more integrated gender identification, which has no place in his society. " 'To be, or not to be" becomes "To be, a man or not to be a *man*." This seems to be the fundamental question. Once the decision is made not to accept the traditional roles prescribed to the masculine male then the pressure is off.

Is there a chance of reconciliation for Hamlet? Is there any evidence that he seeks alternatives to his fate? Near the end of the play when Hamlet and Laertes are brought together for their battle, which is set up as a resolution, Hamlet tries to excuse his behavior by pleading insanity. This plea of innocence justified by his madness is a fantasized resolution to both the difficulty in which he finds himself and a possible excuse for his divided nature, a peaceful resolution of his difficulty.

> Give me your pardon, sir. I have done you wrong,
> But pardon't, as you are a gentleman.
> This presence knows, and you must needs have heard,
> How I am punished with a sore distraction. What I have done
> That might your nature, honor, and exception
> Roughly awake, I here proclaim was madness.
> Was't Hamlet wronged Laertes? Never Hamlet.
> If Hamlet from himself be ta'en away,
> And when he's not himself does wrong Laertes,
> Then Hamlet does it not, Hamlet denies it.
> Who does it then? His madness. If 't be so,
> Hamlet is of the faction that is wronged;
> His madness is poor Hamlet's enemy.
> Sir, in this audience,
> Let my disclaiming from a purposed evil
> Free me so far in you most generous thoughts
> That I have shot my arrow o'er the house
> And hurt my brother.
>
> (5.2.227–244)

Hamlet has divided himself. There are two Hamlets, sane and mad. As he attempts a reconciliation, or at least a pardon, with the above plea, Hamlet also appears to attempt a reconciliation of his conflicted gender roles. Hamlet wishes to return to the state before his father's murder and his mother's marriage to Claudius. In the scene in his mother's bedchamber Hamlet attempts this restoration. He admonishes his mother to "Confess yourself to heaven, / Repent what's past, avoid what is to come" (3.4.153–154). To which the Queen responds, "O Hamlet, thou hast cleft my heart in twain." And

Hamlet answers, "O, throw away the worser part of it, / And live the purer with the other half. Good night—but go not to my uncle's bed. Assume a virtue, if you have it not" (3.4.161–164). In his sarcastic remarks to the King before leaving for England, Hamlet speaks of his fantasized resolution of his difficulty.

> HAMLET: Farewell, dear mother. [to the king]
>
> KING: Thy loving father, Hamlet.
>
> HAMLET: My mother—father and mother is man and wife, man and wife
> is one flesh, and so, my mother. Come, for England!
>
> (4.3.46–49)

Once again Hamlet has fantasized a return to the mother and father. Masculine and feminine can coexist when man and wife are "one flesh."

• • •

Paw Paw,

I remember after you were diagnosed with cancer how I started riding out with you to the country to help you feed your cows. We would go to the "place out on the highway" and feed those cows first, then drive further to the "Nall's place" to feed your cows there. I remember how impatient I was with how slow you drove and how I wouldn't dare say anything bad to you because I didn't want to hurt your feelings. I remember you saying during the final months of your life how you were so proud of me, how you used to think I was lazy and weak but that during the past few months I had really changed. I also remember how you felt like you had really connected with me after all the years I kept you at a distance.

Do you remember how I wouldn't kiss you good-bye when I was little? It became a game, you would say to me as we were leaving your house, "Are you going to give Paw Paw some sugar?" and I would confidently say "No!" and walk out the door. I felt like I made up that denied affection during the last year of your life. I felt so strong and manly feeding those cows for you. I wanted to show you how strong I could be. This strength felt so different from the way that Daddy forced me to do manly things. The work for you I accepted, I enjoyed feeling the strength of my fifteen-year-old body.

You changed during your illness; you were forced to change. Granny said after you died that the final year of your life was the happiest of your marriage; that you had settled down, that the two of you weren't so mean to each other and that at last you had stopped being interested in other women. I think that the reason that you changed was because your illness forced you to be passive. Before your cancer you were always going, doing, working, but during your last year you had to accept being dependent, being passive, being taken care of. I think that is why we were able to reconcile our

*differences. I got to be active, a role you seldom saw me in, and you got to be depen-
dent. I was responsible for you on those trips. I can hardly grasp the idea of you, who
was always so strong and independent, being dependent on a fifteen-year-old me.*

*One of our trips to feed the cows I will never forget. It was near the end when
you were very sick, after the chemotherapy, after the operations. While I was inside
the barn throwing out the bales of hay for the cows you sat on the tailgate of your
pickup. You had the fly of your dark blue overalls open with your penis hanging out.
I thought you were peeing, and I guess you were at least trying to. When I came
out of the barn and walked up to the pickup you pointed down to the ground where
I expected your urine would have fallen and instead there was a double-handful of
clotted blood and pieces of flesh. You looked sickened, shook your head in disgust at
the sight and said, "Son, that came out of me." Your penis, which perhaps was a
symbol of strength for you during your entire life, was now associated with death and
the deterioration of your body. You seemed to be tired of your failing body, disgusted
with your dependence and passivity. Beyond "Oh, Paw Paw," I don't think I said
anything. We got in the pickup and drove home. Two months later you were dead.*

• • •

In the final scene of *Hamlet*, Horatio says, "Now cracks a noble heart. Good
night, sweet prince, / And flights of angels sing thee to thy rest" (5.2.338–
339). This "sweet" epitaph of the devoted Horatio to his now dead prince
contrasts sharply with Fortinbras's adieu only thirty-five lines later:

> Let four captains
> Bear Hamlet like a soldier to the stage,
> For he was likely, had he been put on,
> To have proved most royal; and for his passage
> The soldiers' music and the rite of war
> Speak loudly for him.
>
> (5.2.374–379)

It is significant that Horatio speaks from a private, individual experience.
He no doubt considered his prince and friend "sweet" and thought a band
of angels appropriate accompaniment for his journey to his rest. Fortinbras speaks from a formal, public distance, saying, "Of course he would
have been a great military man if he hadn't died so young, so let's send him
off like one anyway." Fortinbras describes Hamlet's fate as determined by
society, Hamlet = Man = Warrior = Man = Hamlet, while Horatio describes a fate that perhaps Hamlet would have embraced. Even in death

Hamlet could not escape socially prescribed gender roles: Fortinbras made him a man whether he liked it or not.

This reading of Hamlet and *Hamlet* argues that Shakespeare made a strong statement about the construction of gender. I see Shakespeare as exploring the difficulty with which a man is faced in reconciling the masculine and feminine within his personality and the ways this difficulty is compounded by societal pressures. Because Hamlet is not allowed to live and the play is indeed titled *The Tragedy of Hamlet*, Shakespeare, as well as Hamlet, would appear ambivalent at best about the possibility of a reconciling of both masculine and feminine within an individual personality. Though the particular configuration of this dilemma places it in a sixteenth-century Elizabethan context, I know it at the core as a man brought up in the United States, in East Texas, in the twentieth century. I recognize it because it still feels similar in my time and place.

NOTES

1. With only slight variations the logistics of the cockfights I have witnessed are strikingly similar to those described in Clifford Geertz's "Notes on the Balinese Cockfight."

2. During the mid-1970s, some cockfighters began to use poison on the gaffs attached to their rooster's legs. This led to cases of poisoning in the men who handled the roosters during the matches. My father stopped participating for a number of years because he thought this practice dangerous and dishonorable. He returned to fighting when the tide turned and the game "got cleaned up again." It was during this hiatus that I was at the age at which I would have begun to fight cocks myself, which is the reason that I never actually participated in the handling of cocks. By the time my father reentered the sport I was too old to start training to handle. My father continues to fight cocks every weekend during the season.

3. This reading of Hamlet could possibly be substantiated by evidence of Shakespeare's own struggle with gender identity and bisexuality. Hamlet could have been Shakespeare's attempt to comment on such issues as they were played out in Elizabethan England.

4. Hamlet's reaction against his mother's marrying Claudius could then be explained as a reaction to betrayal, not the betrayal of his father by his mother, but instead a betrayal of the ideals Gertrude instilled in Hamlet that he considered worthy, noble, and wise. Hamlet would view Gertrude as compromising these ideals by marrying Claudius.

5. As grade-school-age kids, my sister and I shot blackbirds with our BB guns so we could then nurse them back to health. They always died. I see this as an example

of an action motivated by conflicting gender messages. My sister graduated from nursing school this year.

REFERENCES

Geertz, Clifford. "Notes on the Balinese Cockfight." In *The Interpretation of Cultures*, 412–53. New York: Basic, 1973.

Shakespeare, William. *Hamlet.* In *Norton Critical Edition,* 2nd ed., edited by Cyrus Hoy. New York: Norton, 1992.

MERRILL BLACK

Three Readings of

the Wife of Bath

The Wife expresses a dream of masculine reading that is not antifeminist and a feminine relation to the condition of being read that is not antimasculinist—but she does so
after having been bruised and battered, permanently injured by that clerk Jankyn in their
concussive renovation of patriarchal discourse.
—Carolyn Dinshaw, *Chaucer's Sexual Poetics*

A few years ago a colleague and I were talking about sexual harassment on
the New England campus where we both worked. "Of course," she said,
"no one would try anything like that with us!" Secretly flattered at her inclusion, I said nothing to counter her impression. My feminist colleague
would not have understood the parts of my story I edit out in my work life.

During the four years I was married, I structured my days around not
getting hit. I examined everything I said and did carefully in the hope of
circumventing my husband's rage. We divorced over a decade ago. I don't
look like a "battered wife"—although I would not set myself apart from
the experience of women who fit the stereoptype more readily. I go for
weeks and months now without thinking of it. I've grown accustomed to
a self-imposed silence about these years. I brush away the urge to share this
experience. My life runs more smoothly if people don't know. But a long
thin scar still scores the center of my abdomen, marking my body with the
memory of the only time I fought back.

The Wife of Bath is introduced in the prologue of Chaucer's *Canterbury
Tales* by her marital scar, "she was somdel deef" (445). Her deafness, we learn
later, is a vestige of the night she ripped a page from her cleric husband's
Book of Wikked Wyves, interrupting his lecture on all the sinful failings of
womankind. He knocked her cold.

The pilgrims introduced in the prologue are all male except for the Wife and a submissive nun. They share their stories and their view of the world. With widening hips and voracious gap-toothed curiosity for all things sensual, the Wife elbows her way into the old boy's tale-telling circle of the *Canterbury Tales* prologue. We hear the Wife's sharp and confident voice in the prologue to her tale insisting that her bawdy experience carries more weight than patriarchal authority.

> Experience, though noon auctoritee
> Were in this world, is right y-nogh for me
> To speke of wo that is in marriage:
> For, lordinges, sith I twelf yeer was of age,
> Thonked be God that is eterne on lyve,
> Housbandes at chirch-door I have had fyve.
>
> (1–6)

> Experience rather than written authority
> Is in the world certainly enough for me
> To speak of the woe that is marriage
> For, sirs, since I was twelve years old
> Thanks to eternal God
> I have married five husbands.

The vectors of courage and foolhardiness intersect in her telling—she is both comic and poignant, but she will not be silenced.

I silence myself, by tasteful omission of my "tale" in the public world, but I too am a veteran, a seasoned campaigner in the war between the sexes. My scar is there as one testimony. Every time I see a doctor, share a dressing room, take a new lover, I revisit the experience of whether or not to tell, to gloss this mark on my body.

We were both drunk the night it happened. My hands finally insistent around his thick throat, he panicked, throwing his full weight behind the punch that ruptured my spleen. This did not feel that different from other beatings, except that a mysterious dull ache traveled back and forth between my abdomen and my shoulder. He left me lying on the kitchen floor. I called the local shelter just to talk. I blacked out while I was on the phone. I remember waking up on the floor with the phone in my hand and thinking fleetingly, "They sure didn't cover this at Riverdale Country Day School for Girls on Hudson." Someone came from the shelter and took me to the hospital, where emergency surgery was performed.

Once hitting became part of our relationship's vocabulary, it was a place we would always end up sooner or later. The spans of time varied where we thought it could be different. This job, this opportunity, this big break, we thought, could ultimately soothe the tension that sooner or later spilled over into the shouted insults and heavy pushes that signaled another attack. I would stand outside myself, watching myself become someone else, watching the man I loved become a monster. Sheltering my head or crying afterwards, I analyzed, as if to pass the terrible time, what I had done this time to elicit his outsized response. If I could understand, I could make it stop.

It is this desire to understand, the feeling of attachment to the oppressor that feels so shameful. A few weeks after the splenectomy, when I returned to have the stitches removed, the doctor ripped the bandage off. He looked at me with contempt, "Twenty minutes later and it would have been over." Maybe he'd seen the predictable aftermath of too many domestic incidents. I just wanted to leave the office as quickly as possible. My husband and I separated shortly after this incident, but it took me over a year to finalize the divorce.

People tend to focus on a woman's "going back for more." What is not examined is the intimate, ambiguously complex and explosive context within which the aggression occurs. It makes it so much harder to get help from authorities or even from other women.

The Wife of Bath does not apologize for her attachment to her husband. Jankyn was the husband she loved best, even though he beat her. The pattern of abuse and remorse, the sexual healings that follow the beatings are familiar to the twenty-first-century reader:

> But in oure bed he was so fressh and gay,
> And therewithal so wel koude he me glose,
> Whan that he wolde han my bele chose;
> That thogh he hadde me bete on every boon,
> He coude winne agayn my love anoon.
>
> (508–12)

> In our bed he was so fresh and gay
> And could read me so well
> he could always win my belle chose [literally, "good" or "beautiful thing"]
> Even though he'd beaten me on every bone
> He could again win my love anon

But what is not familiar is the Wife's happy ending in her tale of this marriage. It is with Jankyn that she eventually attains the "sovereigntee" that her tale asserts as the first desire of all women. Sovereignty, a balance struck between intimacy and autonomy, serves as the real life backdrop for her tale, a fable about a rapist-knight sentenced by a court of women to search out what it is women most desire.

My husband was so tender and remorseful after each incident, so attuned and committed to putting us back together after each shattering time, that I was seduced into believing that this time it would be different. We were mutually intoxicated again and again by the promise of the fresh start. I was too ashamed of my collaboration to get help or even to examine the experience. I was exhausted but enthralled by believing in him—his resolve, renewed and more fervent after each episode. We were cleansed and bonded and it would never happen again. We were a tiny nation in what seemed a dangerous world, with an iron pact of mutual protection and solace.

Everyone told me not to marry him. He was uneducated, irascible, frequently unemployed. He was also funny, imaginative, passionate, sensitive, and crazy about me. Always in trouble as a young man growing up in a small rural town, at seventeen he was given the choice of juvenile detention or military service. Three tours of Vietnam made this unformed boy a volatile man. Civilian life cramped him. Stretched too large too early, he was stung by the reception he received as a returning veteran of an unpopular war.

It has taken me this long to come to terms with this experience, one which many of my friends still find distasteful to talk about. I no longer indulge in the victim's quiet shame, or the survivor's defiant pride. Trying to understand this experience has led me to trace how I came to think about being a woman, a lover, and a wife. Oddly, this medieval text and its centuries-old cross-dressed female character from a strictly patriarchal world has reentered my life at different stages, reflecting something different each time.

· · ·

The first time I read the Wife of Bath's tale I was in high school, a private girl's school, where most students were upper middle class and Jewish. The teacher accepted that most students would not connect to this poem from the Middle Ages—ours was the era of relevance in education. But at sixteen I found the poem very relevant: it was about the dynamics between women and men. I was turned off by the Wife's mercenary marriages to her first three husbands, who were older and wealthy, but I was intrigued by her bawdy reveling in her sexual power and prowess. Most of the promising, virginal girls in my class saw the Wife as a laughable cartoon of a middle-aged slut.

It was the late sixties. The girls at my school had professional ambitions and considered themselves beyond Carolyn Dinshaw's observation of the Wife's approach to marriage "gaining control of [her] husband's property by ransoming her sexual favors" (213). Yet they practiced an updated version of the fifteenth-century sexual economics Chaucer has the Wife of Bath describe. "Virgin" was a term of art at our school. Girls would go pretty far, cordoning off only intercourse and the ring finger of the left hand for marriage. Marriage fantasies involved the prospective lawyers or doctors among us, those skinny boys with high SAT scores.

I had no intention of marrying for social position—I had my mother's career as an example of a woman distinguishing herself on her own merits. If I thought then about marriage at all, I thought of it as the deathbed of passion, like the civil companionate marriage my parents shared until I finished high school. Marriage seemed to me an arid lifeless refuge women turned to because they couldn't hold their own economically, selling their *belle chose* short for security's sake.

I was fully sexually active in high school. As the shiksa who "would," I felt both achingly vulnerable and smugly superior. I loved the passage where the Wife condemns with faint praise the purity of saints' virginity compared with the sexual solace that experienced wives could offer. The lines helped me feel like a toothsome loaf of whole wheat on a shelf of "precius" Wonder bread in the burgeoning age of health food.

• • •

The second time I read the Wife of Bath's tale I was in college. I played the Wife and doubled as the loathly lady of the tale for a student-made film. We sat around in heavy costumes under shaky, jury-rigged lights, eating messily out of trenchers and hoisting foaming chargers of beer for take after take.

The women at my college were forming consciousness-raising groups. The serious, angry tone of the women's groups made me feel shallow and inadequate. Sisterhood, as it was practiced at this small Vermont college, seemed to preclude the 100-watt flirtation I enjoyed in the company of men. I was equally taken aback by the men's response, the chilly aftermath of late-night passionate discussions of literature that ended in bed.

Like Emma Goldman, I wanted a free-love revolution where we could dance. The Wife of Bath lectures her fellow pilgrims on the fallacy of celibate men of the church imposing their canonical authority as having more weight than her hands-on experience. Like the Wife, I perceived the censure and ridicule from my peers and it only fueled my defiance. I opposed my experience to the would-be authority of both, men's double standard and women's doctrinaire exclusion.

In the Wife's tale I found a compelling image of marriage not evident in either the old-style oppressive marriages of my parents' generation or the newly minted "equal" liaisons my peers were forming. From another century came the ghost of a promise that men and women could be equal in love and erotically energized. The tale promised a mutual "sovereigntee" between men and women, warmed by a visceral understanding of each other's experience.

The Wife's tale opens with a rape. The rapist-knight is to be beheaded but the queen and her ladies intercede, proposing an alternative sentence. If he can return to court in a year and a day with the right answer to the question "What do women most desire?" his life will be spared. As the Wife is forcibly educated by her husband in the prevailing negative view of women through nightly readings from his *Book of Wyked Wives*, so the rapist-knight is forced, on fear of death, to educate himself about women.

This year and a day exercise in forced empathy brings him to a teachable moment. After nearly a year of interviewing women who told him women most desired gay clothes and flattery, he meets the loathly lady, described as an ugly old woman, an archetype of the wise crone. He is so desperate about his impending settling up with the ladies of the court that he assents when she tells him that she knows women's greatest desire and will tell him, if he agrees to marry her. He hastily agrees and rushes to court with the loathly lady's answer, that women most desire "sovereigntee."

The ladies of the court agree and his life is saved. He then tries to circumvent his bargain with his elderly, unattractive counsel. He is forced, as he forced the maid, when the ladies at court learn of his deal with the loathly lady, to have the price exacted on his body. He must submit to the attentions of someone he did not choose. The knight tries to buy her off, begging "Tak al my good, and lat my body go" (1061).

But unlike the maid, he is given a choice of his hell. The loathly lady poses him the following riddle on their wedding night: would he prefer an ugly but true wife or a trophy wife who must be guarded from the attentions of other men? Utterly undone, the knight defers to his new wife in the Middle English equivalent of "You decide, dear." The loathly lady pulls aside the bedcurtain, revealing herself transformed into a beautiful and true wife for having had her "sovereigntee" conferred by her husband and lord. She will share his bed and his life as a sovereign being. This mythic happy-ever-after ending amplifies the Wife's ending to her prologue, where she closes with a final reconciliation with Jankyn.

A year after our separation, my husband and I went on a date. The evening started out great, but somewhere after the third or fourth drink, the trapdoor dropped out of our good time, as it always did. We argued in the parking lot. He slapped me. Not hard, but we both knew instantly that normal wouldn't ever have our name on it. He rode off on his motorcycle in a rage and later, going over sixty miles an hour, hit the back of a van, rupturing his spleen.

The next day, I stood over him in the intensive care unit, watching the labored rise and fall of his chest and stomach, now stapled closed, a brawny version of my own healing scar. Tears coursed down my face. Since the slap the night before, I knew the relationship was over. But I still felt loyal to his body, trained to his moods, sensations, and experiences. He was not awake yet. I knew from my operation a year earlier that when he did wake it would hurt him even to breathe.

While I was married, I worked in bars. Occasionally I told the truckers and fishermen some of the raunchier *Canterbury Tales*. Sometimes I told the story of the Wife of Bath just to watch my listeners' faces when I told them the punch line: when the story was written.

Women of the Middle Ages had little place in public life and were totally subjected to their husband's will in the home. With no legal or economic recourse, women could not inherit land or represent themselves in court. Yet the patristic readings that form the social backdrop for the *Canterbury Tales* (the text for Jankyn's *Book of Wikked Wyves*, the catalyst of the final battle with the Wife) attribute frightful atavistic power to women's sexuality:

> Thou lykenest eek wommanes love to helle,
> To bareyne lond, ther water may not dwelle.
> Thou lyknest it also to wilde fyr;
> The more it brenneth, the more it hath desyr.
>
> (371–374)

> You liken women's love to hell
> To barren land, where no water may dwell

You liken it also to a wood [forest] fire
The more it burns [consumes], the more it desires.

A powerful loathsome creature with a million vices, she will drain a man dry, rob him of his earthly goods, and make heaven's doors slam shut on him by inciting his uncontrollable lust.

In neighborhood bars like the ones in which I worked, the same stereotypes prevailed. The woman who drains you and deceives you, wielding tremendous power in the home even while she is publicly powerless, is a perennial figure in after-work bar talk and the country music on the jukebox. Misogyny hasn't progressed very far.

When my husband was angry, he would rail against me in ways that made no sense at all. The vision he painted of me in these moments sounds eerily interchangeable with the patristic pronouncements of the fifteenth century. In the twisted lens of his rage I became somebody so powerful, so selfish and harmful to him, that within the logic of the rage the only response was to hit hard, to silence and bully into submission. I let myself believe, or failed increasingly to question, the text of his rages, relinquishing any agency in the shape and quality of my own life.

The Wife of Bath describes a similar passivity in her marriage to Jankyn. In the free-fall of love, she gives up the resources she so painstakingly acquired over the course of her former marriages: the land and riches that provided her a degree of autonomy within a culture and economy where women were invisible. He beats her. She forgives him or reconciles herself to the beatings because of the passionate sexual aftermath. He attempts to isolate her, limiting her "gadding about." She is drawn in again and again by his "disdainful" love.

In my twenties, I was a fringe dweller, accumulating wreckage and the bruised glory of life lived at the edge. Marriage and career were for those others—those satisfied to live life small and safe. Another friend described those experimental years before we recognized that the meter was running, that there are no free miles: "I was always the front runner—way ahead of the crowd in the first lap. But there was no second lap around the track for me." Near thirty, I collapsed under the burden of too much open-ended choice and married eagerly, having a baby right away. Something to structure the next twenty years.

Unlike many women who are stalked indefinitely, or who suffer a deadly response to their leaving, I had married someone with just enough sanity or fear of public censure to fold when I finally took action and solicited support to leave. It took a long time to regain my sense of agency and to trust my own ability to make decisions, to finish a sentence, to disagree with a loved one. I am still ashamed of how easily I could be coaxed and persuaded to try again, of how much I wanted to believe that this time it would be different.

Since we broke up, my ex-husband has been only with women who are survivors of abuse, as though he can only speak the language of recovery with fellow expatriates. My ex-husband is a limited man in some ways, but I am moved by his struggle and thankful for the extent to which we have been able to become, intermittently, safe enough with each other to talk about what happened.

I still hang a fragile hope for men and women on my ex-husband's recovery. Through sobriety, the support of other men who have battered, and his wife's shared experience of abuse, he has developed a broader range of capabilities for dealing with his rage, short-circuiting his own shame and self-loathing. If he offers no other legacy to our son, he offers the cautionary possibility that blinding rage can be forcibly reversed, can be somehow managed or understood, can be overcome, with few resources beyond love and the desire to change.

. . .

In taking a Chaucer seminar in graduate school, in my forties, I was moved almost to tears listening to the professor quietly read the prologue of the *Canterbury Tales*:

> Whan that Aprill with his shoures sote
> The droghte of Marche hath perced to the rote,
> And bathed every veyne in swich licour
> Of which vertu engendred is the flour
>
> (1–4)

It was an auditory madeleine moment, invoking my youth and all the scarring authoritative experience that had passed, bringing me again to hearing these words. I was hearing them again in the company of smart young women with promising futures, now twenty years my junior, leaning into our teacher's scholarly passion for this lilting obscure language.

As a younger reader, I was drawn to the Wife's outlandish appetites and voracious energy. I now found poignant and precipitously close to home the passages in her prologue where she reflects on the surging gradations between the life stages of maid and matron:

But Lord Christ! whan that it remembreth me
Upon my yowthe and on my jolitee,
It tikleth me aboute myn herte rote—
Unto this day it dooth myn herte bote
That I have had my world as in my tyme.
But age, allas! that al wol envenyme,
Hath me biraft my beautee and my pith.
Lat go, farewel! the devel go therwith!
The flour is goon, ther is namore to telle;
The bren, as I best can, now moste I selle;
But yet to be right merye wol I fonde.

(469–479)

But Lord Christ when I remember
my youth and beauty
It tickles me to my heart's root
And even now does my heart good
That I have had my world as in my time.
But age, alas, would poisen everything,
Has bereft me of my beauty and my pith—
Let go, farewell, the devil take all!
The flour is gone, there is no more to tell;
The bran as I best can now must I sell;
But yet to be right merry will I try.

She is defiant, grateful for her checkered past, paradoxically reconciled to having to sell the bran as best she can having had her world and time. The most brilliant colors appear just as the leaf is ready to fall.

Critic Barbara Gottfried reflects on the Wife's "growing awareness both of the impossibility of comprehending the ultimate causes or reasons for things in one's life, and concomitantly, her sense that she has never really been fully in control of her life" (217).

In rereading the tale in the graduate seminar, I tried to solicit the opinions of the young women in my class on whether the Wife can be used as a feminist model. They looked blank—not seeing her as an exemplar, perhaps, of anything worth having. I did not disclose the personal history that fueled my curiosity. How would she be viewed by the next generation of women, who all seemed to me so defiant, smart, and hopeful? Maybe I was afraid of how they would then view me.

The tale is a fable, its happy ending and the Wife's reconciliation with

Jankyn a myth, written by a male author six centuries ago. What draws me in about this character is not that she is a battered wife who returns again but that she is willing to do battle, to be a worthy opponent despite all, fiercely insisting on a relationship that is both equal and mutually transformative. Bloody but unbowed, she insists on her autonomy, her freedom of speech, and her sexual enjoyment of her partner.

Amos Oz, a Middle Eastern writer, described in an interview what he called the Chekhovian versus the Shakespearean victory. In the Shakespearean victory, someone wins, a clear, glorious conquest—the stage is littered with corpses. In the Chekhovian model, there is no clear victor— everyone gets something but must give something dear for it. The curtain falls on the characters sitting around the table clenched, committed. The samovar hums. If we are, as nations, to survive, Oz says, we must learn to embrace the Chekhovian victory.

REFERENCES

Chaucer, Geoffrey. *The Canterbury Tales.* Edited by V. A. Volve and Glending Olson. New York: Norton, 1989.

Dinshaw, Carolyn. *Chaucer's Sexual Poetics.* Madison: University of Wisconsin Press, 1990.

Gottfried, Barbara. "Conflict and Relationship, Sovereignty and Survival: Parables of Power in the *Wife of Bath's Prologue*." *Chaucer Review* 19 (1985): 202–24.

DAVID RICHMAN

Listening to the Images:

My Sightless Insights

into Yeats's Plays

In Yeats's last play, "The Death of Cuchulain," the eponymous legendary Irish hero receives six mortal wounds and has himself bound to a standing stone so that he may die on his feet. An acquisitive blind man enters, the same blind chicken- and bread-stealer who had appeared in another Cuchulain play, "On Baile's Strand." The blind man has been told that he will be given twelve pennies if he fetches the great Cuchulain's head. Kneeling before the wounded man, he gropes up the body, past the knees, thighs, and waist, feeling for the neck. As he does this, Cuchulain remarks:

> I think that you know everything, blind man;
> My mother or my nurse said that the blind
> Know everything.
>
> (*Collected Plays* 444)

The blind man, his inner eye on the main chance, replies:

> No, but they have good sense.
> How could I have got twelve pennies for your head
> If I had not good sense?
>
> (*Collected Plays* 444).

Yeats's bracing, unsentimental depictions of the blind range from the prophet Tiresias to Cuchulain's nameless killer, and they demonstrate, among other things, that the life of the blind is a continuous collaboration. The fool in "On Baile's Strand" remarks to his blind companion, "I would never be able to steal anything if you didn't tell me where to look for it" (*Collected Plays* 161). The blind man, unable himself to look, must trade his special knowledge for the loan of the fool's eyes.

Since I am always borrowing other people's eyes in my difficult, daily negotiations with my blindness, I am drawn to Yeats's acerbic dramatizations of the collaborative relationship. Being a blind theater artist, I am even more powerfully drawn to the sort of theater to which Yeats the theater manager, theater theorist, and playwright gave life and form. It is not simply that blindness is a recurring theme in these plays. What draws me most to Yeats's plays is the value this painter's son sets on the ear. "Write for the ear, I thought, so that you may be instantly understood" (*Essays* 530).

Yeats's great achievement in writing for the ear was unexpectedly brought home to me when I attended a poetry reading of contemporary avant-garde poetry in the spring of 1996. The reading ought to have been one of the high points of my semester, and I felt, still feel, a lack in myself that it was not. Contemporary poetry is rarely produced in Braille or on tape, so years pass before it becomes available for me to listen to, read, and savor. Readings such as this make the material available to me. More important, such readings create an ambience that I value above all others — made up of the speaking voice and the listening ears of attentive auditors. I prefer the rapt silence of an audience to the rapt silence of a solitary reader. Since so much more material is available on tape than in Braille, the act of reading is for me an act of listening. I set a value beyond price on the speaking voice.

My first intimation that this particular reading might not be aimed solely at the ear came when the reader — my former colleague Romana Huk, who reads extraordinarily well — projected transparencies of the poems she was reading for her audience. Have we lost so much of our power to listen that we must have the words in front of us, or we won't be able to absorb them? Through force of habit, I used the word *we* in my thought, even though I could not be included in this "we." Not being able to read the transparency, I would have to depend on my ear. But surely my ability to listen, trained by years of blindness, would be equal to this new poetry?

I was quite wrong. The street-singer in "The Death of Cuchulain" sings in frustration about being unable to get a grip on the thighs of her phantom lovers from the heroic Irish past. After a fashion, I now shared this frustration. I couldn't get a grip on the streams of words. They reminded me of Lucky's monologue in "Waiting for Godot," or of the monologue uttered by the blubbery lips in Beckett's "Not I." But these words lacked the torrential force that Beckett's monologues, if well performed, always achieve. If I worked hard enough, I could memorize these poems as an actor memorizes a script, but listening to them for the first time, it seemed as if they were passing through my ears, through my brain, leaving scarcely an impression. Were the people around me in the audience, simultaneously reading and listening, doing better than I with this seemingly intractable material?

Trained by an inability to take notes with ease, my memory is durable and has served me. I usually can remember details and phrases from verse drama, as well as the shape of the whole, even after only one hearing. "Appease / The misery of the living and the remorse of the dead" ("Purgatory," *Collected Plays* 435). "I call to the eye of the mind / A Well long choked up and dry" ("At the Hawk's Well," *Collected Plays* 136). My first visceral attraction to Yeats's plays, long before I began to study, write about, and direct them, came about because they contain such phrases. It may be my aging memory, but I cannot now remember any phrase from the poems I heard at the reading. I don't recall the name of a single poet. My only vivid memory of the evening is the fact of the transparencies—that is, that these poems needed to be absorbed simultaneously by the ear and the eye. Lacking working eyes, I was the wrong audience for the material.

The dialogue and lyrics of Yeats's plays exert their greatest effects when they are spoken and listened to. "I have spent my life in clearing out of poetry every phrase written for the eye, and bringing all back to syntax that is for ear alone. Let the eye take delight in the form of the singer and the panorama of the stage and be content with that" (*Essays* 529). Is it any wonder that a blind listener and theater artist should take special delight in a poet who writes for the ear? Does the fact of my blindness make me old-fashioned? I value the traditional iambs, spondees, inversions. The inversion is especially powerful when the stressed syllable begins with a plosive—a P or a B: "And I call to the mind's eye / Pallor of an ivory face" ("At the Hawk's Well," *Collected Plays* 136). That P in "pallor," the unexpectedly stressed first syllable of a line following immediately on the spondee that ends the previous line, strikes my ear with sensuous force. These sorts of effects, this playing with traditional meter, this use of spondees and inversions, pyrrhic feet and enjambment, makes verse a delight to my ear and causes it to take permanent root in my memory. The personal emotion is given vigor and permanence by its expression in the varying rhythms created by traditional meter. "All that is personal soon rots. It must be packed in ice or salt. . . . If I wrote of personal love or sorrow in free verse or in any rhythm that left it unchanged amid all its accidents, I would be full of self-contempt because of my egotism and indiscretion and foresee the boredom of my reader"

(*Essays* 522). For me, the avant-garde poetry was left unchanged amid its accidents.

Perhaps, since it wasn't written for the ear alone, I lack the capacity to comprehend and appreciate it—just as I lack the capacity to comprehend and appreciate painting. My ear requires the ice or salt, the always varying yet always expected beat of the traditional lyric meters. Edgar says of blind Gloucester in *King Lear* that his other senses are made imperfect by his eyes' anguish. I don't know if my senses are made keener by my eyes' anguish, but I do know that they require a more intense stimulation. I like Guinness and Laphroaig, strong black coffee, and the sound of powerful plosives in spondees or inversions. "Hoary-headed frosts / Fall in the fresh lap of the crimson rose" gives me a strong, sensuous pleasure no matter how often I hear it. So does "Have not old writers said / That dizzy dreams can spring / From the dry bones of the dead? ("The Dreaming of the Bones," *Collected Plays* 276). The blind don't have a monopoly on such pleasures, but one who depends as strongly as I do on the ear takes special delight in language composed for the ear and the voice.

Theater, even poetic theater, requires a good deal more than words. Yeats knew himself to be thrusting against every theatrical current of his time in his passionate advocacy of the word as the theater's most important element. Early in his career, when the Abbey Theatre was a far-off dream, he wrote, "The theatre began in ritual, and it cannot come to its greatness again without recalling words to their ancient sovereignty" (*Essays* 170). His theatrical career can be described as a prolonged struggle to create a countertruth to the technically elaborate, ever more spectacular theater he perceived to be dominant in Europe and America. Amid the voluminous theoretical and critical writings on the modern and contemporary theater—with their unremitting praise for movement, gesture, dance, backdrop, inarticulate sound—above all with their frightening distrust of the word, I find continued support and nourishment in Yeats's plays, in his vision of a theater dominated by words. I find an ally in this theater director who insists on stilling the stage's restlessness and on commanding his audience to give ear.

The dramatist's insistence on the primacy of the word reaped its rewards. In the fifteen plays he composed and produced between 1916 and his death in 1939, he established himself as the most significant verse dramatist writing in English since Shakespeare's time. T. S. Eliot, in the first Yeats Memorial Lecture delivered at Sligo in 1940, acknowledged the debt that all subsequent verse dramatists owe to Yeats. "Yeats had nothing, and we have had Yeats . . . I do not know where our debt to him as a dramatist ends, and in time it will not end until that drama itself ends" (62).

But Yeats's achievement as a verse dramatist is bound up with paradoxes that I, a blind teacher/director/critic, must find especially disturbing. Isn't verse drama itself an old-fashioned form—a rotting relic of Peter Brook's deadly theater? Knowing full well that I am pushing in my own small way against the same inexorable current that Yeats contended with for forty years, I assert that I must believe that Ibsen, Brecht, Williams, though they did not compose verse drama, were poets as well as playwrights. Even in these increasingly nonverbal times, plays endure, get read, taught, and performed, remain in memory, because of the power of their words. Words memorably express the passion of characters and the terror of situations. "I am burning your child, Thea!" "Erst kommt das Fressen, dann kommt die Moral." "I have always depended on the kindness of strangers."

I must wonder whether the fact of my blindness constrains me to assert the power and primacy of the word in an art in which many of its theorists, from Craig through Artaud to Grotowski, assert that the word is growing ever less important. Mine is a minority position, as was Yeats's. That position is that the power and pleasure afforded by the dance of strong syllables, by the words in their intricate rhythmic patterns spoken from a stage and listened to by an audience, is unlike, and cannot be replaced by, other theatrical pleasures or sources of theatrical power.

It is my good fortune that there is a place for the production and teaching of verse drama in the university. Being blind, I need a theater in which the spoken word is of primary importance, and the university affords one such theater. I have spent more of my life than most people listening to the speaking voice—absorbing its varying rhythms and patterns. My blindness intensified a natural interest. Blessed with talent as a listener, and trained by years of practice, I am able to teach performers, both student and professional, to speak with clarity and passion, and to command an audience's attention. This ability, in which I take pride and which is a source of my livelihood as theater teacher and director of mostly verse plays with mainly student casts, can also be described as the virtue of a defect. I never allowed myself to wonder during the years of graduate school and the first years as an uncertain assistant professor if I was gravitating toward verse drama because my blindness forever closed to me the world of nonverbal theater. If I allowed myself to think too much about my limitations I would have become paralyzed, unable to function. I had to plunge ahead, deliberately blind to my blindness, banking on my developing dramatic imagination, my strength with words, rhythms, and the thought and passion these express.

By the time a growing confidence in my abilities permitted me to probe my limitations and weaknesses, I had come to know the work of Yeats the playwright, theater manager, and theater theorist. The great example of his theatrical career afforded me nourishment and confirmation. There was indeed a place for the sort of theater I loved and valued. If Yeats could spend so lavish a portion of his great life composing plays "which could only fully succeed in a civilisation very unlike ours" (*Variorum Edition* 566), then I could spend a smaller portion of my smaller life teaching and directing verse drama in the relative comfort of the university. Fighting a battle not dissimilar to Yeats's own, I could make myself into a theater director and find an audience.

Yeats battled to make himself into a playwright. He was not a natural dramatist. He slowly and painfully taught himself the arts of the theater—shaping them the while to his own purposes. As with words, he was a fierce traditionalist in many of the theater's arts. This translator of Sophocles thought of drama in terms of the ancient Aristotelian elements—plot, character, dialogue, thought—in an age when other modernists were calling these into question. Yeats's adherence to traditional dramatic forms imposed on his dramaturgy a necessary discipline—a word he valued—as dependable and certain as the discipline imposed by the contrapuntal relations between meter and rhythm. As he never abandoned meter in verse, he never abandoned the Aristotelian elements in drama. As he did with verse itself, Yeats transmuted each of these traditional elements and fused them to create a wholly modern theater that still exerts its influence on contemporary playwrights. I too am a traditionalist, valuing the ancient elements and forms of drama. Does my blindness make me shy away from the contemporary theater with its love of gesture and movement and its concomitant distrust of words?

The act of writing this essay is forcing me to expose and discuss vulnerabilities I have spent my life trying to minimize. My blindness imposes severe limitations on my ability to function professionally as a director of and writer about plays. A substantial part of theatrical art has little to do with the ear and everything to do with the eye. It would be disingenuous not to acknowledge these limitations—foolish, not to say foolhardy, not to try to work around them. But I don't dwell on these limitations with pleasure, and thinking about them too much, even after twenty-five years in

academic theater, increases my anxiety. In my more sanguine moments—
and these outnumber the other variety—I don't think I have been deceiv-
ing myself and others all these years. My productions of plays by Shakespeare, Yeats, and other dramatists have received praise from colleagues,
students, reviewers, and audiences. I am human enough to take pleasure in
this praise. At the same time, a senior colleague, a world-renowned expert
in Renaissance drama at the university where I worked before coming to
New Hampshire, wrote the following assessment of my theater work:

> There is no point in dodging the issue of his blindness. If he had his sight, it
> is reasonable to assume that he would manage the business of stage block-
> ing more effectively than he typically does, and that the general business of
> the stage action in his productions would be a good deal more interesting
> and inventive than it is. . . . But the productions tend to be fairly static, and
> his Shakespearean productions as often as not amount to little more than
> costumed readings of the play.

I recognize that this is not a prevailing opinion of my work, but I recognize also that such an opinion is possible, arguable, and that many may
hold it. Why then did I choose this career? I recall reading or hearing
that Bobby Kennedy suffered from vertigo and therefore forced himself to
climb mountains. Is my choice of career a desperate attempt to prove that
I can indeed do something that I ought not, by all logic, be able to do? I
try not to apply too strictly to my own case Samuel Johnson's notorious
remark: "Sir, a woman's preaching is like a dog's walking on his hind legs.
It is not done well; but you are surprised to find it done at all." I prefer to
conclude that interest and talent have led me to pursue, like Yeats, a theater
where words are dominant. Characters in the plays through which I have
best success are most fully alive, most deeply reveal themselves, through
their words.

> Gallop apace you fiery-footed steeds
> Toward Phoebus' lodging; such a wagoner
> As Phaeton would whip you to the west
> And bring in cloudy night immediately.
> (*Romeo and Juliet* 3.2.1–4)

The desperate inversion at the beginning of this speech, the urgent alliter-
ations on F and W, the strong stress on the verb *whip*, the rhythm of the first
four syllables—stressed, double unstressed, stressed—the hurry, the forc-

ing the sun to move through the sky by an act of will, the need, embodied in the rhythm, for the immediacy of night even though the sun is standing in high heaven, the passionate life burning behind these words: these are the dramatic materials I best work with. I am most rewarded when a student performer speaks words such as these in a production I have directed, and when a hushed audience listens.

I am drawn to Yeats's romantic model of a room full of people who share one lofty emotion. Competing ideas of an audience exist, best known among them being Brecht's model of a theater full of smokers, self-preoccupied and taking in the play with all critical faculties awake. I have no illusions about creating hypnosis, or a state of theatrically induced trance —though I recognize that the tragic ecstasy at which Yeats aimed is close to trance. Yet there are moments of intense listening during which even a smoker, were such a person allowed in our politically correct contemporary theaters, might pause between puffs and listen.

In the theater, as in the life some argue theater imitates, listening is not enough. In the best of all possible worlds, the eye and the ear collaborate — in the audience as well as in collaborating theater artists. Both senses must be appealed to, and the pleasure taken by each sense enriches the pleasure taken by the other. But Yeats came to see that the eye and the ear could be at war with each other. The modern theater, as Yeats diagnosed it, was restless, nervous, full of extraneous movement and spectacle, never allowing for that slowing and stilling that permit tragic reverie. Looking back on his career toward the end of his life, he wrote, "I wanted to get rid of irrelevant movement; the stage must become still that words might keep all their vividness, and I wanted vivid words. When I saw a London play, I saw actors crossing the stage not because the play compelled them but because a producer said they must do so to keep the attention of the audience" (*Essays* 527).

Yeats took pleasure in Sarah Bernhardt, whose pristine economy of gesture and movement he memorably described. He valued a still and quiet style of acting, holding up for particular praise a performance in which he "counted twenty-seven quite slowly before anybody on a fairly well-filled stage moved, as it seemed, so much as an eyelash" (*Explorations* 87). The painter's son never created a theater of talking heads—far from it. Using mask, dance, tapestry, he created—so I hear, read, and believe—a theater of astonishing visual beauty. But Yeats's visual effects were always the servants of the spoken play, never its masters.

For Yeats, the visual element of the theater often presented an alien or competing interest. How was it possible, he argued, to give imaginative attention to a metaphor when distracted by a piece of competing scenery?

> It needed some imagination, some gift for daydreams, to see the horses in the fields and flowers of Colonus, as one listened to the elders gathered about Oedipus, or to see the pendent bed and procreant cradle of the martlet, as one listened to Banquo before the castle of Macbeth. But it needs no imagination to admire a painting of one of the more obvious effects of nature painted by someone who understands how to show everything to the most hurried glance. (*Essays* 168)

Yeats was forever subordinating scenery to the performer's appeal to the emotions and the imagination. "We must from time to time substitute for the movements that the eye sees the nobler movements that the heart sees, the rhythmical movements that seem to flow up into the imagination from some deeper life than that of the individual soul" (*Explorations* 109).

Too close an attention to what the eye sees daily can be a distraction. "A Funeral Elegy for Master William Peter," probably composed by the verse dramatist John Ford in 1612, develops this idea in somber stanzas. Yeats probably did not know this poem, but he would have agreed with these lines, which give precise expression to a principle he would all his life apply to the composition and production of plays:

> The willful blindness that hoodwinks the eyes
> Of men enwrapped in an earthy veil
> Makes them most ignorantly exercise
> And yield to humor when it doth assail,
> Whereby the candle and the body's light
> Darkens the inward eyesight of the mind,
> Presuming still it sees, even in the night
> Of that same ignorance which makes them blind.
> (lines 257–264)

Yeats strove to create a theater that appeals to the inward eyesight of the mind. The imagination to which his plays appeal is nourished by that which the outward eye does not see. Every traveler in this inward world is uncertain, so it is a world in which I need be no more uncertain than any other traveler. Since my travels in the outward world are full of uncertainty, I am naturally drawn by Yeats's inward world and by his strong championing of inward vision. For Yeats, the primary sense through which this inward vision is achieved is the ear, and the mind behind it. In "The Mother of God" Yeats conjures "a fallen flare / Through the hollow of an ear." In his note to these lines, he describes "Byzantine mosaic pictures of the Annunciation, which show a line drawn from a star to the ear of the virgin. She received the word through the ear, a star fell, and a star was born" (*Collected Poems* 536). This description, to apply the sacred to the profane, is apposite to the effect of a verse play on its hearers.

Moving away from that which the outward eye sees, Yeats became what Katharine Worth, in *The Irish Drama of Europe*, describes as a dramatist of the interior (158). But the inward vision Yeats strove for is not wholly unconnected to outward vision. Yeats doubtless saw dry wells and desiccated landscapes, the archetype of which he evokes in the words of "At the Hawk's Well," or the poor fisherman's cottage that becomes the imagined setting for "The Only Jealousy of Emer." In Yeats's plays at their best, however visionary and otherworldly, there is a discernible relation between the world created for the ear and the mind, and the world the playwright and his audience daily observed. When Yeats's plays suffer, as they sometimes do, they suffer through a vagueness, a wandering too far from the observable world of fact. As playwright, Yeats at his best achieves a difficult balance between being able to draw on the outward world, and yet not allowing his plays' inner vision to be darkened by "The willful blindness that hoodwinks the eyes / Of men enwrapped in an earthy veil."

I don't see the world. I have to depend on my other four senses, my imagination and reading, and what others tell me for what knowledge I have of it. In the spirit of the Yeats who is always battling against a visual competing interest, or of the author of "A Funeral Elegy," my inward eye is not blinded by messages from my outward one. But I doubt that I could produce plays to hold the attention of sighted audiences if I did not have direct, firsthand experience of the observable world. Up to the time I was twelve, I had just enough sight to distinguish colors, objects, human forms and faces. I have a memory of these things. I have a notion of color, of the relations of objects to each other. I have a visual memory and the rudiments of a visual imagination. My writing, even in this essay, is full of visual metaphors that I recognize as metaphors. When I speak or write of my views or perceptions, my reader or listener may get a Brechtian shock and realize that one can "view" or "perceive" through a memory of vision, and through senses other than the eye.

I don't know with certainty whether it is possible for one who has never seen color to be given any useful idea of color. The people I know who have been totally blind from birth have no firsthand notion of color or image. My notion of these things, based on my child's memory, must be in the highest degree imperfect. But this notion enables me at least to enter into difficult and complex theatrical collaborations. In preparing productions for the stage, I must always combine my imagination and my memory of vision with the borrowing of someone else's eyes.

My life of coping with blindness outside the theater also requires collaboration. I chafe at my constant need for personal and professional collaboration, and like Yeats, who also chafed, I have come to love and value those with whom I daily collaborate. Peculiarly analogous to my life, theater is a collaborative art. No theater artist can function in isolation, and though the creation of theater can be an unremitting war of egoisms, theater flourishes where respect and mutual affection also flourish.

Yeats's life in the theater was a protracted struggle, and he famously lashed out at "The day's war with every knave and dolt / Theatre business, management of men" ("The Fascination of What's Difficult," *Collected Poems* 104) At the same time, his theatrical career was enriched, made possible, by many collaborations. In letters, notes, autobiographical writings, prefaces, and especially in poems, he pays homage to his many collaborators.

James Flannery, in "W. B. Yeats, Gordon Craig, and the Visual Arts of the Theatre," argues that Yeats's plays required the collaboration of supremely talented artists, and that his "difficulties with actors were notorious" (82). But toward the end of his life, Yeats remembered with joy his many collaborators. Among others, he memorialized "William Fay at the end of 'On Bailes Strand,' Mrs. Patrick Campbell in my 'Deirdre' passionate and solitary, and in later years that great artist Ninette de Valois in 'Fighting the Waves.' These things will, it may be, haunt me on my deathbed" ("On the Boiler," *Explorations* 416). J. M. Synge and Augusta Gregory, his fellow directors of the Abbey Theatre, were always present in his thought and art. When he accepted the Nobel Prize for literature, he remarked that "two forms should have stood one at either side of me — an old woman sinking into the infirmity of age and a young man's ghost" (*Autobiographies* 374). He wrote repeatedly of his complex and unending debt to Augusta Gregory.

> And I am in despair that time may bring
> Approved patterns of women or of men
> But not that self-same excellence again.
> ("The Municipal Gallery Revisited," *Collected Poems* 369)

To the mask-maker and composer Edmund Dulac, Yeats wrote of a revival of "At the Hawk's Well": "Watching Cuchulain in his lovely mask and costume, that ragged old masked man who seems hundreds of years old, that guardian of the well, with your great golden wings and dancing to your music, I had one of those moments of excitement that are the dramatist's reward and decided there and then to dedicate to you my next book of verse" ("Note to 'The Winding Stair,'" *Collected Poems* 536).

The unvarying necessity for collaboration in my personal and professional life attracts me to the constant presence of collaborators in Yeats's theatrical career. Fruitful collaboration is, at the last, an act of friendship. "Think where man's glory most begins and ends, / And say my glory was I had such friends" ("The Municipal Gallery Revisited," *Collected Poems* 370). Yeats's greatest friends were made for him by his plays. My greatest friendships have grown through the theater—Susan Goldin and Doug Tilton, with whom I collaborate on traveling productions of Shakespeare, colleague and fellow theater director John Edwards, the hundreds of professionals and students who act in, design, choreograph, stage-manage, or build productions with me. I first met my wife Susan through the theater. Our artistic collaboration on "The Revenger's Tragedy" and "No Exit" ripened into friendship and love. Every theater artist is a collaborator, but my blindness requires an especially profound and complex collaboration. This personal history gives me special insight into Yeats's theatrical collaborations, and into the special value he placed on them.

However, as with every fact of Yeats's career, his relations with his theatrical collaborators were fraught with conflict. Existing side by side with his generous appreciation of some of his fellow theater artists was a rage against anything that broke in on his artist's solitude. He was by some accounts a terrible theater director. The Dublin diarist and playgoer Joseph Holloway, quoted in William Murphy's *Family Secrets*, presents a vivid portrait of the playwright at work in the theater:

> a more irritating play producer never directed a rehearsal. He's ever flitting about and interrupting the players in the middle of their speeches, showing them by illustration how he wishes it done, droningly reading this passage and that in monotonous preachy sing-song, or climbing up the ladder on the stage and pacing the boards as he would have the players do. Ever and always he was on the fidgets, and made each and all of the players inwardly pray backwards. Frank Fay, I thought, would explode with suppressed rage at his frequent interruptions during the final speeches he had to utter. (175)

My rage has different sources than Yeats's. I must cope with an anger against my body's limitations, with frustration that I will never actually see the productions on which I work. How much easier would my life in the theater be if I could just for one night, for one rehearsal, see and fix all the things that need seeing and fixing? Like Yeats, I need collaborators, appreciate them enormously, and rage against my own limits that make a constancy of collaboration necessary.

When Yeats began to prepare "At the Hawk's Well" for production in a London drawing room in April 1916, he gathered a group of theatrical artists. With some of these, he forged fruitful relationships that he memorialized in notes and prose writings. So pleased was he with the work of Michio Itow, the Japanese dancer who was to create the role of Guardian of the Well, that he excised from the play in its final form lyric passages describing the quality of the guardian's movement. The movement itself, devised by Itow, spoke more eloquently than even Yeats's words could do. Allan Wade, who created the role of the Old Man, was later to become Yeats's bibliographer and editor of the first major collection of Yeats's letters. Edmund Dulac's masks, costumes, and music delighted the playwright for the rest of his life.

The production process was not free of strife—what production process is? Yeats decried a continuing "feud between Dulac and a stupid musician" and was in a constant state of irritation with Henry Ainlee who, as Cuchulain, insisted on "waving his arms like a drowning kitten" (*Letters* 609). Despite these feuds and irritations, the production went off before a small audience and proved one of the century's significant theatrical events.

My own attempt to produce two of Yeats's dance plays, "The Dreaming of the Bones" and "The Only Jealousy of Emer" came about through happy but occasionally irritable collaboration. I created a "Special Topics" course in theatrical production, and the course drew nine students, bound together by an interest in verse drama, in Yeats, in Irish history and literature. Some of the students had a good deal of theatrical experience. For others, the course would be their first foray into performance, but they had an abiding interest in and ear for poetry. In the event, they were to exemplify Yeats's principle that, for productions of these difficult, unpopular plays, those amateurs who know and value verse may have the advantage over professional players.

I devoted most of my personal attention to working with the performers on the speaking of the verse. We strove for passion, clarity, a great emphasis on rhythm of which we hoped Yeats would have approved, but we avoided the sort of stylized chant one can detect in the few surviving recordings of Yeats speaking of his own poetry. The actor playing Bricriu in "The Only Jealousy of Emer" had the uncanny ability to sound sepulchral without evoking the alien idea of a horror movie. Emer and Eithne-Inguba expressed passion through rhythm, and each worked with me on what Frank O'Connor in *My Father's Son* has called "a trained singer's tricks of imperceptible breathing" (213). They didn't break up their lines to weep, gasp, or groan, and achieved, I think, an intensity of tragic reverie of which Yeats might have been proud.

What about the visual elements of the plays? Yeats's dance plays require intimacy, a small audience, no proscenium separating spectators from performers. The more familiar and less theatrical the setting, the stranger and more affecting these strange events will seem. Our setting was ideal: a small theater that had been converted from an ordinary living room. The room held an audience of about fifty—the ideal size for a production of these plays. There was no separating proscenium.

I was blessed, in addition to the student performers, with two colleagues—a scenographer and a choreographer—without whom these performances of the plays would never have occurred. My colleague Brian Sickels made a tapestry suggesting mountains and sky that hung on what became the upstage wall. After the production he made me a gift of the tapestry, and it presently hangs, the only decoration, in my office. He also made a smaller tapestry with a similar pattern, which the performers playing the three musicians folded and unfolded according to Yeats's stage directions. Finally, he made simple half-masks that did not cover the performers' mouths.

The dancelike movements accompanying the ritual folding and unfolding of the cloth, and the extended dances at the center of each play, were choreographed by another colleague, Meggins Kelly, a freelance choreographer with whom I also worked on productions of plays by Shakespeare, Middleton, and William Inge. Meggins attended a number of rehearsals, absorbed a feeling for the plays, asked many searching questions about the action inherent in the words. For "The Dreaming of the Bones" the dance was to communicate the idea that the lovers were inexorably drawn toward each other. They experienced an unremitting sexual desire. Yet, as their lines indicate, the memory of their crime always came between them and drove them apart. The movements must be simple, clear, and their rhythms must support the rhythms of the verse. The speech rhythms of the young revolutionary deliberately echo those of the ghosts who ask his forgiveness. Meggins worked on giving the actor movements that gradually came to resemble those in the ghosts' dance.

For "The Only Jealousy of Emer" Fand must fuse, as Yeats dictates, sexuality with an eerie mechanical quality, and this mechanized sexuality must be shared by the Ghost of Cuchulain. The characters can't look like robots. Meggins and the actors worked for days on this one. Again, the rhythms of the movements must support the iambic tetrameter and the insistent beat of these characters' lines. The movements also must follow the lines. "Old memories / Have pulled my head upon my knees" (*Collected Plays* 191) The two dancers must not touch each other. From conversations with me and with each other, from repeated rehearsals, and out of their own talent, Meggins and the student performers made dances that I never saw, but which those who did see praised with that astonishment by which I am always rewarded.

The other movements were simple and economical. It was in arguing about these movements that most of our strife in rehearsal arose. Even in the most fruitful collaboration, such as this, my blindness occasionally becomes a source of irritation for my collaborators, as well as myself. In this case, all the actors wanted to move and gesture more than I wanted them to. Remembering Yeats's repeated praise of stillness, I wanted to keep them still. They insisted that, if I could see, I wouldn't tolerate such stasis on the stage. I knew that, if I could see, I would tolerate stasis, and that I would be able to find the precise, economical gesture at need. I experienced, as did my fellow artists, moments of Yeatsian rage.

In the event, we compromised. Bricriu, the eerie undersea spirit who possesses the tranced body of Cuchulain, slowly sat up and then even more slowly stood and took a single step toward Emer. Emer, never permitting her gaze to waver, took a step toward Bricriu, arms at sides. She never attempted a warding gesture. Neither her lines nor her actions showed fear—instead, they showed defiance.

In this, as in all productions, I had to couple my imagination to those of my collaborators; I had to borrow their eyes. I worked closely, for example, with the actor playing Eithne-Inguba and with another actor who doubled for this sequence as a sighted assistant director on Eithne's difficult first entrance. The musician comments that Eithne is coming on "hesitating feet" (*Collected Plays* 185) to greet the formidable wife of her seemingly dead lover. "Everything in your body wants to bolt," I said to the performer in the presence of the assistant director. "You are moving as if through some viscous, resisting substance. Only the strength of your will, your desire to see Cuchulain's body, keeps you moving forward." Eithne worked with the assistant director on her walk. "She really looks as if the air is fighting her legs," my sighted collaborator told me. "As her feet fight forward, her upper body is drawing back." "What's making me continue?" asked Eithne. "I want to get away more than I want to come in." "What happens," I asked, "If you turn your head and look at your lover's body?" Eithne did, and the assistant director said, "That works. The body is making her come toward it." Working together, the three of us created an entrance that none of us could have created alone.

Set in a small theater that had once been a living room, with simple masks and dances, a suggestive tapestry as backdrop, performers who spoke with clarity, passion, attention to rhythm, economy of gesture, and much use of stillness, these plays worked for their small audiences. Whose eyes did I borrow? Everyone's. I did not work with a single codirector or assistant director—student or colleague—as I do in most of my play preparation. Instead, everyone who worked on the project, the scenographer, the choreographer, and especially the nine student performers, contributed suggestions about movement and gesture. It was the performer who played Emer who persuaded us that her Emer, after the first shock, would never draw back from Bricriu—never attempt to ward him off. She would stand her ground, and even take a step closer, as her lines suggest. "You people of the wind / Are full of lying speech and mockery. / I have not fled your face" (*Collected Plays* 188).

I would never see the dances, the tapestries, the masks. As with all the productions I work on, my collaborators had to trust in my ability to shape a unified vision of the performance we were creating together. I, in turn, had to trust in their vision and execution. This element of mutual trust must define all my theater work, and that work stands or falls on the strength of that trust.

As the blind man assures Cuchulain, the blind don't know everything. But we are sometimes less disabled by the funeral elegist's bright earthy veil. We can perhaps, from time to time, fix our inner eyes on something worth seeing. Drawing on the outward world but prevented by my blindness from being too much blinded by it, my fellow artists and I attempt to produce pieces of theater sustained by and nourishing the inward eyesight of the mind.

NOTE ON SOURCES

Being blind, I have an unusual relation to books. Of the books I consulted in preparing for this study, only Yeats's *Collected Poems* and *Memoirs* are available in Braille, the former from the Royal National Institute for the Blind, the latter from National Library Service. Yeats's *Collected Plays*, *Essays and Introductions*, and *Autobiographies* are available on tape from Recording for the Blind and Dyslexic. For all the other books and articles referred to, I used live readers, most of them undergraduates at the University of New Hampshire. In recent years, I have made use of "character recognition" software to transform print documents into machine-readable format.

For direct references in this essay, I use only those sources most readily available to me. For example, while the inkprint pagination for Yeats's *Collected Plays* is available to me, the pagniation for the Variorum edition of his plays is not. Whenever I wish to refer to *Variorum Plays*, I must ask a reader to hunt down the page reference—an often time-consuming task. Reader time is infinitely precious to me, and I do not choose to spend more of it than necessary on page hunts. Consequently, whenever I refer to a Yeats play in its final, published version, I use *Collected Plays*. For published variants and notes I use *Variorum Plays*. When I quote from W.S.'s "A Funeral Elegy," I refer to the version posted on-line to the Shakespeare Electronic Discussion Group, rather than to the version subsequently published.

Several massive new Yeats editions are not yet available to me. The complete text of Allan Wade's selection of letters has been read to me over several years, but I do not yet have access to the multivolume edition edited by John Kelly and others.

REFERENCES

Alspach, Russell K., ed. *The Variorum Edition of the Plays of W. B. Yeats*. New York: Macmillan, 1966.

Beckett, Samuel. "Waiting for Godot." In *The Complete Dramatic Works by Samuel Beckett*. London: Faber and Faber, 1986.

———. "Not I." In *The Complete Dramatic Works by Samuel Beckett*.

Eliot, T. S. "Yeats." In *Yeats: A Collection of Critical Essays*, edited by John Unterecker, 50–65. Englewood Cliffs: Prentice-Hall, 1963.

Flannery, James. "W. B. Yeats, Gordon Craig, and the Visual Arts of the Theatre." In *Yeats and the Theatre*, edited by Robert O'Driscoll and Lorna Reynolds, 81–95. Niagara Falls: Maclean, 1976.

Murphy, William M. *Family Secrets: William Butler Yeats and his Relatives*. Syracuse: Syracuse University Press, 1995.

O'Connor, Frank. *My Father's Son*. New York: Knopf, 1969.

S[hakespeare], W[illiam]. "A Funeral Elegy for Master William Peter." London: G. Eld for T. Horpe, 1612.

Shakespeare, William. *Romeo and Juliet*. 1595. *The Riverside Shakespeare*. Boston: Houghton, 1974. 1058–1093.

Wade, Allan, ed. *The Letters of W. B. Yeats*. London: Hart-Davis, 1954.

Worth, Katharine. *The Irish Drama of Europe from Yeats to Beckett*. Atlantic Highlands, N.J.: Humanities, 1978.

Yeats, W. B. *Autobiographies*. London: Macmillan, 1955.

———. *Collected Plays*. London: Macmillan, 1962.

———. *Collected Poems*. London: Macmillan, 1961.

———. *Essays and Introductions*. London: Macmillan, 1961.

———. *Explorations*. London: Macmillan, 1962.

BONNIE TUSMITH

Activist Academic:

Memoir of an

Ethnic Lit Professor

At a national women of color conference (SOCI)[1] a few years ago, I·was sitting among twenty-odd women around a conference table. Next to me was Amy Ling, the late highly respected scholar of Asian American literature. On the other side of Amy sat Barbara, an African American sociologist and someone with whom I had worked to establish SOCI. Across the table from me were two younger Asian Americans and first-timers at a SOCI conference. At one moment in our roundtable discussion, Barbara and I disagreed about something. As the debate continued, Barbara leaned over the table to address me — using her considerable bulk to support her point. I felt Amy stiffen and lean back, allowing Barbara and me to talk around her. The two young women across from me tensed up as well. I made an instinctive decision at that moment. As Barbara got louder and leaned further, I did the same. The two of us kept up our vociferous conversation until, suddenly, Barbara slapped the table and said, "Bonnie, you *must* be black!" Everyone laughed, and the contest was over.

The years I put into SOCI taught me how to negotiate across seemingly incompatible cultures. Asian American women are often physically smaller than African American women. Being soft-spoken, polite, and reserved are traits that seem to emanate from traditional Asian cultures. Outspokenness, expressiveness, and loud assertiveness are more often attributed to African American women. Neither cultural style is necessarily superior. Understanding difference — and the value inherent in such cultural differences — is the beginning of equality. In my interaction with Barbara, I relinquished my culturally ingrained reserve and engaged her on her terms. I instinctively knew that, had I backed down in the exchange and retreated to my Asian-reserve comfort level, I would have given the Asian Americans around me the message that we could never bridge the gap between our respective "races." Taking on Barbara in this instance did not diminish me. Rather, energetic confrontational dialogue as equals was what won her respect. For her to call this Chinese American woman "black" was high praise indeed.

As this incident suggests, I have learned from the wisdom and fortitude of black folks. A significant part of my ongoing education stems from studying literature. As a literary scholar I believe that imaginative writing has potential benefits for society as a whole. Unfortunately, our technological society does not value its literary artists. Instead, it views them as *fàntŏng*, or useless rice barrels (in Mandarin Chinese, a *fàntŏng* stores or "consumes" rice but doesn't generate income). In my view, creative writers can save lives. African American writers have been especially effective in the life-saving business. I say this because I have witnessed the life-altering effects of their work. Two incidents from my early years as a college teacher will show what I mean.

In the first women writers course I taught at a community college in Anchorage, Alaska, I called on Janine, an African American student who often came late and sat outside the discussion circle, to read aloud in class one day.[2] The piece was "Black Man, My Man, Listen!"—an assertive, heartfelt monologue in the voice of a black woman narrator.[3] Janine's rendition, hesitant at first, gradually gained force. By the end of the two pages she owned the work. In subsequent class meetings Janine became noticeably different. For one thing, whereas before her impromptu performance she had often dragged into class disheveled and withdrawn, after that day she started coming to class neatly dressed and even joined her classmates in the circle. Janine successfully completed the course and graduated that year. Two years later I ran into her at a mall. A young woman appeared out of nowhere and gave me a big hug. "You are one fine lady," she declared, to my amazement. Janine had transformed into a vivacious, self-confident person. From reading black women writers, she told me, she had cleaned up her act and gotten out of a second abusive relationship. Now she was supporting her two kids while attending business school. Two pages of fiction triggered this, I thought to myself—and I became committed to literature as a profession.

A few years later I was teaching in the Midwest. In a course on African American women's literature a student wrote, "Well, I hope you don't feel that I'm blowing sunshine up your skirt for points cause that's not my style if you haven't already guessed, but this class has taught me to read."

As an undergraduate, Lori was already a professional singer and had begun cutting albums. It was from her newfound connection to the literary productions of her people, she said, that she recognized her own potential for saving lives. As she put it:

> Well, just last weekend I had a concert in Denver and I had a chance to speak at three different high schools and also had a speaking engagement in a public library. Because of this class I recognized the Willie Lees in the audience. I addressed them and I made a plea to them to stay in school, stay off drugs, and go on to higher education. The response was overwhelming by the students, the parents, and the faculty of these schools. I also agreed to become pen pals with some of them to encourage them. That was just over the weekend. Imagine when my next album comes out and what an impact I'll have on black youths. It's exciting to be able to make a difference.[4]

Lori also said that she had had her doubts about me at first. "Don't let me tell you of the shock of having an Asian teacher. That floored us all," she remarked in another assignment. She went on to explain: "But what cured that shock was the fact that this Asian woman is also a woman of color. She not only understands the material and has great knowledge of African American writers, she also understands the persecution from first-hand encounters." While Lori's initial skepticism was not surprising, it was exciting to see her overcome the pull of essentialism to find value in the subject matter we were studying. Lori's enthusiasm was not simply ethnic pride. Rather, her written observations indicated that she saw the possibilities of cross-cultural understanding through literary study. Calling me a "woman of color" was her way of saying that we had bridged the gap between teacher and student.

The term *woman of color* connotes a specific group experience in the United States. To many people, women of color are welfare mothers, cooks and cleaning ladies, "working girls," and, for some time to come, cannot be visualized anywhere near the Oval Office without mop in hand. So the term identifies the lower social class, education, and income levels that are often attributed to darker-than-"white"-skinned women in North America. It is no wonder that many potential candidates for the position—women from Asian or Latin American countries, for example—don't recognize themselves as candidates at first. It takes a certain gestation period, sometimes leading to years, before a "nonwhite woman" sees herself as a woman of color. For example, I recently came across an essay in an anthology on whiteness. In recommending Alice Walker's term *womanist* as a political paradigm, the author (self-identified as a "Taiwanese diasporic woman") recalls her shock when she first realized that "yellow" had been a derogatory marker in the United States "in the 19th and early 20th centuries" (Lee 280).[5] Moving from the sins of the past to modern-day *womanism*, this author chooses to bypass the historically grounded political term *woman of color*. While I was also born in Taiwan, having grown up in the United States gives me a slightly different perspective on issues of colorism and race. I feel a strong commitment to the history of racial and gender oppression in this country. I believe that my student was acknowledging this when she wrote, "this Asian woman is also a woman of color."

For those of us who own the term *women of color*, I think we identify with a specific quality in this group identification: namely, the ability to transcend being the "*mule* of the world."[6] The knowledge, the instinct that makes someone a woman of color runs deep. For me, Cherríe Moraga's theoretically informed personal essay "La Güera" epitomizes this understanding. In coming to terms with her denial of her brown mother and her own homophobia as a lesbian, this light-skinned Chicana relates how she hit bottom and survived. She had passed through the eye of the storm, so to speak, and emerged more fully human. She accomplished this with ruthless honesty—through a take-no-prisoners examination of her deepest fears and long-concealed prejudices. By presenting her personal journey in unadorned, incisive prose, Moraga teaches us to stare down the "oppressor," the enemy—her message the more urgent when the enemy is, above all, ourselves. The intensity in such writing demands our attention as socially responsible readers, as foot soldiers for social change. In her courageous grappling with buried truths Moraga is, indeed, a woman of color. When I came across her essay in the groundbreaking anthology *This Bridge Called My Back: Writings by Radical Women of Color*, I thought, "*This* person can teach me something."

So, in my experience and worldview, *women of color* and *black* are honorific terms. That "the personal is political"[7]—a bold assertion from the U.S. (mostly European American) women's movement—is a conviction that many people of color and white women still uphold. Scholarship will help to sustain and enhance human life, I believe, to the extent that scholars retain this insight in their work. As a politically disenfranchised group, many women of color comprehend the inevitable connection between art and politics. In her preface to Toni Cade Bambara's posthumous collection *Deep Sightings and Rescue Missions*, Toni Morrison credits her fellow writer with this understanding: "She always knew what her work was for. Any hint that art was over there and politics was over here would break her up into tears of laughter, or elicit a look so withering it made silence the only intelligent response. More often she met the art/politics fake debate with a slight wave-away of the fingers on her beautiful hand, like the dismissal of a mindless, desperate fly who had maybe two little hours of life left" (x). The statement "She always knew what her work was for" suggests that award-winning writers like Bambara and Morrison accept the social responsibility of their talent. Their work is not "art for art's sake" but, rather, art on behalf of the people. This brings me back to the notion that effective writing—"good" literature—can make a real difference in our lives.

Socially responsible literature encourages ethical behavior. As American Indian and other story-centered cultures believe, words have power. By accessing the human imagination, word artists help to shape human thought and feeling. I believe that at least two criteria are central to the creative enterprise: writers must (1) be in control of their craft and (2) be willing and able to confront their fears. Often, the measure of "good" writing is equated with its aesthetic qualities. As a writing instructor once told me, however, technical ability must be accompanied by authenticity of voice. A writer who hides behind skillfully delineated characters, scenes, and images produces technically admirable works that ring false. Because literature operates in the realm of imaginative, "fictional" constructs, it is especially imperative that the writer aims for truth when "lying"—as some folk cultures humorously call the art of storytelling. This understanding enables me to appreciate Oscar Wilde's witticism that if you "give [a man] a mask, he will tell you the truth."[8] The paradox is that the art of lying is an effective way of deriving truth. Activist writers like Bambara and Morrison have no doubts about the ethical aims of their art.

I make no apologies for giving credit to the writer for the saving grace of literary art. In my experience as a critical reader, the insights that make a novel, short story, poem, play, or essay valuable are the result of honest and searching self-examination on the part of the author. What my more advanced students and I enjoy as "aha!" moments in a text are insights derived from such courageous inquiry. When I consider why I continue to study and teach ethnic American literature, I must acknowledge that a combination of fear and courage—the liminal psychic space in which creative writers often operate—is lodged in my own psyche. Evoking my formative years in the streets of New York City might shed some light on these contrasting emotions.

"One guy pulled a knife, and you were standing there with that big cello and all those books," my younger sister insisted. She said that she watched this from our fifth-floor apartment window. "Then what happened?" I asked, curious. Apparently, I had blocked out this particular memory. "Then the light changed, and you ran across the street like a maniac—still carrying all that stuff." In one of our rare family reunions, my three sisters and I stayed up all night exchanging childhood memories. Our individual and collective experiences in life-threatening encounters—four foreign, unprotected, public school latchkey kids—had stamped our personalities and lives in different ways. One sister found a surrogate family among born-again Christians when she transferred to Cornell University. Another sister married into a wealthy Taiwanese family so that she could feel safe—and protect the rest of us if necessary. Our eldest sister, Mona, became a corporate VP who retained the surrogate parent, caregiver role, to the detriment of further professional advancement. In adulthood we went our separate ways. When adversity strikes, however, we tend to reunite. The bond we have is beyond religion, politics, and individual success. I think we recognize one another as survivors—street kids who made good out of well-honed instincts of self-preservation.

While I can't recall the menacing incident that my younger sister remembers so vividly, I do remember several other experiences in my childhood—both in the rat-infested, unpaved streets of Taipei and in the roach-ridden housing of Manhattan and Queens—that were equally hair-raising. Having experienced moments of intense apprehension, I ultimately learned to stare down my fears. I became a stoic. My philosophy was to try anything I disliked or feared at least once. For example, one time Mona and I took the subway to a man's apartment in the middle of Harlem for dinner—someone I had never met and my sister barely knew. As we emerged from the subway station onto the Harlem streets, I suddenly became hyperconscious of our Asian female bodies on a street full of black males. A group of street singers started harassing us, demanding money in exchange for a performance. As fear began to set in, the two of us put on our inscrutable New Yorker expressions and quickened our pace. Don't let your panic show, I told myself, and don't look back. Nothing horrible happened. We managed to find the apartment, had a sociable evening, and made it home in one piece. Mother never knew about that one!

Placing oneself in real danger is foolish. On the other hand, when life isn't all that safe in the first place, choosing discomfort or potential embarrassment once in a while might be the best defense. This approach keeps one's instincts honed. I attribute my relatively intact adult self to this survival strategy. But I also know that if there's a "gutsy" side to my character (as a colleague called me in a department meeting), I did not develop it in a vacuum. Reading the words of others has been invaluable to me. In my formative years, what my physically and emotionally unavailable parents did not teach me I learned from books. It was the special magic of the literary artist that left the deepest impression on me. Life stories filtered through the imagination and artistry of a creative writer can get under one's skin; they can reach places in one's psyche that a sociological treatise can never penetrate.

Teachers used to talk about education's "broadening effect." For me, studying literature in English, Spanish, Chinese, French, and German provided a broadened sense of community. From reading about the lives of others I knew that I was not alone. Whatever adversity I was facing was not unique. Someone else had been there, someone else had made it through okay. This understanding certainly helped to put my life in perspective. So the urge to share the gift of literature—which can be the gift of life— ultimately determined my choice of career. I thought I could help others benefit from an appreciation of literature in a similar way.

I did not have the luxury of following a straight path to the hallowed halls of academe. It took a ten-year detour as secretary, management analyst, language instructor, karate sensei, and other self-supporting jobs before I returned to graduate school for a Ph.D. in American studies. People with my background do not presume that we're entitled to be scholars, much less poets and novelists. M. Evelina Galang's short story "Rose Colored" dramatizes this pragmatic, if potentially self-defeating, point of view. Rose is building a career in the business world while Mina, her cousin and childhood companion, is a professional dancer. Rose has a hard time reconciling their respective career choices:

> "So, do you have a steady job yet?" I ask.
> "I have a job, Rose, I dance."
> You dance, I think, laughing. That's a job? A job is where a person goes to make money. Finds ways to pay the rent and buy the things you need to eat, to wear, to pay electric bills. A job is work, not dancing. I work. I enter that bank every day and sit at my terminal sometimes for ten hours. That's a job. (18)

As a second-generation Filipina with an internalized script of her parents' immigrant work ethic, Rose is an embittered woman. She played by the rules, she thinks, so why is she so miserable? For someone like Rose, the script of "Americanization" (i.e., capitalism, technological advancement, individualism) is overpowering. The dutiful daughter, the good student, the team player—in short, a significant segment of the Asian American population—doesn't have a chance against its commandments. With its intricate design and vivid character analysis, Galang's story is a wake-up call to would-be conformists. The girl who gave up her dream of being an actress because her parents called it a "hobby" looks into the mirror twice in this story. Both times, the first image she sees are the brown-skinned, slant-eyed, thick-lipped features that racists deride. Rose's need to pursue the American dream by working at a *real* job and living in the suburbs is, to a great extent, attributable to this socially constructed self-image. She has internalized the racist message that she is permanently alien and undesirable. In an unguarded moment, though, Rose actually looks at herself through her own eyes and admits that she's "kind of pretty" (23). Then she cries.

The story ends with renewed tears as Rose, in a heap on the kitchen floor after lashing out at Mina, "fold(s) into [herself], crying." Mina instinctively wraps her arms around her cousin, silently comforting her childhood friend. Rose the narrator tells us, "The women in my family have always embraced and understood this silent way" (29). Mina's gesture of empathy reconnects both women to the source of female strength within their ethnic culture. Through this embrace, Rose's inner turmoil is enfolded into a larger whole, so we know that Rose will be okay.

Taking the measure of one's self-loathing—as in Galang's fiction and Moraga's nonfiction—is itself a courageous act. In recent years, I have encountered this bare-boned honesty most often among ethnic American writers, especially in literature by ethnic women of color. Such honesty reflects conscious choice. These writers are certainly capable of wearing a mask for self-protection. After all, the whole idea of tricksterism behind traditional folk and contemporary ethnic cultures is premised on the necessity of outsmarting the dominant culture through tricks. "Tell the joke and slip the yoke" is an aphorism derived from lived experience. The joke is obviously a form of masking. According to Ralph Ellison, masking is an American phenomenon. I wrote about this in an earlier study:

> "America is a land of masking jokers," he [Ellison] informs us. Franklin posed as Rousseau's Natural Man, Hemingway as a nonliterary sportsman, Faulkner as a farmer, and Lincoln as a simple country lawyer—"the 'darky' act makes brothers of us all" (*Shadow*, 70). Ellison is asserting that the smart-man-playing-dumb role is not the unique province of black culture.

Rather, "it is a strategy common to the [American] culture" and "might be more 'Yankee' than anything else." (*All My Relatives* 50)

In observing that whites as well as blacks have practiced the "happy darky" routine, Ellison makes a trenchant comment about American culture. The need to disguise one's identity has everything to do with power. In an earlier era those who had power—the white men—could pretend to divest themselves of it to suit their purposes. Those without power—black slaves, for example—were forced to play dumb to survive (so that powerful white men wouldn't feel threatened).

In today's multicultural, bi-gendered professional environment, the phenomenon of masking is even more complicated. We are not so much invested in playing dumb as in playing smart. The fool's mask no longer serves because, with women and various "races" competing in the professions, white male supremacy can no longer be taken for granted. With the lifetime guarantee of unearned white privilege being challenged, to play the happy darky has become increasingly risky. It behooves the beneficiaries of such privilege to *appear* the most meritorious. Hence, a new mask was introduced in the post–civil rights era in business, politics, and education: the mask of the all-competent professional.

In my experience, the mask of omni-competence runs rampant in institutions of higher learning. Now, I'm not saying that there are no academics who are truly competent, intelligent, and learned. What I am saying is that we have become too invested in appearances. This extends to the way we speak, write, and interact with one another. One of the hardest things for professors to relinquish is our aura of erudition. If we don't "talk the talk," maybe they'll take back that hard-won Ph.D.? Better be vigilant. Always sound educated and intelligent to be safe. If we don't know something, instead of admitting this and then asking questions or researching the topic, our knee-jerk reaction is to cover up and feign knowledge. We rely on abstractions, euphemisms, theoretical jargon, even Greek and Latin phrases to demonstrate our superiority. We dare not say anything straight—using ordinary spoken language, for example—for fear that we will be exposed as not so smart or learned after all. Considering Ellison's point about America's founding fathers, are we not, in fact, sustaining a patriarchal legacy with the professional masks we wear?

I resist this oppressive inheritance as an activist academic. In my teaching and writing, I struggle to destabilize the pervasive practice of the cover-up. To my mind, why not *learn* the subject at hand instead of *pretending* that one already knows it? Having to feign knowledge or competence guarantees a lifetime of unnecessary stress. When I spot a first-year college student perfecting this dubious art instead of making the effort to learn fundamental skills such as reading and writing, I am deeply troubled. It's not only the waste of human potential that I recognize—I can't help but associate this practice with the continuance of racism in the United States because I see the same dynamics at work.

The same habit, the same impulse behind the "cover your ass" mentality also keeps our society bogged down with what some claim to be "the permanence of racism" in America.[9] People of color know that racism has gone underground, making the disease all the more insidious. Politically correct speech and behavior are the masks that Americans wear to hide our continued prejudices. Instead of developing educational programs that will help to eradicate racism through study and open discussion, many college courses treat racism as a taboo subject in the classroom. Instead of looking inward to confront and root out our fear of the other, "We wear the mask that grins and lies / It hides our cheeks and shades our eyes" (Dunbar 498). These two lines from a poem written over a hundred years ago (as a commentary on African Americans' suffering under Jim Crow laws) have renewed relevance today. Only, today, to a large extent we are enslaving ourselves.

Educators who do not believe in constant evasion seek ways to practice what Paulo Freire calls a "pedagogy of hope." According to Freire:

> We are surrounded by a pragmatic discourse that would have us adapt to the facts of reality. *Dreams* and *utopia* are called not only useless, but positively impeding. (After all, they are an intrinsic part of any educational practice with the power to unmask the dominant lies.) . . . But for me, on the contrary, the educational practice of a progressive option will never be anything but an adventure in unveiling. It will always be an experiment in bringing out the truth. (7)

In line with this position, whether the course is basic writing or race-awareness, an education that does not aspire to unveil truth—that offers little more than pseudosophistication or outright sophistry—is not worthy of its name.

Race in the College Classroom: Pedagogy and Politics, a collection of essays that a fellow activist academic and I recently coedited, reflects the commitment of educators who attempt to bring out the truth regarding race. For those of us who believe that teaching responsibly (in whatever discipline) requires an honest and searching examination of race, Freire's stance continues to inspire. As one of our contributors, a Puerto Rican professor of American literature, states, "If Americans were honest with themselves they would agree that racism still thrives in the country, and they would confront it. Denial and evasion are not going to cure this deep-rooted social disease. Awareness of the problem is crucial; we all need to return to the basics of raising consciousness about racism. We must all become agents for change, because the alternatives are destructive and thus unacceptable" (Torres-Padilla 214). This concerned educator points out that as U.S. minority people of color gradually move into a majority position, our deteriorating race relations are likely to contribute to further, and prolonged, interracial violence. It is this fear that keeps some of us pushing toward change in the way Americans view and treat one another.

So, when addressing racial issues, fear explains my persistence. As a person of color who has experienced and continues to experience racism firsthand, I fear for our society. I am appalled by the ostrichlike behavior of people around me who benefit from their white-skin privilege without considering that there might be a day of reckoning. In reflecting on American race relations, the writer David Mura concedes that there is no adequate compensation for the history of genocide, enslavement, and imprisonment of people of color in the United States. What white folks can and should do, Mura argues, is practice listening to nonwhites (151–53). Learning to listen to the "subaltern" is the necessary first step across the color line. By studying literature, I learned to listen to the voices and thoughts of others—and a collective message of humanity came through their words. This helped me to avoid the self-imposed prison house of the ivory tower.

In taking time to listen to America's ethnic minorities through their written words, I became interested in the vexing issue of colorism in U.S. society. My ongoing research on color reflects my need to understand the power that "race"—no matter how socially and politically constructed an idea—continues to have over our lives. As a researcher and scholar who finds racial prejudice unfathomable, I seem to ask one question again and again: Why?

Why does "race,"—or, more accurately, the sociopolitical meaning of human skin tones—continue to excite riots, divide families, and forestall cross-cultural conversation in America? Then again, why did dark-skinned students from Malaysia once tell me that, *of course*, light skin was beautiful? Maybe it was the "of course" that did it. I felt that, sooner or later, I had to get to the bottom of the color thing. Also, I had the grandiose notion that, if a multiethnically informed study on literature and culture could offer a fresh perspective on colorism, self-reflective readers might begin to extricate ourselves from the tyranny of race.

As an Asian American, I feel a responsibility to help generate a sustained, long overdue national dialogue on race. This is especially necessary because yellow and brown people are hardly ever invited to the table as participants in the debate. The assumption that America is either white or black is obviously inaccurate and, in some ways, a liability when it comes to issues of race. Black/white color-coding is the legacy of America's "peculiar institution"[10] of slavery. As a people, we must "transgress"[11] this paradigm, and this means including non-"black," non-"white" individuals and perspectives in the debate. I recall an experience I had many years ago when I attended one of bell hooks's public lectures. Accompanying me was an undergraduate student who had just reconnected with her cultural heritage through the study of ethnic American literature. As the speech wore on, I felt a mounting discomfort that my student seemed to share. What eventually penetrated my consciousness was the speaker's choice of language. In the hour-long talk, *everything* she said referred to black or white Americans. The student and I—a Lumbee Indian and a Chinese American—were essentially erased, rendered nonexistent by this otherwise deeply insightful black woman. We left the event in a somber mood. I remember declaring to the student, perhaps by way of apology, that in the future I would challenge any speaker who did not acknowledge our existence.

Incidents like these made me an activist. For those who defend the status quo this resolution demonstrates where I went wrong. Frankly, being "model minorities" and all, we Asian Americans are not supposed to challenge anybody—black or white. And yet, we *must* do this. Wasn't it James Baldwin who reflected on "the price of the ticket" in relation to his "colored" status in a white world? The gadfly role exacts a high price. Some of us believe, however, that accommodating and conceding at every turn—in exchange for individual perks—exacts an even higher price.

By listening to the prophetic words of our creative writers, I realized that I was part of a larger whole, of a human community. In my desire to help eradicate racism in America I learned that the responsibility for a racist society rests with all its citizens—not only with those who, being dark-skinned, bear the physical marker of "race." How many times a day must a visibly dark-skinned person think about, talk about, be injured and diminished by, racism, while a light-skinned person doesn't have to give white supremacy a second thought? In a purportedly democratic society, such injustice—a daily burden for most visibly ethnic Americans—must be challenged.

When our life stories are fragments of half-recalled, partly imagined experiences, a linear narration would be an artificially imposed construct. My story as an activist academic does seem to have an overall pattern, though: from the personal to the political, from the individual to the communal. Basically, confronting personal fears and having to develop strategies for survival led me to the world of literature. Contrary to popular belief, the study of literature is not necessarily an escape into fantasy or an evasion of personal responsibility. Given that literary artists can and do explore every aspect of life, reading a work of literature can just as well force the reader to confront life as to escape from it. Having found strength and purpose in predominantly nonescapist literature, I seek to help build a community of readers who find value in, benefit from, and take responsibility for what they read. Perhaps the words of one ethnic writer will help us stay focused.

In an interview, John Edgar Wideman contends that his historical novel *The Cattle Killing* is "a love story" (Wideman, *Conversations* 188). Now, how can a novel seemingly replete with illness, death, and self-destruction be a love story? Well, let's listen to its final lines: "Tell me, finally, what is a man. What is a woman. Aren't we lovers first, spirits sharing an uncharted space, a space our stories tell, a space chanted, written upon again and again, yet one story never quite erased by the next, each story saving the space, saving itself, saving us. If someone is listening" (*Cattle* 208). This quiet observation defines love among humans as telling and listening to one another's stories, thus affirming the value of life. The caveat is that someone has to be listening. An imaginative writer practices his or her craft through an act of will, taking a leap of faith that someone does respond to the call. In studying and teaching the writer's creation, lit. professors like me serve as the "someone" who both listens and keeps the story circulating. If it is true that sharing one's story can unveil and disarm unexamined prejudices such as racism, then my chosen profession serves a real purpose. My job is to pass on the story.

A line from an old blues song has stayed with me: "I need someone to help me sing it one more time!" Between Wideman's someone who's listening and this someone who's helping to sing, we might just forge a human community that ensures the survival of us all.

NOTES

1. SOCI is the acronym for the national women of color organization, Sisters of Color International, founded in 1990. The conference cited here took place in Philadelphia in 1992, hosted by the University of Pennsylvania.
2. To protect students' privacy, I am not using their real names in this essay.
3. See Gail Stokes, "Black Man, My Man, Listen!" in *The Black Woman: An Anthology*, ed. Toni Cade Bambara (New York: Penguin, 1970), 111–13.
4. The passages quoted here come from the student's written assignments for my course. "Willie Lee" is the title character in Frenchy Hodges's story "Requiem for Willie Lee." See *Black-Eyed Susans/Midnight Birds*, ed. Mary Helen Washington (New York: Doubleday, 1990), 211–29.
5. It is curious that Wen Shu Lee refers to "the 19th and the early 20th centuries" in relation to the negative connotations of "yellow" in U.S. society — as if this perception no longer applies.
6. Alice Walker attributes this designation to "folklore" and, specifically, to "black women." See *In Search of Our Mothers' Gardens* (San Diego: Harcourt, 1983), 237. Political activists have used the term "mule of the world" in relation to other women of color as well (e.g., see Moraga and Anzaldúa's *This Bridge Called My Back*.)
7. See Carol Hanisch, "The Personal Is Political" in *Feminist Revolution: Redstockings of the Women's Liberation Movement*, ed. Kathie Sarachild (New York: Random, 1978), 204–05.
8. The full line is, "Man is least himself when he talks in his own person. Give him a mask, and he will tell you the truth." This seeming paradox is forcefully explained and argued in relation to imaginative literature in Chinua Achebe's essay "The Truth of Fiction," in his book *Hopes and Impediments: Selected Essays* (New York: Doubleday, 1988), 138–53.
9. See, for example, Derrick Bell, *Faces at the Bottom of the Well: The Permanence of Racism* (New York: HarperCollins, 1992), for an understanding of this perspective.
10. See Kenneth Stampp, *The Peculiar Institution: Slavery in the Ante-Bellum South* (New York: Vintage, 1989), for a detailed account of what slavery was like, what it did to the American people, and how the whole system constituted a nation's "peculiar institution."
11. I use the term *transgress* in accord with Gloria Anzaldúa's understanding in her book *Borderlands/La Frontera: The New Mestiza* (San Francisco: Spinster/Aunt Lute, 1987).

REFERENCES

Dunbar, Paul Laurence. "We Wear the Mask." In *The Heath Anthology of American Literature*, 2d ed., vol. 2, edited by Paul Lauter, 498–99. Lexington: D. C. Heath, 1994.

Freire, Paulo. "Opening Words." Introduction. In *Pedagogy of Hope: Reliving Pedagogy of the Oppressed*, translated by Robert R. Barr, 7–12. New York: Continuum, 1996.

Galang, M. Evelina. "Rose Colored." In *Her Wild American Self*, 13–30. Minneapolis: Coffee House Press, 1996.

Lee, Wen Shu. "One Whiteness Veils Three Uglinesses: From Border-Crossing to a Womanist Interrogation of Gendered Colorism." In *Whiteness: The Communication of Social Identity*, edited by Thomas K. Nakayama and Judith N. Martin, 27–34. Thousand Oaks: Sage, 1999.

Moraga, Cherríe. "La Güera." In *This Bridge Called My Back: Writings by Radical Women of Color*, edited by Cherríe Moraga and Gloria Anzaldúa, 37–34. Watertown, Mass.: Persephone Press, 1981.

Morrison, Toni. Preface. *Deep Sightings and Rescue Missions: Fiction, Essays, and Conversations*, by Toni Cade Bambara. New York: Pantheon, 1996.

Mura, David. "Strangers in the Village." In *The Graywolf Annual Five: Multi-Cultural Literacy*, edited by Rick Simonson and Scott Walker, 135–53. Saint Paul: Graywolf, 1988.

Torres-Padilla, José L. "Confronting the 'Screaming Baboon': Notes on Race, Literature, and Pedagogy." In *Race in the College Classroom: Pedagogy and Politics*, edited by Bonnie TuSmith and Maureen Reddy, 213–25. New Brunswick: Rutgers University Press, 2002.

TuSmith, Bonnie. *All My Relatives: Community in Contemporary Ethnic American Literatures*. Ann Arbor: University of Michigan Press, 1993.

Wideman, John Edgar. *The Cattle Killing*. Boston: Houghton Mifflin, 1996.

———. Interview with Derek McGinty (1996). "John Edgar Wideman." In *Conversations with John Edgar Wideman*, edited by Bonnie TuSmith, 180–94. Jackson: University Press of Mississippi, 1998.

DONALD M. MURRAY

Following the Voice

of the Draft

An individual sits alone in a room, hears unspoken words, and writes them down.

Another individual sits alone in a room, silently reads what was written a continent or a century away, and hears a voice speak from the page.

Writers who are read and remembered, trusted and believed; writers who entertain, persuade, comfort, influence, educate; writers who send messages that inspire action; writers who create worlds; writers who articulate the feelings and thoughts of those who read them—all share the same talent: they write in a voice that is heard by the reader.

The music of writing is the most mysterious, the least discussed, and the most important element in writing. We used to talk about style or stylistics, but we have adopted the writer's term—*voice*—which better describes the heard quality in writing.

I like the term *voice*. Style is what you can buy off the rack: look left, look right, look at my vest. That is style! It represents what you want to be—in my African safari vest I am young, virile, at home in the wilderness—but voice is what you are—an old, portly, ex-professor, talking, talking, talking.

We have many voices. For a time people talked of the individual voice, the "authentic" voice, and soon the permanent, never-to-be-changed, voice as individual as a baby's footprint developed its own cult.

As writers we have to go beyond the single and singular individual voice to what I call the voice of the text. I want to suggest what goes into that voice and demonstrate how one writer, who has tuned his voice to this purpose and this audience, may tune to other situations and perhaps show

how this voice—combining personal and impersonal elements—leads the writer toward meaning.

"Now hear this," the U.S. Navy loudspeaker voice:

It is voice, more than evidence, more than logical thought, more than emotions, more than past knowledge, more than tradition, that leads me to meaning. In voice I hear, then clarify, develop, and document meaning.

Voice—the music we hear as we write—instructs the writer: it reveals the subject and the writer's attitude toward the subject. The voice of the evolving draft reveals meaning and feeling.

Later the voice of the published text—the music we hear when we read—attracts and holds the reader, making the reader trust and believe the writer.

When I write, I am the product of many oral or vocal influences. I hear my family in my voice, see traces of my handwriting and hear my voice in old notes from my father and mother and new notes from a daughter. I can, in the little writing my parents did, see clues to how I write.

In Scotland I hear a way of telling a story, a sense of humor, a pacing that I hear in my voice when I am writing. We have ethnic elements in our voices. And there are regional elements, an ugly just-south-of-Boston tone that has not entirely been lost. And neither have I lost touches that reveal class: lower middle with pretensions: middle, middle.

My storytelling has traces of the stories told from the pulpit by back-and-forth striding, Bible-thumping evangelists.

A daughter is surprised at the maternal voice she hears telling her son what she hated to hear us telling her: that she is "over tired."

Our voices are influenced by our situation, our responsibilities, and professional training. From time to time I hear the newspaperman and the teacher, the academic and the combat paratrooper woven into my draft.

I hear the voice of my generation mingle with the voice of our times—outplacement, interactive. I am back in Miss Leavitt's eleventh-grade English class and hear her voice—"the course of true love never runs smooth"—as well as the voices of Addison and Steele, Hazlitt, Emerson. I am in college and hear Orwell, E. B. White, later Didion and Baldwin and all the other essayists who shaped and continue to shape our tradition.

And there is always the voice of the task—to entertain, persuade, explicate, analyze, inspire, attack, celebrate, and to combine them—the expository anecdote, the persuading narrative—each with its own voice.

As I write my voice blends with the voices of family, friends, neighbors, newscasters, authors, actors, editors. My voice changes into the voice of my characters when I write fiction, as Joan Didion says: "I don't have a very clear idea of who the characters are until they start talking"; I quote others in nonfiction, and I have even "created" the nonfiction voice for politicians and corporate leaders for whom I have ghosted a voice.

All our voices are influenced by the times in which we live and have lived, by the expectations—the traditions—of the messages we write and the forms in which we write them.

When we write we must also write in the voice of our readers, a voice they can hear and trust. That voice is often the imagined—or not yet imagined—voice of the reader. It is, after all, the mission of the writer to articulate the inarticulate thoughts and feelings of our readers. We give our readers voice.

We write in the voice of the institution for whom we speak, either adopting the voice of the university or the newspaper or purposely running against that grain, for effect. I am influenced by the *Boston Globe*'s voice when I write my column and, in turn, I influence the *Globe*'s voice.

To create a heard voice, most of us write out loud, hearing the word, the phrase, the line before it appears on the screen or the page. At first fragments of language are heard away from the desk as I talk to myself or make notes. And that hearing grows louder as I draft. I can even turn off the computer screen and write, hearing the text, but, of course, the screen must be turned on as I revise and edit by eye and ear, listening to the music of the draft and tuning it with eye and hand.

I could demonstrate voice by writing an argument, then history, a report, a petition; I could write from anger, nostalgia, sadness, joy, amusement. I could even write a speech, but, of course, I've done that.

What I am going to do is write without specific purpose or intent to see my voice reveal what I may have to say and what it may mean. I am going to demonstrate some of the different voices I hear as I write by taking one situation—the rooms I lived in when I was in high school—and listening to what my voice tells me about them. Note that the voice in these first-draft autobiographical explorations is different in purpose and therefore tone than the voice of this essay. Voice is not the only writing game I play, but it is the most important.

11 CHESTER STREET: THE VOICES OF MEMORY

• *First, a clear description, one of the hardest tasks a writer can face. The voice seeks clarity. It is practical, unemotional.*

1. From the middle of the eighth grade until I left for college and the war, my home was the second floor of a brown shingled double-decker behind an Amoco gas station in North Quincy, Massachusetts. Our "front" door was on the side of the house and the stairs inside rose to a small hall with a closet.

To the right was my bedroom, an enclosed sleeping porch, and a porch. To the left the room where my grandmother lived, paralyzed. At the foot of her bed, over the stairway, was a large closet with a window, my first writing room. Beyond Grandma's room, the john, and, at the back, my parents' room.

Right ahead when you came up the stairs, was the living room, then the dining room, the kitchen, the pantry and the back hall for the icebox, the stairs down, the back laundry porch.

• *I read some slight hints of my voice in that—the front door on the side—but it is purposefully flat. Now let's add some color and texture with notes that are brighter, a bit unexpected.*

2. I could always hear the key finding the lock, turning, anywhere I was in the house, and the first step on the stairs at 11 Chester Street introduced the character ascending and began his or her narrative.

Mother. The shopping bags swung in and rested on the bottom step, then the slow climbing, good leg, bad leg, good, bad, good, bad, each step slow with disappointment. The hope that the shopping trip would bring what I never knew, but I was familiar with her disappointment at her return to us.

Father. Late at night home from every other week's New York trip or from his virtuous escape to church politics; other nights the fast climb to report on the new job or the slow steps with the irregular pauses. He had told off the boss and was fired. Again.

The uncles, who helped pay the rent because of their mother, had keys. The bachelor uncle bellowed hello; the oldest strode upstairs with dignity; the middle one's step was careful, appropriate for a CPA.

• *A nice choppiness. Appropriate to the key in the lock and what I knew instantly, told in an instant music.*

3. I can hear my feet tripping down the stairs so fast they barely touch each step. Escape. To deliver papers. To the library for books. To my job at Miller's Market. To the vacant lot to play ball. To the corner to hang out at the edge of the older guys. And the slow two-mile walk to school.

• *Again, quickness to match the memory of my steps on the stairs, going out, and the slow music that reveals how I felt about school.*

4. When I was sick I could smell Dr. Bartlett before he made the stairs. Sinful tobacco, hospital ether, damp tweeds, leather.

• *Can you hear a fragment of a tune about a sickly boy I could learn to whistle? I can—softly, in the distance.*

5. I sought sin on the streets, in the back dirty book rooms of Boston bookstores, outside the burlesque houses I was too young to enter, at the door to the girls' locker room that opened then so quickly shut, but it was home alone that I manipulated sin. At night under the covers, in the john. Guilty, excited, terrified, joyfully I confronted evil, the Devil incarnate, and was disappointed each day that the floor did not open, the lightning bolt did not smite when I fearfully opened the bathroom door.

• *In this piece I would have to hear a duet of voices: the voice of the teenager fearing warts on his palm and the voice of the old-timer looking back with humor, perhaps sadness, and, above all, tenderness.*

6. I remember snow on my bed but never sun. Windows were always open to winter, but shades always drawn against sun. Cold made you strong. Scots liked wind and rain, blizzard and nor'easter, high seas and damp, especially damp. Scots feared the sun and heat and humidity that made the races that lived near the equator slow to walk, slow to speak, slow to work, lazy, sensual, Roman Catholic.

• *Once more, a fragment of music that would need listening, orchestration, tuning, but might carry me to a meaning about my childhood and how it shaped me.*

7. I have lived my life—kept jobs, paid my bills—so I would not be sentenced to return to a rented flat with brown rooms, the stink of failure, the silent rage against those who unfairly had cars, a single-family house they owned, the waiting for our ship to come in.

But in my single-family house, living a life that was better than my impossible dreams, I still walk to those brown rooms, my mother stalking the hall in her corset, beating her thighs, chanting "Over these prison walls will I fly." Father at the dining room table, under the orange ceiling light, adding up the day's sales on tiny slips of paper, dreaming of better days knowing they would never come. And Grandma, in her bed, talking to Morison who had gone before her to prepare a mansion in Heaven.

I wake at 5:20 AM, vault out of bed. If I don't get working, I will fail. The sheriff will come. I will be returned to those rented rooms with brown woodwork, brown shades, brown rugs, brown wallpaper, brown silence.

• *The music of anger, resentment, and anxiety, fear, perhaps even terror. And a tonal quality: brown.*

8. I claw my way backwards through memory, hurt, silence, anger to a moment when Mother and I have been hauling Grandma up in her bed and something tickles us. Grandma's slurred laugh that clicks in and out, Mother's whoops, tears running down her cheeks, my barks of laughter, and father, coming to the door, joining in. I do not remember what caused our laughter but those sounds remind me that there were good times as well as bad.

• *I suspect the reader cannot yet hear the laughter, almost hysterical in its release, but if I can, then I may be able to make a reader hear this desperate jollity.*

• *The voice may lie within the word. Note "claw" in the beginning of this description. A word like that is all I need to begin to compose language music that may lead me — and the reader — to meaning.*

• *The voice is often within the phrase, the line, the fragment of language where re-vealing music is contained* between *words. It may be something as simple as "rented rooms" that contains tension, fear, and powerlessness that resonate for me. Another such phrase in "but I did" in the draft that follows.*

9. I am a stranger to that boy I was who believed in a Heaven of single-family wooden homes, ruled by a God who knew my thoughts as well as my actions. I prayed before I was taken to have my appendix removed and remember the weight that lifted from my soul, the end of fear. I would never smoke, but I did; never allow alcohol to touch my lips, but I did; never abuse myself or think of girls in that way, but I did; never doubt the existence of God, but I did; never befriend a Catholic, but I did; never talk back or think back to Grandma, Uncle, Father, Mother, but I did; never leave the Church, the Republican Party, the family, but I did. I

cannot imagine that believing child in whom they placed so much hope, even when I was failing to fulfill their dreams by dreaming larger, private dreams.

• *As a writer I am prepared to be instructed by the tympani beat of "I did" and I am surprised by the hint of a melody in "larger, private dreams."*

10. Each in turn, Father his back to the pantry, Mother her back to the stove, myself facing the pantry, we sat having supper at the half-moon kitchen table, and I remember the sounds of our eating. Each knife in turn would press down on the stick of butter, click when it hit the plate, the whisper as the slice of Wonder bread was buttered, another click as it was cut. The sound of the fork, the cup returned to saucer, the chewing, their dentures, my own teeth. I can hear the sounds of our swallows, the moths against the screen in summer, the steam knocking within the pipes in winter, the silence that pulled us as close as we ever got, the evenings when everyone was wise enough not to share their fears, their dreams, their truths that might cause disapproval, perhaps even argument.

• *I am surprised by the counterbeat of the beginning, the backwards rhythm and the flow of the chorus carrying me forward—Handel, Bach—toward where I do not yet know but my voice tells me there is a destination—if I listen to what the draft tells me to say.*

In closing this exploration of voice, I would like to share two poems written about the world inside 11 Chester Street. I will try to articulate something about the voices I heard while writing these poems, but of course when I wrote them I did not articulate the voices in this way; I just heard the tune and danced.

The first one began when my wife Minnie Mae said she always thought of brown when she thought of my parents. Brown became my music. Brown lines are long; they stretch across the page like the long hours of silence stretched within those brown rooms. Brahms is brown, or can be. A solemn music, a touch of the symphonies, a quintet, perhaps the requiem. It is a rich music, a gravy of music, almost ponderous, a tidal flow of sound. That voice I heard and tuned carried me to an imaginary discovery about my mother that is now true to me. Until this poem she never had—as far as I know—bright silk hidden away in a trunk. The trunk was opened and the silk she never dared to cut revealed by voice.

BROWN

Left alone in a brown house heavy with the smell of Sunday's lamb
I sneak into the forbidden room still filled with night sounds
and thick light made green by drawn curtains. I never turn on
the lamps with the little orange bulbs, but feel my way into his

closet: rough blue serge, half hidden vests, solemn silk ties,
the belt I know so well, the Sunday morning Deacon's suit,
striped pants, black cutaway. He polished his floorwalker brown
shoes—thwack, snap, thwack—so often they reflect remembered

light. Drunk on Father's smell I stagger through shadowed rooms,
dark brown woodwork, beige curtains, light brown wallpaper, brown
lampshades, brown sofas, sideboard, library table with black
Bible, red-brown rug, shiny brown floors, return to Mother's

closet, where I stand, proud with sin, surrounded by the silk
of dresses, breathing the woman smell until I hear a key
probing lock and I run inside a book. Mother is again surprised I am not
at play, chose to stay alone in the brown house she hated, flees

to shop, to church, to pace the block as she said she had after
dark when she was swollen with me. Once alone I found, in my
father's locked drawer, left unclosed, the safes that had kept me
from brothers, sisters, left me an only child. Sneaking

open Mother's drawer I found an old corset, fragrant with her
woman smell, shaped it on their bed into her. I forced the lock
in her brown trunk, touched the silk of scarlet, pink, silk that
swirled flood time rivers of red but was never cut, never sewn.

Not long ago I was waiting for a poem and saw myself reflected in the
glass of one of the large and terrible prints—brown ink of course—that
hung in the living room at 11 Chester Street. These lines are short, the voice
more distant, maybe Bartok or Ives, even Copland: descriptive, perhaps the
voice of a case history written by a social worker, myself, looking back,
reporting. Perhaps a journalist's voice, describing the scene of a yet uncom-
mitted crime.

NIGHT WATCH

From her bed Grandma could turn
her hand mirror to watch us
in the living room or twist it
to see who closed the bathroom door.

I stood on the back porch, watched
Mother in the mirror over the bedroom
dresser as she stood at the kitchen sink,
plate in hand, staring at the wall.

After our silent supper, I stayed
at the table, saw in black night windows,
Father turn from Mother, Mother
turn from him, re-enter her romance.

I crept to the hall where Mother's
shadow stretched from her reading lamp,
stepped on the shadow with all my weight,
saw her watching me, her knowing smile.

In the china cabinet door, I saw Father,
his rimless glasses reflecting me, nod,
turn away from me, from Mother, then
turn back, watching us from the door.

In the framed etching of Tobermoray
I caught the glint of Grandma's mirror
as she watched Father watching
Mother watching me.

CARLA L. PETERSON

Notes of a Native Daughter:

Reflections on Identity

and Writing

STRANGER IN MY HOME

It was a warm sunny day in early fall 1953, a rare event in Geneva, Switzerland, where in the ten months I had been living there gray seemed the only color the sky knew. My father, a doctor working in the field of international public health, had accepted a position at the headquarters of the World Health Organization at the beginning of that year and moved our family to Geneva. He was away on one of his many professional trips abroad, and my mother and grandmother had promised us kids that we would spend the day in the canton, picnicking and buying some of the tart-sweet apple cider made specially at this time of year that I had already come to love. My sisters and I were loading up the car when a man suddenly turned into our driveway and walked toward our house. He was short and dark and had pronounced Negroid features—broad nose, full lips, tight curly hair—and to my child's eye, he seemed sad-looking and somehow otherworldly. He went into the house where my startled mother and grandmother welcomed him and invited him to sit. That day there would be no picnic, no apple cider, no running in the fields with my sisters, only a stranger in my home. It was only years later that I would discover that this stranger was James Baldwin and that he was on his way back to visit that Swiss village in the mountains that he had depicted with such ambiguous feelings in his now-classic essay "Stranger in the Village."

At the time, the meaning of Baldwin's visit seemed simple to my nine-year-old self: a stranger's disruptive intrusion into a long-anticipated family outing. In retrospect, I can see the ways in which this visit encapsulates complex issues of identity that I have struggled with in both my personal life and my scholarship, the direction of which has been somewhat unconventional. My first book, *The Determined Reader: Gender and Culture in the Novel from Napoleon to Victoria*, focused on canonical novels of French and English realism, but since then I have worked almost exclusively in the field of nineteenth-century African American literary culture. In 1995 I published *"Doers of the Word": African-American Women Speakers and Writers in the North (1830–1880)*. Currently, I am working on a study of what I call the African American family romance of the period 1892–1903 as well as on a history of nineteenth-century black New Yorkers centered on my father's family. Remembering Baldwin's visit and rereading his essay have served as an invitation to enter his imaginative world and think about meanings of the "strange" and the "familiar" in both my life and the literary texts I study, and to meditate on how these meanings have shifted over time and place.

The familiar evokes, of course, family and, in its most common usage, family signifies those people to whom one is bound by ties of blood. As a child, I used to think of family primarily as those relatives whom I knew personally and among whom I lived; more recently, I have come to think more genealogically about those from whom I am descended. From a much broader perspective, however, Baldwin recognized that the Swiss village itself was an extended family that offered its inhabitants a sense of belonging rooted most immediately in a sense of place; the village is "very high. . . . The landscape is absolutely forbidding, mountains towering on all four sides, ice and snow as far as the eye can reach" (79–80). Yet, as Baldwin was all too well aware, the villagers' sense of belonging was just as importantly embedded in their sense of a shared nationality, culture, and race that separates familiars from strangers: "For this village, even were it incomparably more remote and incredibly more primitive, is the West, the West onto which I have been so strangely grafted. These people cannot be, from the point of view of power, strangers anywhere in the world; they have made the modern world, in effect, even if they do not know it. . . . They regard me, quite rightly, not only as a stranger in their village but as a suspect latecomer, bearing no credentials, to everything they have—however unconsciously—inherited" (83). For Baldwin himself, finally, what constitutes the familiar is not only the family of his childhood but also an entity that he simply called "home."

I cannot say that I have welcomed this invitation to retrospection unreservedly; indeed, I have resisted thinking about my childhood encounter with Baldwin, knowing it would raise issues of personal identity that are terribly complicated. If I am more willing to do so now, it is because in recent years I have become acutely aware of my own generational position within my family. Looking back, I see my mother, who at the age of ninety-three has lived a full and rewarding life; looking forward, I see my two daughters, young women in their twenties, who have lives rich in possibility still ahead of them. Taken together, these two generations seem to represent the boundaries of my own life; I see myself caught between them, looking back over my past while at the same time trying to imagine my future. But even as I thought when I began writing this essay that I had carved out a fixed position from which to engage in retrospective reflection, I found my life upset in dramatically different ways in the summer and fall of 2001. In helping my mother over the summer to "break up house"—to use a good nineteenth-century expression—and move into a retirement community, I came across a treasure trove of photographs and documents that yielded up to me a family history whose roots in New York City reach as far back as the late eighteenth century. A mere two weeks later, however, the events of 9/11 forced me to confront the vagaries of history and to think about the ways in which historical forces have made, unmade, and remade the neighborhoods of Lower Manhattan where my family's African American life began.

"HOME: WHERE . . . THE TERRAIN IS FAMILIAR"

When Baldwin walked up the driveway of our house, he was a complete stranger to me, not only in the sense of someone I had never met before but also someone I could not really comprehend. I had been living abroad for several years, first in Beirut, Lebanon, where my father had worked for the United Nations Work Relief Agency, and then in Switzerland. For me, the world was divided into two groups: my familiars, or those few members of my own immediate family with whom I lived, and all the others, whether Arabs, Europeans, or the Americans I had left behind. Baldwin's strangeness (to me) stemmed from a complex set of factors that involved not only his strange looks but also his strange behavior: his sudden and unexplained arrival from the United States as well as my vague sense of his utter aloneness and bohemian lifestyle so at odds with my own conventional upbringing. Thus, at the time of our encounter and from my child's perspective it seemed to me that Baldwin and I could only be strangers to each other. The country he called home was by then no longer home to me;

that which was familiar to him was already strange to me and, conversely, that which was strange to him was gradually becoming very familiar to me.

In his 1959 essay "The Discovery of What It Means to Be an American," Baldwin wrote that he left the United States to escape "the fury of the color problem," which for him included the oppressive confinement to the singular identity of "Negro" (171). In Europe, Baldwin hoped to find freedom and romance or, perhaps more accurately, the romance of freedom. To him, this sense of liberation derived not only from relief from the oppressiveness of U.S. racism but also what he termed in his 1954 essay "A Question of Identity" the "irresponsibility" granted to the foreigner who eagerly embraces the unfamiliar (94). Yet as I peruse these and other essays of the 1950s, in particular "Encounter on the Seine: Black Meets Brown," I am struck by the degree to which Baldwin in Europe repeatedly looked back across the Atlantic to "home" as the place where "at least the terrain is familiar," where "questions are not asked" ("Encounter" 38, "Identity" 95). Europe in fact would become the place where he would discover what it meant to be both an American and an American Negro. In Europe Baldwin would become aware that even for the "most incorrigible maverick" "nothing will efface his origins, the marks of which he carries with him everywhere" ("Discovery" 175). He would thus come to recognize the degree to which his own European sojourn had itself been shaped by his American origins, by the fact that he had been born in New York into a lower middle-class family whose roots lay in the southern United States. It was in the Swiss village that Baldwin would begin his journey back to that originary time and place from which he had tried so hard to escape and would find a form of freedom where he least expected it: "It was Bessie Smith, through her tone and her cadence, who helped me to dig back to the way I myself must have spoken when I was a pickaninny. . . . I had never listened to Bessie Smith in America (in the same way that, for years, I would not touch watermelon), but in Europe she helped to reconcile me to being a 'nigger' " ("Discovery" 172).

The United States and its peculiar racial landscape were not familiar terrain to me, however. Hence I could neither look to it as home nor could I recreate it in Europe. My parents made sure that my sisters and I knew we were black Americans. My father was very sensitive to the many accomplishments of African American men and women—from Jackie Robinson and Althea Gibson to George Washington Carver and Charles Drew—and he was acutely aware of his own historical position as one of the first Afri-

can American doctors working in the field of international public health.
He and my mother used the *Time* magazine articles featuring the students
who integrated the Little Rock High School or Martin Luther King Jr.'s
emergence as a race leader as the starting point for lessons about U.S. race
relations and the ensuing turmoil that was erupting back home. I listened
carefully and was in awe of the courage of these social protesters, yet the
swirl of all these ideas and events remained something of an abstraction to
me. Neither could I locate home in the narrower story of my family's African American identity, for my parents had in fact given us few details about
our family's past. My father never told us that his ancestors had come from
England and San Domingue in the first decades of the nineteenth century
to settle in New York and become part of the city's black cultural elite,
immersing themselves as early as the 1860s in European literary traditions
that both Baldwin and I would find ourselves contending with a century
later. And my mother never told us how her mother had left her family and
native island of Jamaica to come to the United States with her daughter in
search of a better life. Instead, what my parents tried to impart to us was
their deeply felt ecumenical belief, so prevalent in the United Nations and
its international agencies in those postwar years, that all nations and races
constitute one universal family.

In contrast, the terrain that was gradually becoming familiar to me
was that of a cosmopolitan European culture. If Baldwin could write in
"Stranger in the Village" that the culture formed by "Dante, Shakespeare,
Michelangelo, Aeschylus, Da Vinci, Rembrandt, and Racine" was one onto
which he had been "so strangely grafted" (83), to me it felt like a home
into which I had been rightfully born. My relationship to European culture was much less self-conscious than was Baldwin's and hence was fraught
with fewer ambiguities. Not only was I a child, but I was a member of a
middle-class family firmly grounded in traditions of literacy, reading, and
the appreciation of musical and visual arts. Taken together, these factors
greatly facilitated my access to the culture that surrounded me. Following
the French curriculum at the International school of Geneva, I was the only
American among students from Switzerland, France, Germany, and other
European countries, but I felt fully at home with my friends as we read
and discussed our class assignments. We immersed ourselves in the French
literary tradition, starting not with *Beowulf* but *La Chanson de Roland* and
proceeding through the centuries to end with Paul Claudel rather than T. S.
Eliot. By high school I was able to write about these authors in a French
that revealed perfect command of such grammatical intricacies as the past

anterior and the subjunctive. My teachers nurtured my intellectual ambitions and in report card after report card encouraged me to pursue a career in the humanities. A comment on one of my high school French compositions, carefully preserved by my mother, reads, "Excellente composition. Sens de la langue, de l'analyse. Je vous félicite." [Excellent essay. Sense of language, of analysis. I commend you.]

My engagement with European culture continued even after my return to the United States in the early 1960s. My studies at Radcliffe College where I majored in French history and literature were an extension of my high school education. My graduate work at Yale University in comparative literature further built on my European experience where I had become accustomed to comparing European cultures to one another and Europe to what I knew of the United States. *The Determined Reader* reflects my continued engagement with European culture. Here I analyzed a series of nineteenth-century French and English novels in which the protagonists—both male and female—are themselves readers of books so that we readers are put in the position of reading about people who read; among the texts I included were Charlotte Brontë's *Jane Eyre*, Dickens's *David Copperfield*, Stendhal's *Le Rouge et le Noir*, and Flaubert's *Madame Bovary*. I examined the ways in which the protagonists' reading refers us back to the authors' own, shapes their sense of personal identity and life destiny, and finally structures the novels we are reading on both a narrative and ideological level. However unconsciously, I am convinced that I was led to this topic largely from a position of identification, recognizing much of my childhood self in these fictional readers and appreciating the degree to which they had mastered the European literary canon much as I had endeavored to do in high school

Yet, in its own way, this version of culture as home could only be but another abstraction, geographically removed from me not by virtue of the Atlantic Ocean but by the confines of the printed page. So ultimately, my real home, what remained most familiar to me throughout my years abroad, was quite simply the family with whom I lived—my parents, my grandmother, and my two older sisters—and with whom I had shared the experience of being African Americans abroad. Looking back, it seems to me that I thought of my immediate family almost as a nation unto itself, freed from geographical moorings as well as historical bonds. The pleasure of such national belonging was that I knew I could count on the loyalty of each of its citizens; the reality was that I belonged to other more complex and heterogeneous communities as well.

"THIS DARK AND DANGEROUS AND UNLOVED STRANGER"

It must have been sometime during my first year at Radcliffe that I had a conversation that would slowly but surely bring me face to face with my memory of Baldwin's visit. In response to my explanation of why and how I had lived in Switzerland for so many years, an acquaintance (a young African American man whose name and face are lost to me) remarked that it must have been painful for me to think of myself as a participant in white European culture when I, as a black American, could in fact never be part of it. His comments upset and unsettled me, for until that moment I had truly believed that this European culture in which I had been so well schooled was my own. Although I had by then discovered Baldwin's identity as the stranger in my home, I had not yet read his essay and so was unaware that my acquaintance was parroting—poorly, as it turned out—Baldwin's ideas. I angrily dismissed the conversation from my mind.

The details are lost to me, but I remember distinctly the shock of recognition when I finally read "Stranger in the Village" in my last year of college. Since then, I have found this essay impossible to dismiss. It has become a touchstone in my thinking about who I am and how issues of personal identity have both shaped and been shaped by my scholarship. First and foremost, I have come to recognize that Baldwin and I were never fully strangers to one another but shared much in common. Looking back, it is now obvious to me that many Europeans also saw me as a stranger in the village; I too was stared and pointed at because of the color of my skin and the texture of my hair. So, as discomforting as it has been, I have tried to see myself from the outside in much the same way the Swiss villagers saw Baldwin and to comprehend the terms on which others have seen me as strange (or familiar, for that matter). Like Baldwin before me, I have worked to understand "this dark and dangerous and unloved stranger [who] is part of [my]self forever" ("Many Thousands Gone" 77).

If Baldwin and I were both strangers abroad (albeit to different degrees), we were equally strangers upon our return home. Baldwin's later essays from the 1960s and 1970s, particularly "The New Lost Generation" and "No Name in the Street," clearly suggest that when he did come back to the United States with his new sense of what it meant to be an American Negro, he nonetheless felt like a stranger. In these essays, Baldwin describes how his European exile had turned him into a "wanderer" and how, upon his return home, he "began to be profoundly uncomfortable. It was a strange kind of discomfort, a terrified apprehension that I had lost my bearings" ("No Name in the Street" 465). But if home had become strange to Baldwin, he was just as strange to those who had remained at home, referring to himself as "the loneliest and most blackly distrusted of men" ("The New Lost Generation" 313). Baldwin's feelings of estrangement can be attributed to many sources, including his sexuality, but the deep distrust of him stemmed foremost, I think, from his deliberate refusal to readjust to life at home, his determination never "to be anybody's nigger again" ("No Name" 465).

Similarly, my years abroad had turned me into a wanderer and made me feel lost at home. College life introduced me to new concepts, ideas, and people on a daily basis: American literary figures such as Emerson and Thoreau (few black authors could be found on our reading lists); comic-book characters like Batman and Superman; social interactions with a variety of classmates, among them blacks, Jews, and WASPs. I was also plunged into a larger, more turbulent world that encompassed the civil rights movement and the Vietnam War. Like many other students, I threw myself into campus activities that revolved around these issues, attending protest meetings that featured speakers such as Stokely Carmichael and teach-ins led by radical student leaders, or traveling to New York and Washington D.C. to participate in demonstrations that would change the course of our national history. But I was acutely aware that I brought to these events a lived experience that was very different from that of most of my classmates. I had never been obliged to live in a segregated neighborhood or attend a segregated school, barred from entering a restaurant, hotel, or swimming pool, or forced to drink from a "Coloreds Only" water fountain; and my knowledge of Vietnam up until that time had been shaped by the tears my seventh-grade French teacher shed the day of the fall of Dien Bien Phu.

If I felt somewhat of a stranger in the midst of these national events, I was to an even greater degree viewed as strange. Classmates and teachers alike could not figure out why this black American girl spoke English with a French accent or needed a dictionary to write her freshman comp papers or used words that simply did not mean what they were supposed to, choosing "note" instead of "grade" or "support" instead of "tolerate," for example. My more formal manner and clothes (I wore suits to class!) were interpreted as signs of snobbishness, and the images of ice and snow that Baldwin had used to evoke the landscape of his Swiss village were now being applied to me: I was the ice princess from Switzerland. In contrast to Baldwin's experience, however, this distrust of me stemmed not from any principled resistance on my part but rather from the fact that I existed between two languages, two cultures, and simply did not know how to translate from one to the other or negotiate the terrain between them. I found nobody around me who had shared the cosmopolitan experience of growing up as a black American abroad, so although I remained deeply appreciative of the European cultures and ecumenical values to which my parents had exposed me, I also came to resent my Swiss childhood. I felt that I had been deprived of a "home," of a sense of belonging to a social group extending beyond immediate family that my parents themselves had had when they were children. I wished that I too had grown up a Negro in America where the terrain would be familiar and questions not asked. Finding home on this side of the Atlantic was a task that still lay ahead of me, one which, like Baldwin, I would accomplish in large part through reading and writing.

Baldwin's writings have also helped me understand the degree to which American distrust of blacks is not just occasioned by personal idiosyncrasies or simply reserved for specific individuals but is a politically charged emotion directed at the race as a whole, serving to remind us of just how tenuous our claim to home really is. Unknown to me as a child, my father had been the target of such distrust at exactly the time of Baldwin's visit to us in Geneva. Although he was on a WHO assignment to the United States at the time, the State Department, playing out the McCarthy hysteria of the moment, had deemed it necessary to confiscate my father's passport and investigate him for subversive activities. Suspicion centered on the fact that my father was on a list of potential lecturers scheduled to speak at an adult education school for black workers—quite possibly the Jefferson School of Social Sciences—that was considered to be communist. It was not only my father's blackness, then, but his continued involvement with the black community that had brought about his government's distrust. One of the ironies of Baldwin's visit is that he had neglected to tell us who had sent him to visit us. Knowing my father's predicament, my mother and grandmother could only guess that he was from the CIA. In reality Baldwin's decision to return to Europe had been precipitated by his desire to escape "the national convulsion of McCarthyism" ("No Name" 464). Only much later did we learn that it was Langston Hughes, a close friend of my aunt's, who had suggested that he look us up. To this day, none of us can quite fathom Baldwin's reticence; why did he not mention Hughes's name to us? If I try to put myself in his place, I can feel the loneliness of this black wanderer and sense his desire to connect with other black Americans living abroad. But I can also imagine that our conventional middle-class lifestyle might have seemed strange to him and that we simply could not make him feel at home.

Amid the confusion of my return to the United States, I continued to feel that my own family remained the one constant in my life. Interestingly enough, I think that despite his highly conflicted familial relationships, family for Baldwin also served as a crucial site from which he could think about the different forms that home so often takes. If "Notes of a Native Son" constitutes a bitter statement of his lifelong alienation from his father, the closing paragraphs of the essay poignantly acknowledge the paternal legacy embedded in "familiar lines" quoted from the Bible that teach Baldwin the values he must follow in order to make America home for black Americans (145). In "The Fire Next Time," published some eight years later, Baldwin himself adopted the role of father in order to pass this spiritual legacy on to his nephew (336). For me, the question has become one of how to think about and through my family in order to understand the many meanings of black Americanness and its place in American society.

WHAT IT MEANS TO BE A (BLACK) AMERICAN

After finishing graduate school, I joined the faculty at the University of Maryland as a professor of English and comparative literature. Reading, teaching, and writing about literary texts have been the focal point of my professional life. On a general level, this at-homeness with literature connects me to Baldwin; more specifically, my critical writings also meditate on the meanings of the strange and the familiar, home and family, and what it means to be a (black) American. Thinking back to my first book, *The Determined Reader*, I believe my college acquaintance was wrong to suggest that as a black American I was necessarily excluded from European culture; as Baldwin himself remarked in "The Discovery of What It Means to Be an American," the fact that "Europe had formed us [white and black Americans], was part of our identity and part of our inheritance" (172). My reading of the nineteenth-century novels I analyzed in *The Determined Reader* has changed over time, however, and I now approach them from a perspective more akin to Baldwin's own when he commented toward the end of "Stranger in the Village" that if "the cathedral at Chartres . . . says something to the people of this village which it cannot say to me . . . it is important to understand that this cathedral says something to me which it cannot say to them" (88–89). Baldwin's comments illustrate his perfect awareness that the cultural sensibility of African Americans is neither black nor white, neither African, European, nor American. Rather, it is an interplay of all these identities that never dissolves into the grayness of a Geneva sky but maintains the distinctive tastes of each, much like the tart-sweet apple cider whose enjoyment Baldwin's visit to my family had deferred.

As an example of my revisionary thinking, I will cite two texts in particular, Mme de Staël's *Corinne* (1807) and Claire de Duras's *Ourika* (1823). In both novels, the heroine's ties to her biological family have been severed and each comes of age in a family from which she is profoundly alienated; each acquires a deep familiarity with European culture but eventually becomes estranged from the society in which she lives; and each dies at the end. In my discussion of Mme de Staël's novel, I focused on how Corinne, positioned in Rome, the cradle of Western civilization, endeavors through literary improvisation and conversation to mediate between, and reconcile, the classic and romantic traditions of Europe. Now, however, I am much more attentive not only to the ways in which Italy is perceived in the novel from a northern perspective as "other," but also to the manner in which Corinne herself is increasingly "Africanized" in appearance and behavior as she travels south to Naples and ultimately becomes a stranger to the city that once celebrated her. Today I would also include in my study Duras's *Ourika*, a text that had not yet been rediscovered when I wrote my book. Brought to Europe from Africa as a slave, Ourika is adopted into an aristocratic French family and begins a process of assimilation into French culture. In adolescence, however, she becomes estranged from French society, an estrangement marked by the impossibility of interracial marriage; to compensate for her loneliness, she seeks to create for herself "une family de choix" (44), but dies prematurely. Through these rereadings, I have been made aware of the degree to which European literature, no less than its American counterpart, is informed by an African presence, its texts constituting, in Toni Morrison's words, "responses to a dark, abiding, signing Africanist presence" (5). And I can now appreciate in ways that I could not earlier Baldwin's vision of the cathedral at Chartres as dominated by "inescapable gargoyles . . . seeming to say that God and the devil can never be divorced" (89).

The year I finished *The Determined Reader* I started work on a new project that would culminate in my second book, *"Doers of the Word": African-American Women Speakers and Writers in the North (1830–1880)*. If my motivation for writing my first book stemmed in part from an unconscious identification with the novels' fictional readers, this second book and its dramatic shift in my scholarship were motivated by one specific event: the death of my grandmother in September 1985 at the age of 101. Although she had had her share of health problems, my grandmother had remained vibrantly alive until the last six months of her life. Growing up, I had taken her presence in our home as my second mother for granted, but as an adult I have come to realize the degree to which she embodied not only my family's history but larger historical forces as well. Her African ancestors had come to the New World as commodities traded across the Atlantic; in Jamaica, they had helped create a creolized population in which black, white, Indian, and Chinese blood commingled freely; and my grandmother herself served as a perfect illustration of that vast migration of peoples at the beginning of the twentieth century who came to the United States through Ellis Island in pursuit of the American dream. In Harlem, my grandmother and mother lived in a tenement house and although my grandmother had only a sixth-grade education and earned very little money as a seamstress, she made sure that my mother would be able to fulfill her aspirations of becoming a doctor by attending Barnard College and Columbia Medical School.

Thinking about my grandmother, I am reminded of Baldwin's comment that in some fashion we all carry history within us and that consequently "history is literally *present*" in us ("White Man's Guilt" 410). But growing up in Switzerland I had not been able to grasp the varied meanings of my grandmother's history. So her death—and my remembrance of her life—led me to the past. Still asking questions of my home that was the United States, I wanted most urgently to understand the historical experience of blacks in the New World, an understanding that I felt my European sojourn had disrupted. I immersed myself in researching the lives of the many nineteenth-century black women who had been the foremothers of the modern civil rights activists whom I had been told about while living in Geneva. To my mind, my grandmother stood in the company of these women.

My musings resulted in *"Doers of the Word."* In the book, I traced the careers of ten antebellum black women activists—among them Sojourner Truth, Mary Ann Shadd Cary, Sarah Parker Remond, Harriet Jacobs, and Frances Harper—and looked at the ways in which they made use of the "word"—specifically public oratory and writing—as they participated in antislavery activities, racial uplift, and other important reform movements of their day. In the process, I hoped to insert myself into this activist literary tradition and in some small fashion become a "doer of the word" as well. Perusing the speeches and writings of these women, I examined how they came to reject any representation of African Americans as strangers in America and insisted on the rights of full citizenship. Yet even as they claimed America as home, these women paradoxically found themselves excluded from positions of leadership within the male-dominated institutions that organized these reform movements; consequently, they sought sites of authority in what I termed the "liminal" spaces of religious evangelicism, travel, public speaking and, finally, fiction-making. The experiences of these women as social activists were, then, highly complex; they suggest both pain and power, radical subversion and a desire for legitimation; above all, they point to the difficulties of finding and being at home.

NEW FOUND GENERATIONS

It is the writing of the present essay that has made me aware of the larger meanings behind my more recent scholarship. In my two current projects, I am still looking for home in and through history, specifically family histories conceived as embodiments of the larger historical processes noted by Baldwin. I have come to this idea not only by remembering my grandmother as ancestral figure but, as I noted at the beginning of this essay, by reflecting on my own genealogical position within my family, my own place within a historical continuum. In the process I have continued to grapple with what it means to be a black American, turning time and time again to Baldwin's writings on home.

In both my teaching and writing I have been thinking about a set of texts that I refer to as the New Negro novels of the nadir, historical romances written by black American authors Frances Harper, Pauline Hopkins, and Charles Chesnutt during the post-Reconstruction years of 1892–1903. I am fascinated by the way in which these novels resolutely look forward to the future, specifically to African Americans' entrance into modernity and to being at home in America. But the novels' protagonists are in fact caught between what has passed and what is yet to come. Yet even as they anticipate the future, they recognize the need to confront what one character in Harper's *Iola Leroy* calls "the mournful past" (273). This movement from retrospection to anticipation is narratively enacted through the reconstitution of the texts' African American families whose genealogical line has been obscured by the disruptive forces of slavery. By the end of Harper's novel, for example, Iola can joyfully assert that she has been able to reconnect "the once-severed branches of our family" (215).

To a greater extent than Harper's novel, both Hopkins's and Chesnutt's works seek to imagine the family of the future, which they define as a racially amalgamated one in which new branches are discovered and hidden racial lineages revealed. In fact, their texts challenge biological concepts of race and underscore the absurdity of racial designations by pointing out the extent to which black blood so often remains invisible and undetectable in external features. For these two novelists the true meaning of being an American—what Chesnutt termed "the future American"—lies precisely in the blending of black, white, and native American blood. I think that it is significant, however, that all these novels ultimately pay homage to an ancestral female figure—former slaves or Africans whose ties to the continent remain intact—who represents the mournful past. These "Old Negro" figures (to whom my grandmother bears some resemblance) do not truly belong to the newly constituted New Negro household, or their relationship to it is at best marginal. Positioned against the protagonists, they appear backward and primitive, characterized by dialect speech, superstitious beliefs, and visionary religious practices; yet all of them speak important racial truths, warning of the ways in which the legacy of slavery is destroying the nation.

In my second project, family is quite literally my own family, as I am using my father's own forefathers as a lens through which to explore the larger social panorama of African American social and cultural life in nineteenth-century New York. Here, I envision family history as a pathway to public history and to the question of how one becomes a (black) American. As I noted at the beginning of this essay, my father never talked much about his family and I have come to believe that this was because he had never been told much about them. I am guessing that his parents, who entered the twentieth century with all the hopes of the New Negro, might well have felt a certain shame about early family members who had been slaves, domestic servants, or victims of the racial violence that erupted so unpredictably in nineteenth-century New York. They felt compelled to suppress the mournful past, unlike the New Negro novelists for whom the mode of fiction perhaps freed them to honor the Old. Researching my family's history in New York's many archives has offered me yet another form of at-handness, opening up a world heretofore unknown to me. Early in my research I came across a page torn from a scrapbook (whose owner is as yet unidentified) on which several newspaper clippings had been carefully pasted: one was an obituary of one of my great-grandfathers, the rest an assortment of poems that provide a kind of gloss on his character, avocations, and domestic life. My initial reaction was one of amazement that somebody had cared enough about this man to memorialize him in this way. From a broader perspective, however, I have also come to see the scrapbook as a metaphor for the project I am undertaking; I am gathering scraps culled from the past—the past of family, community, and city—to stitch them together into a coherent narrative.

Consonant with the rest of my work, I envision this project as a specifically nineteenth-century story and have chosen to focus on three particular family members who span three generations. I consider first my great-great-grandfather, Peter Guignon (1813–85), who attended New York's African Free Schools with Alexander Crummell, James McCune Smith, Henry Highland Garnet, and other young black men who as adults would form part of New York's black leadership; Guignon also became a pharmacist and active participant in St. Philip's Episcopal Church, a parish of Trinity Church that was strongly committed to racial uplift work. I then turn to my great-grandfather, Philip Augustus White (1824–91), who was also a pharmacist and a vestryman at St. Philip's, and the first black appointed to the Brooklyn Board of Education. I conclude with my grandfather, Jerome Bowers Peterson (1859–1943), coeditor of the *New York Age* with T. Thomas Fortune and a black Republican appointment to Puerto Rico and Venezuela early in the twentieth century. I am particularly impressed by how each of these three men was able to put down roots deep in the city's neighborhoods—whether Lower Manhattan or Brooklyn—and acquire a sense of place that I, as a wanderer, never had. In the city I can walk block after block, pause at corner after corner, and tell myself that through all of the historical upheavals that these places have endured, each of them lived, worked, studied, or worshiped here.

I am gathering scraps about these men and their families from many different sources, and the process of finding these scraps will become part of my story. At the New York Historical Society I came across an entry in a ledger written by the treasurer of the Public School Society noting that Philip A. White was paid the sum of three dollars for making fires to keep African Free School #2 warm over a three-month period in the winter of 1839–40; at the New York Academy of Medicine I found an advertisement for White's pharmacy at the corner of Frankfort and Gold streets that ran in the *American Circular and Chemical Gazette* from approximately 1865 to 1880; taking the J train to Cypress Hills Cemetery in Brooklyn one Saturday morning last year, I stumbled across all of the graves; finally, sorting through boxes in my mother's basement this past summer I found photographs that give faces to these figures from the past. Since my research is still incomplete, so is my story. Much of what I have reconstructed so far lies comfortably within familiar paradigms of African American history, but other aspects are more perplexing and border on the strange.

Like the protagonists of the novels of the nadir, I have discovered that my ancestors came to the United States from faraway places. I have not been particularly surprised to find out that some came from England, others from Jamaica, and still others from San Domingue, that some were free and other slaves, but I do not quite know what to make of a great-great-great-grandfather, named Joseph Marshall, who hailed from Maracaibo, Venezuela. I also do not recognize myself in any of the family photographs I have discovered. I am now holding in my hand, for example, a photograph of a great-grandaunt, Mary White Thompson. Captured in profile, she is severe looking: her unsmiling lips are pinched into a thin straight line, her hair is drawn tightly back in a bun and smoothed hard against her scalp, her angular chin juts out as if in warning. To me, she seems the very image of a New England schoolmarm. What was she like? What were her hopes, dreams, aspirations? Were they fulfilled or disappointed? If I put all these family members together, do they suggest Chesnutt's future American family in which black, white, and native American blood are married?

Once settled in New York, my forefathers followed a pattern of success that is quite typically American. Emphasizing education, trade, and hard work, they rose to positions of prominence and became part of New York City's black political and social elite, forerunners of Du Bois's Talented Tenth. Like the leaders of other free black communities in the North, their public activism unfolded on two levels. On the one hand, these men and their colleagues worked to gain the full privileges of citizenship, to overcome that distrust of blacks that Baldwin and my father would still evoke a century later, to make the nation home. On the other hand, confronted with pervasive and systemic patterns of discrimination, they chose to establish separate institutions that would give them a greater degree of autonomy and control over their lives and ultimately create their identity as African Americans. It is in this spirit that they established black churches, schools, literary societies, and newspapers.

As I mine the archives, however, I find still other stories that are unfamiliar and demand that we extend our vision beyond that of black lives confined to the black community. For example, in his daily work my great-grandfather came into contact with whites from varied social classes and these interactions affected his life in profound ways. His drugstore was located in ward four, a mixed neighborhood of blacks and Irish who were often too poor to pay for their medicines, and so my great-grandfather often gave them away freely. An obituary recounts how he refused to leave the drugstore during the Draft Riots of 1863, counting on the protection of his Irish neighbors who in fact defended him against an Irish mob and prevented his property from being destroyed. Such an incident complicates the conventional narrative of the Draft Riots, which insists on pitting aggressive Irish against helpless blacks. Somewhat less dramatically, my great-grandfather's professional and civic life also brought him into contact with prominent men in the city. Edward Squibb was a member of the Pharmaceutical Association that Philip White had joined; John Jay helped my family's church, St. Philip's, gain recognition from the Episcopal diocese; as mayor of Brooklyn, Seth Low appointed my great-grandfather to the Brooklyn Board of Education.

Most surprising to me, however, has been my dawning realization that the cosmopolitanism of my childhood life would not have been totally unfamiliar to my nineteenth-century relatives and that they might not have seen it as particularly strange. For, if they had a strong sense of their local belonging to New York neighborhoods, I believe they also remained aware of their familial roots in England and San Domingue and alive to the possibility of living abroad, which my grandfather in fact did when he was appointed to posts in Puerto Rico and Venezuela. But my ancestors were cosmopolitan even without moving out of their local neighborhoods. In my mother's basement I discovered books from my great-grandfather's and grandfather's library—Longfellow's translation of Dante's *Divine Comedy*, Shakespeare's plays, Macaulay's *History of England*, Carlyle's *The French Revolution*, and many novels translated from the French. These were the texts that Baldwin had claimed as "part of our identity and part of our inheritance" and they were the texts that had been my companions growing up in Geneva. As one of my colleagues noted when I told him of my discovery: "Carla, you were prefigured."

REFERENCES

Baldwin, James. "The Discovery of What It Means to Be an American." In *The Price of the Ticket*, 171–76. New York: St. Martin's/Marek, 1985.
———. "Encounter on the Seine: Black Meets Brown." In *The Price of the Ticket*, 35–40.
———. "The Fire Next Time." In *The Price of the Ticket*, 333–80.
———. "Many Thousands Gone." In *The Price of the Ticket*, 65–78.

———. "The New Lost Generation." In *The Price of the Ticket*, 305–14.

———. "No Name in the Street." In *The Price of the Ticket*, 449–552.

———. "Notes of a Native Son." In *The Price of the Ticket*, 127–46.

———. "A Question of Identity." In *The Price of the Ticket*, 91–100.

———. "Stranger in the Village." In *The Price of the Ticket*, 79–90.

———. "White Man's Guilt." In *The Price of the Ticket*, 409–14.

Chesnutt, Charles. "The Future American: A Complete Race-Amalgamation Likely to Occur." *Boston Evening Transcript*. 1 September 1900. Reprinted in *Charles W. Chesnutt: Essays and Speeches*, edited by Joseph R. McElrath Jr. et al., 131–35. Stanford: Stanford University Press, 1999.

Duras, Claire de. *Ourika*. 1823. New York: The Modern Language Association of America, 1994.

Harper, Frances E. W. *Iola Leroy*. 1892. Boston: Beacon, 1987.

Morrison, Toni. *Playing in the Dark: Whiteness and the Literary Imagination*. New York: Vintage, 1993.

History

DAVID BLEICH

Tribute to Robert D. Marcus

Robert D. Marcus died on 6 October 2000, at age sixty-four, with his boots on. At the time he was chair of the department of history at the State University of New York at Brockport. Previously, he had been the vice president and chief academic officer of that school for about nine years. When he held that office, he observed, "It is the job of the President of the College to speak for the College. It is the job of the Faculty to think for the College. It is the job of the Vice President to prevent the President from thinking, and the Faculty from speaking." I knew him for over thirty years as an admired scholar and friend. I thought he was an extraordinary person, truly a mensch.

He began writing "Journey/man: Hi/s/tory" at a point when he was trying to evaluate his professional life with an eye toward resuming historical scholarship. He had been a standout as a graduate student and junior faculty member, whose promise was marked by his book, *Grand Old Party* (Oxford, 1971), a history of the Republican Party in the nineteenth century. He soon became a dean, however, because he had, as suggested mildly in this essay, an instinct for nurturing: strange as it may sound to those of us who know many deans, this dean's fundamental premise was the question of how much he could contribute to his school. It is surprising indeed how completely his colleagues concur in this view of him: he was truly admired, respected, and loved by those over whose professional lives he presided.

This essay was to have been part of a larger inquiry in which he was going to combine a personal with a public, collective historical interest: recovering the documentation of his father's family's arrival in New York City around the turn of the twentieth century. He suspected that there were, still, undocumented patterns of settling on the part of the immigrant Jewish population, and that, as he was searching for his own family's history, he would simultaneously document the "different" neighborhoods into which many immigrants moved when they arrived in the new country. He had planned to discuss this project in a panel on autobiography and the writing of history at the annual meeting of the American History Association in Boston in January 2001. It is a new path in contemporary historiography, one that the majority of academic historians do not travel.

Those of us who have striven to humanize our academic voices, to include ourselves yet not to distract our colleagues with our preoccupations, are aware that this is no easy task. In this essay, we see both the salutary results of Bob's work as well as the struggle to move back and forth, fairly, between the personal and the public, between the individual and the collective. I think he provides a model for writing history even for those of us who are not historians, and thus an example of how to recognize historicity and collectivity in what was once considered the record of only one life.

ROBERT D. MARCUS

Journey/man: Hi/s/tory

The life of the mind, I used to think, was a form of running away from home. If I became a scientist or mathematician rather than an engineer or actuary I would enter a world more calm and clear, more remote and elegantly impractical, than anything imaginable in my lower-middle-class family. Then in books from neighborhood public libraries I glimpsed a yet richer world, particularly the great Russian and French novels of the nineteenth century, authors not read in high school English classes like Dickens or George Eliot. Finally, in my undergraduate years at Columbia College in the mid-1950s, its expansive general education program seemed to project me directly into this world of ideas. Collecting both the Great Books and my many college mentors, I thought my life's direction was set, buying those golden books in the used book stores that then lined Fourth Avenue and teaching them uptown at Columbia or at St. Johns or some other of the little heavens of academe. High ideas; genteel poverty; interesting friends; interested students: more than enough.

So distinct an education from anything around me. Except for one course in sociology with C. Wright Mills, I can't recall a class that touched on anything then current. The memory of high school social studies kept me from taking any courses in the history department. Philosophy, not offered in high school and apparently closer to mathematics and science, became my field. The department, the soul of general education, didn't offer a strict major. Wanting its undergraduates to learn something to philosophize about first, the program required only a few philosophy courses before the senior year. Then came the opportunity to reflect on it all in seminars held in Claremont Avenue apartments redolent with academic anecdote and sherry. So I learned nothing at all about the nature of academic disciplines, having read no more than a handful of secondary works, but I absorbed great gobs of intellectual history in the form of the classics of literature, philosophy, and political theory. I never quite recovered from all those ideas and movements and grand books in one timeless past-present swirling about my adolescent brain.

My experience immediately after college convinced me that philosophy was not my field. During a confusing year in England I saw at first hand technical philosophy—Oxford linguistic analysis—and wondered how it related to the great questions of my undergraduate classes. I reacted by turning back to the Greek philosophers I had studied in college, learning some Greek and reading Aristotle. But that didn't work for me either. I recalled John Herman Randall Jr., one of my teachers at Columbia, saying that Plato and Aristotle were not abstract thinkers. They were interested in practical questions: how large should a state be; how should it be ruled; how many soldiers did it need? They studied the world around them, not thinkers from millennia before. After the first year of what could have been a continuing fellowship I went home no longer the golden boy of the Columbia philosophy department, probably not a prospective philosopher, just as naive as before, and more confused than ever.

I wanted to be a professor, that was sure, but I simply drifted into the academic discipline of history. Like philosophy, it seemed to have no fixed subject. Everything, after all, has a history. And unlike philosophy, it was resolutely eclectic. The great scavengers of academe, historians picked up methods from wherever, usually as they began to molder. You did not have to believe in history as a field; it did not fall into schools separated by methods; it was a set of tools, some of which were bound to fit a man's hand (sorry, but after high school I never had a class with a woman instructor and thought that way).

History also made more sense to my family, and, reluctant as I was to admit it then, that had begun to matter. They didn't read history, but they cared about it. The events of the 1930s and 1940s still resonated for them in the late 1950s. My parents had lost some of their dreams in the Great Depression. They had a hero in Franklin Delano Roosevelt (the middle name always included). In the early 1940s my father had organized the print shop in which he worked. My mother knew school teachers who were communists. Both parents had been air raid wardens. My brother served in Korea. Philosophy was a luxury. History was real, almost a thing. Forget epistemology; forget ontology. Not problems for historians. They argue on the basis of evidence the way engineers in deciding how to build a bridge (one of my father's unrealized ambitions) argue the physics of stress.

Naive? Yes. Studying the past is full of epistemological tangles. But they did not—and still mostly don't—bother historians. "The overwhelming majority of historians," writes the distinguished cultural historian Michael Kammen, "are utterly indifferent to issues involving epistemology and the philosophy of history" (17). Historians were much like scientists. There's work to be done. Check those theories of knowledge at the door of the archive or laboratory like some fancy garment you might want to wear to a special occasion—perhaps a seminar.

For some years, I fit right into the profession. An essay Martin Duberman wrote in 1965 describes historians in a way that makes me—reading it for the first time in 1999—wince in recognition:

> Historians, to oversimplify, tend not to be interested in personality—other than in its public manifestations. . . . We would all agree that the individual cannot be fully understood apart from his society, but what is too often made to follow, is that apart from his social role, the individual is not worth understanding. Such an attitude converts the historian's inability to examine individuality from a limitation into a virtue.
>
> Further, it confirms those very traits of personality in many historians which first inclined them to join the profession. For historians, almost by definition, are men who shy away from the interior life, who are temperamentally drawn instead to the externals of behavior, to what is verifiable, concrete, susceptible of exact description—everything we sum up in the word "facts." In this regard it is instructive that historians like to use the word "solid" in expressing their admiration for a particular work of history—as if the prime virtue was filling some literal void. (*The Uncompleted Past* 51–52)

Am I Duberman's archetypical historian? Most of my historical writing would say yes.

My first serious excursion into historical writing—becoming my first published article—was a master's essay on the radical abolitionist orator and reformer Wendell Phillips. My account of Phillips left me with the same void Duberman felt about Charles Francis Adams and James Russell Lowell, the subjects of his widely recognized biographies. After all that research and writing, I still couldn't find Phillips's *self*. My thesis title, "Wendell Phillips: The Public Vocation," secretly confessed failure. Then one day I noted a comment in Emerson's journals: "The first discovery I made about Phillips was, that while I admired his eloquence, I had not the faintest wish to meet the man. He had only a *platform*-existence, and no personality" (December 1854, qtd. in Perry 265). In one brief paragraph, Emerson absolved me of my failure. Perhaps beneath that facade of benevolent reformer there was only . . . a benevolent reformer. Or, more likely, the private man was simply unreachable from the historical record. (Since that time, newly found letters between Phillips and his wife give a little more character to the private Phillips, although I still find him remote, unfathomable.)

Apparently I wanted something for myself in my search for Wendell Phillips that I had not succeeded in finding. But I had chosen this Boston Brahmin reformer as my subject just as I had selected history as my discipline. Neither his portrait nor his speeches had suggested a man of intimate reflections. Something about the stentorian public voice and absence of the intimate had attracted me, even as it left me dissatisfied. Duberman, for all his complaints about the discipline of history, had chosen both to be a historian and to tackle the forbidding Charles Francis Adams as his first subject. Historians in fact regularly struggle with such dilemmas. "To lay stress on the personal," wrote Preserved Smith, a historian at Cornell in the early twentieth century, "is to make history unscientific; to omit it altogether is to make our study inhuman" (qtd. in Kammen 7).

History, I now see, was "split at the root" for me, an image from Adrienne Rich ("Split at the Root: An Essay on Jewish Identity"). The narrative I had learned in school and in my professional training was about highly public sayings and doings. That accorded well with what I had heard from my father. His world remained largely a mystery: his parents dead before my birth, their ancestors lost in an unknown history of Eastern Europe, his world largely abandoned for my mother's. I remember from him mostly political heroes with grand names like Alfred Emanuel Smith and Franklin Delano Roosevelt and baseball players with odd ones like Heinie Groh and Mel Ott. My vision of historical scholarship reflected my father's world: cool, distant, abstract, remote from the language of passion. That language I learned from my mother. Most of the family history I knew came from her and her mother. The family's social and emotional life gravitated around my mother's family and her friends. She told me of childhood struggles, rivalries with sisters, contributing at an early age to family finances, conflicts with her mother, later difficulties with relatives and struggles managing home and work. From an age too early for me to remember and continuing for all the decades her powers of recollection endured, I was her audience, fixed in a chair beyond my power to escape, listening to her urgent, repetitive narrative. She offered a dangerous example of a kind of history I feared to write, not only for its passion, even obsession, but for its perpetual irresolution. By the time her mind had resolved these tortuous issues she was in her mid-seventies, my father had died years before, and I was hearing these now-tempered monologues but twice a year in my visits to her in Florida.

My mother and most of her friends were elementary school teachers, so I grew up even more surrounded by maternal authority than my playmates. Brooklyn schoolteachers of the 1940s were typically formidable women of middle years commanding respect more than affection, teachers not only of correct from incorrect spelling and arithmetic, but of right from wrong, acceptable from unacceptable, clean from dirty, smart from stupid. Along with my homework, my mother's cohorts checked my manners and my fingernails. The few times I saw my mother with her students, she presented a powerful image of authority, free from the conflicts of home, something I expected to emulate in my academic life.

These all-knowing teachers were learners as well. I knew my mother had gone to a "training school" for one year after high school—all it took then to qualify for elementary school teaching. More impressive to my young mind was that she was always taking courses. Whatever courses were, I knew that on some days they forced her to arrive home late. She never referred to anything learned in them, but I knew they had to do with teaching. Now I understand that they were routine in-service workshops, but my young mind envisioned a separate and secret professional world she shared with all those formidable women who peopled my school and her life. Lesson plans suggested another mysterious entity occupying her time, something like the secret and important plans that spies were always trying to steal on the radio programs I listened to during World War II. I also heard of secret answer pages in teachers' editions of textbooks. Such perceptions, reinforced by my father's silent membership in a fraternal organization, the Knights of Pythias, prepared me for the ideal of a secular academic priesthood's esoteric knowledge and secret rituals.

Some of my mother's work fit less easily into visions of academic life. In Brownsville, where she taught, the school year began with less urgency about pencils and erasers and wide-lined marbled tablets than about clothing and shoes. Dorothy Marcus and her colleagues were not going to lose students to cold weather when their clothing, particularly their shoes, kept them from school. By the end of the first week of class, she knew what garments in what sizes each poor student needed. Whatever my brother and I no longer used went into the "school bin," a mysterious vessel presumably in her classroom. Her friends searched their closets for castoffs; charities and cajoled Brownsville merchants provided the rest. Magazines, toys, tools, remnants of wallpaper, wrapping paper, thread, tinsel, wires, and metal coat hangers landed as well in the school bin to be recycled into activities, lessons, and projects.

For some years in the mid-1940s, before she amassed the seniority to teach the first-graders she preferred, my mother taught a health class with students K through 8 who experienced serious health problems like tuberculosis or asthma. Every day the students would push aside the furniture, spread out cots, take breaks for milk and snacks, and have their special health needs met. I remember once seeing this enormous classroom with its huge windows opened in all seasons, the flexible tables and chairs instead of desks bolted to the floor, the cots stacked on the side of the room: an island of progressive education in our sea of regimentation.

The school bin with its things to wear and materials for projects and the health class with its cots and special attentions appeared to me as peculiarities of elementary school or of dealing with especially needy students. Without being aware of it, I drew the lesson from both parents that such concerns—and such clientele—were exactly what I was supposed to escape. For her poor struggling students my mother expressed gentle pity, while people who struggled against her instead of against their lives she dismissed as "thick as shit"—not her ordinary teacherly language. "Work with your head, not with your hands," advised my father, a print-shop foreman who had failed in his own printing business during the Depression. Nonetheless some alternative lessons of the school bin filtered through my parents' warnings against doing what they did, enough to prepare me for the interest around me in the 1960s in new audiences for history and to make me an enthusiastic volunteer for experimental programs that crossed disciplines or served new student clienteles like auto union shop stewards or minorities.

Most of what I would later learn about academic life was, in fact, implicit in that school bin: that there is no easy dividing line between the everyday and what you learn in school, no fancy academic subjects, only common life better or less well understood; that education is a form of doing, that a teacher's job is mostly to organize material and experiences in preparation for what students do in a classroom (or library or elsewhere); that education is a social, not an individual process; that the small jobs, like deaning (as I later did) or providing shoes, that enable teachers and students to meet in classrooms under conditions allowing learning are worth doing. I could have learned all this from Dorothy Marcus had that been what she wanted to teach me just as I could have learned it from the books of John Dewey I read at Columbia in the 1950s. But these were not the lessons I was yet prepared to learn as I sought in the historical profession that separate life of the mind that college had promised.

Having glimpsed the larger world of college in the sheltered 1950s, I was learning to be a historian in the 1960s. What did I do during that exciting time? Nothing that sounds exciting. I went to graduate school, wrote my dissertation, found my first two academic jobs and with them my teaching voice, and finished my first book. I married, had two children, and was divorced. None of this sounds particularly marked by the era, although I attended a reasonable number of demonstrations, and had I not moved so many times in the intervening years might still own the collection of rally buttons to prove it.

This relatively quiet life exciting only to me, however, took place against a gaudy backdrop of demonstrations, assassinations, riots, and a bizarre war. The effects were right in front of me: a departmental party in the spring of 1963 interrupted to hear John F. Kennedy finally support the civil rights movement; canceling plans to attend the 1963 March on Washington out of a mix of trivial considerations and vague fears that I still shudder to disentangle; rumors flying about Washington after Kennedy's assassination several months later when I was doing research on my dissertation at the Library of Congress; attending an early teach-in during my first academic job; being unable to teach as my students and I were overwhelmed by the events whipping around us; having semesters end abruptly without final examinations after student rioting; realizing that my late-blooming opposition to the Vietnam War discredited the diplomatic history, and soon virtually all the history, that I had been taught to teach; being told by black students that my use of the term *Negro*, then polite, was unacceptable and had just the day before been officially rejected by SNCC, which was now a black power organization. *The day before!* If only I had read the morning paper.[1] The vague notions that had led me from philosophy to history were sharpening to suspicions that no form of academic life I knew about would realize my adolescent Columbian dreams. Pushing aside my confusions, I simply pursued my degree and career.

Like nearly all my generation of American historians, I was enormously influenced by Richard Hofstadter's deconstruction (a word he would have hated) of the language of American political and historical discourse. In luminous prose, he challenged a whole tradition of interpreting American life that historians generally labeled "progressive." The language of progress and reform, he taught, had not only dominated political vocabulary throughout most of American history but controlled historical interpretation as well. Both political oratory and historical prose, so I read him, had portrayed American history—the American Revolution, the Civil War, and the smaller quarrels—as symbolic battles between progress and reaction, private gain and public good, armies of light and forces of darkness, when in reality the participants on all sides—particularly since the Civil War—had shared many values and goals.[2] Hofstadter's rereading of the rhetoric of American history was subtle. He did not flatten argument into a consistent liberal consensus as some of his contemporaries did, nor did he deny the importance of ideas or even of conflict.[3] Rather, he criticized the simplicity of the ideas both politicians and historians held of the conflicts that had rippled through American history. This essentially ironic and cautionary voice was daring in its historical reach and originality. All of American history was his field; he borrowed freely from both literary criticism and the social sciences.[4] He had ceased early to dig in the archives; he aimed at the general point, not the definitive account, the disturbing insight that would drive others to the archives on new missions. Dealing with the nitty-gritty of American political and intellectual life, he somehow floated above it all, my dream of a professional life. To a graduate student of the 1960s in American history, his presence was inescapable.

Not having met the man and rarely conscious of his presence in my decision making, I was nevertheless constantly under his influence. Early on I had a remote encounter. My master's thesis took off from an essay by Hofstadter on Wendell Phillips. Begun in one professor's seminar and continued the next semester with another, the essay when I sent it in a few semesters later went to Hofstadter, whose turn it was to approve such products. The brevity of his comment and the signs of a quickly abandoned struggle to remove the essay from its complicated folder have led me to doubt that he read it. Certainly my careful revision of what he had written about Phillips did not get his careful attention ("Wendell Phillips: The Patrician as Agitator"). He was, I suppose, the ultimate absent intellectual father. This contrasted sharply with my experience of so many mentors as an undergraduate at Columbia but turned out to be typical of my experience as a historian, where I found brothers now and again, but never a substitute father.

My first choice of a dissertation subject was much less directly under

Hofstadter's influence. Rather, without realizing it then, I was trying to mix into some unlikely stew virtually everything on my plate—including my ambition to become the next Richard Hofstadter. The first quantitative studies of American political history were appearing and I thought I might use my mathematical skills, however rusty since the time I had been captain of my high school math team, to link my old ambitions to the new. I planned to isolate a political subdivision of Brooklyn that had changed rapidly from an older to a newer American ethnic mix in the late nineteenth or early twentieth century to determine how its politics had changed and to what extent earlier political divisions had survived. While I had not settled on a place (indeed that would be a large part of the historical puzzle), my mind was picturing many of the people I had grown up with: Jewish and other immigrants bursting out of Manhattan ghettos and finding lower-middle-class lives across the river. I would enter the world my parents had worked to climb beyond while insulating myself from it with cool mathematical techniques. All circuits would be completed, all paradoxes resolved: I would be on the cutting edge of scholarship yet returning to my old identity of math whiz, to the neighborhoods of my childhood, and even to my parents' childhoods. Now I smile in retrospect that I could have failed to notice how this project connected to my family history.

Robert Wiebe, my dissertation supervisor at Northwestern University, had too many good arguments against such a project. The historical profession looked askance at local history; I would be restricting my range of job possibilities; a topic of national scope would serve me better (all true at the time, although soon to change with the rise of social history).[5] Quantitative studies took forever to complete (certainly true then, and to a considerable extent still true). And they require working through stacks of a type of document—voter rolls, election statistics, and manuscript census—that I would find extremely boring (probably true for me). So I took Wiebe's suggestion and went to the Library of Congress to find out how the Republican Party organized itself nationally in the late nineteenth century, once again leaving only a little reluctantly an old for a new world.

Republican politicians of the Gilded Age didn't seem any more interesting as people than Wendell Phillips. I had been an avid reader of Thomas Wolfe during high school and never forgot his bewilderment over his father's enthusiasm for these Republican leaders (how like my own father's inexplicable enthusiasms): "Garfield, Arthur, Harrison, and Hayes were the lost Americans: their gravely vacant and bewhiskered faces mixed, melted, swam together in the sea-depths of a past intangible, immeasurable, and unknowable. . . . Which had the whiskers, which the burnsides: which was which?" (121). But without quite knowing why I was interested—other than the practical desire to get a Ph.D. and pursue the career I envisioned— I marched into the big country of national history, undoubtedly deriving some motivation from the chance to explore my psychic parallelism with Thomas Wolfe and at the same time take an oblique approach to a little piece of Hofstadter's most famous book, *The Age of Reform*. Whether or not it was precisely the game I wanted to play, it seemed an entrance into the big adult leagues.

Insofar as my dissertation responded to the challenges Hofstadter posed, my approach was extremely indirect. Rather than reinterpreting the language of the past as Hofstadter had done, I avoided taking anyone's language seriously, looking instead at what people did. I ran the equivalent of a nineteenth-century prison in which no one was allowed to speak.

Studying the Republican Party in the late nineteenth century, an institution about which historians widely acknowledged the separation of rhetoric and behavior, I boxed my main characters within the crude machineries of party organization: creating alliances, raising money, promising offices, printing campaign literature, organizing rallies and speaking tours. Some of them had also *written* campaign literature or *made* numerous political speeches or *held* political offices, but this interested me no more than had I discovered them writing poetry or collecting stamps. I sought to lay bare a process and not be led astray by the feints, darts, and shifts of my subjects' language (*Grand Old Party: Political Structure in the Gilded Age, 1880–1896*).

I treated other historians the same way. Taking the patient manner of a fisherman untangling a line, I softened my revisionism by virtually purging the manuscript of argument. Only a few footnotes, buried amid thousands of citations, even hint at controversy: I note with the barest possible elaboration a recent book "for a view . . . directly contradictory of mine" (275 n.45) or comment that another historian "interprets this letter very differently" (290 n.55), always suggesting offhandedly that they are entitled to their opinion. And of course not quoting them at any length. My account is as coldly behavioral as the quantitative study I had once envisioned, or even the game-theory studies in political science that analyze mutual deterrence.[6] Relying only on traditional forms of historical narrative rather than still-controversial statistical methodologies, the book speaks with a voice dispassionately authoritative. It arrived at the right moment to satisfy both historians and political scientists and become a standard work for graduate students.

The quotations fronting the title page illustrate the book's peculiar tone: Eugene McCarthy airily compares politicians to football coaches "smart enough to understand the game but not smart enough to lose interest"; Aristotle in *De Partibus Animalium* justifies the study of creatures "be [they] never so mean." The style suited the academic world it was entering. It was pretty much the style that adults in my family had used to address children: my father's confident misappropriation of what he remembered from reading the *New York Herald Tribune* on the subway in the morning and the *New York World-Telegram* on the same ride at night; my mother's matter-of-fact assurance that she "knew every street in Brooklyn"; her mother's certainty about where every knife, fork, and glass belonged on the dinner table. And it fitted my role in the family drama, the baby of the household who listened silently to what these powerful people said, but who never argued, who found his own involuted ways to avoid the mysterious warfare around him.

Then one day early in the 1970s, I noticed something that had eluded me during the six years in which writing *Grand Old Party* had dominated my life: all the characters in it are men. I was aware of the division in nineteenth-century American life between the feminine world of culture and the masculine sphere of politics and business,[7] a separation I had found convenient rather than troublesome. Neither the documents I read nor the literature I used from either history or political science even noticed the issue. Did it really matter, then? What would change if I took seriously the notion that politicians were all men, operating in a man's world—what I started to call a "male subculture"? What troubled me most was not that I had left women out of my particular story, but that I had done so without noticing it. I was learning the limits of my method and even of my discipline. It scarcely seemed to require proof that men behave differently in male groups than in the presence of women. It had to matter that politics was a male subculture. Not wanting to write about politics again, and not even dreaming of an attempt to unlock the least secret of women's historical experience, I began to look at other male subcultures for comparison. The old Marlene Dietrich song swam through my brain: I would "see what the boys in the back room will have."

Baseball was my choice among nineteenth-century boys' backrooms. While I had always played the game awkwardly, it was my father's sport and he had taught me to appreciate its subtleties. Besides, its peculiar late-nineteenth-century sense of statistical history, pursuit of respectability, and efforts to create long-term loyalties suggested analogies to politics.

Nineteenth-century American men had pored over political almanacs and memorized political statistics just as their sons later quoted batting averages and pitching records. Wanting baseball to be different from less reputable sports like boxing or horse racing, team owners resisted gambling and alcohol consumption at the ballparks, respected the Sabbath where they had to, tried to avoid the most blatant forms of commercialism, which including discouraging players from switching teams, and appealed to local loyalties and patriotic sentiments.[8]

But something happened to me on the way to the ballpark. The parallels between the narrative of baseball and the way I had written about politics became too obvious. Each was a series of contests structured by a set of institutions and rules, highly complex in the case of politics, more transparent in baseball, and both gauged by a set of statistics. Nineteenth-century politics could be thought of as a game. And that was how I had approached it. The party labels and political practices, like the structure of leagues and the rarely changing rules of baseball, lent a sense of timelessness, a linkage to the time before and the time before that made studying them a comfortably distanced intellectual pastime. I could begin anywhere, confident that I had missed nothing, each contest always comparable to the ones before. Nothing was new under the sun; yet there was a lot to talk about. I could write versions of my book again and again forever. Politics, baseball, it didn't matter. And at least on the surface none of it was personal.

"The typical structure of Western autobiography," write the psychologists and students of narrative strategies George C. Rosenwald and Richard L. Ochberg, "is the history of a conversion as modeled by the *Confessions of St. Augustine*" (12). Such, however, was not the secret autobiography I had emplotted in *Grand Old Party*. My new awareness produced no revelation of a new scholarly mission, but something far harder to find a genre in which to express: confusion and paralysis. I became bored with reading the historical monographs in my field, impatient with research in the archives, restless about my teaching, restless about my role in the academy, restless, restless, restless.

Why didn't I make my scholarship into something more personally satisfying? Just what kind of cowardice was at work? To answer the question, I must turn to the possibilities that the historical profession did and did not support. While that will not explain my next steps, it provides a significant context.

Unlike me, Martin Duberman had the courage to go far beyond other historians in search of a personal connection with the subjects he studied.

In 1972 he published *Black Mountain, An Exploration in Community*.[9] Still unique among the writings of professional historians, this book poses most starkly the question of "the autobiographical nature of knowledge" in historical writing.

Between its founding in 1933 and its demise in 1956 Black Mountain College became legendary for nurturing many of what Duberman describes as "the singular, shaping talents" of mid-century America, men (virtually all men) such as John Cage, Charles Olson, Josef Albers, Merce Cummingham, and Buckminster Fuller. Black Mountain was also a college of sorts (never accredited) and a utopian community (also of sorts: always changing and never defined) diversely and often painfully influencing the lives of its small and ever shifting student body and faculty. Interested in "nonauthoritarian education, group process, anarchism, and the possibilities of community" (xi),[10] Duberman for five years in the late sixties and early seventies read the hundred thousand documents on the college in the state archives at Raleigh, North Carolina, generated thousands of pages of transcripts of taped interviews, and solicited and collected written reminiscences, comments, photographs, and other documents.

Remaining the same carefully hidden guide weaving the documents into a narrative as in his previous writings, Duberman began writing a traditional history. Then he recoiled from the chapters he had written "with disgust and disbelief; they seemed very nearly as disembodied as my earlier work." (14). Abandoning the project for a year, he returned to the manuscript in June 1970 and with very little change in what he had already written, proceeded with "a renewed effort to give up the deadly impersonality, the hiding-behind instead of tangling-with, that had characterized the earlier chapters" (14).

This newer writing—over three hundred pages—is a brave pastiche of traditional historical narrative and a number of experiments in which the author inserts his own perspective and self into his text. Most of these insertions are brief dated transcripts from his own journal or direct discussions of an issue in the text. For example, his interpretation of factional battles at Black Mountain, he warns the reader, may be influenced by his attitude toward Princeton that led to his leaving there in 1971 as well as by the "antipathy" he developed for one of the chief protagonists when interviewing him in 1967 (176–78). The archival records and his weaknesses in interviewing, he notes elsewhere, may privilege schisms and anguish over "the *everyday* quality of life at Black Mountain" (216). From a former Black Mountain student "endowed with a larger capacity than I seem to have for appreciating common occurrences" he entices a lengthy reminiscence, and from it extracts a substantial three-page account of "the frequent joy of daily life at Black Mountain" (218–21).

I found two places where the author jumps directly into the narrative. In "A Black Mountain Faculty discussion of teaching, 1936, joined by me, 1971" (110–19), Duberman enters as a participant in what is otherwise a lengthy transcript from the Raleigh archives. If the reader is willing to accept this heresy against historical method, the effect is to make Duberman's opinions carry less authorial weight than had he seized the privilege and authority of commenting in the normal historical third person. The other instance, occupying eight and a half pages (257–65), presents Duberman's struggle to understand the controversies at Black Mountain over the teaching of a psychologist, John L. Wallen. While noting parallels between the quarrels at Black Mountain and those at other intentional communities such as Brook Farm, Duberman argues that the comparison would distort each place more than it would illuminate both (257–58). He sees as well ambitions common to Wallen's teaching and his own but fears that he cannot get close enough to the "nuance and specificity" of Wallen's classes to draw out their meaning or to compare them usefully to his own experiences (258–59). Then, before returning to his account of Wallen's classes at Black Mountain, he offers a "pertinent example, as reconstructed from my journal notes, [of] an unstructured course I offered at Princeton on 'American Radicalism'" in the fall of 1970 (260–65).

From his studies of slavery and abolition Duberman must have known well Stanley Elkins's methodologically daring *Slavery*.[11] Dissatisfied with accounts of the psychology of American slaves, Elkins turns to the writings of World War II Nazi concentration camp survivors to provide an analogy to the way slaves might have experienced the infantilizing effects of slavery. I don't wish to enter into the years of controversy surrounding Elkins's work; my point here is simply the similarity of intention between Elkins's analogy and Duberman's. Wallen's "experiential approach to classes, his fascination with group interaction, his belief that the exchange of information and feelings are always interrelated and that the interrelationship should be consciously explored" created experiences in the classroom that Duberman acknowledges he cannot recreate, so he presents instead his "pertinent example," with no assertion as to exactly how it pertains and certainly no pretense of its being exemplary. Once more the chutzpah of entering the story is, I think, balanced by the modesty of what he does once there: no stunning insights into education; just a pedagogical mix of success and failure and a personal mix of satisfaction and frustration over his classes and the controversies they generated. "It remains true," writes Duberman, "that around the margins Wallen's experience and mine have coincided" (259). No point in pretending that he can get any closer than that.

One personal statement became famous even beyond the historical profession. Duberman later refers to it as his "definitive coming out" (*Cures* 224) and asserts—with, I believe, some exaggeration—that "several of the reviews reacted as if those few coming-out lines constituted the whole of a 578-page book" (*Black Mountain* xii).

In 1945 Robert Wunsch, the rector of the college, "was arrested outside Asheville while parked in a roadster with a marine; the charge was 'crimes against nature'" (224). The Black Mountain board of fellows accepted his proffered resignation with the agreement that he would slip back into the college at one in the morning, pack his things, and leave before dawn. He disappeared, avoiding all further contact with his Black Mountain colleagues, so that Duberman later failed to locate him (224–27).[12]

Duberman ends this story with a paragraph of personal reflection: "It's hard to think well of a place that could cooperate as fully as Black Mountain did in an individual's self-destruction—indeed to have assumed it as foreclosed. But perhaps I exaggerate—a function of my own indignation as a homosexual, a potential victim. It may well be that Wunsch would have had it no other way. And it may well be that communities, no less than individuals, are entitled to their aberrations" (227).

This confession sharply colors Duberman's later perceptions of the reviews of *Black Mountain*. Closely linking his coming out and his use of autobiographical material generally, he understandably blends objections to either of these daring acts. But each was separately shocking to his professional audience. Historians then did not, and with rare exceptions still don't, directly inject themselves into the narrative, even in the playful way Duberman entered the Black Mountain faculty meeting. Reviewers in the major historical journals attacked directly this breach of historical decorum, and I suspect would have done so even had he not announced his homosexuality. In the two most important professional journals, the *American Historical Review* and the *Journal of American History*, the reviewers carefully praised Duberman's traditional scholarship in gathering all the known sources for his history, then utterly condemned his experiments. "Throwing the cardinal principles of historical writing to the winds," writes F. Garvin Davenport Sr. in the *American Historical Review*, "he lets himself become personally involved with his subject in an attempt to write a new kind of history" (524–25). Paul Conkin in the *Journal of American History* is relentless: "The book becomes a confession. He reveals his taste in people, parades his near anarchic and imprecise views on education, . . . bares his own sexual preferences, devotes pages to random notes he compiled on a seminar he taught at Princeton, and even inserts himself as a participant in a transcript of educational debates that took place at Black Mountain. The book becomes embarrassing, pretentious, the very epitome of bad taste" (510–12).

Whether or not his confession added a special edge to such criticism, it is quite certain that *Black Mountain* did not encourage other historians to follow Duberman's self-reflective example. "Most historians, in preface or conclusion, reveal their own tastes," wrote Conkin in concluding his review of *Black Mountain*. "They do not parade them. This is not, as Duberman suggests, a matter of feigned detachment or intellectual cowardice, but rather a product of simple humility" (512). Such sentiments might not be so directly stated now: historians have become a bit sensitive (if a bit proud as well) of how different they are from the other humanities in their rejection of the postmodernist use of the first-person.[13] And even now when articles in historical journals tend to have a few pages of first-person narrative at the beginning or end ("preface or conclusion"), historians remain nervous over even the most limited exposure of their personality. Two recent examples will serve as illustration.

In March 1997 the *Journal of American History* published in lieu of a lead article a highly unusual body of material that elicited strong reactions in the profession. "What We See and Can't See in the Past, A Round Table"[14] consists of an editor's introduction, an unedited article exactly as submitted by a distinguished Southern historian, Joel Williamson, that tries to explain why it took him so many years into his career to discover lynching as a major issue in Southern history, six referee's reports also exactly as submitted, and one later comment (by the only woman round the metaphorical table) on all the previous material.

The editor, David Thelen, offers two goals for this unique project. One is to show readers the editorial process, a goal that Thelen subsequently conceded could not be reached. As correspondents pointed out, the nature of the article made the author's identity obvious to the reviewers and the form of publication abruptly truncated the normal editorial process (*Journal of American History* 84: 748–49). His more interesting reason and his difficulty in stating it indicate that even in 1997 such issues remain dark and mysterious ground for historians: "It is hard to talk about personal experience in ways that engage others. . . . But in the best autobiographical accounts personal experience becomes a threshold, not a destination, as authors transcend themselves and speak to us. The personal rises above the individual." Or again:

> Williamson challenges us to think about what we see and do not see, to reflect on what in our experience we avoid, erase, or deny, as well as what we focus on. . . . He insists that the subjects of history live inside of us and that we as a culture can talk ourselves into not recognizing and confronting dark emotional sides of our past, preferring to leave them silent in the shadows. . . . If as good a historian as Williamson could not see the experience and literature about [lynching]. . . the challenge that keeps scholars from making history add up is not simply specialization of topic, but segregation of historians' life experiences. (*JAH* 83: 1217, 1219)

The September 1997 issue of the journal contains an unprecedented eighteen double-column pages of letters on the roundtable (748–65). Some praise it, in the words of one writer, as "courageous and bold editorial action." Others used it as an exercise for graduate students and in one case even for high school advanced placement students. Another reports on the great unhappiness it provoked at the national meeting of the journal's sponsor, the Organization of American Historians, and urges the editor to apologize to "a membership deeply embarrassed by destructive messages conveyed by the 'Williamson Roundtable.'" Most striking is a letter from a highly distinguished older historian with a keen interest in theoretical issues in historical writing:

> Three years ago, at the close of an A.H.A. [American Historical Association] session on the critique of postmodernism by Appleby, Hunt, and Jacob, *Telling the Truth About History*, a graduate student from the University of Iowa approached me to express her appreciation of the spirit of the session. "I'm so relieved," she exclaimed. "I was afraid that History was going the way of English."
>
> In the glare of the current issue of the *Journal*, my interlocutor may want to think again about where history is going. The editor of our flagship journal, announcing that for years he has tried to get historians to reveal their inner selves, is joined by four knowledgeable and responsible referees [the number that supported publication] in publishing a rambling confessional statement about the history that the author has failed to write. The past is swallowed up in the present. The external world is engulfed in a frac-

tured subjectivity. Ours is indeed a time when personal memoirs flourish
on best-seller lists. But scholars who think they are qualified to probe their
own psyches deserve no encouragement from their professional journals.
(John Higham, "To the Editor" 751)

A radical new historical journal, *Rethinking History*, devoted to experimental writing in history, offers further evidence of how nervous assertions
of the personal make historians. The prospectus meant to guide contributors almost stands as an inadvertent warning about injecting autobiography
into historical writing: "*Rethinking History* wishes to establish a pattern of
themed issues. . . . Themes could encompass the role of narrative in writing
the past, the connections between history and the variety of its media representations, the character of interdisciplinarity within the construction of
the past, and the interventionism of the (autobiographical?) self-reflexive
historian in creating history" (volume 1, 1997). In an editorial in the third
issue of the journal, American editor Robert Rosenstone reflects on writing about the influence of Japan on three nineteenth-century Westerners in
Mirror in the Shrine — the most notable self-reflexive work of history since
Duberman's.[15] "In creating *Mirror in the Shrine* I was working in a vacuum.
There were no models for what I wanted to do, and even good friends in
the profession had difficulty looking me directly in the eye after reading
chapters" (229).[16] He acknowledges as well that the experimental goals of
the journal, its effort to encourage historians "to write History that incor-
porates the techniques or strategies of Twentieth-Century literature, . . .
to engage the diverse literary sensibilities of our time" suffers from "one
small problem . . . [that] it is virtually impossible to find works that carry
out most, even part of such a program" (231).

While Rosenstone is correct that historians avoid use of the first person
and other techniques common in literature and the other humanities, historians of course covertly, even unconsciously emplot autobiography into
their works. A spectacular example of this comes from one of my historical heroes, Perry Miller. Miller's studies of American Puritan thought led
the authors of *Telling the Truth about History*, the discussion of which so encouraged that University of Iowa graduate student, to describe Miller as
"probably this century's greatest historian" (142). Certainly his name would
be on any short list — including mine — for that honor. In a prolific career
in the 1930s, 1940s, and 1950s, Miller pursued a single insistent theme: the
social impact of ideas and the way they are presented. Critical of social
history and economic interpretation on one side, and of formalistic criti-

cism divorced from a base in history on the other, Miller single-mindedly pursued the core of ideas that in his vision dominated the American colonies through their first two centuries. The depth of his penetration into the most complex documents, the thoroughness of his scholarship, the dark passion of his writing made him beyond emulation. Forming no school and having few disciples, he envisioned himself as an atavistic "lone wolf" like Henry Adams, intellectually of an earlier century than that in which he was born. Extravagantly as I and others admired his work, I never knew anyone who dreamed of being the next Perry Miller. There had been none before and, we assumed, would not be another.

In prefaces and introductions to reprints of his articles, Miller made occasional nods to autobiography in the traditional historian's way, but these often disguise more than they reveal. Kenneth S. Lynn, a student and then a colleague and close friend of Miller, was astonished to learn over the years "how many of his direct statements about his life were bogus." Nonetheless, as Lynn notes, "In his scholarship and in his criticism, he talked, in code, about the man he really was" (223).

Although Miller never refers to himself in his historical works, secret autobiography abounds, most powerfully in his complex identification with the greatest of the American Puritan theologians, Jonathan Edwards.[17] There is at least hyperbolic truth in saying that in some recesses of his mind, Perry Miller is Jonathan Edwards. Far too often to ignore, the historian turns to the theologian to make Miller's point about the nature of ideas, of language, even of the theological significance (or lack thereof) of the atomic age ("The End of the World," *Errand into the Wilderness*). Miller's prose is replete with marvelous invocations of Edwards and those with whom he argued in his remote way from his distant perch in the American wilderness (as Miller constantly insists). And with only a change of name, these passages can be about Perry Miller and the respondents to his lofty arguments.

Miller, in a rare prefatory comment about his life, provides in scarcely more than two pages a much quoted account of his intellectual concerns. He tells a now legendary anecdote of his "determination conceived three decades ago at Matadi on the banks of the Congo . . . a sudden epiphany (if the word be not too strong) of the pressing necessity for expounding my American to the twentieth century." He then announces that "those I may call 'social' historians . . . were not getting at the fundamental themes–or anywhere near *the* fundamental theme, assuming that such a theme even exists." He more specifically defines his theme as "the uniqueness of the

American experience" and asserts as a fundamental axiom in his search for it that "the mind of man is the basic factor in human history" (*Errand into the Wilderness* vii–ix).

These themes not only emerge in his many writings on Jonathan Edwards, they become a major part of his interpretation of Edwards's work and life. I take only brief examples from his 1949 biography of Edwards—and many of his essays and other writings are equally rich in this analogy—to suggest the complex linkages the atheist Miller makes with the devout Edwards.[18]

In discussing Edwards's most famous work *A Careful and Strict Enquiry into . . . Freedom of Will* (1754), Miller writes, "Read as a cipher, as all Edwards writings must be, it is a penetrating analysis of modern culture and specifically of the American variant. Which is to say that the writing of it posed for Edwards still more urgently the problem that the Awakening first thrust upon him, the problem of history, and most importantely, the problem of America's role in the sequence of things throughout time, which is what men call history" (263). Thus Miller finds American uniqueness confronting Edwards in Northampton, Massachusetts, just as it caught Miller's imagination "among the fuel drums" whose unloading he was supervising on the banks of the Congo nearly two centuries later.

Similarly, Miller's commentary on Edwards's *A History of the Work of Redemption* becomes ammunition against those mindless social historians: "the idea which determines the coherence of history is not just a whimsical notion of the historian; it would indeed be just that were it a supine induction from evidences (if one surrenders his mind to his footnotes, he can write untold monographs, and call them history!)" (312). And Miller raised the stakes yet higher:

> Arminians [Edwards' disputants], like modern sociologists, clinging to the
> fallacy of a causal sequence with no inner coherence, to a God who must
> mend and patch, write history as an assemblage of accidental conjunctions,
> and can tell nothing of tendency or of development. . . . In this sense,
> Edwards, as opposed to all naturalistic and materialistic versions, to Marx
> no less than to Gibbon, wrote the first truly historical interpretation in
> American literature; and until the contemporary crisis, wherein the non-
> historical has at last been challenged, Edwards' was our only such example.
> (314–15)

This is, I think, enough to suggest that, at the very least, Miller connected his intellectual journey with that of Jonathan Edwards and lodged this analogy deeply in much of his writing. It seems odd, this identification between the urbane and sophisticated Miller who modeled his demeanor after Ernest Hemingway and the wilderness preacher with his eleven children. Were the similarities purely intellectual? "The real life of Jonathan Edwards," reads the famous opening sentence of Miller's biography, "was the life of his mind." Yet there is surely more than this. In analyzing Edwards's expulsion from Northampton in 1750, Miller describes his hero in terms that resembles Kenneth Lynn's characterization of the private Perry Miller in the *American Scholar* article noted above. Edwards fell because he was "proud, overbearing and rash; [and] something more fundamental was at work in him—that trait inherent in his deepest thought, a habit of mystification, a concealment practised until it became second nature. . . . All his works are a code, hiding some secret that would not come out" (xi, 210–11).

Miller's strategy in disclosing himself is far different from Duberman's, yet the impulse behind it seems every bit as powerful as Duberman's in *Black Mountain* and, I think, far more controlling of the text. Miller's form of disclosure is more representative of, as well as far more acceptable in, the historical profession that demands keeping well hidden the directly autobiographical. Revealing the codes, however, would confront us more directly with the autobiographical nature of knowledge in historical scholarship, and that too would tell necessary truths about history. But they were not truths I understood or was ready to tell in the early 1970s. I turned instead to another kind of personal experiment, I became an academic administrator.

Academic administration, odd as this will sound to most faculty members, provided me with much that faculty life lacked. Faculty readily use the word *collegiality*, yet compared with administration, faculty life had been rather isolating. Nothing was more striking or welcome in the move from faculty to administration than the rich web of collaborative relationships with other deans, faculty committees, professional staff, secretaries, even administrators in other institutions. Many faculty have a deep sense of institutional responsibility and most are committed to their students' welfare, but I experienced the same surprise that Jane Tompkins reports in *A Life in School* at the greater knowledge as well as range and depth of concern that many professional staff and administrators had for students (214–15). It would probably also surprise most faculty to discover how much nurturing of faculty and staff administrators can do. Much of the best of the work was the encouraging, consoling, and kibitzing, the many forms of informal counseling. I had taken lessons from a master in this part of the job, my mentor among mentors in college, Sidney Gelber, who had become Academic Vice President at the State University of New York at Stony Brook, where I began my administrative career. Those first years in administration felt as if I were back in college with Sid and new worlds opening. Such emotional rewards carried me through the excessively busy pace, the politics, and the blizzard of Xerox for most of eighteen years until I finally returned to the life of a historian.

Never wholly divorced from the historical profession during those years, I profited from the evolution of the historical profession into a less androcentric enterprise, from the model of my mother's coming to terms with her life, and quite simply from growing older and more willing to learn about myself. I confess that I am very much the person that Duberman described as the typical historian of my generation, one of the boys in the backroom. It seems quite a deflation to find that as I struggle to place myself into a public record, I am now engaged in an almost trivial form of coming out: as a guy and a journeyman teacher-scholar. Essays like this one, and my current work in mixing the history of the educational efforts I have been part of with accounts of both me and students in my collaborative classrooms, use both autobiography and history in somewhat the way that in a salad dressing we combine the oil and vinegar that make it tasty precisely because they do not quite mix. The material I am now collecting for an account of my family of origin will, I expect, produce a mixed-genre work blending straightforward historical reconstruction (complete with footnotes), dialogic interviewing—particularly with my older brother—where it is uncertain who is the interviewer and who the interviewee, memoir, poetry, documents—historic and invented, creatively recreated conversations—some of which occurred and some that someone thinks should have, and who knows what else. So long as the reader knows which is which, my loosened historical conscience is clear. What I thought I went into academic life to escape now calls me. "If we do our work well," writes Jane Flax, " 'reality' will appear even more unstable, complex, and disorderly than it does now" (643). And how like my mother's stories that is.

NOTES

1. Knowing something about the black nationalist tradition might have helped as well. See Theodore Draper, *The Rediscovery of Black Nationalism* (New York: Viking, 1970).

2. Among Hofstadter's books, see especially *The American Political Tradition and the Men Who Made It* (New York: Knopf, 1948); *The Age of Reform: From Bryan to F.D.R.* (New York: Knopf, 1955); *The Progressive Historians: Turner, Beard, Parrington* (New York: Knopf, 1968).

3. See Louis Hartz, *The Liberal Tradition in America: An Interpretation of American Political Thought since the Revolution* (New York: Harcourt Brace, 1955), and Daniel Boorstin, *The Genius of American Politics* (Chicago: University of Chicago Press, 1953).

4. See especially Richard Hofstadter, "History and the Social Sciences," in *The Varieties of History from Voltaire to the Present*, ed. Fritz Stern (New York: Meridian, 1956), 359–70.

5. Both Wiebe's perspicacity and the speed of change were brought home to me while I was writing my dissertation. A book now seen as a landmark of the new social history, Stephan Thernstrom, *Poverty and Progress: Social Mobility in a Nineteenth-Century City* (Cambridge: Harvard University Press, 1964), despite the Harvard University Press imprimatur, received a one-paragraph unsigned review in the "Book Notes" section (since discontinued) of the leading American history journal. Several young historians' verbal complaints to the journal's editor at a conference soon after this issue of the journal appeared led to a full-scale review a few issues later. See *Journal of American History* 51 (March 1965): 777 for the unsigned review and 52 (December 1965): 645–46 for the full—and highly complimentary—review by Constance McLaughlin Green.

6. See, for example, Herman Kahn, *Thinking about the Unthinkable* (New York: Avon, 1968).

7. See Thomas Beer, *Mauve Decade: American Life at the End of the Nineteenth Century* (New York: Knopf, 1926), and George Santayana, *Character and Opinion on the United States* (Garden City: Doubleday, 1956).

8. See David Q. Voigt, *American Baseball: From Gentlemen's Sport to the Commissioners System* (Norman: University of Oklahoma Press, 1966).

9. Unless otherwise indicated, references in the text are to this 1972 edition.

10. Martin Duberman, *Black Mountain*, 2d ed. This is a reprint with a brief new preface.

11. See particularly the section on the psychology of slavery, 81–139.

12. Duberman in earlier chapters carefully describes in traditionally written historical narrative and analysis the community's response to the challenges of incorporating blacks and homosexuals, concluding that "comparatively, at least, Black Mountain did do well, did, within the easily discerned taboos of its culture and the less accessible private fears of its members, show more acceptance than the larger society of 'foreign' people or behavior" (78). Specifically on its inability to tolerate homosexual behavior (which changed considerably in the college's last years in the 1950s), he notes, "There were boundaries to Black Mountain's tolerance of 'deviant' symptoms. It can be argued that some boundaries had to be set if the community was to remain functional. But in fact

'functional' tended to be defined at Black Mountain in the thirties as 'orderly,' with certain kinds of deviation, like homosexuality, considered by its nature, disruptive" (86–87).

13. See, for example, Joyce Appleby et al., *Telling the Truth about History*.

14. *Journal of American History* 83: 1217–72. Remarkably this roundtable was not, as the term would suggest, the published outcome of anyone (other than editors at the journal) meeting around a table of any shape. None of the principals spoke directly to one another.

15. Rosenstone's capsule description of the innovations used is as follows: "Though as well documented as anything I had written (the empiricist lives!), the book at once narrated the past and acknowledged the limitations of its own narrative. Among techniques, it utilized the following: the second person (direct address to the reader and, sometimes to the historical characters); the first person (not of the author but of his subjects); a character named 'the biographer,' who occasionally enters the pages to complain about the problems involved in creating this book; and an occasional fancy shift of time or space within a single sentence, a flash back or forwards or sideways of the kind Latin American novelists undertake with such ease" (*Rethinking History* 1 [1997]: 228–29).

16. Reviews of *Mirror in the Shrine* have been much kinder than those Duberman received a quarter-century before. Reviewers do not outrightly condemn Rosenstone's experiments in voice and generally praise the book, although sometimes in spite of them. See *American Historical Review* 95 (1990): 601–02, by Jane Hunter; *New England Quarterly* 62 (1989): 594–98, by Dan McLeod; and *Reviews in American History* 17 (1989): 619–24, by Fumiko Fujita. I find it remarkable that Rosenstone makes no reference to *Black Mountain*, even in a section of his editorial enumerating the few "historical works that in recent years have indulged in any experiment with form."

17. Miller identifies as well with Thoreau, and, in one painful elegiac essay, with Sinclair Lewis. See *Consciousness in Concord* (Boston, 1958) for Thoreau and "The Incorruptible Sinclair Lewis" (originally published in 1951) in *Responsibility of Mind*. The work of Allen Weinstein offers another interesting example of covertly emplotted autobiography. In 1970 Weinstein published *Prelude to Populism: Origins of the Silver Issue, 1867–1878* (New Haven, Conn.: Yale University Press) on the arguments over whether the nation's currency should be backed with both silver and gold. Then in 1978 he published a book on a dramatically different subject and period, *Perjury: The Hiss-Chambers Case* (New York: Knopf, 1978). The two books have essentially identical plots. Both sort out allegations of conspiracy and counterconspiracy; in each case there really was a conspiracy on one side but not on the other; and in both the real conspirators were on the side supported by cultural elites of the era. In both instances, Weinstein's readings seem plausible. If his books emplot some secret autobiography, he has apparently chosen his subjects well.

18. See Perry Miller, *Jonathan Edwards*, and *Errand into the Wilderness*, especially the

essays "Jonathan Edwards and the Great Awakening," 153–66; "The Rhetoric of Sensation" (particularly thick with such analogies), 167–83; "From Edwards to Emerson," 184–203; and "The End of the World," 217–39.

REFERENCES

Appleby, Joyce et al. *Telling the Truth about History*. New York: Norton, 1994.

Conkin, Paul. Review of *Black Mountain: An Exploration in Community*, by Martin Duberman. *Journal of American History* 60, no. 2 (1973): 510–12.

Davenport, F. Gavin Sr. Review of *Black Mountain: An Exploration in Community*, by Martin Duberman. *American Historical Review* 80, no. 2 (1975): 524–25.

Dewey, John. *The School and Society*. 1899. Carbondale: Southern Illinois University Press, 1980.

———. *The Child and the Curriculum*. Chicago: University of Chicago Press, 1902.

———. *Human Nature and Conduct: An Introduction to Social Psychology*. 1930. New York: Modern Library, 1957.

Duberman, Martin. *The Uncompleted Past*. New York: Random House, 1969.

———. *Black Mountain: An Exploration in Community*. New York: E. P. Dutton, 1972.

———. *Cures: A Gay Man's Odyssey*. New York: Dutton, 1991.

———. *Black Mountain: An Exploration in Community*. 2d. ed. New York: Norton, 1993.

Elkins, Stanley M. *Slavery, A Problem in American Institutional and Intellectual Life*. Chicago: University of Chicago Press, 1959.

Flax, Jane. "Postmodernism and Gender Relations in Feminist Theory." *Signs: Journal of Women in Culture and Society* 12 (1987).

Hofstadter, Richard. "Wendell Phillips: The Patrician as Agitator." *The American Political Tradition*, 135–61. New York: Knopf, 1948.

Kammen, Michael. *Selvages and Biases: The Fabric of History in American Culture*. Ithaca: Cornell University Press, 1987.

Lynn, Kenneth S. "Perry Miller." *American Scholar* 52 (1983): 221–27.

Marcus, Robert D. *Grand Old Party: Political Structure in the Gilded Age, 1880–1896*. New York: Oxford University Press, 1971.

Miller, Perry. *Jonathan Edwards*. New York: William Sloan, 1949.

———. *Errand into the Wilderness*. 1956. New York: Harper Torchbook, 1964.

———. "The Plight of the Lone Wolf." In *The Responsibility of Mind in a Civilization of Machines*. Amherst: University of Massachusetts Press, 1979.

Perry, Bliss. *The Heart of Emerson's Journals*. Boston: Houghton Mifflin, 1926.

Rethinking History 1 (1997).

Rich, Adrienne. "Split at the Root: An Essay on Jewish Identity." In *Blood, Bread, and Poetry: Selected Prose, 1979–1985*, 100–123. New York: Norton, 1986.

Rosenstone, Robert A. *Mirror in the Shrine: American Encounters with Meiji Japan*. Cambridge: Harvard University Press, 1988.

Rosenwald, George C., and Richard L. Ochberg. *Storied Lives: The Cultural Politics of Self-Understanding*. New Haven: Yale University Press, 1992.

Thelan, David. Editor's introduction. *Journal of American History* 84 (1997).

Tompkins, Jane. *A Life in School: What the Teacher Learned*. Reading, Mass.: Addison-Wesley, 1996.

To the Editor [in response to "What We See and Can't See in the Past: A Round Table"]. *Journal of American History* 84 (1997): 748–65.

"What We See and Can't See in the Past: A Round Table." *Journal of American History* 83 (March 1997): 1217–72.

Wolfe, Thomas. "The Four Lost Men." In *From Death to Morning*. New York: Charles Scribner's, 1935.

Religion

JAMES CONE

From *God of the Oppressed*

I was born in Fordyce, Arkansas, a small town about sixty miles south-west of Little Rock. My parents moved to Bearden, fourteen miles from Fordyce, when I was a year old. In Bearden, a small community with approximately eight hundred whites and four hundred blacks, two important realities shaped my consciousness: the black Church experience and the sociopolitical significance of white people.

The black Church introduced me to the essence of life as expressed in the rhythm and feelings of black people in Bearden, Arkansas. At Macedonia African Methodist Episcopal Church (A.M.E.), I encountered the presence of the divine Spirit, and my soul was moved and filled with an aspiration for freedom. Through prayer, song, and sermon, God made frequent visits to the black community in Bearden and reassured the people of his concern for their well-being and his will to bring them safely home. Home was often identified with heaven — that "otherworldly" reality beyond the reach of the dreadful limitations of this world. It was that place on the "other side of Jordan," "down by the riverside," where the streets are gold and the gates are pearl. Home was that eschatological reality where the oppressed would "lay down that heavy load," singing and shouting because "there would be nobody there to turn [them] out." Every Sunday the black brothers and sisters of Macedonia experienced a foretaste of their "home in glory" when God's Spirit visited their worship, and they responded with thankfulness and humility, singing joyfully:

> Sooner-a-will be done with the trouble of this world,
> Sooner-a-will be done with the trouble of this world,
> Going home to live with God.

I responded to the black Church experience by offering myself for membership at Macedonia when I was only ten and by entering the ministry at the early age of sixteen. It was a natural response, a response consistent with the beauty and joy of black life and an expression of my deep yearning for human definitions not bound by this earthly sphere. The black Church taught me how to deal with the contradictions of life and provided a way to create meaning in a society not of my own making. In the larger "secular" black community, this perspective on life is often called the "art of survival"; but in the black Church, we call it the "grace of God." It is called survival because it is a way of remaining physically alive in a situation of oppression without losing one's dignity. We call it *grace* because we know it to be an unearned gift from him who is the giver of "every good and perfect gift." This is what black people mean when they sing: "We've come this far by faith, leaning on the Lord, trusting in his holy Word."

Unfortunately the black Church experience was not my *only* experience in Bearden, Arkansas. The presence of eight hundred whites made me realize, at an early age, that black existence cannot, indeed must not, be taken for granted. White people did everything within their power to define black reality, to tell us who we were — and their definition, of course, extended no further than their social, political, and economic interests. They tried to make us believe that God created black people to be white people's servants. We blacks, therefore, were *expected* to enjoy plowing their fields, cleaning their houses, mowing their lawns, and working in their sawmills. And when we showed signs of displeasure with our so-called elected and inferior status, they called us "uppity niggers" and quickly attempted to put us in our "place."

To be put in one's place, as defined by white society, was a terrible reality for blacks in Bearden. It meant being beaten by the town cop and spending an inordinate length of time in a stinking jail. It meant attending "separate but equal" schools, going to the balcony when attending a movie, and drinking water from a "colored" fountain. It meant refusing to retaliate when called a nigger — unless you were prepared to leave town at the precise moment of your rebellion. You had no name except your first name or "boy"; and if you were past the age of sixty-five, you might attain the dubious honor of being called "uncle" or "auntie."

The white people of Bearden, of course, thought of themselves as "nice" white folks. They did not lynch and rape niggers, and many attended church every Sunday. They honestly believed that they were *Christian* people, faithful servants of God. Their affirmation of faith in Jesus Christ was a source of puzzlement to me, because they excluded blacks not only socially but also from their church services. My brother and I (aspiring young theologues at the time) often discussed the need to confront the white "Christians" of Bearden with the demands of the gospel by invading their Sunday worship service with our presence, making them declare publicly that *all* are not welcome in "God's" house. But the fear of bodily harm prevented us from carrying out that wish.

If Richard Wright is correct in his contention that "expression springs out of an environment" (83), then I must conclude that my theological reflections are inseparable from the Bearden experience. I say with Claude McKay that "what I write is urged out of my blood" and out of the blood of blacks in Bearden and elsewhere who see what I see, feel what I feel, and love what I love. This is why Black Theology differs in perspective, content, and style from the Western theological tradition transmitted from Augustine to Barth. My theology will not be the same as that of my white colleagues at Union Theological Seminary, because our experience is different. They were not born black in Bearden. They did not know about Macedonia A.M.E. Church, and the Black Spirit of God who descended upon that community when folks there gathered for worship and praise to him who had brought them a "mighty long way." They could not know the significance of black prayer, because they had not heard nor felt the invested meaning of those familiar words as Brother Elbert Thrower invited the congregation to pray with him a little while:

> Once more and again, O Lawd, we come to thee, with bowed heads and humble hearts, thankin' thee for watchin' over us last night as we slept and slumbered, and gave us the strength to get up and come to church this mornin'. I thank thee that my last night's sleepin' couch was not my coolin' board and my cover was not my windin' sheet. I thank thee, Lawd, because you have been with me from the earliest rockin' of my cradle up to this present moment. You know my heart, and you know the range of our deceitful minds. And if you find anything that shouldn't be, I ask you to pluck it out and cast it into the sea of forgetfulness where it will never rise to harm us in this world.

As familiar as the words of that prayer were the words of "Amazing Grace." When Sister Ora Wallace raised her melodious voice and filled Macedonia with its rich and resonant tones, the entire congregation joined with her, because "Amazing Grace" spoke to their condition:

Amazing grace! how sweet the sound,
That saved a wretch like me!
I once was lost, but now am found,
Was blind, but now I see.
Thro' many dangers, toils, and snares,
I have already come;
'Tis grace hath bro't me safe thus far,
And grace will lead me home.

Ironically, this song was written by an ex–slave trader; but when the sons and daughters of black slaves sang it, "Amazing Grace" was infused with black power and meaning. For blacks in Bearden, the "dangers, toils, and snares" referred to their daily struggle to survive, the ups and downs of black existence, and the attempt to seize a measure of freedom in an extreme situation of oppression. "Amazing Grace" was the miracle of survival, because it is difficult to explain how we made it through slavery, Reconstruction, and the struggle against oppression in the twentieth century. Blacks in Bearden said: "It must have been the grace of God!"

Because I have lived the Bearden experience, I cannot separate it from my theological perspective. I am a *black* theologian! I therefore must approach the subject of theology in the light of the black Church and what that means in a society dominated by white people. I did not recognize the methodological implication of that assumption until the summer of 1966 when Willie Ricks sounded the cry of "black power" and Stokely Carmichael joined him as the philosophical spokesman. Yet long before that, I knew in the depths of my being that European and American approaches to theology did not deal with the questions arising out of my experience.

Like most college and seminary students of my generation, I faithfully studied philosophy and theology—from the pre-Socratics to modern existentialism and linguistic analysis, from Justin Martyr, Irenaeus, and Origen to Karl Barth, Bultmann, and Tillich. I was an expert on Karl Barth and knew well the theological issues that shaped his theology. I wrote papers in seminary on the Barth and Brunner debates, the knowledge of God in contemporary theology, Bultmann's program of demythologization, the Tillichian doctrine of God as being-itself, and concluded my formal education with a Ph.D. dissertation on Barth's anthropology. But when I left Garrett Theological Seminary and Northwestern University (1963) and began to teach at Philander Smith College in Little Rock, Arkansas, I encountered head-on the *contradictions* of my seminary education as I attempted to inform black students about the significance of theological discourse. What could Karl Barth possibly mean for black students who had come from the cotton fields of Arkansas, Louisiana, and Mississippi seeking to change the structure of their lives in a society that had defined black as nonbeing? What is the significance of Nicea and Chalcedon for those who knew Jesus not as a thought in their heads to be analyzed in relation to a similar thought called God; they knew Jesus as a Savior and a friend, as the "lily of the valley and the bright and morning star"?

Those black students drove me back to the primary art forms of the black religious experience by refusing to accept a prefabricated theology from the lips of James Cone. I began once more to listen to the heartbeat of black life as reflected in the song and speech of black people. As I did so, I asked myself, What is theology? What is the substance of this "reasoning about God" that the Church has undertaken for nearly twenty centuries? And I knew that Calvin and Bultmann could not answer the question for me. Indeed the heart of the problem was the relation of the black religious experience to my knowledge of classical theology.

My concern was intensified during the black insurrection in Detroit in the summer of 1967. I had moved the year before to teach in Adrian, Michigan, just seventy miles from Detroit. I remember the feeling of dread and absurdity as I asked myself, "What has all this to do with Jesus Christ—his birth in Bethlehem, his baptism with and life among the poor, and his death and resurrection?" I intuitively knew that the responses of white preachers and theologians were not correct. The most sensitive whites merely said: "We deplore the riots but sympathize with the reason for the riots." This was tantamount to saying: "Of course we raped your women, lynched your men, and ghettoized the minds of your children, and you have a right to be upset, but that is no reason for you to burn our buildings. If you people keep acting like that, we will never give you your freedom."

I knew that that response was not only humiliating and insulting but wrong. It revealed not only an insensitivity to black pain and suffering but also, and more importantly for my vocation as a theologian, a *theological bankruptcy*. The education of white theologians did not prepare them to deal with Watts, Detroit, and Newark. What was needed was a new way of looking at theology that must emerge out of the dialectic of black history and culture.

Instinctively, I went to the Scriptures as the primary source for this new approach and asked, "What has the biblical message to do with the black power revolution?" My answer is found in my first book, *Black Theology and*

Black Power (Seabury, 1969). My second book, *A Black Theology of Liberation* (Lippincott, 1970), is a continued probing of that question in the light of the classical structures of theology. Although I do not think that those books represent the only possible *answers*, I do think that it is impossible to do Christian theology with integrity in America without asking the *question*, What has the gospel to do with the black struggle for liberation?

Reflecting on those books I realized that something important was missing. They did not show clearly enough the significance of Macedonia A.M.E. Church and the imprint of that community upon my theological consciousness. After all, I was insisting that theology has to arise out of an oppressed community as it seeks to understand its place in the history of salvation.

Therefore I had to inquire about the theological significance of the black experience as reflected in sermon, song, and story.

> O I been rebuked, and I been scorned,
> Done had a hard time sho's you born.
> I don't know what my mother wants to stay here fuh,
> Dis ole worl' ain't been no friend to hugh.
> If de blues was whiskey,
> I'd stay drunk all de time.
> I wrote these blues, gonna sing 'em as I please,
> I wrote these blues, gonna sing 'em as I please,
> I'm the only one like the way I'm singing' 'em,
> I'll swear to goodness ain't no one else to please.

Some of the results of this inquiry were published as *The Spirituals and the Blues* (Seabury, 1972).

The present work deals with the social basis of theology and is concerned with, among other related matters, the problem of the particular and the universal in theological discourse. It is prompted by three considerations. One is that my previous work obliged me to raise certain important problems but did not provide the context for dealing fully with them. Second, I have been overwhelmed in recent years with the seemingly endless theological fertility of the black experience, not merely as a slogan but in all its rich, concrete detail. Finally, there is the need to respond to a certain kind of critical dismissal of Black Theology, typified by the statement of one distinguished theologian that blacks "are not free to violate the canon of exact reflection, careful weighing of evidence, and apt argument, if they want to make a case for other intellectually responsible listeners" (Holmer 211).[1] Because theological discourse is *universal*, I am constrained to reply to this comment, serious despite its patronizing mood, by a fellow theologian. But because theology is also *particular*, my reply is (in brief) that he is wrong, and that he is wrong because his theological perspective is determined by his whiteness. He is saying nothing other than, "Unless you black people learn to think like us white folks, using our rules, then we will not listen to you." And that is bad theology.

For these reasons then—a feeling of unfinished business, a desire to explore further the theological riches of the black experience, and a hope of bridging a gap in the theological community—it seems important to talk about theology and its social sources, beginning with some reflection on the task of the theologian.

Like most theologians, I believe that Christian theology is language about God. But it's more than that, and it is the "more" that makes theology *Christian*. Christian theology is language about the *liberating* character of God's presence in Jesus Christ as he calls his people into being for freedom in the world. The task of the theologian, as a member of the people of God, is to clarify what the Church believes and does in relation to its participation in God's liberating work in the world. In doing this work, the theologian acts in the roles of exegete, prophet, teacher, preacher, and philosopher.

The theologian is *before all else* an exegete, simultaneously of Scripture and of existence. To be an exegete of Scripture means that the theologian recognizes the Bible, the witness to God's Word, as the primary source of theological discourse. To be an exegete of existence means that Scripture is not an abstract word, not merely a rational idea. It is God's Word to those who are oppressed and humiliated in this world. The task of the theologian is to probe the depths of Scripture exegetically for the purpose of relating that message to human existence.

Because the theologian is an exegete, he is also a prophet. As prophet he must make clear that the gospel of God stands in judgment upon the existing order of injustice. This task involves, as Abraham Heschel said, the "exegesis of existence from a divine perspective" (xiv), disclosing that God is not indifferent to suffering and not patient with cruelty and falsehood. But God's power and judgment will create justice and order out of chaos.

As teacher, the theologian is an instructor in the faith, clarifying its meaning and significance for human life. He investigates the past and relates the struggles of the apostles and the Fathers to our present struggles. Thus he becomes the defender of the faith, showing its reasonableness, its "fittingness" for the oppressed community now.

As preacher, the theologian is a proclaimer of the Word, the truth of Jesus Christ as the Liberator of the poor and the wretched of the land. Here the theologian recognizes the *passionate* character of theological language. It is a language of celebration and joy that the freedom promised is already present in the community's struggle for liberation.

As philosopher, the theologian is a keen observer of the alternative in-terpretations of the meaning of life. He knows that the gospel cannot be taken for granted, cannot be accepted without the continued test of life in struggle. The philosophic side of the theological task keeps one intellec-tually honest and open to other perspectives. It guards against dogmatism and provides the groundwork for dialogue with other faiths.

In all roles the theologian is committed to that form of existence aris-ing from Jesus' life, death, and resurrection. He knows that the death of the man on the tree has radical implications for those who are enslaved, lynched, and ghettoized in the name of God and country. In order to do theology from that standpoint, he must ask the right questions and then go to the right sources for the answers. The right questions are always re-lated to the basic question: What has the gospel to do with the oppressed of the land and their struggle for liberation? Any theologian who fails to place that question at the center of his work has ignored the essence of the gospel.

Identifying the right source is more complicated. Of course, the sources include Scripture and tradition as they bear witness to the higher source of revelation as particularized and universalized in Jesus Christ. But also with equal and sometimes greater weight, the sources must include the history and culture of oppressed peoples. In the United States and its cultural de-pendencies that must mean people of color—black, yellow, red, and brown. Here the theologian asks: How have black people understood their history and culture, and how is that understanding related to their faith in Jesus Christ? The place to go for answers is the black sermon, prayer, song, and story. These sources must not be evaluated with the same methods used in analyzing the classical tradition. The methods one employs for analysis must arise from the sources themselves. Only then can one do justice to the complexity of black thought forms and the depth of theological expression found in black life.

It is of course possible to assume that black religion and white religion are essentially the same, since white people introduced "Christianity" to black people. However, that assumption will deprive the theologian of vital insights into black religious thought forms, because it fails to recognize the significant connection between thought and social existence. If Ludwig Feuerbach is correct in his contention that "Thought is preceded by suffering" (qtd. in Marcuse 270) and if Karl Marx is at least partly correct in his observation that "it is not consciousness that determines life but life that determines consciousness" (74–75), then it is appropriate to ask, What is the connection between life and theology? The answer cannot be the same for blacks and whites, because blacks and whites do not share the same life. The lives of a black slave and a white slaveholder were radically different. It follows that their thoughts about things divine would also be different, even though they might sometimes use the same words about God. The life of the slaveholder and others of that culture was that of extending white inhumanity to excruciating limits, involving the enslavement of Africans and the annihilation of Indians. The life of the slave was the slave ship, the auction block, and the plantation regime. It involved the attempt to define himself without the ordinary historical possibilities of self-affirmation. Therefore when the master and slave spoke of God, they could not possibly be referring to the same reality. When the slave spoke of Jesus Christ, he spoke out of the depths of suffering and despair and the pain of "rolling through an unfriendly world."

In order for the theologian to recognize the particularity of black religion, he must imagine his way into the environment and the ethos of black slaves, probing the language and rhythm of a people who had to "feel their way along the course of American slavery," enduring the stress of human servitude, while still affirming their humanity. How could this be? How was it possible for black people to keep their humanity together in the midst of servitude, affirming that the God of Jesus is at work in the world, liberating them from bondage? The record shows clearly that black slaves believed that just as God had delivered Moses and the Israelites from Egyptian bondage, he also will deliver black people from American slavery. And they expressed that theological truth in song.

> Oh Mary, don't you weep, don't you moan,
> Oh Mary, don't you weep, don't you moan,
> Pharaoh's army got drownded,
> Oh Mary, don't you weep.

That truth did not come from white preachers; it came from a liberating encounter with the One who is the Author of black faith and existence. As theologians, we must ask: What is the source and meaning of freedom expressed in this spiritual?

> Oh Freedom! Oh Freedom!
> Oh Freedom, I love thee!
> And before I'll be a slave,
> I'll be buried in my grave
> And go home to my Lord and be free.

Here freedom is obviously a structure of, and a movement in, historical existence. It is black slaves accepting the risk and burden of self-affirmation, of liberation in history. That is the meaning of the phrase, "And before I'll be a slave, I'll be buried in my grave." But without negating history, the last line of this spiritual places freedom beyond the historical context. "And go home to my Lord and be free." In this context, freedom is eschatological. It is the anticipation of freedom, a vision of a new heaven and a new earth. Black slaves recognized that human freedom is transcendent— that is, a constituent of the future—which made it impossible to identify humanity exclusively with meager attainment in history.

If theologians could penetrate the depths of that affirmation, then they could understand the significance of John Cassandra's bold affirmation: "You treat me like a mule and I came out like a man" (qtd. in Baker 116). And they might be able to comprehend the theological significance of my mother's melodious rendition of her favorite song:

> This little light of mine,
> I'm goin' to let it shine;
> This little light of mine,
> I'm goin' to let it shine,
> Let it shine, let it shine.
>
> Everywhere I go,
> I'm goin' to let it shine;
> Everywhere I go,
> I'm goin' to let it shine,
> Let it shine, let it shine.
>
> God give it to me,
> I'm goin' to let it shine;

My God give it to me,
I'm goin' to let it shine,
Let it shine, let it shine.

Here *thought* is connected with the substance of black life, the rhythm and feelings of a people who intuitively recognized that they were more than what had been defined for them in white society. They were human beings—though whites treated them as nonpersons. They were *somebody* despite the humiliating limits placed on their existence.

The same ethos flourished appropriately in the northern ghettos and the Jim Crow south after the end of institutional slavery. After being told six days of the week that they were nothings by the rulers of white society, on the Sabbath, the first day of the week, black people went to church in order to experience another definition of their humanity. Like Mary Magdalene at the tomb, looking for the body of Jesus, folks in Bearden went to Macedonia looking for the One who said, "I am the way, and the truth, and the life" (John 14:6 RSV). And like Mary, they were overjoyed to find him alive and present at Macedonia. That is why they shouted and prayed and why Reverend Hunter preached such fervent sermons, proclaiming Jesus' presence among them. Those six days of wheeling and dealing with white people always raised the anxious question of whether life was worth living. But when blacks went to church and experienced the presence of Jesus' Spirit among them, they realized that he bestowed a meaning upon their lives that could not be taken away by white folks. That's why folks at Macedonia sang: "A little talk with Jesus makes it right": not that "white is right," but that God had affirmed the rightness of their existence, the righteousness of their being in the world. That affirmation enabled black people to meet "the Man" on Monday morning and to deal with his dehumanizing presence the remainder of the week, knowing that white folks could not destroy their humanity.

The power of that insight came to me at an early age, although I did not know what it meant. I only knew that when my mother sang her favorite song, "This little light of mine," she was affirming much more than what was apparent in the lines. And the emotional response of the congregation reinforced my intuitions. The "light" was what illumined her existence, an alternative view of life, different from the current estimations of her being in the world. It was her attempt to make a statement about her life and to say to the world that she is who she is because and only because of the presence of God in her world.

As a child I could not really understand the meaning and depths of my parents' faith. It was only recently that the profundity of their religious affirmation broke through to me. I realized that they and the others of Macedonia possessed something essential to the very survival of black humanity, and it ought not be dismissed or belittled. They were in fact providing me with my only possible theological point of departure.

[Here] I am not writing simply a personal account of my religious faith, though that is partly involved. I am writing about my parents, Lucy and Charlie Cone, and other black people in Bearden and elsewhere who gave me what it takes to deal with life's contradictions and negations. For it was they who introduced me to the man called Jesus, the One whom they said could "lift your feet out of the muck and miry clay and place them on the solid rock of salvation." They sometimes called him that "wheel in the middle of the wheel," the "Rose of Sharon and the Lord of life." He was their "ever present help in time of trouble."

I respect what happened at Nicea and Chalcedon and the theological input of the Church Fathers on Christology, but that source alone is inadequate for finding out the meaning of black folks' Jesus. It is all right to say as did Athanasius that the Son is *homoousia* (one substance with the Father), especially if one has a taste for Greek philosophy and a feel for the importance of intellectual distinctions. And I do not want to minimize or detract from the significance of Athanasius's assertion for faith one iota. But the *homoousia* question is not a black question. Blacks do not ask whether Jesus is one with the Father or divine and human, though the orthodox formulations are implied in their language. They ask whether Jesus is walking with them, whether they can call him up on the "telephone of prayer" and tell him all about their troubles. To be sure Athanasius's assertion about the status of the Logos in the Godhead is important for the church's continued christological investigations. But we must not forget that Athanasius's question about the Son's status in relation to the Father did not arise in the historical context of the slave codes and the slave drivers. And if he had been a black slave in America, I am sure he would have asked a different set of questions. He might have asked about the status of the Son in relation to slaveholders. Perhaps the same is true of Martin Luther and his concern about the ubiquitous presence of Jesus Christ at the Lord's Table. While not diminishing the importance of Luther's theological concern, I am sure that if he had been born a black slave his first question would not have been whether Jesus was at the Lord's Table but whether he was really present at the slave's cabin, whether the slave could expect Jesus to be with him as he tried to survive the cotton field, the whip, and the pistol.

Unfortunately not only white seminary professors but some blacks as well have convinced themselves that only the white experience provides the appropriate context for questions and answers concerning things divine. They do not recognize the narrowness of their experience and the particularity of their theological expressions. They like to think of themselves as *universal* people. That is why most seminaries emphasize the need for appropriate tools in doing theology, which always means *white* tools, i.e., knowledge of the language and thought of white people. They fail to recognize that other people also have thought about God and have something significant to say about Jesus' presence in the world.

My point is that one's social and historical context decides not only the questions we address to God but also the mode or form of the answers given to the questions. That is the central thesis of [*God of the Oppressed*]. And I intend to illustrate it through selected theological themes, with particular reference to the contrasting ways that black and white people think about God.

NOTE

1. See also an important reply to Holmer by Charles S. Rooks in the same issue, "Response to Paul Holmer," 215–18.

REFERENCES

Baker, Houston A. *Long Black Song*. Charlottesville: University Press of Virginia, 1972.
Heschel, Abraham. *The Prophets*. Vol. 1. New York: Harper Torchbooks, 1969.
Holmer, Paul. "Remarks Excerpted from 'The Crisis in Rhetoric.'" *Theological Education* 7, no. 3 (spring 1971): 211.
Marcuse, Herbert. *Reason and Revolution*. Boston: Beacon, 1960.
Marx, Karl, and Friedrich Engels. *On Religion*. New York: Schocken, 1964.
Wright, Richard. *White Man Listen!* New York: Doubleday, 1964.

Philosophy

LAURA DUHAN KAPLAN

Beyond Holocaust Theology: Extending a Hand across the Abyss

For many contemporary middle-aged Jews like myself, envisioning an alternative to Holocaust theology is not easy. As the generation that knows of the Holocaust mainly through oral history, photographs, movies, and books, we have been trying to gain some inkling of the enormity of the slaughter and the behaviors that made it possible. Without any clear focus, we consume images of the Holocaust and find ourselves riveted to the emotions of horror they incite. We feel wounded, scarred, slashed through and through by the anti-Semitism that moved millions of Europeans to collaborate in the murders of our family members. Temporarily safe ourselves from such a massacre, we bask in the luxury of a justified but unfocused anger and reject the possibility of relationship with other ethnic or religious groups. Consciously or unconsciously we view all other groups as actual or potential oppressors of Israel, who deserve neither our understanding nor our aid even in their own times of suffering. Many of our generation extend this same attitude toward God. Because we rightly cannot understand how a God pledged to us by covenant could allow our destruction, we renege on our pledge to God without qualms. We view our covenant with God as an artifact of mere historical interest, dismissing out of hand any possibility of a personal relationship with a living God.

In some ways, we speak and act as though we are suffering from a collective personality disorder. Traumatized in our youth by betrayal and abandonment at the hands of a significant other, we are now unable to form any relationships with others except those based on self-interest. If this were an individual problem, the psychological task would be to find a way of understanding our loss that contains within it the seeds of moving beyond it. That is exactly what I try to do in this essay as I sort through my own experiences, guided by a therapist in the form of Emmanuel Levinas's phenomenology of relationship.

RELATIONSHIP WITH HISTORY

In the summer of 1987 I visited Germany, studying German during the week and touring the country on weekends. Early in the trip, I visited the concentration camp at Dachau. Its proximity to residential neighborhoods shocked me. The story told by a man who walked with me from the train station, an American army veteran who had been among the first to liberate the camp, moved me. The wrought-iron slogan on the gates, *Arbeit macht Frei*, chilled me. But the camp and museum themselves did not unseat me, as I had hoped they would. Instead, they reinforced how much I had already crystallized the Holocaust into a well-packaged event. I had seen the film *The Sorrow and the Pity* when I was nine, read a good share of Holocaust literature in my preteen and teenage years, and stared at endless gritty photographs of ghettos, concentration camps, and mass graves on the Russian front. By the time I got to Dachau, the photos, the bunkers, even the monastery seemed familiar. There was nothing more they could teach me, I thought. The existence of an entity called "the Holocaust" had become a vague node on my choppy timeline of history, taking its place in a long line of by now unsurprising anti-human and anti-Semitic atrocities.

The Holocaust functioned for me as an example of what Levinas calls the "*il y a*," the "there is," the "phenomenon of impersonal being." This impersonal being stands apart from any possibility of human relationship. Its enormity and untouchability evoke only horror. People may try to escape this horror through various "nourishments," that is, diversions, or through "knowledge," the attempt to make the "there is" conform to our representations of it. But none of these attempts can tame the "there is." Its impersonality always returns to confront us. It is a sort of "deafening silence," always making noise, but never saying anything that we find coherent (*Ethics* 57–60).

So the Holocaust appeared to me, until several weeks after my visit to Dachau, when I visited Worms.

My traveling companion, a Christian Ph.D. student in religious studies, was as eager as I to see the small room in which the great Biblical scholar Raschi taught. After a long long walk from the train station along narrow cobblestoned streets, we arrived at the site. A small stone building, two rooms wide, sat atop a tall ziggurat of steps, crowning the former Jewish Quarter of Worms. A group of Israeli tourists was visiting and we listened to their guide translate the docent's lecture into Hebrew. We learned that the building had been rebuilt many times after its destruction by fires, both accidental and intentional. After the tourists left, we visited the small basement museum. We spent considerable time studying lists of Holocaust victims and maps tracing the dispersion of survivors to North and South America. We chatted with the museum volunteers, who explained with bittersweet smiles that a few Jews chose to live in Worms to maintain the Raschihaus site. After buying some souvenirs, we emerged, half-blind, into the summer sunlight.

And into silence. I did not hear a single car, a single shout, a single ball bouncing, a single child crying or laughing. The Jewish Quarter of Worms was dead. Emptied. Silenced. The names we studied downstairs were not mere names. They were people, families, mothers, teachers, grocers, athletes, once upon a time teeming with life, spilling out in joy and sorrow over the narrow streets of Worms.

I sat down on the steps of Raschihaus and cried.

For Levinas, there is only one way to escape the impersonality of the "there is": social relationship with the Other. In an ideal social relationship, each person responds to the Other without appropriating or reducing the identity of the Other. Each person recognizes that the Other offers a continual confrontation with mystery. This mystery has nothing in common with the impersonality of the "there is." It is, instead, a human mystery, calling out for ethical responses to its surprises. Committing oneself to the realm of the ethical enables an overcoming of the horror of impersonal being. At Raschihaus, the ghosts of Worms showed me the possibility of an ethical relationship with the Holocaust. A mysterious Other confronted me, an Other who was not alive, but who teemed with life; an Other who as yet had no particular face, yet who I could imagine by analogy to my own.

Later that same day, close to sunset, my friend and I visited the Jewish cemetery in Worms. Viewed by the Nazis as another historical reminder of the barbarism of their enemies, the cemetery had not been destroyed in the Holocaust. My friend and I wandered its rough hills, squinted at its gravestones spanning hundreds of years, strained to read the Yiddish names, half rubbed out by time and weather, and added to the piles of stones at some sites. We marveled at the good fortune these few corpses had enjoyed. Each had a marker, declaring, "I was here!," a marker noting each person in her or his unique singularity. No longer did I need to imagine the particularity of the ghosts who called to me. Here was solid evidence that the vision I had seen was not a mere fantasy. Without that vision, I doubt the cemetery would have appeared so alive to me. Without the cemetery, I might have been unable to confirm my vision.

I recalled Worms recently, after a funeral, while wandering through the Hebrew Cemetery in my own Southern Bible-Belt city of Charlotte. Our cemetery is a rather bleak affair, on a shadeless plot of land, located in a neighborhood of old warehouses on the outskirts of downtown. It is only marginally maintained. In the cemetery, I saw headstones erected seventy years ago marking the graves of babies and young children. One headstone had a little granite kitten atop it, its face rubbed smooth, its cracks carpeted with soft downy moss. Yet many of these tiny graves lacked the encircling comfort of their parents' graves by their sides, lacked a small pile of stones to indicate their memories were still held dear. Obviously their families moved out of town. Just as obviously, I like to imagine, they have not been forgotten, for a child's death marks a parent forever, transfiguring the future in previously unimaginable ways. I am moved by the analogy between my own fierce love for my babies and the love I imagine was directed at these babies. Standing beside these small graves, I can comprehend the infinite suffering produced by even a single death, an infinity that can hide within statistics reporting millions of deaths.

For Levinas, the connection between parent and child is a particularly close one. He calls that relationship "paternity," not having had the opportunity to learn through experience that the dynamic relationship he identifies also lies at the heart of mothering a growing child. "Paternity," says Levinas, "is a relationship with a stranger who, entirely while being Other, is me" (*Ethics* 71). Paternity/maternity complicates Levinas's claim that social relationship offers human beings the possibility of time, of transcending the stagnation of the "there is." "The Other," says Levinas, "is the future" ("Time" 44). In the case of paternity/maternity, I might add, the Other is not only the future, but also the personal present and the link to the human past. Parents find themselves standing between the traditional, which they hope to transmit, and the unknown, as yet unlived future of their children's lives. They attempt to anchor their children's lives in the past, while preparing them for a surprising future. Parents commit themselves to a project whose end they hope never to see.

Applying the phenomenology of paternity/maternity to the possibility of relating personally to the Holocaust, I might add that the relationship of paternity/maternity need not be understood only in its literal sense, as obtaining between a single generation of parent and child. The relationship of paternity/maternity offers a model for understanding cross-generational connections between human beings, for understanding concepts such as "the human family" or "the Jewish people." We need only interpret the first commandment in the Torah, "Be fruitful and multiply," as a reminder that all humans are connected in an unbroken chain of paternity/maternity. In taking this chain seriously, perhaps I cannot, in good faith, imagine myself a casualty of the Holocaust, wading in filth or awaiting execution. But I certainly can imagine myself a victim of the Holocaust, having all webs of family connection ripped away from me. And I can imagine grief over the rupture of my own chain deepening as I contemplate a rupture in the great chain of human being.

My discussion so far has referred only to awakening a sense of responsibility in the face of the Holocaust by finding a point of connection for those who shrink from its enormity. I have said nothing about gathering knowledge of the Holocaust, getting clear on the basic facts, learning details that might also make it possible to see human faces among the facts. Following Levinas's line of thinking, knowledge is metaphysically less important than ethical response. Knowledge cannot offer an alternative to the impersonality of the "there is." The project of knowing is an attempt to understand the world according to a predetermined "scale." The purpose of knowledge is precisely to destroy the alterity of the Other, to put an end to a phenomenon's existence as a mystery offering continuous surprises. And this is precisely what my childhood knowledge of the Holocaust accomplished for me. I became convinced that the few representative representations I was familiar with had laid out the basic outline of the event. There was nothing new for me to learn, I believed, and so was unmoved when I stood on the very same earth where so many murders, so much torture, and so much distortion had taken place. It took confrontation in the form of relationship with Others whom I recognized as both me and not me to wake me to the cold indifference of my position. Truly there is much to learn about and from the Holocaust, in terms of both facts and values. But without recognition of an ethical commitment born of relationship, I would have no motivation to learn it.

I think I shall advise my own *chavurah*, my own religious collective, to gather this year at the Hebrew Cemetery. The continued existence of our impoverished, simple cemetery will remind us of the strength of the links that connect us with the past. The personal names on the headstones and the list of relationships the deceased left behind will remind us of the infinite suffering a single death can cause. The graves of our own members and their families will remind us of our own experiences of that suffering. I shall stand next to my own beloved husband, father of my children, whose Hebrew name Yishaya Yehezkel, Isaiah Ezekiel, recalls an ancient prophet whose vision steadied the Israelites during a difficult time of passage. With his own hands and fine carpentry skills, my husband has built the simple coffins in which members of our community rest. Paternity/maternity, infinity, suffering, and the practical need to respond to the dead will converge. Perhaps my husband and I and the rest of our community will echo the words of my husband's namesake, the prophet Ezekiel, and say, "Let these bones live!"

RELATIONSHIP WITH THE LIVING

But, spoken to in this fashion, these bones will not live. So far I have spoken only of relationship with the dead, and not of relationship with the living. Grieving for the victims of the Holocaust through the stance of a parent who has lost a child gives us a language but not a solution. As I know from observing my own parents' bereavement after the death of my four-year-old brother, such grief can easily trap parents in the past, paralyzing any movement toward a creative future. They may lose their grasp on one side of the paradox of parenting: while they are still anchored in the past, they are no longer preparing for the unlived future. Their consciousness of possibility, which Jean-Paul Sartre identifies as the foundation for the human capacity to create meaning, may be extinguished. For these parents, and those who identify with them, still face the *il y a*, the "there is," impersonal being. These parents, and those who feel with them, hear the "deafening silence," always making noise, but never saying anything coherent. Consider a song I learned in an Orthodox religious school when I was ten years old:

> Struck, beset with fierce emotion
> Walking on, a legend to become
> Stripped of all *yirat shamayim* [fear of heaven],
> The rebbe lost, a living outcast won.
>
> Once in fields of golden array,
> This passer-by heard a father say,

"Go my son, for *shilooach hakan* [sending away the mother bird before
   taking her eggs]
will bring you joy, and length to your day."

Struck, with warmth and deep devotion
Anxious to fulfill his father's plea
The young lad climbed
Up to the velvet tree.

His hand outstretched, the bird flew away
And in his heart, content began to swell
All at once, he stumbled and fell
Dead and cold, near his father he lay.

Struck, beset with fierce emotion
walking on, a legend to become
Stripped of all *yirat shamayim*
the rebbe lost, a living outcast won.

His faith was shattered,
gone was his *yirah*,
"*Hashem yisborach* [Blessed God], how could you let him go?
Could you not guide him,
maintain his *yirah*,
Hashem yisborach, how could you let him go?"

Oh no my children, I cannot help him,
For fear of the Lord must come from within.
Struck, beset with fierce emotion
Walking on, a legend to become
Stripped of all *yirat shamayim*
The rebbe lost, a living outcast won.

The rebbe had lost his capacity for awe. God had outlined an agreement
with human beings, and God had completely failed to play the divine part.
A transcendentally brilliant God, speaking in person as well as through
learned interpreters, had charged humanity with ethical duties. But this
same God, now morally callous, had forgotten the duties allocated to Itself.
Long ago, God's voice had drowned out the thunder, the lightning, and
the incessant bleating of the shofar at Mount Sinai, declaring, "Honor your
father and your mother, that your days may be long upon the land which

the Lord your God gives you" (Exodus 20: 12). And God's detailed elaboration of duties that followed the original ethical revelation included the rule, "If a bird's nest is before you, you shall not take the mother with the young; you shall let her go, that it may be well with you, and that you may prolong your days" (Deuteronomy 22: 6–7).

The boy the rebbe saw had obeyed both commandments, honoring his father by sending away the mother bird. And his life had been cut short. God's agreements, God's words, meant nothing. No wonder the rebbe's faith was shattered. Instantly, he withdrew from God, suddenly feeling God shrinking away from him at the speed of light. The rebbe found himself in a world bereft of relationship. Foundation, ceiling, sheltering walls were gone. This impersonal world offered no hospitality, extended no hand of help, no hand of meaning.

Yet the song's conclusion does not fault God. God had not abandoned the rebbe; the rebbe had withdrawn his faith. The conclusion leaves it up to the rebbe to extend the hand of meaning to win back a relationship with God. But the rebbe lost, walking on, holding his formerly extended hand close to his body. He became a living outcast, cast out of relationship with God, through the failure of his own hand. The rebbe was no longer naive; he knew how to protect himself. By walking out on the relationship he would not be fooled again. But anguish, forlornness, and despair, to use Sartre's words, would be his lot. I am, we are, my generation is, like the rebbe, bystanders to the Holocaust in empirical fact, participants by existential choice, withdrawn from relationship by way of response. Yes, these are the hard cases: a God who condones the senseless suffering of good people, and beings, human, divine, or diabolical, who bring it about. Perhaps it is best to withdraw from relationship and avoid the risk of betrayal. If we do not extend our hand, we will not be lured into a false sense of security about our position. But then the world becomes once again an *il y a*, a "there is," impersonal being.

Relationship with God is but one way of taking the risk that is the leap into meaning. It is but one of the relationships in which meaning can be obliterated through betrayal, betrayal in which expressions of commitment seem to turn into lies, in which the words of those commitments, perhaps all words in general, come to mean nothing. After all, the concrete betrayal of the Jewish people was carried out not by God, but by our neighbors. Fraught with risk are relationships with persons of other nations, those marked with differences in culture and power. Some contemporary writers on culture and power have recognized the two edges of this risk, betrayal and meaning. For example, bell hooks has described the experience of betrayal many women of color felt in the feminist movement. Early multicultural feminists rightly accused white middle-class feminists of ignoring the impoverished women of color whose labor made it possible for white women to seek liberation, and therefore of crafting theories that speak only to the experiences of the white theorizers. Initially the white feminists replied that their theories described basic realities common to all women's lives, and therefore all were welcome to join the cause of women's liberation as they themselves defined it. But, said some multicultural feminists, if that is the case, then very little in your experiences as women finds parallels in our experiences; perhaps we do not even use the word *woman* in the same sense. An unbridgeable abyss of meaning lies between your feminism and ours; we cannot even talk. But, exploring the other edge of the risk, the creation of meaning, Maria Lugones and Elizabeth V. Spelman argue that women *must* talk with one another, reaching out across the genuine abyss of difference and the very real history of oppression that separate us from one another. Becoming friends, traveling to one another's worlds, are the first steps. Only after that will women be able to create common meanings and theorize together.

The stance many contemporary Jews take toward other nations is precisely that of early multicultural feminist authors: you betrayed us; therefore, there is no possibility of meaningful dialogue, no connection, no relationship. But this withdrawal from friendship, if taken too far, amounts to a withdrawal from the realm of the ethical, leading in practice to abandoning the ideals of an ethical state, a universal care for the oppressed, an openness to healing the world, and a covenant with a living God. Without extending our hand in risk, we lose our grasp on the very commitments that some thinkers see as foundational to Judaism. A philosophy like Levinas's ought not to be applied selectively, its harsh duties avoided out of fear of risk, or, worse, out of the self-indulgence of prolonged grief. To apply it selectively would be to misunderstand his phenomenology of relationship by expecting relationships to rest on an already established ground of meaning. On the contrary, according to Levinas's thought, relationships create a ground of meaning where previously there was none.

My Christian friend took a risk when he traveled with me to Worms. The condition he had originally laid down as the only possible foundation for meaningful dialogue, my acceptance of Jesus Christ as the Lord, had not been satisfied. Yet when we grieved together at Worms, he came to see that I, though entirely Other, was also, in some ways, him. I do not know how my friend would have behaved had he lived in Europe during the war. But for now, we are not in Europe, we are not at war, and we are friends. Here is a place to start. We have both come to recognize that, in the wake of the Holocaust, we need more than just new theologies. We also need new sociologies.

Withdrawal from relationship recreates the *il y a*, impersonal being. Yet relationship is fraught with risk of betrayal, of the terrifying loss of meaning that once again recalls the *il y a*, and seems to make relationship impossible. The only solution I can see to this dilemma is to take the risk and work toward friendship. As Annie Dillard, who sees the living God of the Hebrew Bible everywhere in nature, reminds us, in the risks lie the riches. She writes, "Ezekiel excoriates false prophets as those who have 'not gone up into the gaps.' The gaps are the clifts in the rock where you cower to see the back parts of God; they are the fissures between mountains and cells the wind lances through, the icy narrowing fiords splitting the cliffs of mystery" (268–69).

Relationships are journeys into the gaps of mystery; clearly they are risks, and their paths are not predictable. But in order to break the cycle of withdrawing from the ethical, someone must take a deliberate leap across the abyss in order to form the relationships that will create new meanings. These meanings, both theological and sociological, are needed if the Jewish people are to rise from the ashes of the Holocaust, and finally speak credibly, as we repeat the words of the ancient prophet Ezekiel:

"Let these bones live!"

NOTE

This essay is dedicated to my brother David, who unknowingly taught me the concrete meaning of the term *Holocaust theology*. When asked several years ago what being Jewish meant to him, he replied quite honestly, "It means that if someone makes an anti-Semitic remark, I hit him."

REFERENCES

Arendt, Hannah. *Eichmann in Jerusalem: A Report on the Banality of Evil*. New York: Penguin, 1963.
Cohen, Richard A. Introduction. *Face to Face with Levinas*, edited by Richard A. Cohen, 1–10. Albany: SUNY Press, 1986.
———. Translator's Introduction. *Time and the Other*, by Emmanuel Levinas. Translated by Richard A. Cohen, 1–27. Pittsburgh: Duquesne University Press, 1987.

———. *Elevations: The Height of the Good in Levinas and Rosensweig*. Chicago: University of Chicago Press, 1994.

Dillard, Annie. *Pilgrim at Tinker Creek*. New York: Harper, 1974.

Ellis, Marc H. "Solidarity with the Palestinian People: The Challenge to Jewish Theology." In *Beyond Occupation: American Jewish, Christian, and Palestinian Voices for Peace*, edited by Rosemary Radford Ruether and Marc H. Ellis, 285–88. Boston: Beacon, 1990.

Greenberg, Irving. "The Ethics of Jewish Power." In *Beyond Occupation*, 22–74.

The Holy Scriptures According to the Masoretic Text. Philadelphia: Jewish Publication Society, 1955.

hooks, bell. *Feminist Theory from Margin to Center*. Boston: South End, 1984.

Lerner, Michael. *Jewish Renewal: A Path to Healing and Transformation*. New York: HarperCollins, 1994.

Levinas, Emmanuel. *Ethics and Infinity: Conversations with Philippe Nemo*. Translated by Richard A. Cohen. Pittsburgh: Duquesne University Press, 1985.

———. "Time and the Other." In *The Levinas Reader*, edited by Sean Hand, 37–58, Cambridge: Basil Blackwell, 1989.

Lugones, Maria. "Playfulness, 'World'-Traveling, and Loving Perception." *Hypatia* 2.2 (1987): 3–19.

Lugones, Maria, and Elizabeth V. Spelman. "Have We Got a Theory for You! Feminist Theory, Cultural Imperialism, and the Demand for 'The Woman's Voice.'" In *Women and Values: Readings in Recent Feminist Philosophy*, edited by Marilyn Pearsall, 19–32. Belmont: Wadsworth, 1986.

A Passover Haggadah. [Comments by Elie Wiesel, illustrations by Mark Podwal, and English commentaries edited by Marion Wiesel.] New York: Simon and Schuster, 1993.

Roth, John K., and Michael Berenbaum, eds. *Holocaust: Religious and Philosophical Implications*. New York: Paragon, 1989.

Sartre, Jean-Paul. *Existentialism*. Translated by B. Frechtman. New York: Philosophical Library, 1947.

Ward, Miriam. "The Theological and Ethical Context for Palestinian-Israeli Peace." In *Beyond Occupation*, 171–82.

SARA RUDDICK

Maternal Thinking

From *Maternal Thinking: Toward a Politics of Peace*

In recent decades several philosophers have elaborated a "practicalist" conception of "truth." They have argued negatively that there is no truth by which all truths can be judged nor any foundation of truths nor any total and inclusive narrative of all true statements. Positively they have claimed that distinctive ways of knowing and criteria of truth arise out of practices. I use this general philosophical view—which makes no mention of either women or mothers—to describe the relation between mothering and thinking. I therefore begin by outlining very briefly certain tenets of practicalism that I assume.[1]

THINKING AND PRACTICE

From the practicalist view, thinking arises from and is tested against practices. Practices are collective human activities distinguished by the aims that identify them and by the consequent demands made on practitioners committed to those aims. The aims or goals that define a practice are so central or "constitutive" that in the absence of the goal you would not have that practice. I express this intrinsic dependency when I say that to engage in a practice means to be committed to meeting its demands. People more or less consciously create a practice as they simultaneously pursue certain goals and make sense of their pursuit. Understanding shapes the end even as the practical pursuit of the end shapes the understanding. Horse racing, for example, is defined by the goal of winning a race by means of riding a horse over a finish line. In a particular culture, horse racers refine their concept of the race and the means of victory as questions about meaning or policy arise. A horse racing riderless past the wire, and a jockey slowing her mount in the interests of its beauty are not engaged in horse racing. Natural science is defined by its goal of understanding nature's workings so that they may be explained, predicted, and, insofar as possible, controlled. Central to scientific control is replication by experiment. A chemist who created only beautiful reactions, invented her results, or was uninterested in replicating a reaction would not be doing chemistry.

Individuals need not be enthusiastic or honorable participants to be said to engage in a practice. A rider who drugs her horse is cheating in horse racing but she is still racing her horse. Although an individual scientist hates her work and writes up her experiments with one eye on *General Hospital*, she nonetheless, by dint of her activity, acknowledges that the idea of scientific truth is dependent on replication by experiment. To engage in a practice is, by definition, to accept connections that constitute the practice. To be recognized as a jockey or a scientist means to evince or to pretend a commitment to crossing the finish line or replicating by experiment.

The goals that constitute a practice determine what counts as reasonable within it. Practices in some ways surprisingly alike and in others strikingly divergent give rise to reasons that can be compared and contrasted. Scientific reasoning, for example, is distinct from, though in many of its elements similar to, religious, historical, mathematical, and psychoanalytic reasoning.

To say that thinking depends on practice means that thought is social in at least two senses. First, concepts are defined by shared aims and by rules or means for achieving those aims. An individual may race a horse across a finish line or conduct an experiment. Individuals nonetheless make sense of their activities to themselves by means of concepts and values that are developed socially. Thinking itself is often a solitary activity; its cooperative forms are the dialogue or conversation, not the chorus. Yet the language of solitary thinking is necessarily public in the sense that it is governed by public criteria of meaning and truth. One can think alone, but one cannot "think" "Monday is read asparagus" or "I am Napoleon." Of course, someone could invent an idiosyncratic meaning for the phrase "Monday is read asparagus," but if it is to have any sense, that sense must be sharable. One can claim—as many people have—to be Napoleon; but, except for Napoleon himself, the only public sense of the claim makes it necessarily false.

More important, on the practicalist view, thought does not transcend its social origins. There is no truth to be apprehended from a transcendental perspective, that is, from no perspective at all. Practicalists reject a recurrent philosophic fantasy of finding a language free from the limits of any language in which to speak of the limits of all language. Limit and perspective are intrinsic to language and to thought, not a deficiency of them. In particular, practicalists have been suspicious of attributing to science a privileged relation to reality and making scientific knowledge the paradigm of intellectual accountability against which all other ways of knowing are tested. Science, like any other kind of thinking, presupposes communities of participants, shared goals, and an agreement that some methods of reaching goals are appropriate while others are not. In scientific inquiry, observation is inseparable from theory, and both are inseparable from a commitment to the restraints of experimental inquiry. Both theory and experiment depend on agreement, shared language, and shared actions. Similarly, psychoanalytic, critical, or historical thinking depends on the community of participants in which it arises and their truths are tested by shared criteria.

Truth is perspectival, relative to the practices in which it is made. To say that true statements are relative in this sense does not mean that their truth is a matter of the opinion of communities of speakers. The statement that Mount Baldy is ten feet high is false, whatever any like-minded group of people may think. The point is that it is possible to make the false statement (and the alternative true one) because some people have identified mountains and invented a vocabulary of measurement. To speak, name, and measure means to act in social contexts in which geography and height matter to us. It is true that Margaret Thatcher was reelected prime minister of Great Britain, no matter how much a group of her opponents might wish otherwise, but that truth is dependent on a whole set of institutions in which the meaning of "elect" and "prime minister" have been constituted.

It is only within a practice that thinkers judge which questions are sensible, which answers are appropriate to them, and which criteria distinguish between better and worse answers. The philosopher Peter Winch puts the practicalist point using religious language as an example:

> Job is taken to task for having gone astray by having lost sight of the reality of God; this does not, of course, mean that Job has made any sort of theoretical mistake, which should be put right, perhaps, by means of an experiment. God's reality is certainly independent of what any man may care to think, but what that reality amounts to can only be seen from the religious tradition in which the concept of God is used, and this use is very unlike the use of scientific concepts, say of theoretical entitie. The point is that it is *within* the religious use of language that the conception of God's reality

has its place, though, I repeat, this does not mean that it is at the mercy of what any man cares to say; if this were so, God would have no reality.[2]

In sum, any discipline will distinguish true from false, will take some matters on faith, others on evidence, will judge evidence inadequate or faith misplaced. The practicalist's point is that the criteria for truth and falsity, the nature of evidence, and the role of faith will vary with the practice, whether the practice be religious, scientific, critical — or maternal.

MATERNAL PRACTICE

Maternal practice begins in a response to the reality of a biological child in a particular social world. To be a "mother" is to take upon oneself the responsibility of child care, making its work a regular and substantial part of one's working life.

Mothers, as individuals, engage in all sorts of other activities, from farming to deep sea diving, from astrophysics to elephant training. Mothers as individuals are not defined by their work; they are lovers and friends; they watch baseball, ballet, or the soaps; they run marathons, play chess, organize church bazaars and rent strikes. Mothers are as diverse as any other humans and are equally shaped by the social milieu in which they work. In my terminology they are "mothers" just because and to the degree that they are committed to meeting demands that define maternal work.

Both her child and the social world in which a mother works make these demands. "Demands" is an artificial term. Children demand all sorts of things — to eat ice cream before dinner, stay up all night, take the subway alone, watch the latest horror show on TV. A mother's social group demands of her all sorts of behavior — that she learn to sew or get a high school degree, hold her tongue or speak wittily in public, pay her taxes or go to jail for refusing to do so, sit ladylike in a restaurant or sit in at a lunch counter. A mother will decide in her own way which of these demands she will meet.

But in my discussion of maternal practice, I mean by "demands" those requirements that are imposed on anyone doing maternal work, in the way respect for experiment is imposed on scientists and racing past the finish line is imposed on jockeys. In this sense of demand, children "demand" that their lives be preserved and their growth fostered. In addition, the primary social groups with which a mother is identified, whether by force, kinship, or choice, demand that she raise her children in a manner acceptable to them. These three demands—for *preservation, growth,* and *social acceptability*—constitute maternal work; to be a mother is to be committed to meeting these demands by works of preservative love, nurturance, and training.

Conceptually and historically, the preeminent of these demands is that of preservation. As a species, human children share prolonged physical fragility and therefore prolonged dependence on adults for their safety and well-being. In all societies, children need protective care, though the causes and types of fragility and the means of protection vary widely. This universal need of human children creates and defines a category of human work. A mother who callously endangers her child's well-being is simply not doing maternal work. (This does not mean that she is a bad person. She may sacrifice maternal work out of desperation or in a noble cause.)

The demand for protection is both epistemological and practical. Meeting the demand presupposes a minimal attentiveness to children and an awareness that their survival depends upon protective care. Imaginatively grasping the significance of children's biological vulnerability is necessary but not sufficient for responding to them. The perception that someone is in need of care may lead to caring; but then again it may lead to running away. In the settings where I first encountered polliwogs and goldfish (usually in jars and bowls where I'd managed to put them), they were exceedingly vulnerable. When I was young, I saw that these little creatures were vulnerable and I cared for them. Much later, when I was dealing with my children's attachment to them, I found the vulnerability and total unpredictability of goldfish merely an annoyance. I cared for them because I cared for my children but, given the total inadequacy of our caring, I would have been delighted if my children had forgotten them altogether. Now I almost never think about goldfish and never want to care for one the rest of my life.

Given the passions that we have for children, comparing them to goldfish may seem frivolous. When you *see* children as demanding care, the reality of their vulnerability and the necessity of a caring response seem unshakable. But I deliberately stress the optional character first of perceiving "vulnerability" and then of responding with care. Maternal responses are complicated acts that social beings make to biological beings whose existence is inseparable from social interpretations. Maternal practice begins with a double vision—seeing the fact of biological vulnerability as socially significant and as demanding care. Neither birth nor the actual presence of a vulnerable infant guarantees care. In the most desperate circumstances mothers are more apt to feed their babies than to let them sicken and starve. Yet when infants were dependent solely on mothers' milk, biological mothers could refuse the food their children needed, for example, sending them away to wet-nurses, although this was known to have a high risk of illness and even death.[3] To be committed to meeting children's demand for preservation does not require enthusiasm or even love; it simply means to see vulnerability and to respond to it with care rather than abuse, indifference, or flight. Preserving the lives of children is the central constitutive, invariant aim of maternal practice; the commitment to achieving that aim is the constitutive maternal act.

The demand to preserve a child's life is quickly supplemented by the second demand, to nurture its emotional and intellectual growth. Children grow in complex ways, undergoing radical qualitative as well as quantitative change from childhood to adulthood. They experience intense emotions and varieties of changing, complex sexual desire. As they grow they develop more or less useful ways of coping with other people and their own feelings—adaptive strategies and defenses against anxiety, fear, shame, and guilt. Children's minds also develop gradually, their cognitive capacities and uses of memory becoming different in kind as they move from early childhood through adolescence. In one sense, children grow "naturally," provided favorable conditions for growing. On the other hand, each child grows in her or his distinctive, often peculiar way. Children's desires, defenses, and goals can be hurtful to others and to themselves; their cognitive and emotional development is easily distorted or inhibited. They "demand" nurturance.

This demand to foster children's growth appears to be historically and culturally specific to a degree that the demand for preservation is not. To be aware of children's need for nurturance depends on a belief, prevalent in my social milieu, that children have complicated lives, that their minds and psyches need attending. But even in social groups I know firsthand, some people—in my experience more often men—claim that if children are protected and trained, growth takes care of itself. On the other hand, it is difficult to judge what mothers themselves really believe about the conditions of growth. Some mothers who say that children simply grow and need little nurturance nonetheless act in ways that indicate they believe their children are complex and needy beings.

To say that the demand to foster growth is culturally and historically specific does not mean that the complexity of children's lives is primarily a cultural creation. In cultures dramatically different from middle-class North American culture—where, for example, there are no notions of "adolescence" or "cognitive development"—children's growth is still complex. Only some cultures, and some people within a culture, may believe, as I do, that children's spiritual and intellectual growth requires nurturance. But what I believe, I believe about all children. When others claim that children are simple, naturally growing beings whose growth does not require attentive nurturance, we disagree in our beliefs about *all* children's needs. To believe that only the children of one's own or similar cultures are complex— that their complexity is essentially a cultural creation—is a familiar form of racism. Certainly, some children exist in conditions in which they can do no better than "simply" survive. It seems grotesque to speak of the complex psychological needs of children who are dying of famine. Yet those children, in my view, are as complicated and demanding of nurturance as any others. Where terror or deprivation reduces children to the most basic need for simple survival, they are nonetheless fragile, complicated human creatures who have been so reduced.

In the urban middle-class cultures I know best, mothers who believe that children's development is sufficiently complex to require nurturance shoulder a considerable burden. Many people other than mothers are interested in children's growth—fathers, lovers, teachers, doctors, therapists, coaches. But typically a mother assumes the primary task of maintaining conditions of growth: it is a mother who considers herself and is considered by others to be primarily responsible for arrested or defective growth. The demand to nurture children's growth is not as ineluctable as the demand to ensure their survival. Mothers often find themselves unable to deal with the complexities of their children's experience because they are overwhelmed simply tending to their children's survival or are preoccupied by their own projects or are simply exhausted and confused. Children survive nonetheless.

The third demand on which maternal practice is based is made not by children's needs but by the social groups of which a mother is a member. Social groups require that mothers shape their children's growth in "acceptable" ways. What counts as acceptable varies enormously within and among groups and cultures. The demand for acceptability, however, does not vary, nor does there seem to be much dissent from the belief that children cannot "naturally" develop in socially correct ways but must be "trained." I use the neutral, though somewhat harsh, term *training* to underline a mother's active aims to make her children "acceptable." Her training strategies may be persuasive, manipulative, educative, abusive, seductive, or respectful and are typically a mix of most of these.

A mother's group is that set of people with whom she identifies to the degree that she would count failure to meet their criteria of acceptability as her failure. The criteria of acceptability consist of the group values that a mother has internalized as well as the values of group members whom she feels she must please. Acceptability is not merely a demand imposed on a mother by her group. Indeed, mothers themselves as part of the larger social group formulate its ideals and are usually governed by an especially stringent form of acceptability that nonmothers in the group may not necessarily adhere to. Mothers want their children to grow into people whom they themselves and those closest to them can delightedly appreciate. This demand gives an urgency—sometimes exhilarating, sometimes painful—to mothers' daily lives.

In training their children, mature and socially powerful mothers find opportunities to express their own values as well as to challenge and invigorate dominant creeds. Often, however, a mother is ambivalent about her group's values and feels alienated or harassed by the group's demands on her and her children. Mothers are usually women, and women typically, though to varying degrees, have less power than men of their group. Many mothers are, at least at the beginning of their work, young women. Although they consider failing the group as their own failure, this assessment may be less motivated by moral self-definition than by fear or a need for social survival. If a group demands acceptable behavior that, in a mother's eyes, contradicts her children's need for protection and nurturance, then the mother will be caught in painful and self-fragmenting conflict. Nonetheless, however alienated they feel, mothers seem to recognize the demand to train their children as an ineluctable demand made on them as mothers.

In addition to preservation, growth, and social acceptability there may well be other demands that constitute maternal practices. Certainly there are other ways to categorize maternal commitment. But without any claim to exhaustiveness, I take the goals of preservation, growth, and social acceptability as constitutive of maternal practice.

Although in my view all social groups demand training, all mothers recognize their children's demand to be protected, and all children require some kind of nurturance, it may well be that some cultures do not recognize "children" or "mothers" in my sense of the terms. The concept of "mother" depends on that of "child," a creature considered to be of value and in need of protection. Only in societies that recognize children as creatures who demand protection, nurturance, and training is there a maternal practice that meets those demands. Social historians tell us that in many cultures, it was a normal practice to exploit, neglect, or abuse children.[4] What I call "maternal practice" is probably not ubiquitous, even though what I call "children" exist everywhere.

In any culture, maternal commitment is far more voluntary than people like to believe. Women as well as men may refuse to be aware of or to respond to the demands of children; some women abuse or abandon creatures who are, in all cultures, dependent and vulnerable. All mothers sometimes turn away, refuse to listen, stop caring. Both maternal work and the thinking that is provoked by it are decisively shaped by the possibility that any mother may refuse to see creatures as children or to respond to them as complicated, fragile, and needy.

Among those cultures who do recognize children, perceptions of their fragility and adult responses to it vary enormously and may be difficult for outsiders to understand. As anyone knows who listens to mothers, commonality of childhood demands does not preclude sharp disagreement about children's "nature" and appropriate maternal responses to it. Comparing and contrasting differing strategies of maternal work goes on among mothers all the time. When it is generous and thoughtful, this collective, self-reflective activity is a source of critical and creative maternal thinking.

To protect, nurture, and train—however abstract the schema, the story is simple. A child leans out of a high-rise window to drop a balloon full of water on a passerby. She must be hauled in from the window (preservation) and taught not to endanger innocent people (training), and the method used must not endanger her self-respect or confidence (nurturance). In any mother's day, the demands of preservation, growth, and acceptability are intertwined. Yet a reflective mother can separately identify each demand, partly because they are often in conflict. If a child wants to walk to the store alone, do you worry about her safety or applaud her developing capacity to take care of herself? If you overhear your son hurling insults at a neighbor's child, do you rush to instill decency and compassion in him, or do you let him act on his own impulses in his need to overcome shyness? If your older child, in her competitive zeal, pushes ahead of your younger, smaller child while climbing a high slide, do you inhibit her competitive pleasure or allow an aggressiveness you cannot appreciate? Should her younger brother learn to fight back? And if he doesn't, is he bowing too easily to greater strength? Most urgently, whatever you do, is somebody going to get hurt? Love may make these questions painful; it does not provide the answers. Mothers must *think*.

MATERNAL THINKING

Daily, mothers think out strategies of protection, nurturance, and training. Frequently conflicts between strategies or between fundamental demands provoke mothers to think about the meaning and relative weight of preservation, growth, and acceptability. In quieter moments, mothers reflect on their practice as a whole. As in any group of thinkers, some mothers are more ambitiously reflective than others, either out of temperamental thoughtfulness, moral and political concerns, or, most often, because they have serious problems with their children. However, maternal thinking is no rarity. Maternal work itself demands that mothers think; out of this need for thoughtfulness, a distinctive discipline emerges.

I speak about a mother's thought—the intellectual capacities she develops, the judgments she makes, the metaphysical attitudes she assumes, the values she affirms. Like a scientist writing up her experiment, a critic working over a text, or a historian assessing documents, a mother caring for children engages in a discipline. She asks certain questions—those relevant to her aims—rather than others; she accepts certain criteria for the truth, adequacy, and relevance of proposed answers; and she cares about the findings she makes and can act on. The discipline of maternal thought, like other disciplines, establishes criteria for determining failure and success, sets priorities, and identifies virtues that the discipline requires. Like any other work, mothering is prey to characteristic temptations that it must identify. To describe the capacities, judgments, metaphysical attitudes, and values of maternal thought presumes not maternal achievement, but a *conception* of achievement.

Maternal thinking is one kind of disciplined reflection among many, each with identifying questions, methods, and aims. Some disciplines overlap. A mother who is also a critic may learn something about "reading" a child's behavior from reading texts or learn something about reading itself from her child. A believer's prayer or a historian's sense of causal narrative or a scientist's clear-eyed scrutiny may enliven maternal attentiveness, which in its turn may prepare a mother for prayer, historical insight, or experiment. Disciplines may, on the other hand, be undertaken quite separately without conflicting. An engineer may find the particular kind of reasoning required by engineering almost entirely different from that required by mothering, and each may provide welcome relief from the other. Even though people's behavior is limited by the disciplines they engage in, no one need be limited to a single discipline. No person because she is a woman, no woman or man because they are mothers, should be denied any intellectual activities that attract them. A scientist cannot disregard evidence for the sake of beauty, but she may care differently at different times about both. If a mother is called on to decide an appropriate punishment for a child's misbehavior or to weigh the possible success of a medical treatment against its serious pain, she cannot compose a sonata in response. There is a time for composing and a time for maternal thinking and, on happy days, time for both.

Mothers meeting together at their jobs, in playgrounds, or over coffee can be heard thinking. This does not necessarily mean that they can be heard being good. Mothers are not any more or less wonderful than other people—they are not especially sensible or foolish, noble or ignoble, courageous or cowardly. Mothers, like gardeners or historians, identify virtues appropriate to their work. But to identify a virtue is not to possess it. When mothers speak of virtues they speak as often of failure as of success. Almost always they reflect on the *struggles* that revolve around the temptations to which they are prey in their work. What they share are not virtuous characteristics but rather an identification and a discourse about the strengths required by their ongoing commitments to protect, nurture, and train.

Identifying virtues within maternal thinking should not be confused with evaluating the virtue of maternal thinking itself. Though no less thoughtful, no less a discipline than other kinds of thinking, maternal thinking is also not free from flaws. For example . . . in training children, mothers often value destructive ways of thinking and misidentify virtues. This means that mothers not only fail but in certain respects mischaracterize what counts as success and failure.

If thinking arises in and is tested by practice, who is qualified to judge the intellectual strength and moral character of a practice as a whole? It is sometimes said that only those who participate in a practice can criticize its thinking. Accordingly, it might be argued that it is not possible to evaluate maternal thinking without practicing maternal work or living closely and sympathetically with those who do. When mothers engage in self-criticism, their judgments presuppose a knowledge of the efforts required to respond to children's demands that those unpracticed in tending to children do not have. Maternal criticisms are best left to those who know what it means to attempt to protect, nurture, and train, just as criticism of scientific or—to use a controversial example—psychoanalytic thinking should be left to those who have engaged in these practices.

There are moral grounds for critical restraint. People who have not engaged in a practice or who have not lived closely with a practitioner have no right to criticize. Although any group might make this claim, the point is particularly apt for maternal thinkers. Mothers have been a powerless group whose thinking, when it has been acknowledged at all, has most often been recognized by people interested in interpreting and controlling rather than in listening. Philosophically minded mothers have only begun to articulate the precepts of a thought whose existence other philosophers do not recognize. Surely, they should have time to think among and for themselves.

In the practicalist account of reason, there is also a powerful epistemological check on criticism. Critical vocabularies and standards are themselves embedded in practices from which they arise. Even principles of logical consistency and coherence do not stand outside of practices, although any practice can be assessed in their terms. To many outsiders, contemporary physics, Christian theology, and theories of nuclear defense abound in contradiction. But as experiences with scientists, believers, and defense intellectuals suggest, the intellectual and practical contradictions are interpreted and their weight measured not by the outside observer but by practitioners reflecting on their shared aims.

This is not to say that even an outsider's charge of inconsistency is without force. Unless self-deceived or ignorant of the contradictions their thinking displays, most people find the experience of self-contradiction both disorienting and demoralizing. Indeed, political and philosophical critics charge people with contradictory thinking in the expectation of provoking them to change. I, for example, hope that maternal thinkers will be affected by my claims that certain concepts of maternal thinking that arise from training are inconsistent with other maternal concepts and that preservative love is at least *prima facie* incompatible with maternal militarism. . . . But although my respect for consistency is not connected to mothering, my particular identification of contradictions within maternal thinking arises from my experience of maternal practice, and the effect of my criticism can be measured only by mothers' responses.

One should not, however, conflate epistemological restraint with critical silence. The practical origins of reason do not preclude radical self-criticism. Indeed, developing vocabularies and standards of self-criticism is a central intellectual activity in most practices. More important, although all criticism arises from some practice or other, interpractice criticism is both possible and necessary for change. It is common sense epistemologically that alternative perspectives offer distinctive critical advantages. A historian, medical ethicist, and peace activist—especially if they themselves were conversant with science—might claim to have a better sense than a scientist not only of the limits but also of the character of scientific discipline. Militarists criticize maternal thinkers for insufficient respect for abstract causes, while peacemakers criticize them for the parochial character of maternal commitment.

Interpractice criticism is possible and often desirable; yet there is no privileged practice capable of judging all other practices. To criticize is to act on one's practical commitments, not to stand above them. Maternal thinking is one discipline among others, capable of criticizing and being criticized. It does not offer nor can it be judged from a standpoint uncontaminated by practical struggle and passion.

NOTES

1. The philosophers on whom I draw most closely are Ludwig Wittgenstein, especially *Philosophical Investigations* (New York: Macmillan, 1953) and *On Certainty*, ed. G. E. M. Anscombe and G. H. von Wright (Oxford: Basil Blackwell, 1969), and Peter Winch, especially "Understanding a Primitive Society," in *Ethics and Action* (London: Routledge and Kegan Paul, 1972). In my earliest work on maternal thinking I was directly indebted to Jürgen Habermas, *Knowledge and Human Interests* (Boston: Beacon Press, 1971), and influenced by Jean-Paul Sartre, *Being and Nothingness* (New York: Philosophical Library, 1956). In the last several years, there has been considerable philosophical discussion of the social construction of knowledge and its relation to relativism. An excellent account of some of this discussion is Richard Bernstein, *Beyond Objectivism and Relativism* (Philadelphia: University of Pennsylvania Press, 1983). I have found the following works and discussions of them useful: Richard Rorty, *Philosophy and the Mirror of Nature* (Princeton: Princeton University Press, 1979) and *Consequences of Pragmatism* (Minneapolis: University of Minnesota Press, 1982); Jean-François Lyotard, *The Post-Modern Condition: A Report on Knowledge* (Minneapolis: University of Minnesota Press, 1984). I do not, however, enter into the subtleties of philosophic argument here.
2. Winch, "Understanding a Primitive Society," 12.
3. The example is from Elisabeth Badinter, *Mother Love: Myth and Reality* (New York: Macmillan, 1980).
4. There is considerable controversy about parental attitudes toward children in different historical periods or in different subcultures of North America, particularly over the extent and degree to which children have been exploited and abused. What no one seems to dispute is that there is wide social as well as indi-

vidual variation in the basic understanding of the needs and rights of children. Elisabeth Badinter, *Mother Love*, is a good place to start reading about this issue. Lloyd De Mause has written extensively about the "nightmare" of childhood. See "The Evolution of Childhood," *The History of Childhood Quarterly* (spring 1974): 503–75. For a different perspective see John Demos, *Past, Present, and Personal* (New York: Oxford University Press, 1986).

Africana Studies

KWAME ANTHONY APPIAH

Altered States

From *In My Father's House: Africa in the Philosophy of Culture*

Aban εεgu a, εfiri yam.
If the state is going to fall, it is from the belly.[1]

When I was a child in Asante, there were, I suppose, only about a million of us and there would soon be 10 million Ghanaians, but we knew that Kumasi, the country's second-largest city (built, my father said, like Rome, like so many great cities, on seven hills) had a longer and nobler history than the capital, Accra. Kumasi was a proud, bustling, busy place, a city of gorgeous parks and flowered roundabouts; people all along the west coast knew it as the capital of our famous kingdom, as the "garden city of West Africa." I grew up knowing that I lived in Asante and that the Asantehene was our king. I also grew up singing enthusiastically the Ghanaian national anthem—"Lift High the Flag of Ghana"—and knowing that Nkrumah was, first, our prime minister, then, our president. It did not occur to me as a child that the "we," of which this "our" was the adjective, was fluid, ambiguous, obscure.

I knew my father was, and cared that he was, an Asante man, and that he was, and cared that he was, a Ghanaian nationalist: proud of his role in the struggle for our independence from Britain; committed, nevertheless, to our learning English, not as the tongue of the colonizer but as the unifying language of our new and polyglot nation. It did not occur to me—it never occurred to him—that these identities might be in conflict: though it occurred to others (many of them journalists from Europe and North America) to say that of him when he joined the opposition to his old friend Nkrumah and entered Ghana's first independent parliament in the United party, with J. B. Danquah and Kofi Busia; and it occurred to many in Asante when he did not join Busia's Progress party, as it, in turn, came to power, a coup and a couple of constitutions later, when I was in my teens. I grew up knowing that we were Ghanaian nationalists and that we were Asante.

I grew up also believing in constitutional democracy, or to speak more precisely, believing that what these words stood for was important. When my father and his friends were locked up by Kwame Nkrumah in the early sixties, I was too young to think of it as anything more than a family tragedy. By the time they came out, I knew that the abolition of the legal opposition in 1960 had been a blow against democracy, that it had led naturally to imprisoning those who disagreed with our president and what my father called the "gaping sycophants" who surrounded him, that all this evil owed respect to the chiefs of Asante (indeed, of other regions of Ghana), that their role in controlling the allocation of land, and in the settlement of family disputes, was an essential part of life. I grew up knowing we were democrats and that we respected chieftaincy.

And by the time I was old enough to be *for* democracy, I knew we were also *for* development and modernization; that this meant roads and hospitals and schools (as opposed to paths through the bush, and juju and ignorance); cities (as opposed to the idiocy of rural life); money and wages (as opposed to barter and domestic production). None of which, of course, did we take to rule out the proper pouring of libation to the ancestors, or the complex multilayered practices of the Asante funeral. If you had to wear a white coat to be a doctor, you did not have to give up *ntoma*, the togalike cloth my father wore almost always, in the world outside the hospital. In a slogan: I grew up believing in development *and* in preserving the best of our cultural heritage.

I doubt that these experiences were unusual in the (admittedly itself somewhat unusual) situation of a young person growing up around independence in sub-Saharan Africa in the household of professional people.[2] Yet it is natural enough for someone looking from Europe or North America at the political history of sub-Saharan African states since independence to see this cluster of beliefs and commitments as inconsistent. Perhaps it might be possible to hold together ethnoregional and national allegiances (African American, southern in the United States; Welsh or northern in Britain; perhaps more controversially, Québecois in Canada); perhaps it may even be possible (with enough constitutional theory to paper over the problems) to combine social deference for a hereditary aristocracy with a form of democracy, as in Britain; perhaps postmodernism in the domain of expressive culture gives us reason for skepticism about modernization and development conceived of as inconsistent with older folkways. But few in the industrialized West, I think, have been able to proceed as blithely as we did in ignoring what must be admitted at least to be tensions here, even if they do not amount to outright contradictions.

Of course, Ghana and I have grown uneasy with all of these childhood faiths. Yet, looking back now, I can discern a pattern to these paired adherences, yoked so uneasily together—Ghana, Asante; development, heritage; democracy, chieftaincy—and it is a pattern that makes a sort of sense. For, though we would not have put it this way when I was growing up, I think that we can say that in each case, the first member of the pair was something we took to belong to the sphere of the state, the business of the government in the capital, Accra, while the second belonged to a sphere that we could call society.

But this way of thinking leaves too much obscure. In Western political theory, the state is naturally characterized in terms that it is usual to trace back, once more, to Weber: where there is a state the government claims supreme authority over a territorial domain and the right to back up that authority with coercive force. Taxes and conscription are not voluntary; the criminal law is not an optional code. Imprisonment, the lash, the gallows, stand behind state power. The sphere of society, by contrast, though equally demanding, is bound together by ethical conviction, ties of affection, shared worlds of meaning. Correlative—but, alas for theoretical convenience, only roughly correlative—with these distinctions between state and society are others: between law and custom, private and public life, the obligations of citizenship and the more elective world of communal reciprocity. Perhaps, in our theories, we imagine a state in which only the government regularly coerces—and only in matters of public concern; where personal affection and region and ethnicity play no role in the assignment and execution of state offices; where, in a formula, careers are open to talent. But there is a common currency of state and society, thus conceived, and it is the economy. Whatever the extent of state involvement in the economy (and the collapse of the Soviet empire and its model of the state-managed economy should not lead us to lose sight of the centrality of the state in all functioning economies in the modern world), there will always be enough economically at stake in the operations of the modern state for our social impulses—the call of society—to enter inextricably into the operations of government. Social relations, family relations, cannot always be bought and sold, but even in the most intimate of domestic relationships money has its uses, and in the sphere of the state, social relations—family, ethnicity, regional allegiances, clubs, societies, and associations—provide the materials of alliances.

In the United States (as in Europe) this is an all-too-familiar fact: economic interests, ethnic affiliations, regional alliances, struggle together to shape the operations of the state. In Europe and North America, with powerfully important exceptions (in Ireland and the Basque country, in "Soviet" Lithuania or in Puerto Rico), there is an overwhelming consensus that the claims of the state to the monopoly of coercion are legitimate, and they are, as a result, largely effective. Even where some of the state's specific injunctions do not have that ethical consensus behind them, this fact does not, by and large, threaten its other claims. Recall that in many American cities and states, one of the largest industries is the drug industry, every step of which, from production to distribution to consumption, is illegal. Like the so-called parallel economies of Africa, it involves state functionaries, including police officers; entails bribery and corruption of officials; mobilizes ethnic and family loyalties; and depends on the existence of subcultures whose norms simply do not fit with the legal norms enunciated in law and the pronouncements of officials. Still the majority of Americans who use and trade drugs—and thus question a central norm of the American government—do not go on to question their allegiance to the United States.

But in Ghana (as in the rest of sub-Saharan Africa) something else is going on. In Ghana, for a short period before and after independence, it may well have been true that many urban literate citizens (and some others) shared a similar allegiance to the Ghanaian state. In the high days of postindependence nationalism, many of us shared a sense of the meaning of Ghana because it was clear what it was that we were *against*—namely, British imperialism. But even then Asante had, in the minds of many, legitimate claims—at least in some domains—to obedience. And a formalistic distinction between law (enforceable, in theory, by the police power of the state) and custom (no longer entitled to coerce in spheres where the law held technical sovereignty) would help to explain nothing about how it looked to *us* at all.

Nor, for that matter, could we have made much use of a distinction between an ethnic private and a national public life. Public life in Ghana has consistently involved the ceremonial of chieftaincy; and, conversely, chiefs and heads of families, whose conceptions of obligation do not belong to the modern state, continue to claim real legitimacy and exercise substantial power in matters of marriage, inheritance, and upbringing, and through all these, of wealth.

Yet, for a time, as I say—while we were enthusiastic for national independence and Nkrumah created the first (and last) mass party in Ghana, the CPP, which involved organizations of market women and first-generation-literate "veranda boys," products of the expanding system of primary and secondary education—all these complications failed to diminish our enthusiasm. But the "we" here was, in fact, rather limited. Nkrumah's electoral support in the 1957 preindependence elections in Ghana was a 57 percent majority of half of the population registered to vote, and amounted perhaps to 18 percent of the adult population.[3] Our vision of Nkrumah is in part one of those typical illusions of modernity: Osagyefo Dr. Kwame Nkrumah, the "Redeemer," the organizer of rallies, the charismatic public speaker, the international statesman—even Nkrumah the blind tyrant— was a creature of the modern media and all these roles fit easily into our narratives; we did not see the millions (especially away from the coast) for whom he was almost as mysterious as the colonial governor who had preceded him. (I can still vividly recall the retired watchman, who had been long in service to colonial masters, who visited us annually at Christmas through much of my childhood to inquire after a calendar with photographs of the British queen. In his opinion, it was clear, independence had been a mistake.) By 1966, when the first of our many postindependence coups exiled Nkrumah, the real, if limited, enthusiasm there once had been had largely evaporated and the complications began to take up our attention. When Jerry Rawlings came to power in a coup after our third civilian constitution (itself his own creation) in 1981, his nationalist rhetoric and the resurrection of Nkrumahism generated enthusiasm mostly among students, who had not seen all this before. Cynicism about the state and its rhetoric was the order of the day. It is instructive to reflect on the processes of this disillusion.

• • •

But first we should recognize how surprising it is that there was a moment of "nationalism" at all. The state that inherited Ghana from the British was like most of the twoscore-odd sub-Saharan states of postcolonial Africa. It had a rather wide range of cultures and languages within its borders (despite the fact that much of modern Ghana was at one time or another within the

hegemonic sphere of the Asante empire). There was, for example, the relatively centralized bureaucratic Asante state itself, along with various other
Akan states of lesser size and power (with, in the case of Akuapem, a significant Guan-speaking subordinate ethnicity); there were the much less
centralized Ewe-speaking peoples of the southeast, whose dialects were not
always easily mutually intelligible and whose separation from their fellow
Ewe speakers in Togo was an artifact of the division of Germany's colonial
possessions at the end of the First World War; there were the significantly
urbanized Ga-Adangbe who dominate the region of the capital; there were
miscellaneous small chieftaincies and acephalous societies in what we in
Kumasi called "the North."

In a few cases elsewhere in black Africa—Somalia, Lesotho, Swaziland
—the new national states corresponded to precolonial societies with a
single language; in the case of the latter two, the modern nation-state derived from a precolonial monarchy.[4] In most places, however, the new
states brought together peoples who spoke different languages, had different religious traditions and notions of property, and were politically (and,
in particular, hierarchically) integrated to different—often radically different—degrees. By the end of European decolonization—when more than
80 percent of black Africa's population was in the ten largest sub-Saharan
Africa countries and 2 percent was in the smallest ten—even the states with
the smallest populations were by and large not ethnically homogeneous.

Ghana also had a diverse ecology, ranging from coastal savannah (economically integrated into the world economy by four centuries of sea
trade), through a forest belt (relatively rich from nearly a century of cocoa
production), to the savannah and semiarid tropics of the northern and
upper regions stretching on to Upper Volta (now Burkina Faso) and the
southern fringes of the Sahara. Here, too, it was like many of the anglophone and francophone states of the West African littoral, and many of the
states of East Africa—Kenya, Uganda, Malawi—are similarly economically
and ecologically diverse.

Out of all these diverse cultures, economies, and ecologies, four European states—Britain, France, Portugal, and Belgium—constructed the national geography of contemporary Africa. (Spain never mattered much;
Germany lost its African possessions after the First World War; after the
Second World War, Italy ceased to be a player.) In Ghana, as in almost all
others, the colonial language remained the language of government after
independence, for the obvious reason that the choice of any other indige-

nous language would have favored a single linguistic group. (Even largely monolingual Somalia, as I pointed out in Chapter 1 [of *In My Father's House*], took a while to get around to using Somali.)

If the history of metropolitan Europe in the last century and a half has been a struggle to establish statehood for nationalities, Europe left Africa at independence with states looking for nations. Once the moment of cohesion against the British was over (a moment whose meaning was greatest for those of us—often in the cities—who had had most experience of the colonizers), the symbolic register of national unity was faced with the reality of our differences.

How was Nkrumah's nationalism able to ignore the fact of our diversity? Partly, I think, because at the level of symbolism it was rather oddly unconnected with the Ghanaian state. Nkrumah's nationalist enthusiasms were, famously, Pan-Africanist. In Chapter 1 [of *In My Father's House*] I quoted a speech Nkrumah made in Liberia in 1952: "Africa for the Africans! . . . We want to be able to govern ourselves in this country of ours without outside interference."[5] It was natural for him to speak of "our" country anywhere in (black) Africa. At the level of generality at which Africans are opposed to Europeans, it is easy to persuade us that we have similarities: most of "us" are black, most of "them" white; we are ex-subjects, they are ex-masters; we are or were recently "traditional," they are "modern"; we are "communitarian," they are "individualistic"; and so on. That these observations are, by and large, neither very true nor very clear does not stop them from being mobilized to differentiate, in part because, in the end, "they" are mostly quite rich and "we" are mostly very poor. Only in the richest of sub-Saharan black African countries has the average annual per capita GNP exceeded a thousand dollars (Gabon, with its small population, its oil, and its rich mineral reserves heading the list at about three thousand dollars in 1988). More characteristic are the per capita GNPs of a few hundred dollars in Senegal, Ghana, Kenya, and Zambia.

It was an important part of Nkrumah's appeal, therefore, that he was central to the foundation of the Organization of African Unity, that he represented Africa in the nonaligned movement and at the UN, that he was consistently and publicly preoccupied with the complete liberation of Africa from colonial rule. Being proud to be Ghanaian, for many of us, was tied up with what Nkrumah was doing not for Ghana but for Africa. And so it is not so surprising that as decolonization continued and Ghana, impoverished in part by Nkrumah's international adventures, became less of a figure on the African scene, the post-Nkrumah state was able to appeal less and less successfully to this nationalist register.

• • •

Like the inheritors of the postcolonial state who followed him in other parts of Africa, Nkrumah had extensive ambitions for that state: they were shaped, in part, by Ghana's specific experience with colonialism. And while Ghana's cultural plurality was typical of the new states, the form of colonialism it had known was not found everywhere.

Samir Amin, a leading African political economist and director of the Third World Forum in Dakar, Senegal, has usefully classified sub-Saharan Africa's colonial experiences as falling under three broad headings. Countries like Ghana belong to the "Africa of the colonial trade economy," where the slave trade had been at the heart of initial integration into the world economy, known mineral reserves were not substantial during the colonial era, and tropical agricultural products—cocoa, palm oil, coffee—were the basis of an export-oriented agricultural economy. Nigeria, with perhaps a quarter of the population of black Africa, is the most important such state. In francophone central Africa—Gabon, the Central African Republic, Congo, and Zaire—is "Africa of the concession-owning companies," the creation of France and Belgium. Here low populations and a difficult climate and ecology made the tropical agriculture of West Africa a dubious proposition: concessionary companies dealing in timber, rubber, and ivory practiced a brutal form of exploitation, investing as little as possible and creating, as a result, no local surpluses and offering little in the way of Western education. (At independence in 1960 there were only three Africans among the top 4,700 civil servants in Zaire.)[6] The final colonial sphere was "Africa of the labor reserves"—including the settler plantation economies of German Tanganyika, Kenya, and Rhodesia, and the whole of Africa south of Zaire, where the colonial economy was dominated by mining. In these areas societies were radically disrupted by the institution of new, massive, and not-always-voluntary migration to the mines and plantations.[7]

In the Africa of the colonial trade economy, the development of tropical agricultural cash crops as the heart of the economy—in our case it was cocoa that mattered—made the financing of government a matter of appropriating the agricultural surplus. Influenced as he was by notions of planning that were as likely to be advocated in those days by liberal as by socialist development economists, Nkrumah used the machinery of a national Cocoa Marketing Board (originally a colonial contrivance), with a legal purchasing and trading monopoly and a large agricultural extension division, to supervise the state's extraction of money from the cocoa economy. Production was not nationalized; marketing (and thus access to the foreign exchange value of the commodity) was. In theory the surplus generated by this monopsony was to be used to finance development; in practice it went to the cities. As the predominant source of money profits in our economy, the Cocoa Marketing Board and the state that "owned" it — which is to say all the politicians and bureaucrats who had some sort of leverage — were prime sites for enrichment. In other systems of political economy, different methods of financing the state suggested themselves, often to much the same effect.

But despite the variations in the political economy of empire, the colonial systems had shared a fundamental set of structuring assumptions: in each sphere the dominant economic concern was at the center of metropolitan attention, and all colonies were supposed to be economically self-financing until after the Second World War; this included the financing of their own administration. As a result, once roughly half of the colonial government revenues had been spent on paying for expatriate bureaucrats and another sixth had been spent on servicing loans raised for capital expenditures, many of which were in the interest of control rather than development, there was little left for the cultivation — through education, health, and social services — of human capital. Outside the maintenance of an economic and political order within which tropical agriculture or labor reserves or concessions could develop, colonial management had very limited interests. "The formal agencies transferred to African hands were . . . alien in derivation, functionally conceived, bureaucratically designed, authoritarian in nature and primarily concerned with issues of domination rather than legitimacy," as a recent study observes.[8] The colonial states were made for raising — not spending — government revenues. By 1960 only one in six adults in Africa was literate, and in Belgian and Portuguese possessions there were hardly any university graduates at all.

In view of the limited aims of colonial governance, it is perhaps unsurprising how few were the foreign administrators, the colonialists, who were required to maintain the short-lived colonial hegemony. Just as the British had "ruled" the Indian subcontinent through an Indian Civil Service with under a thousand British members, so the British and French and Portuguese colonial civil services were massively outnumbered by the populations supposedly in their charge. The armies and police forces that kept the colonial peace were officered by Europeans but manned by African subjects.

The apparent ease of colonial administration generated in the inheritors of the postcolonial nation the illusion that control of the state would allow them to pursue as easily their much more ambitious objectives. "Seek ye first the political kingdom," Nkrumah famously urged. But that kingdom was designed to manage limited goals. Once it was turned to the tasks of massive developments in infrastructure—to the building of roads and dams, schools and government offices—and to universal primary education and the enormous expansion of health and agricultural extension services, it proved unequal to the task. When the postcolonial rulers inherited the apparatus of the colonial state, they inherited the reins of power; few noticed, at first, that they were not attached to a bit.

One reason, of course, was that planning and directing an economy requires not only will but knowledge. And economic planning in sub-Saharan Africa has had to rely on very modest statistical bases. But a second crucial reason was exactly the ethnoregional loyalties with which I began.

These were often not especially old, it is important to note, being the product, often—in ways I have discussed and will take up again finally in chapter 9 [of *In My Father's House*]—of responses to colonial and postcolonial experiences. When people from related cultures speaking similar languages arrived in the colonial towns and cities; when they listened to programs on the radio, transmitted in a dialect related to their own; when they realized that there were other parts of their countries where people had different practices, an old and vague body of shared cultural practice was often transformed into a new campaigning ethnicity. In many places, then, newly organized ethnoregional identities are extremely powerful. Here, however, was another point where differences in colonial experience mattered. For British and French colonial administrations were guided by very different theories of empire, and while ethnoregional affiliations are central across the anglophone-francophone divide, one result of these different theories has been a difference not so much in the importance of ethnicity— it is crucial everywhere—as in the role it plays in the postcolonial state.

• • •

British indirect rule maintained "native administrations," attempting to regulate the colonial states' limited interests in taxes and order by using the structures of existing precolonial states. So far as was possible, attempts were made, with the aid of official colonial anthropologists, to understand what came to be called "customary law" and to allow traditional elites to enforce those customs—in marriage and land rights, for example—that were (roughly) consistent with British mores. Buganda—the kingdom at the heart of modern Uganda that gave the new republic its capital—and the northern Moslem states of Nigeria were like Asante in fitting with the monarchical vision of the Indian civil servants from among whom were re-cruited the colonial officers who invented British colonial policy in Africa. (Where there were no traditional rulers to support, as in eastern Nigeria among the Igbo-speaking peoples, the colonial authorities sought to invent a form of "chieftaincy.")

The result of this policy, of course, was that, especially in places—like Asante, in Ghana, Buganda in Uganda, or in the Islamic states of northern Nigeria—where there were strong precolonial state structures on which to build, many local elites were not at all happy at independence to defer to the centralizing impulses of the independent states. This process helped produce in Nigeria, for example, the strong centripetal forces that gave rise to the Nigerian civil war of the late sixties. What began as a pogrom against Igbo traders in northern Nigeria led first to Igbo secession and then to a civil war in which Yoruba people aligned with the North to "save the union."

In Ghana, too, when we have had civilian elections in the period since Nkrumah, parties have usually come with "tribal" labels; labels whose force has little to do with the announced intentions of their leaders. Certainly, the Asante kingdom in which I grew up was a source of resistance to Nkrumah's vision of the nation. The party that came to focus parliamentary opposition to Nkrumah in the late fifties, in the first years after indepen-dence, was the United party, whose founders and electoral support were solidly in Asante. Because of the association of Nkrumah's opposition with Asante, in particular, and the wider sphere of Akan societies in general, Busia's Progress Party in the 1969 elections was seen as Asante; the opposi-tion to Busia, Gbedemah's National Alliance of Liberals, was Ewe (at least, in Asante eyes) because Gbedemah was. Even the tiny United Nationalist party my father founded for the second republic, known by its Akan slogan "Abaa basε," came to be identified with Ga people and the capital. Traveling on public transport in Akan areas of Ghana, in the eighties, one heard (if one understood Twi, the language of most of Ghana's Akan peoples)[9] the present government of Jerry Rawlings, whose mother was Ewe, discussed as an instrument of Ewe domination (an accusation that seems only marginally more reasonable than the allegation that he represents the domination of Scotland, through his father).

The French colonial project, by contrast with the British, entailed the evolution of francophone Africans; its aim was to produce a more homogeneous francophone elite. Schools did not teach in "native" languages, and the French did not assign substantial powers to revamped precolonial administrations. You might suppose, therefore, that the French project of creating a class of black "evolués" had laid firmer foundations for the postcolonial state. To the extent that precolonial political relations were successfully extirpated, they could not be the basis of resistance to the penetration of state power.

And it is certainly true that some of the states of the old French African Empire—in particular, Senegal and Ivory Coast in the West, and Cameroon and Gabon further east—have been relatively stable. But this has not, in my view, been the result of the eradication of ethnicity. The majority of French colonies have chosen to stay connected to France, and all but Guinée (which hardly has had a record of stable progress) have accepted varying degrees of "neocolonial" supervision by the metropole. No military coups have been possible in Ivory Coast, for example, because the defense of the state apparatus is in the hand of French troops stationed there (while reinforcements can be flown in from elsewhere); in Gabon, the French actually removed some soldiers who had the temerity to attempt to install themselves by way of a coup. And while Dahomey (later Benin) had an average of about one coup per year in its first decade of independence, they involved the circulation of power among a small group, usually with the tacit consent of the Quai d'Orsay. (That the French have recently officially withdrawn from this commitment poses problems for a number of states.) The CFA franc, used throughout almost all the former French colonies in West and central Africa, is maintained convertible by France, and this also limits the autonomy of the states, ruling out the sort of massive inflations caused by the printing of money that we witnessed in Ghana in the midseventies under General Acheampong, and thus also helps to maintain political stability.

But the fact is that despite these legacies of the difference between British and French approaches to colonial policy and the politics of decolonization, figures such as Félix Houphouët-Boigny, Ivory Coast's leader since independence, have had to play a complex ethnoregional balancing game in managing the forces that keep them in power. The reason is simple: because, as I have suggested, ethnicities can be new as well as old, merely removing old political institutions—chieftaincy is largely ceremonial in

Ivory Coast—has not wiped out the power of cultural commonalities. (This idea should hardly surprise Americans: African Americans have a politicized ethnicity without any traditional systems of rule.) President Houphouët-Boigny of Ivory Coast hails from a small town in the Baoule region of southeastern Ivory Coast (home, too, you will recall, to Lela Kouakou). In the precolonial era the Baoule were a relatively decentralized group speaking an Akan language, held together by complex affiliations of trade and marriage—certainly not a great kingdom like their Akan neighbors in the Asante state to their east. But because the president is Baoule, and because migrants to Abidjan, the capital, discover the significance of the cultures they bring with them as modes of association in urban life, being Baoule (and, equally importantly, not being Baoule) in a capital where the president *is* Baoule comes to have profound significance. Furthermore, the president, in building his support in regions other than his own, has practiced a careful policy of including representatives of all the country's regions in his party—the Parti Democratique de la Côte d'Ivoire—and in his cabinet.

In the lusophone states of Angola and Mozambique, which achieved independence through long colonial wars in which the resistance was dominated by Marxists, their Marxism—whatever it amounted to—led the United States (acting often in concert with South Africa) and the Soviet Union (acting sometimes through Cuba) to play out their mutual antagonisms with African lives. In each of these countries a major preoccupation of the central government is an opposition that is, in large part, and at least in military terms, the creation—if not the creature—of South Africa and the United States. But here, too, ethnoregional affiliations have played a substantial role in shaping these civil wars; the National Union for the Total Independence of Angola (UNITA), the South African–backed resistance to the government of Angola, for example, is strongest among some southern ethnic groups.

• • •

In all their extremely varied circumstances, those who seek to control the institutions of the African state have to mobilize the standard repertory of the resources of statecraft. They can use the symbolism through which Nkrumah captured the attention of so many; they may offer material rewards and the Hobbesian virtues of security; and (when the carrot fails) they can use the coercive stick.

Deteriorating terms of trade, the oil shocks of the seventies, droughts, and a good deal of mismanagement—some of it careless, some well intentioned, much venally oblivious to the common good—have meant that the states of sub-Saharan Africa have few resources to buy loyalty and few achievements since independence to earn it in symbolic coin. As for coercion, this, too, requires resources for surveillance and enforcement. To the extent that African states have continued to be able to offer both carrot and stick, it has often been because the international community has provided (admittedly limited) financial and military support to regimes, in large part because national governments and multilateral donors have only recently tried to help the citizens of African states without supporting their governments. As a result of notions of international legality, and the widespread acceptance (at least in theory) of the idea that relations between states should respect principles of noninterference in each others' internal affairs, state elites in Africa have been able to resist, in the name of legality, attempts to keep their hands out of the aid pot. But increasingly, under the coordinated instrumentalities of the IMF and the World Bank, programs of so-called structural adjustment have forced elites to accept reduced involvement in the economy as the price of the financial (and technical) resources of international capital.[10] The price of shoring up the state is a frank acknowledgment of its limits: a reining in of the symbolic, material, and coercive resources of the state.

· · ·

Because of the role of the state in mediating between citizens in different countries, there is an obvious role for even the weakened states of contemporary Africa in facilitating the integration of African economies. This is a goal toward which a proliferation of regional organizations is allegedly aimed: the Economic Community of West African states (ECOWAS); the francophone Communauté Economique de l'Afrique de l'Ouest (CEAO); the South African Development Coordination Conference (SADCC); and l'Organisation pour la Mise en Valeur du Fleuve Sénégal (OMVS). These and a host of other organizations—under the broad umbrella of the OAU—have sought such grand goals as free movement of labor (ECOWAS) and the lifting of trade barriers (CEAO), and they have done so, on the whole, without much success. (SADCC has set itself more modest goals and has modestly achieved some of them, united, in part, so far, by their common enmity to and dependence on the apartheid state.)

These international organizations demonstrate the problem—which we also see in the European community, and which Americans should remember from their Civil War—that the integration of states often poses a threat to those states' elites.[11] In fact, far from wanting to facilitate intraregional trade, many African state elites have depended on the existence of barriers to trade and finance as a mechanism for making money, continuing in the long tradition of African rulers who have lived off taxes on trade. One of the most successful patterns of trade in southeastern Ghana in the seventies was the smuggling of cocoa (eventually a majority of the eastern region's production!) into the neighboring Republic of Togo, a mechanism that circumvented the state's attempt to profit both from the difference between the prices it offered to farmers and the world market price and from artificial exchange rates and control of access to foreign exchange. And, conversely, one of the most valued commodities in Ghana at many periods since independence has been the import license, which, given artificial exchange rates and limited foreign exchange, was often more like a license to print money.

• • •

And what of the Hobbesian currency of order? In the midseventies, as the Ghanaian state began its precipitous decline, I was teaching in Ghana. As it happens, one of my tasks at the university was to teach political philosophy, and, in particular, the *Leviathan*. For a Hobbesian, I suppose, the withdrawal of the Ghanaian state, in the face of its incapacity to raise the income to carry out its tasks, should have led to disaster. Yet, despite the extent to which the government was not in control, Ghanaian life was not a brutish war of all against all. Life went on. Not only did people not "get away with murder," even though the police would usually not have been in a position to do anything about it if they did, but people made deals, bought and sold goods, owned houses, married, raised families.

If anything could be said about the role of state officials (including the army and the police), it was that by and large their intervention was as likely to get in the way of these arrangements as to aid them, as likely to be feared and resented as welcomed. For many Ghanaians, and especially those in the culturally more homogeneous world of rural farming people—a world where one language, a mother tongue other than English, the language of our colonizers and the government that succeeded them, was sovereign—what mattered was the regulation of life through the shared and intelligible norms that grew out of the responses of precolonial cultures to their engagement with European imperialism. Disputes in urban as well as in rural areas were likely to end up in arbitration, between heads of families, or in the courts of "traditional" chiefs and queen mothers, in procedures that people felt they could understand and, at least to some extent, manage: once the lawyers and the magistrates and the judges of the colonial (and, now, with little change, the postcolonial) legal system came into play, most people knew that what happened was likely to pass beyond their comprehension and control.[12]

In these circumstances, an argument for the state as the provider of security would rightly have been laughed to scorn. Only in a few extreme situations—among them Uganda, since the depredations of Idi Amin—have things reached a point of Hobbesian crisis. Even in Nigeria, where urban armed robbery and banditry on the highways have become accepted inconveniences, citizens are unlikely to see the state as a solution, since (rightly or wrongly) they seem to suspect that the rulers have allies (or surrogates) through whom they profit from these offenses against order.

Yet despite all their limitations, African states persist, and, so it seems to me, in Ghana, as in a number of other places, the decline has been halted. I am not in a position to judge how much of this can be credited to the policies of structural adjustment whose strictly economic effects have been a good deal less positive than the World Bank has sometimes claimed. But in trying to make sense of what has happened with the return of the state in Ghana, I think it is useful to point to the way in which the government has become a facilitator, rather than a director, mobilizing and enabling social allegiances that are largely autonomous. And it is important to be clear that I am not speaking only of the mobilization of ethnoregional (or "tribal") allegiances.

To explain what I mean, it will help to return to Kumasi.

· · ·

One of the most important organizations in my grandfather's life was the Asante Kotoko society, a modern Asante organization that engaged in various, often charitable, activities. Equally important, I suspect, was the Masonic lodge of which he was master (the picture of him that hangs in my parents' home shows him in his Masonic outfit). All over Africa in the colonial period, new social organizations developed, drawing sometimes, like the Masons, on imported European models, sometimes building on traditional secret societies, guilds, and cults. When people moved to towns, they often formed hometown societies (*associations des originaires*)—like the Umuofia Progressive Union in Chinua Achebe's *No Longer at Ease*; among the most important other forms of organization were many centered on Christian churches and Islamic mosques.[13]

It became clear in the seventies, and increasingly in the eighties, that organizations in Kumasi like the Methodist church (to which my father belonged) and smaller churches (such as my mother's) were becoming more and more central in organizing the financing, building, staffing, and equipping of schools; in supporting the city hospital; and working, often in combination with each other and with the leaders of the Moslem community and the Catholic archbishop, to maintain orphanages and homes for the mentally ill and old people without families to care for them. (Indeed, when he stopped working within state politics in the mid-eighties, it was to his church and its institutional politics that my father, like many others, turned his attention.)

It was not that churches and mosques had not done these things earlier: much of the best secondary schooling in Ghana has been in church schools since my father was a boy, and mission hospitals are a familiar feature of the African landscape. Moslems are obliged as a matter of religious duty to support the poor. What was significant about these changes in the last decade and a half was that they involved explicit recognition that these organizations (and other groups, such as the Rotary Club) were taking over functions formerly reserved to government, and that they were doing so in circumstances where state officials were only too keen to have their aid.

But it has not only been the churches. Chiefs and elders have organized the maintenance of "public" roads; business organizations and other private groups have provided food for "state" schools; citizens groups have bought and imported medical equipment for "government" hospitals. Along with new but ethnically based clubs, universalist religious organizations and transplanted societies like the Masons, the institutions of chieftaincy, in Asante and elsewhere, also began increasingly to carry out what were formerly government functions: mediating between labor and management in industrial disputes, for example.

So that one might say in a general way that allegiances whose salience depends on the ways in which all the various forms of association have economic, affectional, and symbolic rewards—rewards, now often substantially exceeding those formerly available to the state—came to be used to carry out what were formerly state functions, *and that the state acquiesced in this*. The significance of the withdrawal of the state goes beyond official announcements in the capital; local bureaucrats in towns and villages increasingly rely on nonstate associations to carry out their functions. The management of "government" old-people's homes and orphanages in Kumasi depends crucially on "private" support, on the cooperation of chiefs, business people, and community leaders in mobilizing and providing support.

To the extent that the government provides some technical assistance and serves a coordinating function in this process, we can speak, as I said, of the state adopting a role now not as *directing* but as *facilitating* certain functions; this is surely to be welcomed to the extent that it increases the control of citizens over their own lives.[14] As I have suggested, it has always been true that in large parts of Africa, "tribalism"—what, in Ivory Coast, is half humorously called geopolitics, the politics of geographical regions, the mobilization and management of ethnic balancing—far from being an obstacle to governance, is what makes possible any government at all. And we can see this new role as facilitator—acknowledging the associations of society rather than trying to dominate to ignore or to eradicate them—as an extension of this established pattern.

• • •

While it has occurred at different rates and with different effects, the proliferation of nonstate organizations is, if anything is, a universal phenomenon in postcolonial Africa. And it is important to be clear that the ethno-regional and religious associations that I have been focusing on are only first among many. Sports clubs, market-women's groups, professional organizations, trade unions, and farming cooperatives; all provide the multifarious rewards of association. In many of these organizations—whether it be a sports club or a choir or an *association des originaires* or the Asante Kotoko Society—there is a remarkable degree of formality: elections, rules of procedure (in the anglophone world, sometimes even Robert's Rules), and a considerable concern with the responsibility of leaders—those who manage the organization's day-to-day life and, in particular, its finances; a concern with constitutions and procedure is a key feature of churches in Ghana and elsewhere, and where the Catholic church sets antidemocratic procedures for the church itself, it cannot stop the development of lay associations—a proliferation of what we might call paraecclesial organizations—in which the very same phenomena occur. Women's "auxiliaries"—whether they be auxiliary to church or union organizations— allow women, who have, by and large, been much worse treated (and a good deal worse represented) in the postcolonial state, access to the practice of something like democratic participation. This is not an exclusively urban phenomenon, either. Clubs, associations, and cooperatives abound in the rural sector.

These organizations and their experiences with autonomous and relatively democratic organization are, I believe, of tremendous significance for the development of public life in Africa, and for the simplest of reasons: they give people a chance to practice participatory modes of organizing communal life; they offer the experience of autonomy. As a result it will become increasingly difficult for weak states to maintain legitimacy without offering such forms of democratic participation. In 1989 and 1990 there were riots in Ivory Coast and in Kenya (two of the stablest and economically strongest African states), in each case plausibly connected with a sense that the president, in particular, and the elite, more generally, were not responsive to the concerns of his people. We have seen in Eastern Europe how the removal of the army as a mechanism of control leads to resistance to apparently well-established authoritarian states with elaborate security apparatuses and even the appearance of some degree of legitimacy. Many African states have none of these to fall back on.

Democracy in this context is not simply a matter of parliaments and elections—though these would be welcomed by some, though not always the most thoughtful, in every state in Africa—but entails the development of mechanisms by which the rulers can be restrained by the ruled. And in Africa, without such a compact, citizens have few reasons to acquiesce to the wishes (or the whims) of those who claim to rule. Paradoxically, so it seems to me, it is the state that needs democracy, more than the citizen.

But while it is easy to remark the inadequacy of the nation-state model in face of the complex institutions and allegiances through which civil society may be organized, it may be too soon to pronounce on the outcome. Clearly, if the state is ever to reverse recent history and expand the role it plays in the lives of its subjects, it will have to learn something about the surprising persistence of these "premodern" affiliations, the cultural and political fretwork of relations through which our very identity is conferred.

• • •

When I was about eight, I fell very ill. Toward the end of my couple of months in bed in the local hospital, the English queen paid her first post-independence visit to Ghana. She and her husband and the president of Ghana, Osagyefo Dr. Kwame Nkrumah, duly arrived in Kumasi and made their way through the hospital, passing, as they did so, by my bed. The queen, whose mastery of small talk is proverbial, asked me how I was, and I, in a literal fever of excitement at meeting my mother's queen and my father's president all on the same day, mumbled with equal, but perhaps more excusable, fatuousness, that I was quite well. Throughout all this, the president, who had only recently locked up my father, stared at the ceiling tapping his foot (making, as it turned out, a mental note to return my doctor to what was then still Rhodesia). When they had passed through, I went, against the orders of my doctor and to the consternation of the nurses, to the window and looked out in time to see an extraordinary sight: the duke of Edinburgh and the president of Ghana trying, halfheartedly, to pull an ancient Asante sword out of the ground in which it was embedded. The sword, tradition had it, was put there by Okomfo Anokye, the great priest of Asante, who with the first great king, Osei Tutu, had founded the kingdom two and a half centuries earlier. Not long after independence, the colonial "Central Hospital," where I was, had been renamed Okomfo Anokye Hospital. Tradition also said that the great priest had declared that, with all the spells he had spoken, if the sword were ever to be pulled out of the ground, the Asante nation would fall apart into the many units from which he and Osei Tutu had forged it.

It seemed to me, from way up above the crowd of dignitaries, that Nkrumah's tug on the sword was even more halfhearted than the duke's. No Ghanaian ruler could even jestingly simulate an assault on Asante unity here in the heartland. Now, long after Nkrumah has gone to his ancestors, Asante, of course, remains; refashioned, perhaps, but strangely obdurate. The sword, they tell me, has disappeared.

NOTES

1. Akan proverb. (Proverbs are notoriously difficult to interpret, and thus, also to translate. But the idea is that states collapse from within, and the proverb is used to express the sentiment that people suffer as a result of their own weaknesses. My father would never have forgiven the solecism of trying to explain a proverb!)

2. In *Politics and Society in Contemporary Africa*, 81, Naomi Chazan, Robert Mortimer, John Ravenhill, and Donald Rothchild cite from *Afriscope* 7, no. 4 (1977): 24–25, a figure of 150,000 "professionally qualified people" in sub-Saharan Africa.

3. See D. G. Austin, *Politics in Ghana, 1946–1960* (Oxford: Oxford University Press, 1964), 48.

4. Ethiopia, which was never a colony, is one of the world's oldest unitary states,

but the modern boundaries of Ethiopia include Eritrea and the Ogaden, both of them essentially granted to the Ethiopian empire by Western powers.

5. Nkrumah, *Autobiography of Kwame Nkrumah* (London: Panaf, 1973), 153.

6. Peter Duignan and Robert H. Jackson, eds., *Politics and Government in African States, 1960–1985* (London and Sydney: Croom Helm; Stanford; Hoover Institution, 1986), 120–21.

7. Samir Amin, "Underdevelopment and Dependence in Black Africa: Origins and Contemporary Forms." *Journal of Modern African Studies* 10, no. 4 (1972): 503–24.

8. Chazan et al., *Politics and Society in Contemporary Africa* (Boulder, Colo.: Lynn Rienner, 1988), 41.

9. Twi is the generic name for the language spoken (with some variations in accent and vocabulary) in most of the Akan portion of Ghana; the language of Asante is Asante-Twi.

10. This is not to ignore the role of the structural adjustment program (SAP) in strangling the labor movements, which in some places constituted one of society's major antagonists to the state. The SAP has, as intended, played a part in making life easier for capital in other ways as well.

11. In Britain, Mrs. Thatcher's opposition to full European monetary union and a single currency, for example — an opposition that played a part in her departure from the prime ministership — was plainly connected with a sense (threatening in the extreme to anyone with Mrs. Thatcher's sympathies with monetarism) that this would reduce the options for British national monetary policy.

12. Reference to "the essential faith of citizens in Ghana and elsewhere in the established judicial system" — in Chazan et al., *Politics and Society in Contemporary Africa*, 59 — is one of the few points where I am bound to say I find their analysis unconvincing.

13. I have found very helpful the theoretical elaboration of these patterns in Chazan et al., *Politics and Society in Contemporary Africa*, chap. 3 on "Social Groupings."

14. We should not, however, ignore the role of asymmetries of power in the Kumasi and other places in the state's periphery, in structuring who benefits from these arrangements.

Art History

EUNICE LIPTON

History of an Encounter

From *Alias Olympia: A Woman's Search for Manet's Notorious Model & Her Own Desire*

I don't remember when I first saw Victorine Meurent, but I wouldn't have recognized her or known her name at the time. No one would have. She was just another naked woman in a painting. Maybe I remarked that the man who made the picture was called Manet or that the work itself was named *Olympia*, but that would have been it. When I was at college in the late 1950s works of art were considered things of beauty. Period. One would never pay attention to a painting's literal content. One wouldn't even risk noticing that De Kooning's *Woman* II had a woman in it.

Even as I became a professional art historian in the 1960s, the look of *Olympia* did not change. The naked white woman on the bed seemed like any odalisque, Venus, or Danae—idealized flesh made into art. I was taught to appreciate Manet's particularly modern vocabulary, his tonal contrasts, flattened spaces, outlined forms, that is, his fundamentally abstract intentions. It was Manet who was placed first in the pantheon of modernist painting; we were told that before anyone else, he had seen people and events for what they really were: abstract pictorial forms.

But one day in 1970, try as I may, I could not shake the feeling that there was an event unfolding in *Olympia* and that the naked woman was staring quite alarmingly out of the picture. I could not make her recede behind the abstract forms I knew—I had been taught so fervently to believe—were the true content of the work. Her face kept swimming forward, her eyes demanded attention. I saw that unlike other naked woman in paintings, Olympia did not drape herself suggestively upon her bed, or supplicate prospective lovers, or droop resignedly. Nor did she smile flirtatiously. Rather she reigned imperiously, reclining upon silken pillows, her steady gaze a dare, her tight little body and proprietary hand an omen. Now I could see that even the stilted pose of the black maid and overarching cat gave the lie to scenarios of seduction. Olympia, alert and dignified, resembled a noble consort on an Etruscan funerary monument far more than an inviting Greek or Oriental courtesan. This was a woman who could say "yes," *or* she could say "no."

Her contemporaries knew this in the nineteenth century though they didn't say it in so many words. In fact, Manet was greatly distressed over how his painting was received; he even considered destroying it. What happened was this. In May of 1865 *Olympia* was exhibited in the Salon, the official exhibition forum of the time. The press took an instant and bellicose dislike to the work, using words like" "The vicious strangeness of [this] . . . woman of the night"; "a sort of female gorilla, a grotesque . . ." "Such indecency! . . ." (qtd. in Clark 88, 94, and Hamilton 71). Before anyone knew what was happening, respectable Parisians were sweeping through the Salon's drafty halls brandishing walking sticks and umbrellas; they were heading toward *Olympia* with murder on their minds. The authorities were taken aback, and took the unprecedented step of cordoning off the painting. But the damage was done. Manet fled to Spain thinking: Titian had done it, so had Giorgione and Velázquez—he meant painted naked women—why is everyone so angry at me? This may have been the first time in modern history that a painting incited people to such public agitation.

I discovered that Manet painted the same red-headed woman nine times during the years 1862 to 1874, and from the Metropolitan Museum of Art's catalogue of French painting, I learned that her name was Victorine Meurent. In eight of the works Manet made of her, Meurent examines the viewer with Olympia's unflinching gaze. In the *Dejeuner sur l'herbe* (in the Musée d'Orsay), she sits naked in the country with two clothed men. Canny, unflappable, she peers out, oblivious to the near-pornographic promptings of the story. In *Women with a Parrot* (in the Metropolitan Museum), neither Meurent's plush, pink dressing gown nor the strange still-life of parrot and orange distract from the penetration of her look. In *Victorine in the Costume of an Espada* (also at the Metropolitan), her blunt stare and iconic stillness halt the unfolding drama in the bullring.

From each and every canvas I saw that the model surveyed the viewer, resisting centuries of admonition to ingratiate herself. Locked behind her gaze were thoughts, an ego maneuvering. If later on Freud would ask, "What do women want?" then this woman's face answered. You knew what she wanted. Everything. Or rather she wanted, she lacked, nothing. And *that* is why in the spring of 1865 men shook with rage in front of *Olympia*. She was unmanageable; they knew she had to be contained.

These men only meant to persuade her, a single unwieldy woman, to comply. But the plot they hatched, and the map their worries charted, took them way off the road of Art Appreciation and Art History and deep into twentieth-century sexual struggle. Everything was done to silence her. Discourse would bar her presence, indeed would transform her into her opposite—a helpless woman. This is what scholars and writers said about her.

> [She] was a young girl whom Manet met by chance in the middle of a crowd in a room at the Palais de Justice. (Theodore Duret, 1902, 199–200)

> Here [in *Olympia*] in the flesh is a girl whom the artist has put on canvas in her youthful, slightly tarnished nakedness. . . . He has introduced us to Olympia . . . whom we have met in the streets. (Emile Zola, 1867)

> [Victorine Meurent] was, between 1862 and 1874, with long eclipses, because she was whimsical, Manet's preferred model. . . . [She was] like a lot of girls of the lower classes who knew they were beautiful and unable to easily resign themselves to misery. She immediately consented to model. (Adolphe Tabarant, 1937, 73)

> Victorine Meurent disappeared from circulation for several years and was silent about this disappearance that one knows was for romantic reasons. . . . A sentimental folly had taken her to America. (Tabarant, 1947, 221)

> A thin woman with red hair . . . was introduced to me and I was told that she was Marie [Pellegrin]'s intimate friend, and that the two lived together whenever Marie returned to Montmartre. [The red-head] was known as La Glue [*sic*]; her real name was Victorine. She had sat for Manet's picture of Olympe, but that was many years ago. The face was thinner, but I recognized the red hair and the brown eyes, small eyes set closely, reminding me of little glasses of cognac. . . . She lit cigarette after cigarette, and leaned over Marie with her arm about her shoulder. (George Moore, 1920, 54, 55)

> After having attempted, without much success, to give music lessons, [Victorine] tried to paint. She asked for advice . . . from Etienne Leroy, an obscure painter. Soon she thought about exhibiting in the Salon, and the jury was not discriminating. In 1876 she sent them her own portrait and then some historic or anecdotal paintings. Wretched little daubs. (Tabarant, 1921, 299)

[At the café Nouvellas Athenes] going from table to table was a former model of Manet's, Victorine Meurent, nicknamed The Shrimp . . . ; she was showing artists her most recent studies because she had started painting since she was no longer able to pose in the nude. (Georges Riviere, 1931, 32)

[In the] very mediocre salon [of 1879] . . . what a surprise for Manet, that his neighbor in the same room was Victorine Meurent. She was there, smiling, happy, camped in front of her entry, which had brought her such honor, the *Bourgeoise de Nuremberg au XVIe Siecle*. (Tabarant, 1947, 299)

One day [ca. 1895] I was in [Lautrec's] studio and [he] said to me: "Get your cane and your hat, we are going to see '*la*' . . ." I took my hat and cane, intrigued, and attempted to query Lautrec. He put his finger to his lips and murmured mysteriously. . . . At the end of a quarter hour's walk . . . he darted under the porch of an old house on the rue Douai. He climbed . . . five dark flights of steps and reaching the attic . . . said to me again, raising his finger, she is more famous than. . . . Finally, he knocked on a little door. An old woman came to open it and Toulouse-Lautrec introduced me to . . . the Olympia of Manet. (Paul Leclercq, 1954, 54–56)

She tried to sell her drawings to her companions of the night. . . . But she no longer drew very well, and she stopped making them and returned to her guitar playing where she could, and then came the final disgrace. She descended into alcoholism. A painting by Norbert Goeneutte represents her collapsed in a chair against a table on which is located a monkey dressed in red. She grasps in her right hand a guitar and with the other presses down on the neck of a wine bottle. (Tabarant, 1947, 489–90)

To these writers Victorine Meurent is a wretched lower-class model from the streets of Paris. She is promiscuous and alcoholic; she draws and paints unsuccessfully; she is foolish in her persistence and ambitions. She is a sad, failed person—a loser.

I never saw her that way. Was I missing the point, with all my expensive education? I didn't think so. But how was one to explain the competing images: a pathetic female character on the one hand, Manet's cocky, self-contained model on the other? I wondered why none of the writers were surprised that Meurent—this mere model—painted? Why only condescension and contempt? Why was no one captivated by her trip to the United States? Why was it designated romantic folly? And what, finally, was behind all the attention this red-headed model received?

I was bewildered and perturbed, and had no idea what to do with these feelings that were so inappropriate to my profession. Art History, after all, promised serenity and pleasure—it's a gentleman's profession—not emotional excess. Luckily I met an extraordinary woman who helped me. Coincidentally she was a red-head, like Victorine, and something of a character as well. She was an art historian named Linda Nochlin. I had already heard of her in the mid-1960s when I was a graduate student. Even then Nochlin was a celebrity although it was not clear exactly what the parameters of her notoriety were. In fact, I sensed something missing in the stories that circulated. The talk was about her unorthodox dissertation, *Gustave Courbet: A Study in Style and Society*, completed in 1964. In it she proposed that the radical politics of Courbet's time emphatically and specifically informed his paintings. The very subjects he chose—an old man and a child breaking stones, the elaborate Catholic burial of a peasant, the portrait of a socialist—and the compositional schema he used had political meaning.

Reading historical events into the style of works of art was forbidden in Art History. This was most stringently the case in the realm of modern art where abstraction, both as visual content and analytic tool, was sacred. Typical thesis subjects in the field of modern Art History were: "Color in Matisse," "Medieval Sources in Gauguin," "Classical Tendencies in Ingres." But Nochlin drew stylistic considerations into a net of political and social meaning. It was the 1960s. And, it turns out, her Russian-Jewish family had been committed liberals for generations, and she had gone to Vassar, a college noted for encouraging smart girls to speak their minds. She believed in her thoughts; she felt no shyness about her voice. Her prosaic, demystifying questions, her political passions, and her lively, sometimes biting, sometimes poetic prose were harbingers of things to come. Art History was changing. . . .

. . .

Yes, I marveled at the intricate psychological drama surrounding *Olympia*, which on the one hand elicited men's attraction—so many had written *something* about her at a time when models were usually nameless and invisible—but on the other provoked ridicule and contempt. *All that writing about her.* In our own time, in 1977, an entire book on *Olympia* was written by Theodore Reff, and again in 1985, T. J. Clark, the most dazzling bad boy in the Art History community, published a notably long, obfuscating, and tortured essay on *Olympia* in his book on Manet. Every prominent scholar of nineteenth-century art planted himself in front of her, writing paraphernalia at hand. All thought their engagement disinterested, but it wasn't. They circled her from above, close up, on top. What did they mean to do with all those words? Describe her? Analyze her? Situate her? Or: Possess her? Control her? Silence her? No one admitted his emotions, neither the irritation nor the fascination. None could acknowledge what amounted to a professional obsession that spanned a century and a half. And continues. . . .

REFERENCES

Clark, T. J. *The Painting of Modern Life: Paris in the Art of Manet and His Followers*. New York: Knopf, 1985.

Duret, Theodore. *Histoire d'Edouard Manet et de son oeuvre*. Paris: H. Floury, 1902.

Hamilton, George Heard. *Manet and His Critics*. New York: Norton, 1969.

Leclerq, Paul. *Autour de Toulouse-Lautrec*. Geneva: Cailler, 1954.

Moore, George. *Memoirs of My Dead Life*. New York: Boni and Liveright, 1920.

Riviere, Georges. *Renoir et ses amis*. Paris: H. Floury, 1931.

Tabarant, Adolphe. "Celle quifut L'Olympia." In *La Bulletin de la vie Artistique* II, 299. 1921.

———. *Manet, Historie catalographique*. Paris: Editions Montaigne, 1937.

———. *Manet et ses oeuvres*. Paris: Gallimard, 1947.

Zola, Emile. *Edouard Manet, etude biographique et critique*. Paris: E. Dentu, 1867.

Music

PETER HAMLIN

Devouring Music:

Ruminations of a

Composer Who Cooks

RECIPE #1: AN IMPROVISATION

A friend asked me once for the recipe for Thai green beans I had cooked for a potluck dinner. Thai what? Then I vaguely remembered making something that fit that description some months before. It wasn't really a recipe —more like an improvisation. I didn't remember exactly how I had made it. I recalled I had cheated a little by using some Thai hot sauce. Probably some coconut milk was thrown in, too, and some hot peppers. I'm sure I would have tossed in some spices—maybe we had some early coriander in the little spice garden outside the kitchen door? Or something left over that hadn't rotted yet in the vegetable bin. I remember that the green beans benefitted from being invited to a potluck—setting them out a bit let them soak up the sauce without being overcooked. Practical exigencies do not always result in compromises!

That kind of cooking is a bit like playing jazz. You vaguely remember what you did, but you're not exactly sure what it was and whether you could do it again. You usually start with something like a "prepackaged" song or bottle of hot sauce, but you add a great deal of your own personality until the original blends into a new creation that is uniquely yours.

There is much technique and skill involved in improvisation: you need to know how to play blues scales and thirteenth chords and how to slice and sauté and how to thicken a sauce. But when you get to the gig, you really aren't sure exactly what will happen. Heat up the oil in the pan (sounds a little bit like applause, doesn't it?), throw on some onions and garlic (maybe that's the drums sizzling), a few sliced peppers and eggplants (some chords on the piano), chopped tomatoes and hot sauce (that's the bass!), a few riffs of cheese and spices, and finally throw it all on top of some lemon pepper macaroni you've been waiting to use up (just like those old jazz standards you always have sitting on the shelf).

Cooking with a recipe, on the other hand, reminds me of making classical music. The recipe is the score, and all the planning and measurement let you create wondrous large structures like sonatas, fugues, and chocolate cakes. Within the guidelines of the recipe, a good composer-cook can still be spontaneous. New ingredients are added (more chocolate, more butter, more woodwind flourishes), some are reduced (less sugar, a slightly thinner contrapuntal texture), and, in the end, despite the recipe, what you get is a reflection of the personality of the chef. For some reason, I'm mostly a jazz cook and a classical composer. I do play jazz for fun, and I use recipes sometimes. But my professional creative work seems to draw me more naturally to written scores, while my cooking is mostly improvised.

A RECIPE FOR MUSIC

Written music is a kind of frozen improvisation. When it works well, there is a feeling of spontaneity in a performance that the audience members sense, even though they know all the notes are written down. A written score is an improvisation in slow motion. A five-second phrase may actually have taken shape in an hour, and so every note can be studied and considered and turned over and revised until it's just right. But it's more than that, too. It's no accident that classical pieces tend to be longer than much other music, because working out a score lets you deal in an almost architectural way with the musical elements. My improvised cooking is less likely to be structurally magnificent: I can thicken sauces impromptu, for example, but when I feel like baking a cake, out come the cookbook and measuring cups.

The impetus for developing a precise system of musical notation came with the development of contrapuntal music. With notation, a composer could construct a fabric of intertwining melodies that all fit within the required harmonic sound of the piece. It's a kind of musical crossword puzzle, with the melodies ("across") and harmonies ("down") fitting perfectly together. What we mean by compositional technique has a great deal to do with the ability of a composer to create such a web of melodies without compromising either the harmonic or melodic realm. The contrapuntal melodies give the illusion that they are completely free and independent even though they are, in fact, intricately codependent.

A skilled composer makes decisions about how these melodies will interact even before they actually encounter each other in the music. Bach must have known that all three themes in his "St. Anne" fugue would work together when he began composing, even though it sounds to the listener like a miraculous coincidence later in the piece. A good chef similarly knows how preparation in the early stages of making a thousand-layer pastry can have an effect that may not be obvious until the dough is finally shaped and baked.

A common misconception about notation is that the musical score tells you all you need to know about performing the piece. In fact, classical music is not, at heart, a notated tradition at all, but a living oral tradition. The little black dots on the staff tell the performer everything about the music except what is most important: the creative interpretation marinated in years of learning about the many kinds of deeper meanings that lie beneath the surface of the written notes. The score is a carefully measured tennis court and a rulebook, and the performance is when an actual game of tennis springs to life.

Most musical traditions don't rely on notated scores as Western classical music does. A score is often held suspect, as witness the old jazz musician's rejoinder when asked if he can read music: "Sure, but not enough to hurt my playing." But, like a recipe in the hands of a good cook, a score is meant to be a liberating force, not a straitjacket. Each family's Thanksgiving stuffing can have a distinctive personality, even though the recipe came from the same bag of bread crumbs.

The mother of an old family friend was an expert cook. She made a legendary cheesecake. I was excited to hear that she had left a recipe, and waited with anticipation to receive a copy. Alas, the recipe gave only the most basic information. It was a list of ingredients, with approximate measurements ("a pinch of this," "a touch of that"), and only the barest directions about what to do with them. This is more like a musical score than the self-explanatory recipes in cookbooks: it could only be interpreted by someone who is familiar with the unspoken traditions behind the words.

COMPOSING DINNER

Composers love to cook. I heard one reason third-hand from a friend's composition teacher: "Not everyone will enjoy your music, but everyone loves to eat!" The reception of a good curry is often much more satisfying than a yawning and frowning audience at an orchestra premiere. Good cooking skills are also handy assets for the starving composer. I've eaten like a king on ten dollars a week because I could create interesting meals with a few carrots, a jar of peanut butter, and a tortilla.

But beyond practical necessity, the processes of composing and cooking have much in common. My undergraduate composition teacher was always talking about texture, counterpoint, gesture. His cooking shows attention to similar qualities in food. Both activities are sensual: to a musician, the pleasure of a fine meal is one of the few sensations that come close to the effect of musical sound on a receptive soul.

There is more to music and food, though, than the pleasure of taste and sound. These are really only half the story—one might say, only half the brain. There is a more abstract and objective kind of fascination in both that has to do not with pleasure, or expression, or emotion, but with structure and form. Many composers are also theoreticians because we love musical structures. We are not content just to listen to a beautiful piece; we want to understand as much as we can about how it is put together.

I met someone at a dinner once who bragged, "I'm a right-brain sort of person." It was a curious statement, boasting about using only half of her thinking power as if there were something unclean or corrupting about the rational or logical or analytical competencies associated with the "left-brain." One of the marvels of music is that, in its most perfect form, it stimulates so many kinds of thought, including the intellectual and the emotional.

Some new-age music seems that it would appeal to a "right-brain" person. It can be beautiful on the surface, but there are parts of the brain it leaves cold. The paradigm of the left brain/right brain dichotomy seems to have taken hold of the public view of music: art is in the intuitive right side of the brain, while more technical and structural, inartistic kinds of thinking are found in the left. But, like a beautiful cathedral or a magnificent soufflé, great music cannot just be beautiful. It requires a structure to keep from falling down.

I was interested to learn recently, in a book about child development and music, that musical thought seems, indeed, to be located in the right hemisphere of the brain, but when someone is musically trained, brain activity expands to the other half as well (Denckla 228). This reflects the experience we have with individual pieces and whole genres of music: when we first hear a piece or type of music, we may respond to the beautiful tunes or harmonies or the most obvious emotional expression. As our acquaintance grows, we appreciate the music in deeper or more subtle ways, or, if it has nothing more to offer, we begin to lose interest. This also happens in our experience with food. For me, for example, my entrée (so to speak) to sushi was first through the more familiar items like crab and tuna, coming to an appreciation of eel and sea anemone more gradually. Someone experienced with a certain cuisine or musical style may be impatient with a neophyte who seems less adventuresome or sophisticated, while the newcomer may regard the more experienced as snobbish or overly refined. The latter is not snobbishness at all, though, just a demand for a more whole experience with sound, an experience that can reach all corners of the mind: a duet, as researcher Martha Denckla puts it, "between the two sides of the brain." (228). Some twentieth-century classical music has the opposite problem, all structure and no focus on the affective features of the music. Maybe we become too well-trained for our own good, and everything migrates over to the left-brain leaving nothing for the right! Recent classical music has sought to correct this error, and the best of it, as in the works of John Adams, succeeds wonderfully. It is the quality of "whole thought" that defines, in my mind, the very greatest music. Bach is an especially rich example: there are structural complexities that can delight the most observant technical analyst no matter how many times the piece is investigated, and at the same time there is an overpowering expressive beauty that can move an expert listener or a novice. So too with other transcendentally great composers: Brahms, Mozart, Beethoven. Or, closer to home, forget about the haunting beauty and perfect reflection of the words of Gershwin's "The Man I Love" long enough to admire the exquisitely crafted chromatic counterpoint that complements the tune. (Or better yet, in the spirit of whole thinking, admire them all together!) Or revel in the sumptuous and exhilarating sonic spectacle and evocative colors of Joseph Schwantner's *Aftertones of Infinity* while admiring the carefully constructed chord relationships that tie it all together. Beyond the surface pleasure of great art and great food there are nourishing qualities that burrow deeply into the belly and the soul.

RECIPE #2: PFEFFERNÜSSE

I began to cook and compose at about the same time. I think I was in the sixth grade when I decided to bake a batch of Christmas cookies for a class party—a recipe for Pfeffernüsse, I think. My mother, no doubt, offered to make them, or at least to help. But, filled with that wonderfully self-deluded confidence of youth, I decided to make them on my own. I followed the recipe carefully. I was intrigued by not only the combining flavors but the structures forming as the ingredients mixed together. Fresh out of the oven that night, they were spectacular in flavor, texture, and form, and so I spent the next morning in school bragging about how splendidly my Pfeffernüsse had turned out, and what a great experience it would be for everyone to eat them.

At noon I passed them out and looked with anticipation for reactions. Instead of the expected expressions of pleasure, I saw the screwed-up faces of classmates trying unsuccessfully to bite into them. The Pfeffernüsse had become tiny, indestructible chunks of concrete. They were impervious even to the determined teeth of their creator in his futile attempts to show they could at least be appreciated by connoisseurs. I received my first harsh reviews for a creative effort, and an early comeuppance for artistic hubris. A motherly analysis that night revealed a missing ingredient: baking powder. Around the site of my boyhood home in New Jersey, I imagine there are tiny Pfeffernüsse still standing up to the elements while ordinary rocks around them erode to dust.

The Pfeffernüsse did teach me an important lesson in creativity: failure is an indispensable part of the process. Creativity always involves risk taking, and risks, by definition, often fail. On the bright side, most artistic failures, unlike my Pfeffernüsse, are fairly easy to destroy.

I think it was during my Pfeffernüsse period that I started writing short pieces. The first composition I remember was based on an augmented chord that I heard in the score of the classic 1932 Boris Karloff film *The Mummy*. Into my teen years, I wrote many rock 'n' roll songs about surfing, cars, and romantic love, drawing on my extensive lack of experience with all three. I made a naïve attempt at a piano sonata in high school, and then became very excited about experimental music in college and in my twenties.

RECIPE #3: BOSTON EVERYTHING

Soon after college, in 1974, I was living on my own in San Diego. My interest in cooking helped me to meet a ten-dollar weekly food budget. I experimented with lots of variations on favorite recipes. My favorite dish in those days was brown rice, topped with sautéed carrots and onions, smothered with Indonesian peanut sauce. Peanut butter heated in a tortilla was another common meal. I had a Colombian roommate who told me I made it hard for him to figure out what American cooking was. When he asked me to cook an American meal, I was at first stumped. I ended up serving all the "Boston" dishes I could think of: Boston baked beans, Boston brown bread, Boston cream pie. The main dish was hot dogs, which a visiting vegetarian on the rebound devoured at an alarming rate. But I wasn't sure this meal was really any more "American" than what I cooked the rest of the time. It was certainly less natural to me. I had to use a cookbook, which I never did for my more idiosyncratic meals.

I think I was a fairly good cook by the time I was about twenty-one, but I didn't write any music I'm still proud of until I was thirty-two. One of the greatest challenges a composer faces is finding a personal voice without being either derivative or self-consciously mannered. You hear so much music today, representing so many different times and places and cultural traditions, that it is very difficult to find a uniquely personal style. Keeping a healthy balance between learning from the music you hear and developing your own musical voice is an important feature of any creative journey. Until I was in my thirties, I was writing music the way I cooked Boston cream pie, following a recipe and trying too hard to fit into a predefined style. Musical peanut sauce came only later.

RECIPE #4: PEANUT SAUCE

Fry some hot peppers and diced onions in a pan. You can use chili and/or sesame oil, although any oil will work. When the onions and peppers are cooked to your liking, add about two large spoonfuls of chunky peanut butter. After the peanut butter is just hot enough to be stirred, add about a quarter cup of water and/or coconut milk and stir until blended. Gradually add more water/coconut milk until you have a good sauce consistency. Be sure to stir constantly and let the mixture thicken after each addition of liquid. Don't let the sauce ever come to a boil or the peanut butter will separate. You can add turmeric, coriander, cardamom, cayenne, soy sauce, or your favorite hot sauce if you think the flavor will match.

This is a wonderful Indonesian sauce that is perfect on any number of vegetable or meat dishes: on something as simple as steamed broccoli on rice, or as involved as a marinated shish kebab. I like to use huge quantities of the sauce and make sure it's extra spicy.

I can never tell exactly how the peanut sauce will turn out. Sometimes it comes off perfectly, but often there is something about the flavor, color, or texture that isn't quite what I wanted. A composer is used to this kind of experience because no matter how much we write, and how much we study, and how much experience and technique we acquire, we are never sure exactly how well our labors will work out in the end. The final result is always at least a little bit out of our control.

My experience with each composition begins with an initial inspiration in which the basic sound and expressive mood spring to mind. I might find a poem I want to set and almost before reading the poem through I have a notion of the orchestration, the kind of melodic and harmonic language that will be used, and the emotional character and general form. I was asked to write a piece for solo horn recently, and, after spotting a book of palindromes on a friend's coffee table, got the idea of writing a set of pieces that imitate word games (one movement, for example, was written the same forward and backward, in the manner of a word palindrome). A piece for orchestra sprang to mind when I saw a small patch of native prairie in Iowa, and a choral piece took shape in the moments after I had learned of a friend's death. The idea may be longer in coming, but, in any case, somewhere early in the process of writing a piece I experience what seems a kind of cerebral big bang, and, like the big bang of cosmology, it is only after considerable time that the actual materials of the piece begin to take their eventual form.

The initial inspiration is in some ways quite specific. I know that certain chords just don't sound right for the piece, or certain instruments might be more or less appropriate. I feel as if I have a very clear idea of what I want or don't want, and yet, on the other hand, the image is still unformed and incomplete. While the piece is in my head in a certain sense, I can't sit down and write it out yet. The initial inspiration takes place in a flash, but turning it into a score may take months. This all seems very much like Thomas Edison's observation that invention is 2 percent inspiration and 98 percent perspiration.

A great danger for a composer at the early stage of a piece is not starting the hard work (the perspiration) soon enough to capture the fragile image that initiates the piece. I believe in the universality of creativity in people, and I think everyone is capable of the 2 percent flash of inspiration. Like many human capabilities—the ability to see, to hear, to reproduce, to be aware of oneself—it is both miraculous and common.

The process of moving from this internal inspiration to something written out in detail is what our training teaches us to do, and it involves quite a variety of approaches. Sometimes you try planning the overall form of the piece. Other times you sketch melodic ideas. Perhaps a progression of harmonies is a useful thing to explore. You might try working out some contrapuntal ideas. Your work might be very controlled, structured, and abstract or very free and undirected. You might work directly on the score without playing to avoid letting the fingers fall by habit on keyboard clichés, or you might improvise freely. These different approaches match different needs in the piece as well as your own changing moods. You move from busywork (copying a doubled melody in the flute), to crafting (fashioning an accompaniment that best completments a melody), to invention (creating a melodic theme).

It's also important to get your nose out of the score enough so that you can find a fresh perspective on your piece. Take a walk. Eat a leisurely lunch. Sit on the porch and read the paper. Have a good night's sleep and dream lavishly. Get your brain thinking of something else. The subconscious and unconscious parts of the mind keep working on the piece if you can get your conscious thoughts out of the way for a while. Composers need to work hard to be successful, but we shouldn't schedule our work time with no margin for a walk in the woods.

Perhaps composition is 2 percent inspiration, 68 percent perspiration, and 30 percent procrastination.

Moving from inspiration to score is filled with false starts and dead ends. You feel almost afraid of working, fearing that the wonderful idea that has started everything will prove to be a mirage. You can be filled with a terrible sense of insecurity and uncertainty as the piece very slowly begins to unfold. There is much practical work to do. This section of the piece doesn't get to that section smoothly, so I'd better craft a transition. This peanut sauce doesn't quite match the main dish, so I'll add just a little bit of the marinade to it. There are small moments of inspiration throughout the process, but, for the most part, a composer feels much more like an artisan than the popular image of an inspired genius in a mystical trance.

I find that, as I work, I begin to learn the language of my piece. The kinds of chords and melodies become more familiar, and I become more competent in working with them. I almost feel as if I have invented my own language, and, as I write, I am learning better to speak it. I usually become more excited and confident as the piece progresses. When the music is finished, I experience a sense of exhilaration at having found a way to bring this creation to life.

Alas, when I'm done I may have created my finest orchestral work or most perfect peanut sauce, but I can't go back and retrace exactly what I did so it can be done again. It is as if the mind expanded to a complete level of understanding within the world of that one piece, and as soon as it's done, you not only forget what you did but, in a sense, no longer retain even the ability to think in that way again. After the passage of some time, you may feel as if you didn't even write the piece. When you start another composition, you are again alone speaking an unfamiliar tongue that you have not yet invented.

I believe another reason many composers cook is that the creative cycle is completed in a matter of hours, not months, and the final reward of a good meal comes so soon.

TEACHING AND LEARNING COMPOSITION

To most people, cooking is a fairly unremarkable thing. Lots of people do it, and it's considered a common skill. Composition seems quite the opposite: a rare and mystical gift, not an acquired or learned competence. When people learn that I teach composition, they often react with surprise or skepticism: "How do you *teach* composition?" Nobody would ever say in wonder, "How do you *teach* someone to cook a chicken?"

My experience with a wide range of students—children, adults, music majors, nonmajors, students with no musical background at all—shows me that all people have the gift of creativity and can learn how to compose. As with teaching how to cook, you line up a few basic ingredients, explain a few principles, and watch natural human creativity take hold. Perhaps one reason many people assume they can't compose is that the role of creativity in many other kinds of human endeavors—science, business, farming, bantering with friends, cooking, playing basketball—is very much underappreciated. In a way, creativity is the easy part. The last 98 percent is often the crucial challenge.

RECIPE #5: OYSTERS

Get the oysters and eat them raw. To open the shell, you have to stick the knife into a weak spot near the "hinge." Wear protective gloves, because an oyster knife can be nasty.

What we do musically, and what we do in our cooking, springs from a mind that has been profoundly shaped by the culture that surrounds us. An oyster is a delicacy for some, an inedible blob of slime to others. Part of this is personal taste, of course, but much of it is culture. In my family culture, raw oysters and clams were normal food, and we ate them eagerly from an early age. They never seemed problematic to me.

Culture is a vital part of artistic language, and yet defining culture is an exasperating exercise in fuzzy boundaries. Culture helps us define our standards for art as it does for cooking. There is really no such thing, apart from culture, as a beautiful chord or a delicious dish. A well-tuned piano sounds beautiful to us, but it is acoustically out of tune. When today's tuning system was first introduced hundreds of years ago, it offended the ears of many listeners. We have trained ourselves so thoroughly to that artificial standard that hearing an acoustically perfect chord seems at first strangely out of tune. We Americans are so used to cooking fish that we have to work hard to eat it raw in a sushi bar.

I often wonder what a visitor from another country unfamiliar with lobsters must think when seeing those odd creatures being devoured. Eating the guts of what looks like a giant insect must certainly be an acquired taste. How was it ever discovered that the slimy oyster was not only edible but delicious in its raw form? Plants like onions and peppers evolved their spicy flavor to trigger an aversion response in animals to keep from being eaten. How did humans discover this stinging sensation could be pleasurable? People sprinkle cayenne on the garden to keep rabbits away and pour it in chili to get compliments from dinner guests.

ACQUIRED TASTES

Some music challenges our "natural" instincts as much as a raw oyster or hot pepper. We all have experiences with music we don't appreciate. Why do professional musicians like so much music that more casual listeners can find repugnant? As an example, many audiences do not respond well to dissonance. The tang of a dissonant chord is analogous to the sting of a hot pepper. Those who are not accustomed to the spice can't understand its appeal. I once ate a meal called "Angry Dish" at a favorite Thai restaurant. Half of us ordered it, and the other half, watching us sweat and wince, didn't really believe we were enjoying ourselves. In some cultures, spiciness is an acquired taste. So too with dissonant chords. But, with food as with music, once you've acquired a taste for piquancy, it's hard to go back to ordinary flavors. After returning from a visit to Mexico, I found myself putting hot sauce or peppers on just about everything. And I like to pepper my pieces with a little dissonance, too.

An artist is always judged by an audience. I am always inspired by the acts of communication between composer, performer, and listener that bring a piece to life. When one's own particular blend of ingredients doesn't work for listeners, however, a composer has to wonder whether it really is a lousy recipe, or whether the audience just needs a little time to get used to the spices.

EL CHARRO

There's a great little Mexican restaurant in Waterloo, Iowa, called El Charro. They serve real mole sauce at El Charro, an amazing blend of chilies, peanuts, and chocolate. It's the greatest taste in the world, but you can't imagine anyone sitting down and inventing such an unlikely combination. Maybe it's a little bit like Villa-Lobos' inspired combination of Brazilian folk music and Bach, or the blend of pre-Columbian sensibilities and modernism in the work of Carlos Chávez.

RECIPE #6: A RECIPE FROM WHO KNOWS WHERE

Combine spinach and sautéed mushrooms in a white sauce. This works wonderfully as an enchilada filling, but you can roll it in lefse (Norwegian potato flatbread) instead of tortillas. Bake it as little as necessary to get it good and hot.

AUTHENTICITY

In a sense, nothing I do is authentic. I play folk music that I learned from records. I cook food that I picked up and combined from books, travels, friends, family, and who knows where. I write music that almost never relates to the musical environment in which I grew up, and I don't think anyone could guess where I grew up from my cooking. I started to like my own music and cooking when I finally felt able to blend many different influences in natural and personal ways.

In the modern world we don't acquire our cultural identity quite so much by the accident of the time and place in which we were born. We seem more to gather what suits our personalities from many sources, from all possible times and places, available readily to us on radio, in libraries, on compact discs, on the Internet, and through travel. Why was I fascinated as a child by the asynchronized rhythms created by the pneumatic windshield wipers of my uncle's old jeep? It's not surprising that many years later I was drawn to the similar phased rhythms in music by Steve Reich.

Why did a suburban kid from northeast New Jersey have an instant love for the blues and for Ravel? The first time I heard both, I felt as if I had been born into them, but there was nothing in my upbringing that would suggest that. The first time I heard Schubert's Impromptu in A-flat and Beethoven's Third Symphony and the guitar playing of Blind Blake they jumped out of the speakers and took instant hold. Why? Our response to music is certainly conditioned by culture, and yet there is also often an innate rapport with musical styles that are not part of our cultural environment.

I loved Doc Watson when I was in high school and tried to learn some guitar finger-picking from his records. The same kinds of interlocking rhythms appear frequently in my own music, even though it doesn't sound at all like Doc Watson. Related rhythmic techniques from African drumming, medieval dances, rock 'n' roll, and Bach syncopation somehow all contribute to what I think of as my own style. My fascination with evocative orchestral colors goes back to a first-grade hearing of Stravinsky's *Firebird*. I loved *Grand Canyon Suite* when I was a little kid. My uncle had it on a set of bright red 45 RPM records that I played over and over. I was transfixed by the orchestral colors and still use similar techniques in my pieces even though they don't sound anything like Grofé.

Similar things have happened with food. My mother took us to a fancy Spanish restaurant in New York when we were children, and I had my first corn tortilla. I still remember what a great impression it made on me. Why? At that time there was no particular reason from my own life experience, but it certainly was a small premonition of my future love of Mexican music, cuisine, and culture. Where our sensibilities and tastes come from is a fascinating question, and one that cannot receive a simple cultural or ideological answer. Music draws on the power of many influences, often as unlikely and sometimes as inspired as the chilies, peanuts, and chocolate of a Mexican mole sauce.

This wonderful eclecticism so characteristic of today's music and cooking—a mixture of different cultures, aesthetic perspectives, and historical styles—is certainly not a new invention. One thinks of the introduction of spaghetti to Italy from Asia, or Mozart's use of the Turkish cymbal in eighteenth-century Vienna. But technology in our world has dramatically increased the potential for these kinds of intermixtures. Each of us, in our cooking and our art, can create an aesthetic neighborhood that draws not only from our physical neighbors and family but from people in any place and time who excite us with the sounds and flavors of their cultures.

RECIPE #7: A GIFT TO BE SIMPLE

Catch and filet a fish. Dot with a tiny bit of butter and sprinkle with a pinch of seasoning and some lemon juice. Cook it on a grill until it is barely done.

. . .

The one last thing I like to remember in cooking and in composing is never to forget the basics. "Keep it simple" is advice one gives to composition students: don't write a symphony if a string quartet will perfectly convey your idea. See if you can make the strongest statement through the resourceful and creative use of limited materials. See if you can cook something grand with just the few things you have around rather than throwing in every possible ingredient you find at the supermarket.

Jazz musicians talk about the basis of the blues in jazz, and, no matter how sophisticated or advanced the harmonic language of jazz becomes, that inner core remains present. Classical musicians stay grounded by listening to folk music and letting it remind them of how music works at its most fundamental level. A song like "We Shall Overcome," made up of basic scales, harmonies, and forms, can change the world. While we revel in the marvels of a technological world that allows us to transcend the physical limits of our lives, we should also remember the enduring power of a simple flute or the taste of a fresh-picked apple.

RECIPE #8: FINAL WORDS

Eat a strawberry. Sing "Amazing Grace."

REFERENCE

Denckla, Martha B. "The Paradox of the Gifted/Impaired Child." In *The Biology of Music Making: Music and Child Development Proceedings of the 1987 Denver Conference*, edited by Frank R. Wilson and Franz L. Roehmann, 227–40. St. Louis: MMB Music, 1990.

Film

JULIE THARP

When the Body Is

Your Own: Feminist

Film Criticism and

the Horror Genre

On a day in November I was seated in an empire-style conference room at the Marriott Pavillion-St. Louis, professionally attired like the others in the room, carefully attending to the words of several scholars, when the unthinkable happened. I started crying. Had the presenters been speaking of some hideous miscarriage of justice, my tears might have been less noteworthy. Instead, the topic was film studies.

Corey Creekmur of Wayne State University discussed the Louise Brooks cult in film criticism, Craig Fisher of the University of Illinois presented some film history focusing on an early gore-fest film, *Blood Feast*, and Stephanie Tingley from Youngstown State University discussed the effects of test audiences on film endings. It may be testimony to the enthusiasm of the speakers that I was deeply engaged in the discussion, but it was the unplanned convergence of the film clips' subject matter that upset me. Creekmur showed a silent film scene in which Louise Brooks, as a London prostitute, is stalked and terrorized by Jack the Ripper. Fisher showed a scene in which the male killer of *Blood Feast* tears out the tongue of a young woman and eats it while she chokes to death. Tingley showed the alternate endings of *Fatal Attraction* and *Thelma and Louise* to illustrate how test audiences often choose simple endings in which women characters meet violent ends rather than choosing more enigmatic endings. Time elapsed: one hour, thirty minutes. Body count: five women. Certainly a great deal of the session's impact derived from the fact that the clips shown were utterly decontextualized. As such, they magnified Hollywood's penchant for hurting and killing women. Perhaps it also reflected on the demands of capturing and holding overtaxed listeners' attentions at long-winded conferences.

In any event, what interested me was myself. The disjuncture I experienced there was between the critic and the woman. I was mildly disturbed by the first clip, revolted by the second, and shocked and pained by the last two, primarily because I found myself identifying, not with the critics who stood before me, but with the women in the films. I came away wondering what violence we do to ourselves in order to arrive at a cold-blooded analysis of violence toward others. Furthermore, why was I unable to remain dispassionate and what implications did that have for the ways in which I respond to films?

Creekmur's control was, by contrast, admirable. He actually approached this topic in his discussion, speaking of the film critic's need to repress "fan tendencies." He argued that in order for film studies to rise as a discipline, film critics have had to discipline themselves. Within this particular viewing, I would not have been so much repressing "fan tendencies" as repressing visceral response to visual assaults. In order to discipline myself as a critic I would more or less have to disconnect from the visual presentation, perhaps by hiding under a blanket, like I did when I was young. The blanket technique, however, is hardly conducive to rigorous analysis.

Could I, instead, disconnect my body from the body on screen? I have tried to achieve critical distance from horror films, but on my initial viewing of a film it is almost impossible to do so. The response elicited by horror is too physical. It's only on repeated viewings, and especially viewings in which I control the VCR, zipping around in a film, looking for specific bits, that I can completely disconnect from the screen bodies. Control of the clips, then, might have been the critical difference between the Midwest-MLA presenters and me. Not only had the presenters isolated the specific scenes they wanted to show but they also had control of the showing. Furthermore, they all stood or sat next to the monitor, watching the clips from the side. They created the texts; I consumed them. They activated them; I received them. Their view was sidelong; mine frontal.

Where do I sit, however, as a female (and feminist) critic? I will eventually return to the issue of the critic's role, but I need to explore first what it means for me to watch horror films. Before I can excerpt, describe, and critique a given film, I have to watch it. I have to live through the horror with the bodies on screen. Assuming for the moment that it is not possible to watch a horror film without feeling some bodied connection, it is difficult to comprehend the "fun" (or even interest) of horror for women viewers without suspecting masochistic tendencies, as many feminist film critics have noted.

Barbara Ehrenreich suggests in a striking essay titled "Why Don't We

Like the Human Body?" that the increasingly sadistic ways of dispatching bodies in films today can be traced back to larger social trends against sex and food. She says it's "no wonder we enjoy seeing the human body being shredded, quartered, flayed, filleted and dissolved in vats of acid. . . . It's been, let's face it, a big disappointment. May as well feed it to the rats or to any cannibalistically inclined killer still reckless enough to indulge in red meat" (80). This suggests that people participate in the bodied connection of horror films to, at least in part, punish their own bodies for their betrayal. We eat ourselves. Carol Clover describes it as being "both Red Riding Hood and the Wolf" ("Her Body, Himself: Gender in the Slasher Film," 191). We are in a position to be both sadist and masochist, to rehearse the whole gamut of domination.

Myself a survivor of sexual violence, I have felt immediate empathy for the tortured women of horror films. Once made, the connection with the bodies on screen has been difficult to break. The intensity of the action and the relentless buildup of suspense are calculated to hold viewer identification. I can see my cinematic cohorts through any hell, up to, but only halfway through, their deaths. Sadomasochism is, of course, restricted only by death. To illustrate this breaking point: a young woman in one of the *Friday the 13th* films relaxes on a porch swing when suddenly she sees a butcher knife slicing out of her torso. She and I have time to register our shock, to realize that someone is behind the swing, and that we are going to die before I can hastily disconnect from her. But the film has had its shock effect: I have already contemplated my impending demise.

The camera angles in the infamous shower scene from *Psycho* make it clear that Hitchcock fully intended that viewers should identify with the victim right up until clinical death, the point at which the camera zooms in on Marion's vacant, staring eye. The eye fades into a view of water swirling down the drain. Only because of my new disassociation from Marion can I appreciate Hitchcock's visual gag. I'm Not Her, so I can laugh at her life going down the drain, like so much water. In that moment of comic relief, I get not only a temporary reprieve from terror; I also get to join an exclusive club: those who have conquered the body, the ones who have met death and lived. I am, in fact, a critic, appreciating the symbolic qualities of Hitchcock's film work, snickering at its melodrama. Had I not identified with Marion initially, would this new membership be so cozy? Horror films actually train us to be critics, taking our raw emotion and raising it to such a peak that we are forced into critical distance or suffer our own symbolic death.

I have only walked out on one horror film—*Pet Sematary*—not because of the quality of the film, but because I finally felt a threat too great to tolerate. I was nine months pregnant at the time I attended the film and was horrified at a scene in which a two-year-old wanders out onto a highway and is hit by a semitrailer truck.

I am beginning to understand that until that moment I had so successfully detached from female characters' deaths as to be relatively unperturbed over the mutilation of women on screen, but seeing a baby wantonly slaughtered while holding a cherished baby within my belly created a disjuncture that was intolerable. I could not detach from the child's death in time to keep from experiencing the assault personally, because my child was still within my body. I had no perspective, no critical distance from which to view this death. My own overwrought response to this assault revealed to me the sadism inherent in critical distance, particularly as applied to horror films. I was suppressing this kind of pain every time I detached from a female victim at the point of her death. I spent the rest of the film in the lobby.

If the horror film actually teaches us to turn raw emotion into critical detachment, it also teaches other forms of critical analysis. Tania Modleski argues that "insofar as Hitchcock films repeatedly reveal the way women are oppressed in patriarchy, they allow the female spectator to feel an anger that is very different from the masochistic response imputed to her by some feminist critics" (61). Hitchcock films possess a level of sophistication only glimpsed at in most contemporary horror films, but I believe some of the rudiments of patriarchal oppression are transparent in the latter. *Friday the 13th*, *Halloween*, *Nightmare on Elm Street*, and any number of spinoffs, for example, repeatedly equate female sexuality with danger or death. In fact, any horror fan can predict the order in which female characters will be killed by the scarcity of their clothing. In these films, as in many of Hitchcock's, the patriarchal institutions of law/order, of specialized knowledge (psychiatry, for instance), and of religious guidance all fail the victims and in many cases even add another dimension to their oppression. In many slasher films, the serial killer's psychosis is traced back to patriarchy's failure to properly gender him as masculine. If these and other signs of patriarchal oppression are stock characteristics of most horror films (not just Hitchcock's), is it not possible, as Modleski observes, that women, far from responding masochistically only, actually learn a certain cultural analysis through watching these films?

I offer a common example. The "Final Girl," say Laurie from the first two

Halloween flicks, tries to enlist the aid of authorities or warn others of the present danger. The audience knows the danger and so is in agony and rage when Laurie's pleas are ignored or dismissed as silly, girlish fears. The viewers are sympathetic to the female point of view and angered over paternalist dismissal. This is a moment of cultural critique. What Laurie learns, what female viewers learn, is that, because social arrangements are inequitable, we're on our own. We have to draw on internal resources of strength, courage, and ingenuity in order to survive the onslaught of male gender dilemmas. Judith Halberstam further argues in *Skin Shows* that women learn the crucial lesson of paranoia, which is, in the characters' lives as in most real women's lives, an entirely reasonable caution.

The formulaic nature of contemporary horror films suggests that a certain level of analysis is readily available to the average viewer. Promotional materials and reviews announce self-awareness. The campy "Jason Does New York" kind of promo, Hannibal the Cannibal jokes, and even very early horror advertisements that guaranteed to have people fainting in the aisles proclaim the fan's awareness of her own perverse fascination with horror. Several horror films of the 1990s—*Scary Movie*, *Scream* and *Scream 2*, *I Know What You Did Last Summer*—further develop that self-awareness into expressly postmodern irony.

I have been a lover of horror films and novels since adolescence. I understood the violence, empathized with its victims while they were alive and quickly abandoned them once dead to identify solely with the "Final Girl" who survived to foil the killer. I, along with all other viewers, bemoaned the stupidity of the girls who went back in the house, who looked in the closet, who thought themselves safe. To an extent, I learned from them how to blame myself for lack of foresight. If I have suffered from an excess of guilt, of self-blame, I have also taken the advice to heart. Get smart. Pay attention to your environment. Don't let yourself get caught daydreaming. I learned to disconnect from the flesh and blood that the dead girls represent and to connect with the rational mind represented by the survivor. As Isabel C. Pinedo points out in *Women and the Pleasure of Horror Film Viewing*, "the surviving female of the slasher film may be victimized, but she is hardly a victim" (87). I had already realized the former; I wanted to attain the latter.

At the movies, I was the resourceful, bright, chaste girl, a Nancy-Drew-girl-scout, capable of conquering chainsaw-wielding psycho killers with wits and a nail file. If I could conquer Michael, Jason, and Freddy, I could certainly make mincemeat of the men who attacked me in real life. To date, the most thoughtful and sophisticated rendering of this character type is Jodie Foster's portrayal of Clarice Starling in *The Silence of the Lambs*. She asks us to reconsider our definitions of femininity (Dubois). For Clover, the "Final Girl" becomes a masculinized female, with definite use-value for teenage male viewers, but for me she was the intelligent female, the capable, rational female.

Had anyone thought to ask me as a teenager why I liked horror, I would have had to take recourse in autobiographical, viewer-response criticism, drawing on my gender, my sexual experience, my familiarity with pain, and my desire to inflict pain in return. Repressing my bodied experience, disciplining myself, would have and did silence(d) me as a female and as a survivor. That silence further cemented the disconnection from my body.

The textual film critic's self-discipline is a repression, if not punishment, of the body. When I watch the shower scene from *Psycho* for the twelfth time, examining camera angles, for example, I render myself to a degree incapable of understanding the logic of horror films, precisely because I am operating on a similar logic. I repress my identification with Marion and align myself with the critic. I split off mind from body, even stow my body away with Marion's in the trunk of her car. It seems clear to me that the textual critic's body gets displaced onto women's bodies (Louise Brooks, Glenn Close, Susan Sarandon, Geena Davis) in much the same way that pornography and horror displace feeling onto women. In that displacement we simply replicate the horror film's sadomasochistic constructs.

I question, however, whether this initial repression of the body best corresponds to all female viewers' methods of analysis. Mary Anne Doane comes to a kind of dead-end on the topic of female spectatorship in "Film and Masquerade," concluding, "Above and beyond a simple adoption of the masculine position in relation to the cinematic sign, the female spectator is given two options: the masochism of over-identification or the narcissism entailed in becoming one's own object of desire, in assuming the image in the most radical way" (54). Doane's concept of "over-identification" does not strike me as a problem, however, if it actually facilitates women's critical response, as a British study on televised violence would seem to imply.

Researchers focus enormous energy on the question of whether or not contemporary film violence translates into increased personal violence on the part of viewers (although they really mean male viewers). A study published by the British Film Institute and titled *Women Viewing Violence* purported to discover, instead, what effect media representations of violence against women have had on women viewers, on "women's conceptions of themselves—their gender identities" (Schlesinger 3). One of their most striking conclusions was that women from a wide range of ethnic and class backgrounds who had experienced violence in their lives differed markedly in their perceptions of televised violence from those who had not experienced violence:

> Viewers with such life-experience [violence] were more sensitive to televised violence, more subtle and complex in their readings, more concerned about the possible effects and more demanding in their expectations of the producers of such content. . . . There was also a knowledge of all the excuses offered for male violence towards women and a consequential refusal to play the game of exculpation which contrasted with the greater willingness to do so among some of the women with no experience of violence. (165)

What strikes me in this description is the high degree of awareness reported. If many female victims of violence do have a better developed analysis of and sensitivity to media violence, it suggests that these women may both connect more deeply with the bodies on screen and also understand better the dynamics of domination enacted there. Identification, in other words, is not inimical to critical thinking.

My own response to the film clips in the opening example was one of tears rather than terror precisely because I understand the films to be signifying an entrenched misogyny. Thelma and Louise's last, poignant look at one another, before plummeting into the Grand Canyon, expresses the kind of pain I was experiencing in watching these women's lives end.

Thelma and Louise, whatever else it may do, illustrates that women's active desire and positive regard for women's bodies is anomalous in contemporary American culture and therefore threatening. Hollywood cannot imagine a sexually assertive female. Linda Williams argues that the "Final Girl's" increased power, "to the point of appropriating phallic power," is compensation for her sexual self-denial. Power comes at the expense of desire. (Thelma and Louise may have both power and desire for a brief time, but they also have platoons of armed men chasing them through the desert.)

When I act as a textual critic, I tend to replicate this tradeoff. I give up historically based desire in exchange for textual power. If I accept desire as abstract concept only, I can defer investigation into concrete desire's power and perversities, joys and disappointments. Desire becomes a utopian ideal that may in reality undo all my best-laid theories. Desire in the abstract, furthermore, is terribly appealing to people who have been burned or disappointed by the real stuff (and who hasn't?). Acted out, it's messy, so the body gets a bad rap. As Ehrenreich points out, we punish our real physical desires in every sadistic way imaginable.

The horror film's ideological bulwark is, however, corrupted by historically based desire. Actual viewers produce contradictions in films that the textual critic, locked into particular ideological representations, cannot perceive. Clover's work on male adolescent horror fans reveals such an erosion of form. Horror films also offer women the chance to produce contradiction and to rehearse other than "proper forms," particularly in the last battle between the "Final Girl" and the "Psycho Killer."

In any horror film this battle lasts an interminable length of time; it is, in fact, usually set up for us from somewhere near the first scene of the film. The killer, even bludgeoned, knifed, and immolated, still stumbles after our hero. This "prolongation of desire" allows us to play between the two poles of hunter and hunted (Williams 10). For even as I identify with Laurie's abject terror, I also identify with her cunning. I cannot match the violence of my husband's frequent exhortations to "cut off his head" in the final scenes of horror films, but I admit to a certain amused satisfaction with his solution. In this response I "rehearse" a form of violent revenge not "properly" my own.

The film provides a safe brush with deadly danger, but it also provides the thrill of victory over the danger. The problem I originally set out to discuss—of overidentifying with female victims—actually intensifies the pleasure of the ending. I not only have my own life to rejoice over. I also have revenge for my fallen sisters; indeed, as a victim I *am* my sisters. In this conflation of victim and victor, I collapse the dichotomous roles imposed on me as a female. Real desire can to a degree deconstruct the ideology of horror, but there is a cost.

The price of my revenge is my desire for other than violent connection. The "Final Girl" is always led off or carried off in the end by patriarchal emissaries (police officers, psychiatrists, actual fathers), but she is, in an emotional sense, alone. How can she trust these guys, care for them, knowing what she now knows? In many ways, the "Final Girl" is the eminent textual critic. She can read the signs, but she has lost all desire for them. Desire becomes an abstract concept deferred for "some day" when Jason finally dies, when Freddy finally dissolves. It's not coincidental that the "Final Girl" is always chaste, even disgusted by her girlfriends' amours.

One lesson I learn from identifying with Laurie and her cohorts is that I must discipline myself, repress or displace my feelings in order to survive in a world of men. I feel as though I have betrayed my fallen sisters, though; the quest I embarked on has lost its meaning; I am a spy in the enemy camp. Even the mystery is unappealing. I'm Lila Crane, in tight with the psychiatrist, the police, the bereaved fiancé, but I'm a woman alone with little hope. I can't forget the way that psychiatrist described Marion's death to me, sadistically, eyes riveted on mine. He enjoyed the telling.

In my self-discipline, I am disembodied. Ultimately, I become through identification with the "Final Girl" neither an intelligent female nor the masculinized female but a kind of incorporeal individual. I transcend my own body. And transcendance or control over the body is, after all, the compulsion acted out in horror. Being a film critic becomes, under these circumstances, pornographic. Strikingly, it is only as a critic that I can understand the response of some male viewers to particularly gory scenes in horror films. When they cheer the gruesome death of a coed, they are pornographers. They are appreciating new and unusual ways of subduing the physical.

I am frightened by my own ability to adopt this mode of viewing. This mode of viewing the other/female/body may well have led to the assaults I survived. Only through an inclusion of the personal, of historical desire, can I actually resist those messages. Like the fetus in my womb on that evening at the movies, the body held firmly in my mind will not allow me to torture it. Healed of the split, my body and mind can work together to produce a kind of empathetic analysis, one which is hardly painless but one which will at least maintain a degree of integrity. The "Final Girl" understands violence. Indeed, part of her appeal for me is that she is a survivor, but she has only survived to fight another day. If I want to understand desire as well, if I want more than violence, I have to merge these ways of knowing the world. I have to own the knowledge of the body.

A dilemma I face within this reintegrated viewing, however, is my own reduced tolerance for most contemporary film. Given that misogyny runs rampant throughout film, not just in horror, I am less capable of watching it. I find myself limiting my viewing to the films I feel might truly have something new or life-enhancing to offer. I also give myself permission to leave a film midway, to turn the television off, to return the video. Perhaps this makes me a better consumer, but it does little for my role as film critic.

What horror films and pornography, in particular, and film in general help reveal about textual criticism is that it almost inevitably practices a repression and displacement of the bodied self, a process that mirrors the compulsions acted out in horror. Popular film in all of the more bodied

genres, including the suspense/action drama, is actually an informal training camp for critics, guaranteeing that there will never be any lack of demand for or supply of the kind of films that would rightfully cause us pain.

When I watched *The Fugitive*, for example, I fully enjoyed the action-
packed, suspenseful drama, admired Richard Kimble's cunning and Harrison Ford's conditioning. I respected Tommy Lee Jones's performance as a
tough U.S. marshall. It has only occurred to me now, sitting here writing
this essay, that the entire film is centered on the tragedy of a man being
falsely accused of his wife's murder. Not the tragedy of her murder. The film
actually details the growing relationship between two men—the hunted
and the hunter. The dead woman, whom we see shot, bludgeoned, dying,
and dead in numerous flashbacks, is merely a vehicle for the men's relationship. The flashbacks are actually an interesting problem because they
are presented as though they were Richard Kimble's memories and dreams,
even though he does not actually witness her murder. The flashbacks are,
therefore, anomalous to the point of being gratuitous violence. The film
work is far more self-consciously stylized within these segments as well, a
factor that encourages me to disassociate from the woman and to concern
myself instead with the effect of her death on our protagonist. Ironically,
she has been setting the stage to seduce her husband when she is killed. The
film is so well made that I am gladly captivated by its seamless construction
of the universe from a male perspective. But what about the dead woman,
who is, by the way, one of only four small, female parts in a huge cast?

Women viewers' apparent tendency to identify closely with characters
is a strength, as I see it. Feminist film critics, however, need to go one step
further to examine that identification and to determine the world view
subscribed to in a given film. What kind of cultural analysis does it convey? We also need to watch for the cues that teach us critical distance. From
what do we back away? Where do filmmakers draw the line? And on whose
body is the line being drawn? If it's mine, I need to know.

REFERENCES

Benjamin, Jessica. *The Bonds of Love; Psychoanalysis, Feminism, and the Problem of Domi-
nation*. New York: Pantheon, 1988.
Clover, Carol J. "Her Body, Himself: Gender in the Slasher Film." In *Misogyny,
Misandry, Misanthropy*, edited by R. Howard Block and Frances Ferguson, 187–
228. Berkeley: University of California Press, 1989.
———. *Men, Women, and Chain Saws*. Princeton: Princeton University Press, 1992.

Doane, Mary Ann. "Film and the Masquerade: Theorizing the Female Spectator." In *Issues in Feminist Film Criticism*, edited by Patricia Erens, 41–75. Bloomington: Indiana University Press, 1990. Rpt. from *Screen* 23, no. 3 (September–October 1982).

Dubois, Diane. " 'Seeing the Female Body Differently': Gender Issues in The Silence of the Lambs." *Journal of Gender Studies* 10, no. 3 (November 2001): 297–311.

Ehrenreich, Barbara. "Why Don't We Like the Human Body?" *Time* (1 July 1991): 80.

Halberstam, Judith. *Skin Shows: Gothic Horror and the Technology of Monsters*. Durham: Duke University Press, 1995.

Modleski, Tania. "Hitchcock, Feminism, and the Patriarchal Unconscious." In Erens, *Issues in Feminist Film Criticism*, 58–74. Rpt. from *The Women Who Knew Too Much*. New York: Methuen, 1988.

Mulvey, Laura. "Visual Pleasure and Narrative Cinema." In Erens, *Issues in Feminist Film Criticism*, 28–40. Rpt. from *Screen* 16, no. 3 (autumn 1975).

Pinedo, Isabel C. *Women and the Pleasures of Horror Film Viewing*. Albany: SUNY Press, 1997.

Rodowick, D. N. *The Difficulty of Difference: Psychoanalysis, Sexual Difference, and Film Theory*. New York: Routledge, 1991.

Schlesinger, Philip, et al. *Women Viewing Violence*. London: British Film Institute, 1992.

Staiger, Janet. *Interpreting Films: Studies in the Historical Reception of American Cinema*. Princeton: Princeton University Press, 1992.

Williams, Linda. "Film Bodies: Gender, Genre, and Excess." *Film Quarterly* 44, no. 4 (summer 1991): 2–13.

DEBORAH LEFKOWITZ

Filming Point of View

While I was growing up as an American Jew in the 1960s, Germany was located at some considerable distance, both geographic and emotional, from my day-to-day life. For years it remained an unexplored territory surrounded by the silence of my parents' discomfort. Although my immediate family had been safe in America during the rise of National Socialism (all my grandparents having emigrated from Eastern Europe in the decades before 1920), nevertheless Germany became firmly associated in my mind with anti-Semitism, Hitler, and the Final Solution for the Jews.

A trip with my parents when I was fourteen—consisting largely of speeding along the autobahn as we traversed the country from south to north in a single day—did little to enlighten me. I seem to recollect flowers outside the pension where we stayed overnight on the German side of the border with France, and I have a clear image of the centuries-old Jewish cemetery we visited in Worms. My mother also wanted to see the yeshiva in Worms where the famous rabbi and Bible commentator Rashi had studied Talmud in the eleventh century. But the building was locked and my mother's German was not sufficient to understand why the caretaker, who was holding a ring of keys, could not open the door for us. We skipped visits to Frankfurt and Cologne in order to cross the border into Holland by nightfall. My most vivid memory is of my mother's hand moving across her forehead as she repeatedly explained to me, "We just don't feel comfortable here in Germany."

I had little occasion to revise my perceptions of Germany until I met, and then married, a German man. Suddenly Germany shifted from background to foreground, from the distance of historical accounts to the intimacy of family relationships.

My husband, Georg, who had come to the United States for graduate studies, associated very different images with Germany. His were the images of childhood that often featured the smiling figure of his mother, a beautiful landscape of fields and forests traversed by long bicycle rides, as well as the remembered anxieties of a schoolboy submitting to the rigors of his unsmiling teachers. Georg had learned about the Holocaust in school, as had most Germans of his generation. But he had not known any Jews in Germany and had met only one other Jew before me, also an American.

Our relationship challenged both of us to reposition ourselves vis-à-vis Germany as we attempted to bridge the gulf between our separate histories and communities. In 1983, when we traveled to Georg's hometown together for the first time, it was not for the purpose of making a film. Only some years later, my efforts to understand relationships between Jews and non-Jews[1] in postwar Germany, as well as my own role there as an American Jewish woman, led me to make the documentary film *Intervals of Silence: Being Jewish in Germany*.

• • •

After introducing me to his family on our first visit to Germany together, Georg showed me around his hometown. The places he had previously described to me came vividly to life. For example, the bakery located on the corner behind the church became associated with a particular aroma, with the sound of coins being tossed onto the counter, and with the greetings of other customers as the door swung open and closed. But these impressions were no longer isolated in one of Georg's stories about growing up in Germany; they had become firmly anchored in the time and space of my own experiences.

The bakery has a specific location in relation to Georg's parents' home. It takes me ten minutes to walk there, a few minutes less if I cut diagonally across the churchyard. There is a specific time of day to go there, early in the morning, so that the rolls are fresh for breakfast. I now understand that this is an almost daily family ritual, repeated in countless homes in other German cities. And although the ritual retains its quaintness for me, never becoming truly familiar, I nevertheless acquired my own role within it.

This, it seems to me, is a fundamental distinction between traveling to Germany with Georg and traveling with my parents so long ago: the ability to become a character within the stories enacted in Germany as opposed to merely being a spectator. My first response to this discovery was sheer delight. Proud of my ability to speak German and to navigate between two cultures, I slipped comfortably in and out of the place reserved for me in Georg's extended family.

But to what extent did my place in Germany encompass my Jewish identity? Near the beginning of my film, I recount my first meeting with Georg's mother: "I was very nervous about meeting [Georg's family] and I asked Georg if he had told his mother I was Jewish. He said yes but that she had not seemed very surprised. Georg's mother was waiting for us with hot coffee and breakfast. When she came to the door and I saw her smile, I knew I was welcome" (*Intervals of Silence*).

If this welcome was not an explicit answer to my question, it was at least a starting point for further exploration. I wondered how Germans lived with the knowledge, and the memory, of what happened in the past. And I wanted to know what it meant to be Jewish in Germany in the present, including what it meant for me.

These interrelated questions motivated me in 1985 to record on audio-tape more than 150 interviews with residents of my husband's hometown, both Jewish and non-Jewish, ranging in age from high school students to pensioners. I specifically limited my interviews in geographic scope, feeling that the historical and personal aspects of our respective identities met and became enmeshed in Georg's hometown more strongly than in any other German location.[2] It was here, walking the streets of Georg's childhood, that I felt most acutely the need to adjust my image of Germany in order to incorporate Georg's meanings as well as my own. And it was here, walking these same streets with me, that Georg first comprehended the disparity between his own experience, and a Jewish experience, of Germany.

Listening attentively during my interviewing (and again during my editing) for the nuances of experience associated with this particular place, I was struck by speakers' frequent insistence on the word *here*. Sometimes speakers used the word as many as three or four times in a single sentence, or repeated it as a cadence in a series of linked statements. For example, describing his inquiries into the history of the city, one non-Jewish man insisted: "*Here* no surprises occurred. *Here* no escalations occurred either. Uh, it is true there was a work camp *here*, but they also existed elsewhere. *Here* there were no, for that the city was simply too small, *here* there were no special, specially organized activities of the Party" (D-13A).[3] And another non-Jewish man told me emphatically: "*Here* is a different Germany. *Here* are people with political responsibility who are aware of their burden and who are doing everything possible so that the past is kept alive and the correct conclusions are drawn from it" (D-6B).

For the first speaker, *here* refers to the city in which he resides, a specific location distinguishable from all others in Germany. The second speaker refers more generally, in geographic terms, to *here* in Germany. But he emphatically assigns *here* to the present as opposed to the past of some sixty years ago. Whereas for one speaker *here* is a mythological place of past innocence, for the other it is the implication of past guilt that creates a moral imperative for political action.

And for a third non-Jewish speaker, *here* is precisely the location of wrongdoing the other two attempt to minimize. But his concession of past guilt is counterbalanced by the claim that acts of resistance were also committed in the past. Thus he fails to corroborate the versions of Germany's past and present put forward by the first two speakers: "Well, I found out that fascism is not just something that is written about in books. But [I] found out that fascism took place *here*, *here*, right *here* in front of our own door. But that at the same time, not only fascism took place *here*, but that resistance also took place *here*, you know?" (D-39A).

None of these speakers, however, places himself in a personal relationship to his own observations. Despite the insistence conveyed by the repetitive syntax, these statements sound remarkably detached. It is almost as if the speakers were not themselves present, or at the very least, not implicated; as if they were merely observing from a distance.

Ultimately, I understood these remarks to illuminate more about the speakers—and their assumptions about me as a listener—than about the city. Fearing, perhaps, a lack of sympathy on my part, their remarks contain an implicit defense against any accusation of wrongdoing, past or present. Perhaps when these speakers said *here*, part of what they meant was *here* in relation to where they perceived me to be—and I was definitely not there with them, not in any sense of the word.

In my interviews with Jewish speakers, I found a similar emphasis on the word *here* but with quite different associations. For example, one Jewish woman connected deep personal meaning with her location in Germany. *Here* is both a place she knows and, more significantly, feels she is known; a place she has invested with strong emotional ties: "And this is so peculiar, but I think it is also something very typical, that I try to cling to some place *here* in the region that I know; to stay *here*, where I have friends" (D-40B). After telling me this, she began to cry and asked me to temporarily turn off the tape recorder. Why, I wondered, did these particular words move her to the point of tears?

In contrast to all three non-Jewish speakers discussed above, this woman is remarkably present in her statements. She speaks not only in the first person but in an active, as opposed to passive, voice. Yet there appears to be more at stake (as evidenced by her tears) than the words themselves suggest. Fearing, perhaps, a negative judgment on my part, her remarks anticipate the response she has often heard from foreign visitors. This same Jewish woman asserts defensively in my film: "I don't think we should accept the reproaches we always hear in Israel, 'How can you live as a Jew in Germany, of all places?' " (*Intervals of Silence*).

Again, I understood these remarks not only in terms of the speaker's relationship to the city but also in terms of her relationship to me. Another interviewer might have elicited somewhat different remarks, a slightly different phrasing, or a different emphasis.[4] How this speaker positioned herself in relation to living in Germany was clearly linked to what she assumed about me as a Jew *not* living in Germany, whether or not I voiced any criticism (and as it happens, I did not).

In contrast to this staunch defense of Jews living in post-Holocaust Germany, other remarks that I recorded in my interviews reveal a more qualified and tenuous sense of belonging. One Jewish man confessed: "We often, my wife and I, we feel like foreigners. We have no friends. No friends. . . . They are all foreign to us. All foreign. . . . Even though they all know us. They all know us *here*. But they are all foreign to us" (D-31A).

Another Jewish man observed, "We are very much alone *here*. We have no friends whatsoever" (D-5A). Later in the same conversation, he detailed his social life in Germany with understated irony: "Our relations *here* are first rate. We get together about every half year or so with Doctor . . . and his wife for an evening of drinking tea. . . . Yes, or maybe every nine months. . . . And that's it for our circle of acquaintances *here* in [this city]" (D-5B).

It would certainly have been possible to suggest that such pronouncements were representative of Jewish sentiments in Germany. It would also have been possible to find excerpts from other interviews to corroborate this particular line of argument. Either approach, I think, would have been misleading and would have required me to ignore, or to minimize, the distinctiveness of other voices.

My film would have to allow for the possibility of dissension within a community of voices. And while acknowledging the diversity of individual expression, I would also want to draw comparisons between groups of voices. And finally, I would have to locate myself in relation to these voices in Germany.

In all of the excerpts I have discussed thus far, *here* signals the importance of place. Yet speakers are clearly not describing the same place—or the same relationship to place. In fact, I question whether *here* actually refers to physical location; it seems to locate speakers more precisely within the social and psychological space of their own experiences, and this includes the experience of me as a listener.

For most of the Jewish Germans I interviewed, I was both familiar (in my Jewishness) and unfamiliar (as an American). For most of the non-Jewish Germans I interviewed, I was the first Jew they had ever encountered—or, depending on their age, the first Jew since the end of the war. But I had married into a family that had lived in this city for three generations, and was therefore not treated as an outsider.

• • •

I envisioned that my film would speak across the rifts in people's experiences—beginning with my husband and me, extending to the Jewish and non-Jewish residents of his hometown, and ultimately encompassing the German and American viewers of my film. In my editing, therefore, I focused first on the voices. I considered how these voices had spoken to me, how they had spoken about each other, and how they might speak beyond the context of their own lives to my film's audiences.

I did not insist that my interviews present chronological or complete life stories. Instead, I juxtaposed short excerpts from a range of speakers in order to point out similarities, highlight contrasting views, and weave thematically interrelated ideas throughout the film as a whole. My editing began with the identification of themes for selecting and grouping excerpts from the interviews. One organizing theme, for example, was the question of how Jews live in post-Holocaust Germany. Here are some of the responses I received from non-Jewish speakers, as quoted in my film:

- I believe the Jews can now live here well with the Germans. But I also understand those Jews who no longer can or want to live here.

- I hope we are helping them feel at home here again.

- They clearly have the right—they in particular—to be treated lovingly. Above all we should welcome them with open arms.

- I admire those who live here but I simply do not understand how they can feel at ease.

- There is a reason why they stay here. They would not stay if they felt they were living among criminals. We have a state, which is (I think this is obvious, I am almost ashamed to say this) friendly towards Jews. That goes without saying.

- I don't know any Jews. But the fact that people hardly speak about them anymore makes it obvious that our living together is now normal. (*Intervals of Silence*)[5]

These passages sound remarkably alike in the aggregate, almost as if spoken by a single voice. The fact that so many speakers expressed themselves so similarly suggests, to me, that they were not speaking from personal experience. Their repeated usage of the third-person plural is also quite striking; such usage underscores the absence of relationships that would have permitted speaking about Jews as friends, neighbors, or colleagues. The language of intimacy suggested by phrases such as "friendly," "treat lovingly," and "welcome with open arms" thus serves to belie the reality of emotional distance.[6] In speaking about Jews, most of this group resorts to subterfuge or denial; only the last speaker frankly admits her lack of personal acquaintances.

In assembling groups of excerpts around a particular theme, I tried to include a wide range of attitudes. The above group of statements about Jews living in Germany, for example, moves from the thoughtful uncertainty of the first speaker ("I believe the Jews can now live here well") to the vacuous certainty of the last ("our living together is now normal"). But I also observed gradual shifts in meaning beneath the surface of words that sounded very similar. Thus, in the same group of statements, focus gradually shifts from the fact of living together to merely *speaking* about living together.

By comparison, most (but not all) of the Jewish responses to the question about living in Germany stressed the importance of relationships:

- The love for Germany cannot be as great as it once was. You cannot expect this of me. I did not believe one could still live here. But after I came back, I found out there were many Germans who were not Nazis.

- I love Germany, not the Germans.

- My father was liberated and met my mother in those first few days. It was love at first sight. My parents had planned to emigrate, but then I came along.

- My sister and I came here as children. My father was born in Berlin and my mother in Poland.

- I was born in Israel and began growing up there. Then we came to Germany. My parents were originally from Germany.

- This is how it is: I was born in Germany. My parents were born in Germany. My grandparents, my great-grandparents were all born in Germany. When Jews live again today in Germany, it is a second victory over the Nazis. (*Intervals of Silence*)

This group of voices comprises two distinct, yet overlapping patterns of movement. The first is a circular pattern in which the first, third, and last speakers refer explicitly (whereas the other speakers refer only obliquely) to the Nazi past. The second is an associative chain of ideas that begins with the "love for Germany," followed by the "love at first sight" that leads to the founding of a family, and concludes with other family connections to Germany.

In *Intervals of Silence* this group of Jewish voices directly precedes the group of non-Jewish voices discussed above. The juxtaposition serves to counterbalance Jewish and non-Jewish perspectives, while also underscoring resonances and dissonances between the two sets of voices. Distanced remarks in the third-person plural can thus be viewed in relation to intimate references to a "love for Germany." Or the notion that "living together has become normal" can be measured against the claim that Jews living in Germany is "a second victory over the Nazis."

As I began connecting one group of voices with another to form larger sections of the film, my editing began to suggest a dialogue between Jewish and non-Jewish voices. It was as if these voices were responding to each other, and not to me. Having edited out my own voice asking questions, I needed to find some other way to acknowledge my dual role as listener (in the interview context) and as interpreter (in the editing process).

My solution was to intersperse short passages of voice-over narration throughout the film. This narration conveys, incrementally, my own story of growing up Jewish in America, meeting Georg, and reexamining my feelings about Germany in the context of our relationship. Placed at the intersections (although not at every intersection) between groups of text, my narration casts me both as a speaker alongside other speakers and also as an outside commentator on those speakers.

Between the two groups of excerpts discussed above—one containing

Jewish voices and one, non-Jewish voices—I inserted my narration (noted earlier) about my first visit to Germany with Georg to meet his family. My remarks thus serve to link these two groups of voices. Repeating the dominant motif from the Jewish voices, I explain my own presence in Germany in terms of a love relationship. Then, foreshadowing the theme that runs throughout the non-Jewish voices, I express my concern about the response in Germany to my being Jewish—specifically, Georg's mother's response.

Germany's Nazi past, which I do not (but other Jewish speakers do) explicitly acknowledge, provides some of the subtext for my nervousness about meeting Georg's mother (in addition to the usual nervousness associated with meeting one's future mother-in-law). The comments of other Germans might be perceived as the responses I feared (but did not hear) from Georg's mother. But whereas some residents of this city "hardly speak" or are "almost ashamed to say" anything about Jews, Georg did speak with his mother.

Speaking and the ramifications of speaking—as well as the "intervals of silence" when speaking does not occur—are the central issues of my film. I focused on the interviews before considering the film footage, but the visual strategies paralleled the textual strategies in many respects.

. . .

Just as I conducted interviews with a cross section of the city's residents, so too I filmed a broad range of the city's motifs. These motifs included, for example, places of historic interest, places of work, and places of leisure and recreation. I was interested in learning what images people associated with living in this city in order to encompass visually as many different perspectives as I had recorded in the sound track.

The film begins with several unambiguous images: the steeple of a church; the somber, gray facade of a building; a nearly empty residential street. In the film's first voice-over narration I explain: "These are all familiar places from Georg's childhood. This is the church where he was baptized. This is where he went to school. And this is the street where Georg's family lives" (*Intervals of Silence*).

Most of what follows this introduction, however, undermines a one-to-one correlation between text and image. Drawing my film imagery from typical scenes of everyday life, I was aware that visual experiences of the city—those I captured on film—might be shared points of reference for all city residents. But the personal experiences associated with those images would not be the same—nor would they be the same for members of an audience viewing the images in my film.

The image of the church steeple, for example, denotes one of the places in this city with special meaning for Georg. This, at least, is what I say in my narration. But this image actually embodies a more complicated web of meanings. The church is not only the place where Georg was baptized. Situated at the entrance to Georg's street in the heart of the old city, it is clearly visible above the treetops as one approaches the old city from the autobahn. Thus the church steeple signals, for Georg, the proximity of home. But it also signifies, for him, a continuity with Germany's past. As he explained to me: "We still have the same trees. We still have the same cityscape. The street configuration is the same. Even the gutters are the same. The church has remained" (Michels).[7] Georg's idea for the film was to turn the camera on the old buildings, which, in his words, stand as "silent witnesses" of what happened in this city.

From my perspective, however, the prominence of church steeples is an uncomfortable reminder of the domination of Christian symbols—and of the absence of comparable Jewish markers—in this German landscape. My idea for the film was to use the camera as a means of distorting the commonplace by inserting the jagged edges of memory, and thus disrupting the veneer of everyday life in which everything seemed to be in order. I was aware of "looking around and seeing not just the city, but seeing what used to be in the city, what could have been in the city, what isn't in the city" (Michels), and I wanted viewers of my film to have this awareness as well.

Where was a Jewish presence visible in this city? Before the Second World War, residents could have located a number of Jewish sites: Jewish-owned stores, a Jewish school, a synagogue, a community center. But when I asked Georg on our first visit to Germany where I could go to celebrate a Jewish holiday with other Jews, he simply didn't know. After making a number of telephone calls, "he discovered there was a small Jewish congregation in his city and that services were held right around the corner from the school he had attended for nine years" (*Intervals of Silence*).

How could Georg have walked past a Jewish place of worship on a daily basis and not been aware of its existence? During all those years (and in fact, until the spring of 1997), services were held in an ordinary-looking three-story apartment house.[8] Set back from the street, the house could be accessed only from a driveway running between two other buildings. There was no sign visible from the street, or even from the front of the building, to indicate the presence of a Jewish prayer hall.

In other words, one had to be specifically looking for the prayer hall. And even if one were looking, it would not be easy to find. The address and telephone number, for example, were not listed in the telephone book. Considered from this perspective, it is not surprising that non-Jewish residents in this city (including Georg) remained unaware of its location.

In order to simultaneously convey familiar images of German everyday life and acknowledge Jewish absence from these images, I used the processes of optical printing and matte photography to superimpose one image on top of another. The two layers are visually distinct: one color, the other black-and-white; one moving, the other static. But neither layer remains intact: color intrudes into the light areas — and is in turn masked by the dark areas — of the black-and-white image. I then superimposed printed English translations of the spoken German over the dark areas (where the color had been erased) in the composite layered images. The resulting interplay of text and image suggests that fragmentation and omission are essential components of experience from any individual standpoint.

To illustrate how I worked with text/image relationships, let me return to the edited groups of texts discussed above. The entire sequence, as it appears in my film, begins with three color images accompanied by the sounds of birds chirping: a long shot of a field, a medium shot of a flower garden, and a close-up of flowers. The next image, accompanied by Jewish voices speaking about their family connections to Germany, depicts laundry blowing in the wind (color layer), seen in the distance through the opening in a window frame (black-and-white layer). The interior space in front of the window is completely dark, and this is where the English titles appear.

My narration about traveling to Germany to meet Georg's family marks a visual transition: a color image reveals a table, set for family breakfast, in front of a large window. However, the view through the window is overexposed and therefore appears as a blank screen.

Next, non-Jewish voices speak about Jews living in Germany while the white silhouette of a woman can be seen washing a large window. Outside the window, where the view should be, is complete darkness, and this is where the English titles appear. With the wiping motion of the woman's hand across the darkened surface of the window, it appears as if she were erasing, or attempting to erase, the printed text from a chalkboard.

At first glance, the relationship between laundry hanging outside to dry and Jewish voices, or non-Jewish voices and the washing of a window, may not be obvious. And yet the very question about what either of these images has to do with Jews in Germany is exactly the point. Jewish presence is embedded within the everyday life of this city, but it is not easily identified. My initial expectation (and perhaps also the viewer's expectation) was that Jewish life in Germany plays itself out in a series of dramatic episodes against the backdrop of the Holocaust. Present-day reality, however, is far more banal. And so, while a voice proclaims "a second victory over the Nazis," a pink nightgown on the clothesline billows upward in the wind.

The window-washing image can be interpreted along the same lines. And yet in conjunction with non-Jewish voices refusing, for the most part, to see any difficulties for Jews in present-day Germany, the blank window through which nothing can be seen (except a reflection of the speakers' own words) acquires an additional meaning. The specific association of standing behind a window and not seeing (what is happening to Jews) is reinforced by verbal allusions in a later section of the film. In that section, two non-Jewish speakers remember prewar relationships with Jews and also remember witnessing the deportations from behind closed windows:

- One night I woke up and there was horrible shouting out in the street. I ran to the window and called, "Pia, Pia!" I saw her. I recognized her. And then my mother pulled me away from the window because I was screaming. I never saw her again.

- My parents were very much opposed to Nazism. All the same, I ask myself today why my parents, who had such good relations with Jews, did not throw themselves in front of the truck when it came to deport the Jews. I remember my mother standing behind the curtain and crying. (*Intervals of Silence*)

The entire visual sequence I have just discussed revolves around images of windows and the spaces they define: laundry viewed through a window, a table illuminated by a window, a woman washing a window. But it is only in the last image of the window sequence that Jewish presence is finally located in the Jewish prayer hall, as it was for me when I first came to this city with Georg.

A color image of a stained-glass window introduces a series of three close-ups of the interior, while my voice-over narration relates Georg's discovery of the proximity of the prayer hall to his former school. The prayer-hall window, so clearly linked to the Jewish presence suggested by voices heard earlier in the film, was, in fact, one of the few visual indications of this presence I was able to document with my camera.

Windows normally facilitate vision far beyond one's actual physical location, yet so many of the speakers in my film had difficulties seeing beyond the confines of their own experience.[9] Thus, my documentary portrait of a contemporary German city ends up foregrounding the subjectivity, and partiality, of the very act of viewing. In creating a multilayered film structure, I constantly bring two issues to the viewer's attention. First, I acknowledge that responses to presumably straightforward visual phenomena—such as a church steeple, or a window—may be many and varied. Second, I account for what is absent from view because it either no longer exists, or, as in the case of the Jewish prayer hall, one doesn't know where to look for it.

But to renounce any claim to objective vision has implications for the viewing of my film as well as for the making of it. If I accept the multiplicity of perspectives among the residents of my husband's German hometown, then I must also be prepared for the multiplicity of responses from viewers of my film. I hope that by raising the issue of subjectivity I will encourage viewers to consciously question where they stand—in relation to me, and in relation to other speakers in the film—and perhaps to explore a shift in their own position as a result.

· · ·

For me personally, the process of making *Intervals of Silence* allowed me to explore questions I wanted to ask, but for which I was (I recall telling Georg at the outset) afraid to hear the answers. From the distance of my life in America, my questions about Jewish identity in the aftermath of the Holocaust often seemed overwhelming. Georg, I recall, wondered whether I wouldn't be surprised at the banality of most German responses.

The film provided a context, outside the circle of Georg's family, in which to consider my own Jewish presence in Germany. After numerous subsequent visits, I find that I share (with Jewish speakers in my film) the sense that belonging in Germany is not only a matter of family ties and individual choice, but also of societal acceptance.

I am not surprised that many Jewish speakers struggle with the ambivalence and the affinity they feel for Germany. But I am profoundly moved by the non-Jewish speaker who points out, "One might also ask: Why do

Germans, who would love to escape their own history, why do the children of the perpetrators live *here*? I think we cannot escape our historical inheritance" (*Intervals of Silence*).

Ultimately, then, *here* could be as specific a place as the one created during a conversation that succeeds in overcoming the barriers of a divisive past. One speaker—and only one in all my interviews—referred to *here* in this way. This speaker used *we* to mean himself and me, not himself and other Germans, and attempted to include me in a shared experience of being *here*:

> if we really concern ourselves with [the German past] . . . the encounter is perhaps more difficult, or the things which then, uh, after all go into the subconscious, make it more difficult for the individual, let's say, to forget or, uh, to encounter the other openly and freely. That is my wish, that we will not repress [the past] and encounter each other, but will instead simply concern ourselves with it. [And] when we have concerned ourselves with it, we will encounter each other just as we are sitting across from each other here now, and, uh, uh, somehow, let's say, will be humanly happy that we are speaking with one another. (D-45B)

And so I conclude, as I concluded my film, not with unequivocal answers to my questions, but with answers I can live with nonetheless: "When I come to this city, I don't have the feeling that I cannot be Jewish here, although there are other cities that are more comfortable for me as a Jew. Sometimes the presence of other Jewish voices here or the singing of a melody familiar to me from my childhood is enough to give me the feeling that I am at home" (*Intervals of Silence*). And then the Jewish melody "Adon Olam," familiar to me from countless Sabbath services, resounds as the film's credits roll.

NOTES

1. I avoid using the terms *Germans* and *Jews*, which seem to suggest mutually exclusive categories. Since it is possible to be both German and Jewish, I prefer to speak about Jewish or non-Jewish Germans.
2. For purposes of clarity, I state here (and elsewhere) that interviews were limited to residents of my husband's hometown. However, at the time of my interviews (1985–86) a single Jewish congregation served the population of ten neighboring communities. Thus, strictly speaking, my interviews were drawn from the area served by the Jewish congregation. Out of consideration for those speakers who

requested anonymity when the original interviews for *Intervals of Silence: Being Jewish in Germany* were conducted, I have deleted the name of the town whenever it appears in quoted excerpts, replacing it with [this city] or simply [city].

3. Here and throughout this essay, I have translated all excerpts quoted from the original German of the interviews. With only one exception, I refer to my interviews by code number rather than by name in order to protect the anonymity of the speakers.

4. Lakoff and Johnson point out that the meaning of a sentence does not necessarily reside in the sentence itself; "it matters a lot who is saying or listening to the sentence" (12).

5. Note that here as elsewhere in this essay when I quote from *Intervals of Silence*, a bullet indicates a new speaker.

6. Henryk Broder observed a similar, albeit more sinister, relationship between emotional detachment and the language of intimacy in an essay published in the German weekly news magazine *Der Spiegel*: "One could also say the collective of perpetrators doesn't want to let go of the collective of victims, whereby the holding on in this instance takes the form of an emphatic embrace of dead souls" (70). I have translated here from the original German.

7. Before going to Germany to conduct interviews and complete the principal shooting for *Intervals of Silence*, Georg and I recorded several conversations with each other in which we discussed the work we planned to do. Some of Georg's comments from these conversations ended up in the film.

8. When I began research for my film in 1985, the Jewish congregation numbered between seventy and eighty members. Since German reunification, this congregation (along with the Jewish population of Germany as a whole) has experienced extraordinary growth, due primarily to the immigration of Russian Jews. To accommodate an increased membership of more than eleven hundred, a new synagogue building was very publicly dedicated in February 1997.

9. The metaphor of the window appears in many writings by both filmmakers and film theorists to describe documentary film practice. John Grierson, considered by film historian Richard M. Barsam to be "the father of the documentary film movement in the English-speaking world" (77), outlined his principles of documentary in the 1930s. He praised the ability of documentary filmmakers to observe from real life, noting that studio films "largely ignore this possibility of opening up the screen on the real world" (qtd. in Hardy 146). By the 1960s, lightweight, portable sync sound equipment permitted Direct Cinema practitioners in the United States such as Richard Leacock, the Maysles brothers, and D. A. Pennebaker to champion the filmmaker as an "impartial and unobtrusive observer capturing the sight and sound of real life" (Reynolds 403). According to D. A. Pennebaker, a film is "just a window someone peeps through" (qtd. in Winston 43). Nearly two decades later, film theorist Bill Nichols wrote of the need "to rescue documentary from the . . . argument that documentary-equals-reality, and that the screen is a window rather than a reflecting surface" (172).

REFERENCES

Barsam, Richard M. *Nonfiction Film. A Critical History*. Revised and expanded edition. Bloomington: Indiana University Press, 1992.

Broder, Henryk M. "Dabeisein ist alles. Ein Expertenkolloquium berät erneut über ein 'Denkmal für die ermordeten Juden Europas.' Doch die deutsche Gedenk-Industrie muß scheitern." *Der Spiegel* (7 April 1997): 70–74.

D-5. Personal interview conducted by Deborah Lefkowitz. Audiocassette. Sides A and B. Summer 1985.

D-6. Personal interview conducted by Deborah Lefkowitz. Audiocassette. Side B. Summer 1985.

D-13. Personal interview conducted by Deborah Lefkowitz. Audiocassette. Side A. Summer 1985.

D-31. Personal interview conducted by Deborah Lefkowitz. Audiocassette. Sides A and B. Summer 1985.

D-39. Personal interview conducted by Deborah Lefkowitz. Audiocassette. Sides A and B. Summer 1985.

D-40. Personal interview conducted by Deborah Lefkowitz. Audiocassette. Sides A and B. Summer 1985.

D-45. Personal interview conducted by Deborah Lefkowitz. Audiocassette. Side B. Summer 1985.

Hardy, Forsyth, ed. *Grierson on Documentary*. Revised edition. Berkeley: University of California Press, 1966.

Intervals of Silence: Being Jewish in Germany. Directed by Deborah Lefkowitz. Lefkowitz Films, 1990. 16mm, 58 min.

Lakoff, George, and Mark Johnson. *Metaphors We Live By*. Chicago: University of Chicago Press, 1980.

Michels, Georg. D-1. Personal interview conducted by Deborah Lefkowitz. Audiocassette. Sides A and B. 3 April 1985.

Nichols, Bill. *Ideology and the Image: Social Representation in the Cinema and Other Media*. Bloomington: Indiana University Press, 1981.

Reynolds, Charles. "Focus on Al Maysles." *The Documentary Tradition*. Selected, arranged, and introduced by Lewis Jacobs, 400–405. 2d ed. New York: Norton, 1979.

Winston, Brian. "The Documentary Film as Scientific Inscription." In *Theorizing Documentary*, edited by Michael Renov, 37–57. New York: Routledge, 1993.

Anthropology

From *The Broken Cord*

In 1982, while in the Twin Cities to deliver a lecture at the University of Minnesota, I had paid a courtesy call to Stan Shepard, a program officer at the Bush Foundation. The Native American Studies Program at Dartmouth was forever on the lookout for new sources of funding, and Bush had a reputation for having an interest in American Indian higher education. Our conversation produced no grants to my program—the foundation for the most part confined its philanthropic activities to the states of the upper Midwest—but it did result in an invitation that was to have a profound and enduring impact on my understanding of Adam's [Dorris's son] condition.

Stan proposed that I join him on several of his upcoming trips to South Dakota reservations. As a matter of policy, Bush staff members, accompanied by one or two outside consultants, normally did a site interview with each organization that had a pending application for financial support. While I was by no means an expert on tribal matters in South Dakota, I did have academic credentials and some experience in the general area of Indian affairs.

I was glad for the opportunity to visit the West, to take a break from the routine of teaching. I missed being among adult Indians, missed the staccato cadence of speech, the gentle in-jokes, enjoyed the long drives through almost empty country. When you've lived for a while as a part of one tribal community in North America, any reservation can have the feel of home to it. Louise did her writing at our farmhouse, seated at a high stool before a desk made from a spare door. The children were all in school, and so when the Bush invitation came, for the first time in ten years I felt com-

pletely free to accept, with no anxiety or guilt, an interesting job that kept
me away overnight.

. . .

The Holiday Inn in Rapid City might as well be ten thousand miles from
the village of Pine Ridge on the huge Sioux reservation of the same name,
but on good days it takes only two hours to drive between the two. The
road, that early spring morning as Stan and I set out, was the warmest spot
on the land, a wet, black Magic-Marker line upon which the snow had
melted faster than it had on the scruffy range that stretched on either side.
The route south winds through a corner of the Badlands, turns to skate the
edges of jagged arroyos, and undercuts sheer bluffs as barren during seasons
of cold or drought as any desert.

   And yet everywhere there was the rush of life. Prairie dogs stretched
upright like sentries to watch the approach of our rented car, then dove for
cover so late that only a glance in the rearview mirror confirmed their escape. The silhouettes of deer surfaced now and then on the peripheral rises,
fragile dark cutouts outlined by sky. Overhead, eagles and red-tailed hawks
made tangents to the circle of approaching, dissolving horizon which on
the high plains, or at sea, so perfectly describes the curve of the earth. In the
leased fields cattle grazed with their noses pressed to the ground, their satin
lips pulled back into smiles that allowed their teeth to scrape for frozen
grass. Stan and I had been told to watch for antelope, for elk, but saw instead
only the cartoon-flat impressions of rattlers, a stationary parade of snakes.
Hung over from the long winter, lulled by the sun, they had dozed on this
north-south highway and were crushed beneath the wheels of speeding
pickups, dawn delivery trucks, low-slung vintage Pontiacs, peeling from
one out-of-the-way dot on a large map to another.

   The only stations we could receive without static were country and
western or National Public Radio, a curious rivalry of heart and mind that
somehow complemented each other in the steady, uninterrupted turn of
miles. There was time for both. We crossed the reservation boundary, an invisible divide just shy of the Long Branch Saloon in Scenic, the single enterprise along the way. It was a combination bar and emporium that retained,
like a memory that couldn't be reconciled, one sign forbidding Indians to
enter and another offering beadwork for sale within. Behind the building
stretched a tangle of smashed cars, their bright paint turning monochrome
in the constant assault of weather.

   Our destination was a rehabilitation and treatment center for teenagers

with "chemical dependencies," the only such facility, according to its application for Bush assistance, on any reservation in North or South Dakota,
Nebraska, Wyoming, or Montana. Project Phoenix had maximum occupancy of under twenty beds, a capacity far too small for the demand. Its
population arrived as referrals from tribal courts, boys and girls at the end
of their rope at fourteen or fifteen, children addicted not only to alcohol
or conventional drugs, but to those very popular reservation highs, favored
only in communities so poor that nothing else is available: "huffing" (the
inhalation of fumes from a gas tank); glue; clear nail polish; dimestore perfume; Sterno; rubbing alcohol. These were the hard-case kids, the ones
with no place else to go, and there was an ever-expanding waiting list. In
the budget cuts to Indian health care, already begun under the new Reagan administration and soon to double, triple, Project Phoenix was the last
stop. It was go there, or sleep in abandoned cars. It was there or tribal jail,
a single-cell lock-up that housed adults and juveniles together, regardless
of the nature of the offense. It was there or nowhere.

As we drove the county roads toward Kyle, Stan and I reviewed the
nightmare statistics and wondered, could the crisis be this bad? Was this the
language of hyperbole, of a sharp-cookie administrator who knew how to
push the right buttons of a St. Paul foundation? We believed that we had no
illusions about the extreme deprivations on Pine Ridge, Cheyenne River,
Rosebud, and yet . . . the conditions described in the narrative sounded
like something out of *The Inferno*. This was America, this was the Reagan
eighties, the me-decade. Pine Ridge had, in the eyes of the Supreme Court
of the United States, the status of a nation, a government-to-government
relationship with Washington.

We took the turnoff onto a potholed road that led to the jail, a small,
squat modern building with a brick and glass facade. Next door, as if
underlining the words we had just spoken, contradicting the doubts we
had expressed, was a ragtag cluster of battered mobile homes, a prefabricated house, a few parked pickups. Over the entrance, a knocked-together
wooden platform with a mat for wiping muddy boots, was a sign, PROJECT
PHOENIX. The director, a smiling Sioux man of about forty, stepped out
to greet us. He wore glasses, had a breast pocket full of pens clipped onto a
plastic lining to protect his shirt from ink stains. The staff had been worried
about us, he said. They had expected us earlier. They had fixed a dinner in
our honor, and we'd better eat soon or it would be spoiled.

Stan apologized — we had miscalculated the time it would take — and we
followed the man through the door into what he called the common room,

the place alternately used for group counseling and television, for in-take and recreation. The room was empty of people. Its walls were lined with cheap couches, with plastic lounge chairs. Coffee tables were laden with clean ashtrays and neatly stacked magazines. The linoleum floor was spotless: we had indeed been expected. On the panel-board walls were posters —many of them featuring Indian-looking characters—warning against addictions of every type.

There was a noise behind us, and I moved to make room for three young boys, "clients" the director called them, to enter. Ignoring our presence, they turned on the TV, dropped onto chairs and couches, and stared straight ahead.

I stared too. They could have been Adam's twin brothers. They resembled him in every facial feature, in every gesture, in body type. They came from a living situation as different as possible from an eighteenth-century farmhouse in rural New Hampshire; they were bare survivors of family crisis, of violence, of abuse—otherwise they wouldn't be at Project Phoenix—and Adam, after the dislocations of his first three years, had been protected, defined as "special," monitored in his every phase of development. Yet there was something so uncannily familiar to me about these boys, about their facial expressions and posture, their choice of television program, their screening out of all but a few elements in the environment that surrounded them. The correspondences seemed too great for mere coincidence; they were not superficial either. The fact that these boys and Adam shared the same ethnic group was far less central to their similarities than was the unmistakable set of fine tunings that transformed disparate individuals into the same general category. Some common denominator was obvious—clear as it would have been if in a gathering of people only a few had blue skin, were seven feet tall, spoke a language no one else understood.

The director saw my confusion and shot a question mark in my direction.

"I have a son," I told him and reached into my wallet for a photograph.

He examined the picture, nodded, and handed it back. "FAS too, huh?" he asked.

The bureaucratic world of Indian affairs is full of triplicate acronyms—BIA, HEW, JOM—but this was a new one on me.

"FAS?"

"Fetal Alcohol Syndrome," he said. "Most of the kids we get are FAS or FAE—Fetal Alcohol Effect. They come from alcoholic families, mothers who drank. Your wife too?"

"He's adopted," I answered. "And, yes, his mother did drink. But he's been with me since he was very small."

"Doesn't matter. There aren't many FAS who live with their birth mothers after a certain point, or if there are, we don't see them. Whatever the booze does, it happens before the kid is born." He reached for Adam's photograph, which I still held.

"You see the eyes?" he pointed out. "The small head? See how thin he is? He's what, thirteen or fourteen? If you didn't know better, you'd think he was a lot younger."

I saw what the man meant. He was right on every count. I looked back at the boys sprawled on the couch. In their fixated concentration on the program, their mouths gaped in a too-familiar way.

"Do these boys, the ones who come to Project Phoenix, have learning problems?" I asked. "Do they have trouble with things like money?"

The director laughed, not unpleasantly but not with real humor either. "Are you kidding?" he said. "Money. Time. You name it. And the worst thing is, they don't learn from experience. We train them, run them through counseling, set them up with voc-ed, whatever, and in a couple weeks or a couple, three, days the court's petitioning them to come back here. Same story. They stole. They huffed. They didn't report in to their parole officer. They were fooling around with some girl who didn't like it."

"What finally works for them?" I asked, ready to go home and try whatever he suggested.

"What works for them?" he repeated. "What works? Not a goddamn thing."

A woman came out of the kitchen, smiled, and called us to the meal she and others had fixed. Three tables had been pushed together, and on them was laid out a full traditional Thanksgiving dinner: turkey, stuffing, mashed potatoes, cranberry sauce, molded jello salad, sliced bread, and margarine in a bright yellow tub. It was offered with an unassuming largesse and hospitality that bespoke traditional Indian people, a generosity toward guests both ingrained and natural, a celebration of values the more striking because it occurred in this place of overpowering need. Every dish had been prepared with care and tasted delicious, but I had to force myself to eat. I kept glancing through the door at the boys watching television—because of space limitations they would eat their helpings of this meal later with the other clients. And I kept seeing Adam. I didn't know any more about FAS than what the director had volunteered, but I held onto those three letters like clues. When I went back to Dartmouth, I would flesh them out.

• • •

Over the course of the next three years I made many Bush Foundation visits to Dakota reservations—to Pine Ridge, Rosebud, Standing Rock, Turtle Mountain, Devil's Lake, Crow Creek—and the contrast between the grim conditions I observed in the West and the manicured, academic detachment of Dartmouth became increasingly more difficult for me to reconcile. There is a luxury to intellectual neutrality, and also an arrogance. The same sought-after "objectivity" that led a campus ethics committee of which I was a member to formally abjure "immediate" issues stood as a convenient barrier to all confusing intrusions that might disrupt the flow of dispassionate thought. Scholarship by its very nature aspires to be above the ebb and flow of daily events, to take the long view. There is no enduring place for the frantic, the desperate, the hysterical.

The life of the mind is ideally serene, and so when I moved to the classroom from the poverty, the multiplying economic and health crises that defined the existence of northern plains Indians, I protected myself with glib rejoinders. It would do no good to rant at the undergraduates who sat in rows before me. They were by and large the sons and daughters of the privileged, blooming with good health, dressed in the newest fashions. The problems with which they came to me as advisor were for the most part wonderfully solvable. Any sense of reality outside their experience had to be insinuated, couched in unthreatening language, if it was to be heard. Generalized guilt, of course, was easy to engender, but equally easy for students to forget in the stroll to their next lecture, their aerobics class, their enormous dining room. In their heart of hearts these well-intentioned young men and women were irrefutably sure that the miseries of the world were not their fault, and in any case their course schedules ensured that each instructor would barrage them with appeals for the relevance and centrality of his or her concern. They had learned to be wary, to withhold their fervor.

Even the Native American student organization took a measured approach to the demands of crises on distant reservations. The admissions office had perfected its techniques since the early 1970s, and the Indians who matriculated at Dartmouth were now often drawn from more affluent economic backgrounds and were less a contrast with their campus peers. The dropout rate was down, fraternity/sorority membership was up, and many had daily concerns far removed from the anger I felt upon the completion of each round-trip to Rapid City or Pierre. I lost my patience with them, and therefore my credibility, for a year, because of one meeting in which I too passionately exhorted the group to spend the bulk of its activities' budget on an issues-related conference or on a direct donation to a community child-neglect project instead of overfinancing the annual May powwow.

It seemed that the more I delved into the ballooning emergency of fetal alcohol syndrome among Indian people, the more I became unmoored from the internal preoccupations of the Ivy League. For many in Hanover, New Hampshire, the burning question about Indians still, after more than a decade's debate, centered on the nickname formerly given to the athletic teams. Every year new generations of freshmen had to be "educated" to the idea that it was inappropriate to turn the image of an oppressed people into a caricature, a negative *or* positive stereotype, for half-time entertainment. As early as 1974 the Board of Trustees had officially concurred with this assessment and banned any official use of the logo. However, in protest against this supposed restriction of their right to be insensitive if they chose, some alumni and a few students proudly hawked Indian-head paraphernalia: door mats, emblazoned clothing, bumper stickers. They took opinion polls, passed out petitions on street corners, even decorated themselves with jagged stripes of greasepaint to assert their position.

Such willful ignorance was hard for some, Indian and non-Indian, to digest, but, juxtaposed with Pine Ridge, for me it became numbing. I returned from one early-October excursion on a red-eye flight and came directly to campus to prepare for my class. I had spoken to no one since leaving a facility near the village of Porcupine devoted to treating little boys who had been sexually abused by drunken adults. The place was run by a Roman Catholic brother, soon to be transferred by his order for a bureaucratic reason incomprehensible to all concerned, and though the need was great and growing, the shelter would likely soon be closed for lack of funds.

As I rummaged through my lecture notes, trying to construct a two-hour explanation of the political underpinnings of the Iroquois Confederacy, there was a knock at my office door. I opened it to three elderly men, the expressions on their scrubbed faces bright and eager. Still in the mode of reservation protocol, I automatically deferred what I was doing to their advanced age, invited them inside, and offered my hand; but they held their ground.

"Are you Professor Dorris?" the middle one of them asked.

"Yes," I smiled.

"Well," he glanced at his two companions and then, in concert, the trio pulled open their coats to reveal Indian symbol T-shirts and loudly chanted, "Wah Hoo Wah"—the former Dartmouth Indians' football cheer.

We faced each other, not two feet apart, and yet in different universes. The old grads were pleased with themselves: they had risen early, dressed with intent to insult, and bearded their tormentor in his den. Mission accomplished. What did I have to say to *this*, their eyes demanded.

I took a step back and closed the door. I had received in the mail an application from the Rockefeller Foundation for a year-long independent study fellowship, and that day I filled it out, requesting support for full-time research on fetal alcohol syndrome and its impact on some of the reservation communities I had visited. I called Louise for her consent, then formally petitioned the dean for a leave of absence.

· · ·

The following winter I was promoted to full professor, *Love Medicine* was the dark-horse winner of the National Book Critics Circle Award for Fiction, a draft of Louise's second novel, *The Beet Queen*, was completed, and my Rockefeller grant was approved. I was earning an extra paycheck by teaching an advanced aerobics class for fifty participants three times a week at the gym in Hanover, and I had begun my own novel, *A Yellow Raft in Blue Water*.

Louise and I had become involved more and more with each other's writing, from the conception of fictional characters to the final copyediting of a manuscript—though each of us faced the blank page or word processor screen alone. By the time any submission left our house, however, we had achieved—after many a heated literary argument—consensus on every word. As a result, both of us felt responsible for and protective of whatever book, article, poem, review, or story was published, regardless of who got the cover byline. We knew every paragraph by heart, so frequently had it been rewritten and revised.

One April evening after supper, Louise and I unfolded a map of the Midwest and circled the possibilities where we might settle for the twelve months of my fellowship beginning in August. We wanted a location reasonably near to her family and to the reservations I needed to visit, a place with an academic library, with access to an airport, with a good day care center for Persia and Pallas, and, the bottom line, with a quality school system that would benefit Sava and Madeline and where Adam could continue the type of instruction he had begun at Hartford—all of which pointed to a college town. We made circles around Missoula in Montana, Winnipeg in Manitoba, St. Paul, Bemidji, and Northfield in Minnesota, Fargo and Grand Forks in North Dakota, and Rapid City in South Dakota, then contacted friends and associates in those places to see if they could help us find a large, furnished dwelling to lease.

Stan Shepard ultimately provided the best lead: Bill Woerhlin, a history professor at Carleton College in Northfield, an hour south of the Twin Cities, who had worked with the Bush Foundation on several occasions. Bill's wife, Molly, answered the phone when we called, and in a matter of days she had put us in touch with a realty agent who mailed photographs of our ideal house—a huge Victorian a block from campus with six bedrooms and a rent we could afford—and which was available on the exact date we wanted to move in. I talked to the director of special education in the Northfield school system, and she assured me that Adam's current program could be mirrored. Carleton College generously offered us library privileges. We had never spent much time in southern Minnesota, but sight unseen we signed a year's lease, made a down payment on a Dodge Caravan—which would transport all seven of us—and as soon as the Dartmouth summer term was over, we packed our things and headed west.

Less than a month later I was on my way back to Pine Ridge, informed by three years of sporadic textual research on the disability I had first learned about at Project Phoenix. I had reexamined and closely analyzed the record of Adam's medical and psychological examinations, and had reviewed as objectively as possible my memories of his life experience. I had spoken by telephone to some of the most illustrious scientists breaking new ground in the field of teratogens and genetics, and had attended dozens of lectures on the subject of birth disorders. Now I knew at last what questions to ask, and the time had come for me to listen firsthand to the voices of men and women directly involved with the victims and perpetrators of fetal alcohol syndrome.

. . .

In 1968, the year Adam was born, four French scientists published a modest research paper (*Les enfants de parents alcooliques. Anomalies observées*) noting certain recurrent birth defects disproportionately represented among 127 children of alcoholic parents. It was not until 1973, when Adam was five years old and had received his Lakota name, that another team of experts, this one at the University of Washington in Seattle, carried that initial observation a step further. This group, headed by Dr. David W. Smith of the Department of Pediatrics, observed retarded intrauterine growth in ten out of twelve newborn infants of mothers with chronic alcoholism; they ultimately described an apparently consistent pattern of physiological deformities in these children, and gave it a name: fetal alcohol syndrome (FAS). Not instantly recognized as a major breakthrough by most of the academic community, only three scientific or clinical papers on the subject appeared worldwide that year. But it was an idea whose time had come. West German research reports in 1975 and 1976 were followed by Swedish studies in 1975 and 1977, and by 1979, more than 200 FAS-related articles had been published. In 1985, the year Adam was hired at his first part-time job—filling salt and pepper shakers—the annual rate of FAS-related professional documentation had increased to almost 2,000 articles.

The notion that maternal drinking was bad for a baby's health was, of course, not new. The Old Testament of the Hebrew Bible contains a very specific proscription in Judges 13—

> And there was a certain man of Zorah of the tribe of the Nanites, whose name was Mano'ah; and his wife was barren and had no children. And the angel of the Lord appeared to the woman and said to her, "Behold, you are barren and have no children; but you shall conceive and bear a son. Therefore beware, and drink no wine or strong drink, and eat nothing unclean, for lo, you shall conceive and bear a son. No razor shall come upon his head, for the boy shall be a Nazirite to God from birth; and he shall begin to deliver Israel from the hand of the Philistines." Then the woman came and told her husband, "A man of God came to me, and his countenance was like the countenance of the angel of God, very terrible; I did not ask him whence he was, and he did not tell me his name; but he said to me, 'Behold, you shall conceive and bear a son; so then drink no wine or strong drink, and eat nothing unclean, for the boy shall be a Nazirite to God from birth to the day of his death.'" (2–7)[1]

As early as 322 B.C., Aristotle, in his *Problemata*, noted that "foolish, drunken, or hare-brained women for the most part bring forth children like unto themselves, difficult and listless." Plato suggested that alcohol should be barred "to any man or woman who was intending to create children. . . . Children should not be made in bodies saturated with drunkenness." Plutarch (120 A.D.) observed that "one drunkard begats another," and the Babylonian *Talmud* (200–500 A.D., Kehuboth 32b) warned pregnant women: "One who drinks intoxicating liquor will have ungainly children." In ancient Carthage there existed a ban against consuming liquor on the wedding night for fear that a defective child might be conceived.

During the so-called "gin epidemic" in England from 1720–1750, when cheap drink was for the first time widely available, the British Royal College of Physicians warned in a report to Parliament that parental drinking was a "cause of weak, feeble, and distempered children." A century later, another scientific committee advised the House of Commons that the children born to alcoholic mothers had a "starved, shrivelled, and imperfect look." It was even worse than that, according to William Sullivan, a physician for a Liverpool prison. In 1899 he published findings to the effect that alcoholic women had a stillbirth and infant death rate of 56 percent, more than double that of their nondrinking female relatives.[2]

The 1973 Seattle researchers presented their findings in the British journal *Lancet*, identifying a number of newborn traits which they associated with maternal drinking. These included prenatal and postnatal growth deficiency; a particular pattern of facial malformations, including small head circumference, flattened midface, sunken nasal bridge, and a smoothed and elongated philtrum (the groove between the nose and upper lip); central nervous system dysfunction; and varying degrees of organ system malformation.[3] In other words, some infants produced by women who consistently used large amounts of alcohol during their pregnancies were smaller, developed more slowly, and looked different from the babies of mothers who used no alcohol; they also more or less shared certain other health problems which clinically set them apart from the newborn population as a whole.

On the surface, this was a startling, radical, even infuriating assertion to some physicians who, in good conscience, had been long in the habit of actually prescribing a calming glass of wine or beer, or an occasional celebratory drink, to their pregnant clients. There were even instances in which premature labor was forestalled by means of an intravenous injection of an alcohol-based solution.

As recently as 1974, a standard reference and medical school textbook, *Pharmacological Basis of Therapeutics* by Louis Goodman and Alfred Gilman, maintained that "alcohol gains free access to fetal circulation, *but it does not seem to harm the fetus*."[4] Though this misinformation was corrected in the 1980 and subsequent editions of the volume, it was the voice of instruction for many students who are presently now practicing doctors and supported the established habits of many of their patients and colleagues. Social drinking, after all, is considered part of American culture, a basic right, like smoking or hand-gun ownership; a notorious period of national lawbreaking occurred in response to the legal prohibition of liquor sales in the 1920s, and in many states the production of wine or spirits is a major industry and employer. "*Our* mothers drank," protested many indignant dissenters to early FAS warnings, "and look at us."

Such a reaction prompts a number of possible responses, the most benign being that women in their mothers' generation probably didn't, as a class, consume as much as many women do in the 1980s. Statistically, in contemporary North America nine out of ten women of child-bearing age are said to drink occasionally. Reliable figures suggest that seven out of ten of these women drink regularly, on the average of one drink per day. Five to ten percent of the women in this same age group qualify as confirmed alcoholics—and the overall total of women within the population who consume ethanol in any form is dramatically on the upswing. In recent years, the ratio of new female drinkers to male has increased by two to one. Among college students, for instance, the estimated number of male drinkers rose about 3 percent between 1953 and 1974; during the same period, the equivalent figure for females was 12 percent. This disturbing trend (matched by a similar surge in female smoking) may be due to any of several causes, but it undeniably parallels other broad, more positive social changes for women within the same time period. Thanks to concerted political effort, women have made statistical gains vis-à-vis men in such areas as salary parity and education, and have achieved greater leadership roles in business and government. However, the process of discarding oppressive and stereotypical roles has not been universally beneficial: liberated of external sanctions discouraging their participation in what were previously guarded as exclusive "masculine" domains, women are now "free" to do, and increasingly are doing, just as much harm to their bodies by use of drugs and chemicals as their male counterparts. But there is a key, biologically based difference. Drunk expectant fathers may, at least as far as it is currently known, hurt only themselves and those unfortunate enough to get in their way; drunk expectant mothers can grievously and irreparably cause harm to their unborn infants.

For the past two decades, it has become irrefutably evident that alcohol is a teratogen (a word deriving from the Greek roots "*terrato-*" and "*-genés*," literally, "to make monsters"), the scientific expression for a chemical agent that in certain dosages can cause birth defects. Alarming articles in respected, usually staid, professional publications such as the *American Journal of Obstetric Gynecology* have attested to the fact that alcohol passes the placental barrier freely in certain animals, such as rhesus monkeys. Acute intoxication of the embryo has been recorded for both lambs and human beings. The human fetus has a reduced capacity to eliminate alcohol, and therefore concentrations tend to be higher *in utero* than in the rest of the mother's system by the end of her intoxication and are likely to endure there for longer periods. The baby in the womb becomes more drunk than its mother with every drink of liquor, wine, or beer she takes. By the time she feels tipsy and thus socially or physically compelled to refuse a refill, the child she carries could, in effect, have already passed out. And, as Dr. Cortez F. Enloe, editor of *Nutrition Today*, put it in 1980, "for the fetus, the hangover may last a lifetime." [5]

The physiological process by which the damage takes place is not precisely understood, but in general it is fairly uncomplicated. When a person ingests more alcohol than his or her liver can process, the excess is released into the bloodstream to circulate until it can be detoxified. Once the placenta of a pregnant woman is formed, any raw ethanol present in her body envelops the fetus, where it is distributed in the liver, pancreas, kidney, thymus, heart, and brain, concentrating in the gray matter of the developing child. It may interfere with zinc metabolism, with hormonal balance, or with the ability of the placenta to carry oxygen, thus creating anoxia and subsequent brain damage, especially during the first and third trimesters. Alcohol is a dehydrating agent, so it absorbs water. This is the reason it stings abraded tissue, and this may well be the reason that the brain of a newborn whose mother drank appears desiccated, smaller than it should be—water has been sucked out of the developing cells, killing them outright or rendering them functionless. (The ability of the fetus to eliminate alcohol is only about 50 percent of the adult capacity, meaning that the same amount is present twice as long.) The amniotic fluid itself becomes a kind of alcohol reservoir, and as Dr. Enloe observes, "the mental computer that is constantly bathed in ethyl alcohol soon adapts to that milieu. Short circuits develop and no amount of education in later life can realign them." [6]

Despite the clear logic of these arguments, the scientific community was characteristically cautious in creating or applying a new label to describe this and related conditions. A "syndrome" is little more than the name given for a collection of symptoms that seem to regularly coexist but for which there is rarely a single diagnostic feature and no specific biochemical, chromosomal, or pathological test. For a condition of "full" FAS to be identified, a number of highly specific criteria had to be simultaneously present in a candidate, including: (1) significant growth retardation both before and after birth; (2) measurable mental deficit; (3) altered facial characteristics; (4) other physical abnormalities; and (5) documentation of maternal alcoholism. Many of these points, of course, are hard or next to impossible to calculate. What constitutes "normal" size or growth within the human species? How can genetically inherited features such as nose shape and eyelid formation be compared between members of one race and those of another? What constitutes a working definition for "alcoholism"? Other characteristics were hard to pin on alcohol as their single cause.

Many factors such as nicotine, environmental pollution, malnutrition, certain ingredients in over-the-counter medications ingested during pregnancy, or even inherited genetic traits might account for some of the specific side effects (arterial and ventricular septal defects in the heart, aberrant palmar creases, joint abnormalities, convulsions, hydrocephaly, abnormal EEG activity, small teeth with faulty enamel, curvature of the spine, hearing problems, cleft lip, cleft palate, club foot, increased risk of perinatal death, epilepsy) most often associated with FAS. Moreover, various practices known to be dangerous to fetal health, especially smoking, poor diet, and drug ingestion, are often found coterminus with extreme drinking patterns—one study showed that 65 percent of heavy drinking was associated with smoking in excess of one pack of cigarettes a day—and thus undoubtedly exacerbate or complicate the ravages of alcohol poisoning. Can alcohol consumption be isolated and factored out as the causal core of the collective problem?

The answer is unambiguous: a pregnant white rat that doesn't smoke tobacco or marijuana, take pills, or drink caffeinated coffee but that eats a balanced diet will still deliver a predictably deformed offspring if, in a controlled experiment, it takes in enough ethyl alcohol. Auxiliary bad habits undeniably make a condition worse; drinking causes it.

In regard to human beings, a growing handful of researchers argued that it was more than coincidence when the full range of FAS symptoms consistently appeared in the babies of alcoholic mothers. They devised ex post facto diagnostic tests in which photograph albums of children from various ethnic groups—some of them suspected of having fetal alcohol syndrome, some of them assumed to be healthy—were sent without any designation to other scientists and physicians, who were asked to identify by looks alone which individuals were likely to be impaired. The respondents, with only their own past clinical experience upon which to base their guesses, were highly accurate in selecting the photos of the children at risk for FAS. The compilation of these surveys yielded a composite "FAS face," recognizable to anyone—doctor, counselor, teacher, social worker, parent—used to dealing with the victims of maternal drinking.

It was certainly familiar to me when I first saw it in 1979; it could have been the picture of Adam.

Clinically, alcohol is an insult to the fetus that can be manifested in a wide range of symptoms.

But probably mental deficiency, in varying degrees, is the most debilitating aspect of FAS in those children who survive. The mean IQ for such individuals falls, according to various studies, between 65 and 80, from, in the terminology of psychological testing, "mildly retarded" through "borderline" to "dull normal," although individuals with IQs as low as 15 or as high as 105 have been positively diagnosed. FAS children at all ages and stages of growth lag behind their peers in everything from rate of language acquisition to development of academic skills in arithmetic. Often these learning problems are not apparent until considerably after birth, and they seem to appear quite independently of environment.

Whether children are raised in the chaotic households of their unreformed alcoholic biological mothers or nurtured in stable, sober, loving natural or adoptive homes, the disabilities surface with uniformity. Overriding the nature/nurture debate about whether genetic inheritance or environment has the predominant influence on the construction of human personality, the permanent limitations caused by alcohol seem to be fixed *in utero* and modified only slightly and perhaps temporarily by anything that happens after birth.

Problems with brain cells and organization, like the formation of vital organs, joints, and absolute body size, cannot be repaired. A baby enters the world with all the raw equipment he or she is ever going to get. What's lacking at delivery may not be obvious for ten or fifteen years, but like advance birthday remembrances set to be opened only at certain ages, the beautiful boxes may turn out to be empty or half full.

If all this were true only of children having "full" FAS, it would be bad enough, but in fact that population represents only the smallest visible tip of a very large iceberg. The syndrome can be detected at birth only in the most severe cases, usually occurring exclusively in the offspring of truly

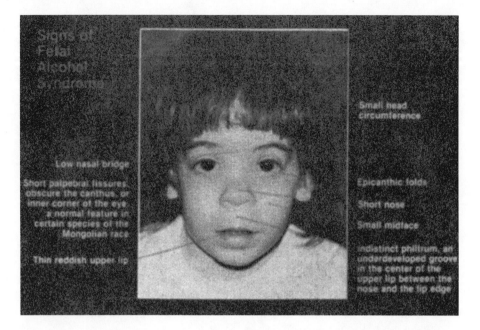

alcoholic women, that is, those who throughout the duration of their pregnancy have regularly consumed more than 100 grams of ethanol each day. That works out to approximately eight beers or slightly less than a pint of whiskey or a bit more than a bottle of wine per day. However, one recent British study[7] has shown that as little as 100 grams per week in the first trimester doubles the risk that the baby will be in less than the tenth percentile for weight compared with nondrinking mothers.

FAS is an equal opportunity affliction. Its victims have been born to women from age fifteen up, of all nationalities and income groups, who ingested every type of liquor, including to some who neither smoked cigarettes nor took any drugs but alcohol during their pregnancies. Rarely will a first baby show signs of full FAS — statistically the average age at birth for the mothers of FAS diagnoses is thirty years, by which time many have borne two to five previous children. As a group, such women rarely seek out prenatal care and often have severe health problems of their own, including, but not confined to, a high incidence of pancreatic and kidney disorders, cirrhosis of the liver, iron deficiency anemia, venereal disease, and general malnutrition. Significantly, many expectant mothers in this category actually lose weight during the course of their pregnancies, since much of their caloric consumption comes from alcohol and is nurturing neither to themselves nor to the child they carry. Underweight women who drink neces-

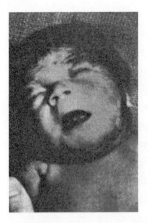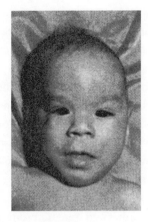

Child with Fetal Alcohol Syndrome photographed at day one, eight months, and four and one half years. This child was diagnosed at birth and has spent all his life in one foster home where the quality of care has been excellent. Despite good school programming, his IQ has remained stable at 40 to 45.

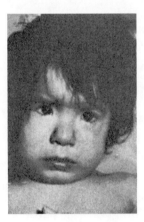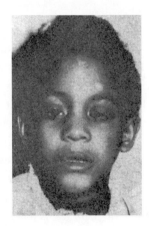

Patients with Fetal Alcohol Syndrome from three racial groups. Photographed at one year, three years and nine months, and two years and six months, respectively.

sarily have higher blood alcohol levels than their heavier counterparts, and protein deficiency might well be due to a lower rate of metabolism and elimination. The cycle of maternal cause and effect is self-perpetuating.

Furthermore, in these women central nervous system (CNS) illnesses, including delerium tremens, are not uncommon. The mothers of those first FAS babies identified in the Seattle study, for instance, were severely at risk themselves, with only about half of the original group surviving more than two years after giving birth. Many factors are important in determining how a particular adult will react to a given dose of alcohol: age, previous pregnancies, duration of drinking history, nutrition, timing (that is, at what stage of pregnancy she consumed specific amounts of ethanol), individual metabolism, or an inherited genetic predisposition related to maternal or paternal drinking behavior. The reaction of each woman to alcohol is unique; the same absolute amount may produce a host of separate outcomes, and different amounts may produce almost identical outcomes, depending on the particular case.

For a woman who imbibes alcoholic beverages more moderately (say, a cocktail or a couple of glasses of white wine several nights a week) or more sporadically (teetotaling, due to morning sickness, for the first trimester; only an occasional beer in the second; then a one-time binge in the third— a critical stage of fetal brain development—in which she consumes five or six drinks in a span of a few hours), the destruction inflicted on the newborn child may be scarcely noticeable to the naked eye, but its effect may still be devastating. Dr. Ronald Forbes, writing in the respected London journal *Public Health* (1984), argues on the basis of several studies that drinking "either before pregnancy or prior to recognition of pregnancy is linked to a variety of neonatal problems, even with an average of only two drinks a day, regardless of whether the drinking is daily or irregular. One ounce of absolute alcohol[8] daily before pregnancy is associated with an average of 91 grams [1–2 ounces] decrease in birth weight.[9]

Fetal Alcohol Effect (FAE), the name given any preparturition alcohol-induced developmental impairment that entails less than the full complement of FAS symptoms, is harder to diagnose, more subtle, but in many respects just as debilitating as the full syndrome—and it is far more widespread within the general population. As Dr. Frank L. Iber points out in a seminal article: "The most exciting recent data reveals new (and disturbing) information about the learning ability of rats and mice born of mothers who have been on diets containing only relatively low levels of alcohol. Anatomically, such infant animals appear in every way to be normal. However, when tested at various stages in later life, it becomes obvious that their learning ability is impaired. . . . It ranges from slight to marked impairment in the ability to learn as demonstrated in such standard tests as shock avoidance maze running, and complex tasks of adaptation experiments that are well characterized in rats."[10] In 1983, Professor V. Cernick announced to a pediatric conference in Canada that only 34 percent of the FAS babies he studied showed the physical deformities considered typical of the syndrome.

At birth, according to Dr. Ann Streissguth and Robin A. LaDue, infants with FAS may be tremulous, irritable, overreactive to sounds, and have feeding difficulties.[11] They typically fail to thrive and show a weak sucking ability. Alcohol effect might surface in a single heart or joint malformation, or it might cause cerebral palsy. In maturing children, the legacy of maternal drinking may become evident in tests that indicate marginal mental retardation or in perception disturbances, short memory span, distractibility, interrupted or unusual sleep patterns, and emotional instability. Later in life, these children may be hyperactive, inattentive, impulsive, fearless, indiscriminate in their reaction to friends and strangers; they may also demonstrate poor motor function or thinking disorders.

In relatively mild cases, FAE might be suggested by a repeated failure to master the multiplication tables, to grasp how to gauge time, or to conform to patterns of social functioning that depend on an internal appreciation of long-term consequences or "morality." It might be indicated by persistent head and body rocking, clumsiness, difficulty with peers, or life management problems. Dr. Forbes reports that FAE children may "show poor judgement and may repeat behaviours that have had bad outcomes in the past. . . . Some of these children have been observed using large vocabularies without really understanding the content of what they are saying. As a result, they may initially sound more capable than they are."[12]

In other words, they don't learn from their mistakes, and they don't know what they're talking about.

Certainly it is true that, considered alone, any one or even two of these deportments might be nothing more than a passing phase of a normal child's development. Certainly, it is true that when grouped in clusters of three or four, these symptoms might be accounted for by any number of causes *other than* or *in addition to* maternal drinking. But when they occur in tandem, when the physical and behavioral anomalies more or less coalesce into a repeated, cumulative set of fixed actions or signs, the alarm bell sounds. The very opposite of deduction by default, a diagnosis of fetal alcohol syndrome or fetal alcohol effect is a reluctant conclusion pressed out by the overpowering weight of connected evidence.

© Michael Dorris 1989

NOTES

1. Dr. Ernest L. Abel, in his fine and comprehensive book *Fetal Alcohol Syndrome and Fetal Alcohol Effects* (New York: Plenum Press, 1984, 1987), argues (2–25) that the subsequent proscriptions against drinking, often cited as evidence that ancient societies recognized the danger of maternal drinking, can be misleading. He makes the valid point that the underlying reasons for these laws and maxims must be understood within the context of the historical period and culture in which they existed. However, the fact remains that though the explanations for these rules may have had other than modern scientific roots, their impact was clearly therapeutic. Before Hebrews grasped the biological concept of trichinosis, they forbade the eating of pork for religious reasons. The end result was the same: it suppressed the incidence of food poisoning. Similarly, no matter why some societies discouraged pregnant or potentially pregnant women from imbibing alcohol, it turned out to be a wise thing for them to do.
2. W. C. Sullivan, "A Note on the Influence of Maternal Inebriety on Offspring," *Journal of Mental Science* (1899) 45: 489–503. This and previous historical references are discussed at length in pp. 1–28 of Abel's *Fetal Alcohol Syndrome and Fetal Alcohol Effects* (1984, 1987).
3. K. L. Jones and D. W. Smith, "Recognition of the Fetal Alcohol Syndrome in Early Infancy," *Lancet* 2 (1973): 999–1001.
4. A. G. Gilman, Louis Goodman, et al., *The Pharmacological Basis of Therapeutics*, 5th ed. (New York: Macmillan, 1975).
5. Cortez F. Enloe, "How Alcohol Affects the Developing Fetus," *Nutrition Today* 15, no. 5 (1980): 15.
6. Ibid., 13.
7. Iain M. Murray-Lyon, "Alcohol and Foetal Damage," *Alcohol and Alcoholism* 20, no. 2 (1985): 185–88.
8. The average drink in a restaurant is rarely less than an ounce and a half, and in clubs it's about two ounces.
9. Ronald Forbes, "Alcohol-Related Birth Defects," *Public Health, London* 98 (1984): 240.
10. Frank L. Iber, "Fetal Alcohol Syndrome," *Nutrition Today* 15, no. 5 (1980): 7.
11. A. P. Streissguth and R. A. LaDue, "Psychological and Behavioral Effects in Children Prenatally Exposed to Alcohol," *Alcohol, Health, and Research World*. A publication of the National Clearinghouse for Alcohol Information, Rockville, MD, 1985.
12. Forbes, "Alcohol-Related Birth Defects," 239.

RUTH BEHAR

Juban América

Shortly before his death in Miami Beach in 1987, my maternal grandfather, Maximo Glinsky, stapled an old photograph onto a small piece of cardboard. On the cardboard, by way of explanation, he wrote the words, "*Recuerdo de Linka de a donde yo nació en 1901 esto era nuestra casa y atras un jardin grande.*" His words were intended for his descendants, now living English-speaking lives in North America: "Souvenir of Linka, where I was born in 1901, this was our house with its garden in back." The picture, indeed, shows a house, or something rather more like a homestead. Three boys in knickers and hats, their faces dim and indistinct, cluster together on one side; perhaps one of them was my grandfather. The ground is covered with snow.

As the good archivist granddaughter I have had this image-text carefully placed on acid-free board, put under glass, and framed in a simple etched wood. Naturally, I removed the staples, which were beginning to rust. The picture now rests in a quiet domestic space, above our used one-hundred-and-fifty-dollar mahogany piano, where I sit almost every night with my kindergarten-age son Gabriel begging him to play his lessons. I had wanted terribly to learn piano as a child in the years after we arrived in the United States from Cuba, but my parents told me they didn't have the space nor the money; besides, they thought it wiser for me to learn to play a more portable instrument, like the accordian or the guitar, an instrument you could take anywhere. I could not understand then how for my parents, who were in their late twenties when they decided to leave Cuba in 1961, all sense of permanence had been ruptured. Though children of immigrants, they had never expected to have to leave Cuba, *nunca en la vida*. The piano in the drawing room—that, for me, is the epitome of a settled, bourgeois existence, the life of people whose citizenship documents are in order and therefore have no reason to harbor immigrant fears, the life of people who don't expect a revolution to come overnight and challenge their hold on the things of the world. And yet, what if, at a moment's notice, I had to leave, what would I take with me? I think of the picture above the piano that traveled through two exiles, from Russia to Cuba and from Cuba to America.

That picture, which by itself would have said very little, became, with the addition of my grandfather's words, an image of displacement, of de-territorialization. The image-text refers to a lost home in Byelorussia, the old country. That this home is undeniably lost is evident not only in my grandfather's use of the past tense, but in the fact that he tells the story of its loss in Spanish, which became the language of his reterritorialization in the New World. The brief, seemingly uncomplicated statement that my grand-father inscribed under the photograph of his origins, in which he locates himself as a minority speaker of Spanish, is redolent with politics and his-tory. His Spanish embodies too many contradictions of territoriality and deterritorialization.[1]

As any educated speaker of Spanish knows, my grandfather's text reflects a nonstandard use of the language. He disregards the difference between the first and third person; as an enunciating subject, my grandfather used the grammatically incorrect, *yo nació*, instead of the grammatically correct, *yo nací*. It seems eerie to me that he placed himself in the interface between the first person and the third person, as if already imagining himself no longer here in the world of the living, no longer speaking as "I" but as "he," being spoken by someone else, edging closer toward the third person of biography, of the narrator, of his own granddaughter's text.

• • •

Spanish was not my grandfather's mother tongue. He was a stepson to the language and yet he claimed it as his own. He spoke Spanish to his children and grandchildren; the Yiddish that he spoke with my grandmother and others of their generation failed to get passed on, while English, learned in a second exile, never entered his veins. My relationship with my grand-father, a man of the Jewish European old world, was lived entirely in Span-ish. To be more exact, it was lived in a combination of Spanish and silence. My grandfather did not talk very much. He was suspicious of people who talked too much. He spoke telegraphically. His most memorable utterances were his jokes, tellable only in Spanish, a Spanish that showed his stepson's precarious kinship to the language. His jokes were really questions, such as "*Como andas?*," which he would answer with "*Con los pies*," or "*Como te sientes?*," to which the reply was "*En la silla.*" These jokes—which were also actual replies that he'd give when asked the Spanish equivalent of "how are you?"—encoded his refusal to say how he was "doing," his refusal to acknowledge that he was "fine, thank you."

It is these refusals, so characteristically part of how he spoke and didn't speak, that make me think that my grandfather was acutely conscious that his was a colonized voice. The "sound" of a colonized voice, it seems to me, carries traces of the effort to resist speaking, to resist speaking "as usual." The locus of enunciation is challenged before speaking even takes place. For the colonized speaker, language is never taken for granted; you cannot go into automatic drive. My grandfather's literal enunciations served as a continual brake on our becoming too comfortable in the language of our colonization—and yet, curiously, these enunciations were so thoroughly rooted in Spanish idiomatic phrases as to be untranslatable. *Después de todo*, Spanish was my grandfather's language, in much the same convoluted way it is mine now.

• • •

As a Russian Yiddish immigrant, my grandfather learned Spanish in his early twenties after arriving in Cuba in 1924. He was one among thousands of Jews from southern and eastern Europe fleeing the legacy of pogroms and the difficult economic conditions that took form in the aftermath of World War I and the collapse of the Hapsburg and Ottoman empires, when the rise of nationalist ideologies increasingly threatened, and undermined, Jewish life. After the United States severely limited Eastern European emigration with its 1924 Immigration and Nationality Act, a growing number of Jews were forced to imagine a future for themselves in the other America south of the border.[2] Some Latin American countries, like Argentina, seeking to whiten their population and find agricultural settlers to make their lands productive, had encouraged Jewish emigration since the turn of the century. But as conditions worsened in Europe, especially by the late 1930s, the United States government acted with supreme hypocrisy, pressuring Latin American countries to absorb the thousands of desperate Jewish emigrants that were being systematically prevented from entering the America north of the border.

Cuba, as the backyard colony of the United States, came under particularly strong pressure to take in Jews, and by 1938 had a Jewish population of about 16,500, mainly settled in Havana, but with about 3,500 scattered in provincial cities and rural towns. In the years when Nazi power was being consolidated and Jews were attempting to flee Europe to any country that would have them, Cuba became the center of a lucrative traffic in visas, landing permits, and other immigration papers. Travel agents bought permits from Cuban officials and then resold them in Europe for three and four times the amount they had paid. Most of these permits left their holders in limbo, allowing them to land in Cuba and remain there until they secured a visa to the United States. As the traffic in Jewish cargo grew in intensity, some xenophobic American observers became concerned that too many Jews were illicitly entering the United States via Cuba. In a strictly confidential document, "European Refugees in Cuba," written in 1939, a consular official warned the authorities in Washington of how "Cuba has long been a base from which aliens are smuggled into the United States." These "aliens," he explained, gained entrance into the country "by means of false visas, Cuban citizenship documents, passports, and birth certificates; by smuggling as stowaways on vessels, by smuggling in small boats hired for the purpose; and attempts have been made to smuggle by airplane."[3]

Many Jewish emigrants had initially viewed Cuba as a way station on route to the United States. After all, wasn't America only ninety miles away? Yet that America which was so omnipresent as a colonial power was, when it pleased, so conveniently distant. By the late 1930s the goal of gaining entrance to the America across the border became less and less pressing for the many Jews who had remade tropical lives for themselves, awakening to the realization that Cuba was to be their America. Jewish Cuban intellectuals came to identify not only with José Martí's stance against racism but with his dialectics of "Our America," as distinct from "the America which is not ours," the America of the U.S. empire.[4] As the situation for Jews grew dim in Europe, those who had found a second home in Cuba, even if it was not quite the America of their expectations, had reason to be grateful. The Jews who stayed in Cuba became "Jewish Robinson Crusoes," stranded by the turns of fate in an island that many years later, in their second exile in the United States after the Cuban Revolution, they would remember nostalgically as a paradise lost. In the words of the Cuban Jewish poet Sarah Luski: "Will I see you again one day, dear Cuba / Or will I spend the rest of my life in exile / Longing for your sky, your beautiful beaches / Oh Cuba! My native land."[5]

As a result of the Cuban Revolution, those same Jewish "aliens" that the consular official in 1939 feared had smuggled their way into the United

States, concealing their "true" Jewish identity behind the mask of a "false" Cuban identity, crossed the border into America after all. History repeated itself in an ironic way: the second time around, the Jews of Cuba gained entrance into America as Cubans, not as Jews. Fidel Castro called the Cubans who deserted the island rather than work to build the Revolution *gusanos*. The Cuban Jews in the United States were doubly wormy. They had not only abandoned the Revolution, as already years before, in the 1940s and 1950s, many had abandoned their early ideals of Jewish communism as they ceased to be peddlers and became deproletarianized members of the Cuban middle class.[6] They had also managed to sneak their way into the United States, worming their way into the American body politic as Cuban refugees. Once in America they would forever have to explain that they were Cubans who also "happened" to be Jewish.

• • •

I need to interrupt this third-person historical interlude to speak, again, as *yo*, at least momentarily. Like my grandfather, I keep wanting to situate myself somewhere between the third-person plural and the first-person singular. Indeed, *yo nació* seems exactly right for getting at the peculiar confluence of identity that is implied in the idea of being Jewish-Cuban, or Juban, as they say in Miami.

It has taken me a long time to reach an obvious conclusion: I am *cubana* because I am Jewish. I am *cubana* because my grandparents were cargo that was unwanted in the United States. I am *cubana* because the border between "our America" and "the America which is not ours" is a real border guarded by guns and decorated with ink. If I am now welcome in the America that is not mine, it is because of my value as symbolic capital, as one of the human spoils of the victory of United States capitalism over impudent Cuban socialism. My parents taught me to be grateful that we ended up with the *yanquis*, because in Cuba I'd be wearing clunky shoes and being told what to study. *Hay que darle gracias a este país* was the incantation I heard all the years I was growing up. So I can't claim too much *cubanidad* for myself. My feet have worn out plenty of good leather and I've studied what I've pleased. My documents are in order, I'm a legal alien, and I have an American passport that warns me, "Certain transactions involving travel to Cuba are prohibited."

On the day I swore my allegiance to the United States, the woman who had examined me on my knowledge of American presidents while chain-smoking in a dingy office offered me a tempting proposition: I could change my name. It wouldn't cost anything extra. No easier time to change your name than when you're being naturalized, she told me. I was eleven at the time and I felt as though this woman had bestowed immense powers upon me. I didn't even consult my parents; I immediately told her to erase that other name of mine, my middle name. I was a child who had been plopped into a New York public school without knowing a word of English, and there was nothing that filled my soul with as much fear as the thought of being ridiculed. I was terrified that one of my schoolmates would discover my middle name on some official slip of paper and make my life insufferable. That name was a deep, dark secret that the insecure emigrant child felt compelled to hide in feeble protection of her dignity.

And so, whenever I'm asked if I have a middle name, I always say I don't have one. This name that I refused, I learned much later, was my grandfather's mother's name. She had been killed in her bed in Byelorussia by Nazi soldiers; that was the story that reached my grandfather in Cuba years afterward. Her name was Fiegele, which means "little bird" in Yiddish, and the translation of that name in Cuba became Fanny, pronounced with a soft vowel sound. But for a chubby emigrant girl in America, that name was unredeemable. I'd become Fanny with the Fat Fanny, forever and ever. It was already bad enough having been made excessively conscious of that part of my body by *el grupo*, whose home movies of the entrance of Fidel Castro into Havana were punctuated with flashes of female backsides. On the verge of adolescence, I was only too glad to be able to strip myself of a name that would have made me even more distressingly aware of my budding sexuality. There seemed no way to liberate the name Fanny from its embarrassing American translation and fly with it—and so I clipped my wings. In Mexico there are those candy skulls that are sold for the Day of the Dead with names like Vicente, Alfredo, Antonia, Catalina, and Esperanza taped onto their foreheads. When I have the blues, I start to imagine myself as a skull with the name Fanny written on my forehead.

The question of my name is on my mind now because I am preparing to visit Cuba at the end of this year, and in order to be able to make that trip I had to acquire a Cuban passport listing my full name as it appears on my Cuban birth certificate. According to Cuban law, you cannot stop being Cuban. Even if you have been naturalized by another nation, you must obtain a Cuban passport to return to Cuba, at a cost of about three hundred dollars. I suppose the purpose of this law is to keep track of the flow of *gusanos* returning to the country while drawing some revenues from them. But I don't feel at all cynical about my Cuban passport; I want to pay my dues for having been spared the clunky shoes and been allowed to study for a career of dubious social value. So I now have a valid Cuban passport, in which I have recovered both a lost middle name and a lost last name. In Cuba I will be Ruth Fanny Behar Glinsky. I will regain the names that link me back to my maternal grandfather.

. . .

I was named Ruth because my great-grandfather, Abraham Levin, my grandmother's father, who did make it to Cuba with my great-grandmother, was reading the Book of Ruth when I was born. I am not surprised that my mother, who was only twenty when she had me, agreed to name her baby girl to satisfy the literary whims of her maternal grandfather. My great-grandfather, the only truly observant Jew on my mother's side of the family, was highly respected, both for his knowledge of the Torah and for his unwillingness to force his religious views on others. The Levin family became a clan in Cuba. After my grandmother married my grandfather in 1929, they worked together with my great-grandfather to bring my great-grandmother and the remaining six children from Poland. Reunited in Cuba, the extended household settled in the small town of Agramonte, in the sugar province of Matanzas, where they ran a general store that sold everything from pins to mattresses. For many years, until another family arrived, they were the only Jewish family in Agramonte and my Aunt Silvia remembers, as a child, that the curtains would be drawn on Passover. But if they were Jews in the wilderness, known to local people as *los polacos*, they were not unhappy. In Agramonte, my grandfather belonged to the Lion's Club and grew roses and *guayabas* in the backyard, while my Aunt Silvia and my mother played with the mayor's children. On many a quiet day, my grandmother would dress up and take her two young daughters to the station to watch, along with everyone else, as the train from Havana made its daily stop in Agramonte.

Eventually my great-aunts and great-uncles moved out of Agramonte as they married and left for more urbane destinies in Matanzas and Havana. For years my grandparents lingered in Agramonte. Only after my grandfather won the lottery in 1946 did they move to Havana, where they opened up a lace shop called "Casa Maximo" in the old part of the city. This little store on Calle Aguacate, which still had its original sign with my grandfather's name when I visited Cuba in 1979, never brought in enough money for my grandparents to become more than insecurely middle class.

It was in Havana that my mother met my father. Their relationship was a

cross-cultural encounter, for my father was a *turco*, who came from a traditional Turkish Sephardic background, in which Ladino, the old Spanish of
the expelled Jews, was still spoken at home. He had grown up street-smart
near the docks of Havana and, though he was a first-generation Cuban
like my mother, his dark black hair and *habanero* style allowed him to pass
more easily as a Cuban. His father was a peddler who worked only half
the day and spent the afternoons playing dominoes with his buddies. If my
mother's family was doing only moderately well, my father's family was
barely making it. Some time in the late 1930s, when my father's family had
gone hungry for several days, my abuelo brought home an excellent cut of
beef. It had been given to him by one of his clients and he presented it with
enormous satisfaction to my grandmother. She refused to accept it because
it wasn't kosher meat. My grandfather insisted she take it, saying it was a
gift and that they were too hungry to be choosy. My grandmother kept
refusing. My grandfather kept insisting. Finally, my grandmother took the
meat from his hands. Holding it in her determined hands, she lifted the
package high above her head and flung it out the window. The argument
that ensued that day must have been momentous, because the story about
the beef that ended up in the street has never been forgotten in my father's
family.

My father has often claimed that it was my mother who taught him to
eat the prohibited foods his mother had so vehemently kept out of her
house. Not that my mother allowed unkosher meat into her house, either.
At home she translated recipes from her Cuban cookbook, *Cocina Criolla*,
itself a creole culinary mix, making kosher *tamales* and kosher *caldo gallego*
by substituting chicken and Hebrew National beef fry for the pork that was
supposed to be in these dishes. But in the street, *en la calle*, it was different;
there, Leviticus gave you license to taste more of the world. Being kosher
stops at your doorstep. That has been our primary dietary rule, our culinary
semiotics, our way of forging a Cuban identity we can live in.

When we were recently at El Rincón Criollo, a Cuban restaurant in New
York where my parents eat almost every weekend, my father adamantly
refused to let me bring home what was left of my *pollo a la plancha*. "But it's
just chicken," I protested. "I don't want it in my house, *y se acabó*, okay?" replied my father. "Case closed," as he likes to say. And yet he and my mother,
like their friends in *el grupo*, will go rushing to El Rincón for *frijoles* and
bistec de palomilla the day after the fast of Yom Kippur. I hope my mother
will forgive me for remembering forever that late-night summer outing

in Puerto Rico when her front tooth, which I had no idea was fake, fell out as she swooned *que rico está este sandwich* while biting into that sweetly pickled ham-and-cheese Cuban special that bears the nostalgic name of *una media noche*.

. . .

In Cuba my mother would have remained a *polaca*, and my father a *turco*; at the least, they would have always been the children of *polacos* and *turcos*. It is in the United States that they have settled into their Cubanness. In this America that is not theirs, they are viewed as Latinos, quirky Latinos, to be sure, but Latinos nonetheless.

My mother says to me, "With my accent, all I have to do is open my mouth and people ask me, 'Where are you from?' When they want to be nice, they say, 'Where are you from *originally*?'" She works in an over-crowded basement of New York University, checking to be sure people's names are spelled correctly on their diplomas. In her office she's now the only Latina, and she finds herself having to straddle between her white American and black American women coworkers. She's neither white nor black in that context, but certainly a little more black than white. It doesn't help her much that she's white and Jewish, because a white Jewish woman in America doesn't usually speak the kind of "broken English" that Latinas and Latinos speak. Her accent and her continuing struggle with the En-glish language are an ever-present reminder that she is an immigrant in an America that is not hers, that her origins are elsewhere. She realizes she's being "othered" all the time and she notices how the black women in the office get the same treatment. And so, as she tells me, "I'm with them, with the women of color." And I say to her, "Ma, don't you see? Here *you* are a woman of color too."

I was speaking to my mother from my own experience. I was denied a position at my university as a minority because it was decided that, given my Jewish heritage, I was not a racially pure Latina. And yet even this im-pure Latina gets counted in as a minority or as a woman of color when the statistics are looking bad for affirmative-action hirings. So I've decided that if I'm going to be counted as a minority, if I'm going to be on the margin, if I'm going to be a woman of color, I'm going to claim that space and speak from it, but in the interests of a politics that challenges the lan-guage of cultural authenticity and racial purity. I'm going to be a Latina, *no a las buenas pero a las malas*, because that's the identity that, exactly inverse to my mother, they're always trying to take away from me, because "I'm white like you, English-speaking like you, right-thinking like you, middle-class-living like you, no matter what I say."[7]

My father gets Latinized not just because of his accent but because of his García Márquez eyebrows and mustache. And he responds with *rumbero* humor, purposely mispronouncing words in English while parading about in a U.S.A. baseball cap and T-shirt. But some of his responses are also tinged with bitterness and an internalized racism that chills me. This past summer, as we cleared up our poolside snacks at an undistinguished Holiday Inn on the northern outskirts of Philadelphia, he said, "Don't leave a mess, okay? *Porque si no van a decir que somos puertoriqueños.*" My father has often been mistaken for Puerto Rican and this bothers him. Being Puerto Rican represents, to him, not making it in America, staying poor, not being a reasonable, white, middle-class, right-thinking person just like you.

Yet it is as a Latino that my father earns his living. As the Latin American sales representative of a textile firm in New York City, it is his job to sell close-outs and other fabric that no one wants to buy on this side of the border to clients in Panama, the Dominican Republic, and Mexico. And, indeed, he sells what the gringos could never sell with remarkable success, for he's an expert border crosser. But when his humor becomes self-deprecating, he says he's a junk salesman, a peddler of *basura*, of *shmates*. He's the Latino smuggled into a company where all the bosses are third-generation American Ashkenazi Jews who drive Jaguars. They're nice enough to my father, but he knows he's not one of the boys. So he takes their smugness with a grain of salt. Each boss, for example, has gotten a nickname. Mr. Sachs, pronounced "Mr. Socks" with a Latino accent, is *La Media*. When things get rough at the office, my father phones my mother at NYU and says, "*Está La Media hoy que apesta*" ("The Sock sure stinks today").

Lately it is Mr. Wolf, *El Lobo*, who is being difficult. And I am to blame. "*El Lobo está que aulla*" ("The Wolf is about to start howling") my father tells me, as I talk in a three-way conversation to him and my mother on the phone from Michigan. And my mother adds, "*Le vira la cara a tu padre. Se lo quiere comer—crudo*" ("He refuses to look at your father in the face. He wants to eat him—raw"). *El Lobo* is angry, you see, because he asked my father to ask me to write a letter of recommendation for his daughter to help get her into the University of Michigan. *El Lobo* describes his own daughter as being indistinguishable from all the other girls in her suburban Long Island high school and tells my father that she needs something a little extra to get her into a place like Michigan. A letter from a professor at Michigan is just the mark of distinction she needs. Surely I will understand. My father dutifully calls me and relays the orders from *El Lobo*. I try to explain that I have no special powers to get *El Lobo*'s daughter accepted into the university. I try to explain that the university is not totally like the business world yet, and that merit still counts for something. I try to explain that it's not a good idea to fake it. And then I flatly say that I will not do it. I will not write a letter on behalf of a young woman in Long Island I have never met in my life. I don't care if she is the daughter of a werewolf who drives a Jaguar. My father starts to get upset, but my mother, who is hovering around waiting to hear my response, gets on the phone and says, "*Te lo dije. Yo sabía que Ruty no lo iba a hacer*" ("I told you. I knew Ruty wouldn't do it").

So *El Lobo* is getting ready to howl. But fortunately it's still *La Manzana*, Mr. Applebaum, who signs the paychecks. And *La Manzana* adores my father. As my mother tells me so I won't feel too guilty, "*Me llama tu padre y me dice, La Manzana me tiene loco hoy dándome besos*" ("Your father calls and says to me, The Apple is driving me crazy today kissing me so much").

• • •

To join together Latin American and Jewish, terms that are not normally joined together, creates a shock effect; as Saúl Sosnowski puts it, one encounters "astonished gazes and conflicting images of the accepted and simple cliches for both."[8] As an Argentine painter once noted, "They say of Linnaeus that when he found an insect which resisted classification, he would crush it immediately."[9] It is not expected for a Jew to have Spanish as a mother tongue, nor for someone from Latin America to lay claim to a Jewish identity. But in the Cuban-Jewish milieu that I have known first-hand, these uncommon expectations exist in a common reality, a Cuban-Jewish sense of identity, of being-in-the-world. It is essential, Sosnowski feels, to "protect the hyphen" in the Latin American–Jewish sense of identity. The hyphen highlights the unease produced by the importation, even smuggling, of the Jew into the monolithic territory of Latin America. It also signals "the inability of language to produce a composite word and of beings to give birth to a gray, melted self."[10] And yet, in the Cuban-Jewish case, there *is* a composite word, "Juban," which gets at a sense of *mestizaje* rooted in a creative amalgam that is different from assimilation. Such an amalgam is possible because of the criollism that is at the center of Cuban culture.

In Latin America, where the traces of the great Nahuatl and Inca civilizations are in permanent tension with the struggles for survival of post-conquest indigenous people, the "other" as well as the "native" has been the Indian. Cuba, like the other islands of the Caribbean, has only a vague prehistoric connection to the indigenous substratum, because its smaller native populations were quickly destroyed by the Spanish conquest, leaving hardly any traces. Positioned much more prominently at the entrance to the New World than the other Caribbean islands, Cuba became a unique crossroads, bustling with the movement of people and goods, but also vulnerable over the centuries to "invasion, depredations, and harassment" that have not yet stopped.[11] Cuban culture was shaped by the exogenous, the foreign. The absence of "aboriginality," as Gustavo Pérez Firmat has pointed out so well, has given to Cuban culture an "originality" that "subsists in and through translation." Like an *ajiaco*, a hearty stew of heterogeneous ingredients, Cuban culture is made up of layers upon layers of migrant displacements and resettlements.[12]

At the beginning of *The Cuban Condition*, Pérez Firmat gives an example, which touches directly upon the theme of this essay, of what he calls the Cuban "translation sensibility." His example is a Cuban-Jewish wedding that took place in Miami, where the Cuban singer Willie Chirino performed a version of the Jewish song "Hava-Nagilah" in guaguancó rhythm, creating a "Havana-gilah," to which people danced "a *horah* with *salsa* steps." For Pérez Firmat, there was "something peculiarly Cuban in that irreverent, creole translation of this Hebrew song."[13] And I agree with him. But there was also, I would add, something peculiarly *Juban* in that irreverent, creole acceptance of Willie Chirino's version as something to which you could dance a *horah con salsa*. If only a Cuban could have done the kind of translation that Chirino did, only a Juban could have had the bicultural fluency to make sense of that creole language—and invent a way to dance to it. Jubans have outdone the *ajiaco* sense of identity. They don't just have a translation sensibility; they are, themselves, translated people.

. . .

Some time after I began writing this piece, I came across Salman Rushdie's essay "Imaginary Homelands," which also begins with an account of an old family photograph. Rushdie's photograph is of the house where he was born in Bombay, which he visited again after living in London for most of his life. Seeing the red roof tiles, the cactuses, and the bougainvillea creepers made him vividly aware of the home and the homeland he had lost. (Yet these are all things not native to Bombay: the red tiles come from Portugal, the cactuses and bougainvillea from Mexico.) Writers who are exiles, emigrants, and expatriates are haunted by the desire to "reclaim, to look back, even at the risk of being mutated into pillars of salt," notes Rushdie. Yet the real distance from the places left behind "almost inevitably means," Rushdie is careful to add, "that we will not be capable of reclaiming precisely the thing that was lost; that we will, in short, create fictions, not actual cities or villages, but invisible ones, imaginary homelands."[14]

This essay has been a first effort on my part to begin to imagine Juba, a Juba that I want to build, salt pillar by salt pillar, from both family stories and my own struggle to reclaim all the little forgotten villages of my *mestiza* identity. Villages, *pueblitos*, mean a good deal to me. I went into anthropology because I thought that the discipline rooted in the foreignness of other worlds would help me to solve the puzzle of my identity. Instead, I ended up spending years of my life in two forgotten villages, one in northern Spain and one in northern Mexico. The village in Spain, called Santa María del Monte after the most Holy Mother, lived up to its name, and everyone went to church, without fail, for Sunday mass. In Santa María I learned to recite the rosary and the credo, to get down on my knees at the appropriate parts of the service, and to cross myself. Yet I never forgot I was a Jew. In the village in Mexico, just five hundred miles away from the U.S.-Mexican border, everyone needed something from *el otro lado*, the other side. Could we bring back a tape recorder, a television, basketball sneakers, a stethoscope? Could we line up some work, any sort of work, over there? I wasn't allowed to forget that I was in Mexico as a gringa with gringa privileges and gringa money. But I also couldn't forget that I had wormed my way into Gringolandia as a *cubana*. When I refused a *compadre*'s request that I claim him as next of kin to help him get across the border, he said to me in a pained voice, "But didn't you tell me that you and your family aren't from there, that you also had to fight to get in?" I was prohibited from forgetting that to become a gringa I had to be legally alienated by the United States.

In addition to these villages, whose dust I have eaten, there is, of course, my grandfather's Linka, the village where he was born, a village that is beyond tasting, beyond remembering. And then there is Agramonte, where I imagine no one remembers anymore *los polocos viejos* who had the general store, but where nonetheless my grandfather's *guayabas* are still fragrant and people continue to wait for the train from Havana that comes in once a day. Then there are the cities — Havana, New York, Miami Beach, Ann Arbor.

In my Juba, there is room for all these villages and cities, and many other places for which I do not yet have names. In Juba there are no aliens. Only people like Lot's wife, who just won't listen.

POSTSCRIPT

I had the Cuban passport, but as 1991 drew to a close I wasn't sure I would make it to Cuba. In the weeks before my trip I became ill with what appeared to be a mysterious flu. I was beyond myself with exhaustion and yet I couldn't sleep. I became jittery, my heart raced constantly, I was dizzy, and could barely eat. I cried, I was overcome with fear. My entire life had curled up into a ball in my throat. Classic anxiety symptoms, I later learned. All I wanted was to retire to my bed and forget everything. Why was I so concerned about Cuba, anyway? Me, this inauthentic Jubana who had been unhinged from Cuba at the age of five, what did I think I would find?

Sure, it didn't help much that I would be leaving Gabriel behind with my parents in New York. They had told me that in case I didn't come back I should leave them all the *papeles*. My mother said, *"Me dejas todo lo del niño, Ruty, por si acaso Fidel Castro no te deja salir."* Fidel Castro, himself, she felt certain, had a vested interest in my not returning to the United States. And my father, *"Ruty, no hables nada nada de política con nadie. Ni una palabra."* Don't talk politics—yes, I had grown up hearing that, had learned early on that talking politics led to arguments, veins throbbing in the neck, and finally those two words "case closed" and silence. I tried to let this paranoia wash over me, but scenarios kept unfolding in my imagination of dear Gabriel being raised by my parents, watching cartoons on television all day, being served breakfast, lunch, and dinner in bed, surrounded by the entire collection of Ninja Turtle and Swamp Thing toys. Me, his mother, I'd be stuck in Cuba, maybe in jail for talking about *política*, or maybe in an insane asylum for doing something crazy, like screaming in the street, saying the unsayable. And his father, the *gringuito*, he'd be running around Cuba, wondering how to save me—that is, if he didn't just get on a plane and leave me there alone, turned into a pillar of salt for daring to look back.

My body turned into a boulder that I dragged all the way to Miami. And then the next day, when we were supposed to leave for Cuba, I learned that my visa had not arrived. I felt a touch of disappointment, wondering whether the Cubans had somehow looked into their crystal ball and learned I was too neurotic to deserve to be let in. But mostly I felt great relief. I thought to myself, oh, well, it wasn't my *destino* to go to Cuba after all. Now I could relax, take a vacation. Yet we kept our suitcases by the door, just in case. And four days later, just after we had given up hope and unpacked our bags, word arrived from Cuba that the visa was ready and I could leave the next morning. I had been warned to adopt a Zen attitude if I wanted to work in Cuba and I now understood why.

When we arrived at the airport at the crack of dawn, there was already *la cola* of people waiting to check in for the daily flight to Havana. There was a man with sad eyes who said in a sad voice that he was going to visit his dying mother whom he hadn't seen in years; there was a woman carrying an oversize shopping bag stuffed with a frilly pink parasol and matching lace basket who was begging the clerk to let her take it onboard; there was a man wearing three hats on his head; there was a woman stuffing beans and sausage under her clothes, because this time she was going to get these things through customs in Cuba; and there were several people carrying portable drugstores, taking enough aspirin for several lifetimes of head-aches. In the midst of this mixture of tenderness and zaniness, I lost all fear of crossing the border into Cuba. Waiting in the airport to board the plane, I knew I was already inside the belly of the monster when I found myself forced to listen four times, twice in English and twice in Spanish, to a U.S. government statement reminding us of the trade embargo against Cuba and the restrictions against giving too many dollars to the enemy.

Entering Cuba with dollars in my purse, I immediately forget the rules of the embargo and rent a spanking new car, red as blood. And in that car I go to Agramonte—a village of one long street, just the way my Aunt Silvia described it. And I learn that they still call the store on one corner *la casa de los polacos nuevos* and the store on the other corner *la casa de los polacos viejos.* You see, there were two Jewish families in Agramonte; but my family got there first, so they became *los polacos viejos* and the others became the *nuevos.*

"Does anybody remember *los polacos viejos?*" I ask, and as we stand around outside the mint green store entrance, a little circle forms around us, and older men begin to utter the names of my great-grandparents, my grandparents, my great-aunts and great-uncles: Abraham, Hannah, Esther, Maximo, Jaime, Dora, Irene . . . Just hearing the names coming from the lips of these men, I feel my lifeline extending, the ball in my throat un-curling. They pose for a photo and a woman who's been standing nearby yells to one of the men to roll down his pant legs, which are folded to the knee, and then she looks at me and says, *"Viniste a retratar los viejos más feos del pueblo!"* ("You came to photograph the ugliest old men in town"). A man who says he's known as El Chiquito tells me to send regards to my great-uncle Jaime and to ask if he doesn't remember all the devilish things they did together. Doctor Pablito, the town doctor who is now ninety, tells me that my great-aunt Dora fell in love with his brother, the lawyer, but the family quickly whisked her away to Havana, fearing she'd marry a non-Jew. Dora is dead, I tell him; and my brother too, he replies.

I forget to ask about the *guayabas* and the train from Havana, but expecting to return soon, I don't worry about it. Having said my last good-bye for now, I am heading toward the car when a young man wearing a baker's hat calls to me. At first I think he's asking me for something, maybe to change dollars like the *jineteros* who now trail after tourists in the hotel zones of Havana, but, no, I have gotten my guard up too quickly. It turns out he simply wants to know if I'd like some *dulces*. There's nothing more I desire at that moment than a sweet ending to my story, and I say yes and he brings out, on a sheet of brown paper, several chunks of glittering rum cake. The drops of sugary rum meander down my chin and fingers and onto the camera hanging from my neck that will die two days later while I am trying to photograph the tomb of a cousin in the Jewish cemetery of Havana. With the taste of that rum cake in my mouth, I begin to know why my family made Cuba their promised land. I begin to know, too, that I must keep reconnecting with the Cuba that my family refused, the Cuba they are afraid of and that I believed I also should fear, the Cuba that dawdled on my visa and almost didn't let me in, the Cuba of the young baker in Agramonte who offered me rum cake because I happened to be walking by. To imagine it all is not enough. The Jubana will have to taste the salt of memory and of loss, but she will also have to make a *rinconcito* for herself in the Cuba of the present.

NOTES

1. His Spanish seemed to be dressed in "a Harlequin costume in which very different functions of language and distinct centers of power are played out, blurring what can be said and what can't be said." See Gilles Deleuze and Félix Guattari, *Kafka: Toward a Minor Literature* (Minneapolis: University of Minnesota Press, 1986), 26. For a feminist rereading of Deleuze and Guattari that I have found very illuminating, see Caren Kaplan, "Deterritorializations: The Rewriting of Home and Exile in Western Feminist Discourse," in Abdul R. Jan Mohamed and David Lloyd, eds., *The Nature and Context of Minority Discourse* (New York: Oxford University Press, 1990), 357–68.
2. For more detailed accounts of this history, see Judith Laikin Elkin, *Jews of the Latin American Republics* (Chapel Hill: University of North Carolina Press, 1980);

Judith Laikin Elkin and Gilbert W. Merkx, eds., *The Jewish Presence in Latin America* (Boston: Allen and Unwin, 1987).

3. Cited in Robert M. Levine, *Tropical Diaspora: Jewish Life in Cuba, 1902–1991*, chapter 4, p. 3, book manuscript, now published as *Tropical Diaspora-Jewish Experience in Cuba* (Gainesville: University Press of Florida, 1993). I am indebted to Robert Levine for kindly allowing me to read his book manuscript, which has helped me to formulate my understanding of the meaning of the Jewish presence in Cuba.
4. José David Saldívar, "The Dialectics of Our America," in Gustavo Pérez Firmat, ed., *Do the Americas Have a Common Literature?* (Durham: Duke University Press, 1990). I owe to Saldívar my concepts of "our America" and "the America which is not ours." The terms originally come from an essay by José Martí, titled "Nuestra América," that, in turn, have been elaborated by the Cuban critic Roberto Fernández Retamar in *Caliban and Other Essays* (Minneapolis: University of Minnesota Press, 1989). Interestingly, in the prerevolutionary period, the Cuban Hebrew Cultural Society established a forum on Martí as seen from a Jewish perspective, publishing the text by Abraham Marcus Matterin, *Martí y las discriminaciones raciales* (Havana: Ediciones de la Agrupación Cultural Hebreo-Cubana, 1953). I want to thank Judith Elkin for kindly lending me her copy of this work.
5. Sander M. Kaplan, "Jewish Robinson Crusoes," *Havaner Lebn*, 12 October 1934, cited in Elkin, *Jews of the Latin American Republics*, 88; Sarah Luski's poem in the original Spanish is cited in Alicia Oberstein, "Cuban Jewish Writers and the Immigrant Experience," *Latino Stuff Review*, (winter 1991): 4. I want to thank Gustavo Pérez Firmat for sending me the Oberstein article.
6. Margalit Bejarano, "The Deproletarianization of Cuban Jewry," *Judaica Latinoamericana: Estudios Históricos-Sociales*, ed. AMILAT (Jerusalem: Editorial Universitaria Magnes, Universidad Hebrea, 1988), 57–67. Some Jews did remain members of the Communist Party and later participated in the Cuban Revolution, staying in Cuba even after the mass exodus of the Jewish community. There are now about a thousand Jews left on the island. Most have intermarried, and those with high-ranking positions tend not to identify as Jewish. During my visit in 1991 I was told that there are only fourteen families currently in Cuba where both husband and wife are of Jewish origin.
7. Rosario Morales, "I Am the Reasonable One," in Aurora Levins Morales and Rosario Morales, *Getting Home Alive* (Ithaca: Firebrand, 1986), 148.
8. Saúl Sosnowski, "Latin American–Jewish Writers: Protecting the Hyphen," in Elkin and Merkx, *The Jewish Presence in Latin America*, 299.
9. The quote is from Kenneth Kemble, and it is cited in Luis Felipe Noe, "Does Art from Latin America Need a Passport?," in Rachel Weiss, with Alan West, *Being América: Essays on Art, Literature, and Identity from Latin America* (New York: White Pine, 1991), 146.
10. Sosnowski, "Latin American–Jewish Writers," 307. Several Latin American

Jewish women writers have sought to go beyond the hyphen, asserting, as does Judit Moschkovich, "I am Latina, Jewish and an immigrant (all at once)." See Judit Moschkovich, "But I Know You, American Woman," in Cherríe Moraga and Gloria Anzaldúa, *This Bridge Called My Back: Writings by Radical Women of Color* (New York: Kitchen Table, Women of Color, 1981), 79. For a detailed exploration of the cross-fertilization of Puerto Rican and Jewish identities, see the lyrical mother-daughter volume by Aurora Levins Morales and Rosario Morales, *Getting Home Alive*, cited above. For a discussion of the generational differences between Cuban exile and Cuban American literary sensibilities, see Eliana S. Rivero, "(Re)Writing Sugarcane Memories: Cuban Americans and Literature," *The Americas Review*, 18, nos. 3–4 (1990): 164–82.

11. Louis A. Pérez Jr., *Cuba: Between Reform and Revolution* (New York: Oxford University Press, 1988), 12.

12. Gustavo Pérez Firmat, *The Cuban Condition: Translation and Identity in Modern Cuban Literature* (New York: Cambridge University Press, 1989), 4, 10, 12.

13. Pérez Firmat, *The Cuban Condition*, 1.

14. Salman Rushdie, "Imaginary Homelands," *Imaginary Homelands: Essays and Criticism, 1981–1991* (New York: Viking Penguin, 1991), 9–10.

LAURA B. DELIND

Close Encounters with a

CSA: The Reflections of

a Bruised and Somewhat

Wiser Anthropologist

In the summer of 1995, my proposal to establish Growing in Place Community Farm (GIP)—an instance of Community Supported Agriculture or CSA—was funded. Like many other food system analysts, I had been advocating decentralized, democratized, community-based approaches to food production, distribution, and consumption. What we needed, I believed (and still believe), was to reduce the distance between people and their food supply, to share the responsibility—to share the risks and rewards, as I was overly fond of saying—of food production. Farmers and eaters not only had to interact, but, in the best of all worlds, all of us needed to involve ourselves directly and physically in the growing of our food and in the care of the natural environment. It was through just such embodied experience, I argued, that we might develop an appreciation (if not an awe) for our elemental dependence on biological processes and ecosystems. We might also through our farming activity reestablish meaningful relationships, personally and socially, to the earth and to a community of place.

The CSA provided a means to engage in this sort of reformation actively. I had grown tired of the academic privilege of observing and critiquing from afar. If learning was to be real, then it had to be grounded, connected in dynamic ways to the reality of our daily lives. Energized by the words and wisdom of David Orr, I thought to separate myself from the cinderblock classroom and the fifty-minute pedagogy. It was time "to walk the talk," and I was ready to roll up my sleeves and take to the field—the field, in this case, being my own backyard. I'd be both a citizen activist and an anthropologist, though the former was clearly in the ascendancy.

That was almost three years ago. Growing in Place still exists and appears to be doing well (though the land has been sold from underneath us, and we will soon need to find a new home—but that's a story in itself). Much, however, has changed, though not necessarily in ways I would have expected or desired. I not only am no longer the board president, I do not even sit on the board. Everyone who originally assumed a leadership role has left the organization, the majority burned out or otherwise disappointed. I too have distanced myself from the intensity of the project. Only now have I begun to reflect on some of what's gone on, and I expect this reflection will continue for a good many years.

From this position of hindsight, I can say that because of my involvement in GIP I now know how to operate a Farmall Cub tractor and a rototiller; I can weed with both hands; I know that squash should not be transplanted, that peppers like Epsom salts, and that spelt hulls over wet newspaper can keep walkways weed free for weeks at a time. I can manage flea beetles, braid garlic, and work twelve hours at a stretch in the summer sun. I can harvest, wash, and crate dozens of vegetables; I can lift eighty pounds of produce, write inspirational newsletters, eat vegetables without washing them, and make a fashion statement of a farmer's tan. I can also lose my temper easily, make demands few others will abide, and cry with frustration and exhaustion. All told, I am reminded of an old Peanuts cartoon I have hanging in my office. In it, Sally is standing at the front of her classroom reading from a piece of paper. She begins, "This is my report on yesterday's field trip which they took us on because it was educational. We were all given sack lunches. . . . Then it rained, and the sack got wet and my lunch fell on the ground. . . . Then the bus backed over it. . . . I never learned so much in all my life!"

WHY TELL A STORY?

First, because I believe, we can (and should) learn from experiences that are less than perfect, that do not unfold according to plan. We as academics and as productive individuals are prone to remove ourselves and our field trips from direct view. We tend to dismiss our stumblings and vulnerabilities and, as a consequence, are inclined to overlook the very matrix of our lives in favor of a more negotiable end result. We favor the abstraction, the pattern, the sanitized rule of thumb, and we present them with an assurance that frequently belies the mental and physical struggles that brought them into being. We find ourselves honoring the fiction of disembodied, objective knowledge and not the fuller, more sensual background that frames who we are, what we know and do.

Second, and quite consistent with this, I think there is a need for us to recognize the subjectivity of our work and for us to express it as best we can. Far from being an admission of deficiency or weakness, it is an expression of engagement, of being alive and human. Experiences and projects that do not work out quite right, that seem to defy our best efforts, invite our self-reflection. They invite us to pay closer attention to our initial assumptions, to the context that surrounds our actions, to those with whom we interact, and to what we observed and did not observe. We start to listen differently when things go wrong; we ask questions and we press against what have become familiar definitions and boundaries. Doubt and the disruption it engenders can move us into new spaces, into as yet unnamed places, in ways that certainty never can.

Third, confronted by new or altered awareness, we (of less than perfect vision) may come to see ourselves and present ourselves with a bit more clarity. The observer can now be the observed, and the observed, both ourselves and others, can now be given voice — describing reality in previously unseen and unheard ways. What we bring with us is always partial, but it grows less partial, less incomplete (though not necessarily any easier to live with) with expanded participation and challenges to prescriptive authority.

In anthropological terms, we can strike down the historical and delusional observer—that all-knowing, expert outsider whose description of a finite reality called culture reproduces himself. It is not the outsider (or the father) who knows best. It is not the insider who fails to comprehend. Natives can speak for themselves. Natives can be activists, and academics can be natives. There are border crossings everywhere, connections, engagements, multiple and shifting identities. We are not simply one thing or another; an oppositional existence does not stand the test of life or time.

For all of us here who work at the margins of agriculture, food, and farming, this is really not difficult to understand. Its logic is essentially organic, ecological, and systemic in nature. For this reason alone, I feel that we who are confronting established mind-sets and institutions, who are forever asking the values questions, should know more (and share more) about ourselves; therein lie clues to inform our work and our lives. For these reasons I offer my story.

THE STORY OF GIP (ABRIDGED)

The Internal Conflict

We began the CSA well aware of its split personality—what Cynthia Cone has referred to as its produce or market orientation vs. its deep eco-value or philosophical nature. We were going to grow good vegetables (in Joan Gussow's sense of the term) as a way to build community. Vegetables were the calling card to bring local residents to an active awareness of each other, their ecosystem, and their food system. GIP was to be a shared experience, an embodied experience, one available to everyone throughout a ten- to fifteen-mile radius of the farm. We embraced the philosophy of the early CSA movement, as expressed by Traugher Groh, that there is a "need to share the experience of farming with everyone who understands that our relationship with nature and the ways that we use the land will determine the future of the earth." We, too, felt that "the problems of agriculture and the environment belong not just to a small minority of active farmers, [but] are the problems of all humanity" (Groh and McFadden xiii) and that CSA was "a way of healing our soils and our souls" (Kirschenmann 107).

Full of high purpose, if not missionary zeal, we began as a not-for-profit corporation. We also began, not as farmers, but as visionaries—academics largely, with twenty acres of dedicated farmland (of which we would use four) and little farming experience among us. This would not matter, we felt, as we and our shareholders would be learning together; in fact, this was the very point of the exercise. And in this, oddly enough, we were correct. It wasn't our lack of farming know-how that proved most difficult, rather, as I see it now, it was the pervasive market mind-set—the tyranny of capital—that overwhelmed us and demoralized organizers and members alike.

Let me stop a moment here and make myself clear. I certainly do not mean to imply that farming organically is a simple proposition, or that it is anything other than the artful application of place-bound, ecologically based knowledge acquired over the course of many lifetimes. What I am saying is that we felt that if nature could forgive (at least up until now) the ravages of industrial agriculture, she wouldn't begrudge the silly efforts of a handful of social activists turned organic gardeners, and she didn't. We were able—by reading books, attending workshops, talking to local farmers, and surfing the net—to grow vegetables adequate, if just barely adequate, to our purpose.

Far less obliging was our own habituated thinking. Despite our non-profit status and guiding philosophy, we trapped ourselves in a classic market dilemma and then argued in circles. How would we manage financially? If we were to hire a farmer or farm manager (something we did not do the first year but did the second), then we would need income. To generate income we would need paying members or produce sales. But the more paying shares we attracted, or the more commercial our products became, the more experienced the farmer we would need to hire and the greater the income we would need to generate. From the start, we set ourselves up to chase the dollar rather than settling in, identifying the resources at hand, and taking the slow route of truly sharing our labor, learning from one other, and accepting the outcome with equal grace.

As a group, we never asked ourselves how we might best work with what we had. Instead, we with middle-class sensibilities kept pondering what we could do if we had more money. If we only had a tractor, if we only had another $10,000, *then* we could hire, or build, or bigger. And the odd thing, looking back on it, even when we found a tractor, took in $10,000, and built ourselves a couple of serviceable outbuildings using scavenged materials, the strain and the wanting never abated. I, typically, found myself the odd woman out. As president, I argued against financial loans and further expansion and for recycled materials and volunteered efforts. I was not popular, but I kept us out of debt. Nonetheless, I came home from board meetings with knots in my stomach and considerable foreboding.

The effect of our orientation was to grow more pronounced over time. Initially, it contributed to our becoming too large too soon. Buoyed by a beginner's euphoria, flattered by an immediate public interest (and the promise of income), we accepted fifty full shares—two times as many as we wanted, four times as many as we needed. Simply put, we were not conservative; we did not know our limits or our competence. As a result, we acquired, along with some eighty households, two-thirds of which had given us between two hundred and four hundred dollars, an instantaneous obligation to produce. And having grabbed the project from the financial end, we framed our obligation in terms of dollars and not in terms of people. We spent far less time asking ourselves whether members (we included) understood the farm as a living enterprise and could visualize their place within it than we did asking ourselves whether they were getting their money's worth. This was the same question newspaper reporters invariably asked us, and it was the same question the state agricultural commissioners asked when they visited the farm (and reluctantly choked down a fresh salad garnished with nasturtium and borage blossoms, wishing all the while for burgers and fries).

But it was the wrong question. It suggested that the value of GIP could be (and should be) found in dollars and cents, and that the farm, to be successful, had to compete with the commercial market on the market's terms. And it fostered ridiculous behavior. I remember, for example, one member complaining that there was too much produce for her to use in a week. Yet when I suggested that she take less or give a portion to another family who might need it, she declined. To do that, she allowed, would mean she'd be paying too much for her vegetables. Such thinking framed the CSA as an alternative market arrangement rather than a partial alternative to the market economy. It submerged community beneath consumption and later beneath convenience. While we who began the farm believed neither should be true, we found ourselves behaving as if both were.

A Dubious Sharing

Those of us who worked, overworked—grossly overworked. We voluntarily exploited ourselves to give those who purchased shares a full return on their investment. How else were we to convince people of the worthiness of the enterprise? What we created, as a consequence, were interpersonal tensions and invidious distinctions. Those who worked in the field— and there were only eight to ten individuals who did so on a predictable basis—disregarded sunburns, bad backs, family obligations, and leisure pursuits to get the ground prepared, the stones picked, the weeds subdued, the gardens planted, the crops harvested, and the membership organized. We kept the heat on in the hoophouse, the frost off the okra, the tools picked up, the porches swept, and the bills paid. We were also the ones who agonized over how to compensate the membership for planting errors or hail-damaged lettuce. Despite the underlying premise that we would share the risks and rewards of the season, we were not willing to do so. We were not willing to share the tough stuff. In classic farmer fashion, we personally absorbed the risk and gave away our labor (and our hearts) in the process.

What this did was to make the raising of good food appear far easier (and less significant) than it truly was. When distributions were made on time and in respectable abundance, when the produce of other area farmers supplemented GIP's own, when extras such as organic apple cider, dried-flower arrangements, homemade cookies, or potted plants were offered as perks, we encouraged (however inadvertently) a disconnect between people and the processes that brought them their food. We absolved them of the need to see and feel the effort for themselves. Members took what we offered. This was the contract. And many never said "Thank you."

Members with full distribution bags would stand in the gardens and talk, often for an hour at a time, without once bending down to pick a weed or deadhead a flower. (They were not reluctant to point out, however, that the basil needed water.) It was ironic and maddening to find midseason when members were asked to cut their own lettuce that the majority did not know where it was planted and literally no one (apart from my family) came to harvest the tons of beets, turnips, collards, kale, rutabagas, and carrots that remained in the gardens after the final distribution.

And yet, even when efforts were made, the lessons drawn were often problematic. I overheard a conversation between a mother and daughter who had come to lend a hand during what we hopefully called a weeding party. "Now that you know how much work this really is," the mother lectured, "you'll appreciate being able to buy your food at Felpausch."

The less members contributed, of course, the more heroic the efforts of the lone few appeared (especially to themselves) and the more resentful they became of others. I was no exception. I remember one remarkable distribution day when only two of us had shown up to harvest. An hour before distribution was to begin and six hours after I began harvesting, two young working women (at least ten years younger than I) appeared to ask if they could pick up their shares early. I explained that there were still some vegetables left to harvest. I would go and pick their shares for them, but perhaps, I nudged, they could thin the carrots or weigh produce or do something, while they waited. No, they reflected, this was not what they had in mind; they'd find a place in town to have coffee and come back in a little while. I know I came close to disemboweling them with my hand trowel, all the while wondering to myself whether I'd earned a Ph.D. in servility and just when it was that I had changed from a fool to a damned fool.

A steady diet of such incidents helped to fuel a slow-burning indignation toward the membership generally, and, sadly, toward those individuals who made an attempt, however tentative, to involve themselves in the farm. The pressure was to produce, to get by from day to day, to anticipate the next "need," to make things work. *And no one ever did enough.* We were operating on mechanical not spiritual energy. Less and less time was spent enjoying the moment, the company of others, or finding reasons to identify with the place. On those occasions when someone did remember to take a breath, read a poem, watch a leopard frog, share a hug or an extra beer, the emotional release was palpable. But for all their potency, these were the exceptional moments.

Would it have been different with a dedicated and skillful farmer—certainly. It would have been far less stressful for some of us and undoubtedly more stable memberwise. There may well have been more smiles and prettier vegetables, important matters to be sure. Still I'm not at all convinced that the internal disjunctures in vision or action would have disappeared or that the community aspect of CSA would have flowered into anything more meaningful. Neither do I think the membership would have grown any more environmentally attentive. Rhetoric aside, as I read accounts of today's working CSAs, few are really sharing the burdens of food production or the embodied experience, but are providing a pleasant and thoroughly necessary brand of subscription farming. They are places where, as one GIP member put it, "You can bring your kids and pet the corn."

This is not a bad situation. It may even be as good as it gets for mainstream America. At the same time, it is not the reason that I threw my middle-aged body into the breach or why I felt it important to work thirty to forty hours a week at the farm. I did it to tap cooperative effort, to invite people to see beyond themselves, and to encourage even small sacrifices for a greater common purpose. The farm was to be a commons and its existence a common responsibility. This, of course, was delusional.

As if to confirm this, one paid member took the time to tell us that she was deeply offended. We should have looked on her money as a resource. We, she felt, had devalued its importance and treated her as a second-class citizen. She hadn't been able to manage her seasonal work requirement— twelve hours over six months—because she had a two-year-old daughter, nor was there any reason why she should be made to feel guilty. Her last CSA had made no such demand and this was not what CSAs were about. If *we* were having labor problems then *we* needed to manage *our* work shares better; *her* money would no doubt help. Another member asked bluntly, "What have you got against hiring a farmer? I have no interest in volunteering on the farm and I am never going to come out and pull weeds. I will support a local farmer, someone who can grow my food for me." She advised that, at the very least, we get help from the experts at the university, people who could tell us how to farm properly. Still others allowed that if fresh produce was available in their neighborhood grocery they wouldn't join a CSA at all. One returned survey simply instructed "concentrate on the vegetables, and stop forcing an artificial community." And therein lies a dilemma.

It is hard to accept that GIP is artificial especially for those who gave their sweat, time, and passion. Yet for all our effort this may well be true.

There is no necessity for GIP to be where it was, in Mason. Our lives and our livelihoods do not depend on its existence. Members can find food else-where—anywhere; they will not starve. Likewise, there is no necessity to abide personal dislikes and discomforts. When pushed too hard, members find no inducement to rethink the offensive remark or behavior, reflect on its wider context, weigh it against a greater need, and negotiate a solution. One woman, after being told to cut the root clump from each head of lettuce before tossing it into the wash tank, soundlessly got up and left the CSA forever. (Whatever else might have been going on at the time will remain forever unknown.) No barns, as Daniel Kemmis points out, were ever raised on such a brittle foundation of interpersonal relationships.

Neither do we have a local tradition or a cultural history to fall back on as do, for example, many rural residents of Finland who without money are using the tradition of "talkoot," or voluntary teamwork, to revitalize community life and craft in the face of industrial development (Pietila). We're much more likely to remove our historic traditions and landmarks to convenient locations, where like butterflies pinned to a board, they can be displayed as very dead specimens or as decorative motifs. Under these conditions, Berry's affection of place, Kirschenmann's love of soil, Illich's sense of the vernacular, or Esteva's sense of *comida* are romantic but hollow notions. Who can afford to give them life, to make them happen?

With little beyond an immediate appreciation for chemical-free, fresh vegetables to bind us together, working members can logically argue (as many did), "I don't need this; I didn't know when I signed up that it would become my life. I'm outta here." With no sense of mutual responsibility around which to build a collective identity how do we realize community and a loyalty to place? As one member put it, "When I want community I can go to my dance community, or my church community, or my teacher colleagues, or I can e-mail my high school buddies. I don't need GIP." We were (and still are) light years away from realizing community in the sense that Selznick had in mind when he wrote, "a group is a community to the extent that it encompasses a broad range of activities and interests and to the extent that participation implicates whole persons rather than seg-mental interests or activities" (199). We were (and still are) dealing with individualized communities and not with communitized individuals.

I have little doubt that, even as CSAs go, GIP's original conception was a bit unusual, an exaggeration perhaps on the community theme, but the circumstances into which it was born were not. We were trying to operate (and we still are) in a society that manufactures greeting cards to console the families of suicide victims (Parsons) and in a state that recently hired the Disney Institute "to help teach Michigan workers not to be grumpy"—that they can "make more money (from tourism) by being nice" ("State Hires"). As members of an industrial society propelled by a capitalist market economy, our more recent traditions permit us to enclose everything we know and own, from land to food to relationships to bodies and emotions. We cater to—we sanctify—the encapsulated individual and the individualized solutions that he or she manipulates to accommodate convenience and the demands of linear time.

Still there are those who contend, and I believe correctly, that CSA members are politically aware, environmentally active, and health conscious, and that by belonging to a CSA, by supporting local food production, members are engaged in social resistance. If this is resistance (and I think it is), it is nonetheless a highly individualized or personalized resistance—a resistance primarily of consumers, not of citizens. The fight remains centered in the marketplace and not in the living place. It is not yet a matter of "right livelihood." Stated somewhat differently, it supports a vision, to quote Gabriel and Lang, that lacks "any wider notion of social solidarity, civic debate, coordinated action or sacrifice. It individualizes the idea of citizenship, as if becoming a citizen is a matter of individual choice alone. In this way, citizenship becomes a life-style, however, praiseworthy and necessary, which can easily degenerate into tokenism and is hardly likely to alter the politics of consumption" (182).

Somewhat Wiser

And this is where I backed myself into a corner. For me it was communities and communities of communities, not individuals, that needed to resist the forces of globalization and commodification. And if we were to build community, we needed to share both the vision and the effort. If it was to be a common enterprise, then it (and we) needed a common language tied to "the project of inhabiting and knowing a place." Consistent with this, I felt that we shouldn't cater to members as customers (and, of late, I have heard CSA advocates use this term, just as I have read about individual farmers selling their CSAs. How, I wonder, can a CSA be individually owned?). To cater to members as customers, I argued, would undermine the basis for community. If, on the other hand, we attended diligently to member comfort and convenience—if we established drop-off sites, hired "real" farmers, grew lovelier vegetables, and threw nicer parties—if, in other words, we didn't push an already food-conscious and environmentally sensitive membership to move beyond their private concerns and engage in new interdependencies, into a more organic existence, where would community come from? As Sanders cautions, "We should not have to wait until our houses are burning [or, I would add, our larders are empty or our horizons asphalted] before we see the wisdom of facing our local needs by joining in common work" (47).

I believed this then and I believe it now. But I could not, for good reason, make it happen. I could not change the world or even that small part in my own backyard. I was, among other things, too impatient, too dogmatic, and too tired. My academic arguments, my raw idealism, and my residual New York manner, while indispensable to the creation of the CSA, also generated considerable Midwest discomfort. Direct confrontation may be honorable, but it doesn't leave room for much long-term cooperation or warm personal friendship.

After two years of self-designed martyrdom, I recognized that I had to step down as board president and allow others to make the decisions and assume the responsibility if Growing in Place was to survive. To my surprise, this was something several members readily agreed to do.

What at first felt like an act of defeat and personal rejection now feels like a constructive solution — the turning over of a new institution to others for local management. And while those currently at the helm come to meetings clutching McDonalds soft drinks and teeny beanie babies and extolling the benefits of Weight Watchers and Sam's Wholesale Buying Club, still no community effort can proceed without them. I've not capitulated, I tell myself; I've merely set my watch to generational, if not ecological, time. To help with this, I remind myself of a harvest day this past season when two little boys, one two and one three, came with their mothers to help wash and pack vegetables. As the sun got warmer and their clothes got wetter, they began discarding them piece by piece. When they were totally unencumbered, they found new and greater purpose. They climbed onto the parked tractor and started to farm. Two naked babies, warm in the sun, sitting proudly on the seat of a fifty-year-old tractor were at ease with themselves and their universe. What better metaphor can there be for growing in place?

Am I better for the experience? I think so. I do not regret the many hours or the spent emotions. I will not deny the experience, and I know absolutely that GIP was (and is) real, not artificial. I know that I am now increasingly interested in the notion of the "commons" and in the nature of common property rights and responsibilities as well as in the history of those few CSAs that appear able to balance "a green space beyond self-interest"(Worpole) with "practical" market demands. I also know that if I had kept my distance, surveyed and observed GIP (or CSAs generally) like any good ethnographer, I would have understood its structural contradictions and operational dilemmas, I would have slept better and written more, but I would not have written from any visceral attachment or passion. We all need to do this from time to time. We need to allow ourselves to become vulnerable and begin to see things, ourselves included, in expanded perspective.

It is at this deeper level that I find myself drawn to words of playwright John Patrick Shanley when he writes in the preface to *Thirteen Plays*:

> "The individual life is a dream." For me personally, this is a most moving idea. It frees me from my fear of death. It puts my ego where it belongs, in a place of secondary importance. It binds me to the human race, and binds the race itself to the atoms in the stars. . . .
>
> I am not a courageous person by nature. I have simply discovered that, at certain key moments in this life, you must find courage in yourself, in order to move forward and live. It is like a muscle and it must be exercised, first a little, and then more and more. All the really exciting things possible during the course of a lifetime require a little more courage than we currently have. A deep breath and a leap.
>
> Writing is acting is directing is living your life. . . . I see no difference between writing a play and living my life. The same things that make a moment in my life succeed, combust, move, these things make a moment in my playwriting have life. And when I move in my writing, I have moved in my life. There is no illusion. It is all the same thing.

This expresses, better than I could ever do, the value of my encounter with GIP. As a strengthening experience it is not limited to my own self-reflexive moments—or even necessarily to CSAs. It can, I hope, invite a conversation and a sharing of lessons learned across other contexts of personal negotiation and community building, contexts in which people globally are trying to cope locally with the circumstances, the indignities, and minor triumphs of advanced capitalism.

NOTE

1. An earlier version of this essay was delivered as the presidential address to the Agriculture, Food, and Human Values Society, San Francisco, June 4–7, 1998; and appeared in *Agriculture and Human Values* 16 (1999): 3–9.

REFERENCES

Berry, Wendell. "The Work of Local Culture." *What Are People For?* San Francisco: North Point, 1990. 153–69.

Cone, Cynthia Abbott, and Ann Kakaliouras. "Community-Supported Agriculture: Building Moral Community or An Alternative Consumer Choice?" *Culture and Agriculture (C&A) Bulletin* 51/52 (1995): 28–31.

Esteva, Gustavo. "Re-embedding Food in Agriculture." *Culture and Agriculture (C&A) Bulletin* 48 (1994): 2–13.

Gabriel, Yiannis, and Tim Lang. *The Unmanageable Consumer: Contemporary Consumption and its Fragmentations.* London: Sage, 1995.

Groh, Traugher, and Steven McFadden. *Farms of Tomorrow Revisited.* Kimberton, Penn.: Biodynamic Farming and Gardening Association, 1997.

Illich, Ivan. *In the Mirror of the Past: Lectures and Addresses, 1978–1990.* New York: Marion Boyars, 1992.

Kemmis, Daniel. "Barn Raising." In *Rooted in the Land: Essays on Community and Place,* edited by William Vitek and Wes Jackson, 167–75. New Haven: Yale University Press, 1996.

Kirschenmann, Frederick. "On Becoming Lovers of the Soil." In *For all Generations: Making World Agriculture More Sustainable,* edited by J. Patrick Madden and Scott G. Chaplowe, 101–14. Glendale: O.M./AWSAA, 1998.

Orr, David. *Ecological Literacy.* Albany: SUNY Press, 1992.

———. *Earth In Mind.* Washington, D.C.: Island Press, 1994.

Parsons, Monique. "New Card Consoles Families of Suicide Victims." *Lansing State Journal* (5 February 1998): 1D.

Pietila, Hilkka. "The Villages in Finland Refuse to Die." *Ecologist* 27, no. 5 (1997): 178–81.

Sanders, Scott Russell. "The Common Life." In Vitek and Jackson, *Rooted in the Land,* 40–49.

Selznick, Philip. "In Search of Community." In Vitek and Jackson, *Rooted in the Land,* 195–203.

Shanley, John Patrick. *13 By Shanley.* New York, Applause: 1992.

"State Hires Disney for Charm Tips." *Lansing State Journal* 8 March 1998: 1C.

Worpole, Ken. "A Green Space Beyond Self-interest." *New Statesman* 30 May 1997: 30–31.

Law

PATRICIA J. WILLIAMS

The Death of the Profane

(a commentary on the

genre of legal writing)

From *The Alchemy of Race and Rights*

Buzzers are big in New York City. Favored particularly by smaller stores and boutiques, merchants throughout the city have installed them as screening devices to reduce the incidence of robbery: if the face at the door looks desirable, the buzzer is pressed and the door is unlocked. If the face is that of an undesirable, the door stays locked. Predictably, the issue of undesirability has revealed itself to be a racial determination. While controversial enough at first, even civil-rights organizations backed down eventually in the face of arguments that the buzzer system is a "necessary evil," that it is a "mere inconvenience" in comparison to the risks of being murdered, that suffering discrimination is not as bad as being assaulted, and that in any event it is not all blacks who are barred, just "17-year-old black males wearing running shoes and hooded sweatshirts."[1]

The installation of these buzzers happened swiftly in New York; stores that had always had their doors wide open suddenly became exclusive or received people by appointment only. I discovered them and their meaning one Saturday in 1986. I was shopping in Soho and saw in a store window a sweater that I wanted to buy for my mother. I pressed my round brown face to the window and my finger to the buzzer, seeking admittance. A narrow-eyed, white teenager wearing running shoes and feasting on bubble gum glared out, evaluating me for signs that would pit me against the limits of his social understanding. After about five seconds, he mouthed "We're closed," and blew pink rubber at me. It was two Saturdays before Christmas, at one o'clock in the afternoon; there were several white people in the store who appeared to be shopping for things for *their* mothers.

I was enraged. At that moment I literally wanted to break all the windows of the store and *take* lots of sweaters for my mother. In the flicker of his judgmental gray eyes, that saleschild had transformed my brightly sentimental, joy-to-the-world, pre-Christmas spree to a shambles. He snuffed my sense of humanitarian catholicity, and there was nothing I could do to snuff his, without making a spectacle of myself.

I am still struck by the structure of power that drove me into such a blizzard of rage. There was almost nothing I could do, short of physically intruding upon him, that would humiliate him the way he humiliated me. No words, no gestures, no prejudices of my own would make a bit of difference to him; his refusal to let me into the store—it was Benetton's, whose colorfully punnish ad campaign is premised on wrapping every one of the world's peoples in its cottons and woolens—was an outward manifestation of his never having let someone like me into the realm of his reality. He had no compassion, no remorse, no reference to me; and no desire to acknowledge me even at the estranged level of arm's-length transactor. He saw me only as one who would take his money and therefore could not conceive that I was there to give him money.

In this weird ontological imbalance, I realized that buying something in that store was like bestowing a gift, the gift of my commerce, the lucre of my patronage. In the wake of my outrage, I wanted to take back the gift of appreciation that my peering in the window must have appeared to be. I wanted to take it back in the form of unappreciation, disrespect, defilement. I wanted to work so hard at wishing he could feel what I felt that he would never again mistake my hatred for some sort of plaintive wish to be included. I was quite willing to disenfranchise myself, in the heat of my need to revoke the flattery of my purchasing power. I was willing to boycott Benetton's, random white-owned businesses, and anyone who ever blew bubble gum in my face again.

My rage was admittedly diffuse, even self-destructive, but it was symmetrical. The perhaps loose-ended but utter propriety of that rage is no doubt lost not just to the young man who actually barred me, but to those who would appreciate my being barred only as an abstract precaution, who approve of those who would bar even as they deny that they would bar *me*.

The violence of my desire to burst into Benetton's is probably quite apparent. I often wonder if the violence, the exclusionary hatred, is equally apparent in the repeated public urgings that blacks understand the buzzer system by putting themselves in the shoes of white storeowners—that, in effect, blacks look into the mirror of frightened white faces for the reality of their undesirability; and that then blacks would "just as surely conclude that [they] would not let [themselves] in under similar circumstances."[2]

(That some blacks might agree merely shows that some of us have learned too well the lessons of privatized intimacies of self-hatred and rationalized away the fullness of our public, participatory selves.)

On the same day I was barred from Benetton's, I went home and wrote the above impassioned account in my journal. On the day after that, I found I was still brooding, so I turned to a form of catharsis I have always found healing. I typed up as much of the story as I have just told, made a big poster of it, put a nice colorful border around it, and, after Benetton's was truly closed, stuck it to their big sweater-filled window. I exercised my first-amendment right to place my business with them right out in the street.

So that was the first telling of this story. The second telling came a few months later, for a symposium on Excluded Voices sponsored by a law review. I wrote an essay summing up my feelings about being excluded from Benetton's and analyzing "how the rhetoric of increased privatization, in response to racial issues, functions as the rationalizing agent of public unaccountability and, ultimately, irresponsibility." Weeks later, I received the first edit. From the first page to the last, my fury had been carefully cut out. My rushing, run-on-rage had been reduced to simple declarative sentences. The active personal had been inverted in favor of the passive impersonal. My words were different; they spoke to me upsidedown. I was afraid to read too much of it at a time—meanings rose up at me oddly, stolen and strange.

A week and a half later, I received the second edit. All reference to Benetton's had been deleted because, according to the editors and the faculty adviser, it was defamatory; they feared harassment and liability; they said printing it would be irresponsible. I called them and offered to supply a footnote attesting to this as my personal experience at one particular location and of a buzzer system not limited to Benetton's; the editors told me that they were not in the habit of publishing things that were unverifiable. I could not but wonder, in this refusal even to let me file an affadavit, what it would take to make my experience verifiable. The testimony of an independent white bystander? (a requirement in fact imposed in U.S. Supreme Court holdings through the first part of the century[3]).

Two days *after* the piece was sent to press, I received copies of the final page proofs. All reference to my race had been eliminated because it was against "editorial policy" to permit descriptions of physiognomy. "I realize," wrote one editor, "that this was a very personal experience, but any reader will know what you must have looked like when standing at that window." In a telephone conversation to them, I ranted wildly about the significance of such an omission. "It's irrelevant," another editor explained in a voice gummy with soothing and patience; "It's nice and poetic," but it doesn't "advance the discussion of any principle. . . . This is a law review, after all." Frustrated, I accused him of censorship; calmly he assured me it was not. "This is just a matter of style," he said with firmness and finality.

Ultimately I did convince the editors that mention of my race was central to the whole sense of the subsequent text; that my story became one of extreme paranoia without the information that I am black; or that it became one in which the reader had to fill in the gap by assumption, presumption, prejudgment, or prejudice. What was most interesting to me in this experience was how the blind application of principles of neutrality, through the device of omission, acted either to make me look crazy or to make the reader participate in old habits of cultural bias.

That was the second telling of my story. The third telling came last April, when I was invited to participate in a law-school conference on Equality and Difference. I retold my sad tale of exclusion from Soho's most glitzy boutique, focusing in this version on the law-review editing process as a consequence of an ideology of style rooted in a social text of neutrality. I opined:

> Law and legal writing aspire to formalized, color-blind, liberal ideals. Neutrality is the standard for assuring these ideals; yet the adherence to it is often determined by reference to an aesthetic of uniformity, in which difference is simply omitted. For example, when segregation was eradicated from the American lexicon, its omission led many to actually believe that racism therefore no longer existed. Race-neutrality in law has become the presumed antidote for race bias in real life. With the entrenchment of the notion of race-neutrality came attacks on the concept of affirmative action and the rise of reverse discrimination suits. Blacks, for so many generations deprived of jobs based on the color of our skin, are now told that we ought to find it demeaning to be hired, based on the color of our skin. Such is the silliness of simplistic either-or inversions as remedies to complex problems.
>
> What is truly demeaning in this era of double-speak-no-evil is going on interviews and not getting hired because someone doesn't think we'll be comfortable. It is demeaning not to get promoted because we're judged "too weak," then putting in a lot of energy the next time and getting fired because we're "too strong." It is demeaning to be told what we find demeaning. It is very demeaning to stand on street corners unemployed and begging. It is downright demeaning to have to explain why we haven't

been employed for months and then watch the job go to someone who is "more experienced." It is outrageously demeaning that none of this can be called racism, even if it happens only to, or to large numbers of, black people; as long as it's done with a smile, a handshake, and a shrug; as long as the phantom-word "race" is never used.

The image of race as a phantom-word came to me after I moved into my late godmother's home. In an attempt to make it my own, I cleared the bedroom for painting. The following morning the room asserted itself, came rushing and raging at me through the emptiness, exactly as it had been for twenty-five years. One day filled with profuse and overwhelming complexity, the next day filled with persistently recurring memories. The shape of the past came to haunt me, the shape of the emptiness confronted me each time I was about to enter the room. The force of its spirit still drifts like an odor throughout the house.

The power of that room, I have thought since, is very like the power of racism as status quo: it is deep, angry, eradicated from view, but strong enough to make everyone who enters the room walk around the bed that isn't there, avoiding the phantom as they did the substance, for fear of bodily harm. They do not even know they are avoiding; they defer to the unseen shapes of things with subtle responsiveness, guided by an impulsive awareness of nothingness, and the deep knowledge and denial of witchcraft at work.

The phantom room is to me symbolic of the emptiness of formal equal opportunity, particularly as propounded by President Reagan, the Reagan Civil Rights Commission, and the Reagan Supreme Court. Blindly formalized constructions of equal opportunity are the creation of a space that is filled in by a meandering stream of unguided hopes, dreams, fantasies, fears, recollections. They are the presence of the past in imaginary, imagistic form—the phantom-roomed exile of our longing.

It is thus that I strongly believe in the efficacy of programs and paradigms like affirmative action. Blacks are the objects of a constitutional omission which has been incorporated into a theory of neutrality. It is thus that omission is really a form of expression, as oxymoronic as that sounds: racial omission is a literal part of original intent; it is the fixed, reiterated prophecy of the Founding Fathers. It is thus that affirmative action is an affirmation; the affirmative act of hiring—or hearing—blacks is a recognition of individuality that re-places blacks as a social statistic, that is profoundly interconnective to the fate of blacks and whites either as subgroups or as one group. In this sense, affirmative action is as mystical and beyond-the-self as an initiation ceremony. It is an act of verification and of vision. It is an act of social as well as professional responsibility.

The following morning I opened the local newspaper, to find that the event of my speech had commanded two columns on the front page of the Metro section. I quote only the opening lines: "Affirmative action promotes prejudice by denying the status of women and blacks, instead of affirming them as its name suggests. So said New York City attorney Patricia Williams to an audience Wednesday."[4]

I clipped out the article and put it in my journal. In the margin there is a note to myself: eventually, it says, I should try to pull all these threads together into yet another law-review article. The problem, of course, will be that in the hierarchy of law-review citation, the article in the newspaper will have more authoritative weight about me, as a so-called "primary resource," than I will have; it will take precedence over my own citation of the unverifiable testimony of my speech.

. . .

I have used the Benetton's story a lot, in speaking engagements at various schools. I tell it whenever I am too tired to whip up an original speech from scratch. Here are some of the questions I have been asked in the wake of its telling:

Am I not privileging a racial perspective, by considering only the black point of view? Don't I have an obligation to include the "salesman's side" of the story?

Am I not putting the salesman on trial and finding him guilty of racism without giving him a chance to respond to or cross-examine me?

Am I not using the store window as a "metaphorical fence" against the potential of his explanation in order to represent my side as "authentic"?

How can I be sure I'm right?

What makes my experience the real black one anyway?

Isn't it possible that another black person would disagree with my experience? If so, doesn't that render my story too unempirical and subjective to pay any attention to?

Always a major objection is to my having put the poster on Benetton's window. As one law professor put it: "It's one thing to publish this in a law review, where no one can take it personally, but it's another thing altogether to put your own interpretation right out there, just like that, uncontested, I mean, with nothing to counter it."[5]

NOTES

1. "When 'By Appointment' Means Keep Out," *New York Times*, December 17, 1986, B1. Letter to the Editor from Michael Levin and Marguerita Levin, *New York Times*, 11 January 1987, E32.
2. *New York Times*, 11 January 1987, E32.
3. See generally *Blyew v. U.S.*, 80 U.S. 581 (1871), upholding a state's right to forbid blacks to testify against whites.
4. "Attorney Says Affirmative Action Denies Racism, Sexism," *Dominion Post*, (Morgantown, West Virginia), 8 April 1988, B1.
5. These questions put me on trial—an imaginary trial where it is I who have the burden of proof—and proof being nothing less than the testimony of the salesman actually confessing yes yes I am a racist. These questions question my own ability to know, to assess, to be objective. And of course, since anything that happens to me is inherently subjective, they take away my power to know what happens to me in the world. Others, by this standard, will always know better than I. And my insistence on recounting stories from my own perspective will be treated as presumption, slander, paranoid hallucination, or just plain lies.

    Recently I got an urgent call from Thomas Grey of Stanford Law School. He had used this piece in his jurisprudence class, and a rumor got started that the Benetton's story wasn't true, that I had made it up, that it was a fantasy, a lie that was probably the product of a diseased mind trying to make all white people feel guilty. At this point I realized it almost didn't make any difference whether I was telling the truth or not—that the greater issue I had to face was the overwhelming weight of a disbelief that goes beyond mere disinclination to believe and becomes active suppression of anything I might have to say. The greater problem is a powerfully oppressive mechanism for denial of black self-knowledge and expression. And this denial cannot be separated from the simultaneously pathological willingness to believe certain things about blacks—not to believe them, but things about them.

    When students in Grey's class believed and then claimed that I had made it all up, they put me in a position like that of Tawana Brawley. I mean that specifically: the social consequence of concluding that we are liars operates as a kind of public absolution of racism—the conclusion is not merely that we are troubled or that I am eccentric, but that we, as liars, are the norm. Therefore, the nonbelievers can believe, things of this sort really don't happen (even in the face of statistics to the contrary). Racism or rape is all a big fantasy concocted by troublesome minorities and women. It is interesting to recall the outcry in every national medium, from the *New York Post* to the *Times* to the major networks, in the wake of the Brawley case: who will ever again believe a black woman who cries rape by a white man? . . . Now shift the frame a bit, and imagine a white male facing a consensus that he lied. Would there be a difference? Consider Charles Stuart, for example, the white Bostonian who accused a black man of murdering his pregnant wife and whose brother later alleged that in fact the brothers had conspired to murder her. Most people and the media not only did not claim but actively resisted believing that Stuart represented any kind of "white male" norm. Instead he was written off as a troubled weirdo, a deviant—again even in the face of spousal-abuse statistics to the contrary. There was not a story I could find that carried on about "who will ever believe" the next white man who cries murder.

English Education

BRENDA DALY

My Father/My Censor:

English Education,

Politics, and Status

From *Authoring a Life: A Woman's Survival in and through Literary Studies*

When Jane Tompkins announces in "Me and My Shadow" her intention to deliberately transgress the public-private hierarchy, which she defines as "a founding condition of female oppression," I immediately want to join the revolution (123). I want to believe, as she and other feminists do, that "the reason I feel embarrassed at my own attempts to speak personally is that I have been conditioned to feel that way. That's all there is to it" (123). And I want to say, as Jane does, "to hell with it!" (123). But for me, although conditioning is certainly a major part of what inhibits me, there's more to it. At this very moment, as I struggle to resist the [paternal] voice inside which tells me to censor personal disclosures that have a profound bearing upon my work in English education, I must confront the powerful emotional inhibitions, the fear and shame, that enforce the conditioning for secrecy. Because Jane Tompkins has read an essay of mine called "Father-Daughter Incest in Hadley Irwin's *Abby, My Love*" in which I did not self-disclose, she will understand my ambivalence in the present essay: I don't want to tell the public (even as I do tell) that my analysis of *Abby, My Love* is based, in part, upon personal experience. At the same time, I know that Jane is absolutely right when she says that "an epistemology which excludes emotions from the process of attaining knowledge radically undercuts women's epistemic authority" (123). As I can testify, my own writing has acquired greater authority as I have acknowledged that my literary analysis of father-daughter incest is not just an academic exercise, but part of an ongoing struggle, through self-therapy, to grow stronger.

The writing process can be excruciatingly painful for survivors of incest. For example, while writing an essay on teenage runaways in Joyce Carol Oates's fiction in the summer of 1988, I twisted my body into such painful

contortions that I had to see a doctor. When I tried to present this paper at
M/MLA in the fall of 1988, I nearly fainted—to the understandable irritation
of the session chair. What I wanted to say then, but couldn't yet, was that
I knew from personal experience that many runaway girls are incest victims. In 1990, after consciously acknowledging the connections between
the sexual victimization of adolescent runaway girls and their lack of narrative authority, I submitted a confused revision of this same paper to the
editors of a collection called *Anxious Power*. While writing "Anxious Power
in the Early Fiction of Joyce Carol Oates," I was as anxious about my own
epistemic authority as I was about Oates's female characters. Fortunately,
despite its flaws, the editors of *Anxious Power* saw the essay's potential, and
in the process of revision I began to confront and overcome the effects
of childhood abuse upon my writing. My struggle to organize the essay,
despite the chaos of my emotions, was one symptom; another symptom
was my tendency to bury the topic sentences of paragraphs. I recognize,
as I write this essay, that I was afraid of self-assertion. In my (unconscious)
mind, self-assertion was analogous to an overt display of sexuality, and,
to many men, an invitation to verbal/sexual attack. What a relief to discover the causes of this inhibition and, finally, in this essay, begin mapping
the emotional terrain of reading and writing, discovering previously hidden connections among my personal, professional, and political selves. This
journey into my own "heart of darkness" is frightening at times, but wonderfully liberating. As I re-assemble my various selves into a stronger and
more coherent writing persona, I feel as if I am writing—to use Emily
Dickinson's wonderful phrase—with my "soul at the white heat."

Until now, for example, I never understood that my concern with social
and professional status can be attributed to the fact that I am the child of
an immigrant: my father came from Norway when he was six years old.
Indeed, it worries me to admit my concern with status because, as everyone knows, such self-disclosure can be risky in a status-conscious academic
world, a world in which what others know about you can be used against
you. In short, it isn't just conditioning—but one's realization about the
actualities of power—that makes self-disclosure risky. To be vulnerable is
to risk the loss of authority. As any classroom teacher knows intuitively: if
I look anxious, students won't respect me; I must look confident, no matter
how afraid I feel. Because part of me does not want to give up my status,
does not want to risk my authority, I would rather not tell you how my
work in English education has roots deep in my nightmarish childhood.
But, following the example of Jane and others, I'm going to say "to hell

with it." After all, I am a newly tenured associate professor of English at Iowa State University, the "second best" university in the state, and I now claim some professional status. And this status, although not apparent in my salary, will soon to be reflected in spatial terms: I have been promised a private office in Ross Hall. For the first time in eighteen years of teaching—seven years at three different high schools, four years as a graduate student teaching associate, and seven years as an assistant professor (five of them at Iowa State)—I will have a room of my own in an English department. I'm enough of a skeptic, however, not to believe in this room until I actually inhabit it.

Furthermore, my status as a professor of English education, not English literature, remains troubling to me for reasons both professional and personal. It is easy to explain the professional dimension of the problem: any association with secondary English teaching is considered, if it is considered at all, as a second- or third-class academic assignment. I think everybody knows this; therefore, I hardly need to add that my problem is neither an individual nor a local one. "A chronic lack of status vis-à-vis other disciplines" is a problem for anyone associated with departments of education, according to John Goodlad, who directs the Center for Educational Renewal at the University of Washington ("Goodlad Tests His Vision" 1). Goodlad argues that education acquired "its stepchild position" because, historically, "teaching was a female occupation in a society that 'didn't value the female intellect'" (1). Little wonder, then, that women who teach in our public high schools report, as Jo Anne Pagano does, on being "troubled by questions of power and authority" (44). She says, "I suspect that a female intellectual of working class background is among those most likely to be troubled by such questions. We know how radically one can be changed by one's education" (44). I share Pagano's preoccupation with questions of power and authority, not only because I am a female with a working-class immigrant background, as she is, but because, as I have said, I experienced the violence of "father rule" as a child. I shall return to this more personal issue, but I will begin with the problem of status in the professional realm.

The College of Education at Iowa State certainly suffers from a chronic lack of status; however, I doubt that Goodlad's solution, which is to give teacher education programs "a position in academe comparable to law schools"(1), will be implemented here at Iowa State University. In fact, a recent survey of department chairs in the College of Liberal Arts and Sciences shows that, of the 46 percent who responded at all, few regard teacher education as part of their department's mission. Some respondents, according to Assistant Dean J. D. Beatty, suggested that a land grant research university should not be in the business of teacher education. I don't know whether my colleagues in the English department share this view; however, teacher education certainly has a problem with visibility in my department, despite the fact that between one-fourth and one-third of our English majors seek admission to our program in secondary teaching. English education's invisibility became obvious during our department's recent external review: specialists in creative writing, linguistics, literature, and rhetoric were invited to evaluate the department's performance, but English education was ignored. As a consequence, and despite my finally successful effort to meet with the evaluating team, English education was mentioned in only one sentence of the report. One consequence of this chronic lack of status is that, as both Catharine Stimpson and Henry Louis Gates have pointed out in the MLA *Newsletter* and in PMLA, respectively, changes in literary studies, such as changes in the canon, are not reaching the high schools. As I see it, the empty rhetoric of George Bush, our so-called Education President, may not be the only impediment to effecting such change; the attitudes of some of my colleagues in the university, including my own department, also impede educational reform.

But my quick course in English education's lack of status among English professors began long before I acquired a tenure-line position. As I was about to begin my job search, a kindly graduate professor counseled me to omit or at least "play down" my experience as a secondary teacher. "It may be important to you," he said, "but hiring committees won't be favorably impressed." However, because jobs were scarce and because I did see some jobs advertised as literature *and* English education positions, I chose to mention—on one unobtrusive line of my vita—my experience teaching high school English. When I interviewed for teaching positions, I hoped to work in both literary studies and English education, not only because I had completed a supporting program in English education, but also because I had a strong commitment to the teaching of English in public schools. Not everyone shares this commitment, as I learned during a one-year position at a liberal arts college. Invited to participate in the department's teacher education committee, I received my second lesson in English education's lack of status. During the first meeting, I heard, to my astonishment, angry resistance from a first-year, tenure-line faculty member who had been placed on the committee, obviously against her wishes. Yes, she acknowledged, she had been a high school teacher, but she had become a college teacher in order to "escape all that." What she meant to escape, I understood immediately, was all that work, all that low status, all that sexism. I sympathized with this woman's anger and with her resistance to serving in the "pink ghetto" of English education; at the same time, I found it painful to experience what felt like rejection from an academic woman who wanted to bury her past—of which I, as a former high school English teacher, had been a part.

As I have said, this professional problem of mine, the status of English education in a university English department, also has roots that reach deeply into the early years of my personal history. It isn't easy to dig up some of these personal roots, exposing them to readers who may prefer not to know. Yet I want to write about this tangle of professional and personal roots, partly out of the hope that it will help me to resolve my ongoing internal debate about status. A public admission of the self-doubt disease may not necessarily lead to a cure, but I believe that writing is a form of therapy that will be good for me, and perhaps for some readers too. Long before I dared think of writing as a form of therapy, I thought of reading as therapy and, in retrospect, I see reading as critical to my emotional and intellectual survival. Indeed, my commitment to reading and writing, and later to English education, probably started in grade school. I enjoyed reading, and I was recognized as a good reader. I remember, for example, that when my sixth grade teacher posted the number of books each of us had completed, I was often at the head of the class. Even then, I liked the status. But in retrospect, I see that I also liked the safety of reading, the escape it provided from the painful realities of my childhood. Reading was a space where I could try to understand myself and my chaotic family, an imaginary place where I had the power to survive bad things, perhaps even imagine changing them. As a child, I certainly didn't have the power to change the terrible things that were happening to my sisters.

Many years later, as I began to write about literature, I did not at first understand that literary analysis enabled me to make sense of my personal past. In fact, analyzing fictional characters allowed me to distance myself from the autobiographical, to find a "cover" for self-analysis. Now that autobiographical criticism has become acceptable (even fashionably controversial among some scholars), I continue to struggle to overcome my resistance. If I propose writing an autobiographical essay, my immediate impulse is to withdraw the proposal, to write something else. I start rationalizing my impulse toward self-censorship. For example, I say to myself, it's easier for Jane Tompkins or Nancy Miller to write autobiographically than it is for me; after all, they don't have such a shameful secret to confess.

That's the voice of the child-victim inside, the voice that cries, "poor me." I have to resist her too. For incest survivors, the writing process is characterized by this impulse toward excessive self-criticism, almost to the point of self-erasure, as Madelon Sprengnether has noted. The inner debate is always: to tell or not to tell, to write or to erase. Yet, even if I acknowledge that it may be more difficult for survivors of sexual abuse to put into practice the slogan "The Personal Is Political," it is no excuse for not trying. For many years, I associated this feminist slogan exclusively with my discontent as an intellectually frustrated, unpaid middle-class housewife; the slogan did not authorize me to speak of the pain and outrage of father-daughter incest. Indeed, if I wrote about incest, I doubted I would ever be admitted into the academy, let alone become a tenured professor. Nevertheless, I was encouraged to write academic essays in the personal voice in graduate school, primarily by feminist scholars at the University of Minnesota—Shirley Nelson Garner, Toni McNaron, and Madelon Sprengnether. Consequently, as I wrote my dissertation, I gradually acquired the courage to focus more explicitly on the problem of fathers and daughters.

The proximity of this topic to my own incest story forced me to invent an imaginary chapter where I could dump "digressive" and deeply disturbing personal material. This survival strategy was fairly effective at the time. If I had stopped for therapy then, I would not have completed my Ph.D., and without the degree I would not have had any chance for employment. I had no other source of financial support because of my divorce; hence, I couldn't afford the luxury of self-disclosure. At that time I also didn't dare risk further loss of status. As everyone knows, a woman's status depends upon her husband's position; when she loses a husband (and mine had the prestige of a Harvard education and an executive position in business), she also loses her place in society. At present, although I haven't recovered my upper-middle-class social status—and never will—I do have a reliable source of income and, having already published an autobiographical essay in *The Intimate Critique*, I can come out of the closet without so great a risk to my well-being. Perhaps even more important, I have begun to experience the exhilaration of genuine creativity, the almost visceral discovery of connections, of mental maps, among once fragmented knowledge. At the same time, I wish I could write in the personal voice without having to use the word *incest*, a word that continues to disturb many people. For example, not long ago at a dinner party when a woman, who had asked about my current research, turned away in embarrassment when I told her that I was writing a book about incest narratives. The word *incest* no longer embarrasses me, and the topic is so much in the news I hadn't expected it to embarrass her. Yet the reluctance to talk about incest remains powerful even in 1992. I have noticed, for example, that some reviews of Jane Smiley's Pulitzer Prize winning novel *A Thousand Acres* avoid comment on its tragic plot, father-daughter incest, even when they emphasize its allusions to Shakespeare's *King Lear*. People who buy the novel expecting another vision of Iowa as a "Field of Dreams" will certainly be surprised.

But I am not innocent of such polite silences myself. Hadn't I, for example, comforted myself for years with the knowledge that my father had, in fact, not actually sexually abused me, but only my three sisters? This refusal to think of the stories of my sisters as part of my own story had made it easier for me to continue my denial. For years, in fact, I feigned naivete about sexual matters—I deliberately resisted understanding the meanings of sexual jokes—largely because I knew that virginal, innocent women have more status in male eyes. But this self-censorship, I came to understand, was a form of betrayal since it left my sisters to bear the shame of their abuse. Indeed, one tragic consequence of society's taboo of speaking about incest is that it leaves children to bear the guilt for crimes committed by fathers (and in rare instances, mothers) against them. At this writing, I am happy to say, I stand with my sisters, all strong and beautiful women who have granted their permission for me to tell our story. Thus, by finally recognizing myself as a victim too, in the sense that my reality was denied, I began to claim strength as a survivor. Yet I had to defend this position recently when a feminist psychoanalytic critic argued that women who criticize Freud for suppressing the truth of the actuality of father-daughter incest are, in her words, "speaking from the place of the victim." I claim authority by writing, not from the place of a victim, I told her, but as a survivor who is critical of Freud's belief that "hysterics lie"—that is, that daughters fantasize their abuse by fathers. She countered that feminists can't "have it both ways," that they can't both criticize Freud and, at the same time, use his theories. But why not? Why do we have to accept the whole package? My hunch is that this woman fears identifying with "victims," preferring instead to identify with the more powerful father-figure, Freud.

This woman's views anger me. Her attitude suggests that feminists, however theoretically sophisticated (or, worse yet, *because* of their theoretical sophistication), are beginning to lose their collective resolve to resist the Law of the Father. If everyone shared her beliefs, I would lose the sense of a feminist community I need in order to write at all. I know, for example, that without a close friend who for many years acted as a sympathetic reader of my many anguished letters, I would never have dared to go on to graduate school. When I told this friend my story, my secret, she did not reject me, and her acceptance gave me hope. While in graduate school, I often began academic papers by writing letters to her, imagining a trusted woman reader in order to start writing for less sympathetic (usually male) professors. (Just a year ago my friend discovered repressed memories of being sexually molested by an uncle at age five; we have yet to explore how this violence has inhibited her writing.) Based on my own difficulties in imagining a sympathetic reader, it has since become evident to me that my father's betrayal has inhibited my ability to write and speak with confidence. Often, when unable to write, I have kept my habit of introspection alive solely through the act of reading, sometimes through imaginative association of literary characters with my family and myself. I remember, for example, the great relief I felt when I read *Crime and Punishment* during the summer after tenth grade: if Dostoevsky's killer could find forgiveness and even love, maybe my father could too. Although I didn't understand it at the time, having been conditioned to think only of my father's needs and not my own, it is likely that my own imaginative identification with violent acts gave me a safe outlet for unarticulated rage. I could imagine myself acting as aggressively as Macbeth, without becoming a tragic figure myself. I could also identify with Macbeth's victims without, at the same time, becoming a victim myself.

In this reading practice, identifying with characters who stand in for both acceptable and unacceptable aspects of my identity, I was illustrating what Jean E. Kennard calls "polar reading," a theory she developed based on views of the "dark" and "light" polarities of identity defined in *Creative Process in Gestalt Therapy* by Joseph Zinker. Kennard says, "One's inner reality consists of both those qualities in one's self that one finds acceptable and those that are unacceptable and therefore hidden and denied" (68). In other words, the habit of reading has allowed me to look within and thereby resist completely censoring the "truth" of my personal experience. Of course, some self-censorship resulted from the fact that, as Judith Fetterley points out in *The Resisting Reader*, I was trained to read as a "man," as were other women of my generation. It did not occur to me until later that my academic training forced me to deny my discomfort about the portrayal of women in literature. Why, I wondered without daring to ask, did the story of Lot place the responsibility for incest on his daughters? And why did Shakespeare encourage us to sympathize more with Macbeth than with Lady Macbeth despite his greater capacity for violence? Traditional literature is one way that our male-dominated culture conditions women not only to sympathize with destructive men, but also to find them attractive. For many years, this conditioning of my sympathies encouraged me to hold my mother accountable for my father's crimes, without taking into consideration her oppression—the oppression of all mothers—in a male-dominated culture.

I did not begin to ask such questions about the politics of gender, or to read with an awareness of gender, until I entered graduate school. Still, I value all those years of reading as a "man" because at least I learned the habit of introspection, the habit of looking at my shadow. This habit of seeking self-knowledge through reading saved me, I am certain, from the practice of denial or repression. By contrast, it was my father's habit of denial that enabled him to abuse my sisters for many years. The same habit also made him ripe for membership in the John Birch Society, a political organization which he joined in the late 1950s and which sanctioned his psychological need to project his own "shadow" onto the communists. Now, as an English educator, I oppose censorship: I stand with people like James Moffett, with members of the National Council of Teachers of English who support "The Right to Read," and with feminists who urge women to "break the silence." I stand against censors like Phyllis Schlafly, the John Birch Society, and my father. In my research on censorship, a topic I address in English methods classes, I have discovered a powerful relationship between my father and me, between "me and my shadow." He tried not to see his shadow, while I have seen my shadow, and his. My father, who should have gone to college, became instead a director of the John Birch Society who resisted "Communism" in his public speeches. By contrast, I achieved his dream of graduating from college, but I resist father rule by writing as a feminist. When, in the register at my father's funeral in 1976, I wrote, "I am my father's daughter," it was the first time I declared myself in public, claiming both my father's authority and his secret as my own.

It took me ten years more to reject what Ursula Le Guin calls the "father tongue" (qtd. in Tompkins 127) and to begin mapping the powerful personal/political connections between English education, the John Birch Society, my father, and me. The revelation of this nexus of relationships enables me to feel more at home in the world of knowledge, and it helps me to recognize that the status of English education is not simply my individual problem, but an issue for all of us who care about good public schools. When critics complain, as David Simpson does, that "the move to autobiography is almost never accompanied by any real analysis of what an individual's position in a culture or society is" (Heller A8), I answer that by writing in the personal, I finally understand my own academic politics: I understand that my father's right-wing politics, a politics which asserts the authority of father rule, frightened me for many years into silence about my experience as his daughter. This fear also dictated my decision to pursue a low status "female" occupation, delaying my entry into higher education, and plaguing me with self-doubt during my job search. Yet during these same years, the feminist movement helped to shape me into the kind of academic I am today: a resistance fighter. Although my resistance to the political right began in my father's house, in silent rebellion against his power to define his daughters as his property, this resistance could not have developed without the feminist movement's collective claim to public power. My mother could not claim such power; her life was exclusively "personal" and domestic. Raised to believe in the rule of the father, she was silently angry for years about the little respect she earned by cleaning my father's house and caring for his children—cooking and sewing and gardening for all of us, her husband and seven children.

She went to bed exhausted, apparently too tired to hear my father visiting my sisters in their bedrooms. One night, however, I remember hearing my mother call my father's name even as my sister, lying next to me, struggled against his sexual advances. My mother's voice did not have the power to stop my father; he called back that he was reading, and she made no further protest. Why, I wonder to this day, wasn't reading enough for my father? Why couldn't he have devoured his books instead of his daughters? The answer, or at least part of the answer, is that my father's reading of right-wing literature allowed him to rationalize "father rule" and to project his own shadow onto the "Communists." By defining U. S. communists as "the enemy within," a phrase often used by John Birchers, my father could avoid looking at the enemy within himself. It must have been a great relief to him to read Robert Welch's words, "For *our* enemy is the Communists, and we do not intend to lose sight of that fact for a minute. We are fighting the Communists—nobody else" (ii). For years my father's "enemy within," his own shadow, escaped detection as he searched for betrayers of our "republic" everywhere. Along with other John Birchers, he was instructed by *The Blue Book of the John Birch Society* to look in the Supreme Court and "Impeach Earl Warren"; to "Investigate Communist Influences at Vassar"; and to document grievances of "Women Against Labor Union Hoodlumism" (Welch 91). Only my sisters saw my father's shadow, looming beside their beds at unpredictable times in the night. One of my sisters told me that, attempting to keep him out of her bed, she wrapped herself tightly in her top sheet.

By analogy, I think of myself as wrapping myself in whatever text I am analyzing, distancing myself from the personal, hiding my vulnerability. But at what point does a sheet/text become more a prison than (an illusion of) protection? Because no space was quite safe in my home, I am hypersensitive to the experience of spatial violation. For this reason, I find it stressful that I don't have my own office yet; however, physical space is not my only concern. The point is that its absence signifies the low status of an English department in a university whose primary focus is science. In some ways, of course, our department benefits from its association with (masculine) science: good things, such as support for research, trickle down to the (feminine) humanities, and I generally teach no more than four courses each year, having been granted a one-course release for research. All tenure-line members of my department must compete for these one-course research releases, and I have not been discriminated against in this competition though I have been careful to balance the literary and pedagogical in my research. Research focused upon pedagogy does not have the status of theory; it's like the difference between "pure" and "applied" science.

As a consequence of my marginal status in an English department, I often feel homeless, as I did as a child. I do not belong in an education department, nor do I wish to go there, but I can't seem to find a place in my own department. This sense of being an orphan is heightened by the fact that I visit student teachers in area secondary schools during one full semester of each year. During this semester, I do not feel at home in either location. The fact that I was once a high school teacher myself adds to this sense of isolation: whereas I was once treated as a colleague by secondary English teachers, I am now regarded with suspicion, as someone who sees herself on a higher plane, as someone from "higher" education. Having felt isolated and marginal all my life—another characteristic of survivors—I am uncomfortable working at the hierarchical borders between these educational institutions. I want to transform these borders, creating more egalitarian and personal relationships with my colleagues in secondary English classrooms, but institutions offer little support for this kind of labor. Whether the work is interdisciplinary or interinstitutional, such border crossing seems to confound the system. At the moment, one of the great frustrations of my life has to do with my "location" as a specialist in English education.

However benign its intentions, my department insists upon defining me in a way that fits its narrowly specialized concepts of scholarship and teaching. Expected to limit myself to fulfill "programmatic need" in English education, I experience a recurrence of my old shrinking man nightmare, a nightmare that woke me repeatedly during the months prior to my graduation from college. In this nightmare, I struggle to keep the man beside me from shrinking. When a crowd jeers at me, I run to the library for protection, but the man running beside me, my twin, shrinks until he is small enough to be carried in my hand. It is a dream, I believe, about trying not to shrink to fit people's expectations of me, about trying to escape a feminine role that makes me a second-class citizen by forcing me to project all my "masculine" traits onto a man. It hasn't helped that I am a small woman, described over the years as "petite" and "cute," words that also imply "trivial." But I fight against trivialization, refusing to shrink. For example, at a Theory/Pedagogy Conference at Indiana University of Pennsylvania in 1991, I opened my talk, "Teaching Alice Walker's *Meridian*," by calling attention to the fact that "theory" was clearly the privileged term at the conference, but I wanted to reverse the hierarchy, beginning my talk with emphasis upon pedagogy, upon actual classroom experience. Calling attention to my subtitle, "Civil Rights According to Mothers," I explained that after teaching Walker's novel in three different college classrooms, I discovered that the theme of motherhood was invisible to young male readers, whereas it was the central theme of the novel for most women. Based upon student responses to Walker's novel, which I cited in my paper, I argued against a phallocentric canon and against "masculine" reading practices, and for inclusion of women's writing as well as attention to a perspective often silenced in our culture: the maternal. "How did you dare to say that?" a woman asked me afterward.

"What is your location?" I asked immediately. She was still in graduate school, she said; that explains it, I told her. My location as a tenure-line professor in a department where feminists are numerically strong means that I can risk making arguments for the inclusion of writing by African American women, I told her. In time, she could do the same. This is the kind of moment that keeps the shrinking man nightmare at bay, the kind of exchange that indicates how my work might make a difference. Sometimes, however, I still despair of ever being heard. At such times, I remind myself that my work in English education—between English and education departments, between universities and high schools, between literature and rhetoric—is a location as rich in possibilities as it is in contradictions. For example, the experience of mentoring future secondary English teachers, at least those willing to risk asking students to genuinely think and feel, can be a most satisfying experience. I warn future teachers to expect censorship, especially on topics such as father-daughter incest, but I encourage them to use novels such as *Abby, My Love*, advising them to make realistic preparations for censorship, not in isolation, but by knowing the policy of their school, or developing one if none exists, and by belonging to state and national professional organizations such as the National Council of Teachers of English. It might be easier to advise students not to teach a novel like *Abby, My Love*; however, I am guided by this fact: if my sisters had known in grade school what they know now—that their bodies belong to them, that they have a right to resist, that they are not to blame—what a difference it would have made in their lives.

My sisters have all become strong women, but their flowering was delayed for years by the abuse they endured as children, abuse that continued largely because my father had too much authority in our family and my mother had too little. It is for this reason that debates over the literary canon, over whose stories are told and whose stories are believed, are not simply "academic" for me. I cheer, for example, when Christine Froula exposes the violence of father rule in literary history. As she argues in "The Daughter's Seduction: Sexual Violence and Literary History": "The relations of literary daughters and fathers resemble in some important ways . . . the family situations of incest victims: a dominating, authoritarian father; an absent, ill, or complicitous mother; and a daughter who, prohibited by her father from speaking about the abuse, is unable to sort out her contradictory feelings of love for her father and terror of him, of desire to end the abuse and fear that if she speaks she will destroy the family structure that is her only security" (112).

Althrough Froula herself does not claim any personal experience of sexual abuse, her clear analysis of paternal power, of "the cultural text that dictates to males and females alike the necessity of silencing women's speech when it threatens the father's power"(112), affirms my efforts to change the canon in universities and high schools where women like my sisters seek educations that will free them from oppression. It is for my sisters, as well as for myself, that I seek to challenge what Froula describes as the authority of "the abusive or seductive father [who] does serious harm to the daughter's mind as well as to her body, damaging her sense of her own identity and depriving her voice of authority and strength" (121).

It is also on behalf of my sisters that I am enthusiastic about teaching a graduate course called "Teaching Literature and the Literature Curriculum." I see this course as a potential site of cultural transformation, a place to enact my commitment to improving education, a place to encourage activism in students who plan to become teachers themselves. In this course, I make assignments that require graduate students to examine the institutions, curricula, and canons where they hope to teach, whether in a high school, community college, or university. Gerald Graff may think that the battle to transform the canon has been won, but this is certainly not the case in Iowa's secondary English classrooms, especially those located in buildings where, throughout the 1980s, pictures of Ronald Reagan were often placed conspicuously in the lobby outside the principal's office. Censorship, though it goes by the name of "excellence," is also evident in Secretary William Bennett's ideal reading list, first published in 1988, a list of American "classics" for grades nine through twelve that recommends writing by only one white woman, Emily Dickinson, and only one black man, Ralph Ellison.

Thus, the question that Henry Louis Gates asked in 1989, "Whose Canon Is It, Anyway?," remains controversial for many secondary English teachers in the 1990s. As one student teacher told me, books by African Americans, ordered in the late sixties and early seventies, now often gather dust in storage rooms while English teachers go "back to the basics" of traditional grammar. I become impatient when I observe teachers who spend hours on prescriptive grammar exercises: for they are not only teaching students the habit of submission to higher authority, they are also practicing an effective form of censorship, keeping students away from literature that might challenge them to think. In fact, right-wing parents want more grammar and less reading because they fear that their children will acquire the ability to think critically. Indeed, if children read stories by women, by daughters and mothers of all races and classes, the authority of fathers, especially upper-class white fathers, will diminish, and society will change. Those who fear change and desire the status quo prefer not to hear the stories of abused daughters, prefer not to know the truth. As James Moffett says, the chief characteristic of the censoring mind is the desire not to know, a characteristic he calls "agnosis." This not wanting to know, this fear of knowing, may be the greatest threat to literacy, according to the editors of *The Right to Literacy*, greater even than the threat of government, schools, or poverty (5). Yet this personal fear of knowing—my own father's "agnosis," his desire not to know—was aided and abetted by his membership in the John Birch Society, an organization that has had a powerful effect upon government and schools.

For example, as I have explained to students in my English methods classes, this desire not to know is evident in an article by Phyllis Schlafly called "Parents Speak Up against Classroom Abuse" in which she identifies journal writing, a common practice in many English classes, as an invasion of the privacy of the home. Schlafly asks, at the end of a long list of parental complaints against teachers who encourage the discussion of suicide, drugs, abortion, and teen pregnancy, "Who are these Typhoid Marys who carry such poison into the classroom?" (1). The implication is that teachers who promote knowledge of such activities stimulate students to try them. "Agnosis," not-knowing, is what Schlafly counsels, the same practice of denial enforced by my father throughout my childhood. Escaping to college, where I could sleep through the night without fear and where I could think without fear, was one of the most wonderful events in my life. In fact, one of the fraternities on campus named me their "Sally Sunshine" during my first year in college, probably because I arrived at my 8 A.M. geology class in such a state of happiness. No one knew why I was so happy, and of course I didn't dare tell them. Nor did I dare think too often about the sisters I had left behind. My older sister was safe, I thought, having married immediately after high school graduation, but I had a difficult time explaining why I was in college when, despite her obvious intelligence, she was not. She graduated from college when she was fifty; I graduated at age twenty-one. The thirty-year difference is easily accounted for: she had been sexually abused, and it took her all those years to deal with the pain.

Had just one teacher behaved as a "Typhoid Mary" (a teacher I will rename "Merciful Mary"), my sister might not have lost all those years. Perhaps it is best that I didn't know, while in college, that my father was also molesting my two younger sisters, both in grade school and still at home. In the early sixties there would have been little I could do to help them: the feminist movement had not yet begun and, at the time (which now seem like the dark ages), most therapists were not trained to listen to and believe the stories of incest survivors. Yet because I had escaped abuse, I suffered from the guilt of the survivor for many years. I had left my sisters behind while I completed a college education that gave me potential for economic independence and, after the changes brought about by feminists in academe, the added potential for mental independence. None of these possibilities was open to my sisters until after they had resolved their struggles with the psychological damage of years—not just a single instance, but years—of sexual violation, and not by a stranger but by the very man who should have protected them from harm.

That is why now, in my teaching and writing, I cannot leave my sisters behind. I will not hide their stories behind the impersonal mask of academic writing. Furthermore, when, under the guise of "family values," the right wing attacks feminists, I continue to resist, not only for my own benefit, but for the benefit of my sisters, and for all vulnerable children. Since the early 1970s the "pro-family" movement has made "frenetic efforts to shore up the father image," as James Moffett says (216), but what the father actually needs, as I know from personal experience, is not "shoring up," but honest confrontation. For example, had I not confronted my father shortly before before his death from cancer in 1976, I might never have found the courage to begin a doctoral program in 1978. The confrontation occurred in the fall of 1975. At the time, I was separated from my husband, and my father tried to counsel me back into my bad marriage. I answered, "Don't play father to me." He looked stricken, and his eyes begged me to rescue him, but I refused. Because he had refused to look within, because of his affliction with "agnosis," he had forced my sisters to bear the burden of his crimes. With other right wingers, my father shared the "masculine" belief that "fighting enemies outside is strength; finding weaknesses inside is itself weakness" (Moffett 221). My father also believed in the sharp division between the personal and the political, the autobiographical and the public: it was this belief that shored up his power and silenced his wife and daughters. That is why, whenever I see a certain kind of impersonal, theoretical writing, the kind that imitates the voice of god the father, I say to hell with it.

POSTSCRIPT, 2001

The status of English education at Iowa State University has changed very little since I wrote "My Father/My Censor" in 1992; however, the needs of students in English education have begun to receive more attention. This change has taken place primarily because of the need to attract students to a literature program that has experienced a sharp decline in majors during the past ten years. As a result, as a colleague recently noted, for the first time in his recollection the literature area had included the needs of future teachers in its discussion of curriculum. I am grateful for such small changes, but I was hoping for even larger changes when I argued for a transformation of the canon and the curriculum in *Authoring a Life: A Woman's Survival in and through Literary Studies* (1998), an autobiographical scholarly book that includes, as chapter 6, "My Father/My Censor." Sadly, even in the year 2001, some faculty in my department remain unaware of, or indifferent to, the political and pedagogical implications of debates over the canon. I am also concerned that the proliferation of books claiming that autobiographical writing has therapeutic value[1] may divert attention for more gender equity in educational institutions, from kindergarten through graduate school. The problem is that authors who claim that writing can be a form of therapy sometimes "forget" that the final step in the process of recovering from trauma is the necessity for survivors to seek social justice. Because I continue to believe the feminist maxim that the personal is political, I counter simplistic claims that writing can be therapeutic by echoing, in both my scholarship and teaching, Judith Lewis Herman's argument that "the remedy for injustice also requires action" (178).

To introduce students to these complex issues—and, in part, to address my own continuing anxiety over self-disclosure—I have designed interdisciplinary seminars that invite students, both graduates and undergraduates, to read trauma narratives and to explore the role of narrative in the process of personal *and* political recovery. In these seminars, I assign narratives such as Dorothy Allison's *Bastard Out of Carolina*, Tim O'Brien's *The Things They Carried*, Art Spiegelman's *Maus II*, Toni Morrison's *Beloved*, and Joyce Carol Oates's *We Were the Mulvaneys* and *What I Live For* along with Judith Lewis Herman's *Trauma and Recovery* and essays from Cathy Caruth's *Trauma: Explorations in Memory*. As Herman explains, only after completing the first step, ensuring the patient's safety, is it possible to begin the second stage: telling the traumatic story in depth and in detail. To have a therapeutic effect, the story must also include the patient's imagery, bodily sensations, and emotional response, and it must be heard by a listener who is not simply neutral, but *affirming*. As survivors confront atrocities, Herman says, the therapist must "affirm a position of moral solidarity with the survivor" (178). However, as students learn, trauma survivors often have multiple and complex audiences, some of whom may not be affirming. For example, while Herman argues that because of the gaps in memory created by trauma both patient and therapist must "develop some degree of uncertainty, even regarding the basic facts of the story" (179), not all psychiatrists, lawyers, or juries agree. In recent years, the controversy over "repressed memory" has created a more skeptical, even hostile reading public; therefore, it is becoming increasingly difficult for survivors to complete the final step in the recovery process: to find a remedy for injustice. I continue to call for such a remedy for injustice—which is as much needed in the classroom as in the courtroom—through the use of the personal in scholarship. The Father continues to censor the stories of survivors of childhood sexual abuse, sometimes through resistance to the use of the personal in scholarship, a form of academic writing that remains controversial.

NOTE

1. For example, Suzette Henke's *Shattered Subjects: Trauma and Testimony in Women's Life Writing* (New York: St. Martin's, 1998) claims that because the act of authorship mimics the therapeutic process, writing alone can heal. In contrast to Henke, Louise DeSalvo warns in *Writing as a Way of Healing* (Boston: Beacon, 1999) that the act of writing cannot always take the place of therapy. The list of books claiming that writing heals continues to grow: *Writing and Healing: Toward an Informed Practice*, edited by Charles M. Anderson and Marian M. MacCurdy (Urbana: National Council of Teachers of English, 2000); *The Writing Cure: Psychoanalysis, Composition, and the Aims of Education* by Mark Bracher (Carbondale: Southern Illinois University Press, 1999); and *Healing Narratives: Women Writers Curing Cultural Dis-ease* by Gay Wilentz (New Brunswick: Rutgers University Press, 2000).

REFERENCES

Bennett, William. "Course Descriptions." *Education Week* (13 January 1988): 28.

Caruth, Cathy, ed. Introduction. *Trauma: Explorations in Memory*. Baltimore: Johns Hopkins University Press, 1995. 3–12.

Daly, Brenda. *Authoring a Life: A Woman's Survival in and through Literary Studies*. Albany: SUNY Press, 1998.

———. "Father-Daughter Incest in Hadley Irwin's *Abby, My Love*: Repairing the Effects of Childhood Sexual Abuse during the Adolescent Years." *Children's Literature Association Quarterly* 17 no. 3 (fall 1992): 5–11.

———. "'How do we [not] become these people who victimize us?' Anxious Power in the Early Fiction of Joyce Carol Oates." In *Anxious Power: Reading, Writing, and Ambivalence in Narrative by Women*, edited by Carol J. Singley and Susan Elizabeth Sweeney, 220–33. Albany: SUNY Press, 1993.

———. "'My Friend, Joyce Carol Oates." In *The Intimate Critique: Autobiographical*

Literary Criticism, edited by Diane Freedman and Olivia Frey, 163–73. Durham: Duke University Press, 1992.

———. "Of Bread and Shadows, Beginnings." In *There Lies a Fair Land: An Anthology of Norwegian-American Writings*, edited by John Solensten, 146–53. Minneapolis: New Rivers Press, 1985.

———. "Teaching Alice Walker's *Meridian*: Civil Rights According to Mothers." In *Narrating Mothers: Theorizing Maternal Subjectivities*, edited by Brenda Daly and Maureen Reddy, 239–57. Knoxville: University of Tennessee Press, 1991.

Fetterley, Judith. *The Resisting Reader: A Feminist Approach to American Fiction*. Bloomington: Indiana University Press, 1978.

Flynn, Elizabeth A., and Patrocinio Schweickart, eds. *Gender and Reading: Essays on Readers, Texts, and Contexts*. Baltimore: Johns Hopkins University Press, 1986.

Freedman, Diane, and Olivia Frey, eds. *The Intimate Critique: Autobiographical Literary Criticism*. Durham: Duke University Press, 1992.

Froula, Christine. "The Daughter's Seduction: Sexual Violence and Literary History." In *Daughters and Fathers*, edited by Lynda E. Boose and Betty S. Flowers, 111–35. Baltimore: Johns Hopkins University Press, 1989.

Gates, Henry Louis Jr. "Whose Canon Is It, Anyway?" *New York Times Book Review*. (26 February 1989): 1 +.

———. "Introduction: Tell Me Sir, . . . What Is 'Black' Literature'?" *PMLA* 105, no. 1 (January 1991): 11–12.

"Goodlad Tests His Vision of Teacher Education." *NCTE Council Chronicle* 1, no. 3 (February 1992): 1, 15.

Graff, Gerald. "Organizing the Conflicts in the Curriculum." *M/MLA* 25, no. 1 (spring 1992): 63–76.

Heller, Scott. "Experience and Expertise Meet in New Brand of Scholarship." *Chronicle of Higher Education* (6 May 1992): A7+.

Herman, Judith Lewis. *Trauma and Recovery*. New York: Basic, 1992.

Kennard, Jean E. "Ourself Behind Ourself: A Theory for Lesbian Readers." In Flynn and Schweickart, *Gender and Reading*, 63–80.

Lunsford, Andrea A., Helene Moglen, and James Slevin, eds. *The Right to Literacy*. New York: Modern Language Association, 1990.

Miller, Nancy K. *Getting Personal: Feminist Occasions and Other Autobiographical Acts*. New York: Routledge, 1991.

Moffett, James. *Storm in the Mountain: A Case Study of Censorship, Conflict, and Consciousness*. Carbondale: Southern Illinois University Press, 1988.

Pagano, Jo Anne. *Exiles and Communities: Teaching in the Patriarchal Wilderness*. Albany: SUNY Press, 1990.

Schlafly, Phyllis, ed. "Parents Speak Up against Classroom Abuse." *Phyllis Schlafly Report* 1, no. 11 (June 1985): 1–5.

Singley, Carol J., and Susan Elizabeth Sweeney, eds. *Anxious Power: Reading, Writing and Ambivalence in Narrative by Women*. Albany: SUNY Press, 1993.

Smiley, Jane. *A Thousand Acres*. New York: Knopf, 1992.

Stimpson, Catharine. "President's Column." *MLA Newsletter* 22, no. 1 (spring 1990): 2.

Tompkins, Jane. "Me and My Shadow." *New Literary History* 19 (1987): 169–78. Rpt. in Freedman and Frey, *The Intimate Critique*, 23–40.

Welch, Robert. *The Blue Book of the John Birch Society*. 4th ed. Belmont, Mass.: Western Islands, 1961.

Zinker, Joseph. *Creative Process in Gestalt Therapy*. New York: Random, 1977.

Research Psychology

NAOMI WEISSTEIN

Adventures of a Woman

in Science

I am an experimental psychologist, doing research in vision. The profession has for a long time considered this activity, on the part of one of my sex, to be an outrageous violation of the social order and against all the laws of nature. Yet at the time I entered graduate school in the early sixties, I was unaware of this. I was remarkably naive. Stupid, you might say. Anybody can be president, no? So, anybody can be a scientist. Weisstein in Wonderland. I had to discover that what I wanted to do constituted unseemly social deviance. It was a discovery I was not prepared for: Weisstein is dragged, kicking and screaming, out of Wonderland and into Plunderland. Or Blunderland, at the very least.

What made me want to become a scientist in the first place? The trouble may have started with *Microbe Hunters*,[1] de Kruif's book about the early bacteriologists. I remember reading about Leeuwenhoek's discovery of organisms too small to be seen with the naked eye. When he told the Royal Society about this, most of them thought he was crazy. He told them he wasn't. The "wretched beasties" were there, he insisted; one could see them unmistakably through the lenses he had so carefully made. It was very important to me that he could reply that he had his evidence: evidence became a hero of mine.

It may have been then that I decided that *I* was going to become a scientist, too. I was going to explore the world and discover its wonders. I was going to understand the brain in a better and more complete way than it had been understood before. If anyone questioned me, I would have my evidence. Evidence and reason: my heroes and my guides. I might add that my sense of ecstatic exploration when reading *Microbe Hunters* has never left me through all the years I have struggled to be a scientist.

As I mentioned, I was not prepared for the discovery that women were not welcome in science, primarily because nobody had told me. In fact, I was supported in thinking—even encouraged to think—that my aspirations were perfectly legitimate. I graduated from the Bronx High School of Science in New York City where gender did not enter into intellectual pursuits; the place was a nightmare for everybody.[2] We were all, boys and girls alike, equal contestants; all of us were competing for that thousandth of a percentage point in our grade average that would allow entry into one of those high-class, out-of-town schools, where we could go, get smart, and lose our New York accents.

I ended up at Wellesley and this further retarded my discovery that women were supposed to be stupid and incompetent: the women faculty members at Wellesley were brilliant. I later learned that they were at Wellesley because the schools that had graduated them—the "very best" schools where you were taught to do the "very best" research—couldn't or did not care to place them in similar schools where they could continue their research. So they are our brilliant unknowns: unable to do research because they labor under enormous teaching loads; unable to obtain the minimal support necessary for scholarship; unable to obtain the foundations for productive research: graduate students, facilities, communication with colleagues.

While I was still ignorant about the lot of women in the academy, others at Wellesley were not. Deans from an earlier, more conscious, feminist era would tell me that I was lucky to be at a women's college where I could discover what I was good at and do it. They told me that women in a man's world were in for a rough time. They told me to watch out when I went on to graduate school. They said that men would not like my competing with them. I did not listen to the deans, however; or, when I did listen, I thought what they were telling me might have been true in the nineteenth century, but not in the late fifties.

So my discovery that women were not welcome in psychology began when I arrived at Harvard, on the first day of class. That day, the entering graduate students had been invited to lunch with one of the star professors in the department. After lunch, he leaned back in his chair, lit his pipe, began to puff, and announced: "Women don't belong in graduate school."

The male graduate students, as if by prearranged signal, then leaned back in their chairs, puffed on their newly bought pipes, nodded, and assented: "Yeah."

"Yeah," said the male graduate students. "No man is going to want you.

No man wants a woman who is more intelligent than he is. Of course, that's not a real possibility, but just in case. You are out of your *natural* roles; you are no longer feminine."

My mouth dropped open, and my big blue eyes (they have since changed back to brown) went wide as saucers. An initiation ceremony, I thought. Very funny. Tomorrow, for sure, the male graduate students will get theirs.

But the male graduate students never were told that they didn't belong. They rapidly became trusted junior partners in the great research firms at Harvard. They were carefully nurtured, groomed, and run. Before long, they would take up the white man's burden and expand the empire. But for me and the other women in my class it was different. We were shut out of these plans; we were *shown* we didn't belong. For instance, even though I was first in my class, when I wanted to do my dissertation research, I couldn't get access to the necessary equipment. The excuse was that I might break the equipment. This was certainly true. The equipment was eminently breakable. The male graduate students working with it broke it every week; I didn't expect to be any different.

I was determined to collect my data. Indeed, I *had* to collect my data. (Leeuwenhoek had his lenses. Weisstein would get her data.) I had to see how the experiment I proposed would turn out. If Harvard wouldn't let me use its equipment, maybe Yale would. I moved to New Haven, collected my data at Yale, returned to Harvard, and was awarded my Ph.D. in 1964. Afterward, I could not get an academic job. I had graduated Phi Beta Kappa from Wellesley; had obtained my Ph.D. in psychology at Harvard in two and one half years, ranked first in my graduate class, and I couldn't get a job. Yet most universities were expanding in 1964, and jobs were everywhere. But at the places where I was being considered for jobs, they were asking me questions like, "How can a little girl like you teach a great big class of men?" At that time, still unaware of how serious the situation was, I replied, "Beats me. I guess I must have talent." At another school, a famous faculty liberal challenged me with, "Who did your research for you?" He then put what I assume was a fatherly hand on my knee, and said in a tone of deep concern, "You ought to get married."

Meanwhile, I was hanging on by a National Science Foundation postdoctoral fellowship in mathematical biology at the University of Chicago, attempting to do some research. Prior to my second postdoctoral year, the University of Chicago began negotiations with me for something like a real job: an instructorship jointly in the undergraduate college and the psychology department. The negotiations appeared to be proceeding in good faith, so I wrote to Washington and informed them that I would not be taking my second postdoctoral year. Then, ten days before classes began, when that option as well as any others I might have taken had been closed, the person responsible for the negotiations called to tell me that because of a nepotism rule — my husband taught history at the University of Chicago — I would not be hired as a regular faculty member. If I wanted to, I could be appointed lecturer, teaching general education courses in the college; there was no possibility of an appointment in psychology. The lectureship paid very little for a lot of work, and I would be teaching material unconnected with my research. Furthermore, a university rule stipulated that lecturers (because their position in the university was so insecure) could not apply for research grants. He concluded by asking me whether I was willing to take the job: ten days before the beginning of classes, he asked me whether I was willing to take the only option still available to me.

I took the job, and "sat in," so to speak, in the office of another dean, until he waived the restriction on applying for research grants. Acknowledging my presence, he told a colleague: "This is Naomi Weisstein. She hates men."

I had simply been telling him that women are considered unproductive precisely because universities do their best to keep women unproductive through such procedures as the selective application of the nepotism rule. I had also asked him whether I could read through the provisions of the rule. He replied that the nepotism rule was informal, not a written statute — flexibility being necessary in its application. Later, a nepotism committee, set up partly in response to my protest, agreed that the rule should stay precisely as it was; that it was a good idea, should not be written out, and should be applied selectively.

Lecturers at major universities are generally women. They are generally married to men who teach at these major universities. And they generally labor under conditions which seem almost designed to show them that they don't belong. In many places, they are not granted faculty library privileges; in my case, I had to get a note from the secretary each time I wanted to take a book out for an extended period. Lecturers' classrooms are continually changed; at least once a month, I would go to my assigned classroom only to find a note pinned to the door instructing me and my class to go elsewhere: down the hall, across the campus, out to Gary, Indiana.

In the winter of my first year, notices were distributed to all those teaching the courses I was teaching, announcing a meeting to discuss the following year's syllabus. I didn't receive the notice. As I was to learn shortly, this is the customary way a profession that prides itself on its civility and genteel traditions indicates to lecturers and other "nuisance personnel" that they're fired: they are simply not informed about what's going on. I inquired further. Yes, my research and teaching had been "evaluated" (after five months: surely enough time), and they had decided to "let me go" (a brilliant euphemism). Of course, the decision had nothing to do with my questioning the nepotism rules and explaining to deans why women are thought unproductive.

I convinced them to "let me stay" another year. I don't know to this day why they changed their minds. Perhaps they changed their minds because it looked like I was going to receive the research grant for which I had applied, bringing in money not only for me, but for the university as well. A little while later, Loyola University in Chicago offered me a job.

So I left the University of Chicago. I was awarded the research grant and found the Psychology Department at Loyola at first very supportive. The chairman, Ron Walker, was especially helpful and enlightened about women at a time when few academic men were. I was on my way, right? Not exactly. There is a big difference between a place like Loyola and a place with a heavy commitment to research—a large state university, for example—a difference that no amount of good will on the part of an individual chairman can cancel out. The Psychology Department was one of the few active departments at Loyola. The other kinds of support one needs to do experimental psychology—machine and electrical shops, physics and electrical engineering departments, technicians, a large computer—were either not available or were available at that time only in primitive form.

When you are a woman at an "unknown" place, you are considered out of the running. It was hard for me to keep my career from "shriveling like a raisin" (as an erstwhile colleague predicted it would). I was completely isolated. I did not have access to the normal channels of communication, debate, and exchange in the profession—those informal networks where you get the news, the comment and the criticism, the latest reports of what is going on. I sent my manuscripts to various people for comment and criticism before sending them off to journals; few replied. I asked others working in my field to send me their prepublication drafts; even fewer responded. Nobody outside Loyola informed me about special meetings in my area of psychology, and few inside Loyola knew about them. Given the snobbery rife in academic circles (which has eased lately since jobs are much harder to find and thus even "outstanding" young male graduates from the "best" schools may now be found at places formerly beneath their condescension), my being at Loyola almost automatically disqualified me from the serious attention of professional colleagues.

The "inner reaches" of the profession, from which I had been exiled, are not just metaphorical and intangible. For instance, I am aware of two secret societies of experimental psychologists in which fifty or so of the "really excellent" young scientists get together regularly to make themselves better scientists. The ostensible purpose of these societies is to allow these "best and brightest" young psychologists to get together to discuss and criticize each other's work; they also function, of course, to define who is excellent and who is not, and to help those defined as excellent to remain so by providing them with information to which "outsiders" in the profession will not have access until much later (if at all).

But the intangibles are there as well. Women are subjected to treatment men hardly ever experience. Let me give you a stunning example. I wrote up an experiment with results I thought were fascinating, and sent the paper to a journal editor whose interests I knew to be close to what was reported in my paper. The editor replied that there were some control conditions that should be run and some methodological loose ends; so they couldn't publish the paper. Fair enough. He went on to say that they had much better equipment over there, and they would like to test my idea themselves. Would I mind? I wrote back, and told them I thought it was a bit unusual, asked if they were suggesting a collaboration, and concluded by saying that I would be most happy to visit with them and collaborate on my experiment. The editor replied with a nasty letter explaining to me that by suggesting that they test my idea themselves, they had merely been trying to help me. If I didn't want their help in this way, they certainly didn't want mine: that is, they had had no intention of suggesting a collaboration.

In other words, what they meant by "did I mind" was: Did I mind if they took my idea and did the experiment themselves? As we know, taking someone else's idea and pretending it's your own is not at all an uncommon occurrence in science. The striking thing about this exchange was, however, that the editor was arrogant enough, and assumed that I would be submissive enough, for him to openly ask me whether I would agree to this arrangement. Would I mind? No, of course not. Women are joyful altruists. We are happy to give of ourselves. After all, how many good ideas do you get in your lifetime? One? Two? Why not *give* them away?

Generally, the justification for treating women in such disgraceful ways is simply that they are women. Let me give another example. I was promised the use of a small digital laboratory computer, which was to be purchased on a grant. The funds from the grant would become available if a certain job position entailing administration of this grant could be filled. I was part of the group which considered the candidates and which recommended appointing a particular individual. During the discussion of future directions of the individual's work, it was agreed that he would, of course, share the computer with me. He was hired, bought the computer, and refused me access to it. I offered to put in money for peripherals which would make the system faster and easier for both of us to work with, but this didn't sway him. As justification for his conduct, the man confessed to the chairman that he simply couldn't share the computer with me: he had difficulty working with women. To back this up, he indicated that he'd been "burned twice." Although the chairman had previously been very helpful and not bothered in the least about women, he accepted that statement as an explanation. Difficulty in working with women was not a problem this man should work out. It was *my* problem. Colleagues thought no worse of him for this problem; it might even have raised him in their estimation. He obtained tenure quickly, and retains an influential voice in the department. Yet if a woman comes to *any* chairman of *any* department and confesses that she has difficulty working with *men*, she is thought pathological.

What this meant for me at the time was that my research was in jeopardy. There were experimental conditions I needed to run that simply could not be done without a computer. So there I was, doing research with stone-age equipment, trying to get by with wonder-woman reflexes and a flashlight, while a few floors below, my colleague was happily operating "his" computer. It's as if we women are in a totally rigged race. A lot of men are driving souped-up, low-slung racing cars, and we're running as fast as we can in tennis shoes we managed to salvage from a local garage sale.

Perhaps the most painful of the appalling working conditions for women in science is the peculiar kind of social-sexual assault women sustain. Let me illustrate with a letter to *Chemical and Engineering News* from a research chemist named McGauley:

> There are differences between men and women . . . just one of these differences is a decided gap in leadership potential and ability . . . this is no reflection upon intelligence, experience, or sincerity. Evolution made it that way. . . . Then consider the problems that can arise if the potential employee, Dr. Y (a woman) [*sic*: he could at least get his chromosomes straight] will be expected to take an occasional business trip with Dr. X. . . . Could

it be that the guys in shipping and receiving will not take too kindly to the lone Miss Y?[3]

Now what is being said here, very simply, and to paraphrase the Bible, is that women are trouble. And by trouble, McGauley means sexual trouble. Moreover, somehow, someway, it is our fault. *We* are provoking the guys in shipping and receiving. Women—no matter who the women are or what they have in mind—are universally assigned by men, first, to sexual categories. Then, women are accused by men of taking their minds away from work. When feminists say that women are treated as sex objects, we are compressing into a single, perhaps rhetorical phrase, an enormous area of discomfort, pain, harassment, and humiliation.

This harassment is especially clear at conventions. Scientific meetings, conferences, and conventions are harassing and humiliating for women because women, by and large, cannot have male colleagues. Conversations, social relations, invitations to lunch, and the like are generally viewed as sexual, not professional, encounters if a woman participates in them. It does not cross many men's minds that a woman's motivation may be entirely professional.

I have been at too many professional meetings where the "joke" slide was a woman's body, dressed or undressed. A woman in a bikini is a favorite with past and perhaps present presidents of psychological associations. Hake showed such a slide in his presidential address to the Midwestern Psychological Association, and Harlow, past president of the American Psychological Association, has a whole set of such slides, which he shows at the various colloquia to which he is invited. This business of making jokes at women's bodies constitutes a primary social-sexual assault. The ensuing raucous laughter expresses the shared understanding of what is assumed to be women's primary function to which we can always be reduced. Showing pictures of nude and sexy women insults us: it puts us in our place. You may think you are a scientist it is saying, but what you really are is an object for our pleasure and amusement. Don't forget it.

I could continue recounting the horrors, as could almost any woman who is in science or who has ever been in science. But I want now to turn to the question of whether or not the commonly held assumptions about women are true. If they are, this would in no way justify the profession's shameful treatment of women, but it might lead us to different conclusions about how to remedy the situation.

I began the inquiry into women's "nature" while I was in graduate school. I wanted to investigate the basis on which the learned men in my field had pronounced me and my female colleagues unfit for graduate study.

I found that the views of the experts reflected, in a surprisingly transparent way, the crudest cultural stereotypes. Erik Erikson wrote:[4]

> Young women often ask me whether they can "have an identity before they know whom they will marry and for whom they will make a home."

He explained (somewhat elegiacally) that:

> Much of a young woman's identity is already defined in her kind of attractiveness and in the selectivity of her search for the man (or men) by whom she wishes to be sought. . . .

Mature womanly fulfillment, for Erikson, rested on this "fact":

> [that a woman's] . . . somatic design harbors an "inner space" destined to bear the offspring of chosen men, and with it, a biological, psychological, and ethical commitment to take care of human infancy.

Bruno Bettelheim, speaking at a symposium on American women in science and engineering, commented:

> We must start with the realization that, much as women want to be good scientists and/or engineers, they want first and foremost to be womanly companions of men and to be mothers.[5]

And Joseph Rheingold, a psychiatrist at the Harvard Medical School, tied the reluctance of women to give in to their true natures to society's problems:

> Woman is nurturance . . . anatomy decrees the life of a woman . . . When women grow up without dread of their biological functions and without subversion by feminist doctrine, and therefore enter upon motherhood with a sense of fulfillment and altruistic sentiment, we shall attain the goal of a good life and a secure world in which to live it.[6]

So the learned men in my field were saying essentially the same thing as the male graduate students, but it still did not sound right to me. Since scientists (supposedly) do not assess the truth or falsity of propositions on the basis of who said them (they look instead for evidence), I decided to look for the evidence on which these eminent men had based their theories. I determined that there is no evidence behind their fantasies of the servitude and childish dependence of women. On the contrary, the idea of human possibility which rests on the accident of sex at conception has strangled and deflected psychology so that it is still relatively useless in describing, explaining, or predicting human behavior. This is true for men as well as women. It becomes especially pernicious when the theories are not only wrong but are proscriptive as well.

I have elsewhere gone through the arguments showing the near uselessness of these kinds of theories of human nature;[7] here, let me just provide the briefest of summaries.

The basic reason that this kind of psychology (i.e., personality theory, and, for the most part, theory from psychotherapists and psychoanalysts) tells us next to nothing about human nature, male as well as female, is that it has been looking in the wrong place. It has assumed that what people do comes from a fixed, rigid, inside directive: sex organs, or fixed cognitive traits, or what happened until, but no later than, the age of five. This assumption has been shown to fail again and again in tests; a person will be assessed by psychologists as possessing a particular constellation of personality traits and then, when different criteria are applied, or someone different is asked to judge, or, more importantly, when that person is in a different kind of social situation, s/he will be thought to exhibit a completely different set of traits.[8]

One might argue, then, that personality is a somewhat subtle and elusive thing, and that it would be difficult to obtain a set of measures that would distinguish personality types. This is a reasonable argument. But even when one looks at what one would expect to be gross differences between a certified schizophrenic, say, and a normal,[9] or between a male homosexual and a male heterosexual,[10] or between a "male" personality and a "female" personality,[11] one finds that the same judges who claim to be able to differentiate human personalities simply cannot distinguish one from the other. In one study,[12] for example, judges who were supposed to be experts at this kind of thing could not tell, on the basis of clinical tests and interviews (in which one is allowed to ask questions such as, "When did you first notice that you had grown antlers?"), which one of a group of people had been classified as schizophrenics and which as normals. Even stranger, some weeks later, when the same judges were asked to judge the same people, in many cases, they reversed their own judgments. Judges (again, allegedly clinical experts), attempting to distinguish between homosexuals and heterosexuals on the basis of what is assumed to be differences in their personalities, have done no better; nor was my graduate class at Harvard able correctly to distinguish stories written by males from those written by females, even though we had just completed a month and a half's study of the differences between men and women. In short, if judges cannot agree on whether a person belongs in a certain personality category, even when those categories are assumed to be as different from each other as normal/crazy, male/female, and straight/gay; if the measurement depends on who is doing the measuring, and on what time of day it is being done, then theories that are based on these personality categories are useless.

The other "test" that has frequently been cited as a way of confirming such theories is the test of therapy. Since most of the theorizing about men and women (and normals and schizophrenics, and homosexuals and heterosexuals) has been done by clinical psychologists, who cite as evidence for their theories "years of intensive clinical experience," one test of their understanding of human personality might be their effectiveness in helping people solve these "problems." Of course, one might question what is going on in these years of intensive clinical practice when clinicians cannot even agree on descriptions; that is, they cannot agree on their categories. But suppose one countered that clinical psychologists really do have an understanding of the depths of human personality, and, although any two clinical psychologists may not be able to agree on a "verbal" level on what categories they are using, nevertheless (so this argument would go), they are operating at an intuitive level which "works" (i.e., they help their patients change their behavior). The fact is that, to the limited extent that therapy may change behavior (if at all), it doesn't matter *which* therapy is used: in general, no one therapy is reported to be any *more* effective than any other, even when the same symptoms are being treated.[13] Since theories upon which different therapies are based are different, and in some cases conflict with each other, the extent to which a particular therapy may work cannot be taken to lend credence to that particular theory.

What all this means for women is that personality theory has given us no idea of what our true "natures" are; whether we were intended from the start to be scientists and engineers and were thwarted by a society that has other plans for us, or whether we were intended, as claimed by some of the learned men in the field, only to be mothers. There are a number of arguments based on selected primates[14] that also purport to show that females are suited only for motherhood (hopefully with a sense of fulfillment and altruistic sentiment). These arguments are even more specious than those from the clinical tradition, as I have discussed elsewhere.[15]

But while personality psychology and clinical psychologists have failed miserably at providing any statements we can trust about women's "true nature," or about anyone's "true nature," the evidence is accumulating from a different area of psychology, *social* psychology: what humans do and when they will do it is highly predictable. What people do and who they believe themselves to be will, in general, be a function of what the people around them expect them to be, and what the overall situation in which they are acting implies that they are. Let me describe three experiments that have made this fact clear.

THE EXPERIMENTER BIAS EXPERIMENTS

These studies[16] have shown that if one group of experimenters has one hypothesis about what they expect to find, and another group of experimenters has the opposite hypothesis, both will obtain results in accord with their differing hypotheses. And this is not because the experimenters lie or cheat or falsify data. In the studies cited, the experimenters are closely observed, and they are made outwardly to behave in identical fashion. The message about their different expectations is somehow picked up by their subjects through nonverbal cues, head nods, ways of communicating expectations that we do not yet know about. The moral here is that, even in carefully controlled conditions, when we are dealing with humans (and in some cases rats),[17] the hypotheses we start with will influence the behavior of the organism we are studying. It is obvious how important this would be when assessing the validity of psychological studies of the differences between men and women.

INNER PHYSIOLOGICAL STATE VERSUS SOCIAL CONTEXT

Subjects[18] were injected with adrenalin, a hormone that tends to make people "speedy"; when placed in a room with another person (a confederate of the experimenter) who acted euphoric, the subject became euphoric. Conversely, if a subject was placed in a room with another person who acted angry, the subject became angry. These data seem to indicate that the far more important determinant to how people will act is not their physiological state, but the social context in which they are acting. Thus, no matter how many physiological differences we may find between men and women, we must be very cautious in assigning any fixed behavioral correlates to the physiological states. The point is made even more strongly, perhaps, in studies of hermaphrodites in whom the genetic, gonadal, hormonal sex, the internal reproductive organs, and the ambiguous appearance of the external genitalia were identical. It was shown that one will consider one's self male or female depending simply on whether one was defined and raised as a male or a female:

> There is no more convincing evidence of the power of social interaction on gender-identity differentiation than in the case of congenital hermaphrodites who are of the same diagnosis and similar degree of hermaphroditism but are differently assigned and with a different postnatal medical and life history.[19]

THE OBEDIENCE EXPERIMENTS

In Milgram's experiments,[20] a subject is told that s/he is administering a learning experiment, and that s/he is to deal out shocks each time another "subject" (who is in fact a confederate of the experimenter) answers incorrectly. The equipment appears to provide graduated shocks ranging upwards from 15 V through 450 V; for each of four consecutive voltages, there are verbal descriptions such as mild shock; danger; severe shock; and finally, for the 435 V and 450 V switches a red xxx marked over the switches. Each time the confederate answers incorrectly, the subject is supposed to increase the voltage. As the voltage increases, the confederate begins to cry out in pain and demands that the experiment be stopped, finally refusing to answer at all. When all responses are stopped, the experimenter instructs the subject to continue increasing the voltage. For each shock administered, the confederate shrieks in agony. Under these conditions, about 62 percent of the subjects administered shocks that they believed to be possibly lethal.

No tested individual differences among subjects predicted who would continue to obey and who would break off the experiment. When forty psychiatrists predicted how many of a group of 100 subjects would go on to give the lethal shock, their predictions were orders of magnitude below the actual percentages; most expected only one or two of the subjects to obey to the end.

But even though psychiatrists have no idea how people will behave in this situation, and even though individual differences do not predict who will and will not obey, it is easy to predict when subjects will be obedient and when they will be defiant. In a variant of Milgram's experiment, two confederates were present in addition to the "victim," working along with the subject in administering electric shocks. When the two confederates refused to continue with the experiment, only 10 percent of the subjects continued to the maximum voltage. This is critical for personality theory. It says that behavior is predicated largely on the social situation, not solely on the individual's history.

To summarize: if subjects under quite innocuous and noncoercive social conditions can be made to kill other subjects, and under other types of social conditions will positively refuse to do so; if subjects can react to a state of physiological arousal by becoming euphoric because there is someone else around who is euphoric, or angry because there is someone else around who is angry; if subjects will act a certain way because experimenters expect them to act in that way, and another group of subjects will act in a different way because experimenters expect them to act in that different way; then it appears obvious that a study of human behavior requires first and foremost a study of the social contexts within which people move, the expectations as to how they will behave, and the authority that tells them who they are and what they are supposed to do.

The relevance to males and females is obvious. We do not know what immutable differences in behavior, nature, ability, or possibility exist between men and women. We know that they have different genitalia and at different times in their lives, different sex hormone levels. Perhaps there are some unchangeable differences; probably there are a number of irrelevant differences. But all these differences are likely to be trivial compared to the enormous influence of social context. And it is clear that, until social expectations for men and women are equal and just; until equal respect is provided for both men and women, our answers to the question of immutable differences, of "true" nature, of who should be the scientist and who should be the secretary, will simply reflect our prejudices.

• • •

I want to stop now and ask: What conclusions can we draw from my experience? What does it all add up to?

Perhaps we should conclude that persistence wins out. Or that life is hard, but cheerful struggle and a "sense of humor" can make it bearable. Or perhaps we should search back through my family, and find my domineering mother and passive father, or my domineering father and passive mother, to explain my persistence. Perhaps . . . but all these conclusions are beside the point. The point is that none of us should have to face this kind of offense. The main point is that we must change this man's world and this man's science.

How will other women do better? One of the dangers of this kind of narrative is that it may validate the punishment as it singles out the few survivors. The lesson appears to be that those (and only those) with extraordinary strength will survive. This is not the way I see it. Many have had extraordinary strength and have *not* survived. We know of some of them, but by definition we will of course never know of most.

Much of the explanation for my own professional survival has to do with the emergence and growth of the women's movement. I am an experimental psychologist, a scientist. I am also a feminist. I am a feminist because I have seen my life and the lives of women I know harassed, dismissed, damaged, destroyed. I am a feminist because without others I can do little to stop the outrage. Without a political and social movement of which I am a part, without feminism, my determination and persistence, my clever retorts, my hours of patient explanation, my years of exhortation amount to little. If the scientific world has changed since I entered it, it is not because I managed to become an established psychologist within it. Rather, it is because a women's movement came along to change its character. It is true that as a member of that movement, I have acted to change the character of the scientific world. But without the movement, none of my actions would have brought about change. And now, as the strength of the women's movement ebbs, the old horrors are returning. This must not happen.

Science, knowledge, the search for fundamental understanding is part of our humanity. It is an endeavor that seems to give us some glimpse of what we might be and what we might do in a better world. To deny us the right to be scientists is to deny us our humanity. We cannot let that happen.

NOTES

Somewhat different versions of this paper have appeared in *Federation Proceedings* 35 (1976), 2226–31; and in *Working It Out*, S. Ruddick and P. Daniels, eds., (New York: Pantheon Books, 1977), 242–50. I wish to thank Tobey Klass for her critical comments and her guidance through the recent literature. I also wish to thank Roger Burton for bringing the Campbell and Yarrow study to my attention.

1. Paul de Kruif, *Microbe Hunters* (New York: Brace & World, 1926).
2. I discovered later on that this in itself was unusual—by high school, if not before, girls are generally discouraged from showing an interest in science.
3. P. J. McGauley, Letter to the Editor, *Chem. Eng. News* 48 (1970): 8–9.

4. Erik H. Erikson, "Inner and Outer Space: Reflections on Womanhood," *Daedalus* 93 (1964): 585–606.

5. From a speech entitled "The Commitment Required of a Woman Entering a Scientific Profession in Present Day American Society," Massachusetts Institute of Technology, 1965.

6. J. Rheingold, *The Fear of Being a Woman* (New York: Grune & Stratton, 1964).

7. Naomi Weisstein, "Psychology Constructs the Female: or the Fantasy Life of the Male Psychologist," *J. Soc. Ed.* 35 (1970): 362–73.

8. J. Block, "Some Reasons for the Apparent Inconsistency of Personality," *Psychol. Bull.* 70 (1968): 210–12; W. Mischel, *Personality and Assessment* (New York: Wiley, 1968); W. Mischel, "Toward a Cognitive Social Learning Reconceptualization of Personality," *Psychological Review* 80 (1973): 252–83.

9. K. B. Little and E. S. Schneidman, "Congruences Among Interpretations of Psychological and Anamnestic Data," *Psychol. Monogr.* 73 (1959): 1–42. See also R. E. Tarter, D. I. Templer, and C. Hardy, "Reliability of the Psychiatric Diagnosis," *Diseases of the Nervous System* 36 (1975): 30–31.

10. E. Hooker, "Male Homosexuality in the Rorschach," *J. Projective Techniques* 21 (1957): 18–31.

11. Naomi Weisstein, "Psychology Constructs the Female."

12. K. B. Little and E. S. Schneidman, "Congruences among Interpretations."

13. Dorothy Tennov, *Psychotherapy* (New York: Abelard-Schuman, 1975); M. L. Smith and G. V. Glass, "Meta-Analysis of Psychotherapy Outcome Studies," *American Psychologist* 32 (1977): 752–60; Sloan, Staples, Cristol, Yorkston, and Whipple, "Short-Term Analytically Oriented Psychotherapy Versus Behavior Therapy," *American Journal of Psychiatry* 132, no. 4 (1975): 373–77.

14. See H. F. Harlow, "The Heterosexual Affectional System in Monkeys," *Am. Psychol.* 17 (1962): 1–9; L. Tiger, *Men in Groups* (New York: Random House, 1969); and L. Tiger, "Male Dominance? Yes. Alas. A Sexist Plot? No.," *New York Times Magazine*, 25 October 1970.

15. Naomi Weisstein, "Psychology Constructs the Female." See also Ruth Hubbard's article, "Have Only Men Evolved?" in *Women Look at Biology Looking at Women*, edited by Ruth Hubbard, Mary Sue Henifin, and Barbara Fried (Boston: G. K. Hall, 1979).

16. R. Rosenthal, "On the Social Psychology of the Psychological Experiment: The Experimenter's Hypothesis as Unintended Determinant of Experimental Results," *Am. Sci.* 51 (1963): 268–83; and R. Rosenthal, *Experimenter Effects in Behavioral Research* (New York: Appleton-Century-Crofts, 1966). A meticulous observation of behavior at a summer camp suggesting the same results is J. D. Campbell and M. R. Yarrow's "Perceptual and Behavioral Correlates of Social Effectiveness," *Sociometry* 24 (1961): 1–20.

17. H. F. Harlow, "The Heterosexual Affectional System."

18. John Money, "Sexual Dimorphism and Homosexual Gender Identity," *Psychol. Bull.* 74 (1970): 6, 425–40; and S. Schachter and J. E. Singer, "Cognitive, Social,

and Physiological Determinants of Emotional State," *Psychol. Rev.* 63 (1962): 379–99.

19. John Money, "Sexual Dimorphism and Homosexual Gender."

20. S. Milgram, "Some Conditions of Obedience and Disobedience to Authority," *Human Relations* 18 (1965): 57–76; and S. Milgram, "Liberating Effects of Group Pressure," *J. Pers. Soc. Psychol.* 1 (1965): 127–34.

Biology

MURIEL LEDERMAN

Through the Looking Glass:

A Feminist's Life in Biology

I was once a college student fascinated with the ability to explain life in its most minute detail. Soon I was a graduate student and postdoctoral fellow who trained to provide these explanations. I became an academic scientist dedicated to creating an laboratory environment in which collaborations could develop toward these goals. Recently, I discovered that the science with which I first fell in love may not really explain the biological phenomena that so fascinated me. Now, I no longer "do" science, which, for me, meant: working at the bench, mentoring students, writing proposals for funding, and learning just how certain processes work. Having become a feminist scientist, I am committed to creating a broader science that defines feminist, social, and political views of science *as* science, rather than as views that are only related to science. This progression was not typical of most scientists; it was influenced by the history of our time, by family, and by the work of other feminist scholars, some of whom also moved from doing science to searching for a whole new sense of science as a field.[1]

NORMAL SCIENCE

In 1965 I was a graduate student in the zoology department at Columbia University, about to begin my dissertation project in molecular biology. A long-standing area of interest in this field was the mechanism by which a gene is turned on to synthesize the enzyme (a kind of protein) it is encoded to produce. I was to study how an enzyme, ß-galactosidase of the bacterium *Escherichia coli*, was made when the bacterium itself uses lactose, a sugar, for growth. François Jacob and Jacques Monod had reported the results of *in vivo* (in living things) experiments showing how the production of ß–galactosidase was regulated within the living cell. My dissertation project would be an expansion of this research. I was to use biochemical and molecular biological techniques *in vitro* (in a glass test tube), using *components of* cells and chemicals, rather than intact cells, to confirm Jacob and Monod's work.[2] I was delighted to be assigned this project. It was "hot," directly at the forefront of research in molecular biology.

Why should the project have been carried out in this particular way? In the introduction to my dissertation, I answered this question—as follows: "The ability to synthesize a readily identifiable protein *in vitro* can permit the study of the control of this synthesis. This would be advantageous since manipulations which might be necessary for a full understanding of a regulatory process, e.g., altering the concentration of the components of a control system, can be done more easily *in vitro* and cannot be done *in vivo*." This meant that I was to devise conditions to produce ß–galactosidase in a test tube in order to see whether I could recreate *in vitro* Jacob and Monod's postulated control circuit, found *in vivo*. If I could do this, it would greatly facilitate the laboratory study of how other genes are regulated to produce protein and how to control the process. In a test tube, I would make an intermediate called mRNA from the ß–galactosidase gene, which would then produce the protein; this sequence of events, called DNA-dependent protein synthesis, had not previously been accomplished. This protocol was necessary because the postulated regulation involves turning on and off the synthesis of mRNA for the enzyme.

My research involved two tests, one for the production of any protein at all and the other for the production of ß–galactosidase. In the first test, I added an amino acid containing a radioactive carbon atom to the tube in which protein synthesis occurred. Amino acids are linked together to produce a protein and even a very small protein will come out of solution in the presence of a very strong acid, trichloroacetic acid (TCA). If the radioactive amino acid became part of a protein that precipitated when TCA is present, I could use a machine to detect and quantify the amount of radioactivity contained in the precipitate. The more radioactivity present, the more protein had been produced, the "better" my results. For the second test, biochemists had already developed a method—the conversion of a colorless compound into a yellow compound—to detect the presence and activity of ß–galactosidase. This test can detect minute amounts. However, in order to do my research, I had to develop conditions under which ß–galactosidase would be synthesized. If these experiments confirmed the genetic evidence, an important concept in molecular biology—how a gene is made to start producing the protein it is encoded to produce—would be on solid ground.

To begin, I had to obtain or produce the ingredients of the laboratory system. I needed DNA containing the gene for ß-galactosidase as well as bacterial cells that were broken to produce a protein-synthesizing extract. Even though it is normally found in the human colon, I grew a well characterized strain of *E. coli* in a liquid containing purchased chemicals. The conditions in the tube had to be just right for DNA to make RNA and for the RNA to make protein; I needed to figure out which chemicals in which quantities must be added for optimal synthesis. When my initial attempts were unsuccessful, I began systematically to change the amount of a single ingredient and look for results. I was inexperienced, but in the laboratory we followed the apprentice system: my mentor and I worked together; I watched him do the manipulations; and then we carried out experiments in parallel, comparing the results we obtained. When mine didn't match his, we figured out what was wrong with my technique. I also learned how to design experiments so that the results could be interpreted and how those results could be considered "positive."

Eventually, I was able to show that the protein synthesized in the *in vitro* system gave the characteristic yellow color indicative of active ß-galactosidase. I was also able to demonstrate that when I added "repressor," a protein that prevented synthesis of mRNA, no yellow color appeared, showing that ß-galactosidase had not been produced (see Lederman and Zubay). This exciting result confirmed the work of Jacob and Monod, corroborating their *in vivo* analysis in what biologists considered to be the most definitive way, through *in vitro* experiments.

After being awarded the doctorate, I won a postdoctoral appointment at the California Institute of Technology because the head of the laboratory there wanted my expertise developing *in vitro* protein-synthesizing systems. Subsequently, both my husband and I were promised positions at a fairly prominent medical school. Though his position materialized, and mine did not, I found another postdoctoral position. Eventually, my husband accepted a faculty appointment at Virginia Tech. I became involved in the full-time care of my very young children. I looked to return to full-time work in science shortly after our second daughter was born. Because of my ability to produce protein in a test tube, I was offered a research associate position in the Anaerobe Laboratory at Virginia Tech. When funding for the project ran out, I moved to the biology department as a research associate because of my skill with *in vitro* protein synthesis. Ultimately, I was offered a tenure-track faculty appointment with all the accompanying teaching and research responsibilities. My current research program, as of 1998, is in the field of agricultural biotechnology. We are developing a novel method, patent pending, to transfer foreign genes into a specific location in a plant chromosome. The technology takes advantage of the biological properties of a virus related to BPV, the human virus adeno-associated virus (AAV). When AAV is used as a gene therapy agent in people with inherited disorders, it transfers a functional gene into a specific site on a specific human chromosome to overcome the genetic abnormality. We have engineered plants to contain the human site that receives AAV and anticipate that we can use AAV to move genes that produce proteins of commercial value into plants.[3]

I cannot stress enough the satisfaction I get just from the handwork involved in carrying out the manipulations of molecular biology. When I work in the laboratory, "at the bench," most of the time I transfer exceedingly small amounts of what appears to be water from one tiny tube to another. I have grown animal cells on plastic dishes, which requires using an enzyme to loosen them from one dish to move them to fresh dishes, where they are less crowded and can continue to grow and divide. This task requires a talent that scientists call "hands." Some people have this ability, while others don't and cannot work at the bench. What is involved in passing cells is observing the shape of the cells under a microscope and sensing how vigorously to shake the dish to break the attachment completely. This talent is not inborn; it demands a particular kind of attention to the subject of the investigation. I learned it by internalizing the changes that occur in the cells, perpetually testing, mentally or actually, assumptions about where the cells are located in the sequence of events that occur during the detachment process. You cannot assume that because it took five minutes for the enzyme to work on Monday, it will take five minutes on Wednesday. (A postdoctoral fellow in my laboratory timed the process once and set a stopwatch the next time she passed cells. Perhaps her undergraduate training as a physicist and her doctoral work in mathematical biology gave her a certain deterministic mind-set that is not consonant with living material.) A comprehending investigator actively watches what the cells are doing, respecting their agency. She remembers that the object of investigation is not inert but an active participant in the research.

Another component of bench work is "eyes." Laboratory scientists focus visually on what the system tells or risk having the experiments not work properly or work at all. For instance, a visiting scholar in the laboratory in which I was doing my dissertation could not reproduce my results. At one point in the course of the experimental protocol, a glob present in the bottom of the tube had to be dispersed in order for the next step to be carried out. I gently flicked the tube with my finger while he used a mechanical mixer that generated a lot of force. Only when he started flicking could he reproduce my results. I wonder now how I knew to flick the tube. I suspect I noted that the glob was a loose aggregate that could be evenly distributed with tiny effort. Here's what I mean when I say that the combination of eye, hand, brain, and experience is critical to the physical side of doing science. We cannot be completely replaced by machines (even though robots are doing more and more routine tasks, such as transferring exceedingly small amounts of what appears to be water from one tiny tube to another). Robots must be programmed, but this may be done only on the basis of human experience.

Another essential part of traditional science, writing proposals for research funding, can be thrilling. In many cases, it is a way to understand just what are the frontiers of research and of discovering which different approaches might be pursued. What usually ends up in the proposal is fiction, a projection of the future. It is walking a path while simultaneously creating the path. I imagine the results that I might obtain, interpret what they mean, and design experiments to test alternative interpretations. This projection can be extremely creative.

Even though these aspects of traditional science remain appealing, their attraction is not strong enough for me to remain a bench scientist, given the current conventions and ideas about science and laboratory research. My having become aware of the inherent limitations of the practice of laboratory science has led me toward revising the ideas and practices of biology.

EPIPHANIES AND UNDERSTANDINGS

By the time I was employed for the third and fourth projects in *in vitro* protein synthesis, the work that had seemed so thrilling when I was a graduate student was becoming routine and tedious. It involved nothing more than changing the chemicals I added and looking for a change in the results. I began to be more thoughtful about my dissertation research, decades after I did the experiments. I began to question how my two tests (one for protein synthesis and the other for a functional protein) related to protein synthesis and the action of ß-galactosidase within a living cell. *Was* protein synthesis in the laboratory strain of bacteria grown in a liquid the same as what oc-curred in the bacterium in its natural environment, the human colon? The bacteria I used were not natural but adapted to and produced in a labora-tory; they were selected in large part so that my results could be confirmed in other laboratories. What criteria made me decide that I had the opti-mal conditions for protein synthesis? Which step along the optimization pathway was "the same" as what occurs in nature?

I concluded that I had no way of knowing how the *in vitro* system re-lated to what occurred *in vivo*. I still remember the almost physical shock when I realized that a major accomplishment in my scientific career was based on an unreliable assumption of correspondence between *in vitro* and *in vivo* processes.

In vitro research functions as a (to me, false) proxy for nature. If these conditions are stand-ins for *in vivo* systems, the "confirming" results ob-tained *in vitro* can turn out to be the conclusion of a self-fulfilling prophecy. Evelyn Fox Keller's distillation of Nancy Cartwright's and Mary Hesse's thoughts capture this idea: "the understanding of the remarkable conver-gences between theory and experiment that scientists have produced re-quires attention . . . to the particular and highly local manipulation of theory and experimental procedure that is required to produce these con-vergences. . . . Scientific laws may be 'true,' but what they are true of is a distillation of highly contrived and exceedingly particular circumstances, as much artifact as nature" (30). Not long ago, I was in my office when I heard a loud whoop of delight from a graduate student across the hall. He shouted, "I made it work!" I can think of no other more telling comment to reinforce the idea that many experiments in molecular biology are artifacts designated as representations of nature.

Eventually, my mistrust of *in vitro* systems expanded to other aspects of science. I suspected the conventions of science in general, especially the ideal that any scientist can develop objective procedures as the fundamen-tal, unbiased, impersonal means to unveil the secrets of nature that yield value-free, accurate descriptions of material processes. Objective science seems to take for granted that the "I" has no part in the doing of sci-ence and that nothing in science is personal. This doubtful ideal is found in other disciplines as well. Susan Krieger observes, "The social science disciplines tend to view the self of the social scientific observer as a con-taminant. The self—the unique inner life of the observer—is treated as something to be separated out, neutralized, minimized, controlled" (1). A female engineering student in my "Gender and Science" course wrote, "objectivity is socially constructed subjectivity." This formulation suggests that collectively held subjectivity—the political and psychosocial agendas of groups of scientists—is concealed by the rules of scientific procedure that reconstruct and rename the collective subjectivity "objectivity." I agree with Frederick Grinnell when he claims that "objectivity is imbedded in the group, not the individual" (B11) and with Ludwik Fleck, who wrote, "Even the simplest observation is conditioned by thought style and is thus tied to a community of thought. I therefore call thinking a supremely social activity which cannot by any means be completely localized within the confines of the individual" (98). In spite of such opinions, increasingly common among scientists and critics of science, the notion of individual autonomy is maintained to permit scientists to keep a false sense of intellectual freedom while they are actually working under collectively held assumptions.

It was during my fourth project of *in vitro* protein synthesis that I became aware of the weight, purpose, and urgency of the feminist critiques of science.[4] This scholarship united in my mind what had seemed to be unrelated elements of my personal life and professional career, such as being a trailing spouse and leaving work to care for sick children on an emergency basis. I understood what it meant for feminists to say that science is political. At my university, struggles for gender equity and the acceptance of feminist perspectives in scholarship brought back the memories of my involvement in the reform wing of the Democratic Party in New York City and in the anti–Vietnam War movement of the 1960s. Some feminist writings spoke to me compellingly about the issue of balancing a scientific career with marriage and parenthood. These writings pointed out how the institutions of science hamper women and some men by making it difficult to balance childbearing, child rearing, and elder care with a life in science (Gornick). When I married, I made the unexamined choice to follow my husband's career path first, which was typical at the time. I had no idea then how deeply this decision would affect my own career. It cemented my status as a second-class citizen trying always to find a position in the same location as my husband. For many of my projects, I had little or no opportunity to select the research I performed. I carried out other people's research agendas when my expertise was useful. True, the availability of my laboratory talents may have influenced the research they chose to pursue. But even when I finally secured a tenure-track appointment, I inherited the subject of the laboratory's research, how bovine parvovirus (BPV) produces copies of itself during an infection.

My way of claiming the importance of the feminist analyses of science while a full faculty member in a traditional science department was to create and teach "Gender and Science," covering feminist analyses of history, philosophy, epistemology, and practice. This undertaking clarified for me that I had long been interested in the social studies of science. Back when I spent a year as a visiting faculty member in the UCLA biology department in the early 1970s, I had volunteered to team-teach a course titled "Biology and Society" in addition to my assignment in molecular biology,

Perhaps the most valuable sense I developed from the feminist analyses was that the formal critique of science was more than just acceptable: it was important and exciting. My affiliation with the women's studies program provided the space in which I could continue to come to terms with my loss of faith in traditional science, which would have been difficult, if not impossible, in the biology department. The feminist critiques validated my conclusion that the experimental design for my dissertation followed the convention of research in molecular biology, which stipulated that *in vitro* experiments must confirm the mechanism by which a natural process occurs. The unexamined premise of this convention is that *in vitro* experiments are an accurate representation of what occurs *in vivo*. Feminist science studies revealed the context in which I could come to this conclusion.

Scientists believe they can study any aspect of nature that they find interesting. In doing so, they use all the information at their disposal to imagine the mechanisms of natural processes. They assume that they are discovering rather than inventing nature, that they are describing and explaining the natural world. Their observations are derived from a particular political framework, and the research is designed, as well, to fit within that framework, the rules by which science progresses. These rules are constructed by the scientists, although most have little awareness of their participation in this process or of the breadth and implications of this construction. They are also unaware that the constraints imposed by the conventions of research affect their choices: they can test only a limited number of ideas, those that link to accepted principles using established methods or newly developed methods that are validated as extensions of current techniques. What counts as a viable hypothesis is defined by the rules, and the rules limit the research that is funded. Ultimately, the interests of funding sources often determine what is done. In response to these constraints, scientists deceive themselves, thinking if it gets funded, it must be good science; if it gets funded it must be creative science. In reality, what is finally carried out is often not creative. Further, because their livelihood depends on this funding, scientists are in no position to mount a critique of the system.

Scientists promulgate the conventions and rules for carrying out research when they train graduate students. "Train" is an example of how scientists themselves define their fields. It implies that there is a correct way to carry out experiments. The rules have practical value for each scientist. Observing established rules yields acceptable answers. Following the rules makes science easy to do. Once a scientist has made an observation, she knows what additional pieces of information must be in hand to convert the observation into a fact. All she has to do is to spend the time and effort necessary to obtain them—it becomes almost make-work. However, sometimes the rules change. New rules come to bear, but they are inextricably linked to the previous sets of rules and become the standard for current and future work, until the process repeats itself. Such changes are claimed to be examples of the self-correcting mechanism of science, one of the hallmarks of objectivity, to make information more certain. The rules are used to construct a view of nature at one particular time that is different from the view at a previous time. As a result, we know a particular version of nature at a particular point in time. Scientific knowledge is historically contingent; most scientists would agree with this assessment, for if all information were completely accurate at time X, they would be out of business.

At the same time, scientists tend to deny that there is anything personal, social, cultural, or political in science, even though some can be truly arrogant and ego-driven people. Scientists tell themselves they are not doing research for personal gain or self-advancement but in the service of objectivity and finding out about the natural world. But scientists mistake reproducibility for objectivity, thinking that if a result is reproduced enough times it may be deemed objectively certain. They insist that a person in New York should be able to carry out an experiment week after week and get the same result each time. A person in Boston should be able to repeat this experiment and get the same outcome. (This is why my dissertation research utilized a uniform, well-characterized strain of *E. coli* rather than the more diverse bacteria from the gut.) A physicist friend says that the speed of light measured on planet X is the same as measured here, given the appropriate conversion factor. But consider: what will the response of objective scientists be if it becomes possible that light can be made to go faster than c (Wang, Kuzmich, and Dogiaru) and that presumed fundamental physical constants, including possibly the speed of light, have changed over time (Webb et al.)?

I imagine science as a spiral composed of dots, each one representing a state of knowledge at a particular time. At close range, each individual dot is visible; at a distance, the pattern is seen, like a pointillist painting. Using my dissertation as an example, the first dot could symbolize Jacob and Monod's *in vivo* work on expression of the ß-galactosidase gene. The second would be my *in vitro* work. The third is the more detailed *in vitro* research examining the state of the regulatory protein, repressor, when bound to the DNA of the gene. A fourth dot represents studies on the location where repressor binds on the DNA. Scientists care about the stages or dots in that path and are rewarded, both personally and professionally, for creating them. Scientists are concerned about the next dot on the spiral, the next step in the pathway, the next result, rather than with the effects of the entirety of their work. For the most part, attention to the impact of one's science outside of the immediate research community is not encouraged. Donna Haraway puts it well when she describes the "god-trick," the view from nowhere, which refers to not assuming responsibility for actions. In contemporary science, such abdication may not be surprising. Bordo terms the Cartesian scientist as "no where" ("Flight" 61). Such lack of location is the ultimate extension of Krieger's description of social scientists' removing themselves from their research (to nowhere?).

The spiral of science can move outward, representing progress. On the other hand, the path might be traced in reverse, moving inward. This is the path I followed after reflecting on the structure and practice of science, progressively losing faith in the authority of science. From my perspective, the spiral implodes inward into nothingness, there's no *there* there, no center or sense of the research as conventionally understood. After I had come to this conclusion, I found that Haraway, too, had reached a similar understanding, "It seems to me that the practices of the sciences—the sciences as cultural production—force one to accept two simultaneous, incompatible truths. One is the historical contingency of what counts as nature for us; the thoroughgoing artificiality of a scientific object of knowledge, that makes it inescapably and radically contingent. You peel away all the layers of the onion and there's nothing in the center" (qtd. in Penley and Ross 2).

AFTERMATH

After coming to the realization of "no there there," I no longer uncover the secrets of nature through the *in vitro* investigations my field expects. My current biotechnology research is applied rather than basic and is as problematic from a feminist perspective as *in vitro* studies. In any event, I also proceed with perhaps greater interest in the project of reviewing scientific values through changes in science education. Sandra Harding maintains:

> Failing to locate any significant critical studies of the sciences in universities, and especially in science departments, indicates to students that no one thinks these studies important to learning to do science or for making reasoned decisions about scientific issues in public life. This is unfortunate, since . . . philosophical, sociological, and historical assumptions form part of scientific understanding about nature. (*Is Science Multicultural?* 329)

I have incorporated the social studies and feminist analyses of science into a science course at Virginia Tech. Here, thoughts *about* the nature of science, its internal culture and rules, are presented to students as already being part of science. Even though these thoughts may have originated in the work of some scholars outside of science, they will no longer be discounted as less rigorous, less objective, or irrelevant. The course I will teach is a sophomore-level cell and molecular biology course for biology majors. Typically, the instructors of the course present the facts resulting from normative investigations—for example, a description of the steps that occur between the time a protein is produced and its leaving the cell. Some go further; one colleague lists the topics "How do we study DNA replication?" and "How do we study transcription?" on the syllabus. She uses "how to think like a scientist" as a guiding principle for her teaching. In doing so, she explicitly transmits the internal culture of science along with the methods and results of scientific inquiry; other instructors do so unconsciously. In my course, I expect to treat the topic of protein export differently, teaching both the generally accepted scheme for this process and the contrast between the *in vivo* work that first suggested it and the *in vitro* experiments that confirmed it. In this picture the *in vitro* work is no longer business as usual but is reconsidered and analyzed, especially from the perspectives of the rules of molecular cell biology: the search for mechanism, the primacy of *in vitro* experimentation, and the relationship of results obtained *in vitro* to what occurs *in vivo*.

Teaching science courses this way may encourage more women to become researchers, mentors, and teachers in biology. The standard answer to the pipeline problem—women continually dropping out of science as they move through education and practice—is to have more females enter the tube. Maria Matyas and Shirley Malcolm raise "the possibility that the pipeline itself and the 'pond' into which it empties may not be neutral" (34). Londa Schiebinger says, "The pipeline model, built on the liberal assumption that women (and minorities) should assimilate into the current practices of science, does not provide insight into how the structure of institutions or the current practices of science need to change before women can comfortably join the ranks of scientists" (64). In other words, the pipeline is not neutral because of the inherent culture of science, the rules of the enterprise. Women are alienated from this culture (Schiebinger; Seymour and Hewitt) by their socialization and by the way science is presented, for example, as ahistoric (Fausto-Sterling, "Race, Gender and Science") or acontextual (Henrion) or boring and isolating (American Association of University Women). Revealing this culture within a science course may give students a perspective by which they may recognize, understand, and challenge their estrangement. If this occurs, it would be similar to the commonly reported epiphany of women whose experiences in women's history courses makes them understand why they were alienated in traditional history courses—they never saw themselves portrayed. If women and men remained in science while being aware of its internal culture, perhaps there is hope for change. I would consider teaching that results in increased retention of women and minorities in science a feminist pedagogy[5] since its result is social justice (Kyle), making participation in science more equitable and science itself less androcentric.

REFLECTIONS

I may be like Alice in *Through the Looking Glass*, moving across the laboratory glass—*in vitro*—to "real life"—*in vivo*—and back. On one side is science, on the other, feminist science studies. Many in the biology department think that feminism is alien to science. I share Anne Fausto-Sterling's experience: her science colleagues find that her "work about science, which they would distinguish from my work in science, is more or less invisible" ("Two-Way Streets" 337). But my department must now acknowledge feminist science studies, since I will be teaching biology majors from this perspective. Accepting these studies as part of science may be more difficult. One faculty member came to a panel on feminist pedagogy in which I participated, looking for "new teaching tools." She did not grasp that feminism in science is not simply an add-on or a tool, but a fundamentally different perspective.

The field of feminist science studies also requires traversing a mirror. One side is science and one side is women's studies. Paraphrasing Fausto-Sterling, my women's studies colleagues may find invisible both my work in science and my work about science, since the latter does not fit with the typical humanities and social sciences orientation of the field. Nevertheless, there were times that women's studies felt like more of a home than the biology department.

I suspect that serendipity has been more influential in my academic career than in most. Even though my profession was not central when my children were young, I was still employed in science. When feminist science studies became compelling, I had the liberty to move in that direction. I made all my choices because they were intellectually exciting at the time. Now I hope to break down the barrier between science and feminist science studies, to introduce previously forbidden topics into science, to shatter the looking glass.

NOTES

I wish to thank the editors and reviewers of this volume and David Bleich, who helped shape the essay into its current form. Steve Fifield and Mike Rosenzweig asked important questions; answering them, with the incisive help of Barbara Reeves, made the work sharper.

1. I am thinking especially of Ruth Hubbard, Evelyn Fox Keller, Donna Haraway, and Bonnie Spanier.

2. For a review of this biology, see Miller and Reznikoff, *The Operon*.

3. Feminists are highly critical of work such as this. Vandana Shiva claims, on a theoretical level, that biotechnology reinforces man's dominion over nature, reifies the primacy of the gene at the expense of all other components of living systems, and reinforces biological determinism. Patenting genetically modified organisms or genes codifies the tradition of viewing mind and body as separate from each other and places human effort in a privileged light. On a practical level, the use of biotechnology in agriculture undermines food production in the Third World, undercutting ecologically sound practices that are culturally the purview of women. How can I, as a feminist, justify an applied biotechnology research program when others, such as Crouch, have abandoned even

basic plant biology research for the reasons put forward by Shiva? On the one hand, I plead guilty to being seduced by the cleverness of the idea and wanting to demonstrate that it can be implemented successfully. On the other hand, I admit that I have not resolved this dilemma.

4. The readings that were most influential were Hubbard's *The Politics of Women's Biology*, in which she claims that scientists are inventing rather than describing nature, and Thomas Kuhn's *Structure of Scientific Revolutions*. Also important were Harding's overt political stance and her discussions of objectivity (*Whose Science, Whose Knowledge?*) and Bordo's analysis of the origin of Descartes' view of a mechanical universe. Bordo's summary line from "The Cartesian Masculinization of Thought," "The otherness of Nature is now what allows it to be known" (453), speaks to scientists' alienation from the material they study, exemplified by the primacy of experimentation. Sue Rosser gives descriptions of the various versions of feminist science in *Women, Science, and Society*.

5. For others' views on feminist pedagogy for the sciences, see Barton; Gilbert; Lederman ("Mutating Virology"); Mayberry and Rose; and Rosser (*Female Friendly Science; Biology and Feminsm; Re-Engineering*). Especially interesting is Gilbert's use of Harding's concept of "strong objectivity" as a "control," in the sense that scientists use the term. To convince scientists of the value of feminist science studies to the teaching of science it may be valuable to use terms and concepts that they understand. However, it strikes me that using the term *control*, which describes part of an experiment designed to confirm the accuracy of the whole, conflicts with the essence of Harding's concept, which is to critique current theory and practice.

REFERENCES

American Association of University Women Educational Foundation. *TechSavvy: Educating Girls in the New Computer Age*. Washington, D.C.: American Association of University Women Educational Foundation, 2000.

Barton, Angela C. *Feminist Science Education*. New York: Teachers College Press, 1998.

Bordo, Susan. "The Cartesian Masculinization of Thought." *Signs: Journal of Women in Culture and Society* 11 (1986): 439–56.

———. "Selections from The Flight to Objectivity." In *Feminist Interpretations of Rene Descartes*, edited by Susan Bordo, 48–69. University Park: Pennsylvania State University Press, 1999.

Crouch, Martha L. "Debating the Responsibilities of Plant Scientists in the Decade of the Environment." *Plant Cell* 2 (1990): 275–77.

Fausto-Sterling, Anne. "Race, Gender, and Science." *Transformations* 2 (1991): 412.

———. "Two Way Streets: The Case of Feminism and Science." *NWSA Journal* 4, no. 3 (1992): 336–49.

Fleck, Ludwik. *Genesis and Development of a Scientific Fact*. Translated by Fred Bradley and Thaddeus J. Tenn. Chicago: University of Chicago Press, 1979.

Gilbert, Scott (with collaboration from the Biology and Gender Study Group). "Mainstreaming Feminist Critiques into the Biology Curriculum." In *Doing Science + Culture*, edited by Roddey Reid and Sharon Traweek, 199–220. New York: Routledge, 2000.

Gornick, Vivian. *Women in Science: Portraits from a World in Transition*. New York: Simon and Schuster, 1983.

Grinnell, Frederick. "The Practice of Science at the Edge of Knowledge." *Chronicle of Higher Education* (24 March 2000): B11.

Haraway, Donna. "Situated Knowledges: The Science Question in Feminism." *Feminist Studies* 14, no. 3 (1988): 575–89.

Harding, Sandra. *Whose Science, Whose Knowledge?* Ithaca: Cornell University Press, 1991.

———. "Is Science Multicultural? Challenges, Resources, Opportunities, Uncertainties." *Configurations* 10 (1994): 310–30.

———. *Is Science Multicultural? Post-Colonialisms, Feminisms, and Epistemologies*. Bloomington: Indiana University Press, 1998.

Henrion, Claudia. *Women in Mathematics: The Addition of Difference*. Bloomington: Indiana University Press, 1997.

Hubbard, Ruth. *The Politics of Women's Biology*. New Brunswick: Rutgers University Press, 1990.

Jacob, François, and Jacques Monod. "Genetic Regulatory Mechanisms in the Synthesis of Proteins." *Journal of Molecular Biology* 3 (1961): 318–56.

Keller, Evelyn Fox. *Secrets of Life, Secrets of Death*. New York: Routledge, 1992.

Krieger, Susan. *Social Science and the Self: Personal Essays on an Art Form*. New Brunswick: Rutgers University Press, 1991.

Kuhn, Thomas S. *The Structure of Scientific Revolutions*. Chicago: University of Chicago Press, 1962.

Kyle, William C. Jr. "Toward a Political Philosophy of Science Education." In *Teaching Science in Diverse Settings: Marginalized Discourses and Classroom Practice*, edited by Angela Calabrese Barton and Margery D. Osborn. New York: Peter Lang, 2001.

Lederman, Muriel. "Mutating 'Virology': How Far to Feminist?" *Feminist Teacher* 13 (2001): 193–201.

Lederman, Muriel, and Geoffrey Zubay. "DNA-Directed Peptide Synthesis. V. The Cell-Free Synthesis of a Peptide with ß-galactosidase Activity." *Biochemical and Biophysical Research Communications* 32 (1968): 710–14.

Matyas, Maria, and Shirley Malcolm. *Investing in Human Potential: Science and Engineering at the Crossroads*. Washington, D.C.: American Association for the Advancement of Science, 1991.

Mayberry, Maralee, and Ellen C. Rose, eds. *Science Education: Meeting the Challenge: Innovative Feminist Pedagogies in Action*. New York: Routledge, 1999.

Miller, Jeffrey H., and William S. Reznikoff, eds. *The Operon*. Cold Spring Harbor, N.Y.: Cold Spring Harbor Laboratory Press, 1978.

Penley, Constance, and Andrew Ross. "Cyborgs at Large: Interview with Donna Haraway." In *Technoculture*, edited by Constance Penley and Andrew Ross, 1–20. Minneapolis: University of Minnesota Press, 1991.

Rosser, Sue V. *Female-Friendly Science: Applying Women's Studies Methods and Theories to Attract Students*. New York: Teachers College Press, 1990.

———. *Biology and Feminism*. New York: Twayne, 1992.

———. *Re-Engineering Female-Friendly Science*. New York: Teachers College Press, 1997.

———. *Women, Science, and Society*. New York: Teachers College Press, 2000.

Schiebinger, Londa. *Has Feminism Changed Science?* Cambridge: Harvard University Press, 1999.

Seymour, Elaine, and Nancy M. Hewitt. *Talking about Leaving*. Boulder: Westview, 1997.

Shapin, Stephen. *The Scientific Revolution*. Chicago: University of Chicago Press, 1996.

Shiva, Vandana. "Democratizing Biology: Reinventing Biology from a Feminist, Ecological, and Third World Perspective." In *Reinventing Biology*, edited by Lynda Birke and Ruth Hubbard, 50–71. Bloomington: Indiana University Press, 1995.

Wang, L. J., A. Kuzmich, and A. Dogiaru. "Gain-Assisted Superluminal Light Propagation." *Nature* 406 (2000): 227–29.

Webb, J. K. et al. "Further Evidence for Cosmological Evolution of the Fine Structure Constant." *Physical Review Letters* 87 (2001): 091301.

Medicine

ALICE WEXLER

That Disorder:

An Introduction

From *Mapping Fate: A Memoir of Family, Risk, and Genetic Research*

For I the Lord your God am an impassioned God, visiting the guilt of the fathers upon
the children, upon the third and upon the fourth generations.
—Exodus 20:5

First there is the grandfather who has died of "nervous trouble" on the back
ward of a state hospital, the uncle who attracts whispers and stares from the
neighbors as he staggers down the street, the doctor who says, "Women do
not get it." Rumors of hereditary insanity linger about the family in question, along with a certain atmosphere of secrecy and suspicion. Divorce,
arrests, abandonment, suicide punctuate the action. There is always a moment of discovery, when the protagonists finally learn the truth, usually
after having had several children. In the end, the characters all come to resemble one another, and the action winds down to a predictably gruesome
close, with no resolution or release and always the promise of more performances to come. This is the drama of families with Huntington's disease
(formerly called Huntington's chorea), played out with minor variations
on stages around the world.

In the summer of 1968, my sister and I discovered that this drama was
also our own, when our fifty-three-year-old mother was diagnosed with
Huntington's disease. In our mid-twenties, we learned for the first time
the hidden history of our family, summed up in the awful word *chorea*. We
learned that our maternal grandfather and all our uncles had died of this
disease and that our mother would repeat their fate. Nancy and I each faced
a fifty-fifty chance of inheriting her disease ourselves.

Back in 1872, the physician George Huntington wrote the classic account of the disease that would become associated with his name. He had

learned about it from his father and grandfather, both physicians, who had seen it among their patients on Long Island, New York. It was "confined to certain and fortunately a few families, and has been transmitted to them, an heirloom from generations away back in the dim past." It was spoken of by those "in whose veins the seeds of the disease are known to exist, with a kind of horror, and not at all alluded to except through dire necessity, when it is mentioned as '*that disorder.*'"

The symptoms began extremely gradually, "by the irregular and spasmodic action of certain muscles, as of the face, arms, etc." The movements grew progressively worse over a period of years "until the hapless sufferer is but a quivering wreck of his former self." In the end, every muscle in the body was affected "(excepting the involuntary ones), and the poor patient presents a spectacle which is anything but pleasing to witness." Nor could the patient hope for remission. "I have never known a recovery or even an amelioration of symptoms in this form of chorea: when once it begins it clings to the bitter end."

Huntington described three notable peculiarities of the disease. One was a marked tendency to insanity and sometimes to suicide. "As the disease progresses the mind becomes more or less impaired, in many amounting to insanity, while in others mind and body both gradually fail until death relieves them of their sufferings." Another was that of late onset: rarely before the age of thirty or forty, "while those who pass the fortieth year *without* symptoms of the disease, are seldom attacked." (In fact, onset may occur both earlier and later.)

The pattern of hereditary transmission was perhaps the most striking aspect of the disorder. If a parent was afflicted, "one or more of the offspring almost invariably suffer from the disease, if they live to adult age. But if by any chance these children go through life *without* it, the thread is broken and the grandchildren and great-grandchildren of the original shakers may rest assured that they are free from the disease." This illness never skipped a generation to reappear in another. For those who were stricken, however, no treatment helped, "and indeed nowadays its end is so well known to the sufferer and his friends, that medical advice is seldom sought. It seems at least to be one of the incurables."[1]

• • •

Our mother's diagnosis in 1968 prompted my father to organize the Hereditary Disease Foundation to support research, and my sister to become a researcher herself. The research in which she participated led to a breakthrough in 1983. That summer, scientists localized the Huntington's gene on the short arm of chromosome 4 by identifying a genetic marker for the disease—a neighboring stretch of DNA indicating the proximity of the Huntington's gene. This event marked the first significant advance in Huntington's research, since the marker would make possible the identification of the gene and, it was hoped, lead to an understanding of how that gene caused brain cells to die. The marker also enabled researchers to identify who would develop the illness years, even decades, in advance of any symptoms. The dream of prediction long cherished by geneticists and counselors and even by affected families became a reality.

The marker discovery reverberated throughout the biomedical community. It demonstrated for the first time the power of a controversial new technology for mapping genes and opened the way to accelerated advances in many areas of human genetics. Never before had this technique been used to locate a disease gene that could have been anywhere on any one of the twenty-three pairs of human chromosomes. Moreover, the localization of the Huntington's gene marked a significant step in the union of human genetics, which had been largely clinical and descriptive, and molecular biology, which had been highly reductionist and focused on mechanics. The coming together of these two worlds fundamentally transformed each of them.[2]

Second, the extensive dialogue that developed around presymptomatic testing for Huntington's has served as a model for thinking about all kinds of genetic testing. The cautions that scientists, doctors, health professionals, and HD activists have built into the procedures for testing have served as examples for those developing ways of testing for other illnesses as well. In a world in which growing numbers of disorders may be diagnosed before symptoms appear, even though there may be no effective therapy for them, the response of the Huntington's disease community has been carefully watched throughout the biomedical world.

Third, the way in which the research on Huntington's has unfolded—through interdisciplinary workshops, collaborative efforts, and a high degree of cooperation between families and investigators—has also served as a model for other research ventures. Although scientists collaborate on all sorts of projects, molecular biology and biomedical research have been arenas of especially fierce competition. The Huntington's Disease Collaborative Research Group, organized under the auspices of the Hereditary Disease Foundation, has been considered by many to be a model of a successful, large-scale collaborative effort in biomedical science.

Fourth, many have seen the status of being at risk for Huntington's as an extreme example of what it means to be at risk for a wide range of other conditions, including AIDS. Huntington's poses stark questions about the meanings of certainty and uncertainty and what it means to occupy a "third space" outside the categories of either-or that we conventionally use to organize experience.[3]

Finally, Huntington's is also about nonscientists playing an active role in science, not only through fund-raising and lobbying but by participating in decision making about which research to support and working with scientists to organize research efforts. By intervening directly in the scientific world, these Huntington's activists have significantly influenced the priorities and practices of biomedical research.

My family's involvement began at a moment when biomedical interest in this disease had already started to revive, on the eve of the recombinant DNA revolution and the blossoming of neurobiology in the late 1960s. The scientific milieu was highly favorable to the intensification of interest in a disease like Huntington's, with its combined neurological and genetic dimensions. At the same time, its late onset made it peculiarly difficult to study, since it was hard to distinguish those who were unaffected from those who might develop the disease later on.

The decade of the 1960s, with its blossoming of social activism, also helped foster a political atmosphere favorable to mobilizing families directly affected by the illness. Civil rights activism, the feminist health movement, and patients' rights movements of the sixties and seventies all created an environment that encouraged families with Huntington's to act on their own behalf. Moreover, Woody Guthrie, the great poet and songwriter of the Dust Bowl, had died of Huntington's in 1967, the year before our mother was diagnosed. His long illness had inspired Marjorie Guthrie, his ex-wife, to start an organization of people with Huntington's in their families. Founded in 1967, the Committee to Combat Huntington's Disease, or CCHD, grew into a national, grassroots organization—later called the Huntington's Disease Society of America, or HDSA—which lobbied Congress, developed services for families, and organized educational campaigns for the public and for health professionals.

Although inspired at the beginning by Marjorie Guthrie and CCHD, my father's deepest commitment was basic research. Imbued with a profound faith in science, he wanted to find a cure. At a time when the disease was of interest primarily to a few neurologists and geneticists, my father and sister helped create a support system—seed money, tissue banks, pedigrees, and workshops—that enticed many basic scientists to study Huntington's. In doing so, they pioneered imaginative ways of working with scientists, and of fostering dialogue among scientists, which would have implications far beyond the Huntington's research community, a community they helped to create.

· · ·

This book [*Mapping Fate*] began as a project of documentation in that heady summer of 1983, when we thought Huntington's might soon come to an end, like polio after the invention of the Salk and Sabin vaccines. As a historian, I wanted to record this first major turning point in the history of an obscure, seemingly hopeless illness and in the development of human neurogenetics. That summer, I began to interview the scientists who had been involved in the marker discovery, as well as others who had been associated with the Hereditary Disease Foundation. I hoped to collect memories before they became too encumbered by myth and before all the publicity in the press began to feed back into the scientists' recollections.

I soon realized that, as a member of a family that had been deeply involved with this effort and had helped to fund it, I could not write as an outsider. Although my own role has been primarily that of an observer, I was too close to the participants to write about their efforts with much critical distance. And, as a person at risk for Huntington's, I was too emotionally involved in the outcome of this research to regard it with much detachment.

I realized further that I did not want to write as an outsider, nor did I wish simply to document an exciting moment in the history of biomedical science. In my early forties and approaching the age at which my mother had begun showing symptoms, I wanted to explore the emotional meanings of being at risk, for my mother as well as for myself. Although my sister and others had studied the psychology of being at risk for Huntington's, few people actually in that position had written personal accounts of their experience outside the context of psychiatric testing, genetic counseling, the neurological exam, or the journalistic interview. As a feminist I particularly wanted to examine the relations between genetics and gender in our family, since I knew it somehow mattered to my own experience of growing up female that my mother—my same-sexed parent—was the parent at risk and that she was the one who had developed the disease. I wanted to see how our lives intersected, the rhythms of her hopes and anxieties informing those of my sister and me. Huntington's, I thought, could even be seen as a metaphor for the fear of many daughters of my 1950s generation—that we would somehow turn into our mothers, that our mothers were mirrors of our future selves—and for that common guilt of our mothers, that they had inflicted suffering on their children. What was the mother-daughter relationship, when viewed through the lens of Huntington's disease? *If the mirror, whose precursor is the mother's face, offers an illusion of wholeness to the child's body of bits and pieces, what then of the daughter who sees the mother imagining herself and imagining her daughter as the fragmented body she fears to become? What psychic map of the body is projected by a mother who recalls her own parent's choreic body? What map of the body is taken in by the daughter who sees chorea memories written on her mother's face?*[4]

Finally, I wanted to explore the meanings of secrecy and silence within our family, the ways in which what could not be said reverberated as loudly as the words that were spoken. Feelings cannot be buried as easily as facts. Denial creates its own emotional force fields, even if the relevant information remains hidden. Secrets, moreover, especially so dramatic a secret as Huntington's, may form part of a family's emotional inheritance, a psychological legacy handed down along with the family Bible, affecting every aspect of family life for generations. Since Huntington's had been a secret in our family, long hidden from my sister and me, our mother's diagnosis had implications far beyond the medical. Learning of our mother's failure for many years to tell our father about Huntington's disease in her family, and discovering our parents' decision not to tell my sister and me of our mother's risk, and therefore our own, meant recasting my entire understanding of our family history.

Our situation, then, had much in common with that of other families whose secrets differed in their content. Certainly any stigmatized condition may be surrounded by webs of secrecy, whose maintenance requires hard work and active effort. As the historian Michel Foucault argued, "Silence itself—the things one declines to say, or is forbidden to name, the discretion that is required between different speakers—is . . . an element that functions alongside the things said, with them and in relation to them . . . we must try to determine the different ways of not saying such things, how those who can and those who cannot speak of them are distributed, which type of discourse is authorized, or which form of discretion is required in either case. There is not one but many silences."[5]

In exploring the impact of secrecy in our family, I also wanted to consider the ways in which our silences were gendered. In recent decades, much feminist writing has addressed the costs for women of socially imposed silence, especially the silencing of our own deepest thoughts and emotions. Feminist historians in particular have described how the female body became the arena in which forbidden speech was acted out through physical symptoms. In our family, much remained unspoken and unspeakable until the day in 1968 when our mother's body spoke that (death) sentence. This book, in part, is my translation. . . .

• • •

In weaving together a personal narrative of a family confronting Huntington's disease with a more detached account of biomedical research, I have utilized several approaches. On the one hand, I have drawn on the traditional resources of the historian and journalist in investigating the past —interviews with many scientists, archival materials, and reports in the scientific, medical, and popular press, as well as personal observation at meetings and workshops. At the same time, I have pored over family papers and photographs, old letters, newspaper clippings, scrapbooks, transcripts, conversations over many years, even dreams and memories, diaries and journals. I hoped my doubled perspective as insider and outsider, as participant and observer, might be a useful position for approaching a topic that is both scientifically significant and emotionally volatile. While my story shares some of the elements of the illness narratives written about cancer and AIDS, it is really less about an illness than about the possibility of an illness, less about the medical dilemma of living with disease than about the existential dilemma of living at risk. . . .

• • •

Human genetics in the 1990s inhabits a volatile space at the intersection of medicine, biology, corporate profits, law, government funding of science, state health programs, private insurance companies, genetic counseling services, schools, courts, and popular culture. Issues of race, gender, and class figure in the discourse of the new genetics, reviving old debates about the distribution of traits such as intelligence and aggression, dominance and disease, within different groups of the population. Genetic engineering is a multibillion-dollar industry, with companies competing for control over diagnostic tests for newly discovered genes or markers of lethal illnesses, whose discoverers are often shareholders and members of the board of directors of the companies that will market the tests. Clearly many groups of people have strong stakes in the technologies that are revolutionizing all of biology.

The new genetics has already opened a vast arena for contests of power over what it means to be human, who has the power to define what is normal, who has access to what resources and when. Who will control the knowledge of our bodies after the Human Genome Project has mapped and sequenced all human genes? How can we ensure that this will not be another project for enforcing narrow norms of "human nature," as the historian of science Donna Haraway has put it, for legislating "genetic destiny"? How can we respect the diversity and difference that the Human Genome Project also establishes as "normal"?

Although Huntington's affects a limited population—some seven to ten people per 100,000, or about 30,000 in the United States, with another 150,000 at risk—it has usefully been considered a prototype for biomedical research since it destroys such a wide range of functions. Understanding Huntington's may shed light on more common inherited, neurological and psychiatric disorders, such as Parkinson's, schizophrenia, and sickle-cell disease.[6] Because it is caused by one gene, however, some have argued that Huntington's may be an inappropriate model for thinking about disease, since most diseases are caused by complex interactions of genes and environment, or by a combination of genes. As the historian of science Evelyn Fox Keller has written, only for very exceptional diseases can "genetic components be considered apart from the environment. For such cases—e.g., cystic fibrosis and Huntington's disease—there is no question that molecular genetics is providing powerful and unambivalently welcome tools. But most diseases are not so simple." Indeed, the ever-expanding category of genetic disease has recently threatened to claim such social conditions as homelessness, while what Keller calls "the geneticization of Health and disease" threatens to move discussions of disease from individuals to their DNA.[7]

But even Huntington's, with its straightforward genetics, may not be entirely reducible to DNA, since the cellular environment and even social milieu may also influence its expression. My hope is that the Huntington's story may suggest the ways in which even this obviously pathological, genetically determined killer may acquire distinct meanings for different individuals, families, and cultures. Biology itself, in this view, is partially shaped by its social, political, and cultural contexts. Moreover, as recent social studies of science have argued, what counts as biological "fact" may be partly a product of cultural struggles over power.[8] Part of the fascination of the new genetics concerns the questions it raises about the construction of knowledge—how, for whom, and for what is this knowledge being constructed? In this context, then, Huntington's disease may serve as a space where many discourses collide and therefore help make visible the hidden stakes in this contest for human survival and identity in which all of us are at risk.

NOTES

1. George W. Huntington, "On Chorea," *Medical Surgical Reporter* 26 (Philadelphia, 1872): 317–21.

2. Robert Mullan Cook-Deegan, "The Human Genome Project: The Formation of Federal Policies in the United States, 1986–1990," in Kathi E. Hanna, ed., *Biomedical Politics* (Washington, D.C.: National Academy, 1991), 102.

3. The literary critic Marjorie Garber has written recently, "The 'third' is a mode of articulation, a way of describing a space of possibility. Three puts in question the idea of one: of identity self-sufficiency, self-knowledge. . . . The third deconstructs the binary of self and other that was itself a comfortable, because commutable, and thus controllable, fiction of complementarity." Garber posits an analogy between the marker for the Huntington's disease gene and the transvestite, or cross-dresser: one points to genetic trouble somewhere else, while the other indicates gender trouble; Marjorie Garber, *Vested Interests* (London: Routledge, 1991), 11–12.

4. See Jacques Lacan, "The Mirror Stage," in *Jacques Lacan, Ecrits: A Selection* (New York: Norton, 1977), 1–7; D. W Winnicott, "Mirror-Role of Mother and Family in Child Development," in *Playing and Reality* (1971; New York: Routledge, 1991), 111–119.

5. Michel Foucault, *The History of Sexuality*, vol. 1 (New York: Pantheon, 1978), 27.

6. Report of the Congressional Commission for the Control of Huntington's Disease and its Consequences, vol. 1 (October, 1977): 7–10.

7. Evelyn Fox Keller, "Genetics, Reductionism, and the Normative Uses of Biological Information," conference paper, "Genes 'R' Us" conference, University of California, Irvine, May 1991. See also Donna Haraway, "When Man Is on the Menu: Technical Products as Social Actors," conference paper, "Genes 'R' US" conference, University of California, Irvine, May 1991.

8. See for example Thomas Laqueur, *Making Sex: Body and Gender from the Greeks to Freud* (Cambridge: Harvard University Press, 1990).

PERRI KLASS

A Textbook Pregnancy

From *A Not Entirely Benign Procedure: Four Years As a Medical Student*

I learned I was pregnant the afternoon of my anatomy exam. I had spent the morning taking first a written exam and then a practical, centered around fifteen thoroughly dissected cadavers, each ornamented with little paper tags indicating structures to be identified.

My classmates and I were not looking very good, our hair unwashed, our faces pale from too much studying and too little sleep. Two more exams and our first year of medical school would be over. We all knew exactly what we had to do next: go home and study for tomorrow's exam. I could picture my genetics notes lying on my desk, liberally highlighted with pink marker. But before I went home I had a pregnancy test done.

My period was exactly one day late, hardly worth noticing—but the month before, for the first time in my life, I had been trying to get pregnant. Four hours later I called for the test results.

"It's positive," the woman at the lab told me.

With all the confidence of a first-year medical student, I asked, "Positive, what does that mean?"

"It means you're pregnant," she told me. "Congratulations."

Somewhat later that afternoon I settled down to make final review notes for my genetics exam. *Down's syndrome*, I copied carefully onto a clean piece of paper, *most common autosomal disorder, 1 per 700 live births*. I began to feel a little queasy. Over the next twenty-four hours, I was supposed to learn the biological basis, symptoms, diagnosis, and treatment of a long list of genetic disorders. Almost every one was something that could conceivably already be wrong with the embryo growing inside me. I couldn't even think about it; I had to put my notes aside and pass the exam on what I remembered from the lectures.

Over the past months, as I have gone through my pregnancy, and also through my second year of medical school, I have become more and more aware of these two aspects of my life influencing each other, and even sometimes seeming to oppose each other. As a medical student, I was spending my time studying everything that can go wrong with the human body. As a pregnant woman, I was suddenly passionately interested in healthy physiological processes, in my own normal pregnancy and the growth of my baby. And yet pregnancy put me under the care of the medical profession—my own future profession—and I found myself rebelling as a mother and a patient against the attitudes that were being taught to me, particularly the attitude that pregnancy is a perilous, if not pathological, condition. The pregnancy and the decisions I had to make about my own health care changed my feelings about medicine and about the worldview of emergency and intervention which is communicated in medical training. My pregnancy became for me a rebellion against this worldview, a chance to do something healthy and normal with my body, something that would be a joyous event, an important event, a complex event, but not necessarily a medical event.

• • •

Medical school lasts four years, followed by internship and residency—three years for medicine, five to seven for surgery. And then maybe a two-year fellowship.

"The fellowship years can be a good time to have a baby," advised one physician. She was just finishing a fellowship in primary care. "Not internship or residency, God knows—that's when everyone's marriage breaks up since you're working eighty hours a week and you're so miserable all the time."

I am twenty-six. After college, I didn't go straight to medical school, but spent two years doing graduate work in biology and one living abroad. I'll probably have reached the fellowship stage by around thirty-three. It seemed like a long time to wait.

The more I thought about it, the more it seemed to me that there was no time in the next seven or so years when it would be as feasible to have a baby as it is now. As a medical student, I have a flexibility that I will not really have further on, a freedom to take a couple of months off or even a year if I decide I need it, and without unduly disrupting the progress of my career. Larry, who is also twenty-six, has just finished his doctoral dissertation on Polish-Vatican relations in the late eighteenth century, and is teaching at Harvard. He also has a great deal of flexibility. Both our lives frequently feel a little frantic, but we don't find ourselves looking ahead to a less complex, less frantic future.

I decided not to take a leave of absence this year. Instead, Larry and I have started on the juggling games which will no doubt be a major feature of the years ahead; I took extra courses last year so I could manage a comparatively light schedule this spring and stay with the baby two days a week while Larry worked at home for the other three. Perfect timing is of course of the essence; happily, we'd already managed to conceive the baby so it would be born between the time I took my exams in December and the time I started work at the hospital in March.

There was one other factor in my decision to have a baby now. All through my first year of medical school, in embryology, in genetics, even in public health, lecturers kept emphasizing that the ideal time to have a baby is around the age of twenty-four. Safest for the mother. Safest for the baby. "Do you think they're trying to tell us something?" grumbled one of my classmates after a particularly pointed lecture. "Like why are we wasting these precious childbearing years in school? It almost makes you feel guilty about waiting to have children."

Ironically, I know no one else my age who is having a baby. The women in my childbirth class were all in their mid-thirties. "Having a baby is a very nineteen-eighties thing to do," said a friend who is a twenty-seven-year-old corporate lawyer in New York. "The only thing is, you and Larry are much too young." In medical school one day last month, a lecturer mentioned the problem of teenage pregnancy, and I imagined that my classmates were turning to look at me.

• • •

In theory, medical education teaches first about normal anatomy, normal physiology, and then builds upon this foundation by teaching the processes of pathology and disease. In practice, everyone—student and teacher alike—is eager to get to the material with "clinical relevance" and the whole thrust of the teaching is toward using examples of disease to illustrate normal body functions by showing what happens when such functions break down. This is the way much of medical knowledge is garnered, after all—we understand sugar metabolism partially because of studies on diabetics, who can't metabolize sugar normally. "An experiment of nature" is the phrase often used.

Although we had learned a great deal about disease, we had not, in our first year of medical school, learned much about the nitty-gritty of medical practice. As I began to wonder more about what was happening inside me and about what childbirth would be like, I tried to read my embryology textbook, but again the pictures of the various abnormal fetuses upset me. So I read a couple of books that were written for pregnant women, not medical students, including *Immaculate Deception* by Suzanne Arms, a passionate attack on the American way of childbirth which argues that many routine hospital practices are psychologically damaging and medically hazardous. In particular, Arms protested the "traditional birth," the euphemism used in opposition to "natural birth." Traditional often means giving birth while lying down, a position demonstrated to be less effective and more dangerous than many others, but convenient for the doctor. An intravenous line is often attached to the arm and an electronic fetal heart monitor strapped to the belly. Traditional almost always means a routine episiotomy, a surgical incision in the perineum to allow the baby's head to emerge without tearing the mother.

In our reproductive medicine course this fall, the issue of home birth came up exactly once, in a "case" for discussion. "BB is a 25-year-old married graduate student . . . ," the case began. BB had a completely normal pregnancy. She showed no unusual symptoms and had no relevant past medical problems. When the pregnancy reached full term, the summary concluded, "no factors have been identified to suggest increased risk." Then, the first question: "Do you think she should choose to deliver at home?"

The doctor leading our discussion section read the question aloud and waited. "No," chorused the class.

"Why not?" asked the doctor.

"Well, there's always the chance of a complication," said one of the students.

Sure enough, after answering the first set of questions, we went on with BB's case, and it turned out that she went two and a half weeks past her due date, began to show signs of fetal distress, and was ultimately delivered by cesarean after the failure of induced labor. It was clear what the lesson was that BB was supposed to teach us. It was hard to read the case without getting the impression that all of these problems were some kind of divine retribution for even considering a home birth.

In fact, Larry and I eventually decided on a hospital birth with a doctor whose orientation was clearly against intervention except where absolutely necessary; he did not feel that procedures that can help in the event of complications should be applied across the board. It pleased me that he volunteered the cesarean and episiotomy figures for his practice, and also that he regarded the issue of what kind of birth we wanted as an appropriate subject for discussion at our very first meeting. ("A low-tech birth?" he said, sounding amused. "You're at Harvard Medical School and you want a low-tech birth?") He seemed to accept that there were consumer issues involved in choosing a doctor—that expectant parents are entitled to an explanation of the doctor's approach early in the pregnancy, when changing doctors is still a reasonable possibility.

At the beginning of my eighth month, we went to the first meeting of a prepared-childbirth class sponsored by the hospital we had decided to use. I had great hopes of this class; I was tired of feeling like the only pregnant person in the world. My medical school classmates had continued to be extremely kind and considerate, but as I moved around the medical school I was beginning to feel like a lone hippopotamus in a gaggle of geese. I wanted some other people with whom Larry and I could go over the questions we discussed endlessly with each other: how do we know when it's time to leave for the hospital? what is labor going to *feel* like? what can we do to make it go more easily?

The prepared-childbirth class met in the hospital. At the first meeting, it became clear that its major purpose was to prepare people to be good patients. The teacher was exposing us to various procedures so we would cooperate properly when they were performed on us. Asked whether a given procedure was absolutely necessary, the teacher said that was up to the doctor.

I found a childbirth class that met at a local day-care center; we sat on cushions on the floor, surrounded by toys and children's artwork. Many members of the class were fairly hostile toward the medical profession; once again I was greeted with remarks like "A medical student and you think you want a natural birth? Don't you get thrown out of school for that?" This class was, if anything, designed to teach people how to be "bad patients." The teacher explained the pros and cons of the various interventions, and we discussed under what circumstances we might or might not accept them.

The childbirth classes not only prepared me well for labor but also provided that sense of community I wanted. Yet they also left me feeling pulled between two poles, especially if I went to medical school during the day to discuss deliveries going wrong in one catastrophic way after another ("C-section, C-section!" my discussion section once chanted when the teacher asked what we would do next) and then later to childbirth class in the evening to discuss ways to circumvent unwanted medical procedures. As a student of the medical profession, I know I am being trained to rely heavily on technology, to assume that the risk of acting is almost always preferable to the risk of not acting. I consciously had to fight these attitudes when I thought about giving birth.

• • •

In our reproductive medicine course, the emphasis was on the abnormal, the pathological. We learned almost nothing about normal pregnancy; the only thing said about nutrition, for example, was said in passing—that nobody knows how much weight a pregnant woman should gain, but "about twenty-four pounds" is considered good. In contrast, I and the other women in my childbirth class were very concerned with what we ate; we were always exchanging suggestions on how to get through those interminable four glasses of milk a day. We learned nothing in medical school about exercise, though exercise books and classes aimed at pregnant women continue to proliferate—will we, as doctors, be able to give valid advice about diet and exercise during pregnancy? We learned nothing about any of the problems encountered in a normal pregnancy; the only thing said about morning sickness was that it could be controlled with a drug—a drug which, as it happens, many pregnant women are reluctant to take because some studies have linked it to birth defects. We learned nothing about the emotional aspects of pregnancy, nothing about helping women prepare for labor and delivery. In other words, none of my medical school classmates, after the course, would have been capable of answering even the most basic questions about pregnancy asked by the people in my childbirth class. The important issues for future doctors simply did not overlap with the important issues for future parents.

I sat with my classmates in our reproductive medicine course in Amphitheater E at Harvard Medical School and listened to the lecture on the disorders of pregnancy. The professor discussed ectopic pregnancy, toxemia, spontaneous abortion, and major birth defects. I was eight months pregnant. I sat there rubbing my belly, telling my baby, don't worry, you're okay, you're healthy. I sat there wishing that this course would tell us more about normal pregnancy, that after memorizing all the possible disasters, we would be allowed to conclude that pregnancy itself is not a state of disease. But I think most of us, including me, came away from the course with a sense that in fact pregnancy is a deeply dangerous medical condition, that one walks a fine line, avoiding one serious problem after another, to reach the statistically unlikely outcome of a healthy baby and a healthy mother.

I mentioned this to my doctor, explaining that I was tormented by fears of every possible abnormality. "Yes," he said, "normal birth is not honored enough in the curriculum. Most of us doctors are going around looking for pathology and feeling good about ourselves when we find it because that's what we were trained to do. We aren't trained to find joy in a normal pregnancy."

I tried to find joy in my own pregnancy. I am sure that the terrors that sometimes visited me in the middle of the night were no more intense than those that visit most expectant mothers: will the labor go well? will the baby be okay? I probably had more specific fears than many, as I lay awake wondering about atrial septal heart defects or placenta previa and hemorrhage. And perhaps I did worry more than I might once have done, because my faith in the normal had been weakened. I too, in my dark moments, had begun to see healthy development as less than probable, as the highly unlikely avoidance of a million abnormalities. I knew that many of my classmates were worrying with me; I cannot count the number of times I was asked whether I had had an amniocentesis. When I pointed out that we had been taught that amniocentesis is not generally recommended for women under the age of thirty-five, my classmates tended to look worried and mutter something about being *sure*.

The climax came when a young man in my class asked me, "Have you had all those genetic tests? Like for sickle-cell anemia?"

I looked at him. He is white. I am white. "I'm not in the risk group for sickle-cell," I said gently.

"Yeah, I know," he said, "but if there's even a one-in-a-zillion chance—"

I see all of us, including myself, absorbing the idea that when it comes to tests, technology, interventions, more is better. There was no talk in the reproductive medicine course about the negative aspects of intervention, and the one time a student asked in class about the "appropriateness" of fetal monitoring, the question was cut off with a remark that there was no time to discuss issues of "appropriateness." There was also no time really to discuss techniques for attending women in labor—except as they related to labor emergencies.

I see us absorbing the attitude, here as in other courses, that the kinds of decisions that have to be made are absolutely out of the reach of nonphysicians. The risks of devastating catastrophe are so constant—how can we let patients take chances like this with their lives? Those dangers which can actually be controlled by the patients, the pregnant women—cigarettes, alcohol—are deemphasized. Instead, we are taught to think in terms of medical emergencies. And gradually pregnancy itself begins to sound like a medical emergency in which the pregnant woman, referred to as "the patient," must be carefully guided to a safe delivery, almost in spite of herself. And as we spend more and more time absorbing the vocabulary of medicine, it becomes harder to think about communicating our knowledge to those who lack that vocabulary.

There have been very positive aspects of having the baby while in medical school. For one thing, the anatomy and physiology and embryology I have learned deepened my awe of the miracle going on inside me. When I looked ahead to the birth, I thought of what we learned about the incredible changeover that takes place during the first minutes of life, about the details of the switch to breathing air, the changes in circulation. I feel that because of what I have learned I appreciated the pregnancy in a way I never could have before, and I am grateful for that appreciation.

Another wonderful thing about having my baby while in medical school was the support and attention from my classmates. Perhaps because having a baby seems a long way off to many of them, there has been some tendency to regard mine as a "class baby." People asked me all the time to promise that I would bring it to lecture; the person who shows the slides offered to dim the lights for a soothing atmosphere if I wanted to nurse in class. My classmates held a baby shower for Larry and me, and presented us with a fabulous assortment of baby items. At the end of the shower, I lay back on the couch with five medical students feeling my abdomen, finding the baby's bottom, the baby's foot.

• • •

Our son, Benjamin Orlando, was born on January 28, 1984. Naturally, I would like to be able to say that all our planning and preparing was rewarded with a perfectly smooth, easy labor and delivery, but of course biology doesn't work that way. The experience did provide me with a rather ironic new wrinkle on the whole idea of interventions. Most of the labor was quite ordinary. "You're demonstrating a perfect Friedman labor curve," the doctor said to me at one point, "you must have been studying!" At the end, however, I had great difficulty pushing the baby out. After the pushing stage had gone on for quite a while, I was absolutely exhausted, though the baby was fine; there were no signs of fetal distress and the head was descending steadily. Still, the pushing had gone on much longer than is usual, and I was aware that there were now two doctors and a number of nurses in the birthing room. Suddenly I heard one of the doctors say something about forceps. At that moment, I found a last extra ounce of strength and pushed my baby out. As I lay back with my son wriggling on my stomach, the birthing room suddenly transformed into the most beautiful place on earth, I heard one of the nurses say to another, "You see this all the time with these birthing-room natural-childbirth mothers—you just mention forceps and they get those babies born."

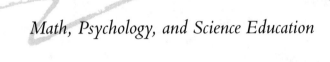

Math, Psychology, and Science Education

Personal Thinking

From *The Children's Machine: Rethinking School in the Age of the Computer*

A course on psychology I took as an undergraduate left little residue in my mind, except for a homily on objectivity delivered in the first lecture. We were warned that many of us might have enrolled under the erroneous impression that the course, being about psychology, would provide an occasion to explore the psychological issues in our own lives. Those who had come for this reason were advised to consider whether they really wanted to be there. The starting point for the study of scientific psychology was, we were told, the skill of distancing oneself from the object of study. We would have to work hard to learn how to keep intuitions based on our own experiences out of our thinking about the psychological issues we would be studying.

Without a doubt there is a need in any discipline for skill in distancing oneself from the object of study. However, the more significant lack in the study of education is quite the opposite: There is too much distancing.

Yearners have tirelessly protested the way that School's curriculum distances knowledge from the individuality of the student. Beyond this, the quest for a science of education has led to ways of thinking about teaching that exclude the teacher as a person, and ways of thinking about education research that exclude the researcher as a person. My protest starts by situating my own work on educational innovation in my life experience.

. . .

My critique of School and yearning for something else began very early. In elementary school I already knew quite clearly that my best intellectual work was done outside the classroom. My resentment of School was mitigated only by the fact that I loved two teachers and had a handful of friends who participated with me in activities I considered to be more valuable. The most important of these was a newspaper produced by a 1930s version of desktop publishing. My printer was a homemade gelatinous block to which ink could be transferred from a glossy master sheet and thence to sheets of absorbent paper. The newspaper was important for me in many ways. Above all, it gave me a sense of identity. Adults asked one another, "What do you do?" and I could think of what I "did" as something more personal and distinctive than "going to school."

Besides this, the newspaper made connections with several areas of intellectual and social development that would shape my high school years and beyond. I developed a sense of myself and a little skill as a chemist. My printing system was initially based on an article in Arthur Mee's *Children's Encyclopedia* but evolved over time and through many experimental variations. I developed a sense of myself as a writer, and I had to shoulder financial and managerial responsibilities that were no less real for being on a very small scale. And, perhaps most important in its subsequent impact on my life, the newspaper slowly drew me into the beginnings of political activism in the highly charged atmosphere of Johannesburg, where I lived from age seven through my mid-twenties.

The particular facts of my story are unique to me as an individual; the general principles it illustrates are not. Reading biographies and interrogating friends has convinced me that all successful learners find ways to take charge of their early lives sufficiently to develop a sense of intellectual identity. A fascinating example is Jean Piaget. The case has a mild irony in that this man, so often quoted as the authority on what children cannot do because they are not at the appropriate stages of development, published his first scientific article at age eleven! What does one make of this? Devotees of Piaget often view it reverently as an early sign of his genius. In fact the short paper, which reports a sighting of a rare bird in the Swiss mountains, does not contain any logical patterns that would be surprising in an average child of eleven. I am inclined to think of the publication as being as much a cause as a consequence of Piaget's exceptional intellectual qualities, though, of course (in what he would have called a dialectical sense), it is surely both.

Piaget's article did not just happen as a consequence of some quality of his mind. He explains it as a simple intentional act. He wanted to be allowed to use the college library in his small Swiss town, and wrote and published the article to make the librarian take him seriously enough to give him permission to do so. What I find most impressive in the story is not that a boy of eleven could write a report about a bird but that this same boy of eleven took himself seriously enough to conceive and carry out this strategy for dealing with the librarian. I see in it young Jean preparing himself to become Piaget. He was practicing taking charge of his own development, something that is necessary not only for those who want to become leading thinkers but for all citizens of a society in which individuals have to define and redefine their roles throughout a long lifetime.

In stark contrast with the image of Piaget the child constructing Piaget the adult, School has an inherent tendency to infantilize children by placing them in a position of having to do as they are told, to occupy themselves with work dictated by someone else and that, moreover, has no intrinsic value—schoolwork is done only because the designer of a curriculum decided that doing the work would shape the doer into a desirable form. I find this offensive in part because I remember how much I objected as a child to being placed in that situation, but mainly because I am convinced that the best learning takes place when the learner takes charge, as the young Piaget did. Thus my antennae are always out for initiatives that will allow the purpose of School as a place for learning to coexist with a culture of personal responsibility.

This must not be confused with the faddish idea that what children learn should be made "relevant"—so, teacher, don't just make them add numbers, pretend you are shopping in the supermarket. Children are not easily duped. If they sense that they are being made to play a silly game, they will be discouraged from taking themselves seriously. I liked a little better what I saw at the Lamplighter School in Dallas, where the fourth-grade children actually had real responsibility for operating an egg business. They bought the feed, cleaned the coops, collected and sold the eggs, and kept the profit, if there was any, at the end of the year. If they ended up with a loss, they had to explain themselves to the next class. But even this allowed very little opportunity for real initiative and only a minor sense of doing something really important.

A deeper sense of doing something important in itself is visible in the project "Kidnet," developed in a collaboration between the National Geographic Society and Robert Tinker, who is responsible for developing some of the best uses of computers for learning science. This project engages middle school students to collect data about acid rain. The individual schools send their data across electronic networks to a central computer where it is integrated and sent back to the local sites, where it can be analyzed and discussed in the context of globally important problems. The project hints at a vision of millions of children all over the world engaged in work that makes a real contribution to the scientific study of a socially urgent problem. In principle, a million children could collect more data about the environment than any socially affordable number of professional scientists.

This is infinitely better than School's ritualistic worksheets and demonstration experiments, if only because the students feel they are engaged in a meaningful and socially important activity they really care about. However, what I like most is the opportunity it offers the students to break out of its own framework to engage in more self-directed activities. One way that students break out quite frequently is to use the expertise acquired in the project to engage in local environmental campaigns. Another example that pleased me particularly was expressed by a student who had worked out a plan to bypass the use of children to collect data by automating these operations. He explained that the children could then devote themselves to more important environmental work! This student could not actually implement this plan with the means provided by his school, but he was close: In a few years such projects will use hardware and software flexible enough for this student's plan to be widely implemented.

A different example of computers giving children the opportunity to develop a sense of doing serious work is that of two fifth-grade boys with very different interests, one in science and the other in dance and music, who came together to create a "screen choreography" by programming a computer set up in the back of the classroom. What they were doing may not have been relevant, but it certainly felt vitally important to these boys and was seen as such by their teacher, who encouraged them to take time from regular class work for their project. Watching them, I was reminded of the newspaper I worked on as a child. I guessed that they were growing as independent intellectual agents, and anyone could see that they were learning what was for their age an unusual amount of mathematics and computer programming.

This discussion, which intermingles learning incidents from my life and Piaget's with incidents from the lives of children in contemporary schools, represents an alternative to the methodology favored by the dominant "scientific" school of thought. Researchers, following the so-called scientific method of using controlled experiments, solemnly expose children to a "treatment" of some sort and then look for measurable results. But this flies in the face of all common knowledge of how human beings develop. Although it is obvious to me that my newspaper played a profound role in my intellectual development, I am pretty sure that no test would have detected its role by comparing my "performance" the day before I started and three months later. The significant effects emerged over a much longer period, to be measured, probably, in years. Moreover, an experiment that gave a hundred children "the experience of producing a newspaper," even if continued for several years, still would miss the point of what happened to me. The significant engagement was too personal to be expected to operate as a mass effect; I fell in love with my newspapering (as I did with mathematics and other areas of knowledge) for reasons that are as personal and in a sense as unreproducible as those that determine any kind of falling in love.

The method of controlled experimentation that evaluates an idea by implementing it, taking care to keep everything else the same, and measuring the result, may be an appropriate way to evaluate the effects of a small modification. However, it can tell us nothing about ideas that might lead to deep change. One cannot simply implement such ideas to see whether they lead to deep change: A megachanged system can come into being only through a slow, organic evolution, and through a close harmony with social evolution. It will be steered less by the outcome of tests and measurements than by its participants' intuitive understanding.

The most powerful resource for this process is exactly what is denied by objective psychology and the would-be science of education. Every one of us has built up a stock of intuitive, empathic, commonsense knowledge about learning. This knowledge comes into play when one recognizes something good about a learning experience without knowing the outcome. It seems obvious to me that every good teacher uses this kind of knowledge far more than test scores or other objective measurements in daily decisions about students. Perhaps the most important problem in education research is how to mobilize and strengthen such knowledge.

One step toward strengthening it is to recognize it. The denial of personal intuitive knowledge has led to a profound split in thinking about learning; the split recalls the theory that each of us has two brains which think in fundamentally different ways. By analogy, one might say that when it comes to thinking about learning, nearly all of us have a School side of the brain, which thinks that School is the only natural way to learn, and a personal side that knows perfectly well it is not.

A second strategy for strengthening the personal side and breaking the stranglehold of the School side is to develop a methodology for reflection about cases of successful learning and especially about one's own best learning experiences. Analogies with two events in the history of aviation—a case of true megachange—will clarify my thinking.

People who dreamed about making flying machines looked at birds in the same spirit as I want to look at examples of successful learning. But it was not enough simply to look and copy. Many were misled into thinking that the essence of bird flight was the flapping of wings. Even the great Leonardo was drawn into the vision of an ornithopter, a machine that would look like a bird and fly by flapping birdlike wings. This was not the way to make a flying machine. Nevertheless, it was the observation of birds that provided the secret. My analogy here concerns John Wilkins, a seventeenth-century bishop, scientist, and founder of the Royal Society. Wilkins could not have been the first to observe that birds could fly without flapping their wings. But he was one of the first to see the importance in this otherwise banal observation. He was right. The simplicity of a gull soaring without a visible movement of its body became the model that eventually led to formulating the principle of lift, the concept underlying both the understanding of natural flyers and the making of artificial flyers. We have to learn to see successful learning through the prism of such powerful ideas.

The second event happened as an indirect result of the first. The year 1903—when a powered airplane first flew successfully—was a turning point in the history of transportation. But the famous flyer made by Wilbur and Orville Wright did not prove itself by its performance. The duration of the best of several flights that day was only fifty-nine seconds! As a practical alternative to the horse-drawn wagon, it was laughable. Yet imaginative minds could see in it the birth of the industry that would lead to the jumbo jet and the space shuttle. Thinking about the future of education demands a similar labor of the imagination. The prevalent literal-minded, "what you see is what you get" approach measuring the effectiveness of computers in learning by the achievements in present-day classrooms makes it certain that tomorrow will always be the prisoner of yesterday. Indeed, the situation in education is often even worse than judging the effectiveness of airplanes by the fifty-nine-second flight. It is more like attaching a jet engine to an old-fashioned wagon to see whether it will help the horses. Most probably it would frighten the animals and shake the wagon to pieces, "proving" that jet technology is actually harmful to the enhancement of transportation.

. . .

I have in my files a large collection of scientific papers reporting experiments that try to measure "the effect of computers on learning." It is like measuring the flight characteristics of the Wrights' flyer to determine "the effect of flying on transportation." The significance of the flyer could be appreciated by hard imaginative work based on understanding the principles, such as "lift," which lay behind the design. In order to find the corresponding principles for learning, we have to look into ourselves as much as at computers: Principles such as "taking charge" and "intellectual identity" and "falling in love" (as I used in talking about my newspaper) have come to play that role in my own thinking as a direct result of observing myself when I seemed to be flying intellectually. The incidents in the rest of this chapter highlight some others.

As I grew up, learning became a hobby. Of course any hobby involves learning, but most people are more interested in what they learn than in how the learning happens. In fact, most learn without giving a thought to learning. I often go to the other extreme. I learned to juggle, to fly a plane, and to cook, not only because I wanted to do these things but also because I wondered what the learning would be like. Though I came to love all these hobbies for their own sake, part of my pleasure in them has always been that of observing myself learn and making up theories about how I do so. A good example of this process is how I learned to make croissants.

When I got croissant making right after many, many failures, I allowed myself some elation but then began to worry about what had happened. One day I couldn't do it, the next day I could! What had changed? In order to reconstruct the moment of transition, I tried to recapture the state of "inability" I had been in the day before. At first I thought in terms of external factors such as the proportions of ingredients, the times of rising and resting, and the temperatures of dough, working surface, and oven. But varying these did not seem to account for my prior uneven results.

When I eventually did relive the key moment, I had learned about much more than making croissants. The difference between before and after lay in feeling the degree of "squishiness" of the butter through the squishiness of the pastry dough and through my heavy marble rolling pin. Trying to capture this deliberately seemed at first like the princess and the pea. I tried many times. It was only when I decided that I had enough and would give up for the day that a breakthrough happened. On my marble slab was a last parcel of butter wrapped in dough. Wondering what to do with it, I playfully flattened it with the rolling pin, relaxed, without trying to do anything in particular—and all of a sudden I felt distinctly the structure of the mass of matter. Once I felt it, I knew "in my fingers" how to make a croissant, and now when I try after an interval of several years, the knack always comes back by the second batch—though if I had to do it on a school test I would fail, because I need the spoiled first try to get the feel for the successful second one.

When I retell such experiences to an audience of educators, I always hope that someone will be annoyed by my talk of croissants and say: "What has this to do with grammar or math or writing business letters? Naturally in cooking you have to learn to feel the relationship of your body to matter. But math is not about feeling relationships of your body to numbers." I like this reaction because it brings out into the open something that lurks in the culture and allows me to confront it.

A few years ago I would have begun with the rejoinder: "You think that math does not have anything to do with the body because you are not a mathematician; if you were you would know that mathematics is full of gut feelings and all sorts of kinesthetics." Today I would say it the other way around: "The reason you are not a mathematician might well be that you think that math has nothing to do with the body; you have kept your body out of it because it is supposed to be abstract, or perhaps a teacher scolded you for using your fingers to add numbers!" This idea is not just metaphysics. It has inspired me to use the computer as a medium to allow children to put their bodies back into their mathematics.

My favorite example is an invention called "the turtle." You can think of this as a drawing instrument whose simplest use will become clear from the following scenario. Imagine that you are looking at a computer screen. On it you see a small turtle, which moves when you type commands in a language called "turtle talk," leaving a line as it goes. The command "Forward 50" causes the turtle to move straight ahead a certain distance. "Forward 100" will make it move in the same direction twice as far. You soon get the idea that the numbers represent the distance it moves; they can be thought of as turtle steps. Now if you want to make it go in a different direction, you give it a command like "Right 90." It stays in the same place but turns on itself, facing east if it had previously been facing north. With this knowledge you should easily be able to make it draw a square. If that's easy for you, you can think about how to draw a circle, and if that's easy, you can try a spiral. Somewhere you will meet your level of difficulty, and when you do I'll give you this piece of advice: Put yourself in the place of the turtle. Imagine yourself moving in a square or a circle or a spiral or whatever it may be. You may resist for a while because you are tense and trying too hard, as I was with my croissants. But when you let yourself go, you will find that there is a richer source of mathematical knowledge in your body than in classroom textbooks.

Learning to speak French was one of my most instructive learning experiences. Although this was not a case of learning for its own sake—I went to live in Paris to complete my doctoral research in mathematics—my professional purpose was interlaced with playful learning experiments. For example, I developed a relationship with an eight-year-old boy who was delighted to be my "professor." He was young enough to be "studying French" at the same time as I was. Although he was a native speaker, he was learning spelling and grammar at school and was acquiring vocabulary at an appreciable rate. I was able to compare the speed and pattern of my progress with his, and in doing so established a curious fact: By any measure I could think of, I was learning faster. I could have attributed the discrepancy between this observation and the common linguistic sluggishness of adults to some kind of special "gift for languages." I didn't. I explain the discrepancy by the fact that I was learning French mostly like a child but could also take advantage of some sophisticated ideas that a child would not know. On the one hand, I was open to playful immersion; on the other, I could make occasional use of formal linguistics. Somewhere between the two was the fact that my learning of French seemed to be facilitated by experimenting (or playing) not only with French but also with learning itself. Studying one's own learning process—as the example of croissant making also shows—can be a powerful method of enhancing learning. In any case, looking back I see an important root of my present ideas in this recognition of the advantages of combining childlike and adultlike ways of learning.

Although my mathematical research in Paris earned me my Ph.D., the Parisian discovery that had the biggest impact on my life was Jean Piaget, who at the time was giving a course at the Sorbonne. I got to know him and was invited to work in his center in Geneva, where I spent the next four years and became passionately interested in children's thinking. If the key ideas in [*The Children's Machine*] first crossed my mind then, however, they were in the most nebulous guise. In particular, I made no connection that I can remember between my own learning and the process of intellectual development of children on which we worked at Piaget's center. The reason is significant: We were all too serious and too formal about children's thinking. Of course we thought about their play; it was Piaget who coined the oft-quoted line that play is child's work. But no one in that environment was looking at the other half of this pithy aphorism: the idea that work (at least serious intellectual work) might be adult's play. We thought of children as "little scientists" but did not think much about the complementary idea of viewing scientists as "big children."

Following the four years in Geneva, I became a professor of mathematics at MIT. Many factors made the move attractive. There was the prospect of access to computers and of working with Marvin Minsky and Warren McCulloch, as well as a wonderful sense of playfulness that I had experienced there on brief visits. When I finally arrived, all this came together in all-night sessions around a PDP-1 computer that had been given to Minsky. It was pure play. We were finding out what could be done with a computer, and anything interesting was worthwhile. Nobody yet knew enough to decree that some things were more serious than others. We were like infants discovering the world.

It was in this situation that I thought about computers and children. I was playing like a child and experiencing a volcanic explosion of creativity. Why couldn't the computer give a child the same kind of experience? Why couldn't a child play like me? What would have to be done to make this possible?

These questions launched me on a new quest guided by the Robin Hood–like idea of stealing technology from the lords of the laboratories and giving it to the children of the world. A first step in the quest was to recognize that one of the sources of the technologists' power was the veil of esoteric mystery woven around the idea of programming. The situation is quite analogous to the way priests of other ages kept power from people by monopolizing the ability to read and write, and by keeping what they considered the most powerful knowledge in languages the common people could not understand. I saw the need to make computer languages that could be "vulgarized"—made available to ordinary people and especially children.

This has turned out to be a long and difficult task. Computer languages, like natural languages, cannot be "made"; they have to evolve. What could be made was a first shot at such a language, named Logo, which would serve as a starting point for a longer evolution that is in fact still continuing.

For the sake of concreteness, the ideas in [*The Children's Machine*] are developed through the story of my own inventions. I make no secret of the fact that I love and value some of them. I believe that some may even have a long-term future. But I repeat that my purpose here is not to tell the reader how to do things right but to provoke and fuel imaginations. In this book my real-life inventions serve the same purpose as the imaginary examples of time travelers and hypothetical nineteenth-century engineers. They are meant to evoke further ideas, to prepare our minds for other, much more exciting inventions still to be made. My purpose could not be further removed from advocating a particular invention as *the* solution to *the* problem of education; rather, each example is meant to serve as a pointer to a vast area of new opportunities for educational invention. My goal in relation to Schoolers—or to anyone who thinks that any form of learning is the right and natural form of learning—is to stir the imagination to invent alternatives. Piaget said that to understand is to invent. He was thinking of children. But the principle applies to all of us.

NOTE ON SOURCES

We list here books and articles excerpted or referred to (in the introduction and elsewhere) in this collection as well as selected texts that demonstrate or authorize the inclusion of autobiography in scholarship across the disciplines. For parallel sorts of bibliographies concentrating on examples of (or theorizing about) autobiographical literary criticism, see our earlier volume (coedited with Frances Murphy Zauhar), *The Intimate Critique: Autobiographical Literary Criticism* (Duke, 1993), and Diane P. Freedman, *An Alchemy of Genres: Cross-Genre Writing by American Feminist Poet-Critics* (University Press of Virginia, 1992).

Anzaldúa, Gloria. *Borderlands/La Frontera: The New Mestiza*. San Francisco: Spinsters/Aunt Lute, 1987.

Appiah, Kwame Anthony. *In My Father's House: Africa in the Philosophy of Culture*. New York: Oxford University Press, 1992.

Aptheker, Bettina. *Tapestries of Life: Women's Work, Women's Consciousness, and the Meaning of Daily Experience*. Amherst: University of Massachusetts Press, 1989.

Atkins, G. Douglas. *Estranging the Familiar: Towards a Revitalized Critical Writing*. Athens: University of Georgia Press, 1992.

Atwan, Robert, ed. *Best American Essays*. 3rd college ed. Boston: Houghton Mifflin, 2001.

Awkward, Michael. *Negotiating Difference: Race, Gender, and the Politics of Positionality*. Chicago: University of Chicago Press, 1995.

Bammer, Angelika, et al. Forum. *PMLA* (October 1996): 1146–169. [Twenty-six comments on the "place, nature, or limits of the personal in scholarship" arranged in two sections, "The Inevitability of the Personal" and "Problems with Personal Criticism." Includes Angelika Bammer, Joseph A. Boone, Terry Caesar, Mary Ann Caws, Jane Gallop, Norman Holland, Joonu Huh, Nellie Y. McKay, David Simpson, Deborah Tannen, Claudia Tate, George T. Wright et al.]

Banks, Anna, and Stephen P. Banks, eds. *Fiction and Social Research: By Ice or Fire.* Thousand Oaks, Calif.: Alta Mira, 1998.

Barrett, Jackie. "Multiple Sclerosis: The Experience of a Disease." *Women's Studies International Forum* 18 (1995): 159–71.

Bauer, Dale. "Personal Criticism and the Academic Personality." In *Who Can Speak? Authority and Critical Identity,* edited by Judith Roof and Robyn Wiegman, 56–69. Urbana: University of Illinois Press, 1995.

Bazerman, Charles. *Shaping Written Knowledge: The Genre and Activity of the Experimental Article in Science.* Madison: University of Wisconsin Press, 1988.

Behar, Ruth. "The Body in the Woman, the Story in the Woman: A Book Review and Personal Essay." *Michigan Quarterly Review* 29, no. 4 (fall 1987): 1–22.

———. *Translated Woman: Crossing the Border with Esperanza's Story.* Boston: Beacon, 1993.

———. "Dare We Say 'I'? Bringing the Personal into Scholarship." *Chronicle of Higher Education* (29 June 1994): B1+.

———. "Juban América." *Poetics Today* 16, no. 1 (spring 1995): 151–70.

———. *The Vulnerable Observer: Anthropology That Breaks Your Heart.* Boston: Beacon, 1997.

Belenky, Mary Field, et al. *Women's Ways of Knowing: The Development of Self, Voice, and Mind.* New York: Basic, 1986.

Bem, Sandra. *An Unconventional Family.* New Haven: Yale University Press, 1998.

Berlin, James. *Rhetoric and Reality: Writing Instruction in American Colleges, 1900–1985.* Carbondale: Southern Illinois University Press, 1987.

Berman, Jeffrey. *Diaries to an English Professor: Pain and Growth in the Classroom.* Amherst: University of Massachusetts Press, 1994.

Bernstein, Susan David. "Confessing Feminist Theory: What's 'I' Got to Do with it?" *Hypatia* 7, no. 2 (1992): 120–47.

Berry, Ellen, and Elizabeth Black. "The Integrative Learning Journal (or Getting Beyond 'True Confessions' or 'Cold Knowledge')." *Women's Studies Quarterly* 12, nos. 3–4 (fall/winter 1987): 59–64.

Bishop, Wendy, ed. *Elements of an Alternate Style.* Portsmouth, N.H.: Boynton/Cook, 1997.

———. *Working Words: The Process of Creative Writing.* Mountain View, Calif.: Mayfield, 1992.

Blackman, Margaret. *Sadie Brower Neakok: An Inupiaq Woman.* Seattle: University of Washington Press, 1989.

Bleich, David. *Readings and Feelings: An Introduction to Subjective Response.* Urbana: NCTE, 1975.

———. "How I Got My Language: Forms of Self-Inclusion." In *Self-Analysis and Literary Study,* edited by Daniel Rancour-Laferriere. New York: New York University Press, 1994.

———. "How Do the Electrons Get across the Two Plates of the Capacitor? Becoming a Writing Teacher." In *Teaching College English and English Education: Reflective Stories,* edited by H. Thomas McCracken et al., 49–62. Urbana: NCTE, 1998.

————. *Know and Tell: Disclosure, Genre, and Membership in the Teaching of Writing and Language Use*. Portsmouth, N.H.: Heinemann-Boynton/Cook, 1998.

Bleich, David, and Deborah Holdstein, eds. *Personal Effects: The Social Character of Scholarly Writing*. Logan: Utah State University Press, 2001.

Bloom, Leslie. *Under the Sign of Hope: Feminist Methodology and Narrative Interpretation*. Albany: SUNY Press, 1998.

Bloom, Lynn. "Freshman Composition as a Middle-Class Enterprise." *College English* 58, no. 6 (October 1996): 654–75.

Bochner, Arthur, and Carolyn Ellis. "Personal Narrative as a Social Approach to Interpersonal Communication." *Communication Theory* 2, no. 2 (1992): 165–72.

Bolter, Jay. *Writing Space: The Computer, Hypertext, and the History of Writing*. Hillsdale, N.J.: Lawrence Erlbaum, 1991.

Brackett, Virginia. *The Contingent Self: One Reading Life*. West Lafayette: Purdue University Press, 2001.

Brandt, Deborah, et al. "Storying Our Lives against the Grain." *College English* 64, no. 1 (September 2001): 41–62.

Brereton, John C., ed. *The Origins of Composition Studies in the American College, 1875–1925: A Documentary History*. Pittsburgh: University of Pittsburgh Press, 1995.

Bridwell-Bowles, Lillian. "Discourse and Diversity: Experimental Writing within the Academy." *College Composition and Communication* 43 (1992): 349–68.

————. *Identity Matters: Rhetorics of Difference*. With Kathleen Sheerin DeVore and Holly Littlefield. Upper Saddle River, N.J.: Prentice Hall, 1997.

Brill, A. A. Introduction. *The Basic Writings of Sigmund Freud*. Edited by A. A. Brill. New York: Random, 1938. 3–32.

Brodkin, Karen. *How Jews Became White Folks and What that Says about Race in America*. New Brunswick: Rutgers University Press, 1998.

Brodribb, Somer. *Nothing Matters: A Feminist Critique of Postmodernism*. New York: New York University Press, 1992.

Brooks, Peter, and Paul Gewirtz, eds. *Law's Stories: Narrative and Rhetoric in the Law*. New Haven: Yale University Press, 1996.

Buck, Gertrude. "Recent Tendencies in the Teaching of English." *Educational Review* 22 (November 1901): 371–82. Rpt. in Brereton, 241–51.

Caesar, Terry. *Conspiring with Forms: Life in Academic Texts*. Athens: University of Georgia Press, 1992.

Capra, Frank [Fritjof]. *The Tao of Physics: An Exploration of the Parallels between Modern Physics and Eastern Mysticism*. Boulder: Shambhala, 1975.

Carr, Claudia, ed. *Feminist Ethics*. Lawrence: University Press of Kansas, 1991.

Cavell, Stanley. *A Pitch of Philosophy: Autobiography Exercise*. Cambridge: Harvard University Press, 1994.

Caws, Mary Ann. *Women of Bloomsbury: Virginia, Vanessa, and Carrington*. New York: Routledge, 1990.

Christian, Barbara. "But What Do We Think We're Doing Anyway: The State of Black Feminist Criticism(s) or My Version of a Little Bit of History." In *Changing Our Own Words: Essays on Criticism, Theory, and Writing by Black Women*, edited by Cheryl A. Wall. New Brunswick: Rutgers University Press, 1989.

Cohen, Anthony P. *Self-Consciousness: An Alternative Anthropology of Identity*. London: Routledge, 1994.

Cohen, Paula Marantz. *The Daughter as Reader: Encounters between Literature and Life*. Ann Arbor: University of Michigan Press, 1996.

Cone, James H. *God of the Oppressed*. New York: Seabury Press, 1975.

Connors, Robert J. "Personal Writing Assignments." *College Composition and Communication* 38 (May 1987): 166–83.

Cook-Lynn, Elizabeth. *Why I Can't Read Wallace Stegner, and Other Essays: A Tribal Voice*. Madison: University of Wisconsin Press, 1996.

Cooper, Lane. "On the Teaching of Written Composition." *Education* 30 (March 1910): 421–20. Rpt. in *Two Views of Education*, by Lane Cooper. New Haven: Yale University Press, 1922: 72–87 and in Brereton, 251–61.

Covington, Dennis. *Salvation on Sand Mountain: Snake Handling and Redemption in Southern Appalachia*. Reading, Mass.: Addison-Wesley, 1995.

Creative Nonfiction. [5501 Walnut Street, Suite 202, Pittsburgh, Penn. 15232.] Issue #1, featuring John McPhee; #2, Poets Writing Prose; #3, Emerging Women Writers; #4, The New Journalism; #19, Diversity Dialogues.

Cronon, William. "A Place for Stories: Nature, History, and Narrative." *Journal of American History* 78, no. 4 (March 1992): 1347–76.

Cutuly, Joan. *Home of the Wildcats: Perils of an English Teacher*. Urbana: NCTE, 1993.

Daly, Brenda. *Authoring a Life: A Woman's Survival in and through Literary Studies*. Albany: SUNY Press, 1998.

———. "I Stand Here Naked, and Best Dressed in Theory: Feminist Refashionings of Academic Discourse." In *Creating Safe Space: Violence and Women's Writing*, edited by Julie Tharp and Tomoko Kuribayashi, 11–26. Albany: SUNY Press, 1997.

Damasio, Antonio. *Descartes' Error: Emotion, Reason, and the Human Brain*. New York: Putnam, 1994.

Davidman, Lynn R. *Growing Up Motherless: Stories of Lives Interrupted*. Berkeley: University of California Press (forthcoming).

Davidson, Cathy. *36 Views of Mount Fuji: On Finding Myself in Japan*. New York: Dutton, 1993.

Davis, Cortney. *I Knew a Woman: The Experience of the Female Body*. New York: Random, 2001.

DeLind, Laura B. "Close Encounters with a CSA: The Reflections of Bruised and Somewhat Wiser Anthropologist." Presidential address to the Organization for Agriculture, Food, and Human Values. *Agriculture and Human Values* 16 (1999): 3–9.

Denton, Lori. "Babies Grasp Idea of Concealed Objects." *Monitor* (October 1990): 8.

DeSalvo, Louise. *Vertigo*. New York: Penguin/Dutton, 1996.

DeShazer, Mary K. "Creation and Relation: Teaching Essays by T. S. Eliot and Adrienne Rich." In *Teaching Writing: Pedagogy, Gender, Equity*, edited by Cynthia Caywood and Gillian K. Overing, 113–22. Albany: SUNY Press, 1987.

Dews, Carlos. "Gender Tragedies: East Texas Cockfighting and Hamlet." *The Journal of Men's Studies* 2, no. 3 (February 1994): 253–67.

Dews, Carlos, and Carolyn Leste Law, eds. *This Fine Place So Far from Home: Voices of Academics from the Working Class*. Philadelphia: Temple University Press, 1995.

Diawara, Manthia. *In Search of Africa*. Cambridge: Harvard University Press, 1998.

Dooley, Deborah Anne. *Plain and Ordinary Things: Reading Women in the Writing Classroom*. Albany: SUNY Press, 1995.

Dorris, Michael. *The Broken Cord*. New York: Harper, 1989.

———. *Morning Girl*. New York: Hyperion, 1992.

Duberman, Martin. "Hidden from History: Reclaiming Gay/Lesbian History, Politics and Culture." In *About Time: Exploring the Gay Past*, edited by Martin Duberman, 436–67. New York: Meridian, 1991.

DuPlessis, Rachel Blau. "Reader, I Married Me: A Polygynous Memoir." In Greene and Kahn, 95–108.

Elbow, Peter. "The Problematics of Academic Discourse." College Composition and Communication Conference. Seattle, 17 March 1989. Later published as "Reflections on Academic Discourse: How it Relates to Freshmen and Colleagues." *College English* 53, no. 2 (February 1991): 135–55.

Eli, Margo, Ruth Vinz, Maryann Downing, and Margaret Anzul. *On Writing Qualitative Research: Living by Words*. Bristol, Penn.: Falmer, 1997.

Elkins, James. *Pictures and Tears: A History of People Who Have Cried in Front of Paintings*. New York: Routledge, 2001.

Ellerby, Janet. *Intimate Reading: The Contemporary Woman's Memoir*. Syracuse: Syracuse University Press, 2001.

Ellis, Carolyn. "Sociological Introspection and Emotional Experience." *Symbolic Interaction* 14, no. 1 (1991): 23–50.

———. *Final Negotiations*. Philadelphia: Temple University Press, 1994.

Ellis, Carolyn, and Arthur P. Bochner, eds. *Composing Ethnography: Alternative Forms of Qualitative Writing*. Thousand Oaks, Calif.: Altamira, 1996.

Faery, Rebecca Blevins. "On the Possibilities of the Essay: A Meditation." *Iowa Review* 20, no. 2 (spring/summer 1990): 19–27.

Farrell, Thomas J. "The Male and Female Modes of Rhetoric." *College English* 40 (1979): 922–27.

Felman, Shoshana. *What Does a Woman Want?: Reading and Sexual Difference*. Baltimore: Johns Hopkins University Press, 1993.

Field, Norma. *In the Realm of a Dying Emperor*. New York: Pantheon, 1991.

Fishkin, Shelley Fisher, and Jeffrey Rubin-Dorsky, eds. *People of the Book: Thirty Scholars Reflect on Their Jewish Identity*. Madison: University of Wisconsin Press, 1996.

Flieger, Jerry Aline. "Growing Up Theoretical: Across the Divide." In Greene and Kahn, 253–66.

"Four Views on the Place of the Personal in Scholarship" (by Michael Berube, Cathy Davidson, Sylvia Molloy, and David Palumbo-Liu). *PMLA* (October 1996): 1063–78.

Freedman, Diane P. "Wild Apple Associations." *Crazyquilt* 2, no. 1 (March 1987): 46–48.

———. "Emily Dickinson: 'Such a little figure . . . visions vast and small.'" *University of Dayton Review* 19, no. 1 (1988): 61–68.

———. "Living on the Borderland: The Poetic Prose of Gloria Anzaldúa and Susan Griffin." *Women and Language* 12, no. 1 (spring 1989): 1–4. Rpt. as "Writing in the Borderlands: The Poetic Prose of Gloria Anzaldúa and Susan Griffin." In *Constructing and Reconstructing Gender: The Links among Communication, Language, and Gender*, edited by Linda Perry, Lynn Turner, and Helen Sterk, 211–17. Albany: SUNY Press, 1992.

———. "Case Studies and Trade Secrets: Allaying Student Fears in 'Litcomp' Class." *College Literature* (February 1991): 77–83.

———. *An Alchemy of Genres: Cross-Genre Writing by American Feminist Poet-Critics.* Charlottesville: University Press of Virginia, 1992.

———. "The Creatively Critical Voice." *The Bucknell Review* (September 1992): 187–95.

———. "A Whale of a Different Color—Melville and the Movies: The Great White Whale and Free Willy." *ISLE* 4, no. 2 (fall 1997): 87–95. Revised and reprinted in *Women Writing Shorewords*, edited by Susan Rosen. Charlottesville: University Press of Virginia, 2003.

———. "Life Work through Teaching and Scholarship." In Bleich and Holdstein, *Personal Effects*, 199–219.

Freedman, Diane P., Olivia Frey, and Frances Murphy Zauhar, eds. *The Intimate Critique: Autobiographical Literary Criticism.* Durham, N.C.: Duke University Press, 1993.

Freedman, Diane P., and Martha Stoddard Holmes, eds. *The Teacher's Body: Embodiment, Authority, and Identity in the Academy.* Albany: SUNY Press, 2003.

Frey, Olivia. "Beyond Literary Darwinism." *College English* 52, no. 5 (September 1990): 507–26. Rpt. in Freedman, Frey, and Zauhar, 41–66.

Fried, Debra. "Andromeda Unbound: Gender and Genre in Millay's Sonnets." *Twentieth-Century Literature* 32, no. 1 (spring 1986): 1–22.

Frye, Marilyn. *The Politics of Reality: Essays in Feminist Theory.* Freedom, Calif.: Crossing, 1983.

Gale, George. *Theory of Science: An Introduction to the History, Logic, and Philosophy of Science.* New York: McGraw-Hill, 1979.

Gallop, Jane. *Thinking Through the Body.* New York: Columbia University Press, 1988.

———. *Around 1981: Academic Feminist Literary Theory.* New York: Routledge, 1992.

———. *Pedagogy: The Question of Impersonation.* Bloomington: Indiana University Press, 1995.

———. *Feminist Accused of Sexual Harassment.* Durham, N.C.: Duke University Press, 1997.

Geertz, Clifford. "Blurred Genres: The Reconfiguration of Social Thought." In *Local Knowledge.*

———. *Local Knowledge: Further Essays in Interpretive Anthropology.* New York: Basic, 1983.

Geisler, Cheryl. "Exploring Academic Literacy: An Experiment in Composing." *College Composition and Communication* 43, no. 1 (1992): 39–54.

Giddens, Anthony. *Modernity and Self-Identity: Self and Society in the Late Modern Age.* Stanford: Stanford University Press, 1991.

Giles, Molly. "Untitled." *Writing on the Edge* 1, no. 2 (spring 1990): 80–94.

Gilligan, Carol. *In a Different Voice: Psychological Theory and Women's Development.* Cambridge: Harvard University Press, 1982.

Goldman, Janice G. "Discursive Autobiography as a Path to Feminist Consciousness." *Journal of Feminist Family Therapy* 4, no. 1 (1992): 69–78.

Gooze, Marjanne E. "The Definitions of Self and Form in Feminist Autobiography Theory." *Women's Studies* 21, no. 4 (1992): 411–29.

Gorra, Michael. "The Autobiographical Turn: Reading the New Academic Autobiography." Rev. of Kaplan, *French Lessons*; Gates, *Colored People*; Freedman et al., *The Intimate Critique*; and others. *Transition* 68 (1995): 143–53.

Gottschalk, Simon. "Postmodern Sensibilities and Ethnographic Possibilities." In Banks and Banks, *Fiction and Social Research*, 205–33.

Greene, Gayle, and Coppelia Kahn, eds. *Changing Subjects: The Making of Feminist Literary Criticism.* New Brunswick: Rutgers University Press, 1993.

Griffin, Gail. *Season of the Witch: Border Lines, Marginal Notes.* Pasadena, Calif.: Trilogy, 1995.

Griffin, Susan. *Woman and Nature: The Roaring Inside Her.* New York: Harper, 1978.

Grumet, Madeline. "The Politics of Personal Knowledge." *Curriculum Inquiry* 17, no. 3 (1987): 319–29.

———. *Bitter Milk: Women and Teaching.* Amherst: University of Massachusetts Press, 1988.

———. "Retrospective: Autobiography and the Analysis of Education Experience." *Cambridge Journal of Education* 20, no. 3 (1990): 321–25.

Hallet, Judith P., and Thomas Van Nortwick, eds. *Compromising Traditions: The Personal Voice in Classical Scholarship.* New York: Routledge, 1997.

Haley, Shelley P. "Black Feminist Thought and Classics: Re-membering, Re-claiming, Re-empowering." In *Feminist Theory and the Classics*, edited by Amy Richlin. New York: Routledge, 1993.

Hamabata, Matthews Masayuki. *Crested Kimono: Power and Love in the Japanese Business Family.* Ithaca: Cornell University Press, 1990.

Hammond, Jeffrey. "Reflections on Milton." *Antioch Review* (winter 1999): 22–37.

Harding, Sandra. "Who Knows? Identities and Feminist Epistemology." In *(En)Gendering Knowledge: Feminists in Academe*, edited by Joan Hartman and Ellen Messer-Davidow, 100–15. Knoxville: University of Tennessee Press, 1991.

Hart, Dianne Walta. *Thanks to God and the Revolution: An Oral History of a Nicaraguan Family.* Madison: University of Wisconsin Press, 1990.

Hedin, Raymond W. *Married to the Church.* Bloomington: Indiana University Press, 1995.

Heller, Scott. "Experience and Expertise Meet in New Brand of Scholarship." *Chronicle of Higher Education* (6 May 1992): A7+.

Henson, Kevin D. *Just a Temp.* Philadelphia: Temple University Press, 1996.

Hewlett, Sylvia Ann. *When the Bough Breaks: The Cost of Neglecting Our Children.* New York: Harper Perennial, 1992.

Heyck, Denis Lynn, ed. *Life Stories of the Nicaraguan Revolution.* New York: Routledge, 1990.

Highwater, Jamake. *The Mythology of Transgression: Homosexuality as Metaphor.* New York: Oxford University Press, 1997.

Hindman, Jane E. "Making Writing Matter: Using 'the Personal' to Recover[y] an Essential[ist] Tension in Academic Discourse." *College English* 64, no. 1 (September 2001): 88–108.

Hines, Thomas S. *William Faulkner and the Tangible Past: The Architecture of Yoknapatawpha.* Berkeley: University of California Press, 1997.

Hirsch, Marianne. *The Mother-Daughter Plot: Narrative, Psychoanalysis, Feminism.* Bloomington: Indiana University Press, 1989.

Hoffman, Roald. *Chemistry Imagined: Reflections on Science.* Washington, D.C.: Smithsonian Institution Press, 1993.

———. *The Same and Not the Same.* New York: Columbia University Press, 1995.

Holloway, Karla. *Codes of Conduct: Race, Ethics, and the Color of Our Character.* New Brunswick: Rutgers University Press, 1996.

hooks, bell. *Talking Back: Thinking Feminist, Thinking Black.* Boston: South End, 1988.

———. *Teaching to Transgress: Education as the Practice of Freedom.* New York: Routledge, 1994.

Hughes, Francesca. *The Architect: Reconstructing Her Practice.* Cambridge: MIT Press, 1996.

Isserman, Maurice. *Dorothy Healey Remembers a Life in the American Communist Party.* New York: Oxford University Press, 1990.

Jackson, Michael. *At Home in the World.* Durham: Duke University Press, 1995.

Jamison, Kay Redfield. *An Unquiet Mind.* New York: Knopf, 1995.

Joeres, Ruth-Ellen Boettcher, and Elizabeth Mittman, eds. *The Politics of the Essay.* Bloomington: Indiana University Press, 1993.

Jouve, Nicole Ward. *White Woman Speaks with Forked Tongue: Criticism as Autobiography.* New York: Routledge, 1992.

Juhasz, Suzanne. *Reading from the Heart: Women, Literature, and the Search for True Love.* New York: Viking, 1994.

Kaplan, Alice. *French Lessons: A Memoir.* Chicago: University of Chicago Press, 1993.

Kaplan, Laura Duhan. "Speaking for Myself in Philosophy." *Philosophy in the Contemporary World* 1, no. 4 (winter 1994): 20–24.

———. *Family Pictures: A Philosopher Explores the Familiar.* Chicago: Open Court, 1997.

Karp, David A. *Speaking of Sadness: Depression, Disconnection, and the Meanings of Illness.* Oxford: Oxford University Press, 1996.

Kaufer, David S., and Cheryl Geisler. "Novelty in Academic Writing." *Written Communication* 6, no. 3 (1989): 286–311.

Kaysen, Carl. *Content and Context: Essays on College Education.* Report prepared by Carnegie Commission on Higher Education. New York: McGraw-Hill, 1973.

Keller, Evelyn Fox. *A Feeling for the Organism: The Life and Work of Barbara McClintock.* New York: Freeman, 1983.

Kent, Deborah. "In Search of a Heroine: Images of Women with Disabilities in Fiction and Drama." In *Women with Disabilities*, edited by Adrienne Asch and Michelle Fine, 90–110. Philadelphia: Temple University Press, 1988.

Kirsch, Gesa E., et al. *Women Writing the Academy: Audience, Authority, and Transformation*. Urbana: NCTE, 1993.

———. *Feminism and Composition: A Critical Sourcebook*. Boston: Bedford/St. Martin's, 2003.

Kitchen, Judith. *Only the Dance: Essays on Time and Memory*. Columbia: University of South Carolina Press, 1994.

Klass, Perri. *A Not Entirely Benign Procedure: Four Years as a Medical Student*. New York: Penguin, 1987.

Klaus, Carl H. "Embodying the Self: Malady and the Personal Essay." *Iowa Review* 25, no. 2 (spring/summer 1995): 176–93.

Knorr-Cetina, K. Karin. *Manufactured Knowledge: An Essay on the Constructivist and Contextual Nature of Science*. New York: Pergamon, 1981.

———. *Epistemic Cultures: How the Sciences Make Knowledge*. Cambridge: Harvard University Press, 1999.

Krieger, Susan. *Social Science and the Self: Personal Essays on an Art Form*. New Brunswick: Rutgers University Press, 1991.

———. *The Family Silver: Essays on Relationships among Women*. Berkeley: University of California Press, 1996.

Krog, Antjie. *The Country of My Skull*. London: Vintage, 1999.

Kroll, Florence R. *Ecotone: Wayfaring on the Margins*. Albany: SUNY Press, 1994.

Lamphere, Louise, Helena Ragone, and Patricia Zavella, eds. *Situated Lives: Gender and Culture in Everyday Life*. New York: Routledge, 1997.

Lee, D. John. *Life and Story: Autobiographies for a Narrative Psychology*. Westport, Conn.: Praeger/Greenwood, 1996.

Lefkowitz, Deborah. "Editing from Life." In *Women in German Yearbook 8: Feminist Studies in German Literature and Culture*, edited by Jeanette Clausen and Sara Friedrichsmeyer, 200–15. Lincoln: University of Nebraska Press, 1992.

Lent, Robin. " 'I Can Relate to That . . .': Reading and Responding in the Writing Classroom." *College Composition and Communication* 44, no. 2 (May 1993): 232–40.

Lentricchia, Frank. *Edge of Night: A Confession*. New York: Random House, 1994.

Levitt, Laura. *Jews and Feminism: The Ambivalent Search for Home*. New York: Routledge, 1997.

Lewin, Ellen, and William L. Leap, eds. *Out in the Field: Reflections of Lesbian and Gay Anthropologists*. Urbana: University of Illinois Press, 1996.

Limerick, Patricia Nelson. "Dancing with Professors: The Trouble with Academic Prose." *New York Times Book Review* (31 October 1993): 3+.

Limon, José E. *Dancing with the Devil: Society and Cultural Poetics in Mexican-American South Texas*. Madison: University of Wisconsin Press, 1994.

Lindemann, Kate. "Philosophy of Liberation in the North American Context: Part I." *Contemporary Philosophy* 14, no. 4 (July/August, 1992): 10–16.

Lipton, Eunice. *Alias Olympia: A Woman's Search for Manet's Notorious Model and Her Own Desire*. 1992. Ithaca: Cornell University Press, 1999.

Locke, John. *An Essay Concerning Human Understanding*. Edited by A. S. Pringle-Pattison. London: Oxford University Press, 1924.

Loftus, Elizabeth, and Katherine Ketcham. *Witness for the Defense.* New York: St. Martin's, 1991.

Lopate, Philip. Introduction. *The Art of the Personal Essay.* New York: Anchor, 1994.

Lugones, Maria. "Playfulness, 'World'-Traveling and Loving Perception." *Hypatia: A Journal of Feminist Philosophy* 2, no. 2 (summer 1987): 3–19.

Lugones, Maria, and Elizabeth V. Spelman. "Have We Got a Theory for You! Feminist Theory, Cultural Imperialism, and the Demand for 'The Woman's Voice.'" *Women's Studies International Forum* 6, no. 6 (1983): 573–81.

Lyndon, Michael. *Writing and Life.* Hanover, N.H.: University Press of New England, 1995.

Mairs, Nancy. *Carnal Acts.* New York: Harper, 1992.

———. *Voice Lessons: On Becoming a (Woman) Writer.* Boston: Beacon, 1994.

Malin, Irving, and Irwin Stark. Introduction. *Breakthrough: A Treasury of Contemporary American-Jewish Literature,* edited by Irving Malin and Irwin Stark, 1–24. New York: McGraw-Hill, 1964.

Marius, Richard. "On Academic Discourse." *Profession 90* (1990): 28–31.

Marshall, Ian. *Story Line: Exploring the Literature of the Appalachian Trail.* Charlottesville: University of Virginia Press, 1998.

———. *Peak Experiences: Walking Meditations on Literature, Nature, and Need.* Charlottesville: University of Virginia Press, 2003.

Mavor, Carol. *Pleasures Taken: Performances of Sexuality and Loss in Victorian Photographs.* Durham: Duke University Press, 1995.

Mayberry, Katherine J., ed. *Teaching What You're Not: Identity and Politics in Higher Education.* New York: New York University Press, 1996.

McMillen, Liz. "The Importance of Storytelling: A New Emphasis by Law Scholars." *Chronicle of Higher Education* (26 July 1996): A10.

Meese, Elizabeth. *(Sem)erotics: Theorizing Lesbian Writing.* New York: New York University Press, 1992.

Michrina, Barry P. *Pennsylvania Mining Families: The Search for Dignity in the Coalfields.* Lexington: University of Kentucky Press, 1993.

Miller, D. A. *Place for Us: Essay on the Broadway Musical.* Cambridge: Harvard University Press, 1999.

Miller, Nancy K. *Getting Personal: Feminist Occasions and Other Autobiographical Acts.* New York: Routledge, 1992.

———. *Bequest and Betrayal: Memoirs of a Parent's Death.* New York: Oxford University Press, 1996.

———. *But Enough About Me: Why We Read Other People's Lives.* New York: Columbia University Press, 2002.

Miller, Susan. *Textual Carnivals: The Politics of Composition.* Carbondale: Southern Illinois University Press, 1991.

Minnich, Elizabeth. *Transforming Knowledge.* Philadelphia: Temple University Press, 1990.

Minnow, Martha, and Gary Bellow, eds. *Law Stories.* Ann Arbor: University of Michigan Press, 1996.

Modleski, Tania. *Old Wives' Tales and Other Women's Stories*. New York: New York University Press, 1998.

Morris, Thomas V., ed. *God and the Philosophers: The Reconciliation of Faith and Reason*. New York: Oxford University Press, 1994.

Nash, Walter. "The Stuff These People Write." *The Writing Scholar: Studies in Academic Discourse*, edited by Walter Nash, 8–30. Newbury Park, Calif.: Sage, 1990.

Nelson, Nancy Owen, ed. *Private Voices, Public Lives: Women Speak on the Literary Life*. Denton: University of North Texas Press, 1995.

Nerburn, Kent. *Neither Wolf nor Dog*. New York: New World Library, 1994.

Newton, Esther. *Margaret Mead Made Me Gay: Personal Essays, Public Ideas*. Durham: Duke University Press, 2001.

Newton, Judith. *Starting Over: Feminism and the Politics of Cultural Critique*. Ann Arbor: University of Michigan Press, 1994.

Ngugi Wa Thiong'o. *Moving the Centre*. Portsmouth, N.H.: Heinemann, 1993.

Niemann, Linda. *Boomer: Railroad Memoirs*. Berkeley: University of California Press, 1990.

Odzer, Cleo. *Patpong Sisters: An American Woman's View of the Bangkok Sex World*. New York: Blue Moon, 1994.

Osborne, Terry. *Sightlines: The View of the Valley through the Voice of Depression*. Middlebury: Middlebury College Press/University Press of New England, 2001.

Ostriker, Alicia. *The Nakedness of the Fathers: Biblical Visions and Revisions*. New Brunswick: Rutgers University Press, 1996.

Oxenhandler, Neil. *Looking for Heroes in Postwar France: Albert Camus, Max Jacob, Simone Weil*. Hanover, N.H.: University Press of New England, 1995.

Paget, Marianne. *A Complex Sorrow: Reflections on Cancer and an Abbreviated Life*. Edited by Marjorie L. Devault. Philadelphia: Temple University Press, 1993.

Paley, Karen. "The Social Construction of Expressivism." "Expressivist Pedagogy: The Politics of Teaching the Personal Narrative." Ph.D. diss. Northeastern University, 1998. 1–61. Rev. and published as *I-Writing: The Politics and Practice of Teaching First-Person Writing*. Carbondale, Ill.: Southern Illinois University Press, 2000.

Palmer, Parker. *To Know as We Are Known: Education as a Spiritual Journey*. San Francisco: Harper, 1983.

———. *The Courage to Teach: Exploring the Inner Landscape of a Teacher's Life*. San Francisco: Jossey-Bass, 1998.

Papert, Seymour. *The Children's Machine: Rethinking School in the Age of the Computer*. New York: Basic, 1993.

Papoulis, Irene. " 'Personal Narrative,' 'Academic Writing,' and Feminist Theory: Reflections of a Freshman Composition Teacher." *Freshman English News* 182 (1990): 9–12.

Patai, Daphne. "Point of View: The Nouveau Solipsism." *Chronicle of Higher Education*. (23 February 1994): A58.

Paul, Deidre Glenn. *Life, Culture, and Education on the Academic Plantation: Womanist Thought and Perspective*. New York: Peter Lang, 2001.

Paul, Sherwin. *Hewing to Experience: Essays and Reviews on Recent American Poetry and Poetics, Nature and Culture*. Iowa City: University of Iowa Press, 1989.

Peritz, Janice Haney. "Making a Place for the Poetic in Academic Writing." *College Composition and Communication* 44, no. 3 (1993): 380–85.

Pettiway, Leon E. *Honey, Honey, Miss Thang: Being Black, Gay, and on the Streets*. Philadelphia: Temple University Press, 1996.

Postman, Neil. *The End of Education: Redefining the Value of School*. New York: Vintage, 1995.

Probyn, Elspeth. "Travels in the Postmodern: Making Sense of the Local." In *Feminism/Postmodernism*, edited by Linda J. Nicholson, 176–89. New York: Routledge, 1990.

Reddy, Maureen. *Crossing the Color Line: Women, Race, and Parenting*. New Brunswick: Rutgers University Press, 1996.

Reed-Danahay, Deborah E., ed. *Auto/Ethnography: Rewriting the Self and the Social*. New York: Berg/New York University Press, 1997.

Reinharz, S. *On Becoming a Social Scientist*. New Brunswick: Transaction, 1984.

Rethinking History. Robert A. Rosenstone, coeditor. A history journal that encourages experimental approaches to history writing, poetic reflections, personal encounters, abstracts for articles yet to be written.

Reynolds, Michelle [Sidney Matrix]. "(Un)Authorized Discourse: Performing in Lesbian: Writing/Lesbian: Theory." Unpublished monograph.

Rich, Adrienne. "Notes Toward a Politics of Location." *Blood, Bread, and Poetry: Selected Prose, 1979–1985*, 210–31. New York: Norton, 1986.

Richards, Joan L. *Angles of Reflection: Logic and a Mother's Love*. New York: W. H. Freeman, 2000.

Richardson, Laurel. *Fields of Play: Constructing an Academic Life*. New Brunswick: Rutgers University Press, 1997.

Richman, David. *Passionate Action: Yeats's Mastery of Drama*. Newark: University of Delaware Press, 2000.

Robillard, Albert R. *The Meaning of a Disability: The Lived Experience of Paralysis*. Philadelphia: Temple University Press, 1999.

Robinson, Julia. "Julia Robinson." In *More Mathematical People: Conversations*, edited by Donald J. Albers et al., 263–80. San Diego: Academic Press, 1990.

Rosaldo, Renato. "Grief and a Headhunter's Rage." *Culture and Truth: Renewing the Anthropologist's Search for Meaning*. Boston: Beacon, 1989.

Rose, Mike. *Lives on the Boundary: A Moving Account of the Struggles and Achievements of America's Educational Underclass*. New York: Penguin, 1989.

Rosenblatt, Louise. *Literature as Exploration*. New York: Appleton-Century, 1938. New York: MLA, 1976.

Ruddick, Sara. *Maternal Thinking: Toward a Politics of Peace*. Boston: Beacon, 1989.

Ruddick, Sara, and Pamela Daniels, eds. *Working it Out: Twenty-Three Women Writers, Artists, Scientists, and Scholars Talk about Their Lives and Their Work*. New York: Pantheon, 1977.

Rudolph, Frederick. *Curriculum: A History of the American Undergraduate Course of Study Since 1636*. San Francisco: Jossey-Bass, 1977.

Russell, David R. *Writing in the Academic Disciplines, 1870–1990: A Curricular History*. Carbondale, Ill.: Southern Illinois University Press, 1991.

Ryan, Michael, and Avery Gordon, eds. *Body Politics: Disease, Desire, and the Family.* Boulder: Westview, 1993.

Saladin, Linda A. *Fetishism and Fatal Women: Gender, Power, and Reflexive Discourse.* New York: Peter Lang, 1994.

Salvio, Paula. "Transgressive Daughters: Student Autobiography and the Project of Self-Creation." *Cambridge Journal of Education* 20, no. 3 (1990): 283–89.

Sarris, Greg. *Mabel McKay: Weaving the Dream.* Berkeley: University of California Press, 1994.

Savigliano, Marta. *Tango and the Political Economy of Passion: From Exoticism to Decolonization.* Boulder: Westview, 1994.

Saxton, Marsha. *With Wings: An Anthology of Literature by and about Women with Disabilities.* Urbana: University of Illinois Press, 1991.

Schama, Simon. *Landscape and Memory.* New York: Knopf, 1995.

Scheese, Don. *Nature Writing: The Pastoral Impulse in America.* Boston: Twayne, 1996.

Slater, Lauren. *Welcome to My Country.* New York: Random, 1996.

Slovic, Scott. *Seeking Awareness in American Nature Writing: Henry Thoreau, Annie Dillard, Edward Abbey, Wendell Berry, Barry Lopez.* Salt Lake City: University of Utah Press, 1992.

Smith, Sidonie. *Subjectivity, Identity, and the Body: Women's Autobiographical Practices in the Twentieth Century.* Bloomington: Indiana University Press, 1993.

Smith, Sidonie, and Julia Watson, eds. *Getting a Life: Everyday Uses of Autobiography.* Minneapolis: University of Minnesota Press, 1996.

Spigelman, Candace. "Argument and Evidence in the Case of the Personal." *College English* 64, no. 1 (September 2001): 63–87.

Spingarn, J. E. "The New Criticism." *Columbia University Lectures on Literature.* 1911. Rpt. in J. E. Spingarn, *Creative Criticism*, 3–38. Port Washington, N.Y.: Kennikat/ Harcourt, 1964.

Steedman, Carolyn. *Landscape for a Good Woman.* New Brunswick: Rutgers University Press, 1987.

Steig, Michael. "Ferdinand and Wee Gillis at Mid-Century." *Children's Literature Association Quarterly* 14 (1989): 118–23.

———. *Stories of Reading: Subjectivity and Literary Understanding.* Baltimore: Johns Hopkins University Press, 1989.

———. "Stories of Reading Pedagogy: Problems and Possibilities." *Reader* 26 (fall 1991): 27–37.

———. "Unearthing Buried Affects and Associations in Reading: The Case of the Justified Sinner." In *Self-Analysis and Literary Study: Exploring Hidden Agendas*, edited by Daniel Rancour-Laferriere. New York: New York University Press, 1994.

Steingraber, Sandra. *Having Faith: An Ecologist's Journey to Motherhood.* Cambridge, Mass.: Perseus, 2001.

Stenross, Barbara. *Missed Connections: Hard of Hearing in a Hearing World.* Philadelphia: Temple University Press, 1999.

Stephenson, Denise. "Blurred Distinctions: Emerging Forms of Academic Writing." Ph.D. diss., University of New Mexico, 1996.

Stivers, Camilla. "Reflections on the Role of Personal Narrative in Social Science." *Signs* 18, no. 2 (winter 1993): 408–25.

Suleiman, Susan Rubin. *Risking Who One Is: Encounters with Contemporary Art and Literature*. Cambridge: Harvard University Press, 1994.

Tallmadge, John. *Meeting the Tree of Life: A Teacher's Path*. Salt Lake City: University of Utah Press, 1997.

Thomas, Jeannie B. *Featherless Chickens, Laughing Women, and Serious Stories*. Charlottesville: University Press of Virginia, 1997.

Todd, Alexandra Dundas. *Double Vision: An East-West Collaboration for Coping with Cancer*. Middletown, Conn.: Wesleyan University Press, 1994.

Tompkins, Jane. *West of Everything: The Inner Life of Westerns*. Oxford: Oxford University Press, 1992.

———. *A Life in School: What the Teacher Learned*. Reading, Mass.: Addison-Wesley, 1996.

Torgovnick, Marianna. "Experimental Critical Writing." *Profession 90* (1990): 27–28.

———. *Crossing Ocean Parkway: Readings by an Italian-American Daughter*. Oxford: Oxford University Press, 1992. Chicago: University of Chicago Press, 1994.

Trebilcot, Joyce. "Ethics of Method: Greasing the Machine and Telling Stories." In *Feminist Ethics*, edited by Claudia Tate. Lawrence: University Press of Kansas, 1991.

Trinh T. Minh-ha. *Woman Native Other: Writing Postcoloniality and Feminism*. Bloomington: Indiana University Press, 1989.

Tsing, Anna Lowenhaupt. *In the Realm of the Diamond Queen: Marginality in an Out-of-the-Way Place*. Princeton: Princeton University Press, 1994.

Veysey, Laurence. *The Emergence of the American University*. Chicago: University of Chicago Press, 1965.

Villanueva, Victor Jr. *Bootstraps: From an American Academic of Color*. Urbana: NCTE, 1993.

Vizenor, Gerald. "Crows Written on the Poplars: Autocritical Autobiographies." In *I Tell You Now: Essays by Native American Writers*, edited by Brian Swann and Arnold Krupat, 99–109. Lincoln: University of Nebraska Press, 1988.

Watkins, Evan. *Work Time: English Departments and the Circulation of Cultural Value*. Stanford: Stanford University Press, 1989.

Weimer, Joan. *Back Talk: Teaching Lost Selves to Speak*. Chicago: University of Chicago Press, 1994.

Weisstein, Naomi. "Adventures of a Woman in Science." In *Women Look at Biology Looking at Women: A Collection of Feminist Critiques*, edited by Ruth Hubbard et al., 188–203. Boston: G. K. Hall, 1979. Rpt. in *Biological Woman—The Convenient Myth: A Collection of Essays and a Comprehensive Bibliography*, edited by Ruth Hubbard, Mary Sue Henifen, and Barbara Fried, 264–81. New York: Schenkman, 1992.

Wexler, Alice. *Mapping Fate: A Memoir of Family, Risk, and Genetic Research*. New York: Random, 1995.

Williams, Patricia. *The Alchemy of Race and Rights*. Cambridge: Harvard University Press, 1992.

Wilson, Robin. "How a Week in the Mountains Can Jump-Start a Dissertation." *Chronicle of Higher Education* (21 July 2000): A10+.

Winawer, Sidney J., with Nick Taylor. *Healing Lessons*. New York: Routledge, 1999.

Woods, Susan. "The Solace of Separation: Feminist Theory, Autobiography, Edith Wharton, and Me." In *Creating Safe Space: Violence and Women's Writing*, edited by Julie Tharp and Tomoko Kuribayashi, 27–46. Albany: SUNY Press, 1998.

Woolf, Virginia. *A Room of One's Own*, 1929. San Diego: Harcourt, 1981.

Wright, George. Forum: "The Inevitability of the Personal." *PMLA* (October 1998): 1159–60.

Yates, Gayle Graham. *Mississippi Mind: A Personal Cultural History of an American State*. Knoxville: University of Tennessee Press, 1990.

Young, Bard. *The Snake of God: A Story of Memory and Imagination*. Montgomery, Ala.: Black Belt Press, 1997.

Zimmerman, Bonnie. "In Academia and Out: The Experience of a Lesbian Feminist Literary Critic." In Greene and Kahn, *Changing Subjects*, 112–20.

KWAME ANTHONY APPIAH is Professor of Philosophy at Princeton University and the author of *Assertion and Conditionals* (1985) and *In My Father's House: Africa in the Philosophy of Culture* (a 1992 *New York Times* Notable Book of the Year), chapter 8 of which is reprinted here. Appiah has also coedited, with Henry Louis Gates Jr., a series of collections on African American authors Alice Walker, Gloria Naylor, Langston Hughes, Toni Morrison, Richard Wright, and Zora Neale Hurston.

RUTH BEHAR is Professor of Anthropology at the University of Michigan, recipient of a MacArthur Foundation award and a John Simon Guggenheim fellowship, and author of *Santa María del Monte: The Presence of the Past in a Spanish Village* (1986), *Translated Woman: Crossing the Border with Esperanza's Story* (1993), and *The Vulnerable Observer: Anthropology that Breaks Your Heart* (1996); she is editor of *Bridges to Cuba* (1995) and coeditor of *Women Writing Culture* (1995). Her essay, "Juban América," reprinted here, first appeared in *Poetics Today*.

MERRILL BLACK runs a writing and research business called Active Voice. She has trained and consulted on desktop publishing, curriculum and publication design, and fund raising to a variety of nonprofits working in economic development, the arts, affordable housing, and health care. She won second place in the 2000 Exoterica Poetry Slam in the Bronx. She holds an M.A. in nonfiction writing from the University of New Hampshire and a B.A. in American studies from Marlboro College, where she wrote a literary biography of a nineteenth-century humorist, a portion of which was published in the *Vermont Historical Quarterly*.

DAVID BLEICH, the author of many books, teaches writing, literature, and teaching at the University of Rochester. His book, *Know and Tell: A Writing Pedagogy of Disclosure, Genre, and Membership*, appeared in 1998, and his coedited collection, *Personal Effects*, was published in 2001.

JAMES CONE, a nationally recognized liberation theologian, is the author of several books on black theology and black culture, including *Risks of Faith* (1999), *Martin &*

Malcolm & America: A Dream or a Nightmare? (1991), and *God of the Oppressed* (1975), the first chapter of which is reprinted here.

BRENDA DALY is Professor of English at Iowa State University and the author of *Lavish Self Divisions: The Novels of Joyce Carol Oates* (1996) and essays on Oates in journals and collections such as *Anxious Power* (1993). Daly's essay "My Father/My Censor" originally appeared, in a slightly different form, in her book *Authoring a Life: A Woman's Survival in and Through Literary Studies* (1998). She has also coedited a collection, *Narrating Mothers: Theorizing Maternal Subjectivities* (1991).

LAURA B. DELIND, past President of the Agriculture, Food, and Human Values Society, is a Senior Academic Specialist in the Department of Anthropology at Michigan State University. Much of her research and writing addresses the social and political impacts of industrial agriculture at the local or community level. She is a proponent of sustainable, organic agriculture and actively works to promote more decentralized, diversified, and democratized systems of food production, distribution, and consumption throughout Michigan and the Midwest. Her essay first appeared in *Agriculture and Human Values* 16 (1999): 3–9.

CARLOS L. DEWS is Associate Professor of Language and Literature at Columbus State University and the founding director of the Carson McCullers Center for Writers and Musicians. He is the editor of *Illumination and Night Glare: The Unfinished Autobiography of Carson McCullers* (1999) as well as (with Carolyn Leste Law) *This Fine Place So Far From Home: Stories of Academics from the Working Class* (1995) and *Out in the South* (2001). His essay here, "Gender Tragedies: East Texas Cockfighting and *Hamlet*," was first published in the *Journal of Men's Studies*.

MICHAEL DORRIS, who held a graduate degree in anthropology from Yale University, founded the Native American Studies Program at Dartmouth College and taught there for fifteen years. He is coauthor of *The Crown of Columbus* (1991) and *A Guide to Research on North American Indians* (1983), and author of the novels *A Yellow Raft in Blue Water* (1987), *Morning Girl* (1992), *Guests* (1994), and *Sees Behind Trees* (1996); *Working Men* (short stories, 1993); *Paper Trail* (essays, 1994); and *The Broken Cord*, excerpted here. He died in 1997.

DIANE P. FREEDMAN (editor) is Associate Professor of English and core faculty member in women's studies at the University of New Hampshire, author of *An Alchemy of Genres: Cross-Genre Writing by American Feminist Poet-Critics* (1992), and a coauthor of *Teaching Prose* (1988); editor of *Millay at 100: A Critical Reappraisal* (1995), coeditor, with Martha Stoddard Holmes, of *The Teacher's Body: Embodiment, Authority, and Identity in the Academy* (2003), and coeditor, with Olivia Frey and Frances Murphy Zauhar, of *The Intimate Critique* (Duke University Press, 1993). Her critical articles, personal essays, reviews, and poetry have also appeared in such publications as *College Literature*, ISLE: *Interdisciplinary Studies in Literature and the Environment*, *Tulsa Studies in Women's Literature*, *The Bucknell Review*, *Personal Effects*, *Anxious Power*, *Constructing and Reconstructing Gender*, *Crazyquilt*, *Sou'wester*, *Wind*, and *Permafrost*.

OLIVIA FREY (editor), retired Professor of English at St. Olaf College, is Lead Administrator at the Village School in Northfield, Minnesota. She is coeditor, with Diane P. Freedman and Frances Murphy Zauhar, of *The Intimate Critique: Autobiographical Literary Criticism* (Duke University Press, 1993) and has published widely in the fields of composition, feminist pedagogy, and peace studies.

PETER HAMLIN, Associate Professor of Music at St. Olaf College, has published and recorded works for orchestra, woodwinds, tuba, guitar, concert band, and voice as well as held residencies with various U.S. symphonies and music festivals.

LAURA DUHAN KAPLAN is Associate Professor of Philosophy and Coordinator of the Women's Studies Program at the University of North Carolina at Charlotte. She is the author of *Family Pictures: A Philosopher Explores the Familiar* (1997) and coeditor of *From the Eye of the Storm: Regional Conflicts and the Philosophy of Peace* (1995) and *Philosophical Perspectives on Power and Domination* (1997). As well as teaching philosophy and other humanities classes, she teaches Hatha Yoga and Hebrew School.

PERRI KLASS is a pediatrician and a writer of fiction and nonfiction. Her fiction includes *Other Women's Children* (1990), *Recombinations* (1995), and *I am Having an Adventure* (1986), and her nonfiction includes essays published in the *New York Times Magazine*, *Vogue*, *Mademoiselle*, and the *Antioch Review* as well as the books *Baby Doctor* (1992) and *A Not Entirely Benign Procedure: Four Years as a Medical Student* (1987), a chapter of which is reprinted here.

MURIEL LEDERMAN is an Associate Professor in the Department of Biology at Virginia Tech, where she teaches virology. Much of her scientific research has been published in the *Journal of Virology*. She is affiliated with the university's Women's Studies Program, where she teaches "Gender and Science." She is coeditor of *The Gender and Science Reader* (2001).

DEBRA LEFKOWITZ has worked as a documentary film maker since 1981. Her award-winning film *Intervals of Silence: Being Jewish in Germany* (1990) has been screened in more than fifty cities in the United States, Germany, Canada, and France. Since 1994 she has also used images from her film footage for the creation of site-specific photographic installations.

EUNICE LIPTON teaches art history at Hunter College and is the author of *Looking into Degas: Uneasy Images of Women and Modern Life* (1986) and *Alias Olympia: A Woman's Search for Monet's Notorious Model and Her Own Desire* (1992), excerpted here.

ROBERT D. MARCUS, who died in October 2000, was Chair of the Department of History at the State University of New York at Brockport. Previously, he had been the vice president and chief academic officer of that school for nine years. He is the author of *Grand Old Party: Political Structure in the Gilded Age, 1880–1895* (1971), among other works.

DONALD MURRAY, retired Professor of English at the University of New Hampshire, is a Pulitzer-prize-winning journalist and the author of several influential books on writing and the teaching of writing, among them *Write to Learn* (1989), *A Writer Teaches Writing* (1968), *Shoptalk* (1990), *Read to Write* (1990), and *The Craft of Revision* (1991). His essay here began as a talk for a UNH conference, "The Call of Story."

SEYMOUR PAPERT is a mathematician and one of the early pioneers of Artificial Intelligence. Additionally, he is internationally recognized as a seminal thinker about ways in which computers can change learning. Born and educated in South Africa, where he participated actively in the antiapartheid movement, Papert pursued mathematical research at Cambridge University from 1954 to 1958. He then worked with Jean Piaget at the University of Geneva from 1958 to 1963. It was this collaboration that led him to consider using mathematics in the service of understanding how children can learn and think. Widely published in academia and the media, Papert is the author of *The Children's Machine: Rethinking School in the Age of the Computer* (excerpted here, 1993), *Mindstorms: Children, Computers, and Powerful Ideas* (1980), and, more recently, *The Connected Family: Bridging the Digital Generation Gap* (1996).

CARLA L. PETERSON is Co-Chair of the Committee on Africa and the Americas, Professor in the Department of English and the Comparative Literature Program, and affiliate faculty of the Women's Studies and American Studies departments at the University of Maryland. She is the author of *"Doers of the Word": African American Women Speakers and Writers in the North (1830–1880)*, published in 1998, and has published numerous essays on nineteenth-century African American literature and literary history. Her current project is a social and cultural history of African American life in nineteenth-century New York City as seen through the lens of family history.

DAVID RICHMAN is Professor of Theater and Humanities at the University of New Hampshire. He is the author of *Laughter, Pain, and Wonder: Shakespeare's Comedies and the Audience in the Theater* (1990) and of a book on Yeats, *Passionate Action* (2000), for which parts of his essay here, "Listening to the Images," serve as the introduction.

SARA RUDDICK is coeditor of *Working it Out: 23 Women Writers, Artists, Scientists, and Scholars Talk of Their Lives and Work* (1977) and *Between Women: Biographers, Novelists, Teachers, and Artists Write about Their Work on Women* (1984) and author of *Maternal Thinking: Towards a Politics of Peace* (1989), a chapter of which is reprinted here. She teaches philosophy and feminist theory at the New School for Social Research in New York City, where she lives.

JULIE THARP is Associate Professor of English at the University of Wisconsin-Marshfield. She has compiled two anthologies of critical essays, *Creating Safe Space: Violence and Women's Writing* (1998) and *This Giving Birth: Pregnancy and Childbirth in American Women's Writing* (2000), in addition to writing numerous articles. She teaches women studies, multicultural literature, and film studies classes. During her recent Fulbright stay in Singapore she became fascinated with Indian film and its relationship to women's roles and status within India.

BONNIE TUSMITH is Associate Professor of English at Northeastern University and past president of the multiethnic literature society, MELUS. Her publications include *All My Relatives: Community in Contemporary Ethnic American Literatures* (1993), *Colorizing Literary Theory: Conversations with John Edgar Wideman* (1998), *American Family Album: 28 Contemporary Ethnic Stories* (2000), and *Race in the College Classroom: Pedagogy and Politics* (2002). As a cultural worker she helped establish academic, community, and campus organizations in Boston and San Francisco as well as in Ohio, Wisconsin, Washington, and Alaska. She considers herself an activist academic who tries to practice what she preaches.

NAOMI WEISSTEIN, author and neuroscientist, is Professor of Psychology at SUNY, Buffalo. She has written extensively on science, feminism, culture and politics as well as worked as activist and comedian. She is best known for her pioneering essay "Kinder, Kirche, Kuche as Scientific Law: Psychology Constructs the Female." Said to have started the discipline of the psychology of women, it has been reprinted over forty-two times in six different languages. A collection commemorating the twenty-fifth anniversary of the article appeared as a special issue of the British journal *Feminism and Psychology* in 1992. Her essay here is reprinted from *Women Look at Biology Looking at Women: A Collection of Feminist Critiques* (1979), edited by Ruth Hubbard et al.

ALICE WEXLER is the author of three books, *Emma Goldman in America* (1984), *Emma Goldman in Exile* (1989), and *Mapping Fate: A Memoir of Family, Risk and Genetic Research* (1996), a section of which appears here. A former Fulbright Scholar to Venezuela, she earned a B.A. in Latin American studies from Stanford and a Ph.D. in history from Indiana University. She has published numerous book reviews and articles in journals such as *Caribbean Studies*, *Feminist Studies*, *Raritan*, and *Rethinking History*. Though she no longer focuses on Latin American history, she returned twice to Venezuela in the 1980s to participate in the International Venezuela Huntington's Disease Collaborative Research Project, headed by her sister, Dr. Nancy Wexler. She has taught history and women's studies at Sonoma State University, Claremont Graduate School, and UCLA, where she is currently a Research Scholar at the Center for the Study of Women. She lives in Los Angeles.

PATRICIA J. WILLIAMS is James L. Dohr Professor of Law at the Columbia University School of Law and author of *The Rooster's Egg* (1997), *Seeing a Color-Blind Future: The Paradox of Race* (1997), and *The Alchemy of Race and Rights* (1991), the third chapter of which is reprinted here. She is also a columnist for *The Nation*.

Library of Congress Cataloging-in-Publication Data

Autobiographical writing across the disciplines :

a reader / with a forword by Ruth Behar ;

edited by Diane P. Freedman and Olivia Frey.

p. cm.

Includes bibliographical references.

ISBN 0-8223-3200-0 (cloth : acid-free paper)

ISBN 0-8223-3213-2 (pbk.: acid-free paper)

1. Readers—Autobiography.   2. English

language—Rhetoric—Problems, exercises, etc.

3. Autobiography—Authorship—Problems,

exercises, etc.   4. Interdisciplinary approach in

education.   5. College readers.   6. Autobiographies.

I. Freedman, Diane P.   II. Frey, Olivia.

PE1127.A9A98   2003

920—dc21   2003012317